IMPORTANT

Y0-CAY-589

HERE IS YOUR REGISTRATION CODE TO ACCESS MCGRAW-HILL
PREMIUM CONTENT AND MCGRAW-HILL ONLINE RESOURCES

For key premium online resources you need THIS CODE to
gain access. Once the code is entered, you will be able to
use the web resources for the length of your course.

Access is provided only if you have purchased a new book.

If the registration code is missing from this book, the registration screen on our
website, and within your WebCT or Blackboard course will tell you how to obtain
your new code. Your registration code can be used only once to establish
access. It is not transferable

To gain access to these online resources

1. **USE** your web browser to go to: **www.mhhe.com/mcshaneESS**

2. **CLICK** on "First Time User"

3. **ENTER** the Registration Code printed on the tear-off bookmark on the right

4. After you have entered your registration code, click on "Register"

5. **FOLLOW** the instructions to setup your personal UserID and Password

6. **WRITE** your UserID and Password down for future reference. Keep it in a safe place.

If your course is using WebCT or Blackboard, you'll be able to use this code to
access the McGraw-Hill content within your instructor's online course.

To gain access to the McGraw-Hill content in your instructor's WebCT or
Blackboard course simply log into the course with the user ID and Password
provided by your instructor. Enter the registration code exactly as it appears to
the right when prompted by the system. You will only need to use this code the
first time you click on McGraw-Hill content.

These instructions are specifically for student access. Instructors are not required
to register via the above instructions.

The **McGraw-Hill** Companies

**McGraw-Hill
Irwin**

Thank you, and welcome to your
McGraw-Hill/Irwin Online Resources.

McShane, Von Glinow
Organizational Behavior
ISBN-13: 978-0-07-322406-0
ISBN-10: 0-07-322406-5

EMKX-BD84-XWYF-F34R-KP8N

REGISTRATION CODE
REGISTRATION CODE

REGISTRATION CODE
REGISTRATION CODE

The **McGraw-Hill** Companies

**McGraw-Hill
Irwin**

>organizationalbehavior

[essentials]

>**organizational**behavior

[essentials]

Steven L. McShane
University of Western Australia

Mary Ann Von Glinow
Florida International University

**McGraw-Hill
Irwin**

Boston   Burr Ridge, IL   Dubuque, IA   Madison, WI   New York
San Francisco   St. Louis   Bangkok   Bogotá   Caracas   Kuala Lumpur
Lisbon   London   Madrid   Mexico City   Milan   Montreal   New Delhi
Santiago   Seoul   Singapore   Sydney   Taipei   Toronto

The McGraw·Hill Companies

 Irwin

ORGANIZATIONAL BEHAVIOR: [essentials]

Published by McGraw-Hill/Irwin, a business unit of The McGraw-Hill Companies, Inc., 1221 Avenue of the
Americas, New York, NY, 10020. Copyright © 2007 by The McGraw-Hill Companies, Inc. All rights reserved.
No part of this publication may be reproduced or distributed in any form or by any means, or stored in a
database or retrieval system, without the prior written consent of The McGraw-Hill Companies, Inc., including,
but not limited to, in any network or other electronic storage or transmission, or broadcast for distance
learning.

Some ancillaries, including electronic and print components, may not be available to customers outside the
United States.

This book is printed on acid-free paper.

1 2 3 4 5 6 7 8 9 0 CCI/CCI 0 9 8 7 6

ISBN-13: 978-0-07-353006-2
ISBN-10: 0-07-353006-9

Editorial director: *John E. Biernat*
Senior sponsoring editor: *Ryan Blankenship*
Senior developmental editor: *Christine Scheid*
Associate marketing manager: *Margaret A. Beamer*
Producer, Media technology: *Janna Martin*
Lead project manager: *Mary Conzachi*
Lead production supervisor: *Michael R. McCormick*
Senior designer: *Kami Carter*
Senior photo research coordinator: *Jeremy Cheshareck*
Photo researcher: *Jennifer Blankenship*
Media project manager: *Joyce J. Chappetto*
Cover design: *Pam Verros, pv design*
Interior design: *Pam Verros, pv design*
Cover image: *© Corbis*
Typeface: *10/12 Times Roman*
Compositor: *ElectraGraphics, Inc.*
Printer: *Courier Kendallville*

Library of Congress Cataloging-in-Publication Data

McShane, Steven Lattimore.
    Organizational behavior : essentials / Steven L. McShane, Mary Ann Von
Glinow.
        p. cm.
    An abridged edition of their comprehensive textbook.
    Various multi-media instructional resources are available to supplement the text.
    Includes index.
    ISBN-13: 978-0-07-353006-2 (alk. paper)
    ISBN-10: 0-07-353006-9 (alk. paper)
    1. Organizational behavior. I. Von Glinow, Mary Ann Young, 1949– . II. Title.
HD58.7.M422 2007
302.3/5—dc22

                                                          2005058547

www.mhhe.com

Dedicated with love and devotion to **Donna**, and to our wonderful daughters, **Bryton** and **Madison**.

—Steven L. McShane

This one is for **Zack**.

—Mary Ann Von Glinow

Steven L. McShane   Steven L. McShane is Professor of Management in the Graduate School of Management at the University of Western Australia (UWA). He has also served on the business faculties at Simon Fraser University and Queen's University in Canada. Steve receives high teaching ratings from MBA and doctoral students both in Perth, Australia, and in Singapore, where he also teaches for UWA.

Steve earned his PhD from Michigan State University in organizational behavior, human resource management, and labor relations. He also holds a Master of Industrial Relations from the University of Toronto and an undergraduate degree from Queen's University in Canada. Steve has served as president of the Administrative Sciences Association of Canada (the Canadian equivalent of the Academy of Management) and director of graduate programs in the business faculty at Simon Fraser University.

Steve is also the author of *Canadian Organizational Behavior,* 6th edition (McGraw-Hill, 2006), Canada's best-selling OB textbook. He is co-author with Professor Tony Travaglione of *Organisational Behaviour on the Pacific Rim* (McGraw-Hill, 2003), which became the second best-selling OB book in that region within its first year of publication. Steve has published several dozen articles and conference papers on informal and structural knowledge management, the socialization of new employees, gender bias in job evaluation, wrongful dismissal, media bias in business magazines, emotions in decision making, and other diverse topics.

Along with teaching and writing, Steve enjoys his leisure time swimming, bodyboard surfing, canoeing, skiing, and traveling with his wife and two daughters.

Mary Ann Von Glinow   Dr. Von Glinow is Director of the Center for International Business Education and Research (CIBER) and Professor of Management and International Business at Florida International University. Previously on the Business School faculty of the University of Southern California, she has an MBA and PhD in Management Science from The Ohio State University. Dr. Von Glinow was the 1994–95 President of the Academy of Management, the world's largest association of academicians in management, and is a Fellow of the Academy and the Pan Pacific Business Association. She sits on 11 editorial review boards and numerous international panels. She teaches in executive programs in Latin America, Central America, the Caribbean region, Asia, and the U.S. She is Department Editor for the Journal of International Business Studies.

Dr. Von Glinow has authored over 70 journal articles and 11 books, including *Organizational Learning Capability* by Oxford University Press, 1999 (in Chinese and Spanish translations), which won a Gold Book Award from the Ministry of Economic Affairs in Taiwan in 2002. She heads an international consortium of researchers delving into "Best International Human Resource Management Practices," and her research in this arena won an award from the American Society for Competitiveness' Board of Trustees.

Mary Ann consults to a number of domestic and multinational enterprises, and serves as a mayoral appointee to the Shanghai Institute of Human Resources in China. Since 1989, she has been a consultant in General Electric's "Workout" and "Change Acceleration Program" including "Coaching to Management." Her clients have included Asia Development Bank, American Express, Burger King, Pillsbury, The Aetna, State of Florida, TRW, Rockwell International, Motorola, N.Y. Life, Amoco, Lucent, and Joe's Stone Crabs, to name a few.

[**brief**contents]

[contents]

>part 3
Team Processes

>part 4
Organizational Processes

12 Organizational Structure 232

13 Organizational Culture 252

14 Organizational Change 270

[preface]

Why We Wrote *Organizational Behavior: [essentials]*

Comprehensive 600- or 700-page textbooks are fine for many courses, but some organizational behavior classes need a resource that slices out the extended or secondary topics so students can drill down to what is really essential to focus on projects, cases, or other course work. That's why we wrote this compact edition, appropriately called *Organizational Behavior: [essentials]*.

Based on our popular comprehensive textbook, *OB: [essentials]* captures the knowledge and practices that we believe are truly important for people who require the foundations of organizational behavior. How did we know what to include and trim out? We surveyed nearly 100 OB instructors about their topic preferences and, along with our own judgment, pruned out material within each chapter that didn't satisfy the definition of "essential." We also found a few chapters that, after pruning, could be combined logically with other chapters.

Although this book is less than two-thirds the length of our comprehensive textbook, it doesn't skimp on classroom support. We don't think it makes sense to cut down the size of an OB book mainly by removing the cases, exercises, and self-assessments. In this era of active learning, critical thinking, and outcomes-based teaching, these supplements are becoming more "essential" than ever, so we kept them in.

We also have a strong commitment to the philosophy of linking theory with practice. By connecting concepts with real-life examples, students are more likely to remember the content and see how it relates to the real world. And, quite frankly, including these examples makes the content even more interesting, thereby motivating students to read on. Consistent with this theory–practice link, we have kept several real-life anecdotes throughout each chapter, including a few captioned photos that add a visual dimension to this connection. And speaking of visual dimension, *OB: [essentials]* fulfills another reasonable expectation in this visual world of ours: it's in full color!

Key Learning Features

Similar to our comprehensive book, *OB: [essentials]* applies four fundamental principles that made the longer version one of the best-selling OB books around the world: linking theory with reality, organizational behavior for everyone, contemporary theory foundation, and active learning support.

- **Linking theory with reality.** *OB: [essentials]* has a strong practical orientation, and this is most evident in the examples that link concepts to real-life incidents in the workplace. For example, you will read how Toyota USA improves team dynamics through an obeya (big room); how W. L. Gore & Associates remains nimble through an organizational structure that has no bosses; and how Indianapolis Power & Light CEO Ann Murtlow keeps her perceptions in focus by interacting with frontline staff.

- **Organizational behavior for everyone.** *OB: [essentials]* is written for everyone in organizations, not just "managers." While this book is certainly relevant to anyone in management, it takes the view that everyone who works in and around organizations needs to understand and make use of organizational behavior knowledge.

- **Contemporary theory foundation.** Scan through the references and you will see that *OB: [essentials]* is as contemporary conceptually as it is practically. This solid literature foundation doesn't translate into dense writing in the book. Rather, we take contemporary research findings and translate them into understandable ideas with clear connections to workplace events. Furthermore, this contemporary approach allows us to bring you leading-edge practices, such as employee engagement, appreciative inquiry, and corporate blogs.

- **Active learning support.** Accreditation associations are encouraging business schools to include more active learning, critical thinking, and outcomes-based teaching. *OB: [essentials]* supports this trend by offering an assortment of cases, exercises, self-assessments, and video cases to aid the learning process. While some books find it easier to cut corners (and pages) by removing these features, we consider them essential to the learning process.

[preface]

Supplement Packages

In addition to the content and learning activities provided within *OB: [essentials]*, we are proud to offer students and instructors further resources to improve the learning experience.

For Instructors

- **Instructor's Manual.** In keeping with the traditions of their comprehensive hardback IM, the IM for *OB: [essentials]* was written by Steve McShane and includes several resources and aids for every chapter that instructors have come to expect from McShane and Von Glinow.

- **Testbank and Computerized Testbank.** Written by Amit Shah, Frostburg State University, the Testbank contains a variety of true/false, multiple-choice, and essay questions, as well as "scenario-based" questions, which are application-based and use a situation described in a narrative, with three to five multiple-choice questions based on that situation. The Computerized Testbank can be found on the instructor's CD-ROM.

- **PowerPoint® slides.** Included is a complete set of well-designed slides for each chapter.

- **Additional cases on the online learning center.** These are useful for additional class discussion or assignments.

- **Video package.** Included is a complete set of videos specifically selected by the authors for their interest and relevance. (To the left is a video still from "Pike Place Fish Market," one of the videos for Part 2.)

- **Group and Video Resource Manual: An Instructor's Guide to an Active Classroom.** This manual was created to help instructors create a more lively and stimulating classroom environment. It contains interactive in-class group exercises to accompany Build Your Management Skills self-assessments found on the Online Learning Center, additional group exercises for each chapter, and comprehensive notes and discussion questions to accompany the Manager's Hot Seat DVD (more on this product under "For Students"). For each exercise, the manual includes learning objectives, unique PowerPoint slides used to implement the exercises, and comprehensive discussion questions to facilitate enhanced learning. Ask your local sales representative how you can get either of these products for use in your classroom.

- **Team Learning Assistant (TLA).** Businesses today demand a workforce with the skills to make an immediate contribution to their organizations. Key among these skills is the ability to work in teams. But teaming in the classroom is rife with challenges, namely team dynamics can sap productive learning time. The Team Learning Assistant is a Web-based set of tools that promotes effective classroom teaming for faculty and students alike. No matter what the course project may be, students in teams learn more when they are held accountable for their behavior and for meeting team learning goals. The TLA offers best practices and *a secure and reliable feedback mechanism* to help students to be more effective and productive and instructors manage precious classroom time. Ask your local sales representative for more information on the Team Learning Assistant.

For Students

The McGraw-Hill/Irwin Online Learning Center (OLC) is the one-stop hub for additional learning resources. Here are the main features that you will find at the student OLC site:

- **Self-scoring self-assessments from the text.** The three-dozen self-assessments summarized in this book are available at the OLC, which allows for rapid self-scoring results, complete with detailed feedback.

- **Additional self-assessments.** From the Build Your Management Skills collection, these assessments are for those students who want to delve deeper into self-awareness, and for professors who'd like to choose additional exercises, along with a matrix to identify the appropriate topic.

- **Additional cases.** Along with the cases provided in this textbook, the OLC offers many others that your instructor might assign for class or assignments.

- **Manager's Hot Seat DVD.** This is an interactive DVD that allows students to watch 15 real managers apply their years of experience in confronting certain management and organizational behavior issues. Students will assume the role of the manager as they watch the video and answer multiple-choice questions that pop up during the segment, forcing them to make decisions on the spot. Students learn from the manager's mistakes and successes; they will then do a report critiquing the manager's approach while defending their reasoning. Ask your local sales representative how you can get the Manager's Hot Seat DVD packaged with the text for your course.

[acknowledgments]

Organizational Behavior: [essentials] symbolizes the power of teamwork. More correctly, it symbolizes the power of a *virtual team* with Mary Ann Von Glinow in Miami, Steve McShane in Perth, Australia, and members of the editorial crew from Chicago, IL, to Valley Forge, PA, to Kingsport, TN.

Superb virtual teams require equally superb team members, and we were fortunate to have this in our favor. Sponsoring editor Ryan Blankenship led the way with enthusiasm and foresight. Christine Scheid (senior developmental editor) demonstrated amazingly cool coordination skills. The keen copy-editing skills of Steve Gomes made *OB: [essentials]* incredibly error-free. Mary Conzachi, our lead project manager, met the challenge of a tight production schedule with superb finesse. Kami Carter delivered a "cool" design with a textbook cover that captures the innovative and essential themes of this book. And we are convinced that Jennifer Blankenship, our photo editor, must have magical powers because she tracked down almost every photo we requested around the planet (from Dubai to New Zealand), even when the odds were incredibly slim. Thanks to you all. This has been an exceptional team effort!

Dozens of instructors took time from their busy lives to offer valuable feedback on which topics to include, where topics could be combined, and what other features should be included in this book. We are indebted to all of you for your guidance in this premiere edition of *OB: [essentials]*. Our reviewers included:

Richard Allen
University of Tennessee–Chattanooga

Barry Armandi
State University of New York at Old Westbury

Kathryn Aten
University of Oregon

Ruth Axelrod
George Washington University

Linda Barrenchea
University of Nevada–Reno

Thomas Begley
Northeastern University

David Bess
University of Hawaii–Manoa

Rex Bishop
College of Southern Maryland

Kevin Bosner
State University of New York at Geneseo

Holly Buttner
University of North Carolina–Greensboro

Suzanne Chan
Tulane University

Sharon Clinebell
University of Northern Colorado

C. Brad Cox
Midlands Technical College

Ray W. Coye
DePaul University

Suzanne Crampton
Grand Valley State University

Joe Daly
Appalachian State University

John N. Davis
Coastal Carolina University

Jeanne Dexter
Florida State University–Panama City

Elizabeth Evans
Concordia University Wisconsin

Erich Dierdorff
DePaul University

Renee Eaton
University of Portland

Sue Eisner
Ramapo College of New Jersey

Elizabeth Evans
Concordia University

Daniel Gallagher
University of Illinois–Springfield

Kay Gilley
North Carolina State and North Carolina Central Universities

David Glew
University of North Carolina–Wilmington

Leonard Glick
Northeastern University

Constance Golden
Lakeland Community College

Kris Gossett
Ivy Tech State College

Jennifer Greene
Maryville College

Selina A. Griswold
University of Toledo

Eileen Higgins
Frostburg State University

Kristin Holmberg-Wright
University of Wisconsin–Parkside

Fred Hughes
Faulkner University

Kendra L. Ingram
Texas A&M University

David Jalajas
Long Island University, C.W. Post Campus

Sheryl Joshua
University of North Carolina–Greensboro

Jordan Kaplan
Long Island University–Brooklyn

John Keiser
State University of New York at Brockport

Sara Kimmel
Belhaven College

Stephen Knouse
University of Louisiana–Lafayette

Jack Kondrasuk
University of Portland

Richard Lebsack
University of Nebraska–Kearney

Laurie Levesque
Suffolk University

Peter Lorenzi
Loyola College of Maryland

Paul Lyons
Frostburg State University

Jim Lyttle
Long Island University–Brooklyn

Elizabeth Malatestinic
Indiana University–Purdue University Indianapolis

Phil Masline
Sinclair Community College

Milton Mayfield
Texas A&M University International

James C. McElroy
Iowa State University

Grace B. McLaughlin
University of California, Irvine

Juhi Mehta
Ramapo College of New Jersey

Edward Miles
Georgia State University

Janice Miller
University of Wisconsin–Milwaukee

Leann Mischel
Susquehanna University

Karthik Namasivayam
Pennsylvania State University–University Park

Arlene J. Nicholas
Salve Regina University

Regina O'Neill
Suffolk University

Dennis Passovoy
University of Texas–Austin

Kenneth Price
University of Texas–Arlington

Douglas Pugh
University of North Carolina–Charlotte

Quenton Pulliam
Nashville State Technical Community College

David Radosevich
Montclair State University

Clint Relyea
Arkansas State University

Charles Riley
Tarrant County College–Northwest

Hannah Rothstein
Baruch College

Holly Schroth
University of California–Berkeley

Mark Seabright
Western Oregon University

Cynthia Simerly
Lakeland Community College

Dennis Slevin
University of Pittsburgh

Karen J. Smith
Columbia Southern University

William B. Snavely
Miami University

Janet Solomon
George Washington University

Christina Stamper
Western Michigan University

Walt Stevenson
Golden Gate University

Paul Swiercz
George Washington University

Karen Tarnoff
East Tennessee State University–Johnson City

Sean Valentine
University of Wyoming

Lynn Walsh
State University of New York at Old Westbury

John Watt
University of Central Arkansas

Jay D. White
University of Nebraska–Omaha

Kathleen Wilch
Bob Jones University

Lynn Wilson
St. Leo University–St. Leo

Marilyn Young
University of Texas–Tyler

Alberto Zanzi
Suffolk University

We would also like to extend our sincerest thanks to several instructors whose cases and exercises appear in *OB: [essentials]*:

Alicia Boisnier
State University of New York at Buffalo

Martha Burkle
Monterrey Institute of Technology

Russell Casey
Clayton State University

Sharon Card
(formerly at) Saskatchewan Institute of Applied Science & Technology

Jeewon Cho
State University of New York at Buffalo

Mary Gander
Winona State University

Cheryl Harvey
Wilfrid Laurier University

Lisa Ho
Prada Shoes, Singapore

Rosemary Maellaro
University of Dallas

Kim Morouney
Wilfrid Laurier University

Joseph C. Santora
Essex County College & TST, Inc.

James C. Sarros
Monash University

Trudy Somers
Pfeiffer University

Christine Stamper
Western Michigan University

Gloria Thompson
University of Phoenix

William Todorovic
Purdue University

Lisa V. Williams
State University of New York at Buffalo

Joana Young
Baylor University

In addition to thanking the reviewers, contributors, and editorial team, Steve McShane would to like to extend special thanks to his students for sharing their learning experiences and assisting with the development of this book. He is also very grateful to organizational behavior colleagues at the Graduate School of Management, University of Western Australia, including (in alphabetical order) Gail Broady, Renu Burr, Ron Cacioppe, Stacy Chappell, Nick Forster, Catherine Jordan, Sandra Kiffin-Petersen, Chris Perryer, David Plowman, Chris Taylor, and Barb Wood. Finally, Steve is forever indebted to his wife Donna McClement and to their wonderful daughters, Bryton and Madison.

Mary Ann Von Glinow would like to thank the contributors, reviewers and the superb editorial team at McGraw-Hill. She would also like to thank Steve McShane, the "energy" from down under, who never ceases to amaze her. In addition, she would like to thank the students and faculty who adopted her and McShane's *Organizational Behavior*, Third Edition. They're the inspiration behind the new *Essentials* book. A special thanks goes to the Center for International Business Education and Research (CIBER) at Florida International University: Tita Kourany, Sonia Verdu, Juan Fernandez, Elsa Villar, and Kranthi Atmakur are simply the best. Mary Ann would also like to acknowledge some essential people in her life: Bill, Karen, Kate, Janet, Peter M., Peter W., Alan, Danny, Jerry, Barb, Joanne, Mary, Linda, and JJ, all very special. Finally, she would like to thank John, Rhoda, Lauren, Lindsay, Christy, Molly, Zack, Emma, and Googun, her family.

>organizational behavior

[essentials]

>part I:

Introduction

[chapter 1]

Introduction to Organizational Behavior

> *Google has leveraged the power of organizational behavior to attract talented employees who want to make a difference in the Internet world.*

>**learning**objectives

After reading this chapter, you should be able to

- Define organizational behavior and give three reasons for studying this subject.

- Discuss the potential benefits and challenges of an increasingly diverse workforce.

- Identify two ways that employers attempt to increase workforce flexibility.

- Explain why values have gained importance in organizations.

- Define corporate social responsibility and argue for or against its application in organizations.

- Identify the five anchors on which organizational behavior is based.

- Diagram an organization from an open systems view.

- Define intellectual capital and describe the knowledge management process.

Friends were puzzled when Rob Pike decided in 2002 to leave his 20-year career at the prestigious Bell Labs in New Jersey to join a Web search start-up in California with a name that sounded like baby talk. The respected computer scientist's move had nothing to do with money. "I took a huge pay cut to come here," says Pike about his decision to join Google. "The reason is, it's an exciting place to work."

Google, the company behind the ubiquitous search engine, has a freewheeling, geeky culture that attracts Rob Pike and other creative thinkers who want to make a difference in the Internet world. Employees are expected to devote a quarter of their time on new ideas of their choosing, and to get those ideas into practice as quickly as possible. "Here, you can have an idea on Monday and have it on the Web site by the end of the week," says Pike, citing Google Maps and Gmail as examples of the company's rapid innovation.

Google's culture has clashed to some extent with its meteoric global growth to 3,000 employees in just six years. In response, the company's chaotic style has been reined in with a more stable structure around teams assigned to projects and functions. "It has scaled [up] pretty well," says Google CEO Eric Schmidt. Meanwhile, Google's unofficial ethical philosophy—Don't be evil—is the guideline by which it refuses to favor paid advertisers in its search results (unlike some other search engines) or to allow Web sites that speak against anyone.

Along with its culture and ethics, Google attracts talent with the Googleplex, the company's campuslike headquarters where high-density team clusters, playful décor, and a legendary cafeteria make everyone feel as though they haven't yet left school. Meetings even start a few minutes after the hour, same as class schedules in a lot of colleges. "That (campus) model is familiar to our programmers," explains Schmidt. "We know it's a very productive environment."

Google chief financial officer George Reyes sums up the main reason for the company's phenomenal success. "We want Google to be the very best place to work for the very best computer scientists in the world," says Reyes. "Google is truly a learning organization."[1]

Google has become a powerhouse on the Internet, but its real power comes from applying organizational behavior theories and practices. More than ever, organizations are relying on organizational behavior knowledge to remain competitive. For example, Google has an engaged workforce through exciting work opportunities, supportive team dynamics, and a "cool" workplace. It attracts talented people through its strong culture, ethical values, and an environment that supports creativity and a learning organization.

This book is about people working in organizations. Its main objective is to help you understand behavior in organizations and to work more effectively in organizational settings. While organizational behavior knowledge is often presented for "managers," this book takes a broader and more realistic view that organizational behavior ideas are relevant and useful to anyone who works in and around organizations. In this chapter, we introduce you to the field of organizational behavior, outline the main reasons you should know more about it, highlight some of the trends influencing the study of organizational behavior, describe the anchors supporting the study of organizations, and introduce the concept that organizations are knowledge and learning systems.

>The Field of Organizational Behavior

Organizational behavior (OB) is the study of what people think, feel, and do in and around organizations. OB researchers systematically study individual, team, and organizational-level characteristics that influence behavior within work settings. By saying that organizational behavior is a field of study, we mean that OB experts have been accumulating a distinct knowledge about behavior within organizations—a knowledge base that is the foundation of this book.

organizational behavior (OB)
The study of what people think, feel, and do in and around organizations.

[3]

organizations
Groups of people who work interdependently toward some purpose.

OB emerged as a distinct field around the 1940s, although people have been studying organizations for centuries.[2] **Organizations** are groups of people who work interdependently toward some purpose.[3] Organizations are not buildings or other physical structures. Rather, they consist of people who interact with each other to achieve a set of goals. Employees have structured patterns of interaction, meaning that they expect each other to complete certain tasks in a coordinated way—in an *organized* way. Organizations also have a collective sense of purpose, whether it's producing oil or creating the fastest Internet search engine. "A company is one of humanity's most amazing inventions," says Steven Jobs, CEO of Apple Computer and Pixar Animation Studios. "It's totally abstract. Sure, you have to build something with bricks and mortar to put the people in, but basically a company is this abstract construct we've invented, and it's incredibly powerful."[4]

Why Study Organizational Behavior?

Unlike accounting, marketing, or most other fields of business, organizational behavior does not have a clearly-defined career path, yet this topic is identified as very important among people who have worked in organizations for a few years. The reason for this priority is that to apply marketing, accounting, and other technical knowledge, you need to understand, predict, and influence behavior (both our own and that of others) in organizational settings (see Exhibit 1.1).

Each one of us has an inherent need to understand and predict the world in which we live. Since much of our time is spent working in or around organizations, OB theories are particularly helpful in satisfying this innate drive to make sense of the workplace. OB theories also give you the opportunity to question and rebuild your personal mental models that have developed through observation and experience. Most of us also need to influence people in organizations, so OB concepts play an important role in performing your job and working more effectively with others. This practical side of organizational behavior is a critical feature of the best OB theories.[5]

Along with helping you as an individual, organizational behavior knowledge is important for the organization's financial health. According to one estimate, firms that apply performance-based rewards, employee communication, work/life balance, and other OB

[**Exhibit 1.1**] Reasons for Studying Organizational Behavior

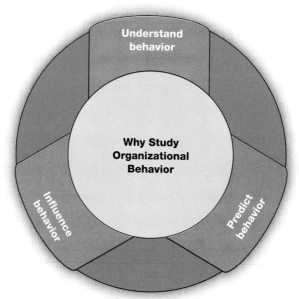

practices have three times the level of financial success as companies where these practices are absent. Another study concluded that companies that earn "the best place to work" awards have significantly higher financial and long-term stock market performance. Essentially, these firms leverage the power of OB practices, which translate into more favorable employee attitudes, decisions, and performance.[6]

Organizational Behavior Is for Everyone

This book takes the view that organizational behavior knowledge is for everyone—not just managers. We all need to understand organizational behavior and to master the practices that influence organizational events. That's why you won't find very much emphasis in this book on "management." Yes, organizations will continue to have managers, but their roles have changed. More important, the rest of us are now expected to manage ourselves, particularly as companies remove layers of management and delegate more responsibilities. In other words, everyone is a manager.

>Organizational Behavior Trends

There has never been a better time to learn about organizational behavior. The pace of change is accelerating, and most of the transformation is occurring in the workplace. Let's take a brief tour through five trends in the workplace: globalization, the changing workforce, evolving employment relationships, virtual work, and workplace values and ethics.

Globalization

Google didn't exist a decade ago, yet today it is one of the best-known names on the Internet around the planet. The Mountain View, California, company offers Web search services in more than 100 languages, and over half of its search engine queries come from outside the United States. One-third of Google's revenue is from other countries, and it is already facing sensitive issues in France, China,

In the late 1980s, 95 percent of Whirlpool's revenue and most of its manufacturing occurred in the United States. Yet executives at the Benton Harbor, Michigan company knew from excursions to other countries that globalization would soon transform the industry. "We came to the conclusion that the industry would become a global one and that someone had to shape it," recalls David Whitwam, Whirlpool's recently retired CEO. Today, Whirlpool is the global leader in the appliance industry, with microwave ovens engineered in Sweden and assembled in China, refrigerators made in Brazil for European consumers, top-loading washers made in Ohio, and front-loading washers made in Germany (shown in photo). This journey toward globalization has required tremendous organizational change. "We need a diverse workforce with diverse leadership," says Whitwam, as well as "strong regional leadership that lives in the culture." Whitwam also believes a global company requires broad-based involvement and an organizational structure that encourages the flow of knowledge.[7]

and other countries that want to censor certain search results. So far, Google has not out-sourced work to contractors in low-wage countries, but it has opened its own research centers in India and Japan.[8]

Google's growth is a rich example of the globalization of business over the past few decades. **Globalization** refers to economic, social, and cultural connectivity with people in other parts of the world. Google and other organizations globalize when they actively participate in other countries and cultures. While businesses have traded goods across borders for centuries, the degree of globalization today is unprecedented because information technology and transportation systems allow a much more intense level of connectivity and interdependence around the planet.[9]

Globalization offers numerous benefits to organizations in terms of larger markets, lower costs, and greater access to knowledge and innovation. At the same time, there is considerable debate about whether globalization benefits developing nations, and whether it is primarily responsible for increasing work intensification, as well as reducing job security and work/life balance in developed countries.[10] Recognizing that globalization is already a reality, OB researchers are examining how leadership, influence, conflict, and other OB topics vary across cultures.

> **globalization**
> Economic, social, and cultural connectivity (and interdependence) with people in other parts of the world.

The Changing Workforce

Walk into the offices of Verizon Communications around the United States and you can quickly see that the communications service giant reflects the communities it serves. Minorities make up 30 percent of Verizon's 200,000 workforce and 18 percent of top management positions. Women represent 43 percent of its workforce and 32 percent of top management. Verizon's inclusive culture has won awards from numerous organizations representing Hispanic, African American, gay/lesbian, people with disabilities, and other groups.[11]

Verizon is a model employer and a striking reflection of the increasing diversity of people living in the United States. Workforce diversity takes many forms, but three of the most prominent are race/ethnicity, gender, and generation (age/work experience).

- *Racial/ethnic diversity.* People with nonwhite or Hispanic origin represent one-third of the American population, and this is projected to increase substantially over the next few decades. The Hispanic population recently replaced African Americans as the second-largest ethnic group. Within the next 50 years, one in four Americans will be Hispanic, 14 percent will be African American, and 8 percent will be Asian American.[12]

- *Women in the workforce.* Women now account for nearly half of the paid workforce in the United States, more than double the participation rate a few decades ago. Gender-based shifts continue to occur within many occupations. For example, the percentage of women enrolled in medical schools has jumped from 9 percent in 1970 to almost 50 percent today.[13]

- *Generational diversity.* A less visible but equally powerful form of diversity is occurring among generational cohorts in the workplace.[14] *Baby boomers*—people born between 1946 and 1964—seem to expect and desire more job security and are more intent on improving their economic and social status. In contrast, *Generation X* employees—those born between 1965 and 1979—expect less job security and are motivated more by workplace flexibility, the opportunity to learn (particularly new technology), and working in an egalitarian and "fun" organization. Meanwhile, some observers suggest that *Generation Y* employees (those born after 1979) are noticeably self-confident, optimistic, adept at multitasking, and more independent than even Gen X co-workers. These statements certainly don't apply to everyone in each cohort, but they do reflect the fact that different generations have different values and expectations.

Diversity offers both direct and indirect benefits to organizations.[15] Directly, a workforce that parallels the characteristics of customers is more likely to understand customer needs. For example, many Vietnamese customers insisted that Southern California Gas Co. field staff remove their steel-toed work boots when entering the customer's home, yet doing so would violate safety regulations. Some of the gas company's Vietnamese employees found a solution; customers would be satisfied if employees wore paper booties over the boots.[16]

Indirectly, companies that support an inclusive workplace potentially increase the pool of talented applicants and reduce employee turnover. A diverse workforce can also improve decision making and team performance on complex tasks. At the same time, workforce diversity presents new challenges, such as conflict, miscommunication, and discrimination in organizations and society.[17] We will explore these diversity issues more closely under various topics throughout this book, such as stereotyping, team dynamics, and conflict management.

Evolving Employment Relationships

Globalization and the changing workforce are two of the forces causing an evolution in employment relationships. Employers today demand more workforce flexibility to remain competitive in the global marketplace, so most have shifted toward a model of **employability**, in which employees are expected to manage their own careers by anticipating future organizational needs and developing new competencies that match those needs. "It's a good idea to stay current with what's out there and take personal responsibility for our own employability," says Rich Hartnett, global staffing director at aerospace manufacturer Boeing."[18]

Companies have also increased workforce flexibility through greater use of **contingent work**, which includes any job without an explicit or implicit contract for long-term employment, or one in which the minimum hours of work can vary in a nonsystematic way. More than 15 percent of the U.S. workforce is employed in some sort of contingent work arrangement, such as temporary or seasonal employees, freelance contractors (sometimes called *free agents*), and temporary staffing agency workers.[19] Contingent work creates a variety of organizational behavior issues related to organizational commitment, feelings of inequity, and organization structure.[20]

Adapting to Emerging Workforce Expectations

While employers are demanding more workforce flexibility, employees are demanding, and receiving, more changes in the workplace to meet their evolving employment expectations. Two decades ago, for example, **work/life balance**—minimizing conflict between work and nonwork demands—was considered a luxury that must be earned through hard work. Today, it is a "must-have" condition in the employment relationship, particularly among Gen X and Gen Y employees. In fact, surveys in several countries consistently report that work/life balance is one of the most important indicators of career success among young employees.[21]

Companies are also adjusting to emerging workforce expectations of a more egalitarian workplace by reducing hierarchy and replacing command-and-control management with facilitating and teacher-oriented leaders. Younger employees tend to view the workplace as a community where they spend a large part of their lives (even with work/life balance), so many companies are accommodating these expectations for more social fulfillment and fun. Google, described at the beginning of this chapter, is a case in point. The company's "Googleplex" headquarters is a campus oasis where, in addition to working, employees play sports, enjoy gourmet meals, and watch first-run movies. Some staff even tried to make headquarters their home, until management advised everyone that residency was against fire regulations.

employability
An employment relationship in which people are expected to continuously develop their skills to remain employed.

contingent work
Any job in which the individual does not have an explicit or implicit contract for long-term employment, or one in which the minimum hours of work can vary in a nonsystematic way.

work/life balance
The minimization of conflict between work and nonwork demands.

Virtual Work

Up to a point, Karen Dunn Kelley follows a familiar routine as a mother and busy executive. She puts her school-aged children on the bus, feeds breakfast to her 19-month-old before handing him off to a nanny, and then heads off to the office. But Kelley's daily commute is different from most; it's just a short walk from her house to the office over her garage. Furthermore, Kelley is an executive with Houston-based AIM Management Group, yet the home office where she oversees 40 staff and US$75 billion in assets is located in Pittsburgh.[22] Karen Dunn Kelley's daily routine is an example of **virtual work**, whereby employees use information technology to perform their jobs away from the traditional physical workplace. Kelly's virtual work, called *teleworking* or *telecommuting,* involves working at home rather than commuting to the office, whereas other employees are connected to the office while on the road or at clients' offices. Nearly 20 percent of Americans work at home at least one day each month.[23]

virtual work
Employees perform work away from the traditional physical workplace using information technology.

Virtual work influences many aspects of organizational behavior. For instance, studies indicate that telecommuting potentially reduces employee stress, increases productivity and job satisfaction, and makes employees feel more empowered. At the same time, unless they regularly visit the office, some virtual workers suffer from loneliness and lack of recognition. Ironically, virtual workers also suffer from work/family stress if they lack sufficient space and resources for a home office.[24]

Virtual Teams

virtual teams
Cross-functional teams that operate across space, time, and organizational boundaries with members who communicate mainly through information technologies.

Another variation of virtual work occurs in **virtual teams**—cross-functional groups that operate across space, time, and organizational boundaries with members who communicate mainly through information technology.[25] Virtual teams exist when some members telework, but also when team members are located on company premises at different sites around the country or world. Teams have varying degrees of virtualness, depending on how often and how many team members interact face-to-face or at a distance. There is currently a flurry of research activity studying the types of work best suited to virtual teams and the conditions that facilitate and hinder their effectiveness, as we will discover later in this book.

Workplace Values and Ethics

Search through most annual reports and you'll soon discover that corporate leaders view values as the *sine qua non* of organizational excellence. For example, as described in the opening story to this chapter, Google places paramount importance on "Don't be evil." **Values** represent stable, long-lasting beliefs about what is important in a variety of situations that guide our decisions and actions. They are evaluative standards that help define what is right or wrong, or good or bad, in the world. Values dictate our priorities, our preferences, and our desires. They influence our motivation and decisions.[26] Although leaders refer to the core values of their companies, values really exist only within individuals, which we call *personal values.* However, groups of people might hold the same or similar values, so we tend to ascribe these *shared values* to the team, department, organization, profession, or entire society.

values
Stable, long-lasting beliefs about what is important in a variety of situations.

Importance of Values in the Workplace

Values have been studied in organizational behavior for a long time, but they have only recently become a popular topic in corporate boardrooms. One reason is that as today's workforce rejects "command-and-control" supervision, leaders are turning to values as a more satisfactory approach to keeping employees' decisions and actions aligned with corporate goals.[27] A second reason is that globalization has raised our awareness of and sensitivity to cultural differences in values and beliefs. This creates an increasing challenge to identify a set of core values acceptable to employees around the world.

The third reason why values have gained prominence is that organizations are under increasing pressure to engage in ethical practices and corporate social responsibility. **Ethics** refers to the study of moral principles or values that determine whether actions are right or wrong and outcomes are good or bad. We rely on our ethical values to determine "the right thing to do." Ethical behavior is driven by our values. Unfortunately, a lot of people give executives low grades on their ethics report cards these days, so ethics and values will continue to be an important topic in OB teaching.[28]

ethics
The study of moral principles or values that determine whether actions are right or wrong and outcomes are good or bad.

Corporate Social Responsibility

More than 30 years ago, economist Milton Friedman pronounced that "there is one and only one social responsibility of business—to use its resources and engage in activities designed to increase its profits." Friedman is a respected scholar, but this argument was not one of his more popular—or accurate—statements. Today, any business that follows Friedman's advice will face considerable trouble. Several studies have reported that employees increasingly want to work for ethical organizations whose decisions benefit the wider community, not just shareholders and employees. Many corporate leaders also expect their business partners to serve this wider constituency. In other words, the public expects organizations to engage in **corporate social responsibility.**[29]

corporate social responsibility (CSR)
An organization's moral obligation toward its stakeholders.

The senior management team at the Department of Economic Development (DED) in the Emirate of Dubai recently devoted several months to identifying the agency's core values: accountability, teamwork, and continuous improvement. Each of these three values is anchored with specific behavior descriptions to ensure that employees and other stakeholders understand their meaning. DED also organized a series of workshops (shown in photo) in which employees participated in a "Values Mystery" exercise to help them recognize values-consistent behaviors. To develop a values-based organization, DED will also use these three values to evaluate employee performance, assess employee competencies, and identify management potential.[30]

stakeholders
Shareholders,
customers, suppliers,
governments, and any
other groups with a
vested interest in the
organization.

Corporate social responsibility (CSR) refers to an organization's moral obligation toward all of its **stakeholders**. Stakeholders are the shareholders, customers, suppliers, governments, and any other groups with a vested interest in the organization.[31] As part of corporate social responsibility, many companies have adopted the *triple bottom line* philosophy. This means that they try to support or "earn positive returns" in the economic, social, and environmental spheres of sustainability. Firms that adopt the triple bottom line aim to survive and be profitable in the marketplace (economic), but they also intend to maintain or improve conditions for society (social) as well as the physical environment.[32]

>The Five Anchors of Organizational Behavior

Globalization, the changing workforce, evolving employment relationships, virtual work, and workplace values and ethics are just a few of the trends that we will explore in this textbook. To understand these and other topics, the field of organizational behavior relies on a set of basic conceptual anchors that guide our thinking about organizations and how to study them (see Exhibit 1.2). Let's look at each of these five beliefs that anchor the study of organizational behavior.

The Multidisciplinary Anchor

Organizational behavior is anchored around the idea that the field should freely borrow knowledge from other disciplines, not just from its own isolated research base. For instance, psychological research has aided our understanding of individual and interpersonal behavior. Sociologists have contributed to our knowledge of team dynamics, organizational socialization, organizational power, and other aspects of the social system. OB knowledge has also benefited from knowledge in emerging fields such as communications, marketing, and information systems. Some OB experts have recently argued that the field suffers from a "trade deficit"— importing far more knowledge from other disciplines than

[**Exhibit 1.2**] Five Conceptual Anchors of Organizational Behavior

it is exporting to other disciplines. While this is a possible concern, organizational behavior has thrived through its diversity of knowledge from other fields.[33]

The Systematic Research Anchor

This anchor states that OB research should rely on the scientific method and related standards of systematic research to advance knowledge in this field. The **scientific method** involves forming research questions, systematically collecting data, and testing hypotheses against those data. This approach relies mainly on quantitative data (numeric information) and statistical procedures to test hypotheses. The idea behind the scientific method is to minimize personal biases and distortions about organizational events. Recently, OB knowledge has also developed through systematic qualitative research methods, such as open-ended interviews and observation of workplace behavior.

scientific method
A set of principles and procedures that help researchers to systematically understand previously unexplained events and conditions.

The Contingency Anchor

People and their work environments are complex, and the field of organizational behavior recognizes this by advocating another important anchor, called the **contingency approach.** This anchor states that a particular action may have different consequences in different situations. In other words, no single solution is best in all circumstances.[34] Of course, it would be so much simpler if we could rely on "one best way" theories, in which a particular concept or practice has the same results in every situation. OB experts do search for simpler theories, but they also remain skeptical about "surefire" recommendations; an exception is somewhere around the corner. Thus, when faced with a particular problem or opportunity, we need to understand and diagnose the situation and select the strategy most appropriate *under those conditions.*[35]

contingency approach
The idea that a particular action may have different consequences in different situations.

The Multiple Levels of Analysis Anchor

This textbook divides organizational behavior topics into three levels of analysis: individual, team, and organization. The individual level includes the characteristics and behaviors of employees as well as the thought processes that are attributed to them, such as motivation, perceptions, personalities, attitudes, and values. The team level of analysis looks at the way people interact. This includes team dynamics, communication, power, influence, conflict, and leadership. The organizational level looks at how people structure their working relationships and on how organizations interact with their environments.

Although an OB topic is typically pegged into one level of analysis, it usually relates to multiple levels.[36] For instance, communication is located in this book as a team (interpersonal) process, but we also recognize that it includes individual and organizational processes. Therefore, you should try to think about each OB topic at the individual, team, and organizational levels, not just at one of these levels.

The Open Systems Anchor

The final anchor is that OB experts view organizations as **open systems**. By open systems, we mean that companies take their sustenance from the environment and, in turn, affect that environment through their output. From this perspective, organizations are viewed as living organisms whose survival and success depend on how well employees sense environmental changes and alter their patterns of behavior to fit those emerging conditions.[37] In contrast, a closed system has all the resources needed to survive without dependence on the external environment. Organizations are never completely closed systems, but monopolies

open systems
Organizations that take their sustenance from the environment and, in turn, affect that environment through their output.

[Exhibit 1.3] Open Systems View of Organizations

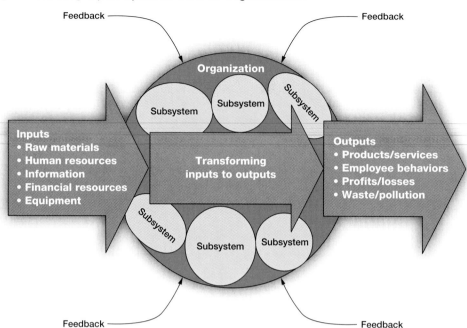

come close because they operate in very stable environments and can ignore stakeholders for a fairly long time without adverse consequences.

As Exhibit 1.3 illustrates, organizations acquire resources from the external environment, including raw materials, employees, financial resources, information, and equipment. Inside the organization are numerous subsystems, such as processes (communication and reward systems), task activities (production, marketing), and social dynamics (informal groups, power dynamics). With the aid of technology (such as equipment, work methods, and information), these subsystems transform inputs into various outputs. Subsystems tend to become more complex as organizations grow, which creates more challenges and potential problems as subsystems need to coordinate with each other in the process of transforming inputs to outputs.

All organizations produce outputs. Some outputs (e.g., products and services) may be valued by the external environment, whereas other outputs (e.g., employee layoffs, pollution) have adverse effects. The organization receives feedback from the external environment regarding the value of its outputs and the availability of future inputs. This process is cyclical and, ideally, self-sustaining, so that the organization may continue to survive and prosper.

As open systems, successful organizations monitor their environments and have the capacity to change their outputs and transformational processes in order to maintain a close fit with the evolving external conditions.[38] Monitoring the environment involves paying attention to stakeholder needs and expectations, because they influence the firm's access to inputs and ability to discharge outputs. Some stakeholders are more important than others, and the relative importance of each stakeholder group fluctuates with other environmental changes. For instance, accounting firms have recently given much more attention to government and professional accounting bodies as professional auditors have come under increasing criticism and scrutiny.

The open systems anchor is an important way of viewing organizations. However, it has traditionally focused on physical resources that enter the organization and are processed into physical goods (outputs). This was representative of the industrial economy but not of the "new economy," where the most valued input is knowledge.

<Knowledge Management

In the opening story to this chapter, Google chief financial officer George Reyes said that his company "is truly a learning organization." Reyes's statement doesn't just refer to the fact that Google is an open system; it also emphasizes that Google is effective as an open system through employees and systems that support **knowledge management**. Knowledge management is any structured activity that improves an organization's capacity to acquire, share, and use knowledge in ways that improve its survival and success.[39]

For instance, Google is a learning organization—it actively applies knowledge management—because it seeks out knowledgeable people (such as Rob Pike), maintains an internal environment (the Googleplex) that supports knowledge sharing and creativity, and encourages employees to quickly transform that knowledge into valuable services, such as Google's search engine, Gmail, Google News, and Google Translate. Even after services have been created, the organization learns from feedback about how the public makes use of those services.

The stock of knowledge that resides in an organization is called its **intellectual capital,** which is the sum of everything that an organization knows that gives it competitive advantage—including its human capital, structural capital, and relationship capital.[40]

- *Human capital.* This is the knowledge that employees possess and generate, including their skills, experience, and creativity.

- *Structural capital.* This is the knowledge captured and retained in an organization's systems and structures. It is the knowledge that remains after all the human capital has gone home.

- *Relationship capital.* This is the value derived from an organization's relationships with customers, suppliers, and other external stakeholders who provide added value for the organization. For example, this includes customer loyalty as well as mutual trust between the organization and its suppliers.

knowledge management
Any structured activity that improves an organization's capacity to acquire, share, and use knowledge in ways that improve its survival and success.

intellectual capital
The sum of an organization's human capital, structural capital, and relationship capital.

Knowledge Management Processes

To maintain a valuable *stock* of knowledge (intellectual capital), organizations depend on their capacity to acquire, share, and use knowledge more effectively. This process is often called **organizational learning** because companies must continuously learn about their various environments in order to survive and succeed through adaptation.[41] The "capacity" to acquire, share, and use knowledge means that companies have established systems, structures, and organizational values that support the knowledge management process.

- *Knowledge acquisition.* This includes the process of extracting information and ideas from its environment as well as through insight. One of the fastest and most powerful ways to acquire knowledge is by hiring individuals or acquiring entire companies. Knowledge also enters the organization when employees learn from external sources, such as discovering new resources from suppliers or becoming aware of new trends from clients. A third knowledge acquisition strategy is through experimentation. Companies receive knowledge through insight as a result of research and other creative processes.[42]

- *Knowledge sharing.* This process refers to how well knowledge is distributed throughout the organization to those who would benefit from that knowledge. Computer intranets are often marketed as complete "knowledge management" systems. While somewhat useful in cataloging where knowledge is located, these electronic storage systems can be expensive to maintain; they also overlook the fact

organizational learning
The knowledge management process in which organizations acquire, share, and use knowledge to succeed.

that a lot of knowledge is difficult to document.[43] Thus, any technological solution needs to be supplemented by giving employees more opportunities for informal online or face-to-face interaction.

- *Knowledge use.* Acquiring and sharing knowledge are wasted exercises unless knowledge is effectively put to use. To do this, employees must realize that the knowledge is available and that they have enough freedom to apply it. This requires a culture that supports learning and change.

Organizational Memory

organizational memory
The storage and preservation of intellectual capital.

Intellectual capital can be lost as quickly as it is acquired.[44] Corporate leaders need to recognize that they are the keepers of an **organizational memory.** This unusual metaphor refers to the storage and preservation of intellectual capital. It includes information that employees possess as well as knowledge embedded in the organization's systems and structures. It includes documents, objects, and anything else that provides meaningful information about how the organization should operate.

How do organizations retain intellectual capital? One way is by keeping good employees. As we noted earlier in this chapter, progressive companies are adapting their employment practices to become more compatible with emerging workforce expectations, including work/life balance, egalitarian hierarchy, and a workspace that generates more fun. A second organizational memory strategy is to systematically transfer knowledge before employees leave. This occurs when new recruits apprentice with skilled employees, thereby acquiring knowledge that is not documented. A third strategy is to transfer knowledge into structural capital. This includes bringing out hidden knowledge, organizing it, and putting it in a form that can be available to others.

>The Journey Begins

This chapter gives you some background about the field of organizational behavior. But it's only the beginning of our journey. Throughout this book, we will challenge you to learn new ways of thinking about how people work in and around organizations. We begin this process in Chapter 2 by presenting a basic model of individual behavior, then introducing

A few years ago, Evercare (formerly Helmac) decided to move its headquarters and manufacturing from Flint, Michigan, to Georgia. The move nearly killed the manufacturer of Lint Pic-up products because none of Evercare's production employees wanted to leave Flint. So when the company's executives arrived in Georgia to set up production, they struggled to rebuild the company's manufacturing and distribution systems from scratch. "Nothing was documented," recalls manufacturing vice president John Moore, shown here with vice president of distribution Barbara Tomaszewski. "All of the knowledge, all of the practices were built in people's heads." The good news was that the rebuilt company seems stronger because employees did not learn some of the past practices that didn't work.[45]

over the next five chapters various stable and mercurial characteristics of individuals that relate to elements of the individual behavior model. Next, this book moves to the team level of analysis. We examine a model of team effectiveness, communication, power and influence, conflict management, and leadership. Finally, we shift our focus to the organizational level of analysis, where the topics of organizational structure, organizational culture, and organizational change are examined in detail.

>chapter summary

Organizational behavior is the study of what people think, feel, and do in and around organizations. Organizations are groups of people who work interdependently toward some purpose. OB concepts help us to predict and understand organizational events, adopt more accurate theories of reality, and influence organizational events. This field of knowledge also improves the organization's financial health.

There are several trends in organizational behavior, including globalization, the changing workforce, evolving employment relationships, virtual work, and workplace values and ethics.

Organizational behavior scholars rely on five anchors to understand and study organizations: OB knowledge should be multidisciplinary; it should be based on systematic research; organizational events usually have contingencies; organizational behavior can be viewed from three levels of analysis (individual, team, and organization); and organizations are open systems.

The open systems anchor suggests that organizations acquire resources from the environment, transform them through technology, and return outputs to the environment. The external environment consists of the natural and social conditions outside the organization.

Knowledge management is any structured activity that improves an organization's capacity to acquire, share, and use knowledge in ways that improve its survival and success. Intellectual capital is knowledge that resides in an organization, including its human capital, structural capital, and relationship capital. Organizations acquire knowledge through hiring, individual learning, and experimentation. Knowledge sharing occurs through various forms of communication, ranging from computer intranets to informal face-to-face gatherings. Knowledge use occurs when employees realize that the knowledge is available and that they have enough freedom to apply it. Organizational memory refers to the storage and preservation of intellectual capital.

>key.terms

contingency approach 11

contingent work 7

corporate social responsibility (CSR) 9

employability 7

ethics 9

globalization 6

intellectual capital 13

knowledge management 13

open systems 11

organizational behavior (OB) 3

organizational learning 13

organizational memory 14

organizations 4

scientific method 11

stakeholders 10

values 9

virtual work 8

virtual teams 9

work/life balance 7

>critical thinking questions

1. A friend suggests that organizational behavior courses are useful only to people who will enter management careers. Discuss the accuracy of your friend's statement.

2. Look through the list of chapters in this textbook and discuss how globalization could influence each organizational behavior topic.

3. Corporate social responsibility is one of the hottest issues in corporate boardrooms these days, partly because it is becoming increasingly important to employees and other stakeholders. In your opinion, why have stakeholders given CSR more attention recently? Does abiding by CSR standards potentially cause companies to have conflicting objectives with some stakeholders in some situations?

4. "Organizational theories should follow the contingency approach." Comment on the accuracy of this statement.

5. A number of years ago, employees of the water distribution department of a major city were put into teams and encouraged to find ways to improve efficiency. The teams boldly crossed departmental boundaries and areas of management discretion in search of problems. Employees working in other parts of the city began to complain about these intrusions. Furthermore, when some team ideas were implemented, the city managers discovered that a dollar saved in the water distribution unit may have cost the organization two dollars in higher costs elsewhere. Use the open systems anchor to explain what happened here.

6. After hearing a seminar on knowledge management, a mining company executive argues that this perspective ignores the fact that mining companies could not rely on knowledge alone to stay in business. They also need physical capital (such as digging and ore-processing equipment) and land (where the minerals are located). In fact, these two may be more important than what employees carry around in their heads. Discuss the merits of the mining executive's comments.

7. At a recent seminar on information technology, you heard a consultant say that more than 30 percent of U.S. companies use software to manage documents and exchange information, whereas firms in Europe are just beginning to adopt this technology. Based on this, the consultant concluded that "knowledge management in Europe is at its beginning stages." In other words, few firms in Europe practice knowledge management. Comment on this consultant's statement.

8. BusNews Corp. is the leading stock market and business news service. Over the past two years, BusNews has experienced increased competition from other news providers. These competitors have brought in Internet and other emerging computer technologies to link customers with information more quickly. There is little knowledge within BusNews about how to use these computer technologies. Based on the knowledge acquisition processes for knowledge management, explain how BusNews might gain the intellectual capital necessary to become more competitive in this respect.

>case study:skillbuilder1.1

Ancol Corp.

Paul Sims was delighted when Ancol Corp. offered him the job of manager at its Lexington, Kentucky, plant. Sims was happy enough managing a small metal stamping plant with another company, but the invitation to apply to the plant manager job at one of the leading metal fabrication companies was irresistible. Although the Lexington plant was the smallest of Ancol's 15 operations, the plant manager position was a valuable first step in a promising career.

One of Sims's first observations at Ancol's Lexington plant was that relations between employees and management were strained. Taking a page from a recent executive seminar that he attended on building trust in the workplace, Sims ordered the removal of all time clocks from the plant. Instead, the plant would assume that employees had put in their full shift. This symbolic gesture, he believed, would establish a new level of credibility and strengthen relations between management and employees at the site.

Initially, the 250 production employees at the Lexington plant appreciated their new freedom. They felt respected and saw this gesture as a sign of positive change from the new plant manager. Two months later, however, problems started to appear. A few people began showing up late, leaving early, or taking extended lunch breaks. Although this represented only about 5 percent of the employees, others found the situation unfair. Moreover, the increased absenteeism levels were beginning to have a noticeable effect on plant productivity. The problem had to be managed.

Sims asked supervisors to observe and record when the employees came or went and to discuss attendance problems with those abusing their privileges. But the supervisors had no previous experience with keeping attendance, and many lacked the necessary interpersonal skills to discuss the matter with subordinates. Employees resented the reprimands, so relations with supervisors deteriorated. The additional responsibility of keeping track of attendance also made it difficult for supervisors to complete their other responsibilities. After just a few months, Ancol found it necessary to add another supervisor position and reduce the number of employees assigned to each supervisor.

But the problems did not end there. Without time clocks, the payroll department could not deduct pay for the amount of time that employees were late. Instead, a letter of reprimand was placed in the employee's personnel file. However, this required yet more time and additional skills from the supervisors. Employees did not want these letters to become a permanent record, so they filed grievances with their labor union. The number of grievances doubled over six months, which required even more time for both union officials and supervisors to handle these disputes.

Nine months after removing the time clocks, Paul Sims met with union officials, who agreed that it would be better to put the time clocks back in. Employee-management relations had deteriorated below the level when Sims had

started. Supervisors were overworked. Productivity had dropped due to poorer attendance records and increased administrative workloads.

A couple of months after the time clocks were put back in place, Sims attended an operations meeting at Ancol's headquarters in Cincinnati. During lunch, Sims described the time clock incident to Liam Jackson, Ancol's plant manager in Portland, Oregon. Jackson looked surprised, then chuckled. He explained that the previous manager at his plant had done something like that with similar consequences six or seven years ago. The manager had left some time ago, but Jackson heard about the earlier time clock incident from a supervisor during his retirement party two months ago. "I guess it's not quite like lightning striking the same place twice," said Sims to Jackson. "But it sure feels like it."

Discussion Questions

1. Use the open systems model to explain what happened when Ancol removed the time clocks.

2. What changes should occur to minimize the likelihood of these problems in the future?

Source: © Copyright 2000 Steven L. McShane. This case is based on actual events, but names and some facts have been changed to provide a fuller case discussion.

>team.exercise:skillbuilder1.2

Human Checkers

Purpose This exercise is designed to help students understand the importance and application of organizational behavior concepts.

Materials None, but the instructor has more information about the team's task.

Instructions

- *Step 1.* Form teams with six students. If possible, each team should have a private location where team members can plan and practice the required task without being observed or heard by other teams.

- *Step 2.* All teams will receive special instructions in class about the team's assigned task. All teams have the same task and will have the same amount of time to plan and practice the task. At the end of this planning and practice, each team will be timed while completing the task in class. The team that completes the task in the least time wins.

- *Step 3.* No special materials are required or allowed for this exercise. Although the task is not described here,

students should learn the following rules for planning and implementing the task:

Rule 1: You cannot use any written form of communication or any props to assist in the planning or implementation of this task.

Rule 2: You may speak to other students in your team at any time during the planning and implementation of this task.

Rule 3: When performing the task, you must move only in the direction of your assigned destination. In other words, you can only move forward, not backward.

Rule 4: When performing the task, you can move forward to the next space, but only if it is vacant (see Exhibit 1).

Rule 5: When performing the task, you can move forward two spaces, if that space is vacant. In other words, you can move around a student who is one space in front of you to the next space if that space is vacant (see Exhibit 2).

Exhibit 1   **Exhibit 2**

          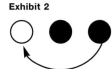

- *Step 4:* When all teams have completed their task, the class will discuss the implications of this exercise for organizational behavior.

Discussion Questions

1. Identify organizational behavior concepts that the team applied to complete this task.

2. What personal theories of people and work teams were applied to complete this task?

3. What organizational behavior problems occurred and what actions were (or should have been) taken to solve them?

>**web**.exercise:**skill**builder**1.3**

Diagnosing Organizational Stakeholders

Purpose   This exercise is designed to help you understand how stakeholders influence organizations as part of the open systems anchor.

Materials   Students need to select a company and, prior to class, retrieve and analyze publicly available information over the past year or two about that company. This may include annual reports, which are usually found on the Web sites of publicly traded companies. Where possible, students should also scan full-text newspaper and magazine databases for articles published over the previous year about the company.

Instructions   The instructor may have students work alone or in groups for this activity. Students will select a company and will investigate the relevance and influence of various stakeholder groups on the organization. Stakeholders will be identified from annual reports, newspaper articles, Web-

site statements, and other available sources. Stakeholders should be ranked in terms of their perceived importance to the organization.

Students should be prepared to present or discuss their organization's rank ordering of stakeholders, including evidence for this rank ordering.

Discussion Questions

1. What are the main reasons certain stakeholders are more important than others for this organization?

2. Based on your knowledge of the organization's environment, is this rank order of stakeholders in the organization's best interest, or should specific other stakeholders be given higher priority?

3. What societal groups, if any, are not mentioned as stakeholders by the organization? Does this lack of reference to these unmentioned groups make sense?

>**team**.activity/**self-assessment**.**skill**builder**1.4**

Does It All Make Sense?

Purpose   This exercise is designed to help you understand how organizational behavior knowledge can help you to understand life in organizations.

Instructions   (*Note:* This activity may be done as a self-assessment or as a team activity.) Read each of the statements below and circle whether each statement is true or false, in your opinion. The class will consider the answers to each question and discuss the implications for studying organizational behavior.

Due to the nature of this activity, the instructor will provide information about the most appropriate answer. The scoring key is not found in Appendix B.

1. True False   A happy worker is a productive worker.

2. True False   Decision makers tend to continue supporting a course of action even though information suggests that the decision is ineffective.

3. True False   Organizations are more effective when they prevent conflict among employees.

4. True False   It is better to negotiate alone than as a team.

5. True False   Companies are more effective when they have a strong corporate culture.

6. True False   Employees perform better without stress.

7. True False   Effective organizational change always begins by pinpointing the source of its current problems.

8. True False Female leaders involve employees in decisions to a greater degree than do male leaders.

9. True False People in Japan value group harmony and duty to the group (high collectivism) more than do Americans (low collectivism).

10. True False The best decisions are made without emotion.

11. True False If employees feel they are paid unfairly, then nothing other than changing their pay will reduce their feelings of injustice.

>self-assessment.skillbuilder1.5

Telework Disposition Assessment

As companies experiment with telecommuting (also called *teleworking*), they are learning that some employees seem to adapt better than others to this new employment relationship. This self-assessment measures personal characteristics that seem to relate to telecommuting and therefore provides a rough indication of how well you would adapt to this employment relationship. The instrument asks you to indicate the degree to which you agree or disagree with each of the statements provided. You need to be honest with yourself for a reasonable estimate of your telework disposition. Please keep in mind that this scale only considers your personal characteristics. Other factors, such as organizational, family, and technological systems support, must also be taken into account.

Find the full self-assessments on the OLC at
www.mhhe.com/mcshaneess

>part II:

Individual Behavior and Processes

[chapter 2]

Individual Behavior, Values, and Personality

>**learning**objectives

After reading this chapter, you should be able to

- Diagram the MARS model.
- Describe three types of ways to match individual competencies to job requirements.
- Identify five types of individual behavior in organizations.
- Define values and describe three types of values congruence.
- Define five main values that vary across cultures.
- List three ethical principles.
- Explain how moral intensity, ethical sensitivity, and the situation influence ethical behavior.
- Identify the Big Five personality dimensions.
- Summarize the personality concepts behind the Myers-Briggs Type Indicator.

Owens Corning is making employee engagement a cornerstone of its business strategy to become a world-class organization.

Shutting down two production furnaces for major repairs effectively idled half of the production employees at Owens Corning's plant in Jackson, Tennessee. But rather than a massive staff layoff, the company rotated everyone through a one-week quality management training program at full pay. This decision had an immediate and powerful effect. "As our employees returned from training, they were more engaged and more aware of waste," says Owens Corning's plant operations leader. This observation was supported a few months later when the plant's employee engagement scores jumped by 12 points from the previous survey.

Employee engagement is getting a lot of attention at Owens Corning and many other organizations. Employee engagement refers to how much employees identify with and are emotionally committed to their work, are cognitively focused on that work, and possess the ability and resources to do so. Royal Bank of Scotland calculated that when its employee engagement scores increase, productivity rises and staff turnover falls. British retailer Marks & Spencer claims that a 1 percent improvement in the engagement levels of its workforce produces a 2.9 percent increase in sales per square foot. "True employee engagement is the key to a world-class operation," says Mark Baroni, manager of Owens Corning's Jackson plant.

Reports from two consulting firms estimate that only about one-quarter of American employees are fully engaged, less than 60 percent are somewhat engaged, and approximately one-fifth are actively disengaged or "checked out" from work. A few years ago, a large percentage of Mutual of Omaha employees fell into the latter categories, prompting executives at the insurance and financial services company to take immediate corrective action. Mutual's managers discussed the survey results with their employees as well as with each other to discover ways to get staff feeling more engaged. "Just that communication in and of itself makes employees feel engaged," says Mutual executive vice president Jane Huerter. Mutual's engagement scores are now well above the national average.

ASB Bank scored well above average in its first employee engagement survey, but that wasn't good enough for the New Zealand financial institution. "We were absolutely shattered," recalls an ASB Bank executive, expecting to be in the top quartile. ASB Bank produced videos showing how managers with the most engaged subordinates perform their jobs. Managers now meet with staff each month and the bank's chief executive personally teaches new employees about the company's customer service vision. Today, ASB Bank's employee engagement scores are in the top 10 percent globally, and the company receives some of the highest ratings in New Zealand for customer service.[1]

///

Employee engagement might seem like the latest management buzz phrase, but this concept actually includes all of the drivers of individual behavior and performance that we will discuss in the first part of this chapter. It refers to the employee's emotional and cognitive (rational) motivation, the ability to perform the job, a clear understanding of the organization's vision and their specific role in that vision, and a belief that they have been given the resources to get their job done. This chapter begins by presenting the MARS model, which outlines these four drivers of individual behavior and results. Next, this chapter briefly looks at the five main types of individual behavior in the workplace. The latter half of this chapter looks at the two most stable characteristics of individuals: values and personality. The section on values looks at Schwartz's model of personal values, various forms of values congruence, the dynamics of cross-cultural values, and key features of ethical values in the workplace. The last section introduces the concept of personality, including two popular personality models: the Big Five personality dimensions and the Myers-Briggs Type Indicator.

employee engagement
How much employees identify with and are emotionally committed to their work, are cognitively focused on that work, and possess the ability and resources to do so.

>MARS Model of Individual Behavior and Results

The MARS model, illustrated in Exhibit 2.1, is a useful starting point to understanding the drivers of individual behavior and results. The model highlights the four factors that directly influence an employee's voluntary behavior and resulting performance—motivation, ability, role perceptions, and situational factors. These four factors are represented by the acronym "MARS" in the model's name.[2] The MARS model shows that these four factors have a combined effect on individual performance. If any factor weakens, employee performance will decrease. For example, enthusiastic salespeople (motivation) who understand their job duties (role perceptions) and have sufficient resources (situational factors) will not perform their jobs as well if they lack sufficient knowledge and sales skill (ability).

Exhibit 2.1 also shows that the four factors in the MARS model are influenced by several other individual variables that we will discuss over the next few chapters. Each of these factors relates to the MARS model in various ways. For example, personal values affect an employee's motivation through emotions and tend to shape role perceptions through the perceptual process.

Employee Motivation

motivation
The forces within a person that affect his or her direction, intensity, and persistence of voluntary behavior.

Motivation represents the forces within a person that affect the direction, intensity, and persistence of voluntary behavior.[3] *Direction* refers to the fact that motivation is goal oriented, not random. People are motivated to arrive at work on time, finish a project a few hours early, or aim for many other targets. *Intensity* is the amount of effort allocated to the goal. For example, two employees might be motivated to finish their project a few hours early (direction), but only one of them puts forth enough effort (intensity) to achieve this goal. Finally, motivation involves varying levels of *persistence,* that is, continuing the effort for a certain amount of time. Employees sustain their effort until they reach their goal or give up beforehand.

Ability

ability
Both the natural aptitudes and learned capabilities required to successfully complete a task.

Ability includes both the natural aptitudes and learned capabilities required to successfully complete a task. *Aptitudes* are the natural talents that help employees learn specific tasks more quickly and perform them better. For example, some people have a more natural ability than others to manipulate small objects with their fingers (called finger dexterity). There are many different physical and mental aptitudes, and our ability to acquire skills is af-

[**Exhibit 2.1**] MARS Model of Individual Behavior and Results

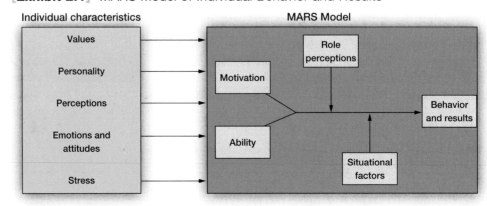

fected by these aptitudes. *Learned capabilities* refer to the skills and knowledge that you have actually acquired. This includes the physical and mental skills you possess as well as the knowledge you acquire and store for later use.

Skills, knowledge, aptitudes, and other personal characteristics that lead to superior performance are bunched together into the concept of **competencies.**[4] Some experts say that competencies also include personality, values, and drives, while others disagree. Competencies typically apply to several jobs or across the entire organizations. The challenge is to match the competencies that people possess with the competencies that each job requires. One strategy is to select applicants whose existing competencies best fit the required tasks. This includes comparing each applicant's competencies with the requirements of the job or work unit. A second approach is to provide training so employees develop required skills and knowledge. The third way to match people with job requirements is to redesign the job so employees are only given tasks within their capabilities.

competencies
The abilities, values, personality traits, and other characteristics of people that lead to superior performance.

Role Perceptions

Employees who feel engaged in their jobs not only have the necessary motivation and competencies to perform their work; they also understand the specific tasks assigned to them, the relative importance of those tasks, and the preferred behaviors to accomplish those tasks. In other words, they have clear *role perceptions*. The most basic way to improve these role perceptions is for staff to receive a clear job description and ongoing coaching. Employees also clarify their role perceptions as they work together over time and receive frequent and meaningful performance feedback.

Situational Factors

With high levels of motivation and ability, along with clear role perceptions, people will perform well only if the situation also supports their task goals. Situational factors include conditions beyond the employee's immediate control that constrain or facilitate his or her behavior and performance.[5] Some situational characteristics—such as consumer preferences and economic conditions—originate from the external environment and, consequently, are beyond the employee's and organization's control. However, other situational factors— such as time, people, budget, and physical work facilities—are controlled by others in the organization. Corporate leaders need to carefully arrange these conditions so employees can achieve their performance potential.

>Types of Individual Behavior in Organizations

Motivation, ability, role perceptions, and situational factors are the main drivers of employee behavior and performance. The organizational behavior literature generally identifies five types of employee behavior and performance: task performance, organizational citizenship, counterproductive work behaviors, joining and staying with the organization, and work attendance.

Task Performance

Task performance refers to goal-directed behaviors under the individual's control that support organizational objectives. Task performance behaviors transform raw materials into goods and services or support and maintain the technical activities.[6] For example, foreign exchange traders make decisions and take actions to exchange currencies. Employees in most jobs have more than one performance dimension. Foreign exchange traders must

task performance
Goal-directed activities that are under the individual's control.

be able to identify profitable trades, work cooperatively with clients and co-workers in a stressful environment, assist in training new staff, and work on special telecommunications equipment without error. Some of these performance dimensions are more important than others, but only by considering all of them can we fully evaluate an employee's contribution to the organization.

Exhibiting Organizational Citizenship

One of the defining characteristics of engaged employees is that they contribute beyond task performance standards or expectations. "They will go the extra step, or maybe even the extra mile, to support the interest of the organization." explains Bill Erikson, vice chairman of consulting firm Kenexa. In short, engaged employees practice **organizational citizenship.** They help others without selfish intent, are actively involved in organizational activities, avoid unnecessary conflicts, perform tasks beyond normal role requirements, and gracefully tolerate impositions.[7]

organizational citizenship
Behaviors that extend beyond the employee's normal job duties.

Counterproductive Work Behaviors

Organizational behavior is interested in all workplace behaviors, including those on the "dark side," collectively known as **counterproductive work behaviors (CWBs).** CWBs are voluntary behaviors that have the potential to directly or indirectly harm the organization. These CWBs can be organized into five categories: abuse of others (e.g., insults and

counterproductive work behaviors (CWBs)
Voluntary behaviors that have the potential to directly or indirectly harm the organization.

Christy Monohan views her job as much more than driving students to school safely and on time. Instead, the Lake Tahoe Unified School District bus driver is also a teacher, friend, and guardian of her young passengers. Recently honored as bus driver of the year by her peers, Monohan practices organizational citizenship. She bought a stuffed dog that sits at the back of the bus to put grumpy students in a more positive mood. When one of the students on her route is featured in a newspaper, she posts the article on her bus and proudly lets everyone know that there is a celebrity on board. "She's made the inside of her bus like a home," says Monohan's supervisor.[8]

nasty comments), threats (threatening harm), work avoidance (tardiness), work sabotage (doing work incorrectly), and overt acts (theft). Counterproductive work behaviors are not minor concerns. One recent study found that units of a fast-food restaurant chain with higher CWBs had significantly worse performance, whereas organizational citizenship had a relatively minor benefit.[9]

Joining and Staying with the Organization

If qualified people don't join and stay with the organization, neither job performance nor organizational citizenship behaviors would occur. Attracting and retaining talented people is particularly important as worries about skills shortages heat up. For instance, NASA projects that U.S. colleges will graduate less than 200,000 engineering and science students to replace 2 million baby boomers who retire from these jobs between 1998 and 2008.[10]

The war for talent includes keeping the best people, not just hiring them. The problem is that one-fifth of American workers voluntarily quit their jobs each year. Although some of this turnover is beneficial, particularly when people leave because they do not fit the job, high turnover disrupts the organization's performance and can undermine morale of those who stay. Furthermore, much of an organization's intellectual capital is the knowledge that employees carry around in their heads, so high turnover can result in a significant loss of organizational memory.[11]

Why do people quit their jobs? One strong influence is how much people like or dislike their jobs or work context. Employees who are unhappy at work tend to be more motivated to search for and join another organization with better conditions. The action of looking for or accepting alternative employment is usually triggered by "shock events," such as the boss's unfair decision or a conflict episode with a co-worker.[12]

Maintaining Work Attendance

Along with attracting and retaining employees, organizations need everyone to show up for work at scheduled times. Situational factors—such as a snowstorm or car breakdown—explain some work absences. Motivation is another factor. Employees who experience job dissatisfaction or work-related stress are more likely to be absent or late for work because taking time off is a way to temporarily withdraw from stressful or dissatisfying conditions. Absenteeism is also higher in organizations with generous sick leave because this benefit limits the negative financial impact of taking time away from work.[13]

The MARS model and the five types of individual behavior and results provide a foundation for the ideas presented over the next few chapters. For the remainder of this chapter, we will look at two of the most stable individual differences: values and personality.

<Values in the Workplace

With 57,000 employees around the world and acquisitions occurring regularly, London-based Vodafone executives wanted to ensure that employees were marching in the same general direction. "[Vodafone] needed a common culture of vision and values," explains Tim Brown, corporate affairs director of the telecommunications giant. "So the chief executive chaired several sessions with 20 of his most senior people around the world, from which they had to generate a vision and set of values that each of them wanted to buy into." Grahame Maher, Vodafone's chief executive in Australia, took the values-driven process a step further by asking more than 40 employee groups to discuss what they value as employees and what they value in a business. Employees said they valued fair dinkum (fairness and honesty), support, excellence and fun. They described Vodafone as gutsy, hungry, and different. With this information, Vodafone began a long process of transformation to improve the congruence of employee and organizational values.[14]

Several best-selling management books conclude that Vodafone is on the right track because successful companies have a deeply entrenched and long-lasting set of core values.[15] **Values** are stable, evaluative beliefs that guide our preferences for outcomes or courses of action in a variety of situations.[16] They are perceptions about what is good or bad, right or wrong. Values tell us what we "ought" to do. They serve as a moral compass that directs our motivation and, potentially, our decisions and actions. Values partly define who we are as individuals and as members of groups with similar values.

People arrange values into a hierarchy of preferences, called a *value system.* Some individuals value new challenges more than they value conformity. Others value generosity more than frugality. Each person's unique value system is developed and reinforced through socialization from parents, religious institutions, friends, personal experiences, and the society in which he or she lives. As such, a person's hierarchy of values is stable and long lasting.[17]

Values belong to individuals, which we call *personal values.* However, groups of people might hold the same or similar values, so we tend to ascribe these *shared values* to the team, department, organization, profession, or entire society. The values shared by people throughout an organization (*organizational values*) will receive attention when we look at corporate culture later in this book. The values shared across a society (*cultural values*) will receive attention later in this chapter.

Before discussing workplace values in more detail, we need to distinguish between espoused and enacted values.[18] *Espoused values* represent the values that we say we use and, in many cases, *think* we use. Corporate leaders might say they value environmentalism, creativity, and politeness, whether or not they really do value these things in practice. Values are socially desirable, so people create a positive public image by claiming to believe in values that others expect them to embrace. Also, corporate values are usually considered espoused values because, although leaders might abide by them, we don't know whether lower level employees share this commitment. *Enacted values,* on the other hand, represent the values we actually rely on to guide our decisions and actions. These values-in-use are apparent by watching people in action.

Types of Values

Values come in many forms, and experts on this topic have devoted considerable attention to organizing them into coherent groups. Exhibit 2.2 illustrates a well-researched and highly regarded model developed by social psychologist Shalom Schwartz.[19] Schwartz reduced dozens of personal values into these 10 broader domains of values and further organized these domains around two bipolar dimensions.

Along the left side of the horizontal dimension in Schwartz's model is *openness to change,* which represents the extent to which a person is motivated to pursue innovative ways. Openness to change includes the value domains of self-direction (independent thought and action) and stimulation (excitement and challenge). *Conservation,* the opposite end of Schwartz's horizontal dimension, is the extent to which a person is motivated to preserve the status quo. Conservation includes the value clusters of conformity (adherence to social norms and expectations), security (safety and stability), and tradition (moderation and preservation of the status quo).

The vertical dimension in Schwartz's model ranges from self-enhancement to self-transcendence. *Self-enhancement*—how much a person is motivated by self-interest— includes the values of achievement (pursuit of personal success) and power (dominance over others). The opposite of self-enhancement is *self-transcendence,* which refers to the motivation to promote the welfare of others and nature. Self-transcendence includes the

values

Stable, long-lasting beliefs about what is important in a variety of situations.

[Exhibit 2.2] Schwartz's Values Circumplex

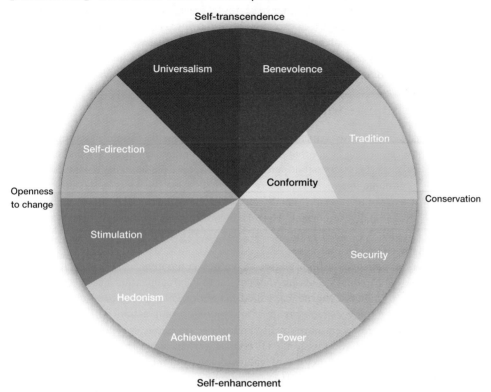

Source: S. H. Schwartz and G. Sagie, "Value Consensus and Importance: A Cross-National Study," *Journal of Cross-Cultural Psychology* 31 (July 2000), pp. 465–97; and S. H. Schwartz, "Universals in the Content and Structure of Values: Theoretical Advances and Empirical Tests in 20 Countries," *Advances in Experimental Social Psychology* 25 (1992), pp. 1–65.

values of benevolence (concern for others in one's life) and universalism (concern for the welfare of all people and nature).

Values and Individual Behavior

Personal values guide our decisions and actions, but this connection isn't as direct as it sounds. Our habitual behavior tends to be consistent with our values, but our everyday conscious decisions and actions apply our values much less consistently. The main reason for the disconnect between personal values and individual behavior is that values are abstract concepts that sound good in theory but are less easily followed in practice. A lot of people say that benevolence is an important value to them, yet they don't think about being benevolent in a lot of situations. Benevolence becomes a "truism" that gets lost in translation in everyday activities.

Benevolence and other values do influence decisions and behavior if three conditions are met.[20] First, a specific value affects our behavior when something makes us mindful (consciously aware) of that value. Co-workers tend to treat each other with much more respect and consideration immediately after a senior executive gives a speech on the virtues of benevolence in the workplace. The speech makes employees temporarily mindful of this value, so they think about it in their behavior towards others. Second, even if a particular value is important and we are mindful of it, we still need to have logical reasons in our head for applying that value. In other words, we tend to apply our values only when we can think of specific reasons for doing so. For example, you will be more motivated to switch your vacation time with a co-worker who needs that time off if you are mindful of your value of benevolence *and* you can think of good reasons why it's good to be benevolent.

The third condition that improves the linkage between our values and behavior is the situation. Work environments shape our behavior, at least in the short term, so they necessarily encourage or discourage values-consistent behavior. The fact is our jobs sometimes require us to act in ways that are inconsistent with our personal values. This incongruence between our personal values and work requirements can also have a powerful effect on employee attitudes and other behaviors, as we'll see next.

Values Congruence

Bill Hetzel's decision a few years ago to join Tom's of Maine was based in part on the personal care products firm's mission to have distinctive products and policies that honor and sustain the natural world. As head of purchasing and supply chain management, Hetzel applies Tom's environmental values every day. "Every decision I make is laced with business, technological, environmental and social factors," explains the MIT chemical engineer and MBA graduate. Equally important, Hetzel is comfortable working within this values framework. "It makes a huge difference every day at work that I share the values of my colleagues and my company," he says.[21]

values congruence
A situation wherein two or more entities have similar value systems.

Bill Hetzel experiences a high degree of **values congruence** in his job at Tom's of Maine because his personal values are very similar to the organization's value system. This particular form of values congruence, called *person-organization values congruence,* is desirable because employees feel less stress and more job satisfaction, while organizations benefit from employees with more loyalty and whose decisions are more consistent with the organization's goals and mission.[22] Of course, perfect congruence is neither possible nor desirable, because some degree of values diversity improves creativity and critical thinking about corporate decisions. However, a more common problem is that employees experience far too much values incongruence. For instance, a recent major survey of MBA students in the United States, United Kingdom, and Canada revealed that half of the respondents anticipate, or have experienced, making business decisions that conflict with their personal values.[23]

Along with person-organization values congruence, corporate leaders need to pay attention to *espoused-enacted values congruence;* that is, how closely the values apparent in their actions (enacted values) are consistent with what they say they believe in (espoused values). Noticeable gaps between espoused and enacted values undermine a person's perceived integrity, a critical feature of effective leaders.[24] Even for nonmanagement staff, espoused-enacted values congruence affects how much co-workers can trust them, which has implications for team dynamics.

A third type of values congruence refers to the compatibility of an organization's dominant values with the prevailing values of the community or society in which it conducts business.[25] For example, an organization originating from one country that tries to impose its value system on stakeholders located in another culture may experience higher employee turnover and have more difficult relations with the communities in which the company operates. Let's look more closely at cross-cultural values.

>Values across Cultures

Anyone who has worked long enough in other countries will know that values differ across cultures. Some cultures value group decisions, whereas others think that the leader should take charge. Meetings in Germany usually start on time, whereas they might be half an hour late in Brazil without much concern. We need to understand differences in cultural values to avoid unnecessary conflicts and misunderstandings between people from different countries.

Individualism and Collectivism

Let's start by looking at the two most commonly mentioned cross-cultural values, individualism and collectivism. **Individualism** is the extent to which we value independence and personal uniqueness. Highly individualist people value personal freedom, self-sufficiency, control over their own lives, and appreciation of the unique qualities that distinguish them from others. **Collectivism** is the extent to which we value our duty to groups to which we belong and group harmony. Highly collectivist people define themselves by their group membership and value harmonious relationships within those groups.[26]

You might think from these definitions that individualism and collectivism are opposites. Until recently, many scholars thought so, too, but the two concepts are actually unrelated, as Exhibit 2.3 reveals.[27] Some people and cultures have both high individualism and high collectivism, for example. Exhibit 2.3 shows that Americans and Canadians with European heritage have relatively high individualism and relatively low collectivism compared with people in most other countries.

individualism
The extent to which people value independence and personal uniqueness.

collectivism
The extent to which people value duty to groups to which they belong as well as group harmony.

Power Distance

A third cross-cultural value that will be mentioned frequently in this book is **power distance.** Power distance is the extent that people accept unequal distribution of power in a society.[28] Those with high power distance accept and value unequal power. They value obedience to authority and are comfortable receiving commands from their superiors without consultation or debate. They also prefer to resolve differences through formal procedures rather than directly. People in Malaysia, the Philippines, and Venezuela tend to have a high power distance value.

power distance
The extent to which people accept unequal distribution of power in a society.

[Exhibit 2.3] Individualism and Collectivism in Selected Countries

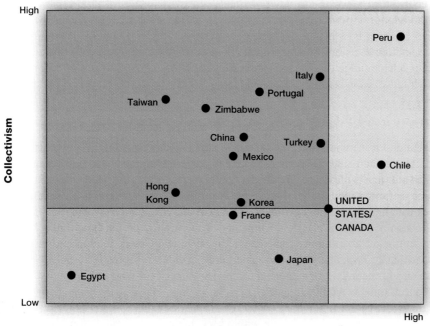

Source: Based on information in D. Oyserman, H. M. Coon, and M. Kemmelmeier, "Rethinking Individualism and Collectivism: Evaluation of Theoretical Assumptions and Meta-Analyses," *Psychological Bulletin* 128 (2002), pp. 3–72. The countries shown here represent only a sample of those in Oyserman's meta-analysis.

A few years ago, several Chinese-born managers living in Silicon Valley were recruited to work in Beijing for Lenovo Group, China's giant computer manufacturer. Most of them quit a year later because, after living in the United States for several years, they had difficulty with China's high power distance culture. Every morning, Lenovo employees had to sing the company song. Their whereabouts in and out of the office had to be accounted throughout the day. Those late for meetings had to stand behind their chair for a minute in humiliation to discourage future tardiness. "It's very militaristic," recalls one former Lenovo employee recruited from the United States. "You just have to do what you're told." Now, as Lenovo takes control of IBM's personal computer business, cross-cultural differences will likely be apparent again for IBM staff in the United States. "We regard cultural integration as the key factor of our eventual success," says Lenovo CEO Yang Yuanqing. While Yang points out the good product fit, he acknowledges that there "will be big cultural conflicts and challenges" bringing together employees from two diverse cultures.[29]

In contrast, people with low power distance expect relatively equal power sharing. They view the relationship with their boss as one of interdependence, not dependence; that is, they believe their boss is also dependent on them, so they expect power sharing and consultation before decisions affecting them are made. Those with low power distance readily approach and contradict their boss. Americans generally have a low power distance value, although it is even lower in Australia and Israel.

Other Cross-Cultural Values

uncertainty avoidance
The degree to which people tolerate ambiguity or feel threatened by ambiguity and uncertainty.

achievement-nurturing orientation
A competitive versus cooperative view of relations with other people.

Cross-cultural researchers have investigated many other values, but the only other two that we will mention are uncertainty avoidance and achievement-nurturing orientation. **Uncertainty avoidance** is the degree to which people tolerate ambiguity (low uncertainty avoidance) or feel threatened by ambiguity and uncertainty (high uncertainty avoidance). Employees with high uncertainty avoidance value structured situations where rules of conduct and decision making are clearly documented. They usually prefer direct rather than indirect or ambiguous communications. People in Japan and Greece tend to have high uncertainty avoidance, whereas very low uncertainty avoidance scores have been reported in past studies for people in Singapore and Jamaica. Americans tend to be around the middle of the uncertainty avoidance range.

Achievement-nurturing orientation reflects a competitive versus cooperative view of relations with other people.[30] People with a high achievement orientation value assertiveness, competitiveness, and materialism. They appreciate people who are tough and favor the acquisition of money and material goods. In contrast, people in nurturing-oriented cultures emphasize relationships and the well-being of others. They focus on human interaction and caring rather than competition and personal success. People in the Netherlands and Sweden score very low on achievement orientation (i.e., they have a high nurturing orientation), whereas people in Japan tend to have high scores on this cultural value. Americans score somewhere around the middle of the pack compared with other countries.

Before leaving this topic, we need to acknowledge two concerns about the cross-cultural values information you have read here.[31] First, the statements about how high or low people in various countries score on power distance, uncertainty avoidance, and achievement-nurturing orientation are based on a survey of IBM employees worldwide more than a quarter century ago. Over 100,000 IBM staff in dozens of countries completed that survey, but it is possible that these IBM employees do not represent the general population. There is also evidence that values have changed quite a bit in some countries since then. A second concern is the assumption that everyone in a society has similar cultural values. This may be true in a few countries, but not in culturally diverse societies such as the United States. By assigning certain values to an entire society, we are engaging in a form of stereotyping that limits our ability to understand the more complex reality of that society.

>Ethical Values and Behavior

When Jim Churchman searched out MBA programs, he was looking for more than courses that develop technical skills; he was also looking for an MBA with a strong ethics orientation. "A leader should make decisions not just from the numbers standpoint, but from an ethical standpoint as well," says the group manager at Sprint in Overland Park, Kansas.[32] **Ethics** refers to the study of moral principles or values that determine whether actions are right or wrong and outcomes are good or bad. People rely on their ethical values to determine "the right thing to do."

ethics
The study of moral principles or values that determine whether actions are right or wrong and outcomes are good or bad.

Three Ethical Principles

Our discussion of ethics begins with three principles: utilitarianism, individual rights, and distributive justice.[33] While you might prefer one principle more than the others based on your personal values, all three should be actively considered to put important ethical issues to the test.

- *Utilitarianism.* **Utilitarianism** advises us to seek the greatest good for the greatest number of people. In other words, we should choose the option providing the highest degree of satisfaction to those affected. This is sometimes known as a *consequential principle* because it focuses on the consequences of our actions, not on how we achieve those consequences. One problem with utilitarianism is that it is almost impossible to evaluate the benefits or costs of many decisions, particularly when many stakeholders have wide-ranging needs and values. Another problem is that most of us are uncomfortable engaging in behaviors that seem, well, unethical, to attain results that are ethical.

utilitarianism
The moral principle stating that decision makers should seek the greatest good for the greatest number of people when choosing among alternatives.

individual rights principle
The moral principle stating that every person is entitled to legal and human rights.

- *Individual rights.* The **individual rights principle** reflects the belief that everyone has entitlements that let him or her act in a certain way. Some of the most widely cited rights are freedom of movement, physical security, freedom of speech, fair trial, and freedom from torture. The individual rights principle includes more than legal rights; it also includes human rights that everyone is granted as a moral norm of society. One problem with this principle is that certain individual rights may conflict with others. The shareholders' right to be informed about corporate activities may conflict with an executive's right to privacy, for example.

distributive justice principle
The moral principle stating that people who are similar should be rewarded similarly, and those dissimilar should be rewarded differently.

- *Distributive justice.* The **distributive justice principle** suggests that people who are similar in relevant ways should receive similar benefits and burdens; those who are dissimilar should receive different benefits and burdens in proportion to their dissimilarity. For example, we expect that two employees who contribute equally in their work should receive similar rewards, whereas those who make a lesser contribution should receive less. A variation of this principle says that inequalities are acceptable where they benefit the least well off in society. Thus, employees in risky jobs should be paid more if this benefits others who are less well off. One problem with the distributive justice principle is that it is difficult to agree on who is "similar" and what factors are "relevant."

Moral Intensity, Ethical Sensitivity, and Situational Influences

Along with ethical principles, we need to consider the moral intensity of the issue, the individual's ethical sensitivity, and situational factors. **Moral intensity** is the degree to which an issue demands the application of ethical principles. Stealing from your employer is usually considered high on moral intensity, whereas borrowing a company pen for personal use is much lower on the scale. Even if an issue has high moral intensity, some employees might not recognize its ethical importance because they have low **ethical sensitivity.** Ethical sensitivity is a personal characteristic that enables people to recognize the presence and determine the relative importance of an ethical issue.[34] Ethically sensitive people are not necessarily more ethical. Rather, they can more accurately estimate the moral intensity of the issue.

moral intensity
The degree to which an issue demands the application of ethical principles.

ethical sensitivity
A personal characteristic that enables people to recognize the presence and determine the relative importance of an ethical issue.

The third important factor explaining why good people do bad things is the situation in which the unethical conduct occurs. Employees say they regularly experience pressure from top management that motivates them to lie to customers, breach regulations, or otherwise act unethically.[35] Situational factors do not justify unethical conduct. Rather, we need to recognize these factors so that organizations can reduce their influence in the future.

Supporting Ethical Behavior

Most large and medium-size organizations in the United States and several other countries have developed and communicate ethical codes of conduct. These statements establish the organization's ethical standards and signal to employees that the company takes ethical conduct seriously. However, written ethics codes alone won't prevent wrongdoing in the workplace.[36] To supplement ethics codes, many firms provide ethics training. For instance, Sun Microsystems puts each of its 35,000 employees worldwide through a basic online ethics training program, and its top 1,200 executives participate in a two-day ethics boot camp. Some firms also have hotlines through which employees can discuss or report wrongdoing.[37]

Long before the scandals at Enron, WorldCom, and Tyco, Molson Coors Brewing Company put together a variety of ethical practices that today makes it one of the best in the United States. A cross-functional team rewrote the Golden, Colorado, brewer's ethics code so it would be clearer and user-friendly. Performance evaluations explicitly consider how well employees model this ethics code. An online training program guides employees through real-world scenarios where they see how the company's ethics principles apply to everyday work situations. The activity is set up as an expedition, where employees progress down a mountain to several "camps," where they must resolve ethics violations. The problems begin with clear violations of the company's ethics code, but later camps have much fuzzier dilemmas requiring more careful thought to underlying values. "The goal of the program is to step beyond rules and guidelines and teach employees how to think, clarify, and analyze situations," says Warren Malmquist, shown here with another Coors ethics leader, Caroline McMichen.[38]

These programs seem to have some influence on ethical conduct, but the most powerful foundation is a culture that supports ethical values and behavior. "If you don't have a culture of ethical decision making to begin with, all the controls and compliance regulations you care to deploy won't necessarily prevent ethical misconduct," warns Devin Brougham, director of Vodafone, the British communications giant. This culture is supported by the ethical conduct and vigilance of corporate leaders. By acting with the highest standards of moral conduct, leaders not only gain support and trust from followers; they serve as role models for the ethical standards that employees are more likely to follow.[39]

>Personality in Organizations

Values are relatively stable characteristics that influence individual behavior. Another individual characteristic that has long-term stability is personality. In fact, there is considerable evidence that values and personality traits are interrelated and reinforce each other.[40] **Personality** refers to the relatively stable pattern of behaviors and consistent internal states that explain a person's behavioral tendencies. We say that personality explains behavioral tendencies because individuals' actions are not perfectly consistent with their personality profile in every situation. Personality traits are less evident in situations where social norms, reward systems, and other conditions constrain our behavior.[41] For example, talkative people remain relatively quiet in a library where "no talking" rules are explicit and strictly enforced.

personality
The relatively stable pattern of behaviors and consistent internal states that explain a person's behavioral tendencies.

Personality and Organizational Behavior

Personality has had a rocky relationship with the field of organizational behavior. Fifty years ago, personality testing was all the rage, but this practice died down by the late 1960s when research indicated that personality traits are too abstract to predict who will be a good employee. Over the past decade, personality has regained some of its credibility in organizational settings. In particular, recent studies have pointed out that specific personality traits predict certain types of behavior fairly well. Also, personality traits seem to help people find the jobs that best suit their needs.[42]

The Big Five Personality Dimensions

Big Five personality dimensions
The five abstract dimensions representing most personality traits: conscientiousness, agreeableness, neuroticism, openness to experience, and extroversion (CANOE)

A few decades ago, researchers pulled thousands of words from *Roget's Thesaurus* and *Webster's Dictionary* that represent personality traits and statistically looked at how they cluster together into meta-categories. The results of their effort is the **Big Five personality dimensions**.[43] These five dimensions, represented by the handy acronym CANOE, are outlined in Exhibit 2.4 and described below:

- *Conscientiousness.* Conscientiousness refers to people who are careful, dependable, and self-disciplined. Some scholars argue that this dimension also includes the will to achieve. People with low conscientiousness tend to be careless, less thorough, more disorganized, and irresponsible.

- *Agreeableness.* This includes the traits of being courteous, good-natured, empathic, and caring. Some scholars prefer the label of "friendly compliance" for this dimension, with its opposite being "hostile noncompliance." People with low agreeableness tend to be uncooperative, short-tempered, and irritable.

- *Neuroticism.* Neuroticism characterizes people with high levels of anxiety, hostility, depression, and self-consciousness. In contrast, people with low neuroticism (high emotional stability) are poised, secure, and calm.

- *Openness to experience.* Experts continue to debate the meaning of this complex dimension, but it generally refers to the extent to which people are sensitive, flexible,

[**Exhibit 2.4**] Big Five Personality Dimensions

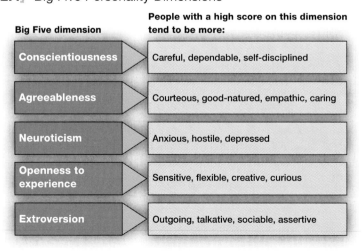

Big Five dimension	People with a high score on this dimension tend to be more:
Conscientiousness	Careful, dependable, self-disciplined
Agreeableness	Courteous, good-natured, empathic, caring
Neuroticism	Anxious, hostile, depressed
Openness to experience	Sensitive, flexible, creative, curious
Extroversion	Outgoing, talkative, sociable, assertive

creative, and curious. Those who score low on this dimension tend to be more resistant to change, less open to new ideas, and more fixed in their ways.

- *Extroversion.* **Extroversion** characterizes people who are outgoing, talkative, sociable, and assertive. The opposite is **introversion,** which refers to those who are quiet, shy, and cautious. Introverts do not necessarily lack social skills. Rather, they are more inclined to direct their interests to ideas than to social events. Introverts feel quite comfortable being alone, whereas extroverts do not.

These five personality dimensions affect work-related behavior and job performance to varying degrees.[44] People with high emotional stability tend to work better than others in high-stressor situations. Those with high agreeableness tend to handle customer relations and conflict-based situations more effectively. However, conscientiousness has taken center stage as the most valuable personality trait for predicting job performance and organizational citizenship in almost every job group. Conscientious employees set higher personal goals for themselves, are more motivated, and have higher performance expectations than do employees with low levels of conscientiousness.

Myers-Briggs Type Indicator

More than half a century ago, the mother and daughter team of Katherine Briggs and Isabel Briggs-Myers developed the **Myers-Briggs Type Indicator (MBTI),** a personality inventory designed to identify individuals' basic preferences for perceiving and processing information. The MBTI builds on the personality theory proposed in the 1920s by Swiss psychiatrist Carl Jung that identifies the way people prefer to perceive their environment as well as obtain and process information. Jung suggested that everyone is either extroverted or introverted in orientation and has particular preferences for perceiving (sensing or intuition) and judging or deciding on action (thinking or feeling). The MBTI is designed to measure these as well as a fourth dimension relating to how people orient themselves to the outer world (judging versus perceiving).[45] Extroversion and introversion were discussed earlier, so let's examine the other dimensions:

- *Sensing/intuition.* Some people like collecting information through their five senses. Sensing types use an organized structure to acquire factual and preferably quantitative details. In contrast, intuitive people collect information nonsystematically. They rely more on subjective evidence as well as their intuition and sheer inspiration. Sensors are capable of synthesizing large amounts of seemingly random information to form quick conclusions.

- *Thinking/feeling.* Thinking types rely on rational cause-effect logic and the scientific method to make decisions. They weigh the evidence objectively and unemotionally. Feeling types, on the other hand, consider how their choices affect others. They weigh the options against their personal values more than rational logic.

- *Judging/perceiving.* Some people prefer order and structure in their relationship with the outer world. These judging types enjoy the control of decision making and want to resolve problems quickly. In contrast, perceiving types are more flexible. They like to spontaneously adapt to events as they unfold and want to keep their options open.

The MBTI questionnaire combines the four pairs of traits into 16 distinct types. For example, ESTJ is one of the most common types for managers, meaning that they are extroverted, sensing, thinking, and judging types. Each of the 16 types has its strengths and weaknesses. ENTJs are considered natural leaders, ISFJs have a high sense of duty, and so on. These types indicate people's preferences, not the way they necessarily behave all of the time.

extroversion
A "Big Five" personality dimension that characterizes people who are outgoing, talkative, sociable, and assertive.

introversion
A "Big Five" personality dimension that characterizes people who are territorial and solitary.

Myers-Briggs Type Indicator (MBTI)
A personality test that measures each of the traits in Jung's model.

Effectiveness of the MBTI

Is the MBTI useful in organizations? Many business leaders think so. The MBTI is one of the most widely used personality tests in work settings and is equally popular for career counseling and executive coaching.[46] Still, evidence regarding the effectiveness of the MBTI and Jung's psychological types is mixed.[47] The MBTI does a reasonably good job of measuring Jung's psychological types. The MBTI predicts preferences for information processing in decision making and preferences for particular occupations. However, other evidence is less supportive regarding the MBTI's ability to predict job performance. Overall, the MBTI seems to improve self-awareness for career development and mutual understanding, but it probably should not be used in selecting job applicants.

Personality and values help us to understand individual behavior in organizations. However, people are also influenced by the environments in which they live and work. These environments are perceived and learned, the two topics presented in the next chapter.

>chapter summary

Individual behavior is influenced by motivation, ability, role perceptions, and situational factors (MARS). Motivation consists of internal forces that affect the direction, intensity, and persistence of a person's voluntary choice of behavior. Ability includes both the natural aptitudes and learned capabilities required to successfully complete a task. Role perceptions are a person's beliefs about what behaviors are appropriate or necessary in a particular situation. Situational factors are environmental conditions that constrain or facilitate employee behavior and performance. Collectively, these four factors are included in the concept of employee engagement.

The five main types of workplace behavior are task performance, organizational citizenship, counterproductive work behaviors, joining and staying with the organization, and work attendance.

Values are stable, evaluative beliefs that guide our preferences for outcomes or courses of action in a variety of situations. People arrange values into a hierarchy of preferences, called a *value system*. Espoused values—the values we say and think we use—are different from enacted values, which are values evident from our actions.

A value influences our decisions and actions when (1) something makes us mindful of it, (2) we can think of specific reasons for applying the value in that situation, and (3) the work environment supports behaviors consistent with the value. Person-organization values congruence refers to the degree that the individual's values are compatible with the organization's values. Espoused-enacted values congruence occurs when our actions are consistent with the values we say we believe in.

Values often differ across cultures. Individualism is the extent to which we value independence and personal uniqueness; collectivism is the extent to which we value our duty to groups to which we belong, and to group harmony. The two values are distinct, not opposite as many have assumed in the past. Power distance is the extent that people accept unequal distribution of power in a society. Uncertainty avoidance is the degree to which people tolerate ambiguity (low uncertainty avoidance) or feel threatened by ambiguity and uncertainty (high uncertainty avoidance). Achievement-nurturing orientation reflects a competitive versus cooperative view of relations with other people.

Three values that guide ethical conduct are utilitarianism, individual rights, and distributive justice. Three factors that influence ethical conduct are the extent that an issue demands ethical principles (moral intensity), the person's ethical sensitivity to the presence and importance of an ethical dilemma, and situational factors that cause people to deviate from their moral values. Companies improve ethical conduct through a code of ethics, ethics training, ethics hotlines, the conduct of corporate leaders, and the organization's culture.

Personality refers to the relatively stable pattern of behaviors and consistent internal states that explain a person's behavioral tendencies. Most personality traits are represented within the Big Five personality dimensions (CANOE): conscientiousness, agreeableness, neuroticism, openness to experience, and extroversion. Conscientiousness is a relatively strong predictor of job performance. The Myers-Briggs Type Indicator measures how people prefer to focus their attention, collect information, process and evaluate information, and orient themselves to the outer world.

>**key.**terms

ability 24

achievement-nurturing orientation 33

Big Five personality dimensions 36

collectivism 31

competencies 25

counterproductive work behaviors (CWBs) 26

distributive justice principle 34

employee engagement 23

ethical sensitivity 34

ethics 33

extroversion 37

individualism 31

individual rights principle 34

introversion 37

moral intensity 34

motivation 24

Myers-Briggs Type Indicator (MBTI) 37

organizational citizenship 26

personality 35

power distance 31

task performance 25

uncertainty avoidance 32

utilitarianism 33

values 28

values congruence 30

>**critical.thinking.**questions

1. This chapter begins by identifying employee engagement as a combination of the four factors in the MARS model. In your opinion, why would all four factors be important? Also, is it possible for employees to have high levels of engagement and be unethical or unproductive?

2. An insurance company has high levels of absenteeism among the office staff. The head of office administration argues that employees are misusing the company's sick leave benefits. However, some of the mostly female staff members have explained that family responsibilities interfere with work. Using the MARS model, as well as your knowledge of absenteeism behavior, discuss some of the possible reasons for absenteeism here and how it might be reduced.

3. Most large organizations spend a lot of money identifying the key competencies for superior work performance. In your opinion, what are the potential benefits and pitfalls associated with identifying competencies? Are there alternatives to selecting employees rather than by identifying their competencies?

4. Executives at a major consumer products company devoted several days to a values identification seminar in which they developed a list of six core values to drive the company forward. All employees attended sessions in which they learned about these values. In spite of this effort and ongoing communication regarding the six values, the executive team concluded two years later that employees were often making decisions and engaging in

behaviors that were inconsistent with these values. Provide three possible explanations why employees have not enacted the values espoused by top management at this company.

5. This chapter discussed the concept of values congruence in the context of an employee's personal values with the organization's values. But values congruence also relates to the juxtaposition of other pairs of value systems. Explain how values congruence is relevant with respect to organizational versus professional values.

6. People in a particular South American country have high power distance and high collectivism. What does this mean, and what are the implications of this information when you (a senior executive) visit employees working for your company in that country?

7. "All decisions are ethical decisions." Comment on this statement, particularly by referring to the concepts of moral intensity and ethical sensitivity.

8. Look over the four pairs of psychological types in the Myers-Briggs Type Indicator and identify the personality type (i.e., four letters) that would be best for a student in this course. Would this type be appropriate for students in other fields of study (e.g., biology, fine arts)?

>case.study:skillbuilder2.1

Cox-2 Inhibitor Drugs

By Christine Stamper,
University of Western Michigan

Treating chronic pain conditions associated with growing older, such as arthritis, has become more important (and more profitable) with the aging of the baby boomers, the largest generation in United States society. Pain medications produced by pharmaceutical companies take many forms, including both over-the-counter (i.e., aspirin, Tylenol, Motrin, Aleve, etc.) and prescription types of medicine. Investment in the research and development of new drugs costs pharmaceutical companies billions of dollars each year, with approximately 4–6 percent of all researched drugs actually achieving the approval of the Food and Drug Administration (FDA), the watchdog governmental agency tasked with maintaining public safety pertaining to medicines. Given this low "to-market" rate, top managers in pharmaceutical companies try to protect the drugs that are on the market at all costs.

Within the last few years, there has been much concern over a class of drugs called Cox-2 inhibitors, such as Vioxx (manufactured by Merck) and both Celebrex and Bextra (both produced by Pfizer). Despite the fact that all of these drugs were approved by the FDA (Celebrex in 1998, Vioxx in 1999, and Bextra in 2001), recent independently conducted research has shown significant negative health effects in people who have taken these medicines long term (more than three months). Specifically, all three drugs have been found to produce an increased risk of heart attack and stroke in patients, and Bextra also may result in sometimes fatal skin reactions. Subsequently, Vioxx was taken off the market by Merck in September 2004, and Pfizer stopped selling Bextra in April 2005 at the request of the FDA. However, Celebrex remains on the market.

When first introduced, Cox-2 inhibitors were hailed as a type of "superaspirin," alleviating the suffering of the patient while causing very little risk. They were also viewed as a preferred alternative to existing NSAIDs, which are nonsteroidal anti-inflammatory drugs like aspirin, naproxen (sold as Aleve and Naprosyn), and ibuprofen (sold as Motrin). When taken for three months or longer, these over-the-counter drugs carry a risk of internal bleeding in the stomach and small intestine areas (approximately 16,000 people die each year). Vioxx, Celebrex, and Bextra were produced to provide pain relief while protecting the lining of the gastrointestinal tract.

Even with the knowledge that Cox-2 inhibitors carry a potentially large cardiovascular health risk, there are chronic pain sufferers who would voluntarily (and happily) continue to take these drugs. For example, it was reported that one gentleman who suffers from chronic knee, hip, and shoulder pain thought, "who do I know who has some but isn't taking it? How can I get as much of it as possible before it disappears from the shelves?" He, and many others, would willingly tolerate the health risks in these medicines instead of living with their chronic pain. The acting director of the FDA's Center for Drug Evaluation and Research has recognized, in light of the new information on health risks, that it is important to balance these risks with the potential benefits of the medicines before deciding whether or not to remove them from the market. However, the associate director for science and medicine at the FDA's Office of Drug Safety argued strongly that the health risks associated with Cox-2 drugs vastly outweigh any potential benefits.

In December 2004 (prior to their request to pull Bextra), the FDA recommended that doctors limit their prescriptions of all Cox-2 inhibitors, including Celebrex, to only those patients at risk for gastrointestinal bleeding. Researchers at Stanford and the University of Chicago argue that millions of patients who did not face this risk were prescribed either

Vioxx or Celebrex by their doctors. Each of these drugs can cost 10–15 times as much as the NSAIDs available to treat the same pain symptoms, and critics of big pharmaceutical companies argue that the Cox-2 inhibitors were marketed too aggressively and deceptively to potential patients. It is not clear whether the increase in prescriptions for the Cox-2 inhibitors in lieu of NSAIDs was due to patients asking their doctors specifically for either Vioxx or Celebrex, or recommendations by physicians that the patients change their medications.

Both Pfizer and Merck maintain the relative safeness of the Cox-2 inhibitors. In February 2005, an FDA advisory panel recommended that Vioxx, Celebrex, and Bextra should continue to be sold despite health risks, because potential benefits of the drugs outweigh the risks for some patients. The doctors on the panel stated that they felt Vioxx posed the greatest risk to consumers and that Celebrex had the fewest side effects. Research estimates indicate that Celebrex increases the risk for heart problems by 1 percent, but only for individuals who routinely take double the normal dosage of 200 milligrams. Also, another recent study indicated that Celebrex may suppress the typical immune function of the body, which may be beneficial to some arthritis sufferers.

The FDA does not always follow the recommendations of its advisory groups, and subsequently it decided to request that Pfizer pull Bextra from the market. A statement released by Pfizer said the company "respectfully disagreed with the FDA's decision on Bextra and that it would work with the agency on Celebrex's label." The FDA has requested a "black box" warning label be placed on Celebrex, which is the strongest warning procedure available in product labeling. However, the FDA also requested black box warnings on NSAIDs like Motrin, Advil, and Aleve. Pfizer has also stopped public advertising of Celebrex, but still argues it should be available to patients who need it, according to a doctor's recommendation. Also, there are two additional Cox-2 drugs waiting for the FDA's approval, one of which is produced by Merck (Arcoxia). Arcoxia has been approved for use in 51 countries worldwide.

At the time of this case, Pfizer had just finished a widely publicized strategic planning meeting addressing the future of the company. In the press releases from this meeting, and prior to the FDA asking Pfizer to remove Bextra from the market, corporate representatives expressed their desire to revitalize the sales of both Celebrex and Bextra in the coming months. With the removal of Bextra from the market, it was predicted by financial analysts that Pfizer's earnings would continue to decline for 2005 and the recent predictions for double-digit earnings growth for 2006 and 2007 would have to be revised. In 2004, sales associated with Bextra were $1.3 billion, and Celebrex's sales were estimated at $3.3 billion. Together, Bextra, Celebrex, and Vioxx totaled more than 50 million prescriptions in the United States in 2004 (Bextra = 13 million, Vioxx = 14 million, and Celebrex = 24 million).

Discussion Questions

1. Should Pfizer voluntarily pull Celebrex off the market, given that the other two drugs in its class have been pulled? What factors are the most important in making this decision? What should the FDA do about Arcoxia?

2. What are the responsibilities, if any, of Merck, Pfizer, and the FDA for the deaths of individuals who took the Cox-2 inhibitors? Who holds primary responsibility?

3. How many deaths per 100,000 people is an acceptable risk for a drug to be viewed as marketable? Should individual patients have the right to determine if the risk is too great for them? What roles do organizations and consumers play in maintaining consumer safety?

Sources: Theresa Agovino, "Pfizer's Outlook Darkens with Bextra Ban," Associated Press, as printed in the *Kalamazoo Gazette,* April 10, 2005; Associated Press, "All Drugs like Vioxx May Cause Problems, Says Merck Official," MSNBC.com, February 16, 2005; Associated Press, "Painkiller Bextra Pulled from Market," MSNBC.com, April 7, 2005; Barnaby J. Feder, "More Lawsuits over Pfizer's Bextra Expected," *The New York Times,* as printed in the *Kalamazoo Gazette,* April 10, 2005; Abby Goodnough, "Consumers Weigh Risks of Painkillers, Life without Them," *The New York Times,* as printed in the *Kalamazoo Gazette,* April 10, 2005; Reuters, "Cox-2 Drugs May Suppress Immune Function," MSNBC.com, April 7, 2005; Reuters, "FDA Rules in Favor of Painkillers," MSNBC.com, February 19, 2005; Reuters, "FDA Should Pull Pain Drugs, Says Group," MSNBC.com, January 24, 2005; Reuters, "FDA Tells Doctors to Limit Painkiller Use," MSNBC.com, December 31, 2004; Reuters, "Pain Killers May Damage Small Intestines," MSNBC.com, January 3, 2005; Reuters, "Researcher Says 139,000 Harmed by Vioxx," MSNBC.com, January 3, 2005; Reuters, "Scientist: No Need for Arthritis Drugs," MSNBC.com, February 17, 2005; Reuters, "U.S. May Pull Painkillers, Researchers Say," MSNBC.com, February 15, 2005; and Reuters, "Vioxx, Celebrex May Be Overprescribed," MSNBC.com, January 24, 2005.

>team.exercise:skillbuilder2.2

Comparing Cultural Values

Purpose This exercise is designed to help you determine the extent that students hold similar assumptions about the values that dominate in other countries.

Instructions

The names in the left column represent labels that a major consulting project identified with businesspeople in a particular country, based on its national culture and values. These names appear in alphabetical order. In the right column are the names of countries, also in alphabetical order, corresponding to the labels in the left column.

- *Step 1:* Working alone, students will connect the labels with the countries by relying on their perceptions of these countries. Each label is associated with only one country, so each label will be connected to only one country, and vice versa. Draw a line to connect the pairs, or put the label number beside the country name.

- *Step 2:* The instructor will form teams of four or five members. Members of each team will compare their results and try to reach consensus on a common set of connecting pairs.

- *Step 3:* Teams or the instructor will post the results for all to see the extent that students hold common opinions about businesspeople in other cultures. Class discussion can then consider the reasons why the results are so similar or different, as well as the implications of these results for working in a global work environment.

Values Labels and Country Names

Country Label	Country Name
1. Affable Humanists	Australia
2. Ancient Modernizers	Brazil
3. Commercial Catalysts	Canada
4. Conceptual Strategists	China
5. Efficient Manufacturers	France
6. Ethical Statesmen	Germany
7. Informal Egalitarians	India
8. Modernizing Traditionalists	Netherlands
9. Optimistic Entrepreneurs	New Zealand
10. Quality Perfectionists	Singapore
11. Rugged Individualists	Taiwan
12. Serving Merchants	United Kingdom
13. Tolerant Traders	United States

Source: Based on R. Rosen, P. Digh, M. Singer, and C. Phillips, *Global Literacies* (New York: Simon & Schuster, 2000).

>team.exercise:skillbuilder2.3

Ethics Dilemma Vignettes

Purpose   This exercise is designed to make you aware of the ethical dilemmas people face in various business situations, as well as the competing principles and values that operate in these situations.

Instructions
The instructor will form teams of four or five students. Team members will read each case below and discuss the extent to which the company's action in each case was ethical. Teams should be prepared to justify their evaluation using ethics principles and perceived moral intensity of each incident.

Case One
An employee at a major food retailer wrote a Weblog (blog) and, in one of his writings, complained that his boss wouldn't let him go home when he felt sick and that his district manager refused to promote him because of his dreadlocks. His blog named the employer, but the employee didn't use his real name. Although all blogs are on the Internet, the employee claims that his was low profile and that it didn't show up when doing a Google search of his name or the company. Still, the employer somehow discovered the blog, figured out the employee's real name,

and fired him for "speaking ill-will of the company in a public domain."

Case Two
Computer printer manufacturers usually sell printers at a low margin over cost and generate much more income from subsequent sales of the high-margin ink cartridges required for each printer. One global printer manufacturer now designs its printers so they only work with ink cartridges made in the same region. Ink cartridges purchased in the United States will not work for the same printer model sold in Europe, for example. This "region coding" of ink cartridges does not improve performance. Rather, this action prevents consumers and gray marketers from buying the product at a lower price in another region. The company says this action allows it to maintain stable prices within a region rather than continually changing prices due to currency fluctuations.

Case Three
For the past few years, the design department of a small (40-employee) company has been using a particular software program, but the three employees who use the software have been complaining for more than a year that the software is out of date and is slowing down their performance. The department agreed to switch to a

competing software program, costing several thousand dollars. However, the next version won't be released for six months and buying the current version will not allow much discount toward the next version. The company has placed advanced orders for the next version. Meanwhile, one employee was able to get a copy of the current version of the software from a friend in the industry. The company has allowed the three employees to use this current version of the software even though they did not pay for it.

>self-assessment.skillbuilder2.4

Identifying Your Dominant Values

Values have taken center stage in organizational behavior. Increasingly, OB experts are realizing that our personal values influence our motivation, decisions, and attitudes. This self-assessment is designed to help you to estimate your personal values and value system. The instrument consists of several words and phrases, and you are asked to indicate whether each word or phrase is highly opposed or highly similar to your personal values, or some point in between these two extremes. As with all self-assessments, you need to be honest with yourself when completing this activity in order to get the most accurate results.

>self-assessment.skillbuilder2.5

Individualism-Collectivism Scale

Two of the most important concepts in cross-cultural organizational behavior are individualism and collectivism. This self-assessment measures your levels of individualism and collectivism with one of the most widely adopted measures. This scale consists of several statements, and you are asked to indicate how well each statement describes you. You need to be honest with yourself to receive a reasonable estimate of your level of individualism and collectivism.

Find the full self-assessments on the OLC at
www.mhhe.com/mcshaneess

[chapter 3]

Perceptions and Learning in Organizations

Indianapolis Power & Light CEO Ann Murtlow keeps her perceptions in focus by visiting line crews in the field.

>learningobjectives

After reading this chapter, you should be able to

- Outline the perceptual process.
- Explain how we perceive ourselves and others through social identity.
- Outline the reasons stereotyping occurs and describe ways to minimize its adverse effects.
- Describe the attribution process and two attribution errors.
- Summarize the self-fulfilling prophecy process.
- Explain how empathy and the Johari Window can help improve our perceptions.
- Define learning and explain how it affects individual behavior.
- Describe the A-B-C model of behavior modification and the four contingencies of reinforcement.
- Describe the three features of social learning theory.
- Summarize the four components of Kolb's experiential learning model.

Indianapolis Power & Light (IPL) was buffeted by customer complaints, staff reductions, low morale, and its acquisition by AES Corp. when Ann Murtlow arrived as CEO in 2002. With such turbulence, some executives would be tempted to remain shuttered in their corporate offices, but Murtlow's style has been to directly find out what's going on. Along with listening to customers and community officials, she regularly visits line crews in the field, sits in on their safety schools, and finds other opportunities to talk with employees throughout the organization. "The plant guys [are] not surprised to see her in a manhole," says Murtlow's executive assistant. "She wants to know what everybody is doing and how it works."

Ann Murtlow is one of a growing number of executives who keep their perceptions focused by "being there" with employees and customers. Some even work alongside their staff. David Neeleman, the founder of New York–based JetBlue, works in the trenches each month with his baggage handlers and ticket takers. "With other aviation companies, upper-level management doesn't like to mingle with employees," says Fred Ramos, JetBlue's ground-operations supervisor. "But David wants to be smack in the middle of everything."

At Domino's Pizza, sending the CEO back to the front lines isn't good enough. The Ann Arbor, Michigan, company has developed a weeklong Pizza Prep School where its administrative and management staff receive 20 hours of classroom instruction in operating a pizza store along with 24 hours of hands-on experience. This arrangement gives everyone a better understanding of how their decisions affect the company's retail outlets.

1-800-GOT-JUNK?, North America's largest rubbish removal company, follows a similar practice. Every new hire in the company's 130 franchises spends an entire week on a junk removal truck to better understand how the business works. "How can you possibly empathize with someone out in the field unless you've been on the truck yourself?" asks CEO and founder Brian Scudamore.[1]

Working in frontline jobs and keeping in close contact with staff and customers is a powerful way for executives to improve their perceptions. **Perception** is the process of receiving information about and making sense of the world around us. It entails deciding which information to notice, how to categorize this information, and how to interpret it within the framework of our existing knowledge. This chapter begins by describing the perceptual process. Social identity theory is then introduced, followed by stereotyping, attribution, self-fulfilling prophecy, and other perceptual issues, as well as strategies to minimize perceptual limitations. Learning follows directly from perceptions, so the latter part of this chapter introduces three perspectives of learning: behavior modification, social learning theory, and experiential learning.

perception
The process of selecting, organizing, and interpreting information in order to make sense of the world around us.

>The Perceptual Process

What we think of as reality is actually filtered through an imperfect perceptual process. Most of the stimuli that bombard our senses are screened out; the rest are organized and interpreted. A nurse working in postoperative care might ignore the smell of recently disinfected instruments or the sound of co-workers talking nearby. Yet, a small flashing red light on the nurse station console is immediately noticed because it signals that a patient's vital signs are failing. This process, called **selective attention**, is influenced by characteristics of the person or object being perceived and of the individual doing the perceiving.[2] People and objects influence whether they get noticed because of their size, intensity, motion, repetition, and novelty. The red light on the nurse station console receives attention because it is bright (intensity), flashing (motion), and a rare event (novelty).

The perceiver's characteristics also influence the selective attention process. Our brain quickly and unconsciously assesses whether sensory information is relevant to us in terms

selective attention
The process of filtering information received by our senses.

of our innate drives. Emotional markers (worry, happiness, anger) are attached to relevant information based on this rapid evaluation, and these emotionally tagged bits of information compete for our conscious attention. Along with our innate drives, our expectations also shape the selective attention process. If you expect to receive an e-mail from someone, it will get noticed more quickly than an unexpected message that may be equally important.[3]

Perceptual Organization and Interpretation

categorical thinking
The mostly unconscious process of organizing people and objects into preconceived categories that are stored in our long-term memory.

People make sense of information even before they become aware of it. This sense making partly includes **categorical thinking**—the mostly unconscious process of organizing people and objects into preconceived categories that are stored in our long-term memory.[4] Most categorical thinking occurs without our awareness, such as filling in missing pieces of a situation (called *closure*) or conceptually grouping people or objects together based on their similarity or proximity to others. We also have a natural tendency to see patterns, even when they are actually random events, such as presumed winning streaks among sports stars or in gambling.[5]

Making sense also involves interpreting incoming information, and this happens just as quickly as selecting and organizing that information. The emotional markers that the brain attaches to incoming information are essentially quick judgments about whether those stimuli are good or bad for us. For instance, studies have found that people who observe very thin slices of video—as little as three two-second snippets—of an instructor's one-hour lecture give that lecturer similar ratings (optimistic, likeable, anxious, active, etc.) as students who attended the entire class in person.[6] In effect, the observers perceived and judged the lecturers very quickly. These studies also suggest that after the judgments are formed, they do not change very much.

Mental Models

mental models
The broad worldviews or "theories in-use" that people rely on to guide their perceptions and behaviors.

People rely on **mental models**, broad worldviews or templates of the mind that provide predictability to the world around them.[7] Without these mental road maps, it would be practically impossible to know how to act safely and purposively. For example, most of us have a mental model about attending a college lecture or seminar. We have a set of assumptions and expectations about how people arrive, arrange themselves in the room, ask and answer questions, and so forth. Mental models allow us to relate to that external world and to fill in missing pieces of the perceptual puzzle. However, mental models also generate expectations that, as we noted earlier, can cause us to overlook important information in the selective attention process.

>Social Identity Theory

social identity theory
States that self-perception and social perception are shaped by a person's unique characteristics (personal identity) and membership in various social groups (social identity).

How we perceive the world is shaped, in large part, by how we perceive ourselves.[8] This process is explained by **social identity theory**, which says that people have both personal identities and social identities. A *personal identity* refers to characteristics that make a person unique and distinct from others in a particular situation. For instance, an unusual achievement that distinguishes you from other people typically becomes a personal identity characteristic. A *social identity,* on the other hand, refers to how people define themselves in terms of the groups to which they belong and have an emotional attachment. For instance, you might have a social identity as an American, a graduate of the University of Vermont, and an employee at IBM (see Exhibit 3.1). Everyone engages in this social categorization process because it helps to make sense of where we fit within the social world.

[Exhibit 3.1] Self-Perception and Social Perception through Social Identity

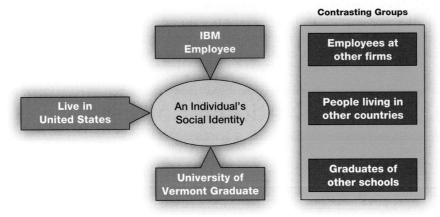

Social identity is a complex combination of many memberships arranged in a hierarchy of importance. Our gender, race, and age are typically prominent social identity characteristics because they are easily identifiable. Most of us want to have a positive self-image, so our social identity also includes our association with groups that have higher status or respect. Medical doctors usually define themselves in terms of their profession because of its high status, for instance.[9]

Perceiving Others through Social Identity

Social identity theory explains more than just how we develop self-perceptions. It also explains the dynamics of *social perception*—how we perceive others.[10] This social perception is influenced by three activities in the process of forming and maintaining our social identity: categorization, homogenization, and differentiation.

- *Categorization.* Social identity is a comparative process, and that comparison begins with categorical thinking—categorizing people into distinct groups. By viewing someone (including yourself) as a Texan, for example, you remove that person's individuality and, instead, see him or her as a prototypical representative of the group called Texans. This categorization then allows you to distinguish Texans from people who live in California and elsewhere.

- *Homogenization.* To simplify the comparison process, we tend to think that people within each group are very similar to each other. For instance, we think Texans collectively have similar attitudes and characteristics, whereas Californians collectively have their own unique brand of characteristics. Of course, we recognize that every individual is unique, but thinking about our social identity and of people in other groups tends to homogenize people within groups.

- *Differentiation.* Social identity fulfills our inherent need to have a distinct and positive identity, in other words, to feel unique and good about ourselves. To achieve this, we do more than categorize people and homogenize them; we also differentiate groups by assigning more favorable characteristics to people in our groups than to people in other groups. This differentiation is usually subtle, but it can escalate into a "good guy-bad guy" contrast when groups are in conflict with each other. Under these conditions, the negative image of opponents preserves our self-image against the threatening outsiders.

To summarize, the social identity process explains how we perceive ourselves and other people, including categorizing people into groups, forming a homogeneous image of people within those groups, and differentiating groups by assigning more favorable features to our own groups. This social identity process makes our social world easier to understand and supports a positive self-image; it is also the basis for stereotyping people in organizational settings, which is discussed next.

>Stereotyping in Organizational Settings

stereotyping
The process of assigning traits to people based on their membership in a social category.

Stereotyping is an extension of social identity theory and a product of our natural process of organizing information.[11] Stereotyping has three elements. First, we develop social categories and assign traits that are difficult to observe. For instance, students might form a stereotype that professors are both intelligent and absent-minded. Personal experiences shape stereotypes to some extent, but they are mainly provided to us through cultural upbringing and media images (e.g., movie characters). Second, we assign people to one or more social categories based on easily observable information about them, such as their gender, appearance, or physical location. Third, people who seem to belong to the stereotyped group are assigned nonobservable traits associated with the group. For example, if we learn that someone is a professor, we might assume the person is also intelligent and absent-minded.

Stereotyping occurs for three reasons.[12] First, as a form of categorical thinking, it is a natural and mostly unconscious energy saving process to simplify our understanding of the world. It is easier to remember features of a stereotype than the constellation of characteristics unique to everyone we meet. Second, we have an innate need to understand and anticipate how others will behave. We don't have much information when first meeting someone, so we rely heavily on stereotypes to fill in the missing pieces. Third, we are particularly motivated to rely on negative stereotypes when others threaten our self-esteem. Stereotypes of aloof, greedy executives often fill employees' minds during layoffs, for instance.

Problems with Stereotyping

Stereotypes are not completely fictional, but neither do they accurately describe every person in that social category. For instance, the widespread "bean counter" stereotype of accountants views people in this profession as "single-mindedly preoccupied with precision and form, methodical and conservative, and a boring joyless character." Although this may be true of some accountants, it is certainly not characteristic of all, or even most, people in this profession.[13]

Another problem with stereotyping is that it lays the foundation for discriminatory behavior. This mostly occurs as *unintentional (systemic) discrimination,* whereby decision makers rely on stereotypes to establish notions of the "ideal" person in specific roles. A person who doesn't fit the ideal tends to receive a less favorable evaluation. In contrast, *intentional discrimination* occurs when people hold unfounded negative emotions and attitudes toward people belonging to a particular stereotyped group. Although this overt discrimination appears to be less common today than a few decades ago, it still exists.[14]

If stereotyping is such a problem, shouldn't we try to avoid this process altogether? Unfortunately, it's not that simple. Categorical thinking (including stereotyping) is mostly an automatic and unconscious process.[15] Also, remember that stereotyping allows us to minimize mental effort, fill in missing information, and support our social identity. The good news is that while it is very difficult to prevent the *activation* of stereotypes, we can min-

Women represent 57 percent of university graduates in the United States but only 19 percent of engineering graduates. A major reason few women enter engineering and sciences seems to be that the stereotypes of people in these fields don't fit the social identities that most women want for themselves. "I think women have a hard time envisioning themselves as a scientist," suggests Jo-Ann Cohen, associate dean at North Carolina State University. "There's a lack of role models." This concern is supported by an Australian report on computer science graduates, which concluded that "the image of the industry is a major problem and is putting girls off." To correct these perceptions, many universities have established summer camps where high school girls meet successful female engineers and discover through hands-on activities that science and math can be fun and fit their self-image. Caltech went one step further five years ago by revising its chemical engineering curriculum to include topics that seem more relevant and appealing, particularly for women (e.g., biochemistry, environmental engineering). Today, nearly half of the Pasadena-based school's chemical engineering class consists of women, including (from left) Shannon Lewis, Michelle Giron, and Haluna Gunterman.[16]

imize the *application* of stereotypic information. In other words, we can avoid using our stereotypes in our decisions and actions toward other people. Later in this chapter, we'll identify a few ways to minimize the problems with stereotyping and other perceptual processes.

<Attribution Theory

One of the most basic hardwired drives in human beings is to make sense of and predict the world around them. This drive explains why we create mental models, and it explains why we attribute the causes of events to people or the situation. These perceptions of causation are guided by the **attribution process**, in which we assign credit or blame for someone's behavior either to their ability or motivation (internal attribution) or to situational influences

attribution process
The perceptual process of deciding whether an observed behavior or event is caused largely by internal or by external factors.

beyond their control (external attribution).[17] If a co-worker doesn't show up for an important meeting, for instance, we infer either internal attributions (the co-worker is forgetful, lacks motivation, etc.) or external attributions (traffic, a family emergency, or other circumstances prevented the co-worker from attending).

Attributions are an essential part of our perceptual world because they link together the various pieces of that world in cause-effect relationships. As a result, our decisions and actions are influenced by our prior attributions. For instance, one study found that students accepted into a graduate program experienced more self-esteem and sense of fairness when they believed their selection was caused by an internal attribution (selected due to their abilities) rather than external attribution (selected due to luck or lack of applicants).[18]

Attribution Errors

People are far from perfect when making attributions. One bias, called **fundamental attribution error**, refers to our tendency to see the person rather than the situation as the main cause of that person's behavior.[19] If an employee is late for work, observers are more likely to conclude that the person is lazy than to realize that external factors may have caused this behavior. Fundamental attribution error occurs because observers can't easily see the external factors that constrain the person's behavior. We also tend to believe in the power of the person; we assume that individuals can overcome situational constraints more than they really can. Research suggests that fundamental attribution error is more common in Western countries than in Asian cultures; most Asians are taught from an early age to pay attention to the context in interpersonal relations and to see everything connected in a holistic way.[20]

Another attribution error, known as **self-serving bias**, is the tendency to attribute our favorable outcomes to internal factors and our failures to external factors. Simply put, we take credit for our successes and blame others or the situation for our mistakes. Self-serving bias is found in corporate annual reports; often in these reports, executives point to their personal qualities as reasons for the company's success and to external factors as reasons for the company's failures.[21]

fundamental attribution error
The tendency to attribute the behavior of other people more to internal than to external factors.

self-serving bias
A perceptual error whereby people tend to attribute their favorable outcomes to internal factors and their failures to external factors.

>Self-Fulfilling Prophecy

Cocoplans is recognized throughout the Philippines as a top-performing insurance company with excellent customer service. This success is due, in part, to the way Cocoplans executives perceive their sales staff. "If you believe that they will not last, your behavior towards them will show it. . . . You get what you expect," explains Cocoplans president Caesar T. Michelena. "It's a self-fulfilling prophecy."[22] **Self-fulfilling prophecy** occurs when our expectations about another person cause that person to act in a way that is consistent with those expectations. In other words, our perceptions can influence reality. Exhibit 3.2 illustrates the four steps in the self-fulfilling prophecy process using the example of a supervisor and subordinate.[23]

self-fulfilling prophecy
Occurs when our expectations about another person cause that person to act in a way that is consistent with those expectations.

1. *Expectations formed.* The supervisor forms expectations about the employee's future behavior and performance. These expectations are sometimes inaccurate, because first impressions are formed from limited information.

2. *Behavior toward the employee.* The supervisor's expectations influence his or her treatment of employees. Specifically, high-expectancy employees (those expected to do well) receive more emotional support through nonverbal cues (e.g., more smiling and eye contact), more frequent and valuable feedback and reinforcement, more challenging goals, better training, and more opportunities to demonstrate their performance.

[**Exhibit 3.2**] The Self-Fulfilling Prophecy Cycle

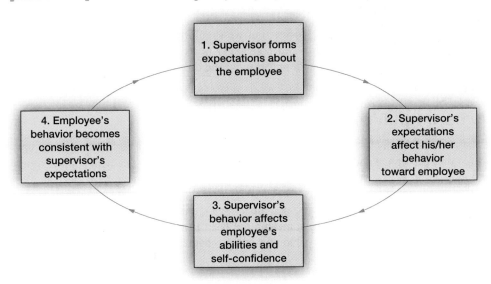

3. *Effects on the employee.* The supervisor's behaviors have two effects on the employee. First, through better training and more practice opportunities, a high-expectancy employee learns more skills and knowledge than a low-expectancy employee. Second, the employee becomes more self-confident, which results in higher motivation and willingness to set more challenging goals.[24]

4. *Employee behavior and performance.* With higher motivation and better skills, high-expectancy employees are more likely to demonstrate desired behaviors and better performance. The supervisor notices this, which supports his or her original perception.

There are plenty of examples of self-fulfilling prophecies in work and school settings.[25] Research has found that women who receive subtle cues that they might not perform as well as men on a math test actually perform worse on the test compared with women who are told the test is gender neutral. Similarly, Israeli Defense Force trainees performed better when their instructors received (fictitious) information that they had high potential to succeed in the boot camp program.

Contingencies of Self-Fulfilling Prophecy

The self-fulfilling prophecy effect is stronger at the beginning of the relationship, such as when employees are first hired. It is also stronger when several people, rather than just one person, hold the same expectations of the individual. In other words, we might be able to ignore one person's doubts about our potential, but not the collective doubts of several people. The self-fulfilling prophecy effect is also stronger among people with a history of low achievement. High achievers can draw upon their past successes to offset low expectations, whereas low achievers do not have these past successes to support their self-confidence. Fortunately, the opposite is also true: low achievers respond more favorably than high achievers to positive self-fulfilling prophecy. Low achievers don't receive this positive encouragement very often, so it probably has a strong effect on their motivation to excel.[26]

The main lesson from the self-fulfilling prophecy literature is that leaders need to develop and maintain a positive, yet realistic, expectation toward all employees.[27] This recommendation is consistent with the emerging philosophy of *positive organizational behavior,* which suggests that focusing on the positive rather than negative aspects of life will improve organizational success and individual well-being.

>Improving Perceptions

We can't bypass the perceptual process, but we should make every attempt to minimize perceptual biases and distortions. Two potentially powerful ways to accomplish this are through meaningful interaction and mutual understanding activities.

Meaningful Interaction

The more we interact with someone in a meaningful way, the less we rely on stereotypes and other perceptual shortcuts to understand that person.[28] This statement sounds simple enough, but it works only under specific conditions. Participants must have close and frequent interaction working toward a shared goal where they need to rely on each other (i.e., cooperate rather than compete with each other). Everyone should have equal status in that context and should be engaged in a meaningful task. Having executives work in frontline jobs, which we described at the beginning of this chapter, tends to create meaningful in-

Every year since 1968, the UPS Community Internship Program (CIP) transports up to 50 UPS managers out of their busy world of package delivery for four weeks and into communities that need their help and are far removed from their own lives. CIP interns help in drug abuse centers, homeless shelters, job-training programs, and other community services in Texas, Tennessee, and New York. For example, this photo shows UPS managers (from left) Dirk Fricke and Dan Sotello assisting bike repairman Ed Matthiack at a bicycle recycling shop and job-training center in Brooklyn. UPS senior vice president Cal Darden explains that CIP is an important part of leadership development at UPS because it creates meaningful interaction that "develops sensitivity to issues that our employees and communities face every day." According to Michael Michalak, who completed CIP last year by assisting the needy in Chattanooga, Tennessee, the experience "brings you back down to earth." The UPS manager from Indiana explains further: "When an issue arises, I am more empathetic in dealing with employees."[29]

teraction because these executives have equal status with other staff, cooperate toward a common goal, and have close and frequent interaction with frontline employees.

Along with reducing reliance on stereotypes, meaningful interaction potentially improves a person's empathy toward others. **Empathy** refers to a person's understanding of and sensitivity to the feelings, thoughts, and situation of others.[30] You have empathy when actively visualizing the other person's situation and feeling that person's emotions in that situation. Empathizing with others improves our sensitivity to external causes of another person's performance and behavior, thereby reducing fundamental attribution error. A supervisor who imagines what it's like to be a single mother, for example, would become more sensitive to the external causes of lateness and other events among these employees.

empathy
A person's ability to understand and be sensitive to the feelings, thoughts, and situations of others.

Mutual Understanding: The Johari Window

Knowing yourself—becoming more aware of your values, beliefs, and biases—is a powerful way to improve your perceptions.[31] The **Johari Window** is a popular model for knowing yourself and increasing mutual understanding with co-workers.[32] Developed by Joseph Luft and Harry Ingram (hence the name Johari), this model divides information about you into four "windows"—open, blind, hidden, and unknown—based on whether your own values, beliefs, and experiences are known to you and to others (see Exhibit 3.3).

The *open area* includes information about you that is known both to you and to others. For example, both you and your co-workers may be aware that you don't like to be near

Johari Window
The model of personal and interpersonal understanding that encourages disclosure and feedback to increase the open area and reduce the blind, hidden, and unknown areas of oneself.

[Exhibit 3.3] Johari Window

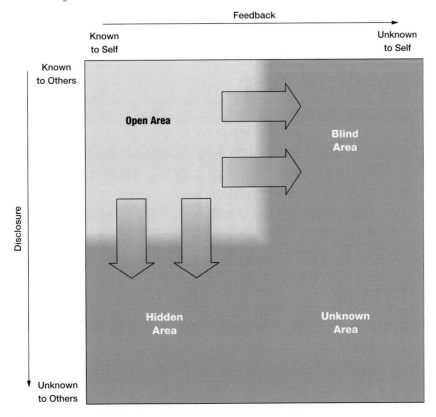

Source: Based on J. Luft, *Group Processes* (Palo Alto, CA: Mayfield, 1984).

people who smoke cigarettes. The *blind area* refers to information that is known to others but not to you. For example, your colleagues might notice that you are self-conscious and awkward when meeting the company CEO, but you are unaware of this fact. Information known to you but unknown to others is found in the *hidden area.* We all have personal secrets about our likes, dislikes, and personal experiences. Finally, the *unknown area* includes your values, beliefs, and experiences that aren't known to you or others.

The main objective of the Johari Window is to increase the size of the open area so that both you and colleagues become more aware of each other's perceptual perspectives and limitations. This is partly accomplished by reducing the hidden area through *disclosure*— informing others of your beliefs, feelings, and experiences that may influence the work relationship.[33] The open area also increases through *feedback* from others about your behavior. This information helps you to reduce your blind area, because co-workers often see things in you that you do not see. Finally, the combination of disclosure and feedback occasionally produces revelations about information in the unknown area.

The Johari Window occurs through frequent open dialogue with co-workers. By communicating with others, we naturally tend to disclose more information about ourselves and eventually feel comfortable providing candid feedback to them. The Johari Window also occurs through the meaningful interaction activities described above. By learning about cultural differences and communicating more with people from different backgrounds, we gain a better understanding of their behavior. "You really have that opportunity to drop your guard and get to know people for who they are," explains Don Wofford, a UPS executive involved for many years in the company's Community Internship Program, which is a powerful form of meaningful interaction with people in the community.[34]

The perceptual process represents the filter through which information passes from the external environment to our brain. As such, it is really the beginning of the learning process, which we discuss next.

>Learning in Organizations

What do employees at Wipro Technologies appreciate most about working at the Indian software giant? Financial rewards and challenging work are certainly on the list, but one of the top benefits is learning. "Wipro provides great learning opportunities," says CEO Vivek Paul. "The core of how employees think about us and value us revolves around training. It simply isn't something we can back off from."[35]

learning
A relatively permanent change in behavior that occurs as a result of a person's interaction with the environment.

Learning is a relatively permanent change in behavior (or behavior tendency) that occurs as a result of a person's interaction with the environment. Learning occurs when the learner behaves differently. For example, we can see that you have "learned" computer skills when you operate the keyboard and windows more quickly than before. Learning occurs when interaction with the environment leads to behavior change. This means that we learn through our senses, such as through study, observation, and experience.

Some of what we learn is *explicit knowledge,* such as reading information in this book. However, explicit knowledge is only the tip of the knowledge iceberg. Most of what we know is **tacit knowledge**.[36] Tacit knowledge is not documented; rather, it is acquired through observation and direct experience. For example, airline pilots learn to operate commercial jets more by watching experts and practicing on flight simulators than through lectures. They acquire tacit knowledge by directly experiencing the complex interaction of behavior with the machine's response.

tacit knowledge
Knowledge embedded in our actions and ways of thinking, and transmitted only through observation and experience.

The rest of this chapter introduces three perspectives of learning tacit and explicit knowledge: reinforcement, social learning, and direct experience. Each perspective offers a different angle for understanding the dynamics of learning.

>Behavior Modification: Learning through Reinforcement

One of the oldest perspectives on learning, called **behavior modification** (also known as *operant conditioning* and *reinforcement theory*), takes the rather extreme view that learning is completely dependent on the environment. Behavior modification does not question the notion that thinking is part of the learning process, but it views human thoughts as unimportant intermediate stages between behavior and the environment. The environment teaches us to alter our behaviors so that we maximize positive consequences and minimize adverse consequences.[37]

> **behavior modification**
> A theory that explains learning in terms of the antecedents and consequences of behavior.

A-B-Cs of Behavior Modification

The central objective of behavior modification is to change behavior (B) by managing its antecedents (A) and consequences (C). This process is nicely illustrated in the A-B-C model of behavior modification, shown in Exhibit 3.4.[38]

Antecedents are events preceding the behavior, informing employees that certain behaviors will have particular consequences. An antecedent may be a sound from your computer signaling that an e-mail has arrived or a request from your supervisor to complete a specific task by tomorrow. These antecedents let employees know that a particular action will produce specific consequences. Notice that antecedents do not cause behaviors. The computer sound doesn't cause us to open our e-mail. Rather, the sound is a cue telling us that certain consequences are likely to occur if we engage in certain behaviors.

Although antecedents are important, behavior modification mainly focuses on the *consequences* of behavior. Consequences are events following a particular behavior that influence its future occurrence. Generally, people tend to repeat behaviors that are followed by pleasant consequences and are less likely to repeat behaviors that are followed by unpleasant consequences or no consequences at all.

Contingencies of Reinforcement

Behavior modification identifies four types of consequences that strengthen, maintain, or weaken behavior. These consequences, collectively known as the *contingencies of reinforcement,* include positive reinforcement, punishment, negative reinforcement, and extinction.[39]

[**Exhibit 3.4**] A-B-Cs of Behavior Modification

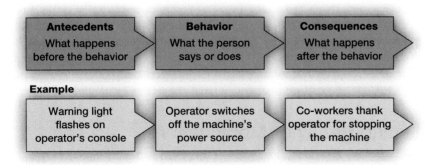

Sources: Adapted from T. K. Connellan, *How to Improve Human Performance* (New York: Harper & Row, 1978), p. 50; F. Luthans and R. Kreitner, *Organizational Behavior Modification and Beyond* (Glenview, IL: Scott, Foresman, 1985), pp. 85–88.

- *Positive reinforcement.* **Positive reinforcement** occurs when the introduction of a consequence increases or maintains the frequency or future probability of a specific behavior. Receiving a bonus after successfully completing an important project is considered positive reinforcement because it typically increases the probability that you use those behaviors in the future.

- *Punishment.* **Punishment** occurs when a consequence decreases the frequency or future probability of a behavior. This consequence typically involves introducing something that employees try to avoid. For instance, most of us would consider a demotion or being ostracized by our co-workers as forms of punishment.

- *Negative reinforcement.* **Negative reinforcement** occurs when the removal or avoidance of a consequence increases or maintains the frequency or future probability of a specific behavior. Supervisors apply negative reinforcement when they *stop* criticizing employees whose substandard performance has improved. When the criticism is withheld, employees are more likely to repeat behaviors that improved their performance. Notice that negative reinforcement is not punishment. It actually reinforces behavior by removing punishment.

- *Extinction.* **Extinction** occurs when the target behavior decreases because no consequence follows it. In this respect, extinction is a do-nothing strategy. Generally, behavior that is no longer reinforced tends to disappear; it becomes extinct. For instance, research suggests that when managers stop congratulating employees for their good performance, that performance tends to decline.[40]

Which contingency of reinforcement should we use in the learning process? In most situations, positive reinforcement should follow desired behaviors and extinction (do nothing) should follow undesirable behaviors. This approach is preferred because relying on punishment and negative reinforcement generate negative emotions and attitudes toward the punisher (e.g., supervisor) and organization. However, some forms of punishment (dismissal, suspension, demotion, etc.) may be necessary for extreme behaviors, such as deliberately hurting a co-worker or stealing inventory. Indeed, research suggests that, under certain conditions, punishment maintains a sense of equity.[41]

Schedules of Reinforcement

Along with considering the contingencies of reinforcement, we need to use the best schedule of reinforcement for the situation.[42] The most effective reinforcement schedule for learning new tasks is *continuous reinforcement*—providing positive reinforcement after every, or nearly every, occurrence of the desired behavior. Employees learn desired behaviors quickly and, when the reinforcer is removed, extinction also occurs very quickly.

The best schedule for reinforcing learned behavior is a *variable ratio schedule* in which employee behavior is reinforced after a variable number of times. Salespeople experience variable ratio reinforcement because they make a successful sale (the reinforcer) after a varying number of client calls. They might make four unsuccessful calls before receiving an order on the fifth one, then make 10 more calls before receiving the next order, and so on. The variable ratio schedule makes behavior highly resistant to extinction because it is never expected at a particular time or after a fixed number of accomplishments.

Evaluating Behavior Modification

Everyone practices behavior modification in one form or another. We thank people for a job well done, are silent when displeased, and sometimes try to punish those who go against our wishes. Behavior modification also occurs in various formal programs to reduce absenteeism, encourage safe work behaviors, and improve task performance.

ExxonMobil seems to win as many safety awards as it produces barrels of oil. The Houston-based energy company relies on extensive safety training and leadership, but it also uses classic behavior modification practices to reinforce safe work behaviors. To some extent, ExxonMobil rewards employees and work units for accident-free milestones and similar *lagging indicators*. In Malaysia, for instance, the company distributes awards to worksites and contractors with zero lost-time injuries. However, ExxonMobil mainly reinforces *leading indicators*—work behaviors that prevent accidents. ExxonMobil's Fawley refinery in the United Kingdom. (shown in photo) introduced a "Behave Safely Challenge" program in which supervisors rewarded employees and contractors on the spot when they exhibited good safety behavior or intervened to improve the safe behavior of co-workers. The company also introduced a system in which co-workers observe each other's safety behaviors.[43]

One concern is that these programs often "incentivize" behavior to the point where bonus money becomes an entitlement rather than a special form of reinforcement.[44] A larger problem, however, is behavior modification's radical view that behavior is learned through personal interaction with the environment and without human thinking as part of that process. This view is no longer accepted; instead, learning experts recognize that people also learn by observing others and logically analyzing what they see. This learning through observation process is explained by social learning theory.

>Social Learning Theory: Learning by Observing

Social learning theory states that much learning occurs by observing others and then modeling the behaviors that lead to favorable outcomes and avoiding behaviors that lead to punishing consequences.[45] This form of learning occurs in three ways: behavior modeling, learning behavior consequences, and self-reinforcement.

- *Behavior modeling.* People learn by observing the behaviors of a role model on the critical task, remembering the important elements of the observed behaviors, and then practicing those behaviors.[46] This is a valuable form of learning because tacit knowledge and skills are mainly acquired from others through observation. As an example, it is difficult to document or verbally explain everything to bake bread professionally. Student chefs also need to observe the master baker's subtle behaviors.

- *Learning behavior consequences.* People learn the consequences of behavior through logic and observation, not just through direct experience. They logically

social learning theory
A theory stating that much learning occurs by observing others and then modeling the behaviors that lead to favorable outcomes and avoiding the behaviors that lead to punishing consequences.

anticipate consequences after completing a task well or poorly. They also learn behavioral consequences by observing the experiences of other people. You might notice how co-workers mock another employee who dresses formally at work. By observing this incident, you learn about the group's preference for wearing casual attire.[47]

self-reinforcement
Occurs whenever someone has control over a reinforcer but delays it until a self-set goal has been completed.

• *Self-reinforcement.* **Self-reinforcement** occurs whenever an employee has control over a reinforcer but doesn't "take" it until completing a self-set goal.[48] For example, you might be thinking about having a snack after you finish reading the rest of this chapter. Raiding the refrigerator is a form of self-induced positive reinforcement for completing this reading assignment. Self-reinforcement takes many forms, such as taking a short walk, watching a movie, or simply congratulating yourself for completing the task.

>Learning through Experience

Along with behavior modification and social learning, employees learn through direct experience. In fact, many organizations are shifting their training and development toward an experiential learning approach because most tacit knowledge and skills are acquired through experience as well as observation. Experiential learning has been conceptualized in many ways, but one of the most enduring perspectives is Kolb's experiential learning model, shown in Exhibit 3.5. This model illustrates experiential learning as a cyclical four-stage process.[49]

Concrete experience involves sensory and emotional engagement in some activity. It is followed by *reflective observation,* which involves listening, watching, recording, and elaborating on the experience. The next stage in the learning cycle is *abstract conceptualization.* This is the stage in which we develop concepts and integrate our observations into logically sound theories. The fourth stage, *active experimentation,* occurs when we test our previous experience, reflection, and conceptualization in a particular context. People tend to prefer and operate better in some stages than in others due to their unique competencies and personality. Still, experiential learning requires all four stages in proper balance.

[Exhibit 3.5] Kolb's Experiential Learning Model

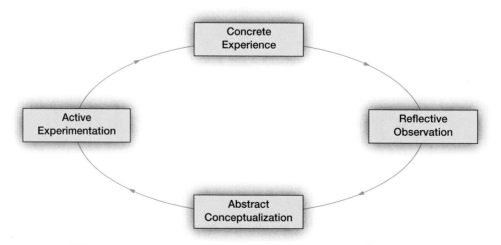

Sources: Based on information in J. E. Sharp, "Applying Kolb Learning Style Theory in the Communication Classroom," *Business Communication Quarterly* 60 (June 1997), pp. 129–134; D. A. Kolb, *Experiential Learning* (Englewood Cliffs, NJ: Prentice Hall, 1984).

Experiential Learning in Practice

Learning through experience works best in organizations with a strong **learning orientation**, which means that they have a commitment to learning, open-mindedness, and a shared vision to guide the learning.[50] Organizations achieve a learning orientation culture by rewarding experimentation and recognizing mistakes as a natural part of the learning process. They encourage employees to question existing practices and to take reasonable risks in discovering new and better ways of doing things.

One application of workplace experiential learning that has received considerable interest, particularly in Europe, is **action learning**. Action learning occurs when employees, usually in teams, investigate and apply solutions to a situation that is both real and complex, with immediate relevance to the company.[51] In other words, the project becomes the source of learning. Kolb's experiential learning model presented earlier is usually identified as the main template for action learning. Action learning requires concrete experience with a real organizational problem or opportunity, followed by "learning meetings" in which participants reflect on their observations about that problem or opportunity. Then, they develop and test a strategy to solve the problem or realize the opportunity. The process also encourages plenty of reflection so the experience becomes a learning process.

This chapter has introduced you to two fundamental activities in human behavior in the workplace: perceptions and learning. These activities involve receiving information from the environment, organizing it, and acting on it as a learning process. Our knowledge about perceptions and learning in the workplace lays the foundation for the next chapter, which looks at workplace emotions and attitudes.

learning orientation
The extent that an organization or individual supports knowledge management, particularly opportunities to acquire knowledge through experience and experimentation.

action learning
Occurs when employees, usually in teams, investigate and apply solutions to a situation that is both real and complex, with immediate relevance to the company.

>chapter summary

Perception involves selecting, organizing, and interpreting information to make sense of the world around us. Selective attention is influenced by characteristics of the person or object being perceived (i.e., their size, intensity, motion, repetition, and novelty) and characteristics of the person doing the perceiving. Perceptual organization engages categorical thinking—the mostly unconscious process of organizing people and objects into preconceived categories that are stored in our long-term memory. To a large extent, our perceptual interpretation of incoming information also occurs before we are consciously aware of it. Mental models—broad worldviews or templates of the mind—also help us to make sense of incoming stimuli.

The social identity process explains how we perceive ourselves and other people. We partly identify ourselves in terms of our membership in social groups. This comparison process includes categorizing people into groups, forming a homogeneous image of people within those groups, and differentiating groups by assigning more favorable features to our own groups than to other groups.

Stereotyping is a derivative of social identity theory, in which people assign traits to others based on their membership in a social category. Stereotyping economizes mental effort, fills in missing information, and enhances our self-perception and social identity. However, it also lays the foundation for intentional and unintentional discrimination. It is very difficult to prevent the activation of stereotyping, but we can minimize the application of stereotypic information in our decisions and actions.

The attribution process involves deciding whether the behavior or event is largely due to the situation (external attributions) or personal characteristics (internal attributions). This process helps us to link together the various pieces of our world in cause-effect relationships, but it is also subject to attribution errors, including fundamental attribution error and self-serving bias. Self-fulfilling prophecy occurs when our expectations about another person cause that person to act in a way that is consistent with those expectations. Essentially, our expectations affect our behavior toward the target person, which then affects the employee's opportunities and attitudes, which then influences his or her behavior.

We can minimize perceptual problems through meaningful interaction and becoming more aware of our values, beliefs, and biases (Johari Window).

Learning is a relatively permanent change in behavior (or behavior tendency) that occurs as a result of a person's interaction with the environment. Some learning results in explicit knowledge, but much of what we learn is tacit knowledge, which is embedded in our actions without conscious awareness.

The behavior modification perspective of learning states that behavior change occurs by altering its antecedents and consequences. Antecedents are environmental stimuli that provoke (not necessarily cause) behavior. Consequences are events following behavior that influence its future occurrence. Consequences include positive reinforcement, punishment, negative reinforcement, and extinction. The schedules of reinforcement also influence behavior.

Social learning theory states that much learning occurs by observing others and then modeling those behaviors that seem to lead to favorable outcomes and avoiding behaviors that lead to punishing consequences. It also recognizes that we often engage in self-reinforcement.

Many companies now use experiential learning because employees do not acquire tacit knowledge through formal classroom instruction. Kolb's experiential learning model is a cyclical four-stage process that includes concrete experience, reflective observation, abstract conceptualization, and active experimentation. Action learning is experiential learning in which employees investigate and act on significant organizational issues.

>**key**.terms

action learning 59

attribution process 49

behavior modification 55

categorical thinking 46

empathy 53

extinction 56

fundamental attribution error 50

Johari Window 53

learning 54

learning orientation 59

mental models 46

negative reinforcement 56

perception 45

positive reinforcement 56

punishment 56

selective attention 45

self-fulfilling prophecy 50

self-reinforcement 58

self-serving bias 50

social identity theory 46

social learning theory 57

stereotyping 48

tacit knowledge 54

>critical.thinking.questions

1. You are part of a task force to increase worker responsiveness to emergencies on the production floor. Identify four factors that should be considered when installing a device that will get every employees' attention when there is an emergency.

2. What mental models do you have about attending a college or university lecture? Are these mental models helpful? Could any of these mental models hold you back from achieving the full benefit of the lecture?

3. Contrast "personal" and "social" identity. Do you define yourself in terms of the university or college you attend? Why or why not? What implications does your response have for the future of your university or college?

4. During a training session on being wary of stereotyping, a manager suggests that stereotypes are a necessary part of working with others. "I have to make assumptions about what's in the other person's head, and stereotypes help me do that," she explains. "It's better to rely on stereotypes than to enter a working relationship with someone from another culture without any idea of what they believe in!" Discuss the merits of and problems with the manager's statement.

5. Several studies have reported that self-serving bias occurs in corporate annual reports. What does this mean and how would it be apparent in these reports? Provide hypothetical examples of self-serving bias in these documents.

6. Describe how a manager or coach could use the process of self-fulfilling prophecy to enhance an individual's performance.

7. Describe a situation in which you used behavior modification to influence someone's behavior. What specifically did you do? What was the result?

8. Why are organizations moving toward the use of experiential approaches to learning? What conditions are required for success?

>case.study:skillbuilder3.1

From Lippert-Johanson Incorporated to Fenway Waste Management

By Lisa V. Williams, Jeewon Cho, and Alicia Boisnier, SUNY at Buffalo

Part One

Catherine O'Neill was very excited to finally be graduating from Flagship University at the end of the semester. She had always been interested in accounting, following from her father's lifelong occupation, and she very much enjoyed the challenging major. She was involved in many highly-regarded student clubs in the business school and worked diligently to earn good grades. Now her commitment to the profession would pay off, she hoped, as she turned her attention to her job search. In late Fall, she had on-campus interviews with several firms, but her interview with the prestigious Lippert-Johanson Incorporated (LJI) stood out in her mind as the most attractive opportunity. That's why Catherine was thrilled to learn she made it to the next level of interviews, to be held at the firm's main office later that month.

When Catherine entered the elegant lobby of LJI's New York City offices, she was immediately impressed by all there was to take in. Catherine had always been one to pay attention to detail, and her acute observations of her environment had always been an asset. She was able to see how social and environmental cues told her what was expected of her, and she always set out to meet and exceed those expectations. On a tour of the office, she had already begun to size up her prospective workplace. She appreciated the quiet, focused work atmosphere. She liked how everyone was dressed: most wore suits and their conservative apparel supported the professional attitudes that seemed to be omnipresent. People spoke to her in a formal, but friendly manner, and seemed enthusiastic. Some of them even took the time to greet her as she was guided to the conference room for her individual interviews. "I like the way this place feels, and I would love to come to work here every day," Catherine thought. "I hope I do well in my interview!"

Before she knew it, Catherine was sitting in a nicely-appointed office with one of the eight managers in the firm. Sandra Jacobs was the picture of a professional woman, and Catherine naturally took her cue from Sandra about how to conduct herself in the interview. It seemed to go very quickly, although the interview lasted an hour. As soon as Catherine left the office, she could not wait to phone her father about the interview. "I loved it there and I just know I'm a good fit!" she told her proud father. "Like them, I believe it is important to have the highest ethical standards and quality of work. Ms. Jacobs really emphasized the mission of the firm, as well as its policies. She did say that all the candidates have an excellent skill set and are well qualified for the job, so mostly, they are going to base their hiring decision on how well they think each of us will fit into the firm. Reputation is everything to an accounting firm. I learned that from you, Dad!"

After six weeks of apprehensive waiting, Catherine's efforts were rewarded when LJI and another firm contacted her with job offers. Catherine knew she would accept the offer from LJI. She saw the firm as very ethical, with the highest standards for work quality, and an excellent reputation. Catherine was grateful to have been selected from such a competitive hiring process. "There couldn't be a better choice for me! I'm so proud to become a member of this company!"

Catherine's first few days at LJI were a whirlwind of a newcomer's experiences. She had meetings with her supervisor to discuss the firm's mission statement, her role in the firm, and what was expected of her. She was also told to spend some time looking at the employee handbook that covers many important policies of the firm, such as dress code, sick time, grievances, the chain of command and job descriptions, and professional ethics. Everyone relied on the handbook to provide clear guidance about what is expected of each employee. Also, Catherine was informed that she would soon begin participating in continuing professional education, which would allow her to update her skills and knowledge in her field. "This is great," thought Catherine. "I'm so glad to know the firm doesn't just talk about its high standards, it actually follows through with action."

What Catherine enjoyed most about her new job were her warm and welcoming colleagues who invited her to their group lunches, beginning her first day. They talked about work and home; they seemed close, both professionally and personally. She could see that everyone had a similar attitude about work: they cared about their work and the firm, they took responsibility for their own tasks, but they also helped one another out. Catherine also got involved in LJI activities outside of work, like their baseball and soccer teams, happy hours, picnics and parties, and enjoyed the chance to mingle with her co-workers. In what seemed like no time at all, Catherine started to really see herself as a fully-integrated member of LJI.

Before tax season started, Catherine attended some meetings of the American Institute of Certified Public Accountants (AICPA) and other professional accounting societies. There, she met many accountants from other firms who all seemed very impressed when she told them where she worked. Catherine's pride and appreciation for being a member of LJI grew as she realized how highly regarded the firm is among others in the accounting industry.

Part Two

Over the past seven years, Catherine's career in New York had flourished. Her reputation as one of the top tax accountants in her company was well established, and was recognized by colleagues outside the firm as well. However, Catherine entered a new chapter of her life when she married Ted Lewis, an oncology intern, who could not turn down an offer of residency at a top cancer center in upstate New York. Wanting to support Ted's once-in-a-lifetime career opportunity, Catherine decided it was time to follow the path of many of her colleagues and leave public accounting for a position that would be more conducive to starting a family. Still, her heart was in the profession, so she took an available position as a controller of a small recycling company located a few miles from Catherine and Ted's new Upstate upstate home. She knew that with this position she could both have children and maintain her career.

Fenway Waste Management is small—about 35 employees. There are about 25 people who work in the warehouse, three administrative assistants, two supervisors, and five people in management. Catherine had trouble adjusting to her new position and surroundings. Often she was asked to perform work that formally belonged to someone else; because it is a smaller company, managers seem to "wear many hats." This was quite different from what she had experienced at LJI. In addition, the warehouse crew often has to work with greasy materials, and sometimes tracks the grease into the offices. Catherine half-laughed and half-worried when she saw a piece of paper pinned to the wall that said, "Clean Up After Yourself!" She supposed that the nature of the business was why the offices are functional, but furnished with old pieces. She couldn't imagine having a business meeting there! Also, for most of the employees, the casual dress matches the causal attitudes. But Catherine continues to wear a dressed-down version of her formal LJI attire, even though her new co-workers consider her overdressed.

With all the changes Catherine has experienced, she has maintained one familiar piece of her past. Although it is not required for her new position, Catherine still attends AICPA meetings and makes a point to continue updating her knowledge of current tax laws. At this year's conference, she told a former colleague, "Being here, I feel so much more like myself—I am so much more connected to these people and this environment than to those at my new job. It's too bad I don't feel this way at Fenway. I guess I'm just more comfortable with professionals who are similar to me."

Discussion Questions

Questions for Part 1

1. Discuss the social identity issues present in this case.

2. What indicated Catherine's positive evaluation of the groups described in Part 1? How did her evaluations foster her social identity?

3. What theory helps us understand how Catherine learned about appropriate behaviors at LJI?

Questions for Part 2

1. Compare and contrast LJI and Fenway.

2. What was Catherine's reaction after joining Fenway Waste Management and why was her level of social identification different from that of LJI Waste Management?

3. Is there evidence that Catherine experienced the categorization-homogenization-differentiation process? What details support your conclusion?

>class.exercise:skillbuilder3.2

The Learning Exercise

Purpose   This exercise is designed to help you understand how the contingencies of reinforcement in behavior modification affect learning.

Materials   Any objects normally available in a classroom will be acceptable for this activity.

Instructions

The instructor will ask for three volunteers, who will then be briefed outside the classroom. The instructor will spend a few minutes briefing the remaining students in the class about their duties. Then, one of the three volunteers will enter the room to participate in the exercise. When completed, the second volunteer will enter the room and participate in the exercise. When completed, the third volunteer will enter the class and participate in the exercise.

For students to gain the full benefit of this exercise, no other information will be provided here. However, your instructor will have more details at the beginning of this fun activity.

>team.exercise:skillbuilder3.3

Who Am I?

Purpose   This exercise is designed to help you understand the elements and implications of social identity theory.

Materials   None.

Instructions

- *Step 1:* Working alone (no discussion with other students), use the form provided here or a piece of paper to write down 12 words or phrases that answer the question "Who am I?" Write your words or phrases describing you as they come to mind; don't worry about their logical order here. Please be sure to fill in all 12 spaces.

- *Step 2:* Circle the S beside the items that define you in terms of your social identity, such as your demographics and formal or informal membership in a social group or institution (school, company, religious group). Circle the P beside the items that define you in terms of your personal identity; that is, unique personality, values, or experiences that are not connected to any particular social group. Next, underline one or more items that you believe will still be a strong characteristic of you 10 years from now.

- *Step 3:* Form small groups. If you have a team project for this course, your project team would work well for

Phrases that describe you	Circle S or P
1. I am _____	S P
2. I am _____	S P
3. I am _____	S P
4. I am _____	S P
5. I am _____	S P
6. I am _____	S P
7. I am _____	S P
8. I am _____	S P
9. I am _____	S P
10. I am _____	S P
11. I am _____	S P
12. I am _____	S P

this exercise. Compare your list with the lists that others in your group wrote about themselves. Discuss the following questions in your group and prepare notes for class discussion and possible presentation of these questions:

1. Among members of this team, what was the typical percentage of items representing the person's social

versus personal identity? Did some team members have many more or less social identity items compared to other team members? Why do you think these large or small differences in emphasis on social or personal identity occurred?

2. What characteristics did people in your group underline as being the most stable (i.e. remaining the same in 10 years from now)? Were these underlined items mostly social or personal identity features? How similar or different were the underlined items among team members?

3. What do these lists say about the dynamics of your group as a team (whether or not your group for this activity is actually involved in a class project for this course)?

Sources: M. H. Kuhn and T. S. McPartland, "An Empirical Investigation of Self-Attitudes," *American Sociological Review* 19 (February 1954), pp. 68–76; C. Lay and M. Verkuyten, "Ethnic Identity and Its Relation to Personal Self-Esteem: A Comparison of Canadian-Born and Foreign-Born Chinese Adolescents," *Journal of Social Psychology* 139 (1999), pp. 288–99; and S. L. Grace and K. L. Cramer, "The Elusive Nature of Self-Measurement: The Self-Construal Scale versus the Twenty Statements Test," *Journal of Social Psychology* 143 (2003), pp. 649–68.

>web.exercise:skillbuilder3.4

Analyzing Corporate Annual Reports

Purpose   This exercise is designed to help you diagnose evidence of stereotyping and corporate role models that minimize stereotyping in corporate annual reports.

Materials   Students need to complete their research for this activity prior to class, including selecting a publicly traded company and downloading the past four or more years of its fully illustrated annual reports.

Instructions

The instructor may have students work alone or in groups for this activity. Students will select a publicly traded company that makes its annual reports available on the company Web site. Ideally, annual reports for at least the past four years should be available, and these reports should be presented in the final illustrated format (typically, PDF replicas of the original hard copy report).

Students will closely examine images in the selected company's recent annual reports in terms of how women, visible minorities, and older employees and clients are

presented. Specifically, students should be prepared to discuss and provide details in class regarding:

1. The percentage of images showing (i.e., visual representation of) women, visible minorities, and older workers and clients. Students should also be sensitive to the size and placement of these images on the page and throughout the annual report.

2. The roles in which women, visible minorities, and older workers and clients are depicted. For example, are women shown more in traditional or nontraditional occupations and nonwork roles in these annual reports?

3. If several years of annual reports are available, pick one that is a decade or more old and compare its visual representation of and role depiction of women, visible minorities, and older employees and clients.

If possible, pick one of the most blatantly stereotypic illustrations you can find in these annual report to show in class, either as a hard copy printout or as a computer projection.

>self-assessment.skillbuilder3.5

Assessing Your Personal Need for Structure

Some people need to "make sense" of things around them more quickly or completely than do other people. This personal need for perceptual structure relates to selective attention as well as perceptual organization and interpretation. This self-assessment is designed to help you to estimate your personal need for perceptual structure. Read each of the statements and decide how much you

agree with each according to your attitudes, beliefs, and experiences. It is important for you to realize that there are no right or wrong answers to these questions. This self-assessment is completed alone so that students rate themselves honestly without concerns of social comparison. However, class discussion will focus on the meaning of need for structure in terms of how we engage differently in the perceptual process at work and in other settings.

>self-assessment.skillbuilder3.6

Assessing Your Perspective-Taking (Cognitive Empathy)

Empathy is an important perceptual ability in social relations, but the degree to which people empathize varies considerably. This self-assessment provides an estimate of one form of empathy, known as *cognitive empathy* or *perspective-taking*. This means that it measures the level of cognitive awareness of another person's situational and individual circumstances. To complete this scale, indicate the degree to which each of the statements presented does or does not describe you very well. You need to be honest with yourself to reasonably estimate your level of perspective taking. The results show your relative position along the perspective-taking continuum and the general meaning of this score.

>self-assessment.skillbuilder3.7

Assessing Your Emotional Empathy

Empathy is an important perceptual ability in social relations, but the degree to which people empathize varies considerably. This self-assessment provides an estimate of one form of empathy, known as emotional empathy. This refers to the extent that you are able to experience the emotions or feelings of the other person. To complete this scale, indicate the degree to which each of the statements presented does or does not describe you very well. You need to be honest with yourself to reasonably estimate your level of emotional empathy. The results show your relative position along the emotional empathy continuum and the general meaning of this score.

Find the full self-assessments on the OLC at
www.mhhe.com/mcshaneess

[chapter 4]

Workplace Emotions, Attitudes, and Stress

Justin Hall (shown) and other staff at Pike Place Fish Market in Seattle practice their Fish! philosophy by tossing fish and joking with customers.

>**learning**objectives

After reading this chapter, you should be able to

- Define emotions.
- Explain how cognitions and emotions influence attitudes and behavior.
- Identify the conditions that require, and the problems associated with, emotional labor.
- Describe the four dimensions of emotional intelligence.
- Summarize the effects of job dissatisfaction in terms of the exit-voice-loyalty-neglect model.
- Discuss the relationships between job satisfaction and performance as well as job satisfaction and customer satisfaction.
- Compare the effects of affective and continuance commitment on employee behavior.
- Describe five strategies to increase organizational commitment.
- Define stress and describe the stress experience.
- Explain why a stressor might produce different stress levels in two people.
- Identify five ways to manage workplace stress.

Layoffs and cutbacks had sapped staff morale at Cooley Dickinson Hospital in Northampton, Massachusetts, and the employee satisfaction team couldn't figure out how to improve the situation. Then, someone mentioned Fish!, a set of principles for creating positive attitudes at work. After viewing the Fish! video during a fish fry, managers and staff started celebrating birthdays, enjoying ice cream breaks, and hosting a Christmas holiday gift-wrapping service. Morale has soared. "The Fish! team is keeping employee satisfaction out front," says Cooley Dickinson's director of guest services. "That stuff doesn't happen by accident."

The Fish! philosophy began at Pike Place Fish Market in Seattle. Fishmongers turned a money-losing, morale-draining business into a world-famous attraction by deciding to have fun at work, such as tossing fish around and joking with customers. Out of this turnaround came four Fish! principles: play, make their day, be there, and choose your attitude. To create an exciting workplace, employees need to learn how to play, just as the fishmongers toss fish. "Make their day" refers to involving others so they, too, have a positive experience. "Be there" means that employees need to be focused (not mentally in several places) and actively engaged to have fun. "Choose your attitude" says that everyone has the power to choose how they feel at work.

The Fish! philosophy has caught on. Human resources staff members at Scope International in Malaysia have fun with color coordination days (where they wear the same color on a particular day). The staff of the Sprint Global Connections Services call center in Kansas City, Missouri, toss around foam toys, walk around in bunny slippers, and dance under a disco ball suspended from the ceiling. Sounds strange, but these antics helped Sprint reduce turnover, improve productivity, and win a Call Center of the Year award. And at Matanuska Valley Federal Credit Union, staff members have a fish parade around the building's exterior before opening. "The winters here in Alaska can get pretty cold and bleak starting in October," explains a manager at the Palmer, Alaska, financial institution. "Fish! has helped boost morale and is just plain fun during those long months"[1]

Whether you work at a hospital in Massachusetts, a credit union in Alaska, or a bank services group in Malaysia, emotions and attitudes are receiving a lot more attention these days. That's because emotions and attitudes can make a huge difference in individual behavior and well-being, as well as in the organization's performance and customer satisfaction. Over the past decade, the field of organizational behavior has experienced a sea change in thinking about workplace emotions, so this chapter begins by introducing the concept and explaining how emotions influence attitudes and behavior. We then consider the dynamics of emotional labor and the popular topic of emotional intelligence. The specific work attitudes of job satisfaction and organizational commitment are then discussed, including their association with various employee behaviors and work performance. The final section looks at work-related stress, including the stress experience, four prominent stressors, individual differences in stress, and ways to combat excessive stress.

>Emotions in the Workplace

Emotions have a profound effect on almost everything we do in the workplace. This is a strong statement, and one that you would rarely find a decade ago in organizational behavior research or textbooks. For most of its history, the field of OB assumed that a person's thoughts and actions are governed primarily by conscious reasoning (called *cognitions*). Yet, groundbreaking neuroscience discoveries have revealed that our perceptions, attitudes, decisions, and behavior are influenced by both cognition and emotion and that the latter often has the greater influence.[2]

emotions
Physiological, behavioral, and psychological episodes experienced toward an object, person, or event that create a state of readiness.

So, what are emotions? **Emotions** are physiological, behavioral, and psychological episodes experienced toward an object, person, or event that create a state of readiness.[3] They are brief events that typically subside or occur in waves lasting a few minutes. Emotions are directed toward someone or something. For example, we experience joy, fear, anger, and other emotional episodes toward tasks, customers, or a software program we are using. This contrasts with *moods,* which are less intense emotional states that are not directed toward anything in particular.

Emotions are experiences regarding how our body responds to the environment. When we are happy or bored, our blood pressure, heart rate, facial muscles, voice tone, and other features change. These bodily changes relate to the fact that emotions put us in a state of readiness. Emotions are also communications to our conscious selves. Some emotions (e.g., anger, surprise, fear) are particularly strong triggers that interrupt our train of thought, demand our attention, and generate the motivation to take action. They make us aware of events that may affect our survival and well-being.[4]

There are dozens of emotions, and experts organize them in terms of whether they are positive or negative as well as how much they activate us (demand our attention). Anger is a negative emotion that definitely demands our attention. Feeling relaxed is a pleasant emotion that has fairly low activation.

Emotions, Attitudes, and Behavior

attitudes
The cluster of beliefs, assessed feelings, and behavioral intentions toward an object.

Emotions influence our thoughts and behavior, but to explain this effect we first need to know about attitudes. **Attitudes** represent the cluster of beliefs, assessed feelings, and behavioral intentions toward a person, object, or event (called an *attitude object*).[5] Attitudes are *judgments,* whereas emotions are *experiences*. In other words, we think about our attitudes, whereas emotions are physiological and behavioral reactions, most of which occur without our awareness. We also experience emotions briefly, whereas our attitude toward someone or something is more stable over time.

Attitudes include three components: beliefs, feelings, and behavioral intentions. Here is a description of each component, using attitude toward mergers as an illustration:

- *Beliefs.* These are your established perceptions about the attitude object—what you believe to be true. For example, you might believe that mergers reduce job security for employees in the merged firms. Or you might believe that mergers increase the company's competitiveness in this era of globalization. These beliefs are perceived facts that you acquire from past experience and other forms of learning.

- *Feelings.* Feelings represent your positive or negative evaluations of the attitude object. Some people think mergers are good; others think they are bad. Your like or dislike of mergers represents your assessed feelings toward the attitude object.

- *Behavioral intentions.* These represent your motivation to engage in a particular behavior with respect to the attitude object. You might plan to quit rather than stay with the company during the merger. Alternatively, you might intend to complain to the company CEO, arguing that this merger was a bad decision.

Until recently, attitude experts assumed that these three attitude components are connected to each other and to behavior only through the cognitive (logical reasoning) process shown on the left side of Exhibit 4.1. Traditional attitude theory assumed that your feelings are "calculated" from your beliefs about the characteristics of that object, person, or event. If you dislike mergers (feelings), it is because you consciously calculated the combined positive and negative effects of mergers, such as that you think (beliefs) mergers cause layoffs and confusion in the organization.

Next, the traditional attitude model says that your feelings influence your behavioral intentions. If your company announces a forthcoming merger and you dislike mergers, you

[Exhibit 4.1] Model of Emotions, Attitudes, and Behavior

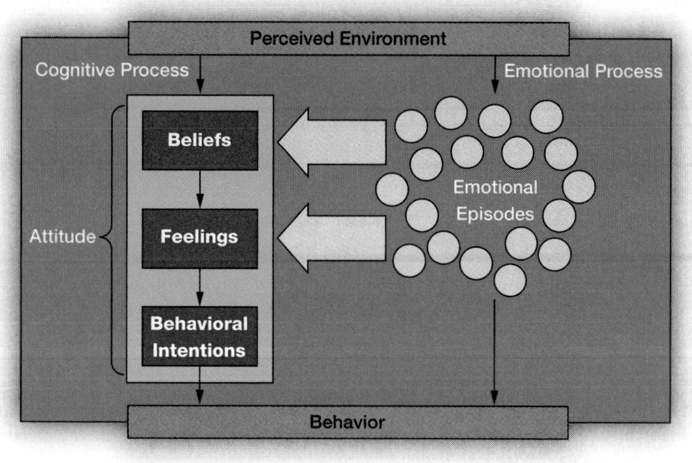

might be motivated to complain to the CEO or quit and join another organization. In the final step, behavioral intentions lead to behavior. Your intention to complain to management about their merger announcement motivates you to engage in that behavior. However, whether you actually do complain depends on the other elements in the MARS model, such as finding the time to write a complaint or figure out the best way to complain to the CEO.

How Emotions Influence Attitudes and Behavior

The traditional cognitive model has dominated attitude research for decades. While it does describe how attitudes are formed and maintained to some extent, we now know that it is only part of the whole picture.[6] According to neuroscience research, incoming information from our senses is routed to the emotional center as well as the cognitive (logical reasoning) center of our brain.[7] We have already described the logical reasoning process, depicted on the left side of Exhibit 4.1. The right side of that diagram offers a simple depiction of how emotions influence our attitudes and behavior.

The emotional side of attitude formation begins with the dynamics of the perceptual process, particularly perceptual interpretation, described in Chapter 3. When receiving incoming information, the emotional center quickly and imprecisely evaluates whether the incoming information supports or threatens our innate drives, then attaches emotional markers to the information. These are not calculated feelings; they are automatic and unconscious emotional responses based on very thin slices of sensory information.[8] For instance, you might experience excitement, worry, or other combination of emotions as soon as you hear that your company intends to merge with a competitor.

The large dots on the right side of Exhibit 4.1 illustrate these multiple emotional episodes triggered by the merger announcement, subsequent thinking about the merger, discussion with co-workers about the merger, and so on. These emotions are transmitted to the logical reasoning process, where they swirl around and ultimately shape our conscious feelings toward the attitude object.[9] Thus, while consciously evaluating the merger—that is, logically figuring out whether it is a good or bad thing—your emotions have already formed an opinion that then sways your analysis of the situation. If you experience worry, frustration, and other negative emotions whenever you think about or discuss the merger, then these emotional episodes will lean your logical reasoning toward negative feelings regarding the merger.

You can see how emotions affect workplace attitudes. When performing our jobs or interacting with co-workers, we experience a variety of emotions that shape our longer-term feelings toward the company, our boss, the job itself, and so on. The more we experience

Wegmans Food Market bends over backward to make sure its employees get plenty of positive emotions at work. Employees enjoy health benefits, an employee assistance program, and a generous scholarship fund, but it's the everyday positive experiences that seem to make the difference. "The atmosphere we work in, the job security we have, it's all great," says Mike O'Brien, a produce clerk in Fayetteville, New York. Bob Staelins, a master chef at Wegmans in Buffalo, likes the freedom to perform his job. "We're empowered to make decisions, to stretch your imagination," says Staelins, who Wegmans sent to the Culinary Institute of America for training. Brenda Hidalgo, who also works at Wegmans in Buffalo, sums up the positive experience: "I've worked at other places that you wake up and you say 'Ech, I have to go to work,'" she recalls. "Now I love to go to work."[10]

positive emotions, the more we form positive attitudes toward the targets of those emotions. This explanation makes sense of popular practices such as Fish!, which was described in the opening story to this chapter. These activities potentially generate more positive emotions in the workplace, which then produce more positive attitudes toward work and the organization.

When Cognitions and Emotions Conflict

The influence of both logical reasoning and emotions on attitudes is most apparent when they disagree with each other. Everyone occasionally experiences this mental tug-of-war, sensing that something isn't right even though they can't think of any logical reason to be concerned. This conflicting experience indicates that our logical analysis of the situation (left side of Exhibit 4.1) can't identify reasons to support the automatic emotional reaction (right side of Exhibit 4.1).[11]

Should we pay attention to our emotional response or our logical analysis? This question is not easy to answer because the emotional and rational processes closely interact with each other. However, some studies indicate that while executives tend to make quick decisions based on their gut feelings (emotional response), the best decisions tend to occur when they spend time logically evaluating the situation.[12] Thus, we should pay attention to both the cognitive and emotional side of the attitude model and hope they agree with each other most of the time.

One last observation about the attitude model in Exhibit 4.1 relates to the arrow leading from the emotional episodes to behavior. This indicates that people have direct behavioral reactions to their emotions. Even low-intensity emotions automatically change your facial expressions. High-intensity emotions can have a more powerful effect, which is apparent when an upset employee bangs a fist on the desk or an overjoyed colleague embraces someone nearby. These actions are not carefully thought out. They are usually automatic emotional responses that serve as coping mechanisms in that situation.

Cognitive Dissonance

Emotions and attitudes usually lead to behavior, but the opposite sometimes happens through the process of **cognitive dissonance**.[13] Cognitive dissonance occurs when we perceive an inconsistency between our beliefs, feelings, and behavior. This inconsistency creates an uncomfortable tension that motivates us to change one or more of these elements. Behavior is usually the most difficult element to change, particularly when it is known to everyone, was done voluntarily, and can't be undone. Thus, we usually change our beliefs and feelings to reduce the inconsistency.

cognitive dissonance
Occurs when people perceive an inconsistency between their beliefs, feelings, and behavior.

>Managing Emotions at Work

Whether giving the friendliest service at Wegmans Foods in Rochester, New York, or the funniest service at Pike Place Fish Market in Seattle, Washington, employees are usually expected to manage their emotions in the workplace. **Emotional labor** refers to the effort, planning, and control needed to express organizationally desired emotions during interpersonal transactions.[14] When interacting with co-workers, customers, suppliers, and others, employees are expected to abide by *display rules*. These rules are norms requiring employees to display certain emotions and withhold others.

emotional labor
The effort, planning, and control needed to express organizationally desired emotions during interpersonal transactions.

Emotional labor is higher in jobs requiring a variety of emotions (e.g., anger as well as joy) and more intense emotions (e.g., showing delight rather than smiling weakly), as well as where interaction with clients is frequent and for longer durations. Emotional labor also increases when employees must precisely rather than casually abide by the display rules. For instance, "Smile: we are on stage" is one of the most important rules at the Ritz-Carlton in San Francisco, so employees must always engage in this form of emotional labor.[15]

Emotional Display Norms across Cultures

How much people are expected to hide or reveal their true emotions in public depends to some extent on the culture in which they live. In some countries—particularly Ethiopia, Korea, Japan, and Austria—cultural values direct people to display a neutral emotional demeanor. In the workplace and other public settings, employees try to subdue their emotional expression and minimize physical contact with others. Even voice intonation tends to be monotonic. In other countries—notably Kuwait, Egypt, Spain, and Russia—cultural values allow or encourage open display of one's true emotions. People are expected to be transparent in revealing their thoughts and feelings, dramatic in their conversational tones, and animated in their use of nonverbal behaviors to get their message across.

These cultural variations in emotional display can be quite noticeable. One survey reported that 83 percent of Japanese believe it is inappropriate to get emotional in a business context, compared with 40 percent of Americans, 34 percent of French, and only 29 percent of Italians. In other words, Italians are more likely to accept or tolerate people who display their true emotions at work, whereas this would be considered rude or embarrassing in Japan.[16]

As one of the world's leading operators of luxury hotels, Four Seasons Hotels and Resorts trains employees and audits hotel performance to ensure that guests consistently experience the highest standards of service quality. Yet Four Seasons also adapts its legendary service to the local culture. "McDonald's is the same all over. We do not want to be that way; we are not a cookie cutter company," says Four Seasons executive David Crowl. One of the most obvious forms of localization is in the way Four Seasons staff are allowed to display emotions that reflect their own culture. "What changes [from one country to the next] is that people do it with their own style, grace, and personality," explains Antoine Corinthios, president of Four Seasons' operations in Europe, Middle East, and Africa. "In some cultures you add the strong local temperament. For example, an Italian concierge has his own style and flair. In Turkey or Egypt you experience different hospitality."[17]

Emotional Dissonance

Emotional labor can be challenging for most of us because it is difficult to conceal true emotions and to display the emotions required by the job. The main problem is that joy, sadness, worry and other emotions automatically activate a complex set of facial muscles that are difficult to prevent and equally difficult to fake. Our true emotions tend to reveal themselves as subtle gestures, usually without our awareness. Meanwhile, pretending to be cheerful or concerned is difficult because several specific facial muscles and body positions must be coordinated. More often than not, observers see when we are faking and sense that we feel a different emotion.[18]

Along with the challenges of hiding and displaying emotions, emotional labor often creates a conflict between required and true emotions, called **emotional dissonance**. The larger the conflict between the required and true emotions, the more employees tend to experience stress, job burnout, and psychological separation from self (called *work alienation*).[19] These negative outcomes of emotional dissonance occur when engaging in *surface acting*—modifying behavior to be consistent with required emotions but continuing to hold different internal feelings. *Deep acting,* on the other hand, involves changing true emotions to match the required emotions. Rather than feeling irritated by a particular customer, you might view the difficult person as an opportunity to test your sales skills. This

emotional dissonance
The conflict between required and true emotions.

change in perspective can potentially generate more positive emotions, which produce friendlier displays of emotion.[20]

Along with teaching employees how to apply deep acting, companies minimize emotional dissonance by hiring people with a natural tendency to display desired emotions. For example, when CiCi's Pizza opens new stores, it looks for job applicants with a "happy, cheery" attitude. The restaurant franchise believes that it is easier to teach new skills than attitudes. "We hire for attitude and train for skill," says one of CiCi's franchisees.[21] In some respects, this also means that CiCi's and other companies look for people with well-developed emotional intelligence, which we discuss next.

Emotional Intelligence

Each year, the U.S. Air Force hires about 400 recruiters, and until recently, up to 100 of them were fired annually for failing to sign up enough people for the service. Selecting and training 100 new recruiters costs $3 million, not to mention the hidden costs of their poor performance. So the Air Force decided to test its 1,200 recruiters on how well they manage their emotions and the emotions of others. The test indicated that the top recruiters were better at asserting their feelings and thoughts, empathizing with others, feeling happy in life, and being aware of their emotions in a particular situation. The next year, the Air Force selected new recruiters partly on their results on this test. The result: Only eight recruiters got fired or quit a year later.[22]

To select the best recruiters, the U.S. Air Force considers more than the cognitive intelligence of job applicants; it also looks at their **emotional intelligence (EI)**. EI is the ability to perceive and express emotion, assimilate emotion in thought, understand and reason with emotion, and regulate emotion in oneself and others.[23] In other words, EI represents a set of *competencies* that allow us to perceive, understand, and regulate emotions in ourselves and in others. Exhibit 4.2 illustrates that EI is organized into four dimensions

emotional intelligence (EI)
The ability to perceive and express emotion, assimilate emotion and thought, understand and reason with emotion, and regulate emotion in oneself and others

[**Exhibit 4.2**] Emotional Intelligence Competencies Model

	Self **(Personal Competence)**	**Other** **(Social Competence)**
Recognition of Emotions	**Self-Awareness** • Emotional self-awareness • Accurate self-assessment • Self-confidence	**Social Awareness** • Empathy • Organizational awareness • Service
Regulation of Emotions	**Self-Management** • Emotional self-control • Transparency • Adaptability • Achievement • Initiative • Optimism	**Relationship Management** • Inspirational leadership • Influence • Developing others • Change catalyst • Conflict management • Building bonds • Teamwork and collaboration

Sources: D. Goleman, R. Boyatzis, and A. McKee, *Primal Leadership* (Boston: Harvard Business School Press, 2002), Chapter 3; D. Goleman, "An EI-Based Theory of Performance," in C. Cherniss and D. Goleman, (Eds.), *The Emotionally Intelligent Workplace* (San Francisco: Jossey-Bass, 2001), p. 28.

representing the recognition of emotions in ourselves and in others, as well as the regulation of emotions in ourselves and in others. Each dimension consists of a set of emotional competencies that people must possess to fulfill that dimension of emotional intelligence.[24]

- *Self-awareness.* Self-awareness refers to having a deep understanding of one's own emotions as well as strengths, weaknesses, values, and motives. Self-aware people are better able to eavesdrop in on their emotional responses to specific situations and to use this awareness as conscious information.[25]

- *Self-management.* This represents how well we control or redirect our internal states, impulses, and resources. It includes keeping disruptive impulses in check, displaying honesty and integrity, being flexible in times of change, maintaining the drive to perform well and seize opportunities, and remaining optimistic even after failure. Self-management involves an inner conversation that guides our behavior.

- *Social awareness.* Social awareness is mainly about *empathy*—having understanding and sensitivity to the feelings, thoughts, and situation of others (see Chapter 3). This includes understanding another person's situation, experiencing the other person's emotions, and knowing that person's needs even though unstated. Social awareness extends beyond empathy to include being organizationally aware, such as sensing office politics and understanding social networks.

- *Relationship management.* This dimension of EI refers to managing other people's emotions. It is linked to a wide variety of practices, such as inspiring others, influencing people's beliefs and feelings, developing others' capabilities, managing change, resolving conflict, cultivating relationships, and supporting teamwork and collaboration.

These four dimensions of emotional intelligence form a hierarchy.[26] Self-awareness is the lowest level of EI because it does not require the other dimensions; instead it is a prerequisite for the other three dimensions. Self-management and social awareness are necessarily above self-awareness in the EI hierarchy. You can't manage your own emotions (self-management) if you aren't good at knowing your own emotions (self-awareness). Relationship management is the highest level of EI because it requires all three other dimensions. In other words, we require a high degree of emotional intelligence to master relationship management because this set of competencies requires sufficiently high levels of self-awareness, self-management, and social awareness.

Most jobs involve social interaction with co-workers or external stakeholders, so employees need emotional intelligence to work effectively. The evidence so far indicates that people with high EI are better at interpersonal relations, perform better in jobs requiring emotional labor, and are more successful in many aspects of job interviews. Teams whose members have high emotional intelligence initially perform better than teams with low EI.[27]

Improving Emotional Intelligence

Emotional intelligence is associated with conscientiousness and other personality traits. However, it can also be learned to some extent, so many companies put employees through EI training programs. "We've developed a seven-hour training program on emotional intelligence," says an executive at BB&T Corp., a large financial services company based in Winston-Salem, North Carolina. "We believe it really helps people grow as employees." In support of the training approach, a recent study reported that business students scored higher on emotional intelligence after taking an undergraduate interpersonal skills course.[28] While training helps, a more effective way to improve EI is through personal coaching, plenty of practice, and frequent feedback. EI also increases with age; it is part of the process called maturity. Overall, emotional intelligence offers considerable potential, but we also have a lot to learn about its measurement and effects on people in the workplace.

So far, this chapter has laid out the model of emotions and attitudes, but we also need to understand specific workplace attitudes. The next two sections of this chapter look at two of the most widely studied attitudes: job satisfaction and organizational commitment.

>Job Satisfaction

Job satisfaction, which is probably the most studied attitude in organizational behavior, represents a person's evaluation of his or her job and work context.[29] It is an *appraisal* of the perceived job characteristics, work environment, and emotional experiences at work. Satisfied employees have a favorable evaluation of their job, based on their observations and emotional experiences. Job satisfaction is really a collection of attitudes about different aspects of the job and work context. You might like your co-workers but be less satisfied with workload, for instance.

job satisfaction
A person's attitude regarding his or her job and work content.

In national polls over the last decade, more than 85 percent of Americans have been satisfied with their jobs. Global surveys place Americans among the top three or four countries for job satisfaction. Can we conclude from these results that Americans are happy at work? Well, maybe to some extent, but probably not as high as these statistics suggest. The problem is that surveys often use a single direct question, such as "How satisfied are you with your job?" Many dissatisfied employees are reluctant to reveal their feelings in a direct question because this is tantamount to admitting that they made a poor job choice and are not enjoying life. In fact, these surveys also report that employees rate almost all aspects of their job lower than their overall score.[30]

Job Satisfaction and Work Behavior

Job satisfaction affects many of the individual behaviors introduced in Chapter 2. A useful template to organize and understand the consequences of job dissatisfaction is the **exit-voice-loyalty-neglect (EVLN) model**. As the name suggests, the EVLN model identifies four ways that employees respond to dissatisfaction:[31]

exit-voice-loyalty-neglect (EVLN) model
The four ways, as indicated in the name, employees respond to job dissatisfaction.

- *Exit.* Exit refers to leaving the organization, transferring to another work unit, or at least trying to exit the dissatisfying situation. Exit usually follows specific "shock events," such as when your boss treats you unfairly.[32] These shock events generate strong emotions that energize employees to think about and search for alternative employment.

- *Voice.* Voice refers to any attempt to change, rather than escape from, the dissatisfying situation. Voice can be a constructive response, such as recommending ways for management to improve the situation, or it can be more confrontational, such as by filing formal grievances. In the extreme, some employees might engage in counterproductive behaviors to get attention and force changes in the organization.

- *Loyalty.* Loyalty has been described in different ways, but the most widely held view is that "loyalists" are employees who respond to dissatisfaction by patiently waiting—some say they "suffer in silence"—for the problem to work itself out or get resolved by others.

- *Neglect.* Neglect includes reducing work effort, paying less attention to quality, and increasing absenteeism and lateness. It is generally considered a passive activity that has negative consequences for the organization.

Which EVLN alternative is used depends on the person and situation. Employees with poor job prospects are less likely to use the exit option. Those who identify with the organization are more likely to use voice rather than exit. People with a high-conscientiousness personality are less likely to engage in neglect and more likely to engage in voice. Finally, past experience influences our choice of action. Employees who were unsuccessful with voice in the past are more likely to engage in exit or neglect when experiencing job dissatisfaction in the future.[33]

Job Satisfaction and Performance

One of the oldest beliefs in the business world is that "a happy worker is a productive worker." Is this statement true? Organizational behavior scholars have waffled on this question for the past century. In the 1980s, they concluded that job satisfaction has a weak or negligible association with task performance. Now the evidence suggests that the popular saying may be correct after all. The most recent studies conclude that there is a *moderate* relationship between job satisfaction and job performance. In other words, happy workers really are more productive workers *to some extent.*[34]

Even with a moderate association between job satisfaction and performance, there are a few underlying reasons why the relationship isn't even stronger. One argument is that general attitudes (such as job satisfaction) don't predict specific behaviors very well. As we learned with the EVLN model, job dissatisfaction can lead to a variety of outcomes rather than lower job performance (neglect). Some employees continue to work productively while they complain (voice), look for another job (exit), or patiently wait for the problem to be fixed (loyalty).

A second explanation is that job performance leads to job satisfaction, rather than vice versa, but only when performance is linked to valued rewards. Higher performers receive more rewards and, consequently, are more satisfied than low-performing employees who receive fewer rewards. The connection between job satisfaction and performance isn't stronger because many organizations are not very good at rewarding good performance. The third explanation is that job satisfaction might influence employee motivation, but this has little influence on performance in jobs where employees have little control over their job output (such as assembly line work). This point explains why the job satisfaction-performance relationship is strongest in complex jobs, where employees have more freedom to perform their work or to slack off.

Job Satisfaction and Customer Satisfaction

Wegmans Food Markets has an unusual motto: Employees first, customers second. As we described in a captioned photo a few pages ago, the grocery chain definitely puts employees on top of stakeholder list, but why not customers first? Wegmans' rationale is that when employees are happy, customers are happy. Virgin Group founder Sir Richard Branson agrees with that theory. "It just seems common sense to me that if you start with a happy, well-motivated workforce, you're much more likely to have happy customers," says Branson.[35]

Research generally supports the idea that job satisfaction has a positive effect on customer satisfaction.[36] There are two main reasons for this relationship. First, employees are usually in a more positive mood when they feel satisfied with their job and working conditions. Employees in a good mood display friendliness and positive emotions more naturally and frequently, which create positive emotions for customers. Second, satisfied employees are less likely to quit their jobs, so they have better knowledge and skills to serve clients. Lower turnover also gives customers the same employees to serve them, which provides more consistent service. There is some evidence that customers build their loyalty to specific employees, not to the organization, so keeping employee turnover low tends to build customer loyalty.[37]

Outback Steakhouse, Inc., has become a phenomenal success in the competitive restaurant industry by following the theory that happy employees make happy customers. "Outback's theory of success is that you hire the right people and take care of them," explained founder Chris Sullivan and three colleagues in a recent journal article. The company hires and creates a culture that supports energized employees who stay with the company and provide excellent service. This service makes customers happy, which brings them back and refers Outback to friends. The result of such customer satisfaction is higher sales, which improve company profits.[38]

>Organizational Commitment

Along with job satisfaction, OB researchers have been very interested in an attitude called organizational commitment. **Organizational commitment** refers to the employee's emotional attachment to, identification with, and involvement in a particular organization.[39] This definition refers specifically to *affective commitment* because it is an emotional attachment—our feelings of loyalty—to the organization.

Along with affective commitment, employees have varying levels of **continuance commitment**. Continuance commitment is a calculative rather than emotional attachment to the organization. In other words, employees stay with the firm because it would be too costly to quit, not because they enjoy working there or identify with the company. Continuance commitment occurs when firms tie employees financially to the organization through low-cost loans, deferred bonuses, high salaries, and other "golden handcuffs."[40]

Consequences of Organizational Commitment

Organizational commitment can be a significant competitive advantage.[41] Loyal employees are less likely to quit their jobs and be absent from work. They also have higher work motivation and organizational citizenship, as well as somewhat higher job performance.

organizational (affective) commitment
The employee's emotional attachment to, identification with, and involvement in a particular organization.

continuance commitment
A bond felt by an employee that motivates him to stay only because leaving would be costly.

Organizational commitment also improves customer satisfaction because long-tenure employees have better knowledge of work practices, and clients like to do business with the same employees. Corporate leaders need to watch out for too much loyalty, which supports a cultlike organization that suppresses constructive conflict. However, most organizations face the challenge of too little rather than too much affective commitment.

While affective commitment is beneficial, research suggests that continuance commitment isn't.[42] In fact, employees with high levels of continuance commitment tend to have *lower* performance ratings and are less likely to engage in organizational citizenship behaviors. Furthermore, unionized employees with high continuance commitment are more likely to use formal grievances, whereas employees with high affective commitment engage in more constructive problem solving when employee–employer relations sour. Although some level of financial connection may be necessary, employers should not confuse continuance commitment with employee loyalty. Employers still need to win employees' hearts (affective commitment) beyond tying them financially to the organization (continuance commitment).

Building Organizational Commitment

There are almost as many ways to increase organizational commitment as topics in this textbook, but the following list highlights the most prominent strategies.

- *Justice and support.* Affective commitment is higher in organizations that fulfill their obligations to employees and abide by humanitarian values, such as fairness, courtesy, forgiveness, and moral integrity. These values relate to the concept of organizational justice that we discuss in the next chapter. Similarly, organizations that support employee well-being tend to cultivate higher levels of loyalty in return.[43]

- *Shared values.* The definition of affective commitment refers to a person's identification with the organization, and that identification is highest when employees believe their values are congruent with the organization's dominant values. Also, employees experience more comfort and predictability when they agree with the values underlying corporate decisions. This comfort increases their motivation to stay with the organization.[44]

- *Trust.* **Trust** is a psychological state comprising the intention to accept vulnerability based upon positive expectations of the intent or behavior of another person. Trust means putting faith in the other person or group. It is also a reciprocal activity: To receive trust, you must demonstrate trust. Employees have higher commitment to the organization the more they trust its leaders. This explains why layoffs are one of the greatest blows to employee loyalty—by reducing job security, companies reduce the trust employees have in their employer and the employment relationship.[45]

- *Organizational comprehension.* Affective commitment is a person's identification with the company, so it makes sense that this attitude is strengthened when employees understand the company, including its past, present, and future. Thus, loyalty tends to increase with open and rapid communication to and from corporate leaders, as well as with opportunities to interact with co-workers across the organization.[46]

- *Employee involvement.* Employee involvement increases affective commitment by strengthening the employee's social identity with the organization. Employees feel that they are part of the organization when they participate in decisions that guide the organization's future. Employee involvement also builds loyalty because giving this power is a demonstration of the company's trust in its employees.

trust
A psychological state comprising the intention to accept vulnerability based upon positive expectations of the intent or behavior of another person.

Organizational commitment and job satisfaction represent two of the most often studied and discussed attitudes in the workplace. Each is linked to emotional episodes and cognitive judgments about the workplace and relationship with the company. Emotions also play an important role in another concept that is on everyone's mind these days: stress. The final section of this chapter provides a brief overview of stress and how it can be managed.

>Work-Related Stress and Its Management

Joe Straitiff realized that his leisure life was in trouble when his boss hung a huge neon sign in the office saying "Open 24 Hours." The former Electronic Arts software developer also received frequent e-mails from the boss to the team, saying that he would see them on the weekend. "You can't work that many hours and remain sane," says Straitiff. "It's just too harsh." Straitiff was eventually fired, but his complaints were not exaggerations. The fiancé of an Electronic Arts video programmer wrote a lengthy diatribe on the Internet describing how her partner was overworked and suffering the consequences. "The love of my life comes home late at night complaining of a headache that will not go away and a chronically upset stomach," she wrote. Within two days, she received more than 1,000 sympathetic messages from people at Electronic Arts and other video game companies.[47]

Employees at Electronic Arts and many other organizations are experiencing increasing levels of work-related stress. **Stress** is an adaptive response to a situation that is perceived as challenging or threatening to the person's well-being.[48] The stress response is a complex emotion that produces physiological changes to prepare us for "fight or flight"—to defend the threat or flee from it. Specifically, our heart rate and perspiration increase, muscles tighten, and breathing speeds up. Our body also moves more blood to the brain, releases adrenaline and other hormones, fuels the system by releasing more glucose and fatty acids, activates systems that sharpen our senses, and uses resources that would normally go to our immune system.

stress
An individual's adaptive response to a situation that is perceived as challenging or threatening to the person's well-being.

We often hear about stress as a negative experience. This is known as *distress*—the degree of physiological, psychological, and behavioral deviation from healthy functioning. However, some level of stress—called *eustress*—is also a necessary part of life because it activates and motivates people to achieve goals, change their environments, and succeed in life's challenges.[49] Our focus will be on the causes and management of distress, because it has become a chronic problem in many societies.

General Adaptation Syndrome

The stress experience is a physiological response called the **general adaptation syndrome** that occurs through the three stages shown in Exhibit 4.3.[50] The *alarm reaction* stage occurs when a threat or challenge activates the physiological stress responses that were noted earlier. The person's energy level and coping effectiveness initially decrease because he or she has not prepared for the stress. The second stage, *resistance,* activates various biochemical, psychological, and behavioral mechanisms that give us more energy and engage coping mechanisms to overcome or remove the source of stress. To focus energy on the source of the stress, the body reduces resources to the immune system during this stage. This explains why people are more likely to catch a cold or other illness when they experience prolonged stress.

general adaptation syndrome
A model of the stress experience, consisting of three stages: alarm reaction, resistance, and exhaustion.

People have a limited resistance capacity and, if the source of stress persists, they will eventually move into the third stage, *exhaustion.* Most of us are able to remove the source of stress or remove ourselves from that source before becoming too exhausted. However, people who frequently reach exhaustion have increased risk of long-term physiological and psychological damage.[51]

[Exhibit 4.3] Selye's General Adaptation Syndrome

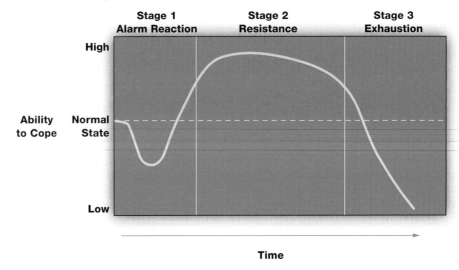

Source: Adapted from H. Selye, *The Stress of Life* (New York: McGraw-Hill, 1956).

Consequences of Distress

Stress takes its toll on the human body.[52] Many people experience tension headaches, muscle pain, and related problems mainly due to muscle contractions from the stress response. Studies have found that high stress levels also contribute to cardiovascular disease, including heart attacks and strokes. They also produce various psychological consequences, such job dissatisfaction, moodiness, depression, and lower organizational commitment. Furthermore, various behavioral outcomes have been linked to high or persistent stress, including lower job performance, poor decision making, and increased workplace accidents and aggressive behavior. Most people react to stress through fight or flight, so increased absenteeism is another outcome because it is a form of flight.[53]

Stressors: The Sources of Stress

The general adaptation syndrome describes the stress experience, but to manage work-related stress, we must understand its causes, known as stressors. **Stressors** include any environmental conditions that place a physical or emotional demand on the person.[54] As you might imagine, people face numerous stressors at work. In this section, we'll highlight three of the most prevalent workplace stressors: harassment, workload, and lack of task control.

Harassment and Incivility

It seems that employees in almost every organization are experiencing some form of psychological harassment these days. **Psychological harassment** includes repeated and hostile or unwanted conduct, verbal comments, actions, or gestures that affect an employee's dignity or psychological or physical integrity and that result in a harmful work environment for the employee. This definition covers a broad landscape of behaviors, from threats and bullying to subtle yet persistent forms of incivility. Psychological harassment has become such a problem that some European governments explicitly prohibit it in the workplace. The Quebec government in Canada recently introduced the first harassment legislation in North America and was swamped with more than 2,500 complaints in the first year alone.[55]

Sexual harassment is a type of harassment in which a person's employment or job performance is conditional on unwanted sexual relations (called *quid pro quo*), or the person

stressors
The causes of stress, including any environmental conditions that place a physical or emotional demand on the person.

psychological harassment
Repeated and hostile or unwanted conduct, verbal comments, actions or gestures, which affect an employee's dignity or psychological or physical integrity and that result in a harmful work environment for the employee.

sexual harassment
Unwelcome conduct of a sexual nature that detrimentally affects the work environment or leads to adverse job-related consequences for its victims.

experiences sexual conduct from others (such as posting pornographic material) that unreasonably interferes with work performance or creates an intimidating, hostile, or offensive working environment (called *hostile work environment*). One study points out that men tend to have a narrower interpretation than do women over what constitutes hostile work environment, so they sometimes engage in this form of sexual harassment without being aware of their transgressions.[56] Sexual harassment sometimes escalates into psychological harassment after the alleged victim complains of the sexual wrongdoing.

Work Overload

A half-century ago, social scientists predicted that technology would allow employees to enjoy a 15-hour workweek at full pay by 2030. So far, it hasn't turned out that way. Americans experience considerable *work overload*—working more hours and more intensely during those hours than they can reasonably cope. Surveys by the Families and Work Institute report that 44 percent of Americans say they are overworked, up from 28 percent who felt this way three years earlier. This work overload is also the main cause of work-family conflicts, because overworked employees have insufficient time to satisfy their nonwork roles of being a parent, spouse, and so forth.[57]

Some writers suggest that the rising workload is caused by globalization and its demands for more work efficiency. Culture is another factor. Working long hours is still considered a badge of honor in some organizations, as well as in many countries, such as Japan. In that country, 20 percent of male Japanese employees chalk up more than 80 hours of overtime each month. The Japanese government is actively discouraging this work overload because of dramatic increases in *karoshi*—death from overwork.[58]

Low Task Control

As a private driver for an executive in Jakarta, Eddy knows that traffic jams are a way of life in Indonesia's largest city. "Jakarta is traffic congestion," he complains. "All of the streets in the city are crowded with vehicles. It is impossible to avoid this distressing fact every day." Eddy's boss complains when traffic jams make him late for appointments, which makes matters even more stressful. "Even watching soccer on TV or talking to my wife doesn't get rid of my stress. It's driving me mad."[59]

Eddy and many other people experience stress due to a lack of task control. Along with driving through congested traffic, low task control occurs where the employee's work is paced by a machine, the job involves monitoring equipment, or the work schedule is controlled by someone else. Computers, cell phones, and other technology also increase stress by limiting a person's control of time and privacy.[60]

The extent to which low task control is a stressor increases with the burden of responsibility the employee must carry. Assembly line workers have low task control, but their stress can also be fairly low if their level of responsibility is also low. In contrast, sports coaches are under immense pressure to win games (high responsibility), yet have little control over what happens on the playing field (low task control). Similarly, Eddy (the Jakarta driver) is under pressure to get his employer to a particular destination on time (high responsibility), yet he has little control over traffic congestion (low task control).

Individual Differences in Stress

People have different stress experiences when exposed to the same stressor due to unique personal characteristics. One reason is that they have different threshold levels of resistance to the stressor. Those who exercise and maintain healthy lifestyles have a larger store of energy to cope with high stress levels. A second reason for varying stress responses is that people use different coping strategies, some of which are more effective than others.

Research suggests that employees who try to ignore or deny the existence of a stressor suffer more in the long run than those who try to find ways to weaken the stressor and seek social support.[61]

Resilience and Stress

A third reason why some people experience less stress than others is that they have higher resilience.[62] **Resilience** is the capability of individuals to cope successfully in the face of significant change, adversity, or risk. Those with high resilience are able to withstand adversity as well as recover more quickly from it. Resilient people possess personality traits (such as high extroversion and low neuroticism) that generate more optimism, confidence, and positive emotions. Resilience also involves specific competencies and behaviors to respond and adapt more effectively to stressors. Research indicates that resilient people have higher emotional intelligence and good problem-solving skills. They also apply productive coping strategies, such as analyzing the sources of stress and finding ways to neutralize these problems.[63]

An emerging view is that resilience is an inner force that motivates us to move forward. This idea is connected to recent OB writing on *workplace spirituality,* which investigates a person's inner strength and how it nurtures and is nurtured by the workplace. Resilience as an inner force has some empirical support. Research has found that resilience is stronger when people have a sense of purpose and are in touch with their personal values.[64]

Managing Work-Related Stress

Some degree of stress is good (eustress), but for the most part employees and employers need to figure out how to minimize distress. Most stress management strategies can be organized into five categories: remove the stressor, withdraw from the stressor, change stress perceptions, control stress consequences, and receive social support.

- *Remove the stressor.* While other stress management strategies try to keep employees "stress-fit," the best solution is to get rid of, or minimize, the conditions that cause high stress. This would include assigning employees to jobs that match their skills and preferences, reducing excessive workplace noise, having a complaint system and corrective action against harassment, and giving employees more control over the work process. Work/life balance initiatives also fall into this category, such as offering flexible work schedules, job sharing, telecommuting, personal leave, and child care support.[65]

- *Withdraw from the stressor.* Employees withdraw from stressors by taking work breaks, days off, vacations, and sabbaticals. In fact, research indicates that leisure time significantly improves the employees' ability to cope with work-related stress.[66]

- *Change stress perceptions.* Earlier, we learned that employees experience different stress levels because they have different levels of resilience, including self-confidence and optimism. Consequently, corporate leaders need to look at ways for employees to strengthen their confidence and self-esteem so that job challenges are not perceived as threatening. A study of newly hired accountants reported that personal goal setting and self-reinforcement can also reduce the stress that people experience when they enter new work settings. Humor can also improve optimism and create positive emotions by taking some psychological weight off the situation.[67]

- *Control stress consequences.* Companies can reduce the adverse consequences of high stress by ensuring that employees maintain healthy lifestyles.[68] Some companies provide onsite subsidize the cost of offsite fitness centers. A few firms, such as AstraZeneca, encourage employees to practice relaxation and meditation

When employees at Liggett-Stashower Inc. need a short break from the daily stresses of work, they retreat to one of three theme rooms specially designed for creativity and respite. Staff at the Cleveland advertising firm can enter the bowling room and knock down a few pins. Or they might try out the Zen room, which serves as a quiet, relaxing place to think. Behind the third door is a karaoke room where frustrated employees can belt out tunes. "The higher the stress level, the more singing there is going on," says Kristen Flynn, a Liggett-Stashower art director.[69]

techniques during the workday. Others offer more comprehensive wellness programs that educate and support employees in better nutrition and fitness, regular sleep, and other good health habits.

• *Receive social support.* Social support occurs when co-workers, supervisors, family members, friends, and others, provide emotional or informational support, or both, to buffer the stress experience. It potentially improves the person's resilience (particularly their optimism and self-confidence) because support makes people feel valued and worthy. Social support also provides information to help employees interpret, comprehend, and possibly remove the stressor. For instance, social support might reduce a new employee's stress because co-workers describe ways to handle difficult customers. Seeking social support is called a "tend and befriend" response to stress, and research suggests that women often follow this route rather than the fight-or-flight response mentioned earlier.[70]

Employee emotions, attitudes, and stress influence employee behavior mainly through motivation. Recall, for instance, that behavioral intentions are judgments or expectations about the motivation to engage in a particular behavior. The next chapter introduces the prominent theories of employee motivation as well as applied practices that increase and support motivation.

>chapter summary

Emotions are physiological, behavioral, and psychological episodes experienced toward an object, person, or event that create a state of readiness. Emotions differ from attitudes, which represent the cluster of beliefs, feelings, and behavioral intentions toward a person, object, or event. Beliefs are a person's established perceptions about the attitude object. Feelings are positive or negative evaluations of the attitude object. Behavioral intentions represent a motivation to engage in a particular behavior with respect to the target.

Attitudes have traditionally been described as a purely rational process in which beliefs predict feelings, which predict behavioral intentions, which predict behavior. We now know that emotions have an equal or greater influence. This dual process is apparent when we internally experience a conflict between what logically seems good or bad and what we emotionally feel is good or bad in a situation. Emotions also affect behavior directly. Behavior sometimes influences our subsequent attitudes through cognitive dissonance.

Emotional labor refers to the effort, planning, and control needed to express organizationally desired emotions during interpersonal transactions. This is more common in jobs requiring a variety of emotions and more intense emotions, as well as where interaction with clients is frequent and for longer durations. It also depends to some extent on the culture in which we live. Emotional dissonance occurs when required and true emotions are incompatible with each other. Deep acting can minimize this dissonance, as can the practice of hiring people with a natural tendency to display desired emotions.

Emotional intelligence is the ability to perceive and express emotion, assimilate emotion in thought, understand and reason with emotion, and regulate emotion in oneself and others. This concept includes four components arranged in a hierarchy: self-awareness, self-management, social awareness, and relationship management. Emotional intelligence can be learned to some extent, particularly through personal coaching.

Job satisfaction represents a person's evaluation of his or her job and work context. The exit-voice-loyalty-neglect model outlines four possible consequences of job dissatisfaction. Job satisfaction has a moderate relationship with job performance and with customer satisfaction. Affective organizational commitment (loyalty) refers to the employee's emotional attachment to, identification with, and involvement in a particular organization. This contrasts with continuance commitment, which is a calculative bond with the organization. Companies build loyalty through justice and support, shared values, trust, organizational comprehension, and employee involvement.

Stress is an adaptive response to a situation that is perceived as challenging or threatening to the person's well-being. Distress represents high stress levels that have negative consequences, whereas eustress represents the moderately low stress levels needed to activate people. The stress experience, called the general adaptation syndrome, involves moving through three stages: alarm, resistance, and exhaustion. Stressors are the causes of stress and include any environmental conditions that place a physical or emotional demand on the person. Three stressors that have received considerable attention are harassment (including incivility), work overload, and low task control.

Two people exposed to the same stressor may experience different stress levels because they have different threshold stress levels or use different coping strategies, People experience less stress when they have high resilience—the capability of individuals to cope successfully in the face of significant change, adversity, or risk. Many interventions are available to manage work-related stress, including removing the stressor, withdrawing from the stressor, changing stress perceptions, controlling stress consequences, and receiving social support.

>**key**.terms

>**critical.thinking**.questions

1. A recent study reported that college instructors are frequently required to engage in emotional labor. Identify the situations in which emotional labor is required for this job. In your opinion, is emotional labor more troublesome for college instructors or for telephone operators working at a 911 emergency service?

2. "Emotional intelligence is more important than cognitive intelligence in influencing an individual's success." Do you agree or disagree with this statement? Support your perspective.

3. Describe a time when you effectively managed someone's emotions. What happened? What was the result?

4. "Happy employees create happy customers." Explain why this statement might be true, and identify conditions in which it might not be true.

5. What factors influence an employee's organizational loyalty?

6. Is being a full-time college student a stressful role? Why or why not? Contrast your response with other students' perspectives.

7. Resilience is an individual characteristic that plays an important role in moderating the effect of stressors. Suppose that you were put in charge of a task force in a large government department to ensure that employees are highly resilient. What would you and your task force do to accomplish this objective?

8. Many stress management sources refer to practices that companies need to apply to minimize employee stress. To what extent, and in what ways, should employees manage their own stress in the workplace?

>**case**.study:**skill**builder**4.1**

New Plant Opening

By Joana Young, Baylor University

The CEO of National Bottling Co., a large beverage manufacturer based in the United States, had recently decided to restructure the organization in order to be more competitive. Historically, National Bottling Co. had maintained only a few corporate-owned facilities with the majority of its plants being owned by franchisees. As a result, several small plants often operated within a relatively limited geographical area. The first phase of the restructuring plan was to buy out most of the franchises in order to better control product consistency, quality, and distribution. The second phase was to build large plants that would house the latest bottling equipment. These new plants would have a production capacity of 45 million cases per year, equal to that of five smaller plants, but at lower operating costs than maintaining the smaller facilities. As a consequence, in some areas, plants would be closed and the workers relocated to one of the new mega-facilities.

Cicero, named after the city in which it's located, would be the first of these giant plants. Employees at all of the plants targeted for consolidation had been told about the imminent closure of their plants in preparation for the opening of the new Cicero mega-plant. However, managers had been evasive about when the plants would close and whether all workers would be transferred to the new plant. Jamie Miller, the corporate head of human resources, was personally overseeing the staffing of Cicero. When Jamie arrived in town he visited the Cicero plant as well as the now obsolete smaller plants in the neighboring towns.

Jamie found the rumor mill on overdrive everywhere he went. Conversation among the line workers stopped whenever he entered a break room or other gathering place. Several employees had been concerned enough to stop him in the halls to express their anxiety about losing their jobs. Jamie tried to be reassuring, but he knew that there was a chance that some people would be let go and he didn't want to lose credibility with the employees by making statements that might turn out to be untrue. At the same time, Jamie knew that continued evasiveness was leading to tension between management and the employees. Without concrete information, employees' imaginations were conjuring up scenarios much worse than the reality. If employees became disgruntled on the basis of what they thought might happen, they could lose motivation or worse become destructive. Jamie must quickly develop both a selection process for bringing workers over to the new plant and a training program for them once they arrived.

Jamie had subcontracted the work to two consulting firms—Hayes Consulting and Temple Associates. Hayes Consulting was a large, well-established consulting firm that would handle development of the employee training program. Temple Associates was a small consultancy that would handle design of the selection process, a communication plan to let employees know what was happening, and actually oversee the selection process. Jamie appointed Corey Chambers, a trainer from headquarters, as the primary liaison in charge of working with Hayes Consulting on developing the training program while Jamie planned to work closely with Temple Associates. Although Temple Associates was a small company, it was headed by Jonathan Temple, a former National Bottling Co. executive, so Jamie had confidence that he understood the issues and would create a plan that was in keeping with National's needs and priorities.

Jamie sat down with Temple to go over the specifics of the situation. He told Temple that Cicero was already over budget on construction costs and would be delayed in opening because of difficulty obtaining the proper permits for such a large facility. The plant must be staffed and ready to run ASAP to recoup losses from the budget overruns and from the delayed opening. All of the plants targeted for closing were previously long-standing franchises run by families who typically hired their friends and relatives and had few hiring standards. Headquarters believed many of these workers did not have the skills necessary to function well in the new plant. One manager from a closing plant estimated that 20 to 30 percent of line workers would have problems with literacy, basic math, or reading English. Although these workers might have been able to get by in the old plants, they would need these skills at a state-of-the-art facility like Cicero. Much of the manufacturing equipment was newly designed to operate by computer touchscreen rather than manually. In addition, Cicero would be the model for the company's new safety program. Correct procedures and safety measures would be printed on placards that would hang from the ceiling and be posted on machinery.

There was also the issue of unionization. Five of the six plants being closed and consolidated were nonunion, but one was unionized. Since the majority of the workforce was not unionized, Cicero could legally be opened as a nonunion plant. However, information about the plant's selection process had to be released carefully as the unionized workers would probably protest the use of anything other than seniority as a method of choosing who would go to the new plant. In addition, instead of having a fixed job assignment, employees would be assigned to either the warehouse or manufacturing team, but they could be required to perform any job within their general area. It was expected that the unionized workers would object to this as well. Headquarters was concerned that the union could bring a suit against National Bottling Co. that would further delay the plant's opening and ultimately lead to Cicero being unionized. Headquarters would find that unacceptable. That was why there has been no communication.

Cicero would employ approximately 350 to 400 of the 450 people currently employed by the plants under consolidation. All management level employees would be transferred to the new plant; however, line employees would be required to reapply for their jobs. If employees were successful in the interview process, they would not return to the same jobs that they had held in the old plants. The new computerized machinery and the elimination of fixed job assignments would make many jobs more complex. Employees would need to understand jobs up and down the production line and across product lines. To meet those new requirements, headquarters would like to weed out current employees who did not have basic skills or did not want to work in the new flexible team approach. The proposed interview process would have three parts: a basic skills test, a team interview, and group problem-solving exercise. However, a passing score on the basic skills test was a prerequisite for proceeding with the rest of the process. Thus employees who could not read English at least at a high school level would be eliminated from the process immediately.

Once the consultants from Temple Associates started appearing in the plants, rumors that they were there to start firing people exploded. The employees at one plant demanded a meeting with Jamie. Herman, a long-time National employee, stood up to speak. "The Bradford family used to own this plant. I worked for them for 31 years. I have put my heart and soul into this place. I can tell you what's wrong with most of this equipment just by listening to it. I have always been proud to work for the Bradfords and for National Bottling. Now, I want to know if you are planning to throw me and guys like me to the side because maybe we had to quit school to support a family." Herman paused and looked around the room at the others nodding in agreement. "I may not be book smart, but nobody works harder than I do. I want to know whether that counts for anything or if I need to be looking for a job right now."

Sensing the volatility of the situation, Jamie told the assembled workers "there is room for everyone at the new plant. There is an interview process, but testing is only part of it." His gaze took in Herman and the rest of the group. "We do not want to lose people like you. You all know who the exemplary workers are and you know those who just skate by. We don't want to bring those slackers with us, but in the process we would never lose a good worker over some test." Jamie wasn't sure what he had just said was completely true, but he felt he had to say something to defuse the situation. After the meeting, Temple Associates devised a communication plan that incorporated that basic message and disseminated it through all of the closing plants.

Discussion Questions

1. What emotions and attitudes do employees feel in this situation? Use the model in Exhibit 4.1 to explain why employees have these particular attitudes.

2. What level of emotional intelligence does Jamie seem to have in this case? Explain your judgment.

3. What information in this case suggests that some employees are experiencing stress from the planned changes at National Bottling? How did employees try to manage this stress? Explain why Jamie's actions in the last paragraph may have reduced this stress to some extent.

>class.exercise:skillbuilder4.2

Stem-and-Probe Interview Activity

Purpose   To help students experience the effects of emotional experiences on behavior.

Materials   None.

Instructions   This simple, yet powerful, exercise consists of students conducting and receiving a detailed stem-and-probe interview with other students in the class. Each student will have an opportunity to interview and be interviewed. However, to increase the variation and novelty of this experience, the student conducting the first interview should *not* be interviewed by the student who was just interviewed. Instead, the instructor should either form groups of four students (two pairs) at the beginning of this exercise or have two pairs of students swap after the first round. Each of the two sets of interviews should take 10 to 15 minutes and use a stem-and-probe interview method. The stem-and-probe method, as well as the topic of the interview, are described next.

Stem-and-probe interviewing.   This interview method attempts to receive more detail from the interviewee than typically occurs in semi-structured or structured interviews.

The main interview question, called the *stem,* is followed by a series of probing questions that encourages the interviewee to provide more details relating to a particular incident or situation. The stem question for this exercise is provided below. There are several probes that the interviewee can use to elicit more detail, and the best probe depends on the circumstances, such as what information has already been provided. Some common probe questions include "Tell me more about that"; "What did you do next?"; "Could you explain that further, please?"; "What else can you remember about that event?" Notice that each of these probes is open-ended, not closed-ended questions such as "Is there anything else you want to tell me" in which a simple yes or no answer is possible. Stem-and-probe interviewing also improves when the interviewer engages in active listening and isn't afraid of silence—giving the interviewee time to think and motivating him or her to fill in the silence with new information.

Interview topic.   In both sets of interviews, the stem question is

> Describe two or three things you did this past week that made someone else feel better.

Through this interview process, the interviewer's task is to receive as much information as possible (that the interviewee is willing to divulge) about the details of these two or three things that the interviewee did over the past week.

Following the two sets of interviews (where each student has interviewed and been interviewed once), the class will discuss the emotional and attitudinal dynamics of this activity.

>self-assessment.skillbuilder4.3

School Commitment Scale

This self-assessment is designed to help you understand the concept of organizational commitment and to assess your commitment to the college you are currently attending. The concept of commitment is as relevant to students enrolled in college courses as it is to employees working in various organizations. This self-assessment adapts a popular organizational commitment instrument so it refers to your commitment as a student to the school where you are

attending this program. Select the response for each statement that best fits your personal belief. This self-assessment is completed alone so that students rate themselves honestly without concerns of social comparison. However, class discussion will focus on the meaning of the different types of organizational commitment and how well this scale applies to the commitment of students toward the college they are attending.

>self-assessment.skillbuilder4.4

Dispositional Mood Scale

This self-assessment is designed to help you understand mood states or personality traits of emotions and to assess your own mood or emotions-based personality. This self-assessment consists of several words representing various emotions that you might have experienced. For each word presented, indicate the extent to which you have felt this way generally across all situations *over the past six months.*

You need to be honest with yourself to receive a reasonable estimate of your mood state or personality trait on these scales. The results provide an estimate of your level on two emotional personality scales. This instrument is widely used in research, but it is only an estimate. You should not assume that the results are accurate without a more complete assessment by a trained professional.

>self-assessment.skillbuilder4.5

Connor-Davidson Resilience Scale

This self-assessment is designed to help you to estimate your personal level of resilience. Please indicate the extent that each statement in this instrument is true for you *over the past month.* It is important for you to realize that there are no right or wrong answers to these questions. This

self-assessment is completed alone so that you can complete this instrument honestly without concerns of social comparison. However, class discussion will focus on the meaning of resilience and how it relates to workplace stress.

>self-assessment.skillbuilder4.6

Perceived Stress Scale

This self-assessment is designed to help you to estimate your perceived general level of stress. The items in this scale ask you about your feelings and thoughts during the

last month. In each case, please indicate how often you felt or thought a certain way. You need to be honest with yourself for a reasonable estimate of your general level of stress.

>self-assessment.skillbuilder4.7

Stress Coping Preference Scale

This self-assessment is designed to help you to identify the type of coping strategy you prefer to use in stressful situations. This scale lists a variety of things you might do when faced with a stressful situation. You are asked how often tend to react in these ways. You need to be honest with yourself for a reasonable estimate of your preferred coping strategy.

**Find the full self-assessments on the OLC at
www.mhhe.com/mcshaneess**

chapter 5

Employee Motivation:
Foundations and Practices

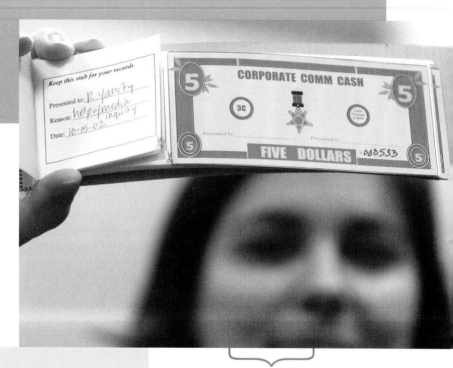

Julie Hans holds up the award coupons that
Progress Energy employees give one another as
recognition for their good work and support.

>**learning**objectives

After reading this chapter, you should be able to

- Describe Maslow's needs hierarchy theory and explain
  why it does not live up to its popularity.

- Describe four-drive theory and explain how these
  drives influence motivation and behavior.

- Diagram the expectancy theory model and discuss its
  practical implications for motivating employees.

- Describe the characteristics of effective goal setting
  and feedback.

- Summarize the equity theory model, including how
  people try to reduce feelings of inequity.

- Discuss the advantages and disadvantages of job
  specialization.

- Diagram the job characteristics model of job design.

- Identify two strategies to increase job enrichment.

- Define empowerment and identify strategies to
  support empowerment.

Bernard McCourt recognized the speaker on his voice mail but was still surprised. Governor Mitt Romney had called to thank the Massachusetts Highway Department manager for a job well done. A resident had called the governor's office, praising McCourt's crew for fixing a culvert, so Romney telephoned McCourt directly to express his compliments. "It certainly is appreciated when you hear from the person at the top," said McCourt, who has replayed Romney's voice mail message for his wife and some skeptical co-workers.

Governor Mitt Romney and other organizational leaders are discovering that one of the best ways to motivate employees is good old-fashioned praise and recognition. Stock options can evaporate and incentive plans often backfire, whereas a few words of appreciation almost always create a warm glow of satisfaction and a renewed energy. "If we can motivate our employees in any way, we find a way to do it," says Ed Ariniello, vice president of operations at G.I. Joe's, a sports retailer in Oregon and Washington. "I do a lot of walking around patting people on the back and I go around the organization and encourage people to do the same. When they do that, the employees feel great."

The challenge of recognition is to "catch" employees doing extraordinary things. Keyspan Corporation chairman Bob Catell resolves this by regularly asking managers for lists of "unsung heroes" at the New England gas utility. He calls an employee every week, often spending the first few minutes convincing the listener that it is really him. "They start by saying, 'Hey, you can't fool me, this isn't Catell!' But once they realize it is me, they are pleased that I would take the time to do this."

Some companies involve co-workers in the motivation-through-recognition process. Staff at the Food Safety and Quality Branch in British Columbia, Canada, posted a large "Appreciation Tree" in the front office and surrounded it with photos of staff members. Branch employees added leaves to the tree that identified specific co-workers and what they specifically did that was valued. Employees at Progress Energy in Raleigh, North Carolina, receive a booklet of coupons resembling currency. The coupons are distributed—up to $25 per award—to colleagues as a show of gratitude. "Everybody needs encouragement, and everybody needs their work to be recognized," says Julie Hans, a member of Progress Energy's communications department.[1]

Perhaps it's a rebellion against the obsession with financial rewards a decade ago, but many companies are rediscovering that motivating employees is more than dangling a paycheck in front of them. Sure, money is important and does motivate employees. But the deepest sources of employee engagement are not put into a bank account. They include recognition, fairness, challenging and interesting work, the opportunity to feel empowered, and many other things that we'll discuss in this chapter.

Recall from Chapter 2 that **motivation** refers to the forces within a person that affect the direction, intensity, and persistence of voluntary behavior.[2] Motivated employees are willing to exert a particular level of effort (intensity), for a certain amount of time (persistence), toward a particular goal (direction). Motivation is one of the four essential drivers of individual behavior and performance and, consequently, is an integral component of employee engagement. An engaged workforce is an important predictor of the organization's competitiveness, so it's easy to see why employee motivation is continuously on the minds of corporate leaders.

We begin this chapter by describing Maslow's needs hierarchy theory and explaining why this incredibly popular theory isn't as sound as the public assumes. We then turn to four-drive theory, which offers more promise. After discussing these needs-based theories, we turn our attention to a rational decision model of employee motivation, called expectancy theory. This is followed by an overview of the key elements of goal setting and feedback as well as equity theory. The latter part of this chapter describes two applied performance practices: job design and empowerment, including specific job design strategies to motivate employees as well as conditions that support empowerment.

motivation
The forces within a person that affect his or her direction, intensity, and persistence of voluntary behavior.

<Employee Needs and Drives

needs
Deficiencies that energize or trigger behaviors to satisfy those needs.

drives
Instinctive or innate tendencies to seek certain goals or maintain internal stability.

Maslow's needs hierarchy theory
A motivation theory of needs arranged in a hierarchy, whereby people are motivated to fulfill a higher need as a lower one becomes gratified.

Motivation begins with individual needs and their underlying drives. **Needs** are deficiencies that energize or trigger behaviors to satisfy those needs. Unfulfilled needs create a tension that makes us want to find ways to reduce or satisfy those needs. The stronger your needs, the more motivated you are to satisfy them. Conversely, a satisfied need does not motivate. **Drives** are instinctive or innate tendencies to seek certain goals or maintain internal stability. Drives are hardwired in the brain—everyone has the same drives—and they most likely exist to help the species survive.[3] Needs are typically produced by drives, but they may also be strengthened through learning (reinforcement) and social forces such as culture and childhood upbringing.

Maslow's Needs Hierarchy Theory

By far, the best-known theory of employee needs and motivation is **Maslow's needs hierarchy theory**. This popularity is rather odd, considering that it has little or no scientific support. Even Maslow, writing in his journals, was surprised that people had accepted his theory wholeheartedly without any critique or investigation.[4] Normally, a theory that fails to live up to its predictions is laid to rest. However, Maslow's model is unique because of its significant historic value, and because Maslow brought a fresh approach to human motivation theories that remains with us today.

Early in Maslow's career, researchers typically studied a specific drive deprivation (such as hunger) and didn't consider the full range of drives or needs in their research. They focused on instinctive motives and relied on animals or people with behavior problems as subjects. In contrast, Maslow called for a more holistic, humanistic, and positive approach to human motivation research. He believed that human behavior is typically motivated by more than one need, so a good theory needs to consider how several needs operate at the same time. He also took the position that need gratification is just as important as deprivation and that higher level needs (such as status) are influenced by social dynamics and culture, not just instincts.[5]

Maslow's needs hierarchy theory takes a holistic approach by condensing the long list of needs into a hierarchy of five basic categories.[6] As Exhibit 5.1 illustrates, physiological needs (need for food, air, water, shelter, etc.) are at the bottom of the hierarchy. Next are safety needs—the need for a secure and stable environment and the absence of pain, threat, or illness. Belongingness includes the need for love, affection, and interaction with other people. Esteem includes self-esteem through personal achievement as well as social esteem through recognition and respect from others. At the top of the hierarchy is **self-actualization**, which represents the need for self-fulfillment—a sense that the person's potential has been realized. In addition to these five, Maslow describes the need to know and need for aesthetic beauty as two needs that do not fit within the hierarchy.

self-actualization
The need for self-fulfillment in reaching one's potential.

Maslow says that we are motivated simultaneously by several needs, but the strongest source is the lowest unsatisfied need at the time. As the person satisfies a lower level need, the next higher need in the hierarchy becomes the primary motivator and remains so even if never satisfied. Physiological needs are initially the most important, and people are motivated to satisfy them first. As they become gratified, safety needs emerge as the strongest motivator. As safety needs are satisfied, belongingness needs become most important, and so forth. The exception to this need fulfillment process is self-actualization; as people experience self-actualization, they desire more rather than less of this need. Thus, while the bottom four groups are *deficiency needs* because they become activated when unfulfilled, self-actualization is a *growth need* because it continues to develop even when fulfilled.

[Exhibit 5.1] Maslow's Needs Hierarchy

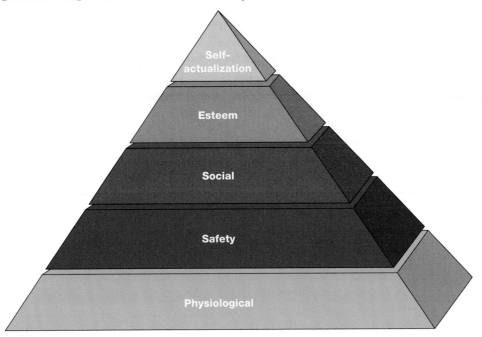

Source: Based on information in A. H. Maslow, "A Theory of Human Motivation," *Psychological Review* 50 (1943), pp. 370–396.

Evaluating Needs Hierarchy Theory

Maslow's needs hierarchy theory has not received much scientific support in several ways.[7] Although Maslow's five need categories are useful ways of thinking about different types of needs, they do not seem to capture the entire variety of needs that people experience. Also, gratification of one need level does not necessarily lead to increased motivation to satisfy the next higher need level. Some people can be very hungry and yet strive to fulfill their social needs; others can self-actualize while working in a risky environment. The theory also assumes that need priorities shift over months or years, whereas the importance of a particular need likely changes more quickly with the situation.

Another explanation why Maslow's model and other needs hierarchy theories don't work is that people don't seem to fit into one universal needs hierarchy. There is increasing evidence that needs hierarchies are unique, not universal, because a person's needs are strongly influenced by his or her values.[8] If your fundamental values lean toward stimulation and self-direction, you probably pay more attention to self-actualization needs. If power and achievement are at the top of your value system, then the status needs might be stronger most of the time. This connection between values and needs suggests that a needs hierarchy is unique to each person and can change over time, just as values change over a lifetime. In summary, we seem to have a personal and somewhat flexible needs hierarchy, not one that is hardwired in human nature, as Maslow's needs hierarchy theory assumes.

Four-Drive Theory

Although motivation experts have mostly abandoned needs hierarchy theories, recent discoveries in neuroscience have prompted them to reconsider a more coherent and integrated approach to innate drives. **Four-drive theory**, proposed by Harvard Business School

four-drive theory
A motivation theory based on the innate drives to acquire, bond, learn, and defend that incorporates both emotions and rationality.

professors Paul Lawrence and Nitin Nohria, captures many of these recent discoveries, yet upholds Maslow's philosophical recommendations.[9] Specifically, four-drive theory is both holistic (it pulls together the various drives and needs) and humanistic (it considers human thought and social influences rather than just instinct).

According to four-drive theory, everyone has the drive to acquire, bond, learn, and defend:

- *Drive to acquire.* This is the drive to seek, take, control, and retain objects and personal experiences. The drive to acquire extends beyond basic food and water; it includes the need for relative status and recognition in society. Thus, it is the foundation of competition and the basis of our need for esteem.
- *Drive to bond.* This is the drive to form social relationships and develop mutual caring commitments with others. Research indicates that people invest considerable time and effort forming and maintaining relationships without any special circumstances or ulterior motives.[10] The drive to bond motivates people to cooperate and, consequently, is a fundamental ingredient in the success of organizations and the development of societies.
- *Drive to learn.* This is the drive to satisfy our curiosity, to know and understand ourselves and the environment around us. When observing something that is inconsistent with or beyond our current knowledge, we experience a tension that motivates us to close that information gap. The drive to learn is related to the self-actualization need described earlier.
- *Drive to defend.* This drive creates a fight-or-flight response in the face of personal danger. The drive to defend goes beyond protecting our physical self. It includes defending our relationships, our acquisitions, and our belief systems. The drive to defend is always reactive—it is triggered by threat. In contrast, the other three drives are always proactive—we actively seek to improve our acquisitions, relationships, and knowledge.

All four drives, which have been well researched prior to this theory, are innate and universal, meaning that they are hardwired in our brains through evolution and are found in everyone. They are also independent of each other, so one drive is not inherently inferior or superior to another drive. Four-drive theory also states that these four drives are a complete set—there are no other fundamental drives excluded from the model. Another key feature is that three of the four drives are proactive, meaning that we regularly try to fulfill them. Thus, any notion of fulfilling drives is temporary, at best.

How Drives Influence Employee Motivation

To understand how these four drives translate into employee motivation, recall from previous chapters that our perceptions of the external world are influenced by our emotions.[11] Every meaningful bit of information we receive is quickly and unconsciously tagged with emotional markers that swirl around our conscious process of logically analyzing that information. Our motivation to act is therefore a result of rational thinking influenced by these emotional markers.[12] In fact, the words "motivation" and "emotion" originate from the same Latin root, meaning "to move."

The four drives fit into this tango of emotionality and rationality because they determine which emotional markers, if any, are attached to the perceived information. For example, suppose your department has just received a new computer program that you are curious to try out (triggered by your drive to learn). However, your boss says that you are too inexperienced to use the new system yet, which makes you somewhat angry (triggered by your drive to defend against the "inexperience" insult). Both the curiosity about the software program and your anger from the boss's beliefs about your experience demand your attention and energize you to act. The key point here is that the four innate drives determine which emotions to generate in each situation.

[Exhibit 5.2] Four-Drive Theory of Motivation

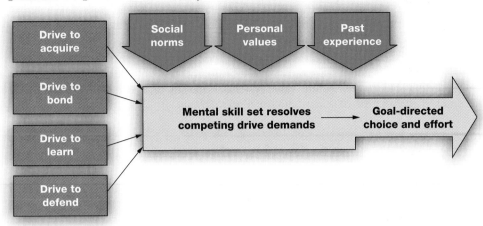

Source: Based on information in P. R. Lawrence and N. Nohria. *Driven: How Human Nature Shapes Our Choices.* (San Francisco: Jossey-Bass, 2002).

Four-drive theory further explains that this process is conscious (humanistic) rather than instinctive, because these drives produce independent and often competing signals that require our attention.[13] As Exhibit 5.2 illustrates, when aware of this internal conflict, we rely on a built-in skill set to resolve the conflict. These skills take into account social norms, past experience, and personal values. The result is goal-directed decision and effort that fits within the constraints of cultural and moral expectations. In other words, our conscious analysis of competing demands from the four drives generates needs that energize us to act in ways acceptable to society and our own moral compass.

Practical Implications of Four-Drive Theory

The main practical implication of four-drive theory is that companies need to ensure that individual jobs and workplaces provide a balanced opportunity to fulfill the drive to acquire, bond, learn, and defend.[14] This recommendation has two parts. First, each of us continuously seeks fulfillment of all four drives, not just some of them. Thus, the best workplaces for motivation and morale provide sufficient rewards, learning opportunities, social interaction, and so forth for all employees.

Second, these four drives must be kept in balance; that is, organizations should avoid too much or too little opportunity to fulfill each drive. The reason for this advice is that the four drives counterbalance each other. Companies that help employees fulfill one drive but

Executives at EnCana Corporation had launched a recognition program called "High Five" in which employees and managers were encouraged to recommend any deserving colleague for a high-five card, which is redeemable for $5.00. The token amount was intended to symbolize their value as an employee and to provide a small financial incentive. But rather than cashing in their cards for money, many employees at the Calgary-based energy company displayed the cards in their offices. The visible symbol of recognition was apparently worth more to many people than the cash value of the card.[15]

not the others will face long-term problems. If a company emphasizes the drive to acquire (such as through highly competitive rewards) without the drive to bond, for instance, it may eventually suffer from organizational politics and dysfunctional conflict.

Another recommendation from the needs/drives-based theories is to offer employees a choice of rewards rather than give everyone the same specific reward. Although we possess the same drives and require their ongoing fulfillment, people differ in their needs at any given time. Due to their unique value systems, some employees generally have a strong need to achieve whereas others are motivated more by social factors.

<Expectancy Theory of Motivation

expectancy theory
The motivation theory based on the idea that work effort is directed toward behaviors that people believe will lead to desired outcomes.

Four-drive and needs hierarchy theory try to explain what motivates employees. But how do these drives and needs translate into specific effort and behavior? One of the best theories to answer this question is **expectancy theory** of motivation. Expectancy theory is based on the idea that work effort is directed toward behaviors that people believe will lead to desired outcomes.[16] As illustrated in Exhibit 5.3, an individual's effort level depends on three factors: effort-to-performance (E-to-P) expectancy, performance-to-outcome (P-to-O) expectancy, and outcome valences (V). Employee motivation is influenced by all three components of the expectancy theory model. If any component weakens, motivation weakens.

- *E-to-P expectancy.* This refers to the individual's perception that his or her effort will result in a particular level of performance. In some situations, employees may believe that they can unquestionably accomplish the task (a probability of 1.0). In other situations, they expect that even their highest level of effort will not result in the desired performance level (a probability of 0.0). In most cases, the E-to-P expectancy falls somewhere between these two extremes.

- *P-to-O expectancy.* This is the perceived probability that a specific behavior or performance level will lead to particular outcomes. In extreme cases, employees may believe that accomplishing a particular task (performance) will definitely result in a particular outcome (a probability of 1.0), or they may believe that this outcome

[**Exhibit 5.3**] Expectancy Theory of Motivation

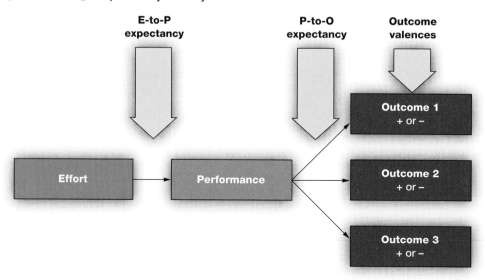

will have no effect on successful performance (a probability of 0.0). More often, the P-to-O expectancy falls somewhere between these two extremes.

• *Outcome valences.* A valence is the anticipated satisfaction or dissatisfaction that an individual feels toward an outcome. It ranges from negative to positive. (The actual range doesn't matter; it may be from –1 to +1, or from –100 to +100.) An outcome valence represents a person's anticipated satisfaction with the outcome.[17] Outcomes have a positive valence when they are consistent with our values and satisfy our needs; they have a negative valence when they oppose our values and inhibit need fulfillment.

Expectancy Theory in Practice

One of the appealing characteristics of expectancy theory is that it provides clear guidelines for increasing employee motivation.[18] Here are some of the main recommendations for each of the theory's three components:

Increasing E-to-P Expectancies

E-to-P expectancies are influenced by the individual's belief that he or she can successfully complete the task. Some companies increase this can-do attitude by assuring employees that they have the necessary competencies, clear role perceptions, and necessary resources to reach the desired levels of performance. Matching employees to jobs based on their abilities and clearly communicating the tasks required for the job is an important part of this process. Similarly, E-to-P expectancies are learned, so behavioral modeling and supportive feedback (positive reinforcement) typically strengthen employee self-confidence.[19]

Increasing P-to-O Expectancies

The most obvious ways to improve P-to-O expectancies are to measure employee performance accurately and distribute more valued rewards to those with higher job performance. P-to-O expectancies are perceptions, so employees need to know how higher performance will result in higher rewards. This occurs by explaining how specific rewards are connected to specific past performance, and by using examples, anecdotes, and public ceremonies to illustrate when behavior has been rewarded.

Increasing Outcome Valences

Everyone has unique values and experiences, which translates into different needs at different times. Consequently, individualizing rather than standardizing rewards and other performance outcomes is an important ingredient in employee motivation. At the same time, leaders need to watch out for countervalent outcomes—consequences with negative valences that reduce rather than enhance employee motivation. For example, peer pressure may cause some employees to perform their jobs at the minimum standard even though formal rewards and the job itself would otherwise motivate them to perform at higher levels.

Overall, expectancy theory is a useful model that explains how people rationally figure out the best direction, intensity, and persistence of effort. It has been tested in a variety of situations and cultures.[20] The main limitation is that expectancy theory ignores the role of emotion in motivation. The valence element of expectancy theory captures some of this emotional process, but only peripherally. Expectancy theory incorrectly assumes that preferences (choices) require conscious inferences (reasoning), but we know from earlier chapters that this isn't true. Many of our preferences form before consciously analyzing the situation. Thus, theorists probably need to redesign the expectancy theory model in light of new information about the importance of emotions in motivation and behavior.

<Goal Setting and Feedback

Walk into almost any call center and you will notice that the organization is obsessed with measured performance. Most call center operations are judged on several metrics such as average time to answer the call, length of time per call, and abandon rates (customers who hang up before the call is handled by a customer service representative). Real-time data on these performance indicators are often displayed on electronic monitors for all employees to see.[21] Associated with these numbers are specific goals, and supervisors conduct goal setting sessions with each employee to help them understand and achieve those objectives. **Goal setting** is the process of motivating employees and clarifying their role perceptions by establishing performance objectives. It potentially improves employee performance in two ways: (1) by stretching the intensity and persistence of effort and (2) by giving employees clearer role perceptions so that their effort is channeled toward behaviors that will improve work performance.

goal setting
The process of motivating employees and clarifying their role perceptions by establishing performance objectives.

Characteristics of Effective Goals

Goal setting is more complex than simply telling someone to "do your best." Instead, it requires the following six conditions.[22]

- *Specific goals.* Employees put more effort into a task when they work toward specific goals rather than "do your best" targets. Specific goals have measurable levels of change over a specific and relatively short time frame, such as "reduce scrap rate by 7 percent over the next six months."

- *Relevant goals.* Goals must also be relevant to the individual's job and within his or her control. For example, a goal to reduce waste materials would have little value if employees don't have much control over waste in the production process.

- *Challenging goals.* Challenging goals (rather than easy ones) cause people to raise the intensity and persistence of their work effort and to think through information more actively. They also fulfill a person's sense of achievement when the goal is

Near the end of a recent financial quarter, Speedera Network's 120 employees in Santa Clara, California, and Bangalore, India, received an enticing challenge from founder and CEO Ajit Gupta: "If we pull together to achieve our business targets [for the next quarter], then we'll all be on a beach in May." Employees at the Internet applications company (now merged with Akamai) even voted on which of four destinations they would prefer (a Hawaiian resort won easily). Speedera would cover employee expenses as well as 50 percent of a spouse's or family member's expenses for four days. Everyone worked feverishly toward the company's goals, which included a hefty increase in revenue. Their motivation was further fueled with constant reminders of the Hawaiian trip. "The offices were transformed to look like tropical islands," says Gupta. Staff also received postcards and brochures with tempting images of the resort and its attractions. Much to everyone's delight, the company achieved its goals and Speedera staff from both countries had a memorable bonding experience on Hawaiian beaches.[23]

achieved. General Electric, Goldman Sachs, and many other organizations emphasize *stretch goals*. These goals don't just stretch your abilities and motivation; they are goals that you don't know how to reach, so you need to be creative to achieve them.[24]

• *Goal commitment.* Ideally goals should be challenging without being so difficult that employees lose their motivation to achieve them.[25] This is the same as the E-to-P expectancy that we learned about in the section on expectancy theory. The lower the E-to-P expectancy that the goal can be accomplished, the less committed (motivated) the employee is to the goal.

• *Goal participation* (sometimes). Goal setting is usually, but not always, more effective when employees participate in setting goals.[26] Participation potentially increases goal commitment compared to goals set alone by the supervisor. Participation may also improve goal quality, because employees have valuable information and knowledge that may not be known to those who initially formed the goal.

• *Goal feedback.* Feedback is another necessary condition for effective goal setting.[27] **Feedback** is any information that people receive about the consequences of their behavior. Feedback lets us know whether we have achieved the goal or are properly directing our effort toward it. Feedback is also an essential ingredient in motivation because our self-actualization and underlying drive to learn can't be satisfied unless we receive information on goal accomplishment. Feedback is so central to goal setting that we will look more closely at it next.

feedback
Any information that people receive about the consequences of their behavior.

Characteristics of Effective Feedback

Feedback is a key ingredient in goal setting and employee performance. It clarifies role perceptions and improves ability by frequently providing information to correct performance problems. Under some conditions, feedback also motivates employees. This is particularly true when feedback is positive, such as the recognition activities described in the opening vignette to this chapter. Even negative (called *constructive*) feedback can be motivating for employees with strong self-esteem, because the less-than-glowing performance feedback motivates them to improve rather than to deny or reject the feedback.[28]

As with goal setting, feedback should be *specific* and *relevant*. It should also be *timely*—available as soon as possible after the behavior or results so employees see a clear association between their actions and the consequences. Feedback should also be *sufficiently frequent*. New employees require more frequent feedback to aid their learning. Some jobs (e.g., executives) necessarily have less frequent feedback because the consequences of their actions take longer than in, say, a cashier's job. Finally, feedback should be *credible,* such as when stated by people with no vested interest or from reliable monitoring devices.

Goal setting represents one of the "tried and true" theories in organizational behavior, so much so that a recent survey of professors identified it as one of the top OB theories in terms of validity and usefulness.[29] This high score is not surprising given the impressive research support and wide application of this concept in a variety of settings. In partnership with goal setting, feedback also has an excellent reputation for improving employee motivation and performance. At the same time, putting goal setting into practice is far from perfect.[30] One concern is that goal setting tends to focus employees on a narrow subset of measurable performance indicators while ignoring aspects of job performance that are difficult to measure. A second problem is that when tied to financial rewards, many employees are motivated to make their goals easy (while making the boss think they are difficult) so they have a higher probability of receiving the bonus or pay increase.

>Equity Theory

Taiwan has legislation guaranteeing gender equality in the workplace, but more than half of the 4,000 working women recently surveyed in that country say men get paid more for doing the same work. "It's unfair," says Hsieh Hsuen-Hui, a senior trade specialist at an export company in Taipei. "Monthly salaries that male colleagues receive are about NT$10,000 ($300) higher than what I get, even though we are doing the same job." Hsieh's boss believes that men should be paid higher wages since they are more flexible when it comes to overseas business travel. Some employers openly say they pay men more because they have a greater need for income as the breadwinners. But Hsieh and other women claim that neither reason justifies the significant pay differences. "We have tried to express our dissatisfaction, but our boss says those are the rules of the game and anyone who doesn't agree can just leave," says Hsieh.[31]

equity theory
A theory that explains how people develop perceptions of fairness in the distribution and exchange of resources.

The feelings that Hsieh Hsuen-Hui and others experience in this situation relate to a perspective of employee motivation that is explained through **equity theory**. According to this theory, feelings of equity or inequity occur when employees compare their own outcome/input ratio to the outcome/input ratio of some other person.[32] The outcome/input ratio is the value of the outcomes you receive divided by the value of inputs you provide in the exchange relationship. Hsieh Hsuen-Hui probably included her level of responsibility, effort, and performance as inputs. Other inputs might include skills, experience, status, and amount of time worked. Outcomes are the things employees receive from the organization in exchange for the inputs. In the case involving Hsieh Hsuen-Hui, the main outcome is the paycheck. Some other outcomes might be promotions, recognition, or an office with a window.

Equity theory states that we compare our outcome/input ratio with a comparison other.[33] In our earlier example, Hsieh Hsuen-Hui compared herself with her male colleagues in similar positions. However, the comparison other may be another person or group of people in the same job, another job, or another organization. Some research suggests that employees frequently collect information on several referents to form a "generalized" comparison other.[34] For the most part, however, the comparison other varies from one person to the next and is not easily identifiable.

Equity Evaluation

We form an equity evaluation after determining our own outcome/input ratio and comparing this with the comparison other's ratio. Let's consider the experience of Hsieh Hsuen-Hui again. Hsieh feels *underreward* inequity because her male counterparts receive higher

[Exhibit 5.4] Equity Theory Model

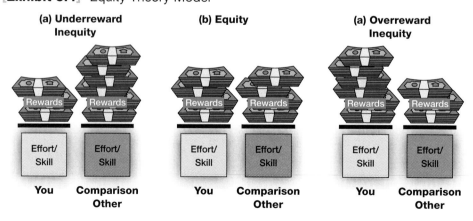

(a) Underreward Inequity	(b) Equity	(a) Overreward Inequity
You Comparison Other	You Comparison Other	You Comparison Other

outcomes (pay) for inputs that are, at best, comparable to what she contributes. This condition is illustrated in Exhibit 5.4a.

In the equity condition, Hsieh would believe that her outcome/input ratio is similar to the ratio of male colleagues. Specifically, if she believes that she provides the same inputs as the male senior trade specialists, then she would feel equity if both job groups received the same pay and other outcomes (see Exhibit 5.4b). If the male senior trade specialists claim they make a greater contribution because they have more flexibility, then they would have feelings of equity only if they receive proportionally more pay than Hsieh and other female trade specialists. It is also possible that some male trade specialists experience *overreward* inequity (Exhibit 5.4c). They would feel that their jobs have the same value as Hsieh's job, yet earn more money. However, overreward inequity isn't as common as underreward inequity, because people tend to quickly change their perceptions to justify the higher rewards.

Motivation to Reduce Inequity Feelings

We experience an emotional tension with perceived inequities, which motivates us to reduce those inequities. But what are we motivated to do to reduce this tension? Here are the main ways that people correct inequity feelings when they are underrewarded compared to a co-worker (comparison other):[35]

- *Reduce our inputs.* Perform at a lower level, give fewer helpful suggestions, engage in less organizational citizenship behavior.
- *Increase our outcomes.* Ask for a pay increase, make unauthorized use of company resources.
- *Increase comparison other's inputs.* Subtly ask the better-off co-worker to do a larger share of the work to justify his or her higher pay or other outcomes.
- *Reduce comparison other's outcomes.* Ask the boss to stop giving favorable treatment to the co-worker (see cartoon).

B. Smaller

"O.K., if you can't see your way to giving me a pay raise, how about giving Parkerson a pay cut?"

Source: The New Yorker Collection 2001

- *Change our perceptions.* Believe the co-worker really is doing more (e.g., working longer hours), or that the higher outcomes (e.g., better office) he or she receives really aren't so much better than what you get.
- *Change the comparison other.* Compare yourself to someone else closer to your situation (job duties, pay scale).
- *Leave the field.* Avoid thinking about the inequity by keeping away from the office where the co-worker is located, taking more sick leave, moving to another department, or quitting the job.

Although the categories remain the same, people who feel overreward inequity would, of course, act differently. For example, overrewarded employees don't usually correct this tension by working harder. Instead, they might encourage the referent to work at a more leisurely pace or, equally likely, change their perceptions to justify why they are given more favorable outcomes.

Evaluating Equity Theory

Equity theory is quite successful at predicting various situations, such as major baseball league salary disputes and perceived fairness of British CEO remuneration.[36] However, equity theory isn't so easy to put into practice because it doesn't identify the "comparison other" and doesn't indicate which inputs or outcomes are most valuable to each employee. The best solution here is for leaders to know their employees well enough to minimize the risk of inequity feelings. Open communication is also the key, so employees can let decision makers know when they feel their decisions are unfair.

One other limitation with equity theory is that it explains our feelings of fairness only to some extent. In fact, some research suggests that a person's sense of fairness is affected just as much by the process of deciding how to divide rewards and resources as in the perceived equity of the actual distribution.[37] In other words, to be fair, we need to pay as much attention to how we go about distributing resources as we do to the relative amounts distributed.

How do companies improve fairness in the *process* of distributing rewards and resources?[38] A good place to start is by giving employees "voice" in the process; encourage them to present their facts and perspectives on the issue. It is also important that the decision maker is unbiased, relies on complete and accurate information, applies existing policies consistently, and has listened to all sides of the dispute. If employees still feel unfairness in the allocation of resources, these feelings tend to weaken if the company has a way of appealing the decision to a higher authority. Finally, people usually feel better when they are treated with respect and are given a full explanation of the decision. If employees believe a decision is unfair, refusing to explain how the decision was made could fuel those feelings of inequity.

>Job Design

How do you build a better job? That question has challenged organizational behavior experts as well as psychologists, engineers, and economists for a few centuries. Some jobs have very few tasks and usually require very little skill. Other jobs are immensely complex and require years of experience and learning to master them. From one extreme to the other, jobs have different effects on work efficiency and employee motivation. The organization's challenge is to find the right combination so work is performed efficiently but employees are motivated and engaged.[39] This challenge requires careful **job design**—the process of assigning tasks to a job, including the interdependency of those tasks with other jobs. To

job design
The process of assigning tasks to a job, including the interdependency of those tasks with other jobs.

understand how jobs affect motivation and performance, let's begin by describing early job design efforts aimed at increasing work efficiency through job specialization.

Job Design and Work Efficiency

Using a pair of tweezers, an employee at Medtronic's assembly line in Minneapolis, Minnesota, loads 275 feedthroughs—tiny needlelike components for pacemakers and neurostimulators—onto a slotted storage block. She fills a block in about 15 minutes, then places the completed block on a shelf, and loads the next block.[40] The Medtronics employee works in a job with a high degree of **job specialization**. Job specialization occurs when the work required to build a pacemaker—or any other product or service—is subdivided into separate jobs assigned to different people. Each resulting job includes a narrow subset of tasks, usually completed in a short time.

For more than two thousand years, philosophers and economists have applauded job specialization for improving work efficiency. People tend to produce more output in jobs with a few simple tasks than in jobs with many complex tasks. One reason is that with fewer tasks to juggle, employees waste less time changing activities. They also require fewer physical and mental skills to accomplish the assigned work, so less time and resources are needed for training. A third reason is that employees practice their tasks more frequently with shorter work cycles, so jobs are mastered quickly. A fourth reason why work efficiency is higher in specialized jobs is that employees with specific aptitudes or skills can be matched more precisely to the jobs for which they are best suited.[41]

Problems with Job Specialization

The popularity of job specialization grew throughout the early 1900s. By the 1970s, however, it became apparent that work efficiency didn't always result in higher performance. The main reason was that highly specialized jobs with simple tasks become tedious, resulting in lower motivation as well as higher turnover and absenteeism. The term *blue-collar blues* became part of the language, and incidents of rebellion on assembly lines brought attention to the problem. Job specialization also reduces work quality because employees see only a small part of the process.[42]

Job Design and Work Motivation

Job specialization gurus of the past may have overlooked the motivational effect of jobs, but it is now the central focus of many job design changes. This motivational perspective is nicely laid out in the **job characteristics model**, shown in Exhibit 5.5.[43] All jobs can be examined in terms of five core dimensions; under the right conditions, employees are more motivated and satisfied when jobs have higher levels of these dimensions.

- *Skill variety.* **Skill variety** refers to the use of different skills and talents to complete a variety of work activities. For example, sales clerks who normally only serve customers might be assigned the additional duties of stocking inventory and changing storefront displays.
- *Task identity.* **Task identity** is the degree to which a job requires completion of a whole or identifiable piece of work, such as assembling an entire computer modem rather than just soldering in the circuitry.
- *Task significance.* **Task significance** is the degree to which the job affects the organization or larger society, or both.
- *Autonomy.* Jobs with high levels of **autonomy** provide freedom, independence, and discretion in scheduling the work and determining the procedures to be used to

job specialization
The result of division of labor in which each job includes a subset of the tasks required to complete the product or service.

job characteristics model
A job design model that relates the motivational properties of jobs to specific personal and organizational consequences of those properties.

skill variety
The extent to which employees must use different skills and talents to perform tasks within their job.

task identity
The degree to which a job requires completion of a whole or an identifiable piece of work.

task significance
The degree to which the job has a substantial impact on the organization and/or larger society.

autonomy
The degree to which a job gives employees the freedom, independence, and discretion to schedule their work and determine the procedures used in completing it.

[Exhibit 5.5] Job Characteristics Model

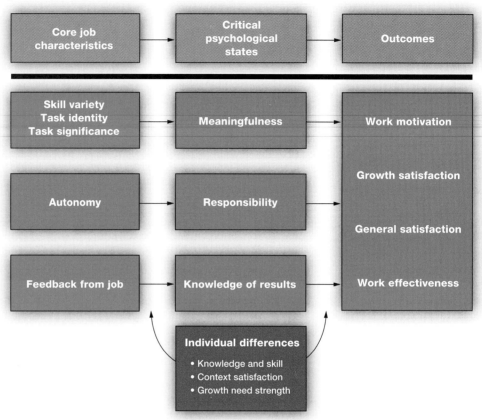

complete the work. In autonomous jobs, employees make their own decisions rather than rely on detailed instructions from supervisors or procedure manuals.

- *Job feedback.* Job feedback is the degree to which employees can tell how well they are doing based on direct sensory information from the job itself. Airline pilots can tell how well they land their aircraft, and road crews can see how well they have prepared the road bed and laid the asphalt.

These five core job characteristics affect employee motivation and satisfaction through three critical psychological states. Skill variety, task identity, and task significance directly influence the job's *experienced meaningfulness*—the belief that one's work is worthwhile or important. Autonomy directly contributes to *experienced responsibility*—where employees feel personally accountable for the outcomes of their efforts. Job feedback affects the third critical psychological state, *knowledge of results.*

Individual Differences

The job characteristics model proposes that increasing these three psychological states will improve employee motivation and satisfaction, but only under certain conditions. Specifically, employees must have the required skills and knowledge to master the more challenging work. Otherwise, job design tends to increase stress and reduce job performance. The original model also suggests that job redesign will not benefit employees who are dissatisfied with their work context (e.g., working conditions, job security) or who have a low growth need strength (i.e., a low need for self-actualization). However, research findings have been mixed, suggesting that employees might be motivated by job design no matter how they feel about their job context or how high or low they score on growth need strength.[44]

Job Enrichment

The job characteristics model is a good template for motivating employees through job redesign. However, OB experts now believe that some of these five dimensions have a stronger effect than others on employee motivation. For instance, simply adding more tasks to a job (i.e., increasing skill variety alone) doesn't motivate employees much. Instead, the evidence points to autonomy as the core dimension to consider when trying to enrich the motivational potential of jobs.[45]

Autonomy is at the heart of **job enrichment**, which occurs when employees are given more responsibility for scheduling, coordinating, and planning their own work.[46] Generally, people in enriched jobs experience higher job satisfaction and work motivation, along with lower absenteeism and turnover. Product and service quality tend to improve because job enrichment increases the jobholder's felt responsibility and sense of ownership over the product or service.[47]

One way to increase job enrichment is by combining highly interdependent tasks into one job. This *natural grouping* approach is much more than increasing skill variety because the "natural" grouping means that tasks are combined to form a meaningful piece of work, such as creating an entire product or large part of it. Video journalists are a good example of natural grouping because they create an entire documentary or news clip by combining the jobs previously performed separately by a camera operator, sound operator, reporter, and editor. By forming natural work units, jobholders have stronger feelings of responsibility for an identifiable body of work. Forming natural work units increases task identity and task significance because employees perform a complete product or service and can more readily see how their work affects others.

A second job enrichment strategy, called *establishing client relationships,* involves putting employees in direct contact with their clients rather than using the supervisor as a go-between. By being directly responsible for specific clients, employees have more information and can make decisions affecting those clients.[48] Establishing client relationships also increases task significance because employees see a line-of-sight connection between their work and consequences for customers. "Before, I never saw a patient; now they have a face," says one medical secretary at a Swedish hospital after her job was redesigned. "I feel I have been useful when I go home."[49]

job enrichment
Occurs when employees are given more responsibility for scheduling, coordinating, and planning their own work.

Traditionally, up to four people are required to shoot a video news clip: a reporter, camera operator, sound operator, and production editor. Now, thanks to technology and innovative thinking about job design in the newsroom, many TV networks are turning staff into video journalists (VJs) who perform all of these tasks in one job. Michael Rosenblum, who became one of the world's first VJs two decades ago, has transformed BBC, NYT-TV, Oxygen, and many other television companies into VJ shops. He also recently trained staff at KRON-TV in San Francisco, which is also making the transition. "The VJ model will empower a new breed of broadcast journalist who will take a story from concept to finished segment," says Mark Antonitis, president and general manager of KRON-TV. "This sort of complete ownership will provide the station with stories that have a singular and unique voice."[50]

Forming natural task groups and establishing client relationships are two ways to enrich jobs, but many companies have taken a broader approach to increasing autonomy. This trend is called *empowerment,* which we discuss next.

>Empowerment Practices

When Clive Beddoe co-founded WestJet Airlines, he wanted to create an organization in which employees had the freedom to serve customers rather than follow strict rules. Beddoe explains that most other airlines in the world have a military mind-set. "Manuals and polices have to be followed exactly and, while that's necessary in the cockpit, it's not the best way when it comes to customer service," says the co-founder of the discount airline in Calgary, Canada. Beddoe emphasizes that WestJet is the opposite. "Here, we empower our employees and encourage them to be free-thinking and to do whatever it takes in whatever way they feel it's appropriate to solve customer problems."[51]

WestJet is one of North America's most successful airlines, in large part because Beddoe and other WestJet leaders create a work environment that makes employees feel empowered. **Empowerment** is a psychological concept represented by four dimensions: self-determination, meaning, competence, and impact of the individual's role in the organization. Empowerment consists of all four dimensions. If any dimension weakens, the employee's sense of empowerment will weaken.[52]

empowerment
A psychological concept in which people experience more self-determination, meaning, competence, and impact regarding their role in the organization.

- *Self-determination.* Empowered employees feel that they have freedom, independence, and discretion over their work activities.
- *Meaning.* Employees who feel empowered care about their work and believe that what they do is important.
- *Competence.* Empowered people are confident about their ability to perform the work well and have a capacity to grow with new challenges.
- *Impact.* Empowered employees view themselves as active participants in the organization; that is, their decisions and actions have an influence on the company's success.

From this definition, you can see that empowerment is not a personality trait, although personality might influence the extent to which someone feels empowered. People also experience degrees of empowerment, which can vary from one work environment to the next.

Supporting Empowerment

Chances are that you have heard corporate leaders say they are "empowering" the workforce. What these executives really mean is that they are changing the work environment to support empowerment. Numerous individual, job design, and organizational or work context factors support empowerment. At the individual level, employees must possess the necessary competencies to be able to perform the work as well as handle the additional decision-making requirements.[53]

Job characteristics clearly influence the dynamics of empowerment.[54] To generate beliefs about self-determination, employees must work in jobs with a high degree of autonomy with minimal bureaucratic control. To maintain a sense of meaningfulness, jobs must have high levels of task identity and task significance. And to maintain a sense of self-confidence, jobs must provide sufficient feedback.

Several organizational and work context factors also influence empowerment. Employees experience more empowerment in organizations where information and other resources are easily accessible. Empowerment also requires a *learning orientation* culture, where employee learning is encouraged and reasonable mistakes are viewed as a natural part of the learning process. Furthermore, empowerment requires corporate leaders who trust employees and are willing to take the risks that empowerment creates.[55]

With the right individuals, job characteristics, and organizational environment, empowerment can have a noticeable effect on motivation and performance. For instance, a study of bank employees concluded that empowerment improved customer service and tended to reduce conflict between employees and their supervisors. A study of nurses reported that empowerment is associated with higher trust in management, which ultimately influences job satisfaction, belief and acceptance of organizational goals and values, and effective organizational commitment.[56] Empowerment also tends to increase personal initiative because employees identify with and assume more psychological ownership of their work.

Empowerment, job design, and the conceptual theories of motivation presented in this chapter provide some indication of the variety of approaches to employee motivation. The topic extends beyond this chapter, however, to how people lead, support or resist organizational change, deal with conflict, and most other topics in this book. Individual decision making also relates to motivation because the decision choice is, in fact, the motivation to take one route or direction over others. Individual decision making is the theme of the next chapter.

>chapter summary

Motivation refers to the forces within a person that affect his or her direction, intensity, and persistence of voluntary behavior in the workplace. Maslow's needs hierarchy groups needs into a hierarchy of five levels and states that the lowest needs are initially most important, but higher needs become more important as the lower ones are satisfied. Although very popular, Maslow's theory lacks research support, partly because it incorrectly assumes that everyone has the same hierarchy.

Four-drive theory states that everyone has four innate drives—the drive to acquire, bond, learn, and defend. These drives generate competing emotions, which we consciously reconcile through a skill set that considers social norms, past experience, and personal values. Four-drive theory recommends that everyone in the workplace needs to regularly fulfill all four drives and that organizations should avoid too much or too little opportunity to fulfill each drive.

Expectancy theory states that work effort is determined by a combination of the individual's effort-to-performance (E-to-P) expectancy, performance-to-outcome (P-to-O) expectancy, and the valences that the person feels for those outcomes. The E-to-P expectancy increases by improving the employee's ability and confidence to perform the job. The P-to-O expectancy increases by measuring performance accurately, distributing higher rewards to better performers, and showing employees that rewards are performance-based. Outcome valences increase by finding out what employees want and using these resources as rewards.

Goal setting is the process of motivating employees and clarifying their role perceptions by establishing performance objectives. Goals are more effective when they are specific, relevant, and challenging; have employee commitment; and are accompanied by meaningful feedback. Participative goal setting is important in some situations. Effective feedback is specific, relevant, timely, credible, and sufficiently frequent.

Equity theory explains why people feel unfairly treated. It includes four elements: outcome/input ratio, comparison other, equity evaluation, and consequences of inequity. The theory also explains what people are motivated to do when they feel inequitably treated. Along with equity of the distribution of resources, companies need to consider fairness in the process of making the resource allocation decision.

Job design refers to the process of assigning tasks to a job, including the interdependency of those tasks with other jobs. Job specialization subdivides work into separate jobs for different people. This increases work efficiency but may also have adverse effects on job performance. The job characteristics model is a template for job redesign that specifies core job dimensions, psychological states, and individual differences. Two ways to enrich jobs are clustering tasks into natural groups and establishing client relationships.

Empowerment is a psychological concept represented by four dimensions: self-determination, meaning, competence, and impact regarding the individual's role in the organization. Job design is a major influence on empowerment, particularly autonomy, task identity, task significance, and job feedback. Empowerment is also supported at the organizational level through a learning orientation culture, sufficient information and resources, and corporate leaders who trust employees.

>key terms

autonomy 103

drives 92

empowerment 106

equity theory 100

expectancy theory 96

feedback 99

four-drive theory 93

goal setting 98

job characteristics model 103

job design 102

job enrichment 105

job specialization 103

Maslow's needs hierarchy theory 92

motivation 91

needs 92

self-actualization 92

skill variety 103

task identity 103

task significance 103

>critical thinking questions

1. Four-drive theory is conceptually different from Maslow's needs hierarchy in several ways. Describe these differences. At the same time, needs are typically based on drives, so the four drives should parallel the seven needs that Maslow identified (five in the hierarchy and two additional needs). Map Maslow's needs onto the four drives in four-drive theory.

2. Research in organizational behavior and other disciplines increasingly recognizes that values play a key role in employee motivation, particularly personal needs. Look at the 10 values dimensions in Schwartz's values model in Chapter 2 and figure out how they might relate to the seven needs identified by Abraham Maslow. Then connect these 10 values to the four drives in four-drive theory.

3. Use all three components of expectancy theory to explain why some employees are motivated to show up for work during a severe storm whereas others make no effort to leave their home.

4. Using your knowledge of the characteristics of effective goals, establish two meaningful goals related to your performance in this class.

5. Several service representatives are upset that the newly hired representative with no previous experience will be paid $3,000 a year above the usual starting salary in the pay range. The department manager explained that the new hire would not accept the entry-level rate, so the company raised the offer by $3,000. All five reps currently earn salaries near the top of the scale ($15,000 higher than the new recruit), although they all started at the minimum starting salary a few years earlier. Use equity theory to explain why the five service representatives feel inequity in this situation.

6. Most of us have watched pizzas being made while waiting in a pizzeria. What level of job specialization do you usually notice in these operations? Why does this high or low level of specialization exist? If some

pizzerias have different levels of specialization than others, identify the contingencies that might explain these differences.

7. This chapter described video journalist as an example of job enrichment through natural grouping of tasks.

Identify examples of this job enrichment practice that might occur in other job clusters, either where you work or in organizations with which you are familiar.

8. Can a manager or supervisor empower an employee? Discuss fully.

>case.study:skillbuilder5.1

Buddy's Snack Company

By Russell Casey, Clayton State University, and Gloria Thompson, University of Phoenix

Buddy's Snack Company is a family-owned company located in the Rocky Mountains. Buddy Forest started the business in 1951 by selling homemade potato chips out of the back of his pickup truck. Now, Buddy's is a $36 million snack-food company that is struggling to regain market share lost to Frito-Lay and other fierce competitors. In the early eighties, Buddy passed the business onto his son, Buddy Jr., who is currently grooming his son, Mark, to succeed himself as head of the company.

Six months ago, Mark joined Buddy's Snacks as a salesperson and after four months was quickly promoted to sales manager. Mark recently graduated from a local university with an M.B.A. in marketing, and Buddy Jr. was hoping that Mark would be able to implement strategies that could help turn the company around. One of Mark's initial strategies was to introduce a new sales performance management system. As part of this approach, any salesperson who receives a below average performance rating would be required to attend a mandatory coaching session with his or her supervisor. Mark Forest is hoping that these coaching sessions will motivate his employees to increase their sales. This case describes the reaction of three salespeople who have been required to attend a coaching session because of their low performance over the previous quarter.

Lynda Lewis

Lynda is a hard worker who takes pride in her work ethic. She has spent a lot of time reading the training material and learning selling techniques, viewing training videos on her own time, and accompanying top salespeople on their calls. Lynda has no problem asking for advice and doing whatever needs to be done to learn the business. Everyone agrees that Lynda has a cheery attitude and is a real team player, giving the company 150 percent at all times. It has been a tough quarter for Lynda due to the downturn in the economy, but she is doing her best to make sales for the company. Lynda doesn't feel that failure to make quota during this past quarter is due to lack of effort, but just bad luck in the economy. She is hopeful that things will turn around in the next quarter.

Lynda is upset with Mark for having to attend the coaching session, because this is the first time in three years that her sales quota has not been met. Although Lynda is willing to do whatever it takes to be successful, she is concerned that the coaching sessions will be held on a Saturday. Doesn't Mark realize that Lynda has to raise three boys by herself and that weekends are an important time for her family? Because Lynda is a dedicated employee she will somehow manage to rearrange the family's schedule.

Lynda is now very concerned about how her efforts are being perceived by Mark. After all, she exceeded the sales quota from the previous quarter yet had not received a "thank you" or "good job" for those efforts. The entire experience has left Lynda unmotivated and questioning her future with the company.

Michael Benjamin

Michael is happy to have his job at Buddy's Snack Company, although he really doesn't like sales work that much. Michael accepted this position because he felt that he wouldn't have to work hard and would have a lot of free time during the day. Michael was sent to coaching mainly because his customer satisfaction reports were low; in fact, they were the lowest in the company. Michael tends to give canned presentations and does not listen closely to the customer's needs. Consequently, Michael makes numerous errors in new sales orders, which delays shipments and loses business and goodwill for Buddy's Snack Company. Michael doesn't really care since most of his customers do not spend much money and he doesn't think it is worth his while.

There has been a recent change in the company commission structure. Instead of selling to the warehouse stores and possibly earning a high commission, Michael is now forced to sell to lower-volume convenience stores. In other words, he will have to sell twice as much product to earn the same amount of money. Michael does not think this change in commission is fair and feels that the coaching session will be a waste of time. He feels that the other members of the sales team are getting all of the good leads and that is why they are so successful. Michael doesn't socialize with others in the office and attributes others' success and promotions to "who they know" in the company rather than the fact that they are hard workers. He feels that no matter how much effort is put into the job, he will never be adequately rewarded.

Kyle Sherbo

For three of the last five years Kyle was the number one salesperson in the division and had hopes of being promoted to sales manager. When Mark joined the company, Kyle worked closely with Buddy Jr. to help Mark learn all facets of the business. Kyle thought this close relationship with Buddy Jr. would assure his upcoming promotion to the coveted position of sales manager and was devastated to learn that Mark received the promotion that he thought was his.

During the past quarter, there was a noticeable change in Kyle's work habits. It had become commonplace for Kyle to be late for appointments, miss them entirely, or not return phone calls or follow up on leads. His sales performance declined dramatically, which resulted in a drastic loss of income. Although Kyle had been dedicated and fiercely loyal to Buddy Jr. and the company for many years, he is now looking for other employment. Buddy's Snacks is located in a rural community, which leaves Kyle with limited job opportunities. He was, however, offered a position as a sales manager with a competing company in a larger town, but Kyle's wife refuses to leave the area because of her strong family ties. Kyle is bitter and resentful of his current situation and now faces a mandatory coaching session that will be conducted by Mark.

Discussion Questions

1. You have met three employees of Buddy's Snacks. Explain how each employee's situation relates to equity theory.

2. Explain the motivation of these three employees in terms of the expectancy theory of motivation.

>team.exercise:skillbuilder5.2

Needs Priority Exercise

Purpose   This class exercise is designed to help you understand the characteristics and contingencies of employee needs in the workplace.

Instructions

- *Step 1:* The table below lists in alphabetical order 14 characteristics of the job or work environment. Working alone, use the far left column to rank order these characteristics in terms of how important they are to you personally. Write in "1" beside the most important characteristic, "2" for the second most important, and so on through to "14" for the least important characteristic on this list.

- *Step 2:* In the second column, rank order these characteristics in the order that you think human resource managers believe are important for their employees.

- *Step 3:* Your instructor will provide results of a recent large-scale survey of employees. When these results are

Importance to You	What HR Managers Believe Are Important to Employees	
_____	_____	Autonomy and independence
_____	_____	Benefits (health care, dental, etc.)
_____	_____	Career development opportunities
_____	_____	Communication between employees and senior mgt
_____	_____	Compensation/pay
_____	_____	Feeling safe in the work environment
_____	_____	Flexibility to balance work/life issues
_____	_____	Job security
_____	_____	Job specific training
_____	_____	Management recognition of employee job performance
_____	_____	Opportunities to use skills/abilities
_____	_____	Organization's commitment to professional development
_____	_____	Relationship with immediate supervisor
_____	_____	The work itself

presented, identify the reasons for any noticeable differences. Relate these differences to your understanding of the emerging view of employee needs and drives in work settings.

>self-assessment.skillbuilder5.3

Measuring Your Equity Sensitivity

Equity theory states that feelings of equity are determined by the perceived outcome/input ratio between yourself and another person or source (the comparison other). However, people have different degrees of equity sensitivity, that is, their reaction to various outcome/input ratios. This self-assessment estimates your level of equity sensitivity. Read each of the statements and indicate the response that best reflects your opinion of that statement. This exercise is completed alone so students assess themselves honestly without concerns of social comparison. However, class discussion will focus on equity theory and the effect of equity sensitivity on perceptions of fairness in the workplace.

>self-assessment.skillbuilder5.4

Measuring Your Growth Need Strength

Abraham Maslow's needs hierarchy theory distinguished between deficiency needs and growth needs. Deficiency needs become activated when unfulfilled, such as the need for food or belongingness. Growth needs, on the other hand, continue to develop even when temporarily fulfilled. Maslow identified self-actualization as the only category of growth needs. Research has found that Maslow's needs hierarchy theory overall doesn't fit reality, but specific elements such as the concept of growth needs are still relevant. This self-assessment is designed to estimate your growth need strength. The instrument asks you to indicate the features of jobs that are most important to you. Please indicate which of the two jobs you personally would prefer if you had to make a choice between them. In answering each question, assume that everything else about the jobs is the same. Pay attention only to the characteristics actually listed.

>self-assessment.skillbuilder5.5

Student Empowerment Scale

Empowerment is a concept that applies to people in a variety of situations. This instrument is specifically adapted to your position as a student at this college or university. Indicate the extent to which you agree or disagree with each statement in this instrument, then request the results, which provide an overall score as well as scores on each of the four dimensions of empowerment. Complete each item honestly to get the best estimate of your level of empowerment.

>self-assessment.skillbuilder5.6

What Is Your Attitude toward Money?

Money is an important part of the employment relationship and, as we read in this chapter, is often mentioned in the context of various motivation theories such as needs/drives, expectancy theory, goal setting, and equity theory. However, people have rather diverse reactions to money, so the effect of financial rewards on motivation can get complicated. This self-assessment is designed to help you to understand the types of attitudes toward money and to assess your attitude toward money. Read each of the statements in this scale and indicate the response that you believe best reflects your position regarding the statement. This exercise is completed alone so students assess themselves honestly without concerns of social comparison. However, class discussion will focus on what money means to people, including the dimensions measured here.

Find the full self-assessments on the OLC at
www.mhhe.com/mcshaneess

chapter 6

Individual Decision Making

The loss of the space shuttle Columbia (shown here lifting off for its final flight) and its crew was caused by more than foam hitting the left wing; it was also due to NASA'S flawed decision making.

>learningobjectives

After reading this chapter, you should be able to

- Explain why people have difficulty identifying problems and opportunities.
- Contrast the rational choice paradigm with how people actually evaluate and choose alternatives.
- Outline how intuition operates.
- Describe four causes of escalation of commitment.
- Identify four contingencies that affect the optimal level of employee involvement.
- Outline the four steps in the creative process.
- Describe the characteristics of employees and the workplace that support creativity.

At 9 A.M. on February 1, 2003, the NASA space shuttle Columbia disintegrated during reentry over Texas and other western states, killing all seven crew members. The physical cause of the accident was that Columbia's left wing was damaged during liftoff by a large piece of foam debris, and the gaping hole allowed superheated gases to melt the wing's aluminum frame during reentry.

Although Columbia's disintegration was caused by a damaged wing, a special accident investigation board also concluded that NASA's damaged decision-making process resulted in several "missed opportunities" to avoid loss of life. The board noted that NASA's middle management resisted attempts to label the foam hit as a problem because they were under intense pressure to keep the shuttle missions on track. One engineer who raised concerns about the foam strike was called "alarmist." Instead, managers relied on a faulty simulation of the foam strike that indicated no problems while questioning other tests suggesting the foam would cause damage.

An engineering team set up to investigate safety concerns about the foam strike sent an e-mail requesting that military satellites take photos of Columbia's wing to assess damage, but the flight director rejected the request 26 minutes later without explanation. In spite of the e-mail evidence, the manager later said she didn't know of any requests for images. When the team detailed their concerns about the foam strike, the flight director replied in an e-mail that their "rationale was lousy."

The Columbia investigation board also noted that acknowledging the foam hit as a problem would have created a huge ethical dilemma for NASA's managers because there were few options for rescuing the crew. In one meeting, Columbia's lead flight director candidly stated, "I don't think there is much we can do, so you know it's not really a factor during the flight because there isn't much we can do about it."

Along with their criticism that NASA management denied the existence of the problem, the Columbia accident investigation board concluded that managers made choices without the level of involvement from engineers required for such complex issues. "They have managers who don't know the technical background, but make decisions without asking the engineers for information," said one accident investigation board member.[1]

The tragic loss of the space shuttle Columbia is a case study in the challenges of decision making in organizational settings. **Decision making** is a conscious process of making choices among one or more alternatives with the intention of moving toward some desired state of affairs.[2] This chapter begins by outlining the rational choice paradigm of decision making. Then, we examine this model more critically by recognizing how people identify problems and opportunities, choose among alternatives, and evaluate the success of their decisions differently from the rational model. Bounded rationality, escalation of commitment, and intuition are three of the more prominent topics in this section. Next, we explore the role of employee involvement in decision making, including the benefits of involvement and the factors that determine the optimal level of involvement. The final section of this chapter examines the factors that support creativity in decision making, including characteristics of creative people, work environments that support creativity, and creativity activities.

decision making
A conscious process of making choices among one or more alternatives with the intention of moving toward some desired state of affairs.

>Rational Choice Paradigm of Decision Making

How should people make decisions? For the past 2,500 years, philosophers, economists, and businesspeople have advocated and assumed that people actually practice rationality and logic—what we now call the *rational choice paradigm* of decision making. Exhibit 6.1 illustrates the stages in this process.[3] First, decision makers identify the problem or recognize an opportunity. A problem is a deviation between the current and the desired situation—the gap between "what is" and "what ought to be." This deviation is a symptom of more fundamental root causes that need to be corrected.[4] An opportunity is a deviation

[Exhibit 6.1] Rational Choice Decision-Making Process

Rational Choice Decision-Making Process

1. Identify problem or opportunity

2. Choose the best decision process

3. Develop alternative solutions

4. Choose the best alternative

5. Implement the selected alternative

6. Evaluate decision outcomes

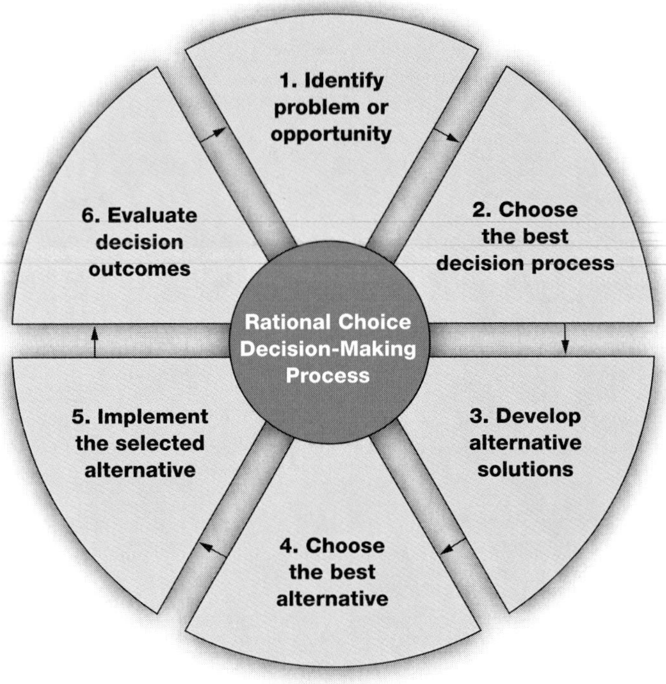

between current expectations and a potentially better situation that was not previously expected. In other words, decision makers realize that certain decisions may produce results beyond current goals or expectations.

The second step involves deciding how to process the decision, such as whether to involve others and whether the decision is unique and therefore requires more attention to searching for and choosing among alternatives.[5] The third step is to develop a list of possible solutions. This usually begins by searching for ready-made solutions, such as practices that have worked well on similar problems. If an acceptable solution cannot be found, then decision makers design a custom-made solution or modify an existing one.

The fourth step is to choose from among the alternatives. The rational choice paradigm assumes that people naturally select the alternative with the highest *subjective expected utility,* meaning that they choose the option with the most favorable outcomes or "highest payoff."[6] According to the rational choice approach, decision makers figure out which alternative has the highest utility by identifying all the outcomes that would occur if the alternative is selected and estimating the amount of satisfaction the person would feel from each of those outcomes. This is incredibly complex, but rational choice assumes that everyone does this calculation without any problem.

The fifth step is to implement the selected alternative. This is followed by the sixth step, evaluating whether the gap has narrowed between "what is" and "what ought to be." Ideally, this information should come from systematic benchmarks, so that relevant feedback is objective and easily observed.

The rational choice paradigm seems so logical, yet it is rarely practiced in reality. One reason is that the model assumes people are efficient and logical information processing machines. But as the next few pages will reveal, people have difficulty recognizing problems; they cannot, or will not, simultaneously process the huge volume of information needed to identify the best solution; and they have difficulty recognizing when their choices have failed. The second reason why the rational model doesn't fit reality is that it completely ignores the fact that emotions also influence, perhaps even dominate, the decision-making process. As we shall discover in this chapter, <u>emotions both support and interfere with our quest to make better decisions.</u>[7] With these points in mind, let's look again at each step of decision making, but this time with a closer look at what really happens.

>Identifying Problems and Opportunities

When Albert Einstein was asked how he would save the world in one hour, he replied that he would spend the first 55 minutes defining the problem and the last 5 minutes solving it.[8] Einstein's point was that problem identification, the first step in decision making, is arguably the most important step. But problems and opportunities are not well-labeled objects when they cross our desk. Instead, we need to translate information into evidence that something is wrong or that an opportunity is available.

To some extent, this discovery process occurs through conscious evaluation of the facts and persuasive arguments by other people. But what is becoming increasingly apparent is that a fair amount of problem recognition actually occurs during the mostly unconscious processes of perceptual selective attention and attitude formation described in earlier chapters.[9] Specifically, we evaluate information as soon as we perceive it by attaching emotional markers (anger, caution, delight, etc.) to that information. The emotional markers are then sent to the rational center where they influence the slower logical analysis of the situation. The result is that both the emotional markers and the logical analysis determine whether you perceive something as a problem, opportunity, or irrelevant.

Problems with Problem Identification

Several problems occur in problem identification.[10] One concern is that people with vested interests try to influence perceptions that there is or is not a problem or opportunity. This persuasion frames the decision maker's view of the situation, which short-circuits a full assessment of the problem or opportunity. A second biasing effect is that under some

The best television commercial in history (as rated by *Advertising Age*) almost never saw the light of day because it was so different from existing mental models of what a good TV ad should look like. The Apple Macintosh "Why 1984 won't be like 1984" clip features a female athlete hurling a sledgehammer at a giant TV screen of an Orwellian Big Brother, liberating thousands of subjugated followers. There was no image of the Macintosh computer and only a brief appearance during the last few seconds of the product's name. Apple founder Steve Jobs and the Macintosh development team liked the concept, so the plan was to launch the Macintosh computer during the 1984 Super Bowl by showing both the 60-second and 30-second versions. But when Apple's board saw rough cuts of the commercial, every outside director despised it. One remarked that it was the worst commercial of all time; another insisted that Apple immediately fire its ad agency. Based on the board's reaction, Apple CEO John Sculley told Chiat-Day, the agency that conceived the ad, to sell off both Super Bowl ad slots that Apple had purchased. Fortunately, the agency claimed it could only sell off the 30-second slot, so Apple had to show the 60-second commercial during the game. That single ad presentation had such a huge effect that TV stations around the country showed it as a news story over the next few days. A month later, Apple's board members applauded the Macintosh team for a successful launch and apologized for their serious misjudgment of the 1984 commercial.[11]

conditions people block out negative information as a coping mechanism. Their brain refuses to see information that threatens self-esteem. A third perceptual challenge is that mental models blind people from seeing opportunities that deviate from the status quo. If an idea doesn't fit the existing mental model of how things should work, then the idea is dismissed as unworkable or undesirable.

A fourth barrier to effective problem identification is that decision makers lack the ability or motivation to diagnose problems.[12] For instance, research has found that leaders are expected to be decisive, and this decisive image motivates them to zero in on a problem without sufficiently analyzing the facts. Another diagnostic error is the tendency to define problems in terms of their solutions. Someone who says "The problem is that we need more control over our suppliers" has fallen into this trap. Notice that this statement focuses on a solution (controlling suppliers), whereas proper diagnosis would determine the cause of symptoms before jumping to solutions. This tendency is consistent with evidence that people form preferences for alternatives as soon as they are identified, rather than after understanding the problem. It occurs mainly because people want to quickly understand and resolve problems.[13]

Identifying Problems and Opportunities More Effectively

Recognizing problems and opportunities will always be a challenge, but the process can be improved through awareness of these perceptual and diagnostic limitations. By recognizing how mental models restrict a person's understanding of the world, decision makers learn to openly consider other perspectives of reality. Perceptual and diagnostic weaknesses can also be minimized by discussing the situation with colleagues. Decision makers discover blind spots in problem identification by hearing how others perceive certain information and diagnose problems. Leaders require considerable willpower to resist the temptation to look decisive when a more thoughtful examination of the situation should occur. Opportunities also become apparent when outsiders explore this information from their different mental models.

>Evaluating and Choosing Alternatives

bounded rationality
Processing limited and imperfect information and satisficing rather than maximizing when choosing among alternatives.

The rational choice paradigm assumes that decision makers evaluate alternatives using well-articulated and agreed-on organizational goals, that they efficiently and simultaneously process facts about all alternatives and the consequences of those alternatives, and that they choose the alternative with the highest payoff. Herbert Simon, who won a Nobel Prize for his writing on decision making, questioned these assumptions half a century ago. He argued that people engage in **bounded rationality** because they process limited and imperfect information and rarely select the best choice.[14] Exhibit 6.2 contrasts rational choice assumptions with observations from Simon and other OB researchers about how people actually evaluate and choose alternatives.

Problems with Goals

We need clear goals to choose the best solution. Goals identify "what ought to be" and, therefore, provide a standard against which each alternative is evaluated. The reality, however, is that organizational goals are often ambiguous or in conflict with each other. For instance, one survey found that 25 percent of managers and employees felt decisions are delayed because of difficulty agreeing on what they want the decision to achieve.[15]

[Exhibit 6.2] Rational Choice Assumptions versus Organizational Behavior Findings about Choosing Alternatives

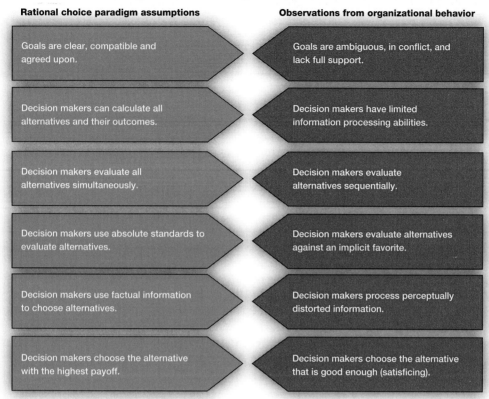

Rational choice paradigm assumptions	Observations from organizational behavior
Goals are clear, compatible and agreed upon.	Goals are ambiguous, in conflict, and lack full support.
Decision makers can calculate all alternatives and their outcomes.	Decision makers have limited information processing abilities.
Decision makers evaluate all alternatives simultaneously.	Decision makers evaluate alternatives sequentially.
Decision makers use absolute standards to evaluate alternatives.	Decision makers evaluate alternatives against an implicit favorite.
Decision makers use factual information to choose alternatives.	Decision makers process perceptually distorted information.
Decision makers choose the alternative with the highest payoff.	Decision makers choose the alternative that is good enough (satisficing).

Problems with Information Processing

People do not make perfectly rational decisions because they don't process information very well. One problem is that decision makers can't possibly think through all of the alternatives and the outcomes of those alternatives. Consequently, they look at only a few alternatives and only some of the main outcomes of those alternatives.[16] For example, there may be dozens of computer brands to choose from and dozens of features to consider, yet people typically evaluate only a few brands and a few features.

A related problem is that decision makers typically look at alternatives sequentially rather than all at the same time. As a new alternative comes along, it is compared to an alternative that the decision maker prefers, called an **implicit favorite**. The implicit favorite is formed unconsciously and early in the decision process, so it might not be the best choice. Another concern is that people tend to defend their implicit favorite by distorting information and changing the importance of decision criteria.[17]

implicit favorite
The decision maker's preferred alternative against which all other choices are judged.

Problems with Maximization

Decision makers tend to select the alternative that is acceptable or "good enough" rather than the one with the highest payoff (i.e., the highest subjective expected utility). In other words, they engage in **satisficing** rather than maximizing. Satisficing occurs because it isn't possible to identify every alternative, and information about available alternatives is imperfect or ambiguous. Satisficing also occurs because, as mentioned already, decision makers tend to evaluate alternatives sequentially, not all at the same time. They evaluate each

satisficing
Selecting a solution that is satisfactory, or "good enough," rather than optimal, or "the best."

alternative against the implicit favorite and eventually select an option that is good enough to satisfy their needs or preferences.[18]

Emotions and Making Choices

Herbert Simon and others demonstrated that people evaluate alternatives imperfectly, but they neglected to mention another glaring weakness with the rational choice paradigm—it completely ignores the effect of emotions in human decision making. The emotional marker process described earlier and in previous chapters also determines our preferences for each alternative when making choices. Basically, our brain attaches specific emotions to information about each alternative when we receive that information. Our logical thought process might add more information through memory recall or logical interpretation, but the emotional process basically determines whether we like or dislike a particular alternative. In fact, people with damaged emotional brain centers have difficulty making choices.

Emotions also affect how we go about making choices. We pay more attention to details when in a negative mood than when in a good mood, for example, possibly because a negative mood signals that there is something wrong that requires attention. When feeling angry, decision makers are more likely to speed up the choice process and tend to be more optimistic about the success of risky alternatives.[19]

The third effect of emotions is that people "listen in" on their emotions to provide guidance when making choices.[20] Most emotional experiences remain below the radar screen of awareness, but sufficiently intense emotions are picked up consciously and figured into our decision. These gut feelings are given more weight by some people than others (see the Myers-Briggs Type Indicator in Chapter 2) and under different circumstances.[21] But all of us listen in on our emotions to some degree. This "emotions-as-information" phenomenon ties directly into our next topic, intuition.

Intuition and Making Choices

Linda, a trainee nurse in the neonatal intensive care unit of a hospital, was responsible for Melissa, a premature baby with no problems other than needing support to grow out of her sensitive condition. One day, Melissa was a little less fussy than normal and was a bit lethargic during feeding. A spot on her heel where a blood sample had been taken was bleeding slightly, but that might be due to a sloppy needle prick. Melissa's temperature had also dropped slightly over several checks, but was still within the normal range. None of these conditions would seem unusual to most people, including Linda. But when Darlene, an experienced nurse, happened to walk by, she immediately sensed that Melissa "just looked funny," as she put it. After looking at Melissa's charts and asking Linda a few questions, Darlene rushed to call a physician with the details. The physician immediately prescribed antibiotics to correct what a blood test later confirmed was sepsis.[22]

intuition
The ability to know when a problem or opportunity exists and select the best course of action without conscious reasoning.

The gut instinct that helped Darlene save this baby's life is known as **intuition**—the ability to know when a problem or opportunity exists and to select the best course of action without conscious reasoning.[23] Intuition is both an emotional experience and a rapid unconscious analytic process. The gut feelings we experience are emotional signals that warn us of impending danger, such as a sick baby, or motivate us to take advantage of an opportunity. Some intuition also directs us to preferred choices relative to other alternatives in that situation.

While all gut feelings are emotional signals, not all emotional signals are intuition. False intuition occurs when we have emotional reactions without relevant experience, whereas real intuition involves rapidly comparing what we see or otherwise sense with mental patterns or templates implicitly learned over time.[24] We quickly match these templates with the current situation, and this pattern matching process generates emotions that motivate us to act. These images are mental models because they usually include anticipated cause-effect relationships, allowing us to anticipate future events from current observations. Darlene's years of experience produced templates of unhealthy babies that matched what she saw on that fateful day. Studies have also found that chess masters receive emotional signals when they sense an opportunity through quick observation of a chessboard. They can't immediately explain why they see a favorable move on the chessboard—they just feel it.

Making Choices More Effectively

It is very difficult to get around the human limitations of making choices, but a few strategies may help. Decisions tend to have a higher failure rate when leaders are decisive rather than contemplative. By systematically evaluating alternatives, decision makers minimize the implicit favorite and satisficing problems that occur when relying on general subjective judgments. Intuition still figures into this analysis, but so does careful consideration of relevant information.[25]

Another issue is how to minimize the adverse effects of emotions on the decision process. The first recommendation here is that we need to be constantly aware that decisions are influenced by both rational and emotional processes. With this awareness, some decision makers deliberately revisit important issues so they look at the information in different moods and have allowed their initial emotions to subside. Others practice **scenario planning**, in which they anticipate emergencies long before they occur, so that alternative courses of action are evaluated without the pressure and emotions that occur during real emergencies.[26]

scenario planning
A systematic process of thinking about alternative futures and what the organization should do to anticipate and react to those environments.

>Evaluating Decision Outcomes

Contrary to the rational choice paradigm, decision makers aren't completely logical when evaluating the effectiveness of their decisions. The most widely studied evidence of this is called **escalation of commitment**—the tendency to repeat an apparently bad decision or allocate more resources to a failing course of action.[27] There are plenty of escalation examples, including the overexpenditure on such projects as Scotland's new parliament building, a subway extension project in Tokyo, an automated baggage handling system at Denver International Airport, and development of the Concorde supersonic airliner. (Some people still refer to escalation of commitment as the "Concorde fallacy.").[28]

Why are people led deeper and deeper into failing projects? There are several reasons, including self-justification, prospect theory effect, perceptual blinders, and closing costs.

escalation of commitment
The tendency to repeat an apparently bad decision or allocate more resources to a failing course of action.

- *Self-justification.* Individuals are motivated to maintain their course of action when they have a high need to justify their decision. This self-justification is particularly evident when decision makers are personally identified with the project and have staked their reputations to some extent on the project's success.[29]

- *Prospect theory effect.* Researchers have discovered that we dislike losing a particular amount more than we like gaining the same amount. We also take fewer risks to receive gains and take more risks to avoid losses. This effect, called **prospect theory**, is a second explanation for escalation of commitment. Stopping a project is a certain loss, which is more painful to most people than the uncertainty of success associated with continuing to fund the project. Given the choice, decision makers choose the less painful option.[30]

- *Perceptual blinders.* Escalation of commitment sometimes occurs because decision makers do not see the problems soon enough. They unconsciously screen out or

prospect theory
An effect in which losing a particular amount is more disliked than gaining the same amount.

explain away negative information to protect self-esteem. Serious problems initially look like random deviations along the trend line to success. Even when they see that something is wrong, the information is sufficiently ambiguous that it can be misinterpreted or justified.

• *Closing costs.* Even when a project's success is in doubt, decision makers will persist because the costs of ending the project are high or unknown. Terminating a major project may involve large financial penalties, a bad public image, or personal political costs.

These four conditions make escalation of commitment look selfish or foolhardy. Usually it is, but there are exceptions. Recent studies suggest that throwing more money into a failing project is sometimes a logical attempt to further understand an ambiguous situation. This strategy is essentially a variation of testing unknown waters. By adding more resources, the decision maker gains new information about the effectiveness of these funds, which provides more feedback about the project's future success. This strategy is particularly common where the project has high closing costs.[31]

Evaluating Decision Outcomes More Effectively

One of the most effective ways to minimize escalation of commitment is to separate decision choosers from decision evaluators. This minimizes the self-justification effect because the person responsible for evaluating the decision is not connected to the original decision. A second strategy is to publicly establish a preset level at which the decision is abandoned or reevaluated. However, conditions are often so complex that it is difficult to identify an appropriate point to abandon a project.[32] Finally, projects might have less risk of escalation if several people are involved. Co-workers continuously monitor each other and might notice problems sooner than someone working alone on the project. Employee involvement offers these and other benefits to the decision-making process, as we learn next.

>Employee Involvement in Decision Making

Sending people into outer space is an incredibly complex job. Most tasks require knowledge and perspectives far beyond the capability of a single decision maker. So it isn't surprising, as we read at the beginning of this chapter, that at least one member of the space shuttle Columbia accident investigation board criticized NASA's managers for making decisions without adequately involving, and encouraging involvement from, its engineers during the days leading up to the accident.

employee involvement
The degree to which employees influence how their work is organized and carried out.

Employee involvement, also called *participative management,* refers to the degree to which employees influence how their work is organized and carried out.[33] At the lowest level, participation involves asking employees for information. They do not make recommendations and might not even know what the problem is about. At a moderate level of involvement, employees are told about the problem and provide recommendations to the decision maker. At the highest level of involvement, the entire decision-making process is handed over to employees. They identify the problem, choose the best alternative, and implement their choice.

Involving employees in decision making offers a number of potential advantages.[34] It improves problem identification because employees are usually the first to know when something goes wrong with production, customer service, or many other subsystems within the organization. In a well-managed meeting, employee involvement also creates synergy that can generate more and better solutions than when these people work alone. A third ad-

At Boeing Co., staying competitive requires the brainwork of every employee, so the aerospace company is pushing decisions down to the level closest to the activity. Every employee now has the opportunity and accountability for the design, execution, and continuous improvement of his or her work. At Boeing's subassembly plant in Macon, Georgia (shown here), for example, employees identify ways to improve work effectiveness and track their own goals and performance metrics. "We encourage employees to be proactive," says Macon site leader Obie Jones. "When they see a problem or have an idea about process improvements, they take the initiative to start the process improvements, they take the initiative to start the corrective action process or incorporate improvement ideas through the proper channels." Partly due to this high level of employee involvement, *Industry Week* magazine recently named Boeing's Macon facility as one of the 10 best manufacturing plants in the United States.[35]

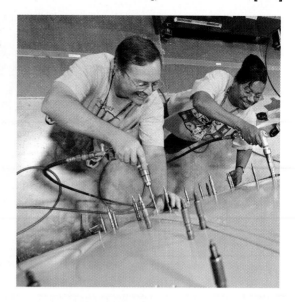

vantage of employee involvement is that people collectively tend to be better than individuals at picking the best alternative when they have diverse perspectives and backgrounds. Along with improving decision quality, employee involvement usually strengthens employee commitment to the decision. Rather than viewing themselves as agents of someone else's decision, staff members feel personally responsible for its success.

Contingencies of Employee Involvement

If employee involvement is so wonderful, why don't companies leave all decisions to employees further down the hierarchy? The answer is that a number of factors can undermine employee involvement or render it unnecessary, so we need to consider the following contingencies:

- *Decision structure.* Employee involvement is unnecessary when the problem is routine; that is, the problem has occurred in the past and a ready-made solution is known from that previous experience. Instead, the benefits of employee involvement increase with the novelty and complexity of the problem or opportunity.

- *Source of decision knowledge.* Subordinates should be involved in some level of decision making when the leader lacks sufficient knowledge and subordinates have additional information to improve decision quality. In many cases, employees are closer to customers and production activities, so they often know where the company can save money, improve product or service quality, and realize opportunities.[36]

- *Decision commitment.* As was mentioned above, participation tends to improve employee commitment to the decision. If employees are unlikely to accept a decision made without their involvement, then some level of participation is usually necessary.

- *Risk of conflict.* Two types of conflict undermine the benefits of employee involvement. First, if employee goals and norms conflict with the organization's goals, then only a low level of employee involvement is advisable. Second, the degree of involvement depends on whether employees will reach agreement on the preferred solution. If conflict is likely, then high involvement (i.e., where employees make the decision alone) would be difficult to achieve.

Employee involvement is an important component of the decision-making process. To make the best decisions, we need to involve people who have the most valuable information and who will increase commitment to implement the decision. Another important component of decision making is creativity, which we discuss next.

>Creativity

Procter & Gamble (P&G) has discovered a magic formula that is putting its products back into customers' shopping carts. It's called creativity. When Alan G. Lafley became CEO a few years ago, the consumer products giant was suffering from flat sales and losing its clout to increasingly powerful retailers. To regain momentum, P&G had to create new products that customers really want. So, while laying off thousands of employees in some areas, P&G was also hiring product designers from other companies and pairing them with P&G's existing research and development staff. P&G staff in diverse areas were grouped together to create innovative products that applied their combined expertise (such as using Mr. Clean with mops). Lafley also modeled the new creative focus by visiting people in their homes to talk about and watch how they used products.[37]

> **creativity**
> The development of original ideas that make a socially recognized contribution.

Procter & Gamble has rediscovered that innovation begins with creativity. **Creativity** is the development of original ideas that make a socially recognized contribution.[38] Although there are unique conditions for creativity that we discuss over the next few pages, it is really part of the decision-making process described earlier in the chapter. We rely on creativity to find problems, identify alternatives, and implement solutions.

The Creative Process Model

One of the earliest and most influential models of creativity is shown in Exhibit 6.3.[39] The first stage is *preparation*—the person's or group's effort to acquire knowledge and skills regarding the problem or opportunity. Preparation involves developing a clear understanding of what you are trying to achieve through a novel solution, then actively studying information seemingly related to the topic.

The second stage, called *incubation,* is the time in which we engage in reflective thought. We put the problem aside, but our mind is still working on it in the background.[40] The important condition here is to maintain a low-level awareness by frequently revisiting the problem. Incubation does not mean that we forget about the problem or issue. Incubation assists **divergent thinking**—reframing the problem in a unique way and generating different approaches to the issue. This contrasts with convergent thinking—calculating the conventionally accepted "right answer" to a logical problem. Divergent thinking breaks us away from existing mental models so we can apply concepts or processes from completely different areas of life.

> **divergent thinking**
> Reframing a problem in a unique way and generating different approaches to the issue.

Insight, the third stage of creativity, refers to the experience of suddenly becoming aware of a unique idea.[41] These bits of inspiration occur at any time and are fleeting; they

[**Exhibit 6.3**] The Creative Process Model

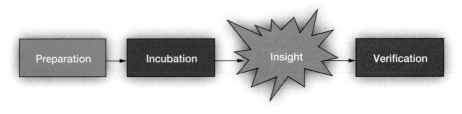

Preparation → Incubation → Insight → Verification

are quickly lost if not documented. Insights are merely rough ideas. Their usefulness still requires *verification* through conscious evaluation and experimentation. Thus, although verification is the final stage of creativity in the model, it is really the beginning of a long process of experimentation and further creativity.

Characteristics of Creative People

Everyone is creative, but some people seem to be more creative than others. Four of the main features of creative people are intelligence, persistence, subject-matter knowledge and experience, and inventive thinking style. First, creative people have above-average intelligence to synthesize information, analyze ideas, and apply their ideas.[42] Like the fictional sleuth Sherlock Holmes, creative people recognize the significance of small bits of information and are able to connect them in ways that no one else could imagine. Then, they have the capacity to evaluate the potential usefulness of their ideas.

Persistence is the second feature of creative people. The fact is, innovations derive more from trial and error than from intelligence and experience, and persistence drives creative people to continue developing and testing after others have given up. In other words, people who develop more creative products and services are those who develop more ideas that don't work. Thomas Edison emphasized this point in his famous statement that genius is 1 percent inspiration and 99 percent perspiration. Edison and his staff discovered hundreds of ways not to build a light bulb before they got it right. This persistence is based on a high need for achievement and moderate or high degree of self-confidence.[43]

A third feature of creative people is that they possess sufficient knowledge and experience on the subject.[44] Creativity experts explain that discovering new ideas requires knowledge of the fundamentals. For example, 1960s rock group the Beatles produced most of their songs only after they had played together for several years. They developed extensive experience singing and adapting the music of other people before their creative talents soared.

Although knowledge and experience may be important in one sense, they can also undermine creativity because people develop mental models that lead to "mindless behavior," whereby they stop questioning their assumptions.[45] This is possibly why Procter & Gamble CEO Alan G. Lafley hired a legion of designers from other companies. They brought "fresh eyes," that is, different ways of seeing and questioning things, that longtime P&G employees had stopped questioning.

The fourth characteristic of creative people is that they have an inventive thinking style. Creative types are divergent thinkers and risk takers. They are not bothered about making mistakes or working with ambiguous information. They take a broad view of problems, don't like to abide by rules or status, and are unconcerned about social approval of their actions.[46]

Organizational Conditions Supporting Creativity

Hiring creative people is only part of the creativity equation. Organizations also need to maintain a work environment that supports the creative process for everyone.[47] One of the most important conditions is that the organizations have a *learning orientation;* that is, they have a commitment to learning, open-mindedness, and a shared vision to guide the learning. In particular, companies with a learning orientation reward experimentation and recognize mistakes as a natural part of the learning process.

Motivation from the job itself is another important condition for creativity.[48] Employees tend to be more creative when they believe their work has a substantial impact on the organization or larger society (i.e., task significance) and when they have the freedom to pursue novel ideas without bureaucratic delays (i.e., autonomy). Creativity is about changing things, and change is possible only when employees have the authority to experiment.

Radical Entertainment, a division of Vivendi Universal Games, pulls out all the stops to support employee creativity. "Hit games are made by people who have the freedom and support to put unconventional ideas in motion," explains Ian Wilkinson, founder and CEO of the electronic games developer in Vancouver, Canada. "So we give our employees the autonomy to drive real change, whatever their role in the company. No other game developer offers this level of creative freedom." To drive home this creative focus, Wilkinson (third from right in this photo) lunches with a group of employees, listening to their suggestions and reinforcing company values, including "Take risks, always learn." Radical also encourages employees to cross-pollinate ideas through a monthly "game fair" day, in which teams show off their products and make presentations to other employees. The result of this creative environment is a series of game hits, including *The Incredible Hulk* and *The Simpsons: Hit and Run.*[49]

Along with supporting a learning orientation and intrinsically motivating jobs, companies foster creativity through open communication and sufficient resources. They also provide a reasonable level of job security, which explains why creativity suffers during times of downsizing and corporate restructuring.[50] To some degree, creativity also improves with support from leaders and co-workers. One recent study reported that effective product champions provide enthusiastic support for new ideas. Other studies suggest that co-worker support can improve creativity in some situations, whereas competition among co-workers improves creativity in other situations.[51] Similarly, it isn't clear how much pressure should be exerted on employees to produce creative ideas. Extreme time pressures are well-known creativity inhibitors, but lack of pressure doesn't seem to produce the highest creativity either.

Activities That Encourage Creativity

Along with hiring creative people and giving them a supportive work environment, organizations have introduced numerous activities that crank up the creative potential. One set of activities encourages employees to *redefine the problem,* such as by revisiting old projects, which tend to be seen in a new light as time passes.[52] Asking people unfamiliar with the issue (preferably with different expertise) to explore the problem with you is another way to redefine problems. You would state the objectives and give some facts, then let the other person ask questions to further understand the situation. By verbalizing the problem, listening to questions, and hearing what others think, you are more likely to form new perspectives on the issue.[53]

A second set of creativity activities, known as *associative play,* range from art classes to impromptu storytelling. Honda Motor Co. hosts an annual gathering of teams from its North American supplier companies, in which participants tie balloon hats and put on skits to display their creative prowess. At TBWA\Chiat\Day in Playa del Rey, California, staff members get the creative juices flowing with a fun game of football played along the main corridor (called "Main Street"). "The worst thing you can do [if you're blocked] is sit and stare at each other or at a blinking cursor," advises the ad agency's creative director Joe Shands. "When you do something else, your brain starts kicking in."[54]

Another associative play activity, called *morphological analysis,* involves listing different dimensions of a system and the elements of each dimension, then looking at each combination. This encourages people to carefully examine combinations that initially seem nonsensical. Tyson Foods, the world's largest poultry producer, applied this activity to identify new ways to serve chicken for lunch. The marketing and research team focused on three categories: occasion, packaging, and taste. Next, the team worked through numerous combinations of items in the three categories. This created unusual ideas, such as cheese chicken pasta (taste) in pizza boxes (packaging) for concessions at baseball games (occasion). Later, the team looked more closely at the feasibility of these combinations and sent them to customer focus groups for further testing.[55]

A third set of activities that encourages creativity in organizations is known as *cross-pollination*.[56] Many creative firms mix together employees from different past projects so they share new knowledge with each other. IDEO, the California-based product design company, does this by encouraging employees to consider how features of one product they've worked on might be relevant to another. Cross-pollination also occurs through formal events during which employees from different parts of the organization share their knowledge through presentations.

Cross-pollination highlights the fact that creativity rarely occurs alone. Some creative people may be individualistic, but most creative ideas are generated through teams and informal social interaction. This probably explains why Jonathon Ive, the award-winning designer of Apple Computer products, always refers to his team's creativity rather than anything that he alone might have thought up. "The only time you'll hear [Jonathan Ive] use the word 'I' is when he's naming some of the products he helped make famous: iMac, iBook, iPod," says one writer.[57] The next chapter introduces the main concepts in team effectiveness and high-performance teams.

>chapter summary

Decision making is a conscious process of making choices among one or more alternatives with the intention of moving toward some desired state of affairs. The rational choice paradigm of decision making includes identifying problems and opportunities, choosing the best decision style, developing alternative solutions, choosing the best solution, implementing the selected alternative, and evaluating decision outcomes.

Persuasion by stakeholders, perceptual biases, and poor diagnostic skills affect our ability to identify problems and opportunities. We can minimize these challenges by being aware of the human limitations and discussing the situation with colleagues.

People have difficulty evaluating and choosing alternatives because organizational goals are ambiguous or in conflict, human information processing is incomplete and subjective, and we tend to satisfice rather than maximize. Emotions shape our preferences for alternatives and the process we follow to evaluate alternatives. Intuition—the ability to know when a problem or opportunity exists and to select the best course of action without conscious reasoning—is both an emotional experience and a rapid, unconscious analytic process of pattern matching. People generally make better choices by systematically evaluating alternatives and engaging in scenario planning long before problems arise.

Escalation of commitment, throwing good money after bad, is mainly caused by self-justification, the prospect theory effect, perceptual blinders, and closing costs. These problems are minimized by separating decision choosers from decision evaluators, establishing a preset level at which the decision is abandoned or reevaluated, relying on more systematic and clear feedback about the project's success, and involving several people in decision making.

Employee involvement, or participation, refers to the degree that employees influence how their work is organized and carried out. It often leads to higher decision quality and commitment, but several contingencies need to be considered, including the decision structure, source of decision knowledge, decision commitment, and risk of conflict.

Creativity is the development of original ideas that make a socially recognized contribution. The four creativity stages are preparation, incubation, insight, and verification. Incubation assists divergent thinking, which involves reframing the problem in a unique way and generating different approaches to the issue. Four of the main features of creative people are intelligence, subject-matter knowledge and experience, persistence, and inventive thinking style. Creativity is also strengthened for everyone when the work environment supports a learning orientation, the job has high intrinsic motivation, the organization provides a reasonable level of job security, and project leaders provide appropriate goals, time pressure, and resources. Three types of activities that encourage creativity are redefining the problem, associative play, and cross-pollination.

>key.terms

bounded rationality 116

creativity 122

decision making 113

divergent thinking 122

employee involvement 120

escalation of commitment 119

implicit favorite 117

intuition 118

prospect theory 119

satisficing 117

scenario planning 119

>critical.thinking.questions

1. A management consultant is hired by a manufacturing firm to determine the best site for its next production facility. The consultant has had several meetings with the company's senior executives regarding the factors to consider when making the recommendation. Discuss the decision-making problems that might prevent the consultant from choosing the best site location.

2. You have been asked to personally recommend a new travel agency to handle all airfare, accommodation, and related travel needs for your organization of 2,000 employees. One of your colleagues, who is responsible for the company's economic planning, suggests that the best travel agent could be selected mathematically by inputting the relevant factors for each agency and the weight (importance) of each factor. What decision-making approach is your colleague recommending? Is this recommendation a good idea in this situation? Why or why not?

3. Intuition is both an emotional experience and an unconscious analytic process. One problem, however, is that not all gut feelings signaling that there is a problem or opportunity represent intuition. Explain how we would know if our emotional response to a situation is intuition, and if not intuition, suggest what might be causing them.

4. A developer received financial backing for a new business financial center along a derelict section of the waterfront, a few miles from the current downtown area of a large European city. The idea was to build several high-rise structures, attract major tenants to those sites, and have the city extend transportation systems out to the new center. Over the next decade, the developer believed that others would build in the area, thereby attracting the regional or national offices of many financial institutions. Interest from potential tenants was much lower than initially predicted, and the city did not build transportation systems as quickly as expected. Still, the builder proceeded with the original plans. Only after financial support was curtailed did the developer reconsider the project. Using your knowledge of escalation of commitment, discuss three possible reasons why the developer was motivated to continue with the project.

5. Ancient Book Company has a problem with new book projects. Even when others are aware that a book is far behind schedule and may engender little public interest, sponsoring editors are reluctant to terminate contracts with authors whom they have signed. The result is that editors invest more time with these projects rather than on more fruitful projects. As a form of escalation of

commitment, describe two methods that Ancient Book Company can use to minimize this problem.

6. Employee involvement applies just as well to the classroom as to the office or factory floor. Explain how student involvement in classroom decisions typically made by the instructor alone might improve decision quality. What potential problems may occur in this process?

7. Think of a time when you experienced the creative process. Maybe you woke up with a brilliant, but usually sketchy and incomplete, idea, or the solution to a baffling problem came to mind while you were doing something else. Describe this incident to your class and explain how the experience followed the creative process.

8. Two characteristics of creative people are that they have relevant experience and are persistent in their quest. Does this mean that people with the most experience and the highest need for achievement are the most creative? Explain your answer.

>case.study:skillbuilder6.1

Employee Involvement Cases

Case 1: The Sugar Substitute Research Decision

You are the head of research and development (R&D) for a major beer company. While working on a new beer product, one of the scientists in your unit seems to have tentatively identified a new chemical compound that has few calories but tastes closer to sugar than current sugar substitutes. The company has no foreseeable need for this product, but it could be patented and licensed to manufacturers in the food industry.

The sugar substitute discovery is in its preliminary stages and would require considerable time and resources before it would be commercially viable. This means that it would necessarily take some resources away from other projects in the lab. The sugar substitute project is beyond your technical expertise, but some of the R&D lab researchers are familiar with that field of chemistry. As with most forms of research, it is difficult to determine the amount of research required to further identify and perfect the sugar substitute. You do not know how much demand is expected for this product. Your department has a decision process for funding projects that are behind schedule. However, there are no rules or precedents about funding projects that would be licensed but not used by the organization.

The company's R&D budget is limited and other scientists in your work group have recently complained that they require more resources and financial support to get their projects completed. Some of these other R&D projects hold promise for future beer sales. You believe that most researchers in the R&D unit are committed to ensuring the company's interests are achieved.

Case 2: Coast Guard Cutter Decision Problem

You are the captain of a 200-foot Coast Guard cutter, with a crew of 16, including officers. Your mission is general at-sea search and rescue. At 2:00 A.M. this morning, while en route to your home port after a routine 28-day patrol, you received word from the nearest Coast Guard station that a small plane had crashed 60 miles offshore. You obtained all the available information concerning the location of the crash, informed your crew of the mission, and set a new course at maximum speed for the scene to commence a search for survivors and wreckage.

You have now been searching for 20 hours. Your search operation has been increasingly impaired by rough seas, and there is evidence of a severe storm building. The atmospherics associated with the deteriorating weather have made communications with the Coast Guard station impossible. A decision must be made shortly about whether to abandon the search and place your vessel on a course that would ride out the storm (thereby protecting the vessel and your crew but relegating any possible survivors to almost certain death from exposure) or to continue a potentially futile search and the risks it would entail.

Before losing communications, you received an update weather advisory concerning the severity and duration of the storm. Although your crew members are extremely conscientious about their responsibility, you believe that they would be divided on the decision of leaving or staying.

Discussion Questions (for both cases)

1. To what extent should your subordinates be involved in this decision? Select one of the following levels of involvement:

   - *No involvement.* You make the decision alone without any participation from subordinates.

   - *Low involvement.* You ask one or more subordinates for information relating to the problem, but you don't ask for their recommendations and might not mention the problem to them.

   - *Medium involvement.* You describe the problem to one or more subordinates (alone or in a meeting) and ask for any relevant information as well as their recommendations on the issue. However, you make the final decision, which might or might not reflect their advice.

   - *High involvement.* You describe the problem to subordinates. They discuss the matter, identify a solution without your involvement (unless they invite your ideas), and implement that solution. You have agreed to support their decision.

2. What factors led you to choose this level of employee involvement rather than the others?

3. What problems might occur if less or more involvement occurred in this case (where possible)?

Sources: The Sugar Substitute Research Decision is written by Steven L. McShane, © 2002. The Coast Guard cutter case is adapted from V. H. Vroom and A. G. Jago, *The New Leadership: Managing Participation in Organizations* (Englewood Cliffs, NJ: Prentice Hall, 1988), © 1987 V. H. Vroom and A. G. Jago. Used with permission of the authors.

>class.exercise:skillbuilder6.2

For What It's Worth

Purpose   This exercise is designed to help you understand issues with making perfectly rational decisions.

Materials   The instructor will either bring to class or show as a computer image three products. Students will need their social security number (a driver's license or other piece of identity with several numbers can substitute).

Instructions

- *Step 1:* The instructor will show the three products (or image of the products) to the class and describe the features of each product so students are sufficiently informed of their features and functions. The instructor will *not* provide any information about the price paid or market value of these products.

- *Step 2:* Working alone, each student will write down at the top of the calculation sheet below (Exhibit 1) the last two digits of his or her social security number (or driver's license or other identification if a social security number is not available). Each student will also write down in the left column of Exhibit 1 the name of each product shown by the instructor. Then, each student will circle yes or no in Exhibit 1 for each product, indicating whether he or she would be willing to pay the dollar equivalent of the two-digit number for each product if looking to purchase such a product.

- *Step 3:* In the right-hand column of the calculation sheet (Exhibit 1), each student (still working alone) will write down the maximum dollar value he or she would be willing to pay for each product if he or she were looking to purchase such a product.

- *Step 4:* After completing their calculations alone, students will be organized into four or five groups as specified by the instructor. Group size is unimportant, but the instructor's criterion for organizing teams is very important and must be followed. Each team will calculate the average price that students within that group were willing to pay for each product. The team will also calculate the percentage of people within the group who indicated yes (willing to purchase at the stated price) for each product.

- *Step 5:* Each team will report its three average maximum willingness-to-pay prices as well as percentage of students in the team who indicated yes for each product. The instructor will outline a concept relevant to rational decision making and how that concept relates to this exercise.

[**Exhibit 1**]   For What It's Worth Calculation Sheet

Two-Digit Number: ____ ____

Product Name (write in product names below)	Willing to Pay Two-Digit Number Price for This Product? (circle your answer)		Maximum Willingness to Pay for This Product
_____	No	Yes	$ ___ ___ ___:00
_____	No	Yes	$ ___ ___ ___:00
_____	No	Yes	$ ___ ___ ___:00

Source: Based on information in D. Ariely, G. Loewenstein, and D. Prelec, "'Coherent Arbitrariness': Stable Demand Curves without Stable Preferences," *Quarterly Journal of Economics,* February 2003, pp. 73–105.

>class.exercise:skillbuilder6.3

Creativity Brainbusters

Purpose This exercise is designed to help students understand the dynamics of creativity and problem solving.

Instructions

This exercise may be completed alone or in teams of three or four people. If teams are formed, students who already know the solutions to one or more of these problems should identify themselves and serve as silent observers. When finished (or, more likely, time is up), the instructor will review the solutions and discuss the implications of this exercise. In particular, be prepared to discuss what you needed to solve these puzzles and what may have prevented you from solving them more quickly (or at all).

1. Double Circle Problem

Draw two circles, one inside the other, with a single line and with neither circle touching the other (as shown below). In other words, you must draw both of these circles without lifting your pen (or other writing instrument).

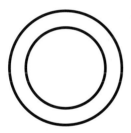

2. Nine Dot Problem

Below are nine dots. Without lifting your pencil, draw no more than four straight lines that pass through all nine dots.

3. Nine Dot Problem Revisited

Referring to the nine dot exhibit above, describe how, without lifting your pencil, you could pass a pencil line through all dots with three or fewer straight lines.

4. Word Search

In the following line of letters, cross out five letters so that the remaining letters, without altering their sequence, spell a familiar English word.

C F R I V E E L A T E T I T E V R S E

Burning Ropes

You have two pieces of rope of unequal lengths and a box of matches. In spite of their different lengths, each piece of rope takes one hour to burn; however, parts of each rope burn at unequal speeds. For example, the first half of one piece might burn in 10 minutes. Use these materials to accurately determine when 45 minutes has elapsed.

>self-assessment.skillbuilder6.4

Measuring Your Creative Personality

This self-assessment is designed to help you to measure the extent to which you have a creative personality.

Our creative potential depends on our personality, values, and competencies. This self-assessment estimates your level of creative potential as a personality characteristic. It consists of an adjective checklist with 30 words that may or may not describe you. You are asked to indicate which words you think accurately describe you. Please *do not* select the boxes for words that do not describe you. This exercise is completed alone so students assess themselves without concerns of social comparison. However, class discussion will focus on how this scale might be applied in organizations, and the limitations of measuring creativity in work settings.

>self-assessment.skillbuilder6.5

Testing Your Creative Bench Strength

This self-assessment takes the form of a self-scoring quiz. It consists of 12 questions that require divergent thinking to identify the correct answers. For each question, type in your answer in the space provided. When finished, look at the correct answer for each question, along with the explanation for that answer.

>self-assessment.skillbuilder6.6

Inventory of Decision-Making Style

People have different styles of decision making that are reflected in how they identify problems or opportunities and make choices. This self-assessment estimates your decision-making style through a series of statements describing how individuals go about making important decisions. Please indicate whether you agree or disagree with each statement.

Answer each item as truthfully as possible so that you get an accurate estimate of your decision-making style. This exercise is completed alone so students assess themselves honestly without concerns of social comparison. However, class discussion will focus on the decision-making style that people prefer in organizational settings.

Find the full self-assessments on the OLC at
www.mhhe.com/mcshaneess

>part III:

Team Processes

chapter 7

Team Dynamics

Employees at Fifth Third Securities as well as other investment firms are discovering the benefits of teamwork.

>**learning**objectives

After reading this chapter, you should be able to

- Define teams.
- Outline the model of team effectiveness.
- Identify six organizational and team environmental elements that influence team effectiveness.
- Explain the influence of the team's task, composition, and size on team effectiveness.
- Describe the five stages of team development.
- List six factors that influence team cohesiveness.
- Discuss the limitations of teams.
- Identify two characteristics of self-directed work teams (SDWTs).
- Explain why virtual teams have become more common in organizations.
- Identify four problems facing teams when making decisions.
- Describe ways to improve team decision making, including three team decision-making structures.

A few years ago, Paul Tramontano was typical of most Wall Street advisers by single-handedly providing advice to hundreds of clients. Not any more. The Smith Barney financial consultant realized that clients needed a wider variety of services than any one person can deliver, so he and two other partners formed an 11-person team, including technical specialists to complement his own focus on financial, estate planning, and advisory business. "By definition, higher-net-worth clients require different and greater levels of service," says Tramontano. "That's why I think the team approach is the model for what this industry will look like."

Firms throughout the securities industry are placing more emphasis on teams rather than individual "stars" to provide better customer service and investment performance. Merrill Lynch has organized more than half of its financial advisers into 3,000 teams. Around 40 percent of Smith Barney advisers are assigned to teams. When Mark Mobius, the head of the Templeton Emerging Markets Fund, was asked whether individual fund managers are the real "brands" for a mutual fund, Mobius quickly replied, "The funds are actually run by teams of people and do not depend on one person."

In spite of the hoopla, getting these professionals to actually engage in teamwork has not been easy. Robert Fischer, a securities rep with Legg Mason in Richmond, Virginia, has had his share of frustrations, particularly the extra time required to maintain teams as new members are added. As a team leader, "you spend time trying to get other people to do stuff," warns Fischer. "There's a cost to that—the time, the planning element, the learning curve."

Another problem is that financial experts who worked alone in the past don't like to share their precious client list with co-workers. "Trust administrators, for example, won't let financial advisers near their clients just to sell them something," admits Jordan Miller, a senior executive at Fifth Third Securities in Cincinnati. In spite of this barrier, Fifth Third has improved team dynamics by literally moving team members into the same room. "It took a lot of work collaborating and co-locating these officers into teams," says Miller.[1]

Corporate leaders in the securities industry and elsewhere are discovering that people working alone often lack sufficient knowledge or capacity to achieve organizational objectives. Instead, they need to work in teams to make more effective decisions, serve clients more fully, and manufacture products more efficiently. This chapter looks at the conditions that make teams more or less effective in organizational settings. We begin by explaining why organizations rely on teams and why people join informal groups. We then introduce a model of team effectiveness and examine each of its elements: team and organizational environment, team design, and team processes. Next, two special types of teams—self-directed work teams and virtual teams—are discussed. The final section of this chapter looks at the challenges and strategies for making better decisions in teams.

>Teams and Groups

Teams are groups of two or more people who interact and influence each other, are mutually accountable for achieving common goals associated with organizational objectives, and perceive themselves as a social entity within an organization.[2] All teams exist to fulfill some purpose, such as assembling a product, providing a service, designing a new manufacturing facility, or making an important decision. Team members are held together by their interdependence and need for collaboration to achieve common goals. All teams require some form of communication so members can coordinate and share common objectives. Team members also influence each other, although some members are more influential than others regarding the team's goals and activities. Exhibit 7.1 briefly describes various types of (usually) formal work teams in organizations. Later in this chapter we'll

teams
Groups of two or more people who interact and influence each other, are mutually accountable for achieving common objectives, and perceive themselves as a social entity within an organization.

[Exhibit 7.1] Several Types of Formal Teams in Organizations

Team Type	Description
Departmental teams	Employees have similar or complementary skills located in the same unit of a functional structure; usually minimal task interdependence because each person works with employees in other departments.
Production/service and leadership teams	Typically multiskilled (employees have diverse competencies), team members collectively produce a common product/service or make ongoing decisions; production/service teams typically have an assembly line type of interdependence, whereas leadership teams tend to have tight interactive (reciprocal) interdependence.
Self-directed work teams	Similar to production/service teams except (1) they produce an entire product or subassembly that has low interdependence with other work units and (2) they have very high autonomy (no supervisors) and usually control inputs, flow, and outputs.
Advisory teams	Entities that provide recommendations to decision makers; such as committees, advisory councils, work councils, and review panels; may be temporary, but often permanent, some with frequent rotation of members.
Task force (project) teams	Usually multiskilled, temporary entities whose assignment is to solve a problem, realize an opportunity, or develop a product or service.
Skunkworks	Multiskilled entities that are usually located away from the organization and relatively free of its hierarchy; these teams are often initiated by an entrepreneurial team leader *(innovation champion)* who borrows people and resources *(bootlegging)* to create a product or develop a service.
Virtual teams	Formal teams whose members operate across space, time, and organizational boundaries and are linked through information technologies to achieve organizational tasks; may be a temporary task force or permanent service team.
Communities of practice	Formally designed or informally created groups bound together by shared expertise and passion for a particular activity or interest; often similar to virtual teams in that many rely on information technologies as main source of interaction; purpose is to share information, not make a product or provide a service.

look more closely at two types of teams that get a lot of attention among academics and practitioners: self-directed work teams and virtual teams.

groups
Two or more people with a unifying relationship.

All teams are **groups** because they consist of people with a unifying relationship. But not all groups are teams; some groups are just people assembled together without any necessary interdependence or organizationally focused objective. Along with formal work teams, organizations consist of *informal groups.* Informal groups are not initiated by the organization and usually do not perform organizational goals (thus they are "informal"). Instead, they exist primarily for the benefit of their members. The groups you meet for lunch and chat with in the hallway are informal groups. In each case, you associate with these groups for your own benefit.

Why Rely on Teams?

Executives at Merrill Lynch, Smith Barney, and other investment firms mentioned in the opening story have put a lot of energy into transforming their organizations into team-based structures. Why all the fuss about teams? The answer is that a considerable body of literature has found that under the right conditions, teams potentially make better decisions, develop better products and services, and create a more energized workforce compared with employees working alone.[3]

As a form of employee involvement, teams are generally more successful than individuals working alone at identifying problems, developing alternatives, and choosing from those alternatives. Similarly, team members can quickly share information and coordinate tasks, whereas these processes are slower and prone to more errors in traditional departments led by supervisors. As many investment firms have discovered, teams can provide superior customer service because they have more breadth of knowledge and expertise than individual "stars" can offer to customers.

Why People Belong to Informal Groups

Employees are not required to join informal groups, yet they exist throughout organizations. One reason is that human beings are social animals. Experts suggest that our drive to bond is hardwired through evolutionary development, which includes the drive to belong to informal groups.[4] This is evident by the fact that people invest considerable time and effort forming and maintaining social relationships without any special circumstances or ulterior motives. A second explanation is provided by social identity theory, which states that individuals define themselves by their group affiliations. Thus, we join informal groups—particularly groups viewed favorably by others and that are similar to our existing values—because they shape and reinforce our self-image.[5]

A third reason why people join informal groups is to accomplish tasks that cannot be achieved by individuals working alone. For example, employees will sometimes form a group to oppose organizational changes because the group collectively has more power than individuals complaining alone. A fourth explanation for informal groups is that in stressful situations we are comforted by the mere presence of other people and are therefore motivated to be near them. When in danger, people congregate near each other even though it serves no apparent purpose. Similarly, employees tend to mingle more often when hearing rumors that the company might be sold.[6]

>A Model of Team Effectiveness

You might have noticed that we hedged our glorification of teams by saying that they are "potentially" better than individuals "under the right conditions." The reason for this cautious writing is that many organizations have introduced team structures that later became spectacular failures. Why are some teams effective while others fail? This question has challenged organizational researchers for some time, and, as you might expect, numerous models of team effectiveness have been proposed over the years.[7]

Let's begin by clarifying the meaning of **team effectiveness**. Team effectiveness refers to how the team affects the organization, individual team members, and the team's existence.[8] First, effective teams achieve their objectives relating to the organization or other system in which the group operates. Second, team effectiveness relates to the satisfaction and well-being of its members. People join groups to fulfill their personal needs, so effectiveness is partly measured by this need fulfillment. Third, team effectiveness relates to the team's ability to survive. It must be able to maintain the commitment of its members, particularly during the turbulence of the team's development. Without this commitment, people leave and the team will fall apart. This element of team effectiveness also includes the ability to secure sufficient resources and find a benevolent environment in which to operate.

There are several pieces to the team effectiveness puzzle, but Exhibit 7.2 organizes them into a few convenient categories: organizational and team environment, team design, and team process.

team effectiveness
The extent to which a team achieves its objectives, achieves the needs and objectives of its members, and sustains itself over time.

[Exhibit 7.2] Model of Team Effectiveness

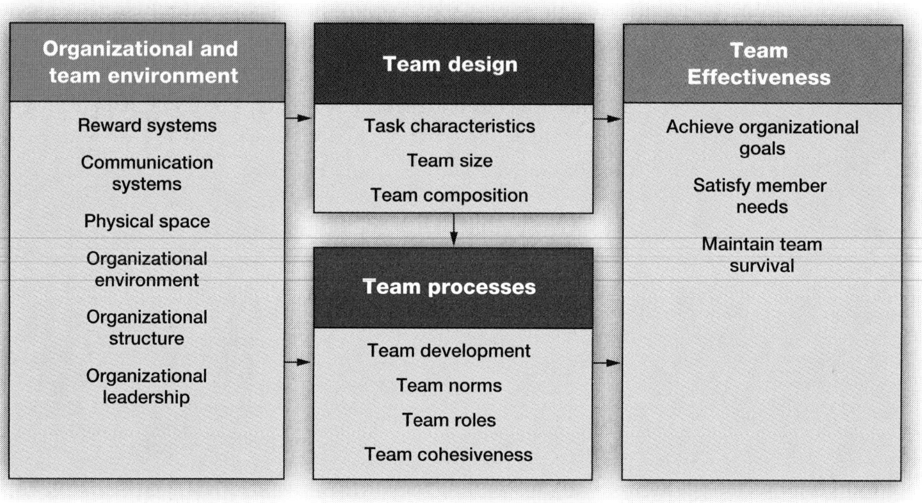

Organizational and team environment	Team design	Team Effectiveness
Reward systems Communication systems Physical space Organizational environment Organizational structure Organizational leadership	Task characteristics Team size Team composition	Achieve organizational goals Satisfy member needs Maintain team survival

Team processes

Team development
Team norms
Team roles
Team cohesiveness

>Organizational and Team Environment

Our discussion of team effectiveness logically begins with the contextual factors that influence the team's design, processes, and outcomes.[9] Six of the most important contextual factors are reward systems, communication systems, physical space, organizational environment, organizational structure, and organizational leadership.

- *Reward systems.* Team members tend to work together more effectively when they are at least partly rewarded for team performance.[10] This doesn't mean that everyone on the team should receive the same amount of pay based on the team's performance. Instead, rewards should at least partially align each person's interests to the team's goals.

- *Communications systems.* A poorly designed communication system can starve a team of valuable information and feedback, or it may swamp it with information overload. Communication systems are particularly important when team members are geographically dispersed.

- *Physical space.* The layout of an office or manufacturing facility assists team communication and shapes employee perceptions about being together as a team. This explains why, as mentioned in the opening story, Fifth Third Securities improved team dynamics after moving team members into the same room. Toyota also follows this strategy by putting everyone involved in product design in a large room (called an obeya) so they have a sense of being a team and can communicate more quickly and effectively.

- *Organizational environment.* Team success depends on the company's external environment. If the organization cannot secure resources, for instance, the team cannot fulfill its performance targets. Similarly, high demand for the team's output creates feelings of success, which motivates team members to stay with the team. A competitive environment can motivate employees to work together more closely.

- *Organizational structure.* Many teams fail because the organizational structure does not support them. Teams work better when there are few layers of management and teams are given autonomy and responsibility for their work. This structure encourages interaction with team members rather than with supervisors. Teams also flourish when employees are organized around work processes rather than specialized skills. This structure increases interaction among team members.[11]

• *Organizational leadership.* Teams require ongoing support from senior executives to align rewards, organizational structure, communication systems, and other elements of team context. They also require team leaders or facilitators who provide coaching and support.

>Team Design Features

The three main elements to consider when designing an effective team are task characteristics, team size, and team composition. As we saw earlier in the team effectiveness model (Exhibit 7.2), these design features influence team effectiveness directly as well as indirectly through team processes, described later.

As with most automakers, Toyota relies on engineers, design stylists, suppliers, assembly workers, and marketing people to help design new vehicles. But rather than have these people meet every week to identify and assess new product features, Toyota moves these three dozen people out of their departments and into one big room as a team. About the size of a basketball court, the *obeya* (Japanese for "big room") arrangement has cut Toyota's product development time and costs by 25 and 50 percent, respectively. "The reason *obeya* works so well is that it's all about immediate face-to-face human contact," explains Atsushi Niimi, president of Toyota Motor Manufacturing North America. Max Gillard, who oversees Toyota's *obeya* in Melbourne, Australia, adds that everyone in the *obeya* can hear conversations between a few people, which encourages others to join the discussion. "There is a hubbub," says Gillard. "You can go there and feel the excitement of the place. It is not like an office environment where people sit quietly tapping away at their computers."[12]

Task Characteristics

Experts are still figuring out the best types of work for teams. Some evidence says that teams are more effective when their tasks are well structured because the clear structure makes it easier to coordinate work among several people. But other research indicates that teams flourish more on complex tasks because the complexity motivates them to work together as a team.[13] Task structure and task complexity aren't opposites, but it can be difficult to find complex work that is well structured.

One task characteristic that is definitely important for teams is **task interdependence**—the extent that team members must share common inputs to their individual tasks, need to interact in the process of executing their work, or receive outcomes (such as rewards) that are partly determined by the performance of others. The higher the level of task interdependence, the greater the need for teams rather than individuals working alone. Employees tend to be motivated and more satisfied working on teams when their tasks are highly interdependent. However, this motivation and satisfaction occurs only when team members have the same job goals, such as serving the same clients or collectively assembling the same product.[14]

task interdependence
The degree to which a task requires employees to share common inputs or outcomes, or to interact in the process of executing their work.

Team Size

Team size plays a role in team effectiveness, but the optimal team size depends on a few things. Larger teams are typically less effective because members consume more time and effort coordinating their roles and resolving differences. At the same time, small teams can undermine team effectiveness if they don't provide enough staffing to fulfill the team's objectives. The general rule is that teams should be large enough to provide the necessary competencies and perspectives to perform the work, yet small enough to maintain efficient coordination and meaningful involvement of each member.

Team Composition

When Hewlett-Packard Co. (HP) hires new talent, it doesn't just look for technical skills and knowledge. The computer manufacturer looks for job applicants who fit into a team environment. "It's important for candidates to prove to us that they can work well with others," explains business-development manager Bill Avey. "We're looking for people who value the different perspectives that each individual brings to a team." Avey describes how HP recruiters will ask applicants to recall a time they worked in a group to solve a problem. "Successful candidates tend to show how they got differences out in the open and reached a resolution as a team," says Avey.[15]

Hewlett-Packard has a strong team orientation, so it carefully selects people with the necessary motivation and competencies for teamwork. Teams require members who are motivated to work together rather than alone, abide by the team's rules of conduct, and buy in to the team's goals. Effective team members also possess valuable skills and knowledge for the team's objectives, and are able to work well with others. Notably, research suggests that high-performing team members demonstrate more cooperative behavior toward others and generally have more emotional intelligence.[16]

Team Diversity

homogeneous teams
Teams that include members with common technical expertise, demographics (age, gender), ethnicity, experiences, or values.

heterogeneous teams
Teams that include members with diverse personal characteristics and backgrounds.

Another important dimension of team composition is the diversity of team members. **Homogeneous teams** include members with common technical expertise, demographics (age, gender), ethnicity, experiences, or values, whereas **heterogeneous teams** have members with diverse personal characteristics and backgrounds. Both have advantages and disadvantages, and their relative effectiveness depends on the situation.[17] Heterogeneous teams experience more conflict and take longer to develop. They are susceptible to "fault lines," hypothetical dividing lines that may split a team into subgroups along gender, ethnic, professional, or other dimensions. In contrast, members of homogeneous teams experience higher satisfaction and less conflict. They have similar mental models to begin with, so develop more quickly as a team. Consequently, homogeneous teams tend to be more effective on tasks requiring a high degree of cooperation and coordination, such as emergency response teams.

Although heterogeneous teams are more difficult to develop and maintain, they are generally more effective than homogeneous teams in situations involving complex problems requiring innovative solutions. One reason is that people from different backgrounds see a problem or opportunity from different perspectives. A second reason is that they usually have a broader knowledge base. For example, Wall Street investment teams are able to serve clients better when each member brings unique expertise to the group than when they all have the same skills. A third reason favoring heterogeneous teams is that the diversity provides representation to the team's constituents, such as other departments or clients from similarly diverse backgrounds. When a team represents various professions or departments, those constituents are more likely to accept and support the team's decisions and actions.

>Team Processes

The third set of team effectiveness elements, collectively known as team processes, include team development, norms, roles, and cohesiveness.

Team Development

Team members pass through several stages of development before emerging as an effective work unit. They must get to know each other, understand their respective roles, discover appropriate and inappropriate behaviors, and learn how to coordinate their work or social activities. The longer that team members work together, the better they develop common mental models, mutual understanding, and effective performance routines to complete the work. A popular and generally representative model of team development includes five stages: forming, storming, norming, performing, and eventually adjourning.[18]

1. *Forming.* The first stage of team development is a period of testing and orientation in which members learn about each other and evaluate the benefits and costs of continued membership. People tend to be polite during this stage and will defer to the existing authority of a formal or informal leader who must provide an initial set of rules and structures for interaction. Members try to find out what is expected of them and how they will fit into the team.

2. *Storming.* This stage is marked by interpersonal conflict as members become more proactive and compete for various team roles. Coalitions may form to influence the team's goals and means of goal attainment. Members try to establish norms of appropriate behavior and performance standards. This is a tenuous stage in the team's development, particularly when the leader is autocratic and lacks the necessary conflict-management skills.

3. *Norming.* During the norming stage, the team develops its first real sense of cohesion as roles are established and a consensus forms around group objectives. Members have developed relatively similar mental models, so they have common expectations and assumptions about how the team's goals should be accomplished. They have developed a common team-based mental model that allows them to interact more efficiently so they can move into the next stage, performing.

4. *Performing.* The team becomes more task-oriented in the performing stage. Team members have learned to coordinate and resolve conflicts more efficiently. Further coordination improvements must occasionally be addressed, but the greater emphasis is on task accomplishment. In high-performance teams, members are highly cooperative, have a high level of trust in each other, are committed to group objectives, and identify with the team.

5. *Adjourning.* Most work teams and informal groups eventually end. During this stage, members shift their attention away from task orientation to a socioemotional focus as they realize that their relationship is ending.

This five-stage model is a useful framework for understanding how teams develop.[19] Teams pass through each stage as members get to know each other and work together. We need to keep in mind that team development is a continuous process. Teams cycle back to earlier stages in the developmental process when new people join the team, the team's task is altered, or the team develops internal conflicts that were previously hidden.

Team Norms

Have you ever noticed how employees in one branch office practically run for the exit door the minute the workday ends, whereas their counterparts in another office seem to be competing for who can stay at work the longest? These differences are partly due to **norms**, the informal rules and shared expectations that groups establish to regulate the behavior of their members. Norms apply only to behavior, not to private thoughts or feelings. Moreover, norms exist only for behaviors that are important to the team.[20]

norms
The informal rules and expectations that groups establish to regulate the behavior of their members.

Norms are enforced in various ways. Co-workers grimace if we are late for a meeting or make sarcastic comments if we don't have our part of the project completed on time. Norms are also directly reinforced through praise from high-status members, more access to valued resources, or other rewards available to the team. But team members often conform to prevailing norms without direct reinforcement or punishment because they identify with the group and want to align their behavior with the team's values. The more tightly the person's social identity is connected to the group, the more the individual is motivated to avoid negative sanctions from that group.[21]

How Team Norms Develop

Norms develop as soon as teams form because people need to anticipate or predict how others will act. Even subtle events during the team's formation, such as how team members initially greet each other and where they sit in the first meetings, can initiate norms that are later difficult to change. Norms also form as team members discover behaviors that help them function more effectively (such as the need to respond quickly to e-mail). In particular, a critical event in the team's history can trigger formation of a norm or sharpen a previously vague one. A third influence on team norms is the past experiences and values that members bring to the team. If most people who join a new team value work/life balance, then norms are likely to develop that discourage long hours and work overload.[22]

Preventing and Changing Dysfunctional Team Norms

Team norms often become deeply anchored, so the best way to avoid norms that undermine organizational success or employee well-being is to establish desirable norms when the team is first formed. As was just mentioned, norms form from the values that people bring to the team, so one strategy is to select people with appropriate values. If organizational leaders want their teams to have strong safety norms, then they should hire people who already value safety.

Another strategy is to clearly state desirable norms as soon as the team is created. For instance, when Four Seasons Hotels & Resorts opens a new hotel, it forms a 35-person task force consisting of staff from other Four Seasons hotels. The task force "Four Seasonizes" the new recruits by training them and watching for behaviors and decisions that are inconsistent with the Four Seasons way of doing things. "The task force helps establish norms [in the new hotel]," explains a Four Seasons manager who has served on these task forces.[23]

One of the first and last tasks of the day at The Container Store is for staff to gather for the "huddle." At The Container Store outlet in White Plains, New York, floor leader Scott Buhler (shown in photo) starts the morning huddle by declaring the day's sales target. Then he asks the group about the store's vision and today's product tip. "We always highlight a product or do a quiz to make sure employees are familiar with new products," Buhler says. The Container Store institutionalized huddle sessions to educate employees, create a team environment, and reinforce norms that the company wants to instill in employees. "The spirit was to keep people on the same page," explains Garrett Boone, co-founder and chairman of the Dallas-based seller of customized storage products.[24]

The suggestions so far refer to new teams, but how can organizational leaders change dysfunctional norms in older teams? One way is to explicitly discuss the counterproductive norm with team members using persuasive communication tactics. Team-based reward systems can also weaken counterproductive norms; however, studies report that employees might continue to abide by team norms (such as limiting output) even though the compliant behavior reduces their paycheck. Finally, if dysfunctional norms are deeply ingrained and the previous solutions don't work, it may be necessary to disband the group and replace it with people having more favorable norms.

Team Roles

Every work team and informal group has various roles necessary to coordinate the team's task and maintain the team's functioning.[25] Some roles help the team achieve its goals; other roles maintain relationships so the team survives and team members fulfill their needs. Some team roles are formally assigned to specific people. For example, team leaders are usually expected to initiate discussion, ensure that everyone has an opportunity to present their views, and help the team reach agreement on the issues discussed. But team members often take on various roles informally based on their personality, values, and expertise. These role preferences are usually worked out during the storming stage of team development, but in a dynamic environment, team members often assume various roles temporarily as the need arises.[26]

Team Cohesiveness

Team cohesiveness—the degree of attraction people feel toward the team and their motivation to remain members—is considered an important ingredient in a team's success.[27] Employees feel high cohesion when they believe the team will help them achieve their personal goals, fulfill their need for affiliation or status, or provide social support during times of crisis or trouble. Cohesiveness is an emotional experience, not just a calculation of whether to stay or leave the team. It exists when team members make the team part of their social identity. Cohesiveness is the glue or *esprit de corps* that holds the group together and ensures that its members fulfill their obligations.

team cohesiveness
The degree of attraction people feel toward the team and their motivation to remain members.

Influences on Team Cohesiveness
Several factors influence team cohesiveness: member similarity, team size, member interaction, difficult entry, team success, and external competition or challenges. For the most part, these factors reflect the individual's social identity with the group and beliefs about how team membership will fulfill personal needs.

- *Member similarity.* Earlier in this chapter we learned that highly diverse teams potentially create fault lines that can lead to factious subgroups and higher turnover among team members. Other research has found that people with similar values have a higher attraction to each other. Collectively, these findings suggest that homogeneous teams are more cohesive than heterogeneous teams. However, not all forms of diversity reduce cohesion. For example, teams consisting of people from different job groups seem to gel together just as well as teams of people from the same job.[28]
- *Team size.* Smaller teams tend to be more cohesive than larger teams because it is easier for a few people to agree on goals and coordinate work activities. The smallest teams aren't always the most cohesive, however, if they lack enough members to perform the required tasks. Thus, team cohesiveness is potentially greatest when teams are as small as possible, yet large enough to capture the diverse skills and perspectives required for the assignment.

- *Member interaction.* Teams tend to have higher cohesion when their members interact with each other fairly regularly. This occurs when team members perform highly interdependent tasks and work in the same physical area.

- *Somewhat difficult entry.* Teams tend to be more cohesive when entry to the team is restricted. The more elite the team, the more prestige it confers on its members, and the more they tend to value their membership in the unit. Existing team members are also more willing to welcome and support new members after they have "passed the test," possibly because they have shared the same entry experience. The exception to this principle occurs when the initiation is severe. Extreme initiations create negative emotions that team members continue to associate with the team, thereby weakening their attachment to the group.[29]

- *Team success.* Cohesiveness increases with the team's level of success because people feel more connected to teams that fulfill their goals. Furthermore, individuals are more likely to attach their social identity to successful teams than to those with a string of failures.

- *External competition and challenges.* Team cohesiveness tends to increase when members face external competition or a challenging objective that is valued. Under these conditions, employees value the team's ability to overcome the threat or competition if they can't solve the problem individually. They also value their membership as a form of social support. However, severe external threats can undermine team cohesiveness when the resulting stress undermines the team's ability to function well.[30]

Consequences of Team Cohesiveness

Every team must have some minimal level of cohesiveness to maintain its existence. People who belong to high-cohesion teams are motivated to maintain their membership and to help the team perform effectively. Compared to low-cohesion teams, high-cohesion team members spend more time together, share information more frequently, and are more satisfied with each other. They provide each other with better social support in stressful situations. Members of high-cohesion teams are generally more sensitive to each other's needs and develop better interpersonal relationships, thereby reducing dysfunctional conflict. When conflict does arise, members tend to resolve these differences swiftly and effectively.[31]

With better cooperation and more motivation, high-cohesion teams usually perform better than low-cohesion teams. However, the relationship is a little more complex than that. Exhibit 7.3 illustrates how the effect of cohesiveness on team performance depends on the extent that team norms are consistent with organizational goals. Cohesive teams will likely have lower task performance when norms conflict with organizational objectives, because cohesiveness motivates employees to perform at a level more consistent with group norms.[32]

>The Trouble with Teams

The investment firms mentioned in the story that began this chapter are placing a lot more emphasis on teams these days. But are teams really necessary? Earlier, we pointed out a number of compelling reasons companies should introduce teams. Still, the reality is that teams aren't always needed.[33] Some tasks are performed just as easily and effectively by one person as by a group.

process losses
Resources (including time and energy) expended toward team development and maintenance rather than the task.

Even if teams are somewhat useful, they tend to require more care and feeding than individuals working alone. Scholars call these **process losses**—resources (including time and energy) expended toward team development and maintenance rather than the task.[34] As Robert Fischer at investment firm Legg Mason mentioned in the opening story, process

[Exhibit 7.3] Effect of Team Cohesiveness on Task Performance

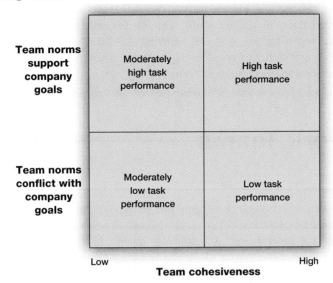

losses are particularly noticeable when adding new people to the team. The software industry even has a name for this. "Brooks's law" says that adding more people to a late software project only makes it later.[35]

A third problem is that teams require the right environment to flourish. Many companies forget this point by putting people in teams without changing anything else. As we noted earlier, teams require appropriate rewards, communication systems, team leadership, and other conditions. Without these, the shift to a team structure could be a waste of time and huge frustration for those involved. Overall, though, we need to determine whether changing these environmental conditions to improve teamwork will cost more than benefits for the overall organization.[36]

Social Loafing

Perhaps the best-known limitation of teams is the risk of productivity loss due to **social loafing**. Social loafing occurs when people exert less effort when working in groups than when working alone.[37] Social loafing is more likely to occur in large teams where individual output is difficult to identify. This includes situations in which team members work alone toward a common output pool, such as collectively serving customers or making the same product. Under these conditions, employees aren't as worried that their performance will be noticed. Social loafing tends to be lower when the task is interesting, because individuals have a higher intrinsic motivation to perform their duties. It is also less common when the group's objective is important, possibly because individuals experience more pressure from other team members to perform well. Finally, social loafing occurs less frequently among members with a strong collectivist value, because they value group membership and believe in working toward group objectives.

By understanding these causes, we can identify ways to minimize social loafing.[38] One approach is to split the team into several smaller groups so each person's performance becomes more noticeable and important for team performance. Second, give each team member a different work activity; this tends to reduce social loafing because each person's contribution stands out. Third, social loafing is minimized when each member's contribution is measured. Fourth, make the job more interesting—apply the job enrichment principles discussed in Chapter 5—so employees are inherently motivated to perform their share of the work. The

social loafing
A situation in which people exert less effort (and usually perform at a lower level) when working in groups than when working alone.

fifth recommendation is to choose people who are inherently motivated to perform the work or who have a collectivist orientation so they are motivated not to let the group down.

The team effectiveness model is a useful template for understanding how teams work, and don't work, in organizations. With this knowledge in hand, let's briefly investigate two types of teams that have received considerable attention among academics and practitioners: self-directed work teams and virtual teams.

>Self-Directed Work Teams

Surrounded by tall prairie grass, Harley-Davidson's assembly plant near Kansas City, Missouri, has no supervisors. Instead, natural work teams of 8 to 15 employees make most day-to-day decisions through consensus. An umbrella group, representing teams and management, makes plantwide decisions. "There is more pressure on employees here because they must learn to do what supervisors did," admits the general manager of Harley-Davidson's Kansas City operations. Still, Harley-Davidson is taking teamwork far beyond the traditional workplace. "There's a lot of work being done to empower the workforce," says the Kansas City manager. "But there are very few examples of where they've taken the workforce to run the factory. And that's what we've done."[39]

self-directed work teams (SDWTs)
Cross-functional work groups, organized around work processes, that complete an entire piece of work requiring several interdependent tasks and that have substantial autonomy over the execution of those tasks.

Harley-Davidson and many other organizations have adopted a form of work structure that relies on **self-directed work teams (SDWTs)**. SDWTs are defined by two distinctive features. First, they complete an entire piece of work requiring several interdependent tasks.[40] This work arrangement is important because it clusters the team members together (high task interdependence) and minimizes their interdependence with employees outside the team.

Second, SDWTs have substantial autonomy over the execution of their tasks. In particular, these teams plan, organize, and control work activities with little or no direct involvement of a higher-status supervisor. They tend to control most work inputs, flow, and output, such as working directly with suppliers and customers. The team's autonomy extends to their responsibility for correcting workflow problems as they occur. With substantial autonomy and responsibility, SDWTs also receive plenty of team-level feedback and rewards.

Self-Directed Work Team Effectiveness and Challenges

Numerous studies have found that self-directed work teams can be significantly more productive than traditional departmental teams. A decade ago, Canon Inc. introduced self-directed teams at all 29 of its Japanese plants. The camera and copier company claims that a self-directed team of a half-dozen people can now produce as much as 30 people in the old assembly line system. One study found that car dealership service garages with self-directed teams were significantly more profitable than service garages where employees work without a team structure. Another study reported that both short- and long-term measures of customer satisfaction increased after street cleaning employees in a German city were organized into SDWTs.[41]

Although SDWTs can be effective, they can be difficult to implement. One sizable challenge is management resistance. Executives and supervisors alike worry about losing power when employees gain power through empowered teams.[42] Supervisors, in particular, need to make the difficult transition from being hands-on controllers to hands-off facilitators. Research suggests that supervisors are less likely to resist self-directed work teams

When Standard Motor Products (SMP) introduced self-directed work teams at its Edwardsville, Kansas, plant, supervisors had a tough challenge replacing their command-and-control management style with something closer to being a mentor or facilitator. "It wasn't easy for managers who were raised in the top-down authority model," recalls Darrel Ray, the nationally recognized consultant who worked with the auto parts company during the transition. "It is far easier to be a tyrant than it is to be a psychologist or a teacher," explains distribution manager Don Wakefield. Steve Domann was one of the managers who had difficulty adjusting. "I thought about quitting when the changes were announced," says Domann, who now oversees plant work teams as a team developer. "Some of the old management team couldn't conform to the team, but I'm glad I did."[43]

when they have personally worked in a high-involvement workplace and receive considerable training in their new facilitation role.[44]

A second challenge is that SDWTs are less compatible with high power-distance cultures.[45] Employees in these cultures are more comfortable when supervisors give them directions, whereas low power-distance employees value their involvement in decisions. One study reported that employees in Mexico (which has a high power-distance culture) expect managers to make decisions affecting their work, whereas SDWTs emphasize self-initiative and individual responsibility within teams. Some writers also suggest that SDWTs are more difficult to implement in cultures with low collectivism because employees are less comfortable collaborating and working interdependently with co-workers.[46]

>Virtual Teams

PricewaterhouseCoopers (PwC) is a global accounting firm whose learning and education (training) department in the United States consists of 190 employees spread across 70 offices in dozens of cities. One in four PwC's training staff telecommutes. In spite of this radical dispersion, PwC's training employees regularly work in project teams ranging from 5 to 50 people from several offices. Some of these teams also include subject experts—consultants, professors, and training vendors—who are usually located in yet another part of the country. "Virtual teaming is the norm for us," says Peter Nicolas, PwC's learning solutions manager in Florham Park, New Jersey.[47]

Employees in PwC's learning and education unit get plenty of experience working in **virtual teams**. Virtual teams are teams whose members operate across space, time, and organizational boundaries and are linked through information technologies to achieve organizational tasks.[48] As with all teams, virtual teams are groups of two or more people who interact and influence each other, are mutually accountable for achieving common goals associated with organizational objectives, and perceive themselves as a social entity within an organization. However, virtual teams differ from traditional teams in two ways: (1) they are not usually co-located (work in the same physical area), and (2) due to their lack of co-location, members of virtual teams depend primarily on information technologies rather than face-to-face interaction to communicate and coordinate their work effort.

virtual teams
Teams whose members operate across space, time, and organizational boundaries and are linked through information technologies to achieve organizational tasks.

Why Companies Form Virtual Teams

Virtual teams are one of the most significant developments in organizations over the past decade. According to one estimate, more than 60 percent of employees in professions are members of a virtual team at some point during the year. One reason is that information technologies have made it easier than ever to communicate and coordinate with people at a distance. For instance, virtual teams in PwC's training unit are connected together using computer-based video conferences, virtual calendars, intranet databases, and good old-fashioned e-mail and telephones. The shift from production-based to knowledge-based work has also made virtual teamwork feasible. Knowledge work, such as writing software code, designing products, and making strategic decisions, is easily transferable across time and distance, whereas production work is not.

Information technologies and knowledge-based work make virtual teams possible, but two other factors—knowledge management and globalization—make them increasingly necessary. Virtual teams represent a natural part of the knowledge management process because they allow and encourage employees to share and use knowledge where geography limits more direct forms of collaboration. PwC virtual teams include experts outside the organization, which is much more difficult in traditional face-to-face team settings. Globalization also makes virtual teams necessary because companies increasingly have talent spread around the world rather than just in one building. They are also forming joint ventures and other partnerships that require project work with people from multiple organizations located in far-flung locations.

Improving Virtual Team Performance

Virtual teams have all of the challenges of traditional teams as well as the vagaries of distance and time. Technology plays a vital role to help virtual teams work more effectively, but so far no technology completely solves the distance problem. Team members misunderstand messages that face-to-face teams more quickly resolve. Time differences among team members can prevent the team from becoming highly cohesive. The lack of instant feedback makes it more difficult for virtual teams to work on ambiguous and complex tasks. The problems with larger teams discussed earlier are amplified in virtual teams due to the limitations of existing technology.

Fortunately, researchers in organizational behavior and other fields have been keenly interested in virtual teams, and their studies are now yielding ways to improve virtual team effectiveness. Here are three of the clearest recommendations:[49]

- *Virtual team competencies.* Virtual team members require competencies beyond those needed in traditional teams. They should have the ability to communicate easily through technology, strong self-leadership skills to motivate and guide their behavior without peers or bosses nearby, and higher emotional intelligence so they can decipher the feelings of teammates from e-mail and other limited communication media.

- *Flexible information technologies.* Researchers have found that corporate leaders like to impose technology on virtual teams rather than allow them to adopt technology that suits their needs. The best situation occurs where virtual teams have a toolkit of communication methods, which gain and lose importance over different parts of the project.

- *Occasional face-to-face interaction.* This may seem contrary to the entire notion of virtual teams, but so far no technology has replaced face-to-face interaction for high-level bonding and mutual understanding. This direct interaction is particularly valuable when virtual teams first form. "I always try to do the kickoff meeting face-to-face," says Scott Patterson, PwC's e-learning manager in Atlanta. "We also try to bring the group back together for major milestones in a project." Patterson explains that bringing virtual team members together once in a while is the best way to "build enthusiasm and to get clear about everyone's roles and responsibilities."[50]

>Team Decision Making

Self-directed work teams, virtual teams, and practically all other groups are expected to make decisions. Under certain conditions, teams are more effective than individuals at identifying problems, choosing alternatives, and evaluating their decisions. To leverage these benefits, however, we first need to understand the constraints on effective team decision making. Then, we look at specific team structures that try to overcome these constraints.

Constraints on Team Decision Making

Anyone who has spent enough time in the workplace can reel off several ways in which teams stumble in decision making. Four of the best-known problems are time constraints, evaluation apprehension, pressure to conform, and groupthink.

Time Constraints

There's a saying that "committees keep minutes and waste hours." This reflects the fact that teams take longer than individuals to make decisions.[51] Team members need time to learn about each other and build rapport. They need to manage an imperfect communication process so that there is sufficient understanding of each other's ideas. They also need to coordinate roles and rules of order within the decision process. Most decision-making teams also suffer from the problem of **production blocking**—the limitation that only one person can speak at a time.[52] Production blocking inhibits idea generation because team members need to pay attention to the conversation to find a good time to speak up, and this monitoring makes it difficult for them to concentrate on their own ideas. Also, ideas are fleeting, so the longer they wait to speak up, the more likely these flickering ideas will die out.

production blocking
A time constraint in team decision making due to the procedural requirement that only one person may speak at a time.

Evaluation Apprehension

Individuals are reluctant to mention ideas that seem silly because they believe, often correctly, that other team members are silently evaluating them.[53] This **evaluation apprehension** is based on the individual's desire to create a favorable self-presentation and need to protect self-esteem. It is most common in meetings attended by people with different levels of status or expertise, or when members formally evaluate each other's performance throughout the year (as in 360-degree feedback). Creative ideas often sound bizarre or illogical when presented, so evaluation apprehension tends to discourage employees from mentioning them in front of co-workers.

evaluation apprehension
When individuals are reluctant to mention ideas that seem silly because they believe (often correctly) that other team members are silently evaluating them.

Pressure to Conform

High cohesion motivates employees to conform to the team's norms. This control keeps the group organized around common goals, but it may also cause team members to suppress their dissenting opinions, particularly when a strong team norm is related to the issue. When someone states a point of view that violates the majority opinion, other members might punish the violator or try to persuade him or her that the opinion is incorrect. Conformity can also be subtle. To some extent, we depend on the opinions that others hold to validate our own views. If co-workers don't agree with us, then we begin to question our own opinions even without overt peer pressure.

[Exhibit 7.4] Symptoms of Groupthink

Groupthink Symptom	Description
Ilusion of invulnerability	The team feels comfortable with risky decisions because possible weaknesses are suppressed or glossed over.
Assumption of morality	There is such an unquestioned belief in the inherent morality of the team's objectives that members do not feel the need to debate whether their actions are ethical.
Rationalization	Underlying assumptions, new information, and previous actions that seem inconsistent with the team's decision are discounted or explained away.
Stereotyping outgroups	The team stereotypes or oversimplifies the external threats upon which the decision is based; "enemies" are viewed as purely evil or moronic.
Self-censorship	Team members suppress their doubts in order to maintain harmony.
Illusion of unanimity	Self-censorship results in harmonious behavior, so individual members believe that they alone have doubts; silence is automatically perceived as evidence of consensus.
Mindguarding	Some members become self-appointed guardians to prevent negative or inconsistent information from reaching the team.
Pressuring dissenters	Members who happen to raise their concerns about the decision are pressured to fall into line and be more loyal to the team.

Source: Based on I. L. Janis, *Groupthink: Psychological Studies of Policy Decisions and Fiascoes,* 2nd ed. (Boston: Houghton Mifflin, 1982), p. 244.

Groupthink

groupthink
The tendency of highly cohesive groups to value consensus at the price of decision quality.

Groupthink is the tendency of highly cohesive groups to value consensus at the price of decision quality.[54] Groupthink goes beyond the problem of conformity; it includes all of the elements listed in Exhibit 7.4. Although the term *groupthink* is now part of everyday language, the concept is apparently too messy for researchers to find much support for it. Indeed, some elements of groupthink actually improve rather than undermine the team decision-making process in some situations.[55] Some pieces of groupthink are still valid concerns, however. One recent study reported that highly confident teams are less attentive in decision making than moderately confident teams. This is consistent with previous evidence that overconfident executive groups make sloppy decisions because they are complacent and have a false sense of invulnerability.[56]

Team Structures to Improve Creativity and Decision Making

There is plenty of research revealing problems with team decision making, but several solutions also emerge from these bad-news studies. Team members need to be confident in their decision making, but not so confident that they collectively feel invulnerable. Team norms should encourage critical thinking, and teams should have sufficient diversity to support multiple viewpoints. Team leaders and other powerful members can sway the rest of the group, so checks and balances need to be in place to avoid the adverse effects of this power. Another practice is to maintain an optimal team size. The group should be large enough that members possess the collective knowledge to resolve the problem, yet small enough that the team doesn't consume too much time or restrict individual input.

constructive conflict
Occurs when team members debate their different perceptions about an issue in a way that keeps the conflict focused on the task rather than people.

Team structures also help to minimize the problems described over the previous few pages. Three team structures that potentially improve creativity and decision making in team settings are constructive conflict, brainstorming, and nominal group technique.

Constructive Conflict

Constructive conflict occurs when team members debate their different perceptions about an issue in a way that keeps the conflict focused on the task rather than people. This conflict is called *constructive* because participants pay attention to facts and logic and avoid statements that generate emotional conflict. The main advantage of this debate is that it presents different points of view, which encourages everyone to reexamine their assumptions and logic. One problem with constructive conflict is that healthy debate too often slides into personal attacks, which may explain why the evidence of constructive conflict on team decision making is inconsistent. Some research indicates that debate, even criticism, can be good for team decision making, whereas other research concludes that all forms of conflict can be detrimental to team dynamics. Until this issue gets sorted out, constructive conflict should be used cautiously.[57]

Brainstorming

Brainstorming tries to leverage the creative potential of teams by establishing four simple rules: (1) speak freely—describe even the craziest ideas; (2) don't criticize others or their ideas; (3) provide as many ideas as possible—the quality of ideas increases with the quantity of ideas; and (4) build on the ideas that others have presented. These rules are supposed to encourage divergent thinking while minimizing evaluation apprehension and other team dynamics problems. Lab studies using university students concluded many years ago that brainstorming isn't so effective, largely because production blocking and evaluation apprehension still interfere with team dynamics.[59]

The ill-fated flight of the space shuttle Columbia was a wake-up call for how NASA's mission management team makes decisions. The Columbia accident investigation team concluded that concerns raised by engineers were either deflected or watered down because the mission management team appeared to be "immersed in a culture of invincibility" and hierarchical authority discouraged constructive debate. If top decision makers had more fully considered the extent of damage during takeoff, they might have been able to save Columbia's seven crew members. To foster more open communications and constructive debate, the mission management team's assigned seating at a rectangular table has been replaced by a C-shaped arrangement where people sit wherever they want (shown in photo). None of the 24 members stands out above the others in the new setup. Around the walls of the room are pearls of wisdom reminding everyone of the pitfalls of team decision making. "People in groups tend to agree on courses of action which, as individuals, they know are stupid," warns one poster.[58]

However, brainstorming may be more beneficial than the earlier studies indicated.[60] The earlier lab studies measured the number of ideas generated, whereas recent investigations within companies using brainstorming indicate that this team structure results in more *creative* ideas, which is the main reason companies use brainstorming. Also, evaluation apprehension is less of a problem in high-performing teams that embrace a learning orientation culture than for students brainstorming in lab experiments. Another overlooked advantage of brainstorming is that participants interact and participate directly, thereby increasing decision acceptance and team cohesiveness. Finally, brainstorming sessions often spread enthusiasm, which tends to generate more creativity. Overall, while brainstorming might not always be the best team structure, it seems to be more valuable than some of the earlier research studies indicated.

Electronic brainstorming is a recent form of brainstorming that relies on networked computers to submit and share creative ideas. After receiving the question or issue, participants enter their ideas using special computer software. The ideas are distributed anonymously to other participants, who are encouraged to piggyback on those ideas. Team members eventually vote electronically on the ideas presented. Face-to-face discussion usually follows. Electronic brainstorming can be quite effective at generating creative ideas with minimal production blocking, evaluation apprehension, or conformity problems.[61]

brainstorming
A freewheeling, face-to-face meeting where team members aren't allowed to criticize, but are encouraged to speak freely, generate as many ideas as possible, and build on the ideas of others.

electronic brainstorming
Using special computer software, participants share ideas while minimizing the team dynamics problems inherent in traditional brainstorming sessions.

Despite these numerous advantages, electronic brainstorming seems to be too structured and technology-bound for some executives. Some leaders may also feel threatened by the honesty of statements generated through this process and by their limited ability to control the discussion.

Nominal Group Technique

nominal group technique
A structured team decision-making process whereby team members independently write down ideas, describe and clarify them to the group, and then independently rank or vote on them.

Nominal group technique is a variation of traditional brainstorming that tries to combine the benefits of team decision making without the problems mentioned earlier.[62] The method is called *nominal* because participants form a group in name only during two of its three stages. After the problem is described, team members silently and independently write down as many solutions as they can. In the second stage, participants describe their solutions to the other team members, usually in a round-robin format. As with brainstorming, there is no criticism or debate, although members are encouraged to ask for clarification of the ideas presented. In the third stage, participants silently and independently rank order or vote on each proposed solution. Nominal group technique tends to generate a higher number of better-quality ideas compared with traditional interacting and possibly brainstorming groups.[63] Due to its high degree of structure, nominal group technique usually maintains a high task orientation and relatively low potential for conflict within the team. However, production blocking and evaluation apprehension still occur to some extent.

>chapter summary

Teams are groups of two or more people who interact and influence each other, are mutually accountable for achieving common objectives, and perceive themselves as a social entity within an organization. All teams are groups, because they consist of people with a unifying relationship; not all groups are teams, because some groups do not have purposive interaction.

Teams have become popular because they tend to make better decisions, support the knowledge management process, and provide superior customer service. Employees belong to informal groups for four reasons: (1) people have an innate drive to bond, (2) group membership shapes our self-image, (3) some personal goals are accomplished better in groups, and (4) individuals are comforted in stressful situations by the mere presence of other people.

Team effectiveness includes the group's ability to survive, achieve its system-based objectives, and fulfill the needs of its members. The model of team effectiveness considers the team and organizational environment, team design, and team processes. Six elements in the organizational and team environment that influence team effectiveness are reward systems, communication systems, physical space, organizational environment, organizational structure, and organizational leadership.

Three team design elements are task characteristics, team size, and team composition. Teams tend to be more effective when they work on well-structured or complex tasks. The need for teamwork increases with task interdependence. Teams should be large enough to perform the work, yet small enough for efficient coordination and meaningful involvement. Effective teams are composed of people with the competencies and motivation to perform tasks in a team environment. Heterogeneous teams operate best on complex projects and problems requiring innovative solutions.

Teams develop through the stages of forming, storming, norming, performing, and eventually adjourning. Teams develop norms to regulate and guide member behavior. These norms may be influenced by initial experiences, critical events, and the values and experiences that team members bring to the group. Team members also have roles—a set of behaviors they are expected to perform because they hold certain positions in a team and organization. Cohesiveness—the degree of attraction people feel toward the team and their motivation to remain members—increases with member similarity, smaller team size, higher degree of interaction, somewhat difficult entry, team success, and external challenges.

Teams are not always beneficial or necessary. Moreover, they have hidden costs, known as process losses, and require particular environments to flourish. Social loafing is another potential problem with teams.

Self-directed work teams complete an entire piece of work requiring several interdependent tasks and have substantial autonomy over the execution of these tasks. SDWTs are more productive than traditional teams in many situations. However, they are sometimes threatened by management resistance, and are more difficult to implement in high-power-distance cultures.

Virtual teams are teams whose members operate across space, time, and organizational boundaries and are linked through information technologies to achieve organizational tasks. Information technology and knowledge-based work make it easier to operate virtual teams. Knowledge management and globalization make virtual teams increasingly necessary. Three factors to consider when improving virtual team effectiveness are team competencies, flexible information technologies, and occasional face-to-face interaction.

Team decisions are impeded by time constraints, evaluation apprehension, conformity to peer pressure, and some elements of groupthink. To minimize decision-making problems, teams should be moderately (not highly) confident, ensure that the team leader does not dominate, maintain an optimal team size, and ensure that team norms support critical thinking. Three team structures that potentially improve team decision making are constructive conflict, brainstorming (as well as electronic brainstorming), and nominal group technique.

>key.terms

brainstorming 149

constructive conflict 149

electronic brainstorming 149

evaluation apprehension 147

groups 134

groupthink 148

heterogeneous teams 138

homogeneous teams 138

nominal group technique 150

norms 139

process losses 143

production blocking 147

self-directed work teams (SDWTs) 144

social loafing 143

task interdependence 137

team cohesiveness 141

team effectiveness 135

teams 133

virtual teams 145

>critical.thinking.questions

1. Informal groups exist in almost every form of social organization. What types of informal groups exist in your classroom? Why are students motivated to belong to these informal groups?

2. You have been asked to lead a complex software project over the next year that requires the full-time involvement of approximately 100 people with diverse skills and backgrounds. Using your knowledge of team size, how

can you develop an effective team under these conditions?

3. You have been put in charge of a cross-functional task force that will develop enhanced Internet banking services for retail customers. The team includes representatives from marketing, information services, customer service, and accounting, all of whom will move to the same location at headquarters for three months. Describe the behaviors you might observe during each stage of the team's development.

4. You have just been transferred from the Kansas City office to the Denver office of your company, a national sales organization of electrical products for developers and contractors. In Kansas City, team members regularly called customers after a sale to ask whether the products arrived on time and whether they are satisfied. But when you moved to the Denver office, no one seemed to make these follow-up calls. A recently hired co-worker explained that other co-workers discouraged her from making those calls. Later, another co-worker suggested that your follow-up calls were making everyone else look lazy. Give three possible reasons why the norms in Denver might be different from those in the Kansas City office, even though the customers, products, sales commissions, and other characteristics of the workplace are almost identical.

5. You have been assigned to a class project with five other students, none of whom you have met before. To what extent would team cohesiveness improve your team's performance on this project? What actions would you recommend to build team cohesiveness among student team members in this situation?

6. Management guru Peter Drucker said a few years ago, "The now-fashionable team in which everybody works with everybody on everything from the beginning rapidly is becoming a disappointment." Discuss three reasons why Drucker and others are disappointed with teams.

7. Suppose the instructor for this course assigned you to a project team consisting of three other students who are currently taking similar courses in Ireland, India, and Brazil. All students speak English and have similar expertise of the topic. Use your knowledge of virtual teams to discuss the problems that your team might face, compared with a face-to-face team of local students.

8. Carmel Technologies wants to use brainstorming with its employees and customers to identify new uses for its technology. Advise Carmel's president about the potential benefits of brainstorming, as well as its potential limitations.

>case.study:skillbuilder7.1

The Shipping Industry Accounting Team

For the past five years, I have been working at McKay, Sanderson, and Smith Associates, a midsized accounting firm in Boston that specializes in commercial accounting and audits. My particular specialty is accounting practices for shipping companies, ranging from small fishing fleets to a couple of the big firms with ships along the East Coast.

About 18 months ago, McKay, Sanderson, and Smith Associates became part of a large merger involving two other accounting firms. These firms have offices in Miami, Seattle, Baton Rouge, and Los Angeles. Although the other two accounting firms were much larger than McKay, all three firms agreed to avoid centralizing the business around one office in Los Angeles. Instead, the new firm—called Goldberg, Choo, and McKay Associates—would rely on teams across the country to "leverage the synergies of our collective knowledge" (an often-cited statement from the managing partner soon after the merger).

The merger affected me a year ago when my boss (a senior partner and vice president of the merger firm)

announced that I would be working more closely with three people from the other two firms to become the new shipping industry accounting team. The other team members were Elias in Miami, Susan in Seattle, and Brad in Los Angeles. I had met Elias briefly at a meeting in New York City during the merger but have never met Susan or Brad, although I knew that they were shipping accounting professionals at the other firms.

Initially, the shipping team activities involved e-mailing each other about new contracts and prospective clients. Later, we were asked to submit joint monthly reports on accounting statements and issues. Normally, I submitted my own monthly reports, which summarize activities involving my own clients. Coordinating the monthly report with three other people took much more time, particularly since different accounting documentation procedures across the three firms were still being resolved. It took numerous e-mails and a few telephone calls to work out a reasonable monthly report style.

During this aggravating process, it became apparent, to me at least, that this "teams" business was costing me more time than it was worth. Moreover, Brad in Los Angeles didn't have a clue as to how to communicate with the rest of us. He rarely replied to e-mails. Instead, he often used the telephone voice-mail system, which resulted in lots of telephone tag. Brad arrives at work at 9:30 A.M. in Los Angeles (and is often late!), which is early afternoon in Boston. I typically have a flexible work schedule, from 7:30 A.M. to 3:30 P.M., which allows me to chauffeur my kids after school to sports and music lessons. So Brad and I have a window of less than three hours to share information.

The biggest nuisance with the shipping specialist accounting team started two weeks ago when the firm asked the four of us to develop a new strategy for attracting more shipping firm business. This new strategic plan is a messy business. Somehow, we have to share our thoughts on various approaches, agree on a new plan, and write a unified submission to the managing partner. Already, the project is taking most of my time just writing and responding to e-mails and talking in conference calls (which none of us did much before the team formed).

Susan and Brad have already had two or three misunderstandings via e-mail about their different perspectives on delicate matters in the strategic plan. The worst of these disagreements required a conference call with all of us to resolve. Except for the most basic matters, it seems that we can't understand each other, let alone agree on key issues. I have come to the conclusion that I would never want Brad to work in my Boston office (thank goodness, he's on the other side of the country). While Elias and I seem to agree on most points, the overall team can't form a common vision or strategy. I don't know how Elias, Susan, or Brad feel, but I would be quite happy to work somewhere that did not require any of these long-distance team headaches.

Discussion Questions

1. Use the team effectiveness model to identify the strengths and weaknesses of this team's environment, design, and processes.

2. Assuming that these four people must continue to work as a team, recommend ways to improve the team's effectiveness.

Copyright © 2004 Steven L. McShane.

>team.exercise:skillbuilder7.2

Team Tower Power

Purpose   This exercise is designed to help you understand team roles, team development, and other issues in the development and maintenance of effective teams.

Materials   The instructor will provide enough Lego pieces or similar materials for each team to complete the assigned task. All teams should have identical, or very similar, number and shapes of pieces. The instructor will need a measuring tape and stopwatch. Students may use writing materials during the design stage (Step 2 below). The instructor will distribute a Team Objectives Sheet and Tower Specifications Effectiveness Sheet to all teams.

Instructions

- *Step 1:* The instructor will divide the class into teams. Depending on class size and space available, teams may have between four to seven members, but all should be approximately equal size.

- *Step 2:* Each team is given 20 minutes to design a tower that uses only the materials provided, is freestanding, and provides an optimal return on investment. Team members may wish to draw their tower on paper or flip chart to assist the tower's design. Teams are free to practice building their tower during this stage. Preferably, teams are assigned to their own rooms so the design can be created privately. During this stage, each team will complete the Team Objectives Sheet distributed by the instructor. This sheet requires the Tower Specifications Effectiveness Sheet, also distributed by the instructor.

- *Step 3:* Each team will show the instructor that it has completed its Team Objectives Sheet. Then, with all teams in the same room, the instructor will announce the start of the construction phase. The time elapsed for construction will be closely monitored and the instructor will occasionally call out time elapsed (particularly if there is no clock in the room).

- *Step 4:* Each team will advise the instructor as soon as it has completed its tower. The team will write down the time elapsed that the instructor has determined. It may be asked to assist the instructor by counting the number of blocks used and height of the tower. This information is also written on the Team Objectives Sheet. Then, the team calculates its profit.

- *Step 5:* After presenting the results, the class will discuss the team dynamics elements that contribute to team effectiveness. Team members will discuss their strategy, division of labor (team roles), expertise within the team, and other elements of team dynamics.

Source: Several published and online sources describe variations of this exercise, but there is no known origin to this activity.

>self-assessment.skillbuilder7.3

Team Roles Preferences Scale

Teams depend on their members to fulfill several roles related to the task and maintenance of the team. This self-assessment is designed to help you to identify your preferred roles in meetings and similar team activities. Read each of the statements in this instrument and indicate the response that you believe best reflects your position regarding each statement. This exercise is completed alone so students assess themselves honestly without concerns of social comparison. However, class discussion will focus on the roles that people assume in team settings. This scale only assesses a few team roles.

>self-assessment.skillbuilder7.4

The Team Player Inventory

How much do you like working in teams? Some of us avoid teams wherever possible; others tolerate team work; still others thrive in team environments. This exercise is designed to help you estimate the extent to which you are positively predisposed to work in teams. Read each statement in this scale and indicate the extent to which you agree or disagree with that statement. This exercise is completed alone so students assess themselves honestly without concerns of social comparison. However, class discussion will focus on the characteristics of individuals who are more or less compatible with working in teams.

Find the full self-assessments on the OLC at
www.mhhe.com/mcshaneess

chapter 8

Communicating in Teams and Organizations

Sun Microsystems president Jonathan Schwartz says that blogs have a lot to offer as a communication medium in organizations.

>**learning**objectives

After reading this chapter, you should be able to

- Explain the importance of communication and diagram the communication process.
- Describe problems with communicating through electronic mail.
- Identify two ways in which nonverbal communication differs from verbal communication.
- Identify two conditions requiring a channel with high media richness.
- Identify several common communication barriers.
- Discuss the degree to which men and women communicate differently.
- Outline the key elements of active listening.
- Summarize four communication strategies in organizational hierarchies.

Having a conversation with 90,000 staff in 48 countries is a monumental challenge for any chief executive. Yet Intel CEO Paul Otellini comes close to this goal by writing his own weblog for employees. Blogs (as weblogs are commonly called) are online journals or diaries. Otellini writes in his blog every few weeks, including thoughts on Intel's future and its competitors. His blog, which is restricted to Intel employees, also includes a forum where employees can add their views.

"[Paul's] blog was a good idea," wrote an Intel employee on Otellini's blog forum. "One of Intel's biggest problems today is its sprawling hugeness . . . with little top-down communication. The blog does 'top-down' one step better. It's almost like a subordinate brown bag luncheon with the top dog."

One of the strongest advocates of corporate blogs is Sun Microsystems president Jonathan Schwartz. "We believe this kind of communication creates community, and that a solid community around a company is not a threat—it's an ideal," suggests Schwartz, whose own public blog attracts 200,000 readers each month. "There's an immediacy of interaction you can get with your audience through blogging that's hard to get any other way, except by face-to-face communication." Schwartz writes his blog for the developer community, but it is equally valuable for employees who want to know what top management is thinking.

"At the end of the day, the job of any good leader at any corporation is to communicate," says Schwartz.

Sun, IBM, and a few other companies also provide resources for employees to create their own personal blogs. IBM has several outward-facing blogs for customers, but its inward-facing (i.e., restricted to IBM employees) BlogCentral hosts more than 3,000 personal blogs created by employees who want to share their thoughts and experiences with co-workers. "Because BlogCentral is searchable and because you can easily see the latest postings across BlogCentral as a whole, it can help you discover colleagues throughout the company with interests similar to your own," explains IBM researcher Dan Gruen.

Meanwhile, Children's Hospital and Regional Medical Center in Seattle is applying blogs in another way to improve corporate communication. Rather than having professionals write employee newsletters or e-zines, the hospital keeps employees up-to-date through volunteer bloggers scattered throughout the organization. Dozens of Children's Hospital staff are authorized to post news and events in their departments to a central blog site that employees visit to learn what's happening. "The distributed authorship of people from different departments means the content is fresher" than the hospital's previous newsletter or e-zine, says Children's Hospital web services manager Christian Watson.[1]

It's almost a cliché to say that information technologies have transformed communication in organizations. Yet we may still be at the beginning of this revolution. Wire cables and telephones introduced a century ago are giving way to e-mail, instant messaging, weblogs, and podcasting. Each of these inventions creates fascinating changes in how people interact with each other in the workplace. **Communication** refers to the process by which information is transmitted and understood between two or more people. The word *understood* is emphasized because transmitting the sender's intended meaning is the essence of good communication. Intel, Sun Microsystems, and other large organizations require innovative strategies to keep communication pathways open. Smaller businesses may have fewer structural bottlenecks, but they, too, can suffer from subtle communication barriers.

Effective communication is vital to all organizations because it coordinates work, fulfills employee needs, supports knowledge management, and improves decision making.[2] First, the ability to exchange information is an essential part of the coordination process, allowing employees to develop common mental models that synchronize their work. Second, communication is the glue that holds people together. The internal blogs at IBM, for example, are valuable because they help employees to satisfy their drive to bond.

Communication is also a key driver in knowledge management. It brings knowledge into the organization and distributes it to employees who require that information. Fourth, communication influences the quality of decision making. Individuals rarely have enough

communication
The process by which information is transmitted and understood between two or more people.

information alone to make decisions on the complex matters facing businesses today. Instead, problem solvers require information from co-workers, subordinates, and anyone else with relevant knowledge.

By improving decision making, knowledge management, employee needs, and coordination, workplace communication has a significant effect on organizational performance.[3] One report estimates that a company's market value increases by more than 7 percent when it improves its "communications integrity." Another identifies the leader's communication skills as an important influence on company performance. Communication is also a key ingredient in employee satisfaction and loyalty.

This chapter begins by presenting a model of the communication process. Next, the different types of communication channels, including computer-mediated communication, are described, followed by media richness as a factor to consider when choosing a communication medium. A discussion of several communication barriers follows, including cross-cultural and gender differences in communication. This chapter then outlines strategies to improve interpersonal communication, followed by a look at some options for communicating in organizational hierarchies, and concludes with a description of the pervasive organizational grapevine.

>A Model of Communication

The communication model presented in Exhibit 8.1 provides a useful conduit metaphor for thinking about the communication process.[4] According to this model, communication flows through channels between the sender and receiver. The sender forms a message and encodes it into words, gestures, voice intonations, and other symbols or signs. Next, the encoded message is transmitted to the intended receiver through one or more communication channels (media). The receiver senses the incoming message and decodes it into something meaningful. Ideally, the decoded meaning is what the sender had intended.

In most situations, the sender looks for evidence that the other person received and understood the transmitted message. This feedback may be a formal acknowledgment, such as "Yes, I know what you mean," or indirect evidence from the receiver's subsequent actions.

[**Exhibit 8.1**] The Communication Process Model

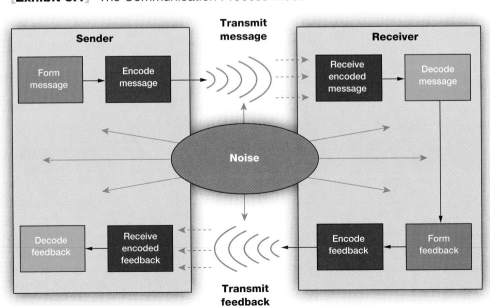

Notice that feedback repeats the communication process. Intended feedback is encoded, transmitted, received, and decoded from the receiver to the sender of the original message.

This model recognizes that communication is not a free-flowing conduit. Rather, the transmission of meaning from one person to another is hampered by *noise*—the psychological, social, and structural barriers that distort and obscure the sender's intended message. If any part of the communication process is distorted or broken, the sender and receiver will not have a common understanding of the message.

>Communication Channels

A critical part of the communication model is the channel or medium through which information is transmitted. There are two main types of channels: verbal and nonverbal. Verbal communication includes any oral or written means of transmitting meaning through words. Nonverbal communication, which we discuss later, is any part of communication that does not use words.

Verbal Communication

Different forms of verbal communication should be used in different situations. Face-to-face interaction is usually better than written methods for transmitting emotions and persuading the receiver. This is because nonverbal cues accompany oral communications, such as voice intonations and use of silence. Furthermore, face-to-face interaction provides the sender with immediate feedback from the receiver and the opportunity to adjust the emotional tone of the message accordingly. Ideas are easier to follow when written down than when communicated aurally, so written communication is more appropriate for recording and presenting technical details. Traditionally, written communication has been slow to develop and transmit, but electronic mail, weblogs, and other computer-mediated communication channels have significantly improved written communication efficiency.

Electronic Communication

Electronic mail (e-mail) is revolutionizing the way we communicate in organizational settings. It has also become the medium of choice in most workplaces because messages are quickly formed, edited, and stored. Information can be appended and transmitted to many people with a simple click of a mouse. E-mail is asynchronous (messages are sent and received at different times), so there is no need to coordinate a communication session. This technology also allows fairly random access to information; you can select any message in any order, skip to different parts of a message, and search for any word in any message on your computer.

E-mail works well for basic forms of coordination, such as confirming a meeting and for transmitting well-defined information. It has definitely changed how we communicate. Specifically, e-mail has increased the volume of communication, reduced some face-to-face and telephone communication, and increased communication with people further up the hierarchy.[5]

Problems with E-Mail
In spite of the wonders of e-mail, anyone who has used this communication medium knows its limitations. Here are the top four complaints:

1. *Poor medium for communicating emotions.* People rely on facial expressions and other nonverbal cues to interpret the emotional meaning of words, and e-mail lacks this parallel communication medium. E-mail aficionados try to clarify the

For the past 800 years, citizens in the port city of Liverpool, England, have relied on face-to-face communication to conduct trade and resolve their differences. But e-mail has weakened the noble practice of dialogue to such an extent that Liverpool City Council banned e-mail on Wednesdays. "We'd seen a doubling in internal e-mails and found a lot of e-mails were unnecessary," says Liverpool City Council chief executive David Henshaw. "A lot of the stuff could be dealt with over the phone, or by getting up and walking to the person next to you." While banning e-mail for one day each week may seem strong medicine, John Caudwell became so fed up with this form of communication that he took more extreme measures. The founder and CEO of British cell phone company Phones 4U banned his 2,500 employees from e-mailing each other at any time! E-mail is allowed only sparingly when communicating with customers. Caudwell's draconian action was triggered when his head office and retail store staff "were beginning to show signs of being constrained by e-mail proliferation. The ban brought an instant, dramatic, and positive effect," claims Caudwell.[7]

emotional tone of their messages by inserting graphic faces called emoticons (smileys), but they definitely do not replace the full complexity of the human face.

2. *Reduces politeness and respect.* E-mail messages are often less diplomatic than written letters because individuals can post e-mail messages before their emotions subside. Also, e-mail is impersonal, so people are more likely to write things that would never be said verbally in face-to-face conversation. Fortunately, research has found that **flaming** decreases as teams move to later stages of development and when explicit norms and rules of communication are established.[6]

flaming
The act of sending an emotionally charged e-mail to others.

3. *Poor medium for ambiguous, complex, and novel situations.* E-mail requires a moderate level of mutual understanding between the sender and receiver. Coordinating through e-mail in ambiguous, complex, and novel situations, on the other hand, requires communication channels that quickly send a larger volume of information and offer equally rapid feedback. In other words, when the issue gets messy, stop e-mailing and start talking, preferably face-to-face.

4. *Contributes to information overload.* As mentioned earlier, the volume of communication has definitely increased with the introduction of e-mail. This occurs because e-mails can be easily created and copied to thousands of people through group mailbox systems. There is good news on the horizon: The number of e-mail messages will probably decrease as people become more familiar with it.

Other Computer-Mediated Communication

Intranets, extranets, Blackberry wireless, instant messaging, blogging, podcasting, and other forms of computer-mediated communication are fueling the hyperfast world of corporate information sharing.[8] As described in the opening story to this chapter, companies are beginning to use blogs (weblogs) as a way for executives to communicate more personally with employees. Most blogs are started by employees because it gives them freedom of expression and a vehicle to share ideas with a large audience.

Employees at IBM, Sun Microsystems, and some other companies now use *instant messaging* (IM) almost as much as e-mail to transmit information quickly with co-workers. IM is more efficient than e-mail because messages are brief (usually just a sentence or two with acronyms and sound-alike letters for words) and appear on the receiver's screen as soon as they are sent. IM also creates real-time communities of practice as employees form clustered conversations around specific topics and fields of expertise. This clustered conversation (each group in a different window) produces yet another advantage—employees can carry on several conversations at the same time.[9]

Nonverbal Communication

Nonverbal communication includes facial gestures, voice intonation, physical distance, and even silence. This communication channel is necessary where noise or physical distance prevents effective verbal exchanges and the need for immediate feedback precludes written communication. But even in quiet face-to-face meetings, most information is communicated nonverbally. Rather like a parallel conversation, nonverbal cues signal subtle information to both parties, such as reinforcing their interest in the verbal discussion or demonstrating their relative status in the relationship.[10]

Nonverbal communication differs from verbal communication in a couple of ways. First, it is less rule-bound than verbal communication. We receive a lot of formal training on how to understand spoken words, but very little on understanding the nonverbal signals that accompany those words. Consequently, nonverbal cues are generally more ambiguous and susceptible to misinterpretation. At the same time, many facial expressions (such as smiling) are hardwired and universal, thereby providing the only reliable means of communicating across cultures.

The other difference is that verbal communication is typically conscious, whereas most nonverbal communication is automatic and unconscious. We normally plan the words we say or write, but we rarely plan every blink, smile, or other gesture during a conversation. Indeed, as we just mentioned, many of these facial expressions communicate the same meaning across cultures because they are hardwired unconscious or preconscious responses to human emotions.[11] For example, pleasant emotions cause the brain center to widen the mouth, whereas negative emotions produce constricted facial expressions (squinting eyes, pursed lips, etc.).

>Media Richness

Probably the most important question to ask when attempting to transmit information is "What communication channel is most appropriate in this situation." We partly answered this question in the previous section by identifying advantages and disadvantages of the various communication channels. However, a critical factor to consider when selecting a communication channel is **media richness**. Media richness refers to the medium's data-carrying capacity—the volume and variety of information that can be transmitted during a specific time.[12]

Exhibit 8.2 illustrates various communication channels arranged in a hierarchy of richness. This hierarchy is determined by three factors. First, rich media simultaneously use multiple communication media. For instance, face-to-face communication scores high on media richness because it includes both verbal and nonverbal information exchange. Second, rich media allow immediate feedback from receiver to sender. Third, rich media allow the sender to customize the message to the receiver. Face-to-face conversations are developed specifically for one or a few people, whereas financial reports have low media richness because one size fits all—everyone gets the same information.

Rich media are better than lean media when the communication situation is nonroutine and ambiguous. In nonroutine situations (such as a problem that you haven't come across before), the sender and receiver have little common experience, so they need to transmit a large volume of information with immediate feedback. Lean media work well in routine

media richness
The data-carrying capacity of a communication medium, including the volume and variety of information it can transmit.

[Exhibit 8.2] Media Richness Hierarchy

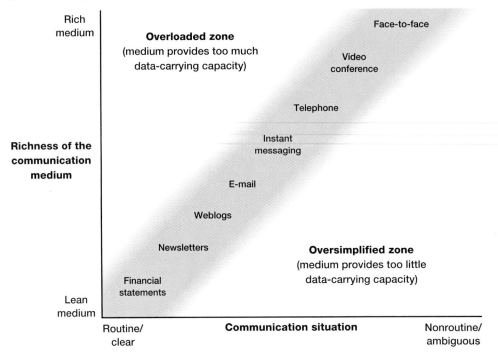

Source: Based on R. Lengel and R. Daft, "The Selection of Communication Media as an Executive Skill," *Academy of Management Executive* 2, no. 3 (August 1988), p. 226; R. L. Daft and R. H. Lengel, "Information Richness: A New Approach to Managerial Behavior and Organization Design," *Research in Organizational Behavior,* 1984, p. 199.

situations because the sender and receiver have common expectations through shared mental models. Ambiguous situations also require rich media because the parties must share large amounts of information with immediate feedback to resolve multiple and conflicting interpretations of their observations and experiences.[13]

Choosing the wrong level of media richness for the situation can make the communication experience less effective in different ways. When the situation is routine or clear, using a rich medium—such as holding a special meeting—would seem like a waste of time. On the other hand, if a unique and ambiguous issue is handled through e-mail or another lean medium, then issues take longer to resolve and misunderstandings are more likely to occur.

>Communication Barriers (Noise)

In spite of the best intentions of sender and receiver to communicate, several barriers (called *noise* earlier in Exhibit 8.1) inhibit the effective exchange of information. As author George Bernard Shaw wrote, "The greatest problem with communication is the illusion that it has been accomplished." Shaw has good reason to be skeptical about how well people actually receive the intended message. Figuratively speaking, communication noise can be deafening at times.

To being with, the sender's message often gets distorted or lost completely due to the receiver's imperfect perceptual process. We don't listen as well as people expect us to, and our needs and expectations influence what signals get noticed and ignored. Even if the perceptual process is well tuned, messages sometimes get filtered on their way up or down the corporate hierarchy. Filtering may involve deleting or delaying negative information or using less harsh words so the message sounds more favorable.[14] Filtering is most common where the organization rewards employees who communicate mainly positive information and among employees with strong career mobility aspirations.

Language Barriers

Language problems can be a huge source of communication noise. Recall from Exhibit 8.1 that the sender encodes the message and the receiver decodes it. To make this process work, both parties need to have the same "codebook"; that is, they need to have a mutual understanding of what the words or other symbols being sent mean. The language barrier is obvious when the parties speak different tongues, such as English and Mandarin. But even when both people speak English, they might interpret words and phrases differently. If someone says "Would you like to check the figures again?" he or she may be politely *telling* you to double-check the figures, or might be merely *asking* if you want to do this.

Also, people who generally speak the same language might not understand specific jargon within that language. **Jargon** consists of technical language and acronyms as well as recognized words with specialized meaning in specific organizations or social groups. Some jargon can improve communication efficiency when both sender and receiver understand this specialized language. But technical experts (including organizational behavior teachers!) sometimes use jargon without realizing that listeners don't have the codebook to translate those special words.

jargon
Technical language and acronyms, as well as recognized words with specialized meanings, in specific organizations or groups.

Information Overload

According to a recent survey, employees receive an average of 54 e-mail messages every day. Add in voice mail, cell phone text messages, Web site scanning, PDF file downloads, hard-copy documents, and other sources of incoming information, and you have a perfect recipe for **information overload**.[15] Information overload occurs when the volume of information received exceeds the person's capacity to get through it. Employees have a certain *information processing capacity*—the amount of information that they are able to process in a fixed unit of time. At the same time, jobs have a varying *information load*—the amount of information to be processed per unit of time.[16]

information overload
A condition in which the volume of information received exceeds the person's capacity to process it.

Information overload is a barrier to effective communication because information gets overlooked or misinterpreted when people can't process it fast enough. It has also become a common cause of workplace stress. These problems can be minimized by increasing information processing capacity, reducing the job's information load, or through a combination of both. Information processing capacity increases when we learn to read faster, scan through documents more efficiently, and remove distractions that slow information processing speed. Time management also increases information processing capacity. When information overload is temporary, information processing capacity can increase by working longer hours.

Three strategies can reduce information load: buffering, omitting, and summarizing.[17] Microsoft chairman Bill Gates applies all three and, as a result, reads only about 30–40 e-mail messages each day. First, Gates receives approximately 300 e-mails daily from Microsoft addresses that are outside a core group of people; these e-mails are buffered— routed to an assistant who reads each and sends Gates only those considered essential reading. Second, Gates applies the omitting strategy by using software rules to redirect e-mails from distribution lists, nonessential sources, and junk mail (spam). These e-mails are

Patricia Oliveira made several cultural adjustments when she moved from Brazil to Australia. One of the more humorous incidents occurred in the Melbourne office where she works. A co-worker would stick his thumbs up when asked about something, signaling that everything was OK. But the gesture had a totally different meaning to Oliveiri and other people from Brazil. "He asked me why I was laughing and I had to explain that in Brazil, that sign means something not very nice," recalls Oliveiri. "After that, everyone started doing it to the boss. It was really funny."[22]

dumped into preassigned folders to be read later, if ever. Third, Gates likely relies on the summarizing strategy by reading executive summaries rather than entire reports.

Cross-Cultural Communication Barriers

As globalization and cultural diversity increase, you can be sure that cross-cultural communication problems will also increase. Words are easily misunderstood in verbal communication, either because the receiver has a limited vocabulary or the sender's accent distorts the usual sound of some words. The problem discussed earlier of ambiguous language becomes amplified across cultures. For example, a French executive might call an event a *catastrophe* as a casual exaggeration, whereas someone in Germany usually interprets this word literally as an earth-shaking event.[18]

Communication includes silence, but its use and meaning vary from one culture to another.[19] A recent study estimated that silence and pauses represented 30 percent of conversation time between Japanese doctors and patients, compared with only 8 percent of the time between American doctors and patients. In Japan, silence symbolizes respect and indicates that the listener is thoughtfully contemplating what has just been said.[20] In contrast, most people in the United States view silence as a *lack* of communication and often interpret long breaks as a sign of disagreement. Similarly, talking while another person is speaking is considered rude in Japan, whereas it is usually interpreted as a sign of interest and involvement in Brazil.

Nonverbal Differences

Nonverbal communication represents another potential area for misunderstanding across cultures. Many unconscious or involuntary nonverbal cues (such as smiling) have the same meaning around the world, but deliberate gestures often have different interpretations. For example, most of us shake our head from side to side to say "No," but a variation of head shaking means "I understand" to many people in India. Filipinos raise their eyebrows to give an affirmative answer, yet Arabs interpret this expression (along with clicking one's tongue) as a negative response. Most Americans are taught to maintain eye contact with the speaker to show interest and respect, whereas people in some other cultures learn at an early age to show respect by looking down when an older or more senior person is talking to them.[21]

Gender Differences in Communication

After reading popular-press books on how men and women communicate, you might come to the conclusion that they are completely different life forms.[23] In reality, men and women have similar communication practices, but there are subtle distinctions that can occasionally lead to misunderstanding and conflict. One distinction is that men are more likely than women to view conversations as negotiations of relative status and power. They assert their power by directly giving advice to others (e.g., "You should do the following") and using combative language. There is also evidence that men dominate the talk time in conversations with women, as well as interrupt more and adjust their speaking style less than do women.[24]

Men engage in more "report talk," in which the primary function of the conversation is impersonal and efficient information exchange. Women also do report talk, particularly when conversing with men, but conversations among women have a higher incidence of relationship building through "rapport talk." Rather than asserting status, women use indirect requests such as "Have you considered . . . ?" Similarly, women apologize more often and seek advice from others more quickly than do men. Finally, research fairly consistently indicates that women are more sensitive than men to nonverbal cues in face-to-face meetings.[25]

Both men and women usually understand each other, but these subtle differences are occasional irritants. For instance, female scientists have complained that adversarial interaction among male scientists makes it difficult for women to participate in meaningful dialogue.[26] Another irritant occurs when women seek empathy but receive male dominance in response. Specifically, women sometimes discuss their personal experiences and problems to develop closeness with the receiver. But when men hear problems, they quickly suggest solutions because this asserts their control over the situation. As well as frustrating a woman's need for common understanding, the advice actually says, "You and I are different; you have the problem and I have the answer." Meanwhile, men become frustrated because they can't understand why women don't appreciate their advice.

>Improving Interpersonal Communication

Effective interpersonal communication depends on the sender's ability to get the message across and the receiver's performance as an active listener. In this section, we outline these two essential features of effective interpersonal communication.

Getting Your Message Across

This chapter began with the statement that effective communication occurs when the other person receives and understands the message. To accomplish this difficult task, the sender must learn to empathize with the receiver, repeat the message, choose an appropriate time for the conversation, and be descriptive rather than evaluative.

- *Empathize.* Recall from earlier chapters that empathy is a person's ability to understand and be sensitive to the feelings, thoughts, and situation of others. In conversations, this involves putting yourself in the receiver's shoes when encoding the message. For instance, be sensitive to words that may be ambiguous or trigger the wrong emotional response.

- *Repeat the message.* Rephrase the key points a couple of times. The saying "Tell them what you're going to tell them; tell them; then tell them what you've told them" reflects this need for redundancy.

- *Use timing effectively.* Your message competes with other messages and noise, so find a time when the receiver is less likely to be distracted by these other matters.

- *Be descriptive.* Focus on the problem, not the person, if you have negative information to convey. People stop listening when the information attacks their self-esteem. Also, suggest things the listener can do to improve rather than point to him or her as a problem.

[Exhibit 8.3] Active Listening Process and Strategies

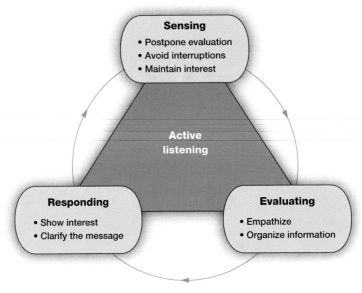

Active Listening

"Nature gave people two ears but only one tongue, which is a gentle hint that they should listen more than they talk."[27] To follow this sage advice, we need to recognize that listening is a process of actively sensing the sender's signals, evaluating them accurately, and responding appropriately. These three components of listening—sensing, evaluating, and responding—reflect the listener's side of the communication model described at the beginning of this chapter. Listeners receive the sender's signals, decode them as intended, and provide appropriate and timely feedback to the sender (see Exhibit 8.3). Active listeners constantly cycle through sensing, evaluating, and responding during the conversation and engage in various activities to improve these processes.[28]

Sensing
Sensing is the process of receiving signals from the sender and paying attention to them. Active listeners improve sensing in three ways. First, they postpone evaluation by not forming an opinion until the speaker has finished. Second, they avoid interrupting the speaker's conversation. Third, they remain motivated to listen to the speaker.

Evaluating
This component of listening includes understanding the message meaning, evaluating the message, and remembering the message. To improve their evaluation of the conversation, active listeners empathize with the speaker—they try to understand and be sensitive to the speaker's feelings, thoughts, and situation. Evaluation also improves by organizing the speaker's ideas during the communication episode.

Responding
Responding, the third component of listening, is feedback to the sender, which motivates and directs the speaker's communication. Active listeners accomplish this by maintaining sufficient eye contact and sending back channel signals (e.g., "I see"), both of which show interest. They also respond by clarifying the message—rephrasing the speaker's ideas at appropriate breaks ("So you're saying that . . . ?").

>Communicating in Organizational Hierarchies

So far we have focused on microlevel issues in the communication process, namely, the dynamics of sending and receiving information between two people in various situations. But in this era where knowledge is competitive advantage, corporate leaders also need to maintain an open flow of communication up, down, and across the organization. In this section, we discuss four organization-wide communication strategies: workspace design, e-zines/blogs/wikis, employee surveys, and direct communication with top management.

Workspace Design

The ability and motivation to communicate is, to some extent, influenced by the physical space in which employees work. The location and design of hallways, offices, cubicles, and communal areas (cafeterias, elevators) all shape whom we speak to as well as the frequency of that communication. Some companies try to encourage communication within the team by organizing employees into clusters. The cluster approach is used at product design firm IDEO. The physical space literally groups employees together so face-to-face communication within the team is easy, whereas interaction with people in other teams is minimized.

Another increasingly popular workspace strategy is to replace traditional offices with open space arrangements, where all employees, including management, work in the same open area. Anecdotal evidence suggests that people do communicate more often with fewer walls between them. However, research also suggests that open office design potentially increases employee stress due to the loss of privacy and personal space. According to an analysis of 13,000 employee surveys in 40 major organizations, the most important function of workspace is to provide a place to concentrate on work without distraction. The second most important function is to support informal communication with co-workers.[29] In other words, workspace needs to balance privacy with opportunities for social interaction.

E-Zines, Blogs, and Wikis

For decades, employees have received official company news through hard-copy newsletters and magazines. Many firms still use these communication devices, but most have supplemented or replaced them completely with web-based information sources. Web-based or PDF-only format newsletters, called *e-zines,* are inexpensive and allow companies to post new information quickly. However, information from e-zines tends to be brief because many employees have difficulty reading long articles on a computer screen.[31]

Communication was a top priority when Pixar Animation Studios designed its new campus in Emeryville, California, a few years ago. The animation company that brought us *The Incredibles, Finding Nemo,* and other blockbuster films created work areas that cluster team members and encourage ongoing informal communication. At the same time, the campus is designed such that employees share knowledge through happenstance interactions with people on other teams. Pixar executives call this the "bathroom effect," because team members must leave their isolated pods to fetch their mail, have lunch, or visit the restroom. The building also invites staff to mingle in the central airy atrium. "It promotes that chance encounter," says Pixar creative director John Lasseter. "You run into people constantly. It worked from the minute we arrived. We just blossomed here."[30]

The opening story to this chapter described how *blogs* are entering the corporate world as another communication vehicle. Blogs written by senior executives offer direct communication to employees and, if written casually, have a personal touch that makes the information more credible than formal magazines. Executive blogs also allow employees to submit their comments, which isn't possible in e-zines or newsletters. In addition to executive blogs, Children's Hospital in Seattle and a few other firms are creating blogs in which employees in each work unit post updates of events in their area.

Wikis are a collaborative variation of blogs in which anyone in a group can write, edit, or remove material from the website. Wikipedia, the popular online encyclopedia is a massive example of a wiki. Although still rare in organizations, wikis might eventually generate a treasure trove of corporate knowledge that attracts employee attention for its collective wisdom and high involvement.[32]

Employee Surveys

Most of America's "best" companies to work for conduct regular employee opinion surveys. Most of them survey employees to monitor worker morale, particularly as part of broader measures of corporate performance. For example, Eaton Corp. surveys its 55,000 employees in 21 countries on a variety of topics, including business ethics, values, employee engagement, employee relations, manager effectiveness, and strategic vision. "The responses from our employees really do drive action, and they are as much a component of our business as strategic, financial, or succession planning," says an executive at the Cleveland-based industrial manufacturing firm.[33]

Direct Communication with Top Management

"The best fertilizer in any field is that of the farmer's footsteps!" This old Chinese saying means that farms are most successful when the farmers spend time in the fields directly observing the crop's development. In an organizational context, this means that to fully understand the issues, senior executives need to get out of the executive suite and meet directly with employees at all levels and on their turf. Nearly 40 years ago, people at Hewlett-Packard coined a phrase for this communication strategy: **management by walking around (MBWA)**.[34]

management by walking around (MBWA)
A communication practice in which executives get out of their offices and learn from others in the organization through face-to-face dialogue.

Along with MBWA, executives are communicating directly with employees through "town hall meetings," where large groups hear about a merger or other special news directly from the key decision makers. Others attend employee roundtable forums to hear opinions from a small representation of staff about various issues. All of these direct communication strategies potentially minimize filtering because executives listen directly to employees. They also help executives acquire a deeper meaning and quicker understanding of internal organizational problems. A third benefit of direct communication is that employees might have more empathy for decisions made further up the corporate hierarchy.

>Communicating through the Grapevine

grapevine
An unstructured and informal communication network founded on social relationships rather than organizational charts or job descriptions.

No matter how much corporate leaders try to communicate through e-zines, blogs, MBWA, and other means, employees will still rely on the oldest communication channel: the corporate **grapevine**. The grapevine is an unstructured and informal network founded on social relationships rather than organizational charts or job descriptions. What do employees think about the grapevine? Surveys of employees in two firms—one in Florida, the other in California—provide the answer. Both surveys found that almost all employees use the grapevine, but very few of them prefer this source of information. The Californian survey also reported that only one-third of employees believe grapevine information is credible. In other words, employees turn to the grapevine when they have few other options.[35]

Grapevine Characteristics

Research conducted several decades ago reported that the grapevine transmits information very rapidly in all directions throughout the organization. The typical pattern is a cluster chain, whereby a few people actively transmit rumors to many others. The grapevine works through informal social networks, so it is more active where employees have similar backgrounds and are able to communicate easily. Many rumors seem to have at least a kernel of truth, possibly because they are transmitted through media-rich communication channels (e.g., face to face) and employees are motivated to communicate the information. Nevertheless, the grapevine distorts information by deleting fine details and exaggerating key points of the story.[36]

Some of the grapevine characteristics identified in these old studies might still be true, but other features of the grapevine would have changed due to the dramatic effects of information technologies in the workplace. E-mail, instant messages, and even blogs have replaced the traditional water cooler as sources of gossip. Social networks have expanded as employees communicate with each other around the globe, not just around the next cubicle. Public blogs and web forums have extended gossip to anyone, not just employees connected to social networks.

Grapevine Benefits and Limitations

Should the grapevine be encouraged, tolerated, or quashed? The difficulty in answering this question is that the grapevine has both benefits and limitations.[37] One benefit, as was mentioned earlier, is that employees rely on the grapevine when information is not available through formal channels. It is also a means through which organizational stories and other symbols of the organization's culture are communicated. A third benefit of the grapevine is that this social interaction relieves anxiety. This explains why rumor mills are most active during times of uncertainty.[38] Finally, the grapevine is associated with the drive to bond. Being a recipient of gossip is a sign of inclusion, according to evolutionary psychologists. Trying to quash the grapevine is, in some respects, an attempt to undermine the natural human drive for social interaction.[39]

While the grapevine offers these benefits, it is not the preferred communication medium. Grapevine information is sometimes so distorted that it escalates rather than reduces employee anxiety. Furthermore, employees develop more negative attitudes toward the organization when management is slower than the grapevine in communicating information. What should corporate leaders do with the grapevine? The best advice seems to be to listen to the grapevine as a signal of employee anxiety, then correct the cause of this anxiety. Some companies also listen to the grapevine and step in to correct blatant errors and fabrications. Most important, corporate leaders need to view the grapevine as a competitor and eventually win the challenge to inform employees before they receive the news through the grapevine.

>chapter summary

Communication refers to the process by which information is transmitted and *understood* between two or more people. Communication supports work coordination, employee well-being, knowledge management, and decision making. The communication process involves forming, encoding, and transmitting the intended message to a receiver, who then decodes the message and provides feedback to the sender. Effective communication occurs when the sender's thoughts are transmitted to and understood by the intended receiver.

Electronic mail (e-mail) is an increasingly popular way to communicate, and it has changed communication patterns in organizational settings. However, e-mail is ineffective channel for communicating emotions, tends to reduce politeness and respect, is an inefficient medium for communicating in ambiguous, complex, and novel situations, and contributes to information overload. Instant messaging, blogs, and podcasts are also gaining popularity in organizations.

Nonverbal communication includes facial gestures, voice intonation, physical distance, and even silence. Unlike verbal communication, nonverbal communication is less rule-bound and is mostly automatic and unconscious. Media richness refers to the medium's data-carrying capacity—the volume and variety of information that can be transmitted during a specific time. Nonroutine and ambiguous situations require rich media.

Several barriers create noise in the communication process. People misinterpret messages because of perceptual biases. Some information is filtered out as it gets passed up or down the hierarchy. Language barriers such as ambiguity and jargon undermine effective communication. Information overload causes people to overlook or misinterpret information because they can't process it fast enough.

Cross-cultural communication barriers include language and accent differences, different meanings of silence and conversation overlaps, and different interpretations of conscious nonverbal signals. There are also some communication differences between men and women, such as the tendency for men to exert status and engage in report talk in conversations, whereas women use more rapport talk and are more sensitive than are men to nonverbal cues.

To get a message across, the sender must learn to empathize with the receiver, repeat the message, choose an appropriate time for the conversation, and be descriptive rather than evaluative. Listening includes sensing, evaluating, and responding. Active listeners support these processes by postponing evaluation, avoiding interruptions, maintaining interest, empathizing, organizing information, showing interest, and clarifying the message.

Some companies try to encourage informal communication through workspace design, although open offices run the risk of increasing stress and reducing the ability to concentrate on work. Many larger organizations also rely on e-zines to communicate corporate news. Employee surveys are widely used to measure employee attitudes or involve employees in corporate decisions. Some executives also meet directly with employees, either through management by walking around or other arrangements, to facilitate communication across the organization.

In any organization, employees rely on the grapevine, particularly during times of uncertainty. The grapevine is an unstructured and informal network founded on social relationships rather than organizational charts or job descriptions. Although early research identified several unique features of the grapevine, some of these features may be changing as the Internet plays an increasing role in grapevine communication.

>key.terms

communication 157

flaming 160

grapevine 168

information overload 163

jargon 163

management by walking around (MBWA) 168

media richness 161

>critical.thinking.questions

1. A company in a country that is just entering the information age intends to introduce electronic mail for office staff at its three buildings located throughout the city. Describe two benefits as well as two potential problems that employees will likely experience with this medium.

2. Corporate and employee blogs might become increasingly popular over the next few years. What are the advantages and disadvantages of this communication medium?

3. Compare and contrast e-mail with instant messaging. Under what conditions is one more effective than the other?

4. This chapter states that rich media are more effective than lean media when the situation is ambiguous or novel. In your opinion, what circumstances might allow two people to use fairly lean media (such as e-mail) in spite of the novelty or ambiguity of the situation?

5. Under what conditions, if any, do you think it is appropriate to use e-mail to notify an employee that he or she has been laid off or fired? Why is e-mail usually considered an inappropriate channel to convey this information?

6. Explain why men and women are sometimes frustrated with each other's communication behaviors.

7. In your opinion, has the introduction of e-mail and other information technologies increased or decreased the amount of information flowing through the corporate grapevine? Explain your answer.

8. Wikis are collaborative websites where anyone in the group can post, edit, or delete any information. Where might this communication technology be most useful in organizations?

>case.study:skillbuilder8.1

Bridging the Two Worlds— The Organizational Dilemma

By William Todorovic, Purdue University

I had been hired by Aluminum Elements Corp. (AEC), and it was my first day of work. I was 26 years old, and I was now the manager of AEC's customer service group, which looked after customers, logistics, and some of the raw material purchasing. My superior, George, was the vice president of the company. AEC manufactured most of its products from aluminum, the majority of which were destined for the construction industry.

As I walked around the shop floor, the employees appeared to be concentrating on their jobs, barely noticing me. Management held daily meetings, in which various production issues were discussed. No one from the shop floor was invited to these meetings, unless there was a specific problem. Later, I also learned that management had separate washrooms, separate lunchrooms, as well as other perks that floor employees did not have. Most of the floor employees felt that management, although polite on the surface, did not really feel they had anything to learn from the floor employees.

John, who worked on the aluminum slitter, a crucial operation required before any other operations could commence, had a number of unpleasant encounters with George. As a result, George usually sent written memos to the floor in order to avoid a direct confrontation with John.

Because the directions in the memos were complex, these memos were often more than two pages in length.

One morning, as I was walking around, I noticed that John was very upset. Feeling that perhaps there was something I could do, I approached John and asked him if I could help. He indicated that everything was just fine. From the looks of the situation, and John's body language, I felt that he was willing to talk, but John knew that this was not the way things were done at AEC. Tony, who worked at the machine next to John's, then cursed and said that the office guys only cared about schedules, not about the people down on the floor. I just looked at him, and then said that I only began working here last week but thought I could address some of their issues. Tony gave me a strange look, shook his head, and went back to his machine. I could hear him still swearing as I left. Later I realized that most of the office staff were also offended by Tony's language.

On the way back to my office, Lesley, a recently hired engineer from Russia, approached me and pointed out that the employees were not accustomed to management talking to them. Management only issued orders and made demands. As we discussed the different perceptions between office and floor staff, we were interrupted by a very loud lunch bell, which startled me. I was happy to join Lesley for lunch, but she asked me why I was not eating in the office lunchroom. I replied that if I was going to understand how AEC worked, I had to get to know all the people better. In addition, I realized that this was not how things were done and wondered about the nature of this apparent division between the management and the floor. In the lunchroom, the other workers were amazed to see me there, commenting that I was just new and had not learned the ropes yet.

After lunch, when I asked George, my supervisor, about his recent confrontation with John, George was surprised that John got upset and exclaimed, "I just wanted John to know that he did a great job, and as a result, we will be able to ship on time one large order to the West Coast. In fact, I thought I was complimenting him."

Earlier, Lesley had indicated that certain behavior was expected from management and therefore from me. I reasoned that I do not think that this behavior works, and besides it is not what I believe or how I care to behave. For the next couple of months, I simply walked around the floor and took every opportunity to talk to the shop floor employees. Often when the employees related specific information about their workplaces, I felt that it went over my head. Frequently I had to write down the information and revisit it later. I made a point of listening to them, identifying where they were coming from, and trying to understand them. I needed to keep my mind open to new ideas. Because the shop employees expected me to make requests and demands, I made a point of not doing any of that. Soon enough, the employees became friendly and started to accept me as one of their own, or at least as a different type of a management person.

During my third month of work, the employees showed me how to improve the scheduling of jobs, especially those on the aluminum slitter. In fact, the greatest contribution was made by John, who demonstrated better ways to combine the most common slitting sizes and reduce waste by retaining some of the common-sized material for new orders. Seeing the opportunity, I programmed a spreadsheet to calculate and track inventory. This, in addition to better planning and forecasting, allowed us to reduce our new order turnarounds from four to five weeks to in by 10 A.M. out by 5 P.M. on the same day.

By the time I was employed for four months, I realized that members from other departments came to me and asked me to relay messages to the shop employees. When I asked why they were delegating this task to me, they stated that I spoke the same language as the shop employees. Increasingly, I became the messenger for the office to floor shop communication.

One morning, George called me into his office and complimented me on the levels of customer service, and the improvements that have been achieved. As we talked, I mentioned that we could not have done it without John's help. "He really knows his stuff, and he is good," I said. I suggested that we consider him for some type of a promotion. Also, I hoped that this would be a positive gesture that would improve the communication between the office and shop floor.

George turned and pulled a flyer out of his desk. "Here is a management skills seminar. Do you think we should send John to it?"

"That is a great idea," I exclaimed, "Perhaps it would be good if he were to receive the news from you directly, George." George agreed, and after discussing some other issues, we departed company.

That afternoon, John came into my office, upset and ready to quit. "After all my effort and work, you guys are sending me for training seminars. So, am I not good enough for you?"

Discussion Questions

1. What barriers to effective communication existed in Aluminum Elements Corp.? How did the author deal with these? What would you do differently?

2. Identify and discuss why John was upset at the end of the case. What do you recommend the writer should do at this time?

>web.exercise:skillbuilder8.2

Analyzing the Blogosphere

Purpose   This exercise is designed to help you understand the dynamics of corporate blogs as a way to communicate around organizations.

Instructions

This activity is usually conducted in between classes as a homework assignment. The instructor will divide the class into teams (although this can also be conducted as individuals). Each team will identify a corporate blog (written by a company or government executive and aimed for customers, employees, or the wider community). The team will analyze content on the selected blog and answer the following questions for class (preferably with brief samples where applicable).

1. Who is the main intended audience of the selected blog?

2. To what extent do you think this blog attracts the interest of its intended audience? Please explain.

3. What are the main topics in recent postings about this organization? Are they mostly good or bad news? Why?

>team.exercise:skillbuilder8.3

Cross-Cultural Communication Game

Purpose   This exercise is designed to develop and test your knowledge of cross-cultural differences in communication and etiquette.

Materials   The instructor will provide one set of question/answer cards to each pair of teams.

Instructions

- *Step 1:* The class is divided into an even number of teams. Ideally, each team would have three students. (Teams may have more or less than three students if matched with an equal-sized team.) Each team is then paired with another team and the paired teams (team A and team B) are assigned a private space away from other matched teams.

- *Step 2:* The instructor will hand each pair of teams a stack of cards with the multiple-choice questions face down. These cards have questions and answers about cross-cultural differences in communication and etiquette. No books or other aids are allowed.

- *Step 3:* The exercise begins with a member of team A picking up one card from the top of the pile and asking the question on that card to students on team B. The information given to team B includes the question and all alternatives listed on the card. Team B has 30 seconds after the question and alternatives have been read to give an answer. Team B earns one point if the correct answer is given. If team B's answer is incorrect, however, team A earns that point. Correct answers to each question are indicated on the card and, of course, should not be revealed until the question is correctly answered or time is up. Whether or not team B answers correctly, it picks up the next card on the pile and asks it to members of team A. In other words, cards are read alternatively to each team. This procedure is repeated until all of the cards have been read or no time remains. The team receiving the most points wins.

Important note: The textbook provides very little information pertaining to the questions in this exercise. Rather, you must rely on past learning, logic, and luck to win.

© 2001 Steven L. McShane.

>self-assessment.skillbuilder8.4

Active Listening Skills Inventory

This self-assessment is designed to help you estimate your strengths and weaknesses on various dimensions of active listening. Think back to face-to-face conversations you have had with a co-worker or client in the office, hallway, factory floor, or other setting. Indicate the extent that each item in this instrument describes your behavior during those conversations. Answer each item as truthfully as possible so that you get an accurate estimate of where your active listening skills need improvement. This exercise is completed alone so students assess themselves honestly without concerns of social comparison. However, class discussion will focus on the important elements of active listening.

Find the full self-assessments on the OLC at
www.mhhe.com/mcshaneess

[chapter 9]

Power and Influence in the Workplace

Through excessive power and influence, former WorldCom CEO Bernard Ebbers (left), Scott Sullivan (right), and other executives perpetrated one of the largest cases of accounting fraud in history

>learningobjectives

After reading this chapter, you should be able to

- Define the meaning of power and counterpower.
- Describe the five bases of power in organizations.
- Explain how information relates to power in organizations.
- Discuss the four contingencies of power.
- Summarize the eight types of influence tactics.
- Discuss three contingencies to consider when deciding which influence tactic to use.
- Distinguish influence from organizational politics.
- Describe the organizational conditions and personal characteristics that support organizational politics.
- Identify ways to minimize organizational politics.

Bernie Ebbers built WorldCom, Inc. (now MCI, Inc.). into one of the world's largest telecommunications firms. Yet he and chief financial officer (CFO) Scott Sullivan have become better known for creating a massive corporate accounting fraud that led to the largest bankruptcy in U.S. history. Two investigative reports and subsequent court cases concluded that WorldCom executives were responsible for billions in fraudulent or unsupported accounting entries. How did this mammoth accounting scandal occur without anyone raising the alarm? Evidence suggests that Ebbers and Sullivan held considerable power and influence that prevented accounting staff from complaining, or even knowing, about the fraud.

Ebbers's inner circle held tight control over the flow of all financial information. The geographically dispersed accounting groups were discouraged from sharing information. Ebbers's group also restricted distribution of company-level financial reports and prevented sensitive reports from being prepared at all. Accountants didn't even have access to the computer files where some of the largest fraudulent entries were made. As a result, employees had to rely on Ebbers's executive team to justify the accounting entries that were requested.

Another reason employees complied with questionable accounting practices was that CFO Sullivan wielded immense personal power. He was considered a "whiz kid" with impeccable integrity who had won the prestigious "CFO Excellence Award." Thus, when Sullivan's office asked staff to make questionable entries, some accountants assumed Sullivan had found an innovative, and legal, accounting loophole. If Sullivan's expert power didn't work, other executives took a more coercive approach. Employees cited incidents where they were publicly berated for questioning headquarters' decisions and intimidated if they asked for more information. When one employee at a branch refused to alter an accounting entry, WorldCom's controller threatened to fly in from WorldCom's Mississippi headquarters to make the change himself. The employee changed the entry.

Ebbers had similar influence over WorldCom's board of directors. Sources indicate that his personal charisma and intolerance of dissension produced a passive board that rubber-stamped most of his recommendations. As one report concluded, "The Board of Directors appears to have embraced suggestions by Mr. Ebbers without question or dissent, even under circumstances where its members now readily acknowledge they had significant misgivings regarding his recommended course of action."[1]

The WorldCom saga illustrates how power and influence can have profound consequences for employee behavior and the organization's success. Although this story has an unhappy ending, power and influence can equally influence ethical conduct and improve corporate performance. The reality is that no one escapes from organizational power and influence. They exist in every business and, according to some writers, in every decision and action.

This chapter unfolds as follows: First, we define power and present a basic model depicting the dynamics of power in organizational settings. We then discuss the five bases of power, as well as information as a power base. Next, we look at the contingencies necessary to translate those sources into meaningful power. The latter part of this chapter examines the various types of influence in organizational settings as well as the contingencies of effective influence strategies. The final section of this chapter looks at situations in which influence becomes organizational politics, as well as ways of minimizing dysfunctional politics.

>The Meaning of Power

power
The capacity of a person, team, or organization to influence others.

Power is the capacity of a person, team, or organization to influence others.[2] Power is not the act of changing others' attitudes or behavior; it is only the potential to do so. People frequently have power they do not use; they might not even know they have power.

[Exhibit 9.1] Dependence in the Power Relationship

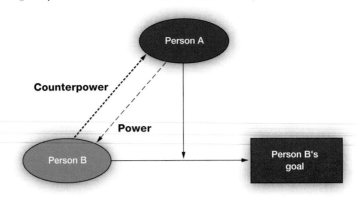

The most basic prerequisite of power is that one person or group believes it is dependent on another person or group for something of value.[3] This relationship is shown in Exhibit 9.1, where person A has power over person B by controlling something that person B needs to achieve his or her goals. You might have power over others by controlling a desired job assignment, useful information, important resources, or even the privilege of being associated with you! Furthermore, power is ultimately a perception, so people might gain power simply by convincing others that they have something of value. Thus, power exists when others believe that you control resources that they want.[4]

Although power requires dependence, it is really more accurate to say that the parties are interdependent. One party may be more dependent than the other, but the relationship exists only when each party has something of value to the other. Exhibit 9.1 shows a dashed line to illustrate the weaker party's (person B's) power over the dominant participant (person A). This **counterpower**, as it is known, is strong enough to maintain person A's participation in the exchange relationship. For example, executives have power over subordinates by controlling their job security and promotional opportunities. At the same time, employees have counterpower by controlling the ability to work productively and thereby creating a positive impression of the supervisor to his or her boss. Counterpower usually motivates executives to apply their power judiciously, so that the relationship is not broken.

counterpower
The capacity of a person, team, or organization to keep a more powerful person or group in the exchange relationship.

>Sources of Power in Organizations

Power derives from several sources and a few contingencies that determine the potential of those power sources.[5] Three sources of power—legitimate, reward, and coercive—originate mostly from the powerholder's formal position or informal role. In other words, the person is granted these power bases formally by the organization or informally by co-workers. Two other sources of power—expert and referent—originate from the powerholder's own characteristics; that is, the individual brings these power bases to the organization. Sources of power are connected to the power interdependence relationship described above because these sources are resources that the dependent person needs to achieve his or her goals. For example, your expertise is a source of power when others need that expertise to accomplish their objectives.

legitimate power
The capacity to influence others through formal authority.

Legitimate Power

Legitimate power is an agreement among organizational members that people in certain roles can request certain behaviors of others. This perceived right partly comes from formal job descriptions as well as informal rules of conduct. This legitimate power extends to employees, not just managers. For example, an organization might give employees the right to request customer files if this information is required for their job. Legitimate power depends on more than job descriptions. It also depends on mutual agreement from those expected to abide by this authority. Your boss's power to make you work overtime partly depends on your agreement to this authority. Thus, legitimate power operates within a "zone of indifference," the range within which people are willing to accept someone else's authority.[6]

The size of this zone of indifference (and, consequently, the magnitude of legitimate power) increases with the extent that the powerholder is trusted and makes fair decisions. Some people are also more obedient than others to authority, particularly those who value conformity and tradition. People in high-power-distance cultures (i.e., those who accept an unequal distribution of power) also tend to have higher obedience to authority compared with people in low-power-distance cultures. The organization's culture represents a third factor. A 3M scientist might continue to work on a project after being told by superiors to stop working on it because the 3M culture supports an entrepreneurial spirit, which includes ignoring your boss's authority from time to time.[7]

Reward Power

Reward power is derived from the person's ability to control the allocation of rewards valued by others and to remove negative sanctions (i.e., negative reinforcement). Managers have formal authority that gives them power over the distribution of organizational rewards such as pay, promotions, time off, vacation schedules, and work assignments. Employees also have reward power over their bosses through the use of 360-degree feedback systems. Employee feedback affects supervisors' promotions and other rewards, so they tend to behave differently toward employees after 360-degree feedback is introduced.

Coercive Power

Coercive power is the ability to apply punishment. In the opening story to this chapter, WorldCom executives demonstrated their coercive power by reprimanding employees and threatening to fire them. Employees also have coercive power, ranging from sarcasm to ostracism, to ensure that co-workers conform to team norms. Many firms also rely on the coercive power of team members to control co-worker behavior. For instance, Mittal's Weirton Steel plant in West Virginia relies on coercive power from co-workers to ensure that all employees are pulling their weight. "There is some degree of peer pressure," admits Weirton's union leader. "You don't want to be the weakest link." This peer pressure is supported by a bonus system that rewards the entire group for production output, so everyone has an incentive to discourage co-workers from slacking off.[8]

Expert Power

For the most part, legitimate, reward, and coercive power originate from the position. In contrast, expert power originates from within the person. It is an individual's or work unit's capacity to influence others by possessing knowledge or skills that they value. The opening story described how Scott Sullivan had expert power at WorldCom, which caused employees to unquestioningly accept his demands for dubious accounting entries. Employees are also gaining expert power as our society moves from an industrial to a knowledge-based economy.[9] The reason is that employee knowledge becomes the means of production and is ultimately outside the control of those who own the company. And without this control over production, owners are more dependent on employees to achieve their corporate objectives.

Referent Power

People have **referent power** when others identify with them, like them, or otherwise respect them. Like expert power, referent power comes from within the person. It is largely a function of the person's interpersonal skills and usually develops slowly. Referent power is usually associated with charismatic leadership. *Charisma* is often defined as a form of interpersonal attraction whereby followers develop a respect for and trust in the charismatic individual.[10]

Information and Power

Information is power.[11] This phrase is increasingly relevant in a knowledge-based economy. Information power exists in two forms. First, people gain information power when they control the flow of information to others. These information gatekeepers can alter perceptions of the situation and restrict information as a resource that others need to accomplish their work. For example, supervisors tend to have more information power in a centralized hierarchy where information flows through them to employees. But when information systems (such as intranets and corporate blogs) bypass supervisors, their information power declines.

Second, information power is higher for those who seem to be able to cope with organizational uncertainties. Organizations value the ability to cope with environmental uncertainties because it allows them to more easily secure resources, introduce more efficient work processes, and estimate demand for their outputs. In other words, coping increases the organization's adaptability to its environment. Individuals and work units gain power by offering one or more of the following ways to cope with uncertainty, with the first being the most powerful:[12]

- *Prevention.* The most effective strategy is to prevent environmental changes from occurring. For example, financial experts acquire power by preventing the organization from experiencing a cash shortage or defaulting on loans.

- *Forecasting.* The next best strategy is to predict environmental changes or variations. In this respect, marketing specialists gain power by predicting changes in consumer preferences.

People who can forecast the future are worth their weight in gold. The reason is this: Information about the future helps companies to cope with environmental uncertainties. Corporate leaders can ramp up production to cash in on growing demand, and they can take corrective action to minimize damage from falling demand. "It's good to have advance-warning radar about what's happening among consumers," says London-based trendspotter Zoe Lazarus. Lazarus and Richard Welch (shown together in this photo) jointly lead a trend analysis unit in New York for Lowe Worldwide, one of several ad agencies that have recently introduced trend analysis teams that peer into the future. Along with scanning offbeat magazines (*Sleazenation, Relax*), Lazarus and Welch anticipate social changes by listening to more than 500 bartenders, photographers, disc jockeys, architects, journalists, designers, and other "influencers" in 52 cities across several countries. "[We're] looking for leading-edge trends that will eventually filter into the mainstream in one to two years' time, changing patterns in leisure behavior, holiday destinations, music choices, as well as fashion trends," Lazarus explains.[13]

• *Absorption.* People and work units also gain power by absorbing or neutralizing the impact of environmental shifts as they occur. An example is the ability of maintenance crews to come to the rescue when machines break down and the production process stops.

>Contingencies of Power

Let's say that you have expert power by virtue of your ability to forecast and possibly even prevent dramatic changes in the organization's environment. Does this expertise mean that you are influential? Not necessarily, because the sources of power operate at full capacity only under certain conditions. Four important contingencies of power are substitutability, centrality, discretion, and visibility.[14]

Substitutability

Substitutability refers to the availability of alternatives. Power is strongest when someone has a monopoly over a valued resource. Conversely, power decreases as the number of alternative sources of the critical resource increases. If only you have expertise across the organization on an important issue, you would be more powerful than if several people in your company possess this valued knowledge. Substitutability refers not only to other sources that offer the resource but also to substitutions of the resource itself. For instance, labor unions are weakened when companies introduce technologies that replace the need for their union members.

Nonsubstitutability is strengthened by controlling access to the resource. For instance, labor unions and professions are more powerful when they control knowledge, tasks, or labor to perform important activities. For instance, the medical profession is powerful because governments give it exclusive rights to perform specific medical procedures. Labor unions that dominate an industry effectively control access to labor needed to perform key jobs. Employees become nonsubstitutable when they possess knowledge (such as operating equipment or serving clients) that is not documented or readily available to others. Nonsubstitutability also occurs when people differentiate their resource from the alternatives. Some people claim that consultants use this tactic. They take skills and knowledge that many consulting firms can provide and wrap them into a package (with the latest buzz words, of course) so it looks like a service that no one else can offer.

substitutability
The extent to which people dependent on a resource have alternatives.

Centrality

Centrality refers to the degree and nature of interdependence between the powerholder and others.[15] Airline pilots have high centrality because their actions affect many people and because their actions quickly affect other people. Think about your own centrality for a moment: If you decided not to show up for work or school tomorrow, how many people would be affected, and how much time would pass before they are affected? If you have high centrality, most people in the organization would be adversely affected by your absence, and they would be affected quickly.

centrality
The degree and nature of interdependence between the powerholder and others.

Discretion

The freedom to exercise judgment—to make decisions without referring to a specific rule or receiving permission from someone else—is another important contingency of power in organizations. Consider the plight of first-line supervisors. It may seem that they have legitimate and reward power over employees, but this power is often curtailed by specific rules.

This lack of discretion makes supervisors largely powerless even though they may have access to some of the power bases described earlier in this chapter. "Middle managers are very much 'piggy-in-the-middle,'" complains a middle manager at Britain's National Health System. "They have little power, only what senior managers are allowed to give them."[16]

Visibility

Several years ago as a junior copywriter at advertising agency Chiat/Day, Mimi Cook submitted an idea for a potential client to her boss, who then presented it to co-founder Jay Chiat. Chiat was thrilled with the concept, but Cook's boss "never mentioned the idea came from me," recalls Cook. Cook confronted her boss, who claimed the oversight was unintentional. But when a similar incident occurred a few months later, Cook left the agency for another firm.[17]

Mimi Cook, who has since progressed to associate creative director at another ad agency, knows that power does not flow to unknown people in the organization. Those who control valued resources or knowledge will yield power only when others are aware of these power bases, in other words, when they are visible. One way to increase visibility is to take people-oriented jobs and work on projects that require frequent interaction with senior executives. Employees also gain visibility by being, quite literally, visible. Some people strategically move into offices or cubicles where co-workers pass most often (such as closest to the elevator or office lunchroom). Many professionals display their educational diplomas and awards on office walls to remind visitors of their expertise. Others spend more time at work and show that they are working productively.

Networking and Power

networking
Cultivating social relationships with others to accomplish one's goals.

"It's not what you know, but who you know that counts!" This often-heard statement reflects the reality that employees get ahead not just by developing their competencies, but by **networking**—cultivating social relationships with others to accomplish one's goals. Networking increases a person's power in three ways. First, networks consist of people who trust each other, which increases the flow of knowledge among those within the network.[18] Second, people tend to identify more with partners within their own networks, which increases referent power among people within each network. This network-based referent power may lead to more favorable decisions by others in the network. Finally, effective networkers are better known by others in the organization, so their talents are more readily recognized.[19] For example, these people might play a central role in distributing information to others in the network.

>Influencing Others

influence
Any behavior that attempts to alter another person's attitudes or behavior.

Thus far, we have focused on the sources and contingencies of power. But power is only the capacity to influence others. It represents the potential to change someone's attitudes and behavior. **Influence**, on the other hand, refers to any behavior that attempts to alter someone's attitudes or behavior.[20] Influence is power in motion. It applies one or more power bases to get people to alter their beliefs, feelings, and activities. Consequently, our interest in the remainder of this chapter is on how people use power to influence others.

Influence tactics are woven throughout the social fabric of all organizations. This is because influence is an essential process through which people coordinate their effort and act in concert to achieve organizational objectives. Indeed, influence is central to the definition of leadership. Influence operates down, across, and up the corporate hierarchy. Executives ensure that subordinates complete required tasks. Employees influence co-workers to help them with their job requirements. Subordinates engage in upward influence tactics so corporate leaders make decisions compatible with subordinates' needs and expectations.

Types of Influence Tactics

Organizational behavior researchers have devoted considerable attention to the various types of influence tactics found in organizational settings. They do not agree on a definitive list, but the following influence tactics have been identified in the most recent literature: silent authority, assertiveness, information control, coalition formation, upward appeal, ingratiation and impression management, persuasion, and exchange.[21] The first five are known as *hard influence tactics* because they force behavior change through position power (legitimate, reward, and coercion). The latter three—ingratiation and impression management, persuasion, and exchange—are called *soft influence tactics* because they rely more on personal sources of power (referent, expert) and appeal to the target person's attitudes and needs (see Exhibit 9.2).

Silent Authority

The silent application of authority occurs where someone complies with a request because of the requester's legitimate power as well as the target person's role expectations. We often refer to this condition as *deference to authority.*[22] This deference occurs when you comply with your boss's request to complete a particular task. If the task is within your job scope and your boss has the right to make this request, then this influence strategy operates without negotiation, threats, persuasion, or other tactics. Silent authority is the most common form of influence in high-power-distance cultures.[23]

Assertiveness

In contrast to silent authority, assertiveness might be called *vocal authority* because it involves actively applying legitimate and coercive power to influence others. Assertiveness includes persistently reminding the target of his or her obligations, frequently checking the

[Exhibit 9.2] Types of Influence Tactics in Organizations

Influence Tactic	Description
Hard influence tactics	
Silent authority	Influencing behavior through legitimate power without explicitly referring to that power base
Assertiveness	Actively applying legitimate and coercive power by applying pressure or threats
Information control	Explicitly manipulating someone else's access to information for the purpose of changing their attitudes or behavior, or both
Coalition formation	Forming a group that attempts to influence others by pooling the resources and power of its members
Upward appeal	Gaining support from one or more people with higher authority or expertise
Soft influence tactics	
Ingratiation/impression management	Attempting to increase liking by, or perceived similarity to, some targeted person
Persuasion	Using logical arguments, factual evidence, and emotional appeals to convince people of the value of a request
Exchange	Promising benefits or resources in exchange for the target person's compliance

target's work, confronting the target, and using threats of sanctions to force compliance. Assertiveness typically applies or threatens to apply punishment if the target does not comply. Explicit or implicit threats range from job loss to losing face by letting down the team. Extreme forms of assertiveness include blackmailing colleagues, such as by threatening to reveal the other person's previously unknown failures unless he or she complies with your request.

Information Control

Information control involves explicitly manipulating others' access to information for the purpose of changing their attitudes or behavior, or both. As described in the opening vignette for this chapter, this tactic was used by WorldCom's executive team to ensure that employees made illegal accounting entries. With limited access to vital information, accounting staff often did not realize that the entries violated accounting rules. Even employees who were suspicious had to trust explanations from headquarters that any irregularities were corrected elsewhere in the organization.

The WorldCom story is an extreme example of information control, but milder applications of this influence tactic are quite common. Almost half of employees in one major survey believe people keep their colleagues in the dark about work issues if it helps their own cause. Employees also influence executive decisions by screening out (filtering) information flowing up the hierarchy. Indeed, one recent study found that CEOs also influence their board of directors by selectively feeding information to board members.[24]

Coalition Formation

coalition
A group that attempts to influence people outside the group by pooling the resources and power of its members.

When people lack sufficient power alone to influence others in the organization, they might form a **coalition** of people who support the proposed change. A coalition is influential in three ways.[25] First, it pools the power and resources of many people, so the coalition potentially has more influence than any number of people operating alone. Second, the coalition's mere existence can be a source of power by symbolizing the legitimacy of the issue. In other words, a coalition creates a sense that the issue deserves attention because it has broad support. Third, coalitions tap into the power of the social identity process introduced in Chapter 3. A coalition is essentially an informal group that advocates a new set of norms and behaviors. If the coalition has a broad-based membership (i.e., its members come from various parts of the organization), then other employees are more likely to identify with that group and, consequently, accept the ideas proposed by the coalition.

Upward Appeal

upward appeal
A type of coalition in which one of the members is someone with higher authority or expertise.

Have you ever had a disagreement with a colleague in which one of you eventually says "I'm sure the boss (or teacher) will agree with me on this. Let's find out!" This tactic, called **upward appeal**, ranges from a formal alliance to the perception of informal support from someone with higher authority or expertise. Upward appeal also includes relying on the authority of the firm as an entity without approaching anyone further up the hierarchy. For instance, one study reported that Japanese managers remind employees of their obligation to support the organization's objectives.[26] By reminding the target that your request is consistent with the organization's overarching goals, you are implying support from senior executives without formally involving anyone with higher authority in the situation.

Ingratiation and Impression Management

ingratiation
Any attempt to increase the extent to which a target person likes us or perceives that he or she is similar to us.

Silent authority, assertiveness, information control, coalitions, and upward appeals are somewhat (or very) forceful ways to influence other people. At the opposite extreme is a soft influence tactic called ingratiation. **Ingratiation** includes any attempt to increase liking by, or perceived similarity to, some targeted person.[27] Flattering your boss in front of others, helping co-workers with their work, exhibiting similar attitudes (e.g., agreeing with your boss's proposal to change company policies), and seeking the other person's counsel (e.g., asking for his or her "expert" advice) are all examples of ingratiation. Collectively, ingratiation behaviors are better than most other forms of influence at predicting career success (performance appraisal feedback, salaries, and promotions).[28]

Ingratiation is potentially influential because it increases the perceived similarity of the source of ingratiation to the target person, which causes the target person to form more favorable opinions of the ingratiator. However, people who are obvious in their ingratiation risk losing any influence because their behaviors are considered insincere and self-serving.[29]

Ingratiation is part of a larger influence tactic known as impression management. **Impression management** is the practice of actively shaping our public images.[30] These public images might be crafted as being important, vulnerable, threatening, or pleasant. For the most part, employees routinely engage in pleasant impression management behaviors to satisfy the basic norms of social behavior, such as the way they dress and how they behave toward colleagues and customers. Impression management is a common strategy for people trying to get ahead in the workplace. For instance, almost all job applicants in a recent study relied on one or more types of impression management. As with ingratiation, employees who use too much impression management tend to be less influential because their behaviors are viewed as insincere.[31]

impression management
The practice of actively shaping our public image.

Persuasion

Along with ingratiation, **persuasion** is one of the most effective influence strategies for career success. The ability to present facts, logical arguments, and emotional appeals to change another person's attitudes and behavior is not just an acceptable way to influence others; in many societies, it is a noble art and a quality of effective leaders. The effectiveness of persuasion as an influence tactic depends on characteristics of the persuader, message content, communication medium, and the audience being persuaded.[32] People are more persuasive when listeners believe they have expertise and credibility, such as when the persuader does not seem to profit from the persuasion attempt and states a few points against the position.[33]

persuasion
Using logical arguments, facts, and emotional appeals to encourage people to accept a request or message.

The message is more important than the messenger when the issue is important to the audience. Persuasive message content acknowledges several points of view so the audience does not feel cornered by the speaker. The message should also be limited to a few strong arguments, which are repeated a few times, but not too frequently. The message should use emotional

Wearing his trademark black turtleneck and faded blue jeans, Apple Computer co-founder and CEO Steve Jobs is famous for stirring up crowds with evangelical fervor as he draws them into his "reality distortion field." A reality distortion field occurs when people are caught in Steve Jobs's visionary headlights. Apple Computer manager Bud Tribble borrowed the phrase from the TV series *Star Trek* to describe Jobs's overwhelming persuasiveness. "In his presence, reality is malleable," Tribble explained to newly hired Andy Hertzfeld in 1981. "He [Steve Jobs] can convince anyone of practically anything. It wears off when he's not around, but it makes it hard to have realistic schedules." As one journalist wrote, "Drift too close to Jobs in the grip of one of his manias and you can get sucked in, like a wayward asteroid straying into Jupiter's gravitational zone."[34]

appeals (such as graphically showing the unfortunate consequences of a bad decision), but only in combination with logical arguments and specific recommendations to overcome the threat. Finally, message content is more persuasive when the audience is warned about opposing arguments. This **inoculation effect** causes listeners to generate counterarguments to the anticipated persuasion attempts, which makes the opponent's subsequent persuasion attempts less effective.[35]

Two other considerations when persuading people are the medium of communication and characteristics of the audience. Generally, persuasion works best in face-to-face conversations and through other media-rich communication channels. The personal nature of face-to-face communication increases the persuader's credibility, and the richness of this channel provides faster feedback that the influence strategy is working. With respect to audience characteristics, it is more difficult to persuade people who have high self-esteem and intelligence, as well as those whose targeted attitudes are strongly connected to their self-image.[36]

inoculation effect
A persuasive communication strategy of warning listeners that others will try to influence them in the future and that they should be wary about the opponent's arguments.

Exchange

Exchange activities involve the promise of benefits or resources in exchange for the target person's compliance with your request. This tactic also includes reminding the target of past benefits or favors with the expectation that the target will now make up for that debt. The norm of reciprocity is a central and explicit theme in exchange strategies. According to the norm of reciprocity, individuals are expected to help those who have helped them.[37] Negotiation is also an integral part of exchange influence activities. For instance, you might negotiate your boss for a day off in return for working a less desirable shift at a future date. Networking is another form of exchange as an influence strategy. Active networkers build up "exchange credits" by helping colleagues in the short term for reciprocal benefits in the long term.

Networking as an influence strategy is a deeply ingrained practice in several cultures. The Chinese term *guanxi* refers to special relationships and active interpersonal connectedness. It is based on traditional Confucian values of helping others without expecting future repayment. However, modern guanxi seems to implicitly include long-term reciprocity, which can slip into cronyism. As a result, some Asian governments are discouraging guanxi-based decisions, preferring more arm's-length transactions in business and government decisions.[38]

Consequences and Contingencies of Influence Tactics

Now that we've covered the main strategies used to influence people, you are probably asking: Which influence tactics are best? The best way to answer this question is to identify the three ways that people react when others try to influence them: resistance, compliance, or commitment.[39] *Resistance* occurs when people or work units oppose the behavior desired by the influencer and consequently refuse, argue, or delay engaging in the behavior. *Compliance* occurs when people are motivated to implement the influencer's request at a minimal level of effort and for purely instrumental reasons. Without external sources to prompt the desired behavior, it would not occur. *Commitment* is the strongest form of influence, whereby people identify with the influencer's request and are highly motivated to implement it even when extrinsic sources of motivation are no longer present.

Research has found that people generally react more favorably to soft than to hard tactics (see Exhibit 9.3). Soft tactics tend to build commitment to the influencer's request. For example, co-workers tend to buy in to your ideas when you apply moderate levels of ingratiation and impression management tactics or use persuasion based on expertise. In

[Exhibit 9.3] Consequences of Hard and Soft Influence Tactics

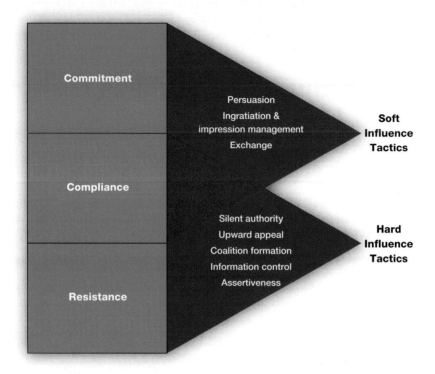

contrast, hard influence tactics tend to produce compliance or, worse, resistance. Hard tactics also tend to undermine trust, which can hurt future relationships. For example, coalitions are often successful, but their effect may be limited when the group's forcefulness is threatening.[40]

Upward, Downward, or Lateral Influence

Aside from the general preference for soft rather than hard tactics, the most appropriate influence strategy depends on a few contingencies. One consideration is whether the person being influenced is higher, lower, or at the same level in the organization. Employees have some legitimate power over their boss, but they may face adverse career consequences by being too assertive with this power. Similarly, it may be more acceptable for supervisors to control information access than for employees to control what information they distribute to co-workers and people at higher levels in the organization.

Influencer's Power Base

A second contingency is the influencer's power base. Those with expertise tend to be more successful using persuasion, whereas those with a strong legitimate power base are usually more successful applying silent authority.[41]

Personal and Cultural Values

Studies indicate that personal values guide our preference for some influence methods more than others.[42] The general trend in North America and elsewhere is toward softer influence tactics because younger employees tend to have more egalitarian values compared with those near retirement. As such, silent authority and assertiveness are tolerated less than a few decades ago. Acceptance of influence tactics also varies across cultures. American managers and subordinates alike often rely on ingratiation because it minimizes conflict and supports a trusting relationship. In contrast, managers in Hong Kong and other high-power-distance cultures rely less on ingratiation, possibly because this tactic disrupts the more distant roles that managers and employees expect in these cultures. Instead, influence through exchange tends to be more common and accepted in Asian cultures than in the United States because of the importance of interpersonal relationships (guanxi).

>Influence and Organizational Politics

organizational politics
Behaviors that others perceive as self-serving tactics for personal gain at the expense of other people and possibly the organization.

You might have noticed that **organizational politics** has not been mentioned yet, even though some of the practices or examples described over the past few pages are usually considered political tactics. The phrase was carefully avoided because, for the most part, organizational politics is in the eye of the beholder. You might perceive a co-worker's attempt to influence the boss as normal behavior, whereas someone else might perceive the co-worker's tactic as brazen organizational politics.

This perceptual issue explains why OB experts increasingly discuss influence tactics as behaviors and organizational politics as perceptions.[43] The influence tactics described earlier are labeled as organizational politics when observers view the tactics as self-serving behaviors at the expense of others and sometimes contrary to the interests of the entire organization or work unit. Organizational politics usually has negative consequences for co-workers, including lower job satisfaction, organizational commitment, and organizational citizenship, as well as high levels of work-related stress. And when political tactics really are self-serving, they divert resources away from the organization's effective functioning.[44]

Conditions Supporting Organizational Politics

Organizational politics flourishes under the right conditions.[45] One of those conditions is scarce resources. When budgets are slashed, people rely on political tactics to safeguard their resources and maintain the status quo. Office politics also flourishes when resource allocation decisions are ambiguous, complex, or lack formal rules. This occurs because decision makers are given more discretion over resource allocation, so potential recipients of those resources use political tactics to influence the factors that should be considered in the decision. Organizational change encourages political behaviors for this reason. Change creates uncertainty and ambiguity as the company moves from an old set of rules and practices to a new set. During these times, employees apply political strategies to protect their valued resources, position, and self-image.[46]

Personal Characteristics

Several personal characteristics affect a person's motivation to engage in organizational politics.[47] Some people have a strong need for personal as opposed to socialized power. They seek power for its own sake and use political tactics to acquire more power. People who believe they can control their environment are more likely than those with an external locus of control to engage in political behaviors. This does not mean that internals are naturally political; rather, they are more likely to use influence tactics when political conditions are present because, unlike externals, they feel very much in charge of their own destiny.

Machiavellian values
The belief that deceit is a natural and acceptable way to influence others.

Some individuals have strong **Machiavellian values.** Machiavellianism is named after Niccolò Machiavelli, the sixteenth-century Italian philosopher who wrote *The Prince,* a famous treatise about political behavior. People with high Machiavellian values are comfortable with getting more than they deserve, and they believe that deceit is a natural and acceptable way to achieve this goal. They seldom trust co-workers and tend to use cruder influence tactics, such as bypassing their boss or being assertive, to get their own way.[48]

A rogue group of foreign currency exchange traders at National Australia Bank (NAB) in Melbourne and London amassed a staggering US$275 million in losses within a few months by betting the wrong way on the Australian dollar and hiding their losses by falsifying transaction records. Former employees say that the group's leader, Luke Duffy (shown in photo), was a Machiavellian individual who used assertiveness and deceitful political tactics to get his way. He and a few other senior traders were "untouchables," claims Dennis Gentilin, one of two junior traders who eventually alerted NAB's senior management. "They just created this power base where they were laws unto themselves." Gentilin recounted how Duffy would threaten and mock staff into submission. "If you want to stay in the team, I demand loyalty and don't want you going to [my boss] about what's happening in the team," Duffy warned Gentilin in a fit of anger. In court, Duffy admitted that he called a co-worker in London "the London stench boy" because he "was always making a stink about things whether they were going on both good and bad, and you could smell the stink coming from London." Vanessa McCallum, the other junior trader who alerted senior management, was terrified. "My greatest fear was, if nothing is wrong I'm going to have to leave the desk because you had to be loyal to Luke [Duffy]," she said.[49]

Minimizing Organizational Politics and Its Consequences

The conditions that fuel organizational politics also give us some clues about how to control dysfunctional political activities.[50] One strategy to keep organizational politics in check is to introduce clear rules and regulations to specify the use of scarce resources. Organizational politics can become a problem during times of organizational change, so politics can be minimized through effective organizational change practices. Leaders also need to actively manage group norms to curtail self-serving influence activities. In particular, they can support organizational values that oppose political tactics, such as altruism and customer-focus. One of the most important strategies is for leaders to become role models of organizational citizenship rather than examples of successful organizational politicians.

Along with minimizing organizational politics, companies can limit the adverse effects of political perceptions by giving employees more control over their work and keeping them informed of organizational events. Research has found that employees who are kept informed of what is going on in the organization and who are involved in organizational decisions are less likely to experience stress, job dissatisfaction, and absenteeism as a result of organizational politics.

>chapter summary

Power is the capacity to influence others. It exists when one party perceives that he or she is dependent on the other for something of value. However, the dependent person must also have counterpower—some power over the dominant party—to maintain the relationship.

There are five power bases. Legitimate power is an agreement among organizational members that people in certain roles can request certain behaviors of others. Reward power is derived from the ability to control the allocation of rewards valued by others and to remove negative sanctions. Coercive power is the ability to apply punishment. Expert power is the capacity to influence others by possessing knowledge or skills that they value.

People have referent power when others identify with them, like them, or otherwise respect them.

Information plays an important role in organizational power. Employees gain power by controlling the flow of information that others need and by being able to cope with uncertainties related to important organizational goals.

Four contingencies determine whether these power bases translate into real power. Individuals and work units are more powerful when they are nonsubstitutable, that is, there is a lack of alternatives. A second contingency is centrality. People have more power when they have high centrality, that is, the number of people affected is large and people are quickly affected by their actions. Discretion, the third contingency of power, refers to the freedom to exercise judgment. The fourth contingency, visibility, refers to the idea that power increases to the extent that a person's or work unit's competencies are known to others.

Networking involves cultivating social relationships with others to accomplish one's goals. This activity increases an individual's expert and referent power as well as visibility and possibly centrality.

Influence refers to any behavior that attempts to alter someone's attitudes or behavior. The most widely studied influence tactics are silent authority, assertiveness, information control, coalition formation, upward appeal, ingratiation and impression management, persuasion, and exchange. Soft influence tactics such as friendly persuasion and subtle ingratiation are more acceptable than hard tactics such as upward appeal and assertiveness. However, the most appropriate influence tactic also depends on the influencer's power base; whether the person being influenced is higher, lower, or at the same level in the organization; and personal and cultural values regarding influence behavior.

Organizational politics refers to influence tactics that others perceive to be self-serving behaviors at the expense of others and sometimes contrary to the interests of the entire organization or work unit. Organizational politics is more prevalent when scarce resources are allocated using complex and ambiguous decisions. Individuals with a high need for personal power, a belief that they control their environment, and strong Machiavellian values have a higher propensity to use political tactics. Organizational politics can be minimized by providing clear rules for resource allocation, engaging in effective organizational change, supporting team norms and a corporate culture that discourage dysfunctional politics, and having leaders who role model organizational citizenship rather than political savvy.

>key.terms

centrality 179

coalition 182

counterpower 176

impression management 183

influence 180

ingratiation 182

inoculation effect 184

legitimate power 176

Machiavellian values 186

networking 180

organizational politics 186

persuasion 183

power 175

referent power 178

substitutability 179

upward appeal 182

>critical.thinking.questions

1. What role does counterpower play in the power relationship? Give an example of your own encounter with counterpower at school or work.

2. Several years ago, the major league baseball players association went on strike in September, just before the World Series started. The players' contract expired in the springtime, but they held off the strike until September when they would lose only one-sixth of their salaries. In contrast, a September strike would hurt the owners financially because they earn a larger portion of their revenue during the playoffs. As one player explained, "If we strike next spring, there's nothing stopping [the club owners] from letting us go until next June or July because they don't have that much at stake." Use your knowledge of the sources and contingencies of power to explain why the baseball players association had more power in negotiations by walking out in September rather than March.

3. You have just been hired as a brand manager of toothpaste for a large consumer products company. Your job mainly involves encouraging the advertising and production groups to promote and manufacture your product more effectively. These departments aren't under your direct authority, although company procedures indicate that they must complete certain tasks requested by brand managers. Describe the sources of power you can use to ensure that the advertising and production departments will help you make and sell toothpaste more effectively.

4. How does networking increase a person's power? What networking strategies could you initiate now to potentially enhance your future career success?

5. List the eight influence tactics described in this chapter in terms of how they are used by students to influence college instructors. Which influence tactic is applied most often? Which is applied least often, in your opinion? To what extent is each influence tactic considered legitimate behavior or organizational politics?

6. How do cultural differences affect the following influence factors: (*a*) silent authority and (*b*) upward appeal?

7. A few years ago, the CEO of Apple Computer invited Steve Jobs (who was not associated with the company at the time) to serve as a special adviser and raise morale among Apple employees and customers. While doing this, Jobs spent more time advising the CEO on how to cut costs, redraw the organization chart, and hire new people. Before long, most of the top people at Apple were Jobs's colleagues, who began to systematically evaluate and weed out teams of Apple employees. While publicly supporting Apple's CEO, Jobs privately criticized him and, in a show of nonconfidence, sold 1.5 million shares of Apple stock he had received. This action caught the attention of Apple's board of directors, who soon after decided to replace the CEO with Steve Jobs. The CEO claimed Jobs was a conniving backstabber who used political tactics to get his way. Others suggest that Apple would be out of business today if he hadn't taken over the company. In your opinion, were Steve Jobs's actions examples of organizational politics? Justify your answer.

8. This book frequently emphasizes that successful companies engage in knowledge management. How do political tactics interfere with knowledge management objectives?

>case.study:skillbuilder9.1

Rhonda Clark: Taking Charge at the Smith Foundation

By Joseph C. Santora

Dr. Rhonda Clark was ecstatic as she hung up the telephone. Bennett Mitchell, chairperson of KLS Executive Search firm, had just informed her that she landed the coveted position of chief executive officer (CEO) at the Smith Foundation, a nonprofit organization whose mission was to fund public awareness campaigns and research programs about eye care. Clark knew that she had just pulled off a major coup.

Her appointment to this new, challenging position would indeed be *the* high point in a long arduous climb to the executive suite. As an organizational outsider—one with no work experience within the hiring organization—she assumed that her appointment as CEO signaled a strong desire by the board to shake up the organizational status quo. However, she heard from a very reliable inside source that the very board that hired her and charged her with the responsibility of transforming the foundation was extremely fragmented. The often rambunctious board had forced the last five CEOs to resign after very short tenures. Clark's feeling of exhilaration was rapidly being replaced by cautious optimism. As a new CEO, she pondered the rather thorny question: How could she take charge of the board of directors to ensure the mission of the organization would be accomplished?

Background

Charlie Smith, an industrialist and philanthropist, founded the Smith Foundation 40 years ago with a multimillion dollar endowment. Despite this generous financial start-up capital and additional income derived from several financial investments and major corporate donations, in recent years, the foundation's endowment has been slowly dwindling as a result of rather significant funding awards to academics, community organizations, and smaller, less well funded foundations. Board members have held some preliminary discussions about developing new innovative strategies to strengthen the balance sheet of the organization. Currently, the foundation operates on an annual budget of slightly less than $1,500,000.

In the last five years, some foundation board members have begun to abandon many of their fiduciary responsibilities. Over the past few months, several board meetings have been canceled because the meetings lacked a quorum. In general, this 13-member board seemed to drift aimlessly in one direction or another. The board has been operating at only 70 percent capacity for the past two years with nine active board members—five men and four women.

Challenges

Dr. Rhonda Clark believed she was the one who could lead the Smith Foundation. She had great academic credentials and management experience that would help her tackle her new position as the foundation head. In the last 30 years, the 54-year old Clark, who holds a PhD in political science and policy analysis from a major U.S. West Coast university, has gained an enviable amount of managerial experience in the nonprofit and public sectors. Past professional experiences included a graduate school professorship; a director of research for a major statewide political office holder, the director of planning in a large metropolitan hospital, and the director of programs at a small foundation.

Immediately upon taking office, Clark was astounded to learn that a small but active and influential faction on the board had withdrawn its initial verbal promise to assist her in working closely with the corporate community. Essentially, she was informed that she was solely responsible for all external corporate relations. Clark thought to herself, "I wonder if they hired me because they thought they would get a 'do-nothing' female leader. These folks want me to either sink or swim on my own. Perhaps they set me up for failure by giving me a one-year appointment." She lamented, "I won't let this happen. I really need to learn about the key decision makers and stakeholders on the board and in the larger community, and fast."

At the last board meeting Clark detailed the major elements of her latest proposal. Yet, several board members seemed totally unfazed by it. Soon she began to encounter stiff resistance from some male board members. Jim Jackson, in particular, told Clark, "We are disappointed that you failed to win a city contract to conduct a feasibility study to determine if we can erect a facility in another section of town. We're not certain if you have the right stuff to run this foundation, and we certainly won't help you to gain financial support for the foundation by using our personal, corporate, or political contacts." Jackson thought to himself, We've removed CEOs before, we can remove Clark, too.

After hearing Jackson's comments, Clark decided to take another tack. She began to focus her attention on making external and internal inroads that she believed could result in some modest gains for the foundation. For example, she identified and developed a close relationship with a few well-connected city agency executives, persuaded some supporters to nominate her for membership on two very influential boards, and forged a relationship with two key foundation decision makers and political power brokers. She reconfigured the internal structure of the foundation to increase maximum productivity from the staff, and she tightened budgetary controls by changing some fiscal policies and procedures.

Clark also sought the support of Susan Frost, a board member who likely had been instrumental in Clark's appointment as CEO. Clark said to herself, If I can develop a strong symbiotic relationship with some female board members, like Sue, to support my plan, then maybe I can get some traction. To do this Clark held a number of late-evening meetings with Sue and another female board member. They indicated their willingness to help her, but only if she would consider implementing a few of their ideas for the foundation as well as recommending their close friend for a current staff vacancy. Clark knew they were trying to exercise their political influence; yet she believed that everyone could benefit from this quid quo pro relationship. She said to herself, I guess it's a matter of you scratch my back, and I scratch yours. She eagerly agreed to move their agenda along. In a matter of a few weeks, as promised, they began working on a couple of relatively "sympathetic" board members. One day Clark got a very terse but critical telephone call from Sue. "Several of us support you. Proceed!"

Once she heard this, Clark began to move at lightning speed. She formed a 15-member coalition of community, educational, and quasi-governmental agencies that would apply for a collaborative federal grant to create a public awareness eye campaign for children. Through the dissemination of various media, coalition members would help to inform the community at large about various eye diseases that afflict young school-age children. Shortly afterward, Clark received notification from a federal agency that this multi-agency project would be awarded a million dollar grant. Clark would serve as the administrative and fiscal agent of the grant, and as a result, she would be able to earmark a considerable amount of the administrative oversight dollars for the foundation's budget. For her efforts at coordinating this project, Clark received high marks from coalition and community members alike.

Yet despite this important initial accomplishment, Clark had the unpleasant task of notifying the full board that, due to some unforeseen problems and their lack of support on certain key initiatives, the foundation would still experience a financial deficit. She heard several rumors that her next employment contract would not be renewed by the executive committee of the board. At this point, she thought about directly confronting the obstructionists on the board by telling them that they were unreasonable and in fact that they were the cause the foundation had not recovered during the past year; but she hesitated: She had signed on to do a job, and she was unsure if was the wisest course of action to take at this time.

Despite this latest conflict between herself and certain board members, she paused to reflect on what she believed to have been a tumultuous year as CEO.

Discussion Questions

1. Does Clark have any sources of power and any contingencies of power? If so, list and discuss them.

2. To what degree were Clark's methods of influencing board members the most effective possible under the circumstances presented in the case?

3. Do you think her methods to get things done at the foundation were ethical? Why or why not?

The names and some managerial actions in this case have been altered to preserve the integrity and anonymity of the organization. This case is intended to be used as a basis for class discussion rather than to illustrate either effective or ineffective handling of a management situation.

© Joseph C. Santora.

>team.exercise:skillbuilder9.2

Budget Deliberations

Purpose   This exercise is designed to help you understand some of the power dynamics and influence tactics that occur across hierarchical levels in organizations.

Materials   This activity works best where one small room leads to a larger room, which leads to a larger area.

Instructions
These exercise instructions are based on a class size of about 30 students. The instructor may adjust the size of the first two groups slightly for larger classes. The instructor will organize students as follows: A few (three or four) students are assigned the position of executives. They are preferably located in a secluded office or corner of a large classroom. Another six to eight students are assigned positions as middle managers. These people will ideally be located in an adjoining room or space, allowing privacy for the executives. The remaining students represent the nonmanagement employees in the organization. They are located in an open area outside the executive and management rooms.

Rules
Members of the executive group are free to enter the space of either the middle management or nonmanagement groups and to communicate whatever they wish, whenever they wish. Members of the middle management group may enter

the space of the nonmanagement group whenever they wish, but they must request permission to enter the executive group's space. The executive group can refuse the middle management group's request. Members of the nonmanagement group are not allowed to disturb the top group in any way unless specifically invited by members of the executive group. The nonmanagement group does have the right to request permission to communicate with the middle management group. The middle management group can refuse the lower group's request.

Task
Your organization is in the process of preparing a budget. The challenge is to balance needs with the financial resources. Of course, the needs are greater than the resources. The instructor will distribute a budget sheet showing a list of budget requests and their costs. Each group has control over a portion of the budget and must decide how to spend the money over which they have control. Nonmanagement has discretion over a relatively small portion and the executive group has discretion over the greatest portion. The exercise is finished when the organization has negotiated a satisfactory budget, or until the instructor calls time out. The class will then debrief with the following questions and others the instructor might ask.

Discussion Questions
1. What can we learn from this exercise about power in organizational hierarchies?

2. How is this exercise similar to relations in real organizations?

3. How did students in each group feel about the amount of power they held?

4. How did they exercise their power in relations with the other groups?

Source: Written by Sharon Card.

>self-assessment.skillbuilder9.3

Upward Influence Scale

Trying to influence people at higher levels of the organization is as old as organizations themselves (a very long time!). But not everyone uses, or likes to use, the same tactics. This instrument identifies the influence strategies that you prefer and avoid when influencing your boss and others in higher positions. Read each of the statements and select the response that you believe best indicates how often you engaged in that behavior over the past six months. This exercise is completed alone so students assess themselves honestly without concerns of social comparison. However, class discussion will focus on the types of influence in organizations and the conditions under which particular influence tactics are most and least appropriate.

>self-assessment.skillbuilder9.4

Guanxi Orientation Scale

Guanxi, which is translated as interpersonal connections, is an important element of doing business in China and some other Asian countries with strong Confucian cultural values. Guanxi is based on traditional Confucian values of helping others without expecting future repayment. This instrument estimates your guanxi orientation, that is, the extent to which you accept and apply guanxi values. This self-assessment is completed alone so that students rate themselves honestly without concerns of social comparison. However, class discussion will focus on the meaning of guanxi and its relevance for organizational power and influence.

>self-assessment.skillbuilder9.5

Machiavellianism Scale

Machiavellianism is named after Niccolò Machiavelli, the 16th-century Italian philosopher who wrote *The Prince,* a famous treatise about political behavior. Out of Machiavelli's work emerged this instrument that estimates the degree to which you have Machiavellian values. Indicate the extent to which you agree or disagree that each statement in this instrument describes you. Complete each item honestly to get the best estimate of your level of Machiavellianism.

>self-assessment.skillbuilder9.6

Perceptions of Politics Scale (POPS)

Organizations have been called *political arenas*— environments in which political tactics are common because decisions are ambiguous and resources are scarce. This instrument estimates the degree to which you believe the school where you attend classes has a politicized culture. This scale consists of several statements that might or might not describe the school where you are attending classes. These statements refer to the administration of the school, not the classroom. Please indicate the extent to which you agree or disagree with each statement.

Find the full self-assessments on the OLC at
www.mhhe.com/mcshaneess

chapter 10

Conflict Management

While Arthur Andersen employees put up a united front during the firm's dying days (as this photo shows), the accounting firm suffered from internal battles.

>learningobjectives

After reading this chapter, you should be able to

- Outline the conflict process.
- Distinguish constructive from socioemotional conflict.
- Discuss the advantages and disadvantages of conflict in organizations.
- Identify six sources of organizational conflict.
- Outline the five interpersonal styles of conflict management.
- Summarize six structural approaches to managing conflict.
- Compare and contrast the three types of third-party dispute resolution.

To outsiders, Arthur Andersen's "One Firm" policy was solid. The Chicago-based accounting firm provided the same quality of work anywhere in the world by the same type of people trained the same way. But when Barbara Toffler joined Andersen as an ethics consultant in 1996, she discovered plenty of infighting. Arthur Andersen is now gone, the result of accounting fraud at its client, Enron, but internal conflict may have also contributed to the accounting firm's demise.

Much of the dysfunctional conflict was caused by Arthur Andersen's fee structure, which generously rewarded one engagement partner (the person in charge of the overall project) at the expense of other partners who provided services to the client. To maximize fees, executives fought over who should be the project's engagement partner and played games that would minimize the fees going to other groups. "While I was at Arthur Andersen, the fight for fees defined my existence," recalls Toffler.

In one incident, a partner demanded that he should be the engagement partner because he made the initial connection with a client, even though the project relied mainly on expertise from Toffler's ethical practices group. The two argued all the way to the airport and in several subsequent "violent" phone arguments. In another client proposal, Toffler flew to Japan, only to spend two days of that time negotiating through a translator with Andersen's Japanese engagement partner over how to split fees.

In a third incident, several Arthur Andersen partners met with a potential client supposedly to discuss their services. Instead, the partners openly criticized each other during the pitch so the client would spend more money on their particular specialization. A couple of partners also extended the length of their presentations so other partners would have less time to convince the client of their particular value in the project. "Eventually, I learned to screw someone else before they screwed me," says Toffler. "The struggle to win fees for your office and your group—and *not* someone else's—came to define the firm."[1]

Backstabbing and infighting over fees at Arthur Andersen illustrates the problems that can result from conflict in organizations. **Conflict** is a process in which one party perceives that its interests are being opposed or negatively affected by another party.[2] Arthur Andersen's partners experienced conflict because they saw each other as competitors vying for the same scarce resources (client fees) on projects where they had to work interdependently. This chapter looks at the dynamics of conflict in organizational settings. We begin by describing the conflict process and discussing the consequences and sources of conflict in organizational settings. Five conflict management styles are then described, followed by a discussion of the structural approaches to conflict management. The last section of this chapter looks at third-party resolution to conflict, such as when managers intervene in disputes between employees.

conflict
The process in which one party perceives that its interests are being opposed or negatively affected by another party.

>The Conflict Process

When describing an incident involving conflict, we are usually referring to the observable part of conflict—the angry words, shouting matches, and actions that symbolize opposition. But this manifest conflict is only a small part of the conflict process. As Exhibit 10.1 illustrates, the conflict process begins with the sources of conflict.[3] Incompatible goals, different values, and other conditions lead one or both parties to perceive that conflict exists. We will look closely at these sources of conflict later in this chapter because understanding and changing them is the key to effective conflict management.

[Exhibit 10.1]   The Conflict Process

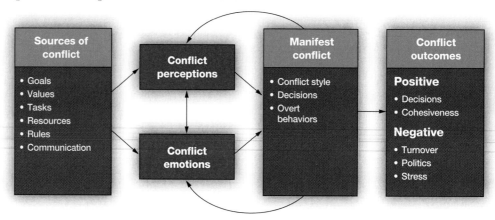

Conflict Perceptions and Emotions

At some point, the sources of conflict lead one or both parties to perceive that conflict exists. They become aware that one party's statements and actions are incompatible with their own goals. These perceptions usually interact with emotions experienced about the conflict. The battle over fees at Arthur Andersen was riddled with emotions, including anger during heated arguments over allocation of client ownership.

Manifest Conflict

Conflict perceptions and emotions usually manifest themselves in the decisions and overt behaviors of one party toward the other. These conflict episodes may range from subtle nonverbal behaviors to warlike aggression. Particularly when people experience high levels of conflict emotions, they have difficulty finding the words and expressions that communicate effectively without further irritating the relationship.[4] Conflict is also manifested by the style each side uses to resolve the conflict. Some people tend to avoid the conflict, whereas others try to defeat those with opposing views. Conflict management styles will be described later in this chapter. At this point, you should know that these styles influence the other party's perceptions and actions regarding the conflict, which then either diffuse or further escalate the conflict.

Conflict Escalation Cycle

The conflict process in Exhibit 10.1 shows arrows looping back from manifest conflict to conflict perceptions and emotions. These loops represent the fact that the conflict process is really a series of episodes that potentially link in an escalation cycle or spiral.[5] It doesn't take much to start this conflict cycle—just an inappropriate comment, a misunderstanding, or an action that lacks diplomacy. These behaviors communicate to the other party in a way that creates a perception of conflict. Even if the first party did not intend to demonstrate conflict, then the second party's response may create that perception.

If the conflict remains focused on perceptions, both parties can often resolve it through logical analysis. However, the communication process has enough ambiguity that a wrong look or word may trigger strong emotions and set the stage for further conflict escalation. These distorted beliefs and emotions reduce each side's motivation to communicate, making it more difficult for them to discover common ground and ultimately resolve the conflict. The parties then rely more on stereotypes and emotions to reinforce their perceptions of the other party. Employees who are more confrontational and less diplomatic also tend to escalate conflict.[6]

Conflict Outcomes

The opening vignette illustrates some of the dysfunctional consequences of conflict: verbal barbs from both parties, lack of cooperation, poor customer service. Conflicts can distract employees from their work, reduce their organizational commitment and job satisfaction, and increase levels of stress and turnover. At the intergroup level, conflict with people outside the team may cause the team to become more insular—increasing their cohesiveness while distancing themselves from outsiders who are critical of the team's past decisions.[7]

Given these problems, it's not surprising that people normally associate **conflict management** with reducing or removing conflict. However, conflict management refers to interventions that alter the level and form of conflict in ways that maximize its benefits and minimize its dysfunctional consequences. This sometimes means increasing the level of **constructive conflict** (also known as *task-related conflict*).[8] Recall from Chapter 7 that constructive conflict occurs when team members debate their different perceptions about an issue in a way that keeps the conflict focused on the task rather than people. This form of conflict tests the logic of arguments and encourages participants to reexamine their basic assumptions about the problem and its possible solution.

The challenge is to engage in constructive conflict without having it escalate into **socioemotional conflict** (also known as *relationship conflict*). When socioemotional conflict dominates, differences are viewed as personal attacks rather than attempts to resolve an issue. The parties become defensive and competitive toward each other, which motivates them to reduce communication and information sharing. This socioemotional conflict was evident in the opening story regarding Arthur Andersen.

Minimizing Socioemotional Conflict

The solution here seems obvious: encourage constructive conflict for better decision making and minimize socioemotional conflict in order to avoid dysfunctional emotions and behaviors. This sounds good in theory, but recent evidence suggests that separating these two types of conflict isn't easy. Most of us experience some degree of socioemotional conflict during or after any constructive debate.[10] In other words, it is difficult to suppress

conflict management
Interventions that alter the level and form of conflict in ways that maximize its benefits and minimize its dysfunctional consequences.

constructive conflict
Occurs when team members debate their different perceptions about an issue in a way that keeps the conflict focused on the task rather than people.

socioemotional conflict
Any situation where people view their differences as personal attacks rather than attempts to resolve an issue.

Jim Syme knows a thing or two about making effective decisions in meetings. Recently voted QBE Insurance Chairperson of the year, the New Zealand executive chairs several boards, including Kiwi Income Property Trust, Waste Management, Abano (formerly Eldercare), and Software of Excellence. Syme is considered a "gentleman" with high integrity in his boardroom behavior, but he is quick to point out that being polite and respectful doesn't mean shying away from constructive conflict. "The relationships need to be strong enough to support rigorous and constructive debate by all directors and to ensure there is a strong and effective relationship between the board and the chief executive," says Syme. He explains that actively debating an issue encourages directors on the board to think more carefully through the logic and analysis of the situation. "It is critical that an important issue in front of us is well debated so that we get the right decision," Syme advises.[9]

defensive emotions when trying to resolve conflicts calmly and rationally. Fortunately, conflict management experts have identified three strategies that might reduce the level of socioemotional conflict during constructive conflict episodes:[11]

- *Emotional intelligence.* Socioemotional conflict is less likely to occur, or is less likely to escalate, when team members have high levels of emotional intelligence. Emotionally intelligent employees are better able to regulate their emotions during debate, which reduces the risk of escalating perceptions of interpersonal hostility. People with high emotional intelligence are also more likely to view a co-worker's emotional reaction as valuable information about that person's needs and expectations rather than as a personal attack.

- *Cohesive team.* Socioemotional conflict is suppressed when the conflict occurs within a highly cohesive team. The longer people work together, get to know each other, and develop mutual trust with each other, the more latitude they give to each other to show emotions without being personally offended. Strong cohesion also allows each person to know about and anticipate the behaviors and emotions of his or her teammates. Another benefit is that cohesion produces a stronger social identity with the group, so team members are motivated to avoid escalating socioemotional conflict during otherwise emotionally turbulent discussions.

- *Supportive team norms.* Various team norms can hold socioemotional conflict at bay during constructive debate. When team norms encourage openness, for instance, team members learn to appreciate honest dialogue without personally reacting to any emotional display during the disagreements. Other norms might discourage team members from displaying negative emotions toward co-workers. Team norms also encourage tactics that diffuse socioemotional conflict when it first appears. For instance, research has found that teams with low socioemotional conflict use humor to maintain positive group emotions, which offsets negative feelings team members might develop toward some co-workers during debate.

>Sources of Conflict in Organizations

Manifest conflict is really the tip of the proverbial iceberg. What we really need to understand are the sources of this conflict, which lie under the surface. The six main conditions that cause conflict in organizational settings are incompatible goals, differentiation, task interdependence, scarce resources, ambiguous rules, and communication problems.

Incompatible Goals

A common source of conflict is goal incompatibility.[12] Goal incompatibility occurs when personal or work goals seem to interfere with another person's or department's goals. This source of conflict was apparent in the infighting over fees at Arthur Andersen, described at the beginning of this chapter. Two partners serving the same client experienced directly conflicting goals—each wanted to be the engagement partner in order to earn the bulk of the fees from that client.

Differentiation

Another source of conflict emerges from unique training, values, beliefs, and experiences. This differentiation tends to produce different perspectives and mental images of ideal goals. Consequently, heterogeneous teams are more likely than homogeneous teams (where people have similar values and backgrounds) to disagree with each other regarding the best decisions and actions.

Differentiation is apparent in mergers where employees bring divergent corporate cultures into the new combined organization. Employees fight over the "right way" to do things because of their unique experiences in the separate companies. A rapidly growing retail clothing chain experienced another variation of differentiation-based conflict when the founder and CEO hired several senior managers from larger organizations to strengthen the experience levels of its senior management group. The new managers soon clashed with executives who had been with the company for some time. "We ended up with an old team and a new team and they weren't on the same wavelength," explains the company owner, who eventually fired most of the new managers.

Along with conflict generated from cultural diversity, many companies are experiencing the rising incidence of cross-generational conflict.[13] Younger and older employees have different needs, different expectations, and somewhat different values, which sometimes produces conflicting preferences and actions. Generational gaps have always existed, but this source of conflict is more common today because employees across age groups work together more than ever before.

Task Interdependence

Conflict tends to increase with the level of task interdependence. Task interdependence exists when team members must share common inputs to their individual tasks, need to interact in the process of executing their work, or receive outcomes (such as rewards) that are partly determined by the performance of others. The higher the level of task interdependence, the greater the risk of conflict, because there is a greater chance that each side will disrupt or interfere with the other side's goals.[14]

Other than complete independence, employees tend to have the lowest risk of conflict when working with others in a pooled interdependence relationship. Pooled interdependence occurs where individuals operate independently except for reliance on a common resource or authority. The potential for conflict is higher in sequential interdependence work relationships, such as an assembly line. The highest risk of conflict tends to occur in reciprocal interdependence situations. With reciprocal interdependence, employees are highly dependent on each other and, consequently, have a higher probability of interfering with each other's work and personal goals.

Scarce Resources

Resource scarcity generates conflict because higher scarcity reduces the ability of each person to fulfill his or her goals without undermining others. Arthur Andersen partners wouldn't have fought over fees if everyone had received what they wanted or needed. The reality, however, was that Arthur Andersen consultants had to share scarce resources. The result was that each group's goals interfered with the goals of other groups because there wasn't enough of the resource for everyone.

Ambiguous Rules

Ambiguous rules—or the complete lack of rules—breed conflict. This occurs because uncertainty increases the risk that one party intends to interfere with the other party's goals. Ambiguity also encourages political tactics, and, in some cases, employees enter a free-for-all battle to win decisions in their favor. This explains why conflict is more common during mergers and acquisitions. Employees from both companies have conflicting practices and values, and few rules have developed to minimize the maneuvering for power and resources.[15] When clear rules exist, on the other hand, employees know what to expect from each other and have agreed to abide by those rules.

Communication Problems

Conflict often occurs due to the lack of opportunity, ability, or motivation to communicate effectively. Let's look at each of these causes. First, when two parties lack the opportunity to communicate, they tend to use stereotypes to explain past behaviors and anticipate future actions. Unfortunately, stereotypes are sufficiently subjective that emotions can negatively distort the meaning of an opponent's actions, thereby escalating perceptions of conflict. Furthermore, without direct interaction, the two sides have less psychological empathy for each other. Second, some people lack the necessary skills to communicate in a diplomatic, nonconfrontational manner. When one party communicates its disagreement in an arrogant way, opponents are more likely to heighten their perception of the conflict. This may lead the other party to reciprocate with a similar conflict management style.[16]

Ineffective communication can also lead to a third problem: less motivation to communicate in the future. Socioemotional conflict is uncomfortable, so people avoid interacting with others in a conflicting relationship. Unfortunately, less communication can further escalate the conflict because there is less opportunity to empathize with the opponent's situation and opponents are more likely to rely on distorted stereotypes of the other party. In fact, conflict tends to further distort these stereotypes through the process of social identity (see Chapter 3). We begin to see competitors less favorably as a way to protect our self-image during these uncertain times.[17]

>Interpersonal Conflict Management Styles

win–win orientation
The belief that the parties will find a mutually beneficial solution to their disagreement.

win–lose orientation
The belief that conflicting parties are drawing from a fixed pie, so the more one party receives, the less the other party will receive.

The six structural conditions described above set the stage for conflict. The conflict process identified earlier in Exhibit 10.1 illustrated that these sources of conflict lead to perceptions and emotions. Some people enter a conflict with a **win–win orientation.** This is the perception that the parties will find a mutually beneficial solution to their disagreement. They believe that the resources at stake are expandable rather than fixed if the parties work together to find a creative solution. Other people enter a conflict with a **win–lose orientation.** They adopt the belief that the parties are drawing from a fixed pie, so the more one party receives, the less the other party will receive.

Conflict tends to escalate when the parties develop a win–lose orientation because they rely on power and politics to gain advantage. A win–lose orientation may occasionally be appropriate when the conflict really is over a fixed resource, but few organizational conflicts are due to perfectly opposing interests with fixed resources. Some degree of win–win orientation is usually advantageous, that is, believing that each side's goals are not perfectly opposing. One possibility is that each party needs different parts of the resource. Another possibility is that various parts of the shared resource have different levels of value to each side.

Consider the example of a supplier and customer resolving a disagreement over the price of a product. Initially, this seems like a clear win–lose situation—the supplier wants to receive more money for the product, whereas the customer wants to pay less money for it. Yet further discussion may reveal that the customer would be willing to pay more if the product could be provided earlier than originally arranged. The vendor may actually value that earlier delivery because it saves inventory costs. By looking at the bigger picture, both parties can often discover common ground.[18]

Adopting a win–win or win–lose orientation influences our conflict management style, that is, how we act toward the other person. The five conflict resolution styles described below can be placed in a two-dimensional grid reflecting the person's degree of concern for

[Exhibit 10.2] Interpersonal Conflict Management Styles

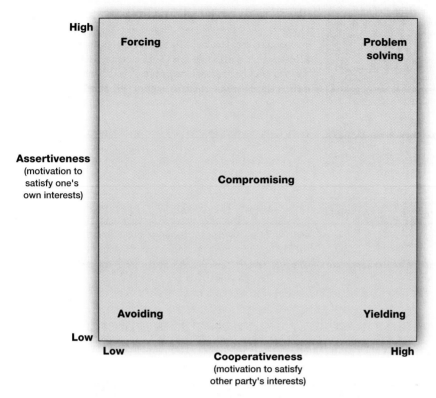

Source: C. K. W. de Dreu, A. Evers, B. Beersma, E. S. Kluwer, and A. Nauta, "A Theory-Based Measure of Conflict Management Strategies in the Workplace," *Journal of Organizational Behavior* 22 (2001), pp. 645–68. For earlier variations of this model, see T. L. Ruble and K. Thomas, "Support for a Two-Dimensional Model of Conflict Behavior," *Organizational Behavior and Human Performance* 16 (1976), p. 145.

his or her own interests and concern for the other party's interests (see Exhibit 10.2). Problem solving is the only style that represents a purely win–win orientation. The other four styles represent variations of the win–lose approach.

- *Problem solving.* Problem solving tries to find a mutually beneficial solution for both parties. Information sharing is an important feature of this style because both parties collaborate to identify common ground and potential solutions that satisfy both (or all) of them.

- *Avoiding.* Avoiding tries to smooth over or avoid conflict situations altogether. It represents a low concern for both self and the other party; in other words, avoiders try to suppress thinking about the conflict. For example, some employees will rearrange their work area or tasks to minimize interaction with certain co-workers.[19]

- *Forcing.* Forcing tries to win the conflict at the other's expense. This style, which has the strongest win–lose orientation, relies on some of the hard influence tactics described in Chapter 9, particularly assertiveness, to get one's own way.

- *Yielding.* Yielding involves giving in completely to the other side's wishes, or at least cooperating with little or no attention to your own interests. This style involves making unilateral concessions and unconditional promises, as well as offering help with no expectation of reciprocal help.

- *Compromising.* Compromising involves looking for a position in which your losses are offset by equally valued gains. It involves matching the other party's concessions, making conditional promises or threats, and actively searching for a middle ground between the interests of the two parties.[20]

Bob Goodenow (left in photo), the Detroit-based agent who led the National Hockey League Players' Association (NHLPA) over the past 15 years, has been called the Darth Vader of hockey. His never-give-in forcing style catapulted NHL player salaries from an average of $210,000 in the early 1990s to $1.3 million today. But while Goodenow's uncompromising approach rewarded players handsomely, critics say it also helped sink the public's image of NHL players, priced professional hockey out of smaller markets, and contributed to the cancellation of the entire 2004–05 season. Goodenow stepped down when players agreed to the NHL owners' request to cap team salaries. Taking his place is Ted Saskin (right in photo), whose diplomatic problem-solving conflict resolution style couldn't be more different from Goodenow's. "We've got to be able to work more cooperatively (with the NHL) in the future," Saskin announced on the day he took over. NHL board of governors chairman Harley Hotchkiss thinks Saskin's approach to resolving differences is good for the sport's future. "I will say nothing bad about Bob Goodenow," insists Hotchkiss. "I just think that in any business you need a spirit of cooperation to move forward, and I think Ted Saskin will handle that well."[21]

Choosing the Best Conflict Management Style

Most of us have a preferred conflict management style, but the best style varies with the situation.[22] The problem-solving style is a good approach for resolving conflict in many situations because it is the only one that actively tries to achieve gains for both parties. However, this style only works well when the parties do not have perfectly opposing interests and when they have enough trust and openness to share information.

You might think that avoiding is an ineffective conflict management strategy, but it is actually the best approach where conflict has become socioemotional or where negotiating has a higher cost than the benefits of conflict resolution.[23] At the same time, conflict avoidance should not be a long-term solution where the conflict persists because it increases the other party's frustration. The forcing style of conflict resolution is usually inappropriate because organizational relationships rarely involve complete opposition. However, forcing may be necessary where you know you are correct and the dispute requires a quick solution. For example, a forcing style may be necessary when the other party engages in unethical conduct because any degree of unethical behavior is unacceptable. The forcing style may also be necessary where the other party would take advantage of more cooperative strategies.

The yielding style may be appropriate when the other party has substantially more power or the issue is not as important to you as to the other party. On the other hand, yielding behaviors may give the other side unrealistically high expectations, thereby motivating them to seek more from you in the future. In the long run, yielding may produce more conflict rather than resolve it. The compromising style may be best when there is little hope for mutual gain through problem solving, both parties have equal power, and both are under time pressure to settle their differences. However, compromise is rarely a final solution and may cause the parties to overlook options for mutual gain.

Cultural and Gender Differences in Conflict Management Styles

Cultural background affects the preferred conflict management style.[24] Some research suggests that people from collectivist cultures—where group goals are valued more than individual goals—are motivated to maintain harmonious relations and, consequently, are more likely than those from low collectivism cultures to manage disagreements through avoidance or problem solving. However, this view may be somewhat simplistic because people in some collectivist cultures are also more likely to publicly shame those whose actions conflict with expectations.[25]

Some writers suggest that men and women also tend to rely on different conflict management styles.[26] Generally speaking, women pay more attention than do men to the relationship between the parties. Consequently, they tend to adopt a problem-solving style in business settings and are more willing to compromise to protect the relationship. Men tend to be more competitive and take a short-term orientation to the relationship. Of course, we must be cautious about these observations because gender has a weak influence on conflict management style.

>Structural Approaches to Conflict Management

Conflict management styles refer to how we approach the other party in a conflict situation. But conflict management also involves altering the underlying structural causes of potential conflict. The main structural approaches are emphasizing superordinate goals, reducing differentiation, improving communication and understanding, reducing task interdependence, increasing resources, and clarifying rules and procedures.

Emphasizing Superordinate Goals

Superordinate goals are common objectives held by conflicting parties that are more important than the departmental or individual goals on which the conflict is based. By increasing commitment to corporatewide goals, employees place less emphasis and therefore feel less conflict with co-workers regarding competing individual or departmental-level goals. They also potentially reduce the problem of differentiation by establishing a common frame of reference. For example, research indicates that the most effective executive teams frame their decisions as superordinate goals that rise above each executive's departmental or divisional goals.[27]

superordinate goal
A common objective held by conflicting parties that is more important than their conflicting departmental or individual goals.

Reducing Differentiation

Another way to minimize dysfunctional conflict is to reduce the differences that produce the conflict in the first place. The more employees think they have common backgrounds or experiences with co-workers, the more motivated they are to coordinate activities and resolve conflict through constructive discussion with those co-workers.[28] One way to increase this commonality is by creating common experiences. The Manila Diamond Hotel in the Philippines accomplishes this by rotating staff across different departments. Multinational peacekeeping forces reduce differentiation among troops from the representative nations by providing opportunities for them to socialize and engage in common activities, including eating together.[29]

Improving Communication and Understanding

A third way to resolve dysfunctional conflict is to give the conflicting parties more opportunities to communicate and understand each other. This recommendation relates back to the contact hypothesis described in Chapter 3. Specifically, the more meaningful interaction we have with someone, the less we rely on stereotypes to understand that person.[31] This

Employees at Toyota Motor Sales U.S.A. are drumming their way to a common bond and cooperation. Over the past three years, more than 3,000 Toyota employees have visited the automaker's training center (University of Toyota) in Torrance, California, to participate in drum circles. Typically in groups of 15 to 50 from one department, employees would begin banging on one of the 150 percussion instruments available in the drum room. Few have played a percussion instrument before, so the first attempt usually produces noise. "At first, it sounds pretty terrible, with everyone competing to be the loudest" admits Ron Johnson, Toyota's resident drum guru and a training center manager in Torrance. But most groups soon find a common beat without any guidance or conductor. Johnson recalls his first drum circle experience: "I'll never forget the spirit that came alive inside me. In a matter of moments, perfect strangers came together in synchronistic rhythm to share a common vision." By the end of the hour-long event, most groups have formed a special bond that apparently increases their cooperation and sense of unity when they return to their jobs.[30]

positive effect is more pronounced when people work closely and frequently together on a shared goal or a meaningful task where they need to rely on each other (i.e., cooperate rather than compete with each other). Another important ingredient is that the parties have equal status in that context.

There are two important caveats regarding the communication-understanding strategy. First, this strategy should be applied only *after* differentiation between the two sides has been reduced. If perceived differentiation remains high, attempts to manage conflict through dialogue might have the opposite effect because defense mechanisms are more likely to kick into action. These self-preservation forces increase stereotyping and tend to distort incoming sensory information. In other words, when forced to interact with people who we believe are quite different and in conflict with us, we tend to select information that reinforces that view.[32] Thus, communication and understanding interventions are effective only when differentiation is sufficiently low.

Second, resolving differences through direct communication with the opposing party is a distinctly Western strategy that is not as comfortably applied in most parts of Asia and in other collectivist cultures.[33] As noted earlier, people in high collectivism cultures prefer an avoidance conflict management style because it is the most consistent with harmony and face-saving. Direct communication is a high-risk strategy because it easily threatens the need to save face and maintain harmony.

Talking Circles

Where avoidance is ineffective in the long run, some collectivist groups engage in structured forms of dialogue that enable communication with less risk of upsetting harmony. One such practice in Native American culture is the talking circle.[34] A talking circle is an ancient group process used to educate, make decisions, and repair group harmony due to conflict. Participants sit in a circle and often begin with song, prayer, shaking hands with the next person, or some other communal activity. Then they share their experiences, information, and stories relating to the issue.

A talking stick or other natural object (rock, feather) is held by the person speaking, which minimizes interruptions and dysfunctional verbal reactions by others. Talking circles are not aimed at solving problems through negotiated discussion. In fact, talking circle norms usually discourage participants from responding to someone else's statements. Rather, the emphasis is on healing relationships and restoring harmony, typically through the circle's communal experience and improved understanding of each person's views.

Reducing Task Interdependence

Conflict increases with the level of interdependence so minimizing dysfunctional conflict might involve reducing the level of interdependence between the parties. If cost effective, this might occur by dividing the shared resource so that each party has exclusive use of part of it. Highly interdependent jobs might be combined so less coordination is needed. For example, rather than have one employee serve customers and another operate the cash register, each employee could handle both customer activities alone. Buffers also help to reduce task interdependence between people. Buffers include resources, such as adding more inventory between people who perform sequential tasks.

Increasing Resources

An obvious way to reduce conflict due to resource scarcity is to increase the amount of resources available. Corporate decision makers might quickly dismiss this solution because of the costs involved. However, they need to carefully compare these costs with the costs of dysfunctional conflict arising out of resource scarcity.

Clarifying Rules and Procedures

Conflicts that arise from ambiguous rules can be minimized by establishing rules and procedures. Armstrong World Industries, Inc., applied this strategy when consultants and information systems employees clashed while working together on development of a client-server network. Information systems employees at the flooring and building materials company thought they should be in charge, whereas consultants believed they had the senior role. Also, the consultants wanted to work long hours and take Friday off to fly home, whereas Armstrong employees wanted to work regular hours. The company reduced these conflicts by having both parties agree on specific responsibilities and roles. The agreement also assigned two senior executives at both companies to establish rules if future disagreements arose.[35]

>Third-Party Conflict Resolution

Most of this chapter has focused on people directly involved in a conflict, yet many disputes in organizational settings are resolved with the assistance of a manager or other third party. **Third-party conflict resolution** is any attempt by a relatively neutral person to help the parties resolve their differences. There are generally three types of third-party dispute resolution activities: arbitration, inquisition, and mediation. These activities can be classified by their level of control over the process and control over the decision (see Exhibit 10.3).[36]

third-party conflict resolution
Any attempt by a relatively neutral person to help the parties resolve their differences.

- *Arbitration.* Arbitrators have high control over the final decision but low control over the process. Executives engage in this strategy by following previously agreed rules of due process, listening to arguments from the disputing employees, and making a binding decision. Arbitration is applied as the final stage of grievances by unionized employees, but it is also becoming more common in nonunion conflicts.

[Exhibit 10.3]   Types of Third-Party Intervention

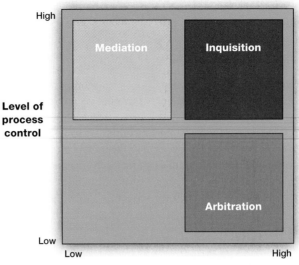

• *Inquisition.* Inquisitors control all discussion about the conflict. Like arbitrators, they have high decision control because they choose the form of conflict resolution. However, they also have high process control because they choose which information to examine and how to examine it, and they generally decide how the conflict resolution process will be handled.

• *Mediation.* Mediators have high control over the conflict management process. In fact, their main purpose is to manage the process and context of interaction between the disputing parties. However, the parties make the final decision about how to resolve their differences. Thus, mediators have little or no control over the conflict resolution decision.

Choosing the Best Third-Party Intervention Strategy

Team leaders, executives, and co-workers regularly intervene in disputes between employees and departments. Sometimes they adopt a mediator role; other times they serve as arbitrators. However, research suggests that people in positions of authority (e.g., managers) usually adopt an inquisitional approach whereby they dominate the intervention process as well as making a binding decision.[37] Managers like the inquisition approach because it is consistent with the decision-oriented nature of managerial jobs, gives them control over the conflict process and outcome, and tends to resolve disputes efficiently.

However, the inquisitional approach to third-party conflict resolution is usually the least effective in organizational settings.[38] One problem is that leaders who take an inquisitional role tend to collect limited information about the problem using this approach, so their imposed decision may produce an ineffective solution to the conflict. Also, employees often view inquisitional procedures and outcomes as unfair because they have little control over this approach.

Which third-party intervention is most appropriate in organizations? The answer partly depends on the situation, such as the type of dispute, the relationship between the manager and employees, and cultural values such as power distance.[39] But generally speaking, for everyday disputes between two employees, the mediation approach is usually best because this gives employees more responsibility for resolving their own disputes. The third-party representative merely establishes an appropriate context for conflict resolution. Although not as efficient as other strategies, mediation potentially offers the highest level of employee satisfaction with the conflict process and outcomes.[40] When employees cannot resolve their differences, arbitration seems to work best because the predetermined rules of evidence and other processes create a higher sense of procedural fairness. Moreover, arbitration is preferred where the organization's goals should take priority over individual goals.

>chapter summary

Conflict is the process in which one party perceives that its interests are being opposed or negatively affected by another party. The conflict process begins with the sources of conflict. These sources lead one or both sides to perceive a conflict and to experience conflict emotions. This, in turn, produces manifest conflict, such as aggressive words or behaviors toward the other side. The conflict process often escalates through a series of episodes.

Conflict management maximizes the benefits and minimizes the dysfunctional consequences of conflict. Constructive conflict, a possible benefit of conflict, occurs when team members debate their different perceptions about an issue in a way that keeps the conflict focused on the task rather than people. Socioemotional conflict, a negative outcome, occurs when differences are viewed as personal attacks rather than attempts to resolve an issue. Socioemotional conflict tends to emerge in most constructive conflict episodes, but it is less likely to dominate when the parties are emotionally intelligent, have a cohesive team, and have supportive team norms. The main problems with conflict are that it may lead to job stress, dissatisfaction, and turnover.

Conflict tends to increase when people have incompatible goals, differentiation (different values and beliefs), interdependent tasks, scarce resources, ambiguous rules, and problems communicating with each other.

People with a win–win orientation believe the parties will find a mutually beneficial solution to their disagreement. Those with a win–lose orientation adopt the belief that the parties are drawing from a fixed pie. The latter tends to escalate conflict. Among the five interpersonal conflict management styles, only problem solving represents a purely win–win orientation. The four other styles—avoiding, forcing, yielding, and compromising—adopt some variation of a win–lose orientation. Women and people with high collectivism tend to use a problem-solving or avoidance style more than men and people with high individualism.

Structural approaches to conflict management include emphasizing superordinate goals, reducing differentiation, improving communication and understanding, reducing task interdependence, increasing resources, and clarifying rules and procedures. These elements can also be altered to stimulate conflict.

Third-party conflict resolution is any attempt by a relatively neutral person to help the parties resolve their differences. The three main forms of third-party dispute resolution are mediation, arbitration, and inquisition. Managers tend to use an inquisition approach, although mediation and arbitration are more appropriate, depending on the situation.

>key.terms

conflict 195	superordinate goals 203
conflict management 197	third-party conflict resolution 205
constructive conflict 197	win–lose orientation 200
socioemotional conflict 197	win–win orientation 200

>critical.thinking.questions

1. Distinguish constructive conflict from socioemotional conflict and explain how to apply the former without having the latter become a problem.

2. The chief executive officer of Creative Toys, Inc., read about cooperation in Japanese companies and vowed to bring this same philosophy to the company. The goal is to avoid all conflict, so that employees would work cooperatively and be happier at Creative Toys. Discuss the merits and limitations of the CEO's policy.

3. This chapter explains that it is a challenge to encourage constructive conflict without having the experience generate too much socioemotional conflict. What characteristics of team dynamics (see Chapter 7) can potentially minimize socioemotional conflict while team members debate their differences?

4. Conflict among managers emerged soon after a French company acquired a Swedish firm. The Swedes perceived the French management as hierarchical and arrogant, whereas the French thought the Swedes were naive, cautious, and lacking an achievement orientation. Describe ways to reduce dysfunctional conflict in this situation.

5. This chapter describes three levels of task interdependence that exist in interpersonal and intergroup relationships. Identify examples of these three levels in your work or school activities. How do these three levels affect potential conflict for you?

6. Jane was just appointed purchasing manager of Tacoma Technologies Corp. The previous purchasing manager, who recently retired, was known for his winner-take-all approach to suppliers. He continually fought for more discounts and was skeptical about any special deals proposed by suppliers. A few suppliers refused to do business with Tacoma Technologies, but senior management was confident that the former purchasing manager's approach minimized the company's costs. Jane wants to try a more problem-solving approach to working with suppliers. Will her approach work? How should she adopt a more problem-solving approach in future negotiations with suppliers?

7. You are a special assistant to the commander-in-chief of a peacekeeping mission to a war-torn part of the world. The unit consists of a few thousand peacekeeping troops from the United States, France, India, and four other countries. The troops will work together for approximately one year. What strategies would you recommend to improve mutual understanding and minimize conflict among these troops?

8. Managers tend to use an inquisitional approach to resolving disputes between employees and departments. Describe the inquisitional approach and discuss its appropriateness in organizational settings.

>case.study:skillbuilder10.1

Conflict in Close Quarters

A team of psychologists at Moscow's Institute for Biomedical Problems (IBMP) wanted to learn more about the dynamics of long-term isolation in space. This knowledge would be applied to the International Space Station, a joint project of several countries that would send people into space for more than six months. It would eventually include a trip to Mars taking up to three years.

IBMP set up a replica of the Mir space station in Moscow. They then arranged for three international researchers from Japan, Canada, and Austria to spend 110 days isolated in a chamber the size of a train car. This chamber joined a smaller chamber in which four Russian cosmonauts had already completed half of their 240 days of isolation. This was the first time an international crew was involved in the studies. None of the participants spoke English as their first language, yet they communicated throughout their stay in English at varying levels of proficiency.

Judith Lapierre, a French Canadian, was the only female in the experiment. Along with holding a PhD in public health and social medicine, Lapierre studied space sociology at the International Space University in France and conducted isolation research in the Antarctic. This was her fourth trip to Russia, where she had learned the language. The mission was supposed to have a second female participant from the Japanese space program, but she was not selected by IBMP.

The Japanese and Austrian participants viewed the participation of a woman as a favorable factor, says Lapierre. For example, to make the surroundings more comfortable, they rearranged the furniture, hung posters on the wall, and put a tablecloth on the kitchen table. "We adapted our environment, whereas the Russians just viewed it as something to be endured," she explains. "We decorated for Christmas, because I'm the kind of person who likes to host people."

New Year's Eve Turmoil

Ironically, it was at one of those social events, the New Year's Eve party, that events took a turn for the worse. After drinking vodka (allowed by the Russian space agency), two of the Russian cosmonauts got into a fistfight that left blood splattered on the chamber walls. At one point, a colleague hid the knives in the station's kitchen because of fears that the two Russians were about to stab each other. The two cosmonauts, who generally did not get along, had to be restrained by other men. Soon after that brawl, the Russian commander grabbed Lapierre, dragged her out of view of the television monitoring cameras, and kissed her aggressively—twice. Lapierre fought him off, but the message didn't register. He tried to kiss her again the next morning.

The next day, the international crew complained to IBMP about the behavior of the Russian cosmonauts. The Russian institute apparently took no action against any of the aggressors. Instead, the institute's psychologists replied that the incidents were part of the experiment. They wanted crew members to solve their personal problems with mature discussion, without asking for outside help. "You have to understand that Mir is an autonomous object, far away from anything," Vadim Gushin, the IBMP psychologist in charge of project, explained after the experiment had ended in March. "If the crew can't solve problems among themselves, they can't work together."

Following IBMP's response, the international crew wrote a scathing letter to the Russian institute and the space agencies involved in the experiment. "We had never expected such events to take place in a highly controlled scientific experiment where individuals go through a multistep selection process," they wrote. "If we had known . . . we would not have joined it as subjects." The letter also complained about IBMP's response to their concerns.

Informed of the New Year's Eve incident, the Japanese space program convened an emergency meeting on January 2 to address the incidents. Soon after, the Japanese team member quit, apparently shocked by IBMP's inaction. He was replaced with a Russian researcher on the international team. Ten days after the fight—a little more than a month after the international team began the mission—the doors between the Russian and international crew's chambers were barred at the request of the international research team. Lapierre later emphasized that this action was taken because of concerns about violence, not the incident involving her.

A Stolen Kiss or Sexual Harassment

By the end of the experiment in March, news of the fistfight between the cosmonauts and the commander's attempts to kiss Lapierre had reached the public. Russian scientists attempted to play down the kissing incident by saying that it was one fleeting kiss, a clash of cultures, and a female participant who was too emotional.

"In the West, some kinds of kissing are regarded as sexual harassment. In our culture it's nothing," said Russian scientist Vadim Gushin in one interview. In another interview, he explained, "The problem of sexual harassment is given a lot of attention in North America but less in Europe. In Russia it is even less of an issue, not because we are more or less moral than the rest of the world; we just have different priorities."

Judith Lapierre says the kissing incident was tolerable compared to this reaction from the Russian scientists who conducted the experiment. "They don't get it at all," she complains. "They don't think anything is wrong. I'm more frustrated than ever. The worst thing is that they don't realize it was wrong."

Norbert Kraft, the Austrian scientist on the international team, also disagreed with the Russian interpretation of events. "They're trying to protect themselves," he says. "They're trying to put the fault on others. But this is not a cultural issue. If a woman doesn't want to be kissed, it is not acceptable."

Discussion Questions

1. Identify the different conflict episodes that exist in this case? Who was in conflict with whom?

2. What are the sources of conflict for these conflict incidents?

3. What conflict management style(s) did Lapierre, the international team, and Gushin use to resolve these conflicts? What style(s) would have worked best in these situations?

4. What conflict management interventions were applied here? Did they work? What alternative strategies would work best in this situation and in the future?

Sources: The facts of this case are pieced together by Steven L. McShane from the following sources: G. Sinclair Jr., "If You Scream in Space, Does Anyone Hear?" *Winnipeg Free Press,* May 5, 2000, p. A4; S. Martin, "Reining in the Space Cowboys," *Globe & Mail,* April 19, 2000, p. R1; M. Gray, "A Space Dream Sours," *Maclean's,* April 17, 2000, p. 26; E. Niiler, "In Search of the Perfect Astronaut," *Boston Globe,* April 4, 2000, p. E4; J. Tracy, "110-Day Isolation Ends in Sullen . . . Isolation," *Moscow Times,* March 30, 2000, p. 1; M. Warren, "A Mir Kiss?" *Daily Telegraph* (London), March 30, 2000, p. 22; G. York, "Canadian's Harassment Complaint Scorned," *Globe & Mail,* March 25, 2000, p. A2; and S. Nolen, "Lust in Space," *Globe & Mail,* March 24, 2000, p. A3.

>team.exercise:skillbuilder10.2

Ugli Orange Role Play

Purpose   This exercise is designed to help you understand the dynamics of interpersonal and intergroup conflict as well as the effectiveness of negotiation strategies under specific conditions.

Materials   The instructor will distribute roles for Dr. Roland, Dr. Jones, and a few observers. Ideally, each negotiation should occur in a private area away from other negotiations.

Instructions

- *Step 1:* The instructor will divide the class into an even number of teams of three people each, with one participant left over for each team formed (e.g., six observers if there are six teams). One-half of the teams will take the role of Dr. Roland and the other half will be Dr. Jones. The instructor will distribute roles after these teams have been formed.

- *Step 2:* Members within each team are given 10 minutes (or other time limit stated by the instructor) to learn their roles and decide negotiating strategy.

- *Step 3:* After reading their roles and discussing strategy, each Dr. Jones team is matched with a Dr. Roland team to conduct negotiations. Observers will receive observation forms from the instructor, and two observers will be assigned to watch the paired teams during prenegotiations and subsequent negotiations.

- *Step 4:* As soon as Roland and Jones reach agreement or at the end of the time allotted for the negotiation (which ever comes first), the Roland and Jones teams report to the instructor for further instruction.

- *Step 5:* At the end of the exercise, the class will congregate to discuss the negotiations. Observers, negotiators and instructors will then discuss their observations and experiences and the implications for conflict management and negotiation.

Source: This exercise was developed by Robert J. House, Wharton Business School, University of Pennsylvania. A similar incident is also attributed to earlier writing by R. R. Blake and J. S. Mouton.

>self-assessment.skillbuilder10.3

The Dutch Test for Conflict Handling

There are many ways to handle a conflict situation, but we tend to prefer one conflict handling style over others. This instrument measures your preference for each of five conflict handling styles. Read each of the statements and select the response that you believe best reflects your position regarding each statement. This exercise is completed alone so students assess themselves honestly without concerns of social comparison. However, class discussion will focus on the different conflict management styles and the situations in which each is most appropriate.

**Find the full self-assessments on the OLC at
www.mhhe.com/mcshaneess**

[chapter 11]

Leadership in Organizational Settings

>**learning**objectives

After reading this chapter, you should be able to

- Define leadership.
- List seven competencies of effective leaders.
- Describe the people-oriented and task-oriented leadership styles.
- Outline the path-goal theory of leadership.
- Contrast transactional with transformational leadership.
- Describe the four elements of transformational leadership.
- Explain how perceptions of followers influence leadership.
- Discuss similarities and differences in the leadership styles of women and men.

A few days after becoming CEO of Procter & Gamble (P&G), Alan George Lafley walked unannounced into a dinner party of former P&G employees who had moved to other companies. This act was highly symbolic because the household goods giant famously promoted from within and treated anyone who left the company before retirement as outcasts. P&G was in trouble—it lacked new products and its existing offerings were under siege from competitors—so Lafley's visit to P&G alumni (the first such visit by a P&G CEO) quickly signaled that the company would embrace ideas and people from outside the organization.

In addition to greeting former employees, Lafley incessantly communicates the mantra that "The consumer is boss" and that the company's future depends on creativity. Far from the heroic charismatic style of P&G's previous CEO, who failed to turn the company around and was ousted in just 18 months, Lafley is distinctly "unassuming" with "a humble demeanor that belies his status." Says one industry observer: "If there were 15 people sitting around the conference table, it wouldn't be obvious that he was the CEO."

Yet Lafley has transformed P&G where others could not. His calm self-assurance, consistent vision, and symbolic and strategic actions toward a more customer-friendly and innovative organization have provided the direction and clarity that the company lacked. Importantly, Lafley also walks the talk; his behavior is closely aligned with the message that he conveys. He restructured the company, pruned costs, made significant acquisitions (Gillette and Clairol), and rekindled a spirit of innovation through special creativity teams. Lafley is also out in the field 10 to 15 days each year, meeting with customers and closely observing what they like and don't like about the company's and competitor's products.

To instill the creative spirit at the top, Lafley took P&G's entire 40-person leadership council to a one-day innovation workshop in San Francisco led by design firm IDEO. IDEO also built an innovation center (called "the Gym") where P&G staff learn brainstorming, prototyping, observation, and other ways to become more innovative. Lafley revamped the executive offices into an open-space plan that improves information sharing. He has also hired an army of creative types from other organizations and paired them with long-service P&G staff. The result: P&G has become the industry's hotspot for innovation, its market share and profitability have experienced sustained growth, and its stock price has soared.[1]

A. G. Lafley might have been an unlikely image of an effective leader a few years ago, but the world is discovering that charisma and leadership do not necessary go hand-in-hand. What, then, is leadership? Not long ago, 54 leadership experts from 38 countries reached a consensus that **leadership** is about influencing, motivating, and enabling others to contribute toward the effectiveness and success of the organizations of which they are members.[2] Leaders apply various forms of influence—from subtle persuasion to direct application of power—to ensure that followers have the motivation and role clarity to achieve specified goals. Leaders also arrange the work environment—such as allocating resources and altering communication patterns—so that employees can achieve corporate objectives more easily.

leadership
Influencing, motivating, and enabling others to contribute toward the effectiveness and success of the organizations of which they are members.

Leadership isn't restricted to the executive suite. Anyone in the organization may be a leader in various ways and at various times.[3] This view is variously known as *shared leadership* or the *leaderful organization*. Successful organizations empower their employees to take leadership roles. "We're quite serious when we talk about leadership even to a bench worker on the assembly line," says an executive at General Semiconductor, a global high-technology company. "Lots of people will say, 'Oh, I'm not a leader,' but when we point out that the essence of leadership is influence, they realize everyone has leadership qualities and responsibilities."[4]

Effective self-directed work teams, for example, consist of members who share leadership responsibilities or otherwise allocate this role to a responsible coordinator. Consider W. L. Gore & Associates, the Newark, Delaware–based manufacturer of fabrics (Gore-Tex), electronics, industrial, and medical products. Gore is organized around self-directed work teams and, consequently, has few formal leaders. Yet when asked in the company's annual survey "Are you a leader?" more than 50 percent of Gore employees answer yes.[5]

>Perspectives of Leadership

Leadership has been contemplated since the days of Greek philosophers, and it is one of the most popular research topics among organizational behavior scholars. This has resulted in an enormous volume of leadership literature, most of which can be organized into the five perspectives shown in Exhibit 11.1.[6] Although some of these perspectives are currently more popular than others, each helps us to more fully understand this complex issue.

Some research studies have examined leadership competencies, whereas others have focused on leadership behaviors. More recent studies have looked at leadership from a contingency approach by considering the appropriate leader behaviors in different settings. Currently, the most popular perspective is that leaders transform organizations through their vision, communication, and ability to build commitment. Finally, an emerging perspective suggests that leadership includes a perceptual bias. We distort reality and attribute events to leaders because we feel more comfortable believing that a competent individual is at the organization's helm. This chapter explores each of these five perspectives of leadership. In the final section, we also briefly consider cross-cultural and gender issues in organizational leadership.

>Competency (Trait) Perspective of Leadership

Since the beginning of recorded civilization, people have been interested in personal characteristics that distinguish great leaders from the rest of us. A major review in the late 1940s concluded that no consistent list of traits could be distilled from the hundreds of studies conducted up to that time. A subsequent review suggested that a few traits are con-

[**Exhibit 11.1**] Perspectives of Leadership

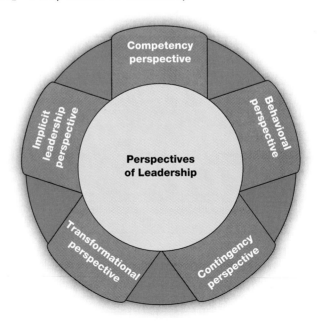

sistently associated with effective leaders, but most are unrelated to effective leadership.[7] These conclusions caused many scholars to give up their search for personal characteristics that distinguish effective leaders.

Over the past decade, leadership researchers and consultants have increasingly returned to the notion that leadership requires specific *competencies*. These competencies enable companies to select future leaders and to provide leadership development programs.[8] Competencies encompass a broader range of personal characteristics—such as knowledge, skills, abilities, and values—that were not considered by earlier studies on leadership traits. The recent leadership literature identifies seven competencies that are characteristic of effective leaders.[9]

- *Emotional intelligence.* Effective leaders have a high level of emotional intelligence.[10] They have the ability to perceive and express emotion, assimilate emotion in thought, understand and reason with emotion, and regulate emotion in themselves and others (see Chapter 4). They possess the ability to empathize with others and possess the social skills necessary to build rapport as well as network with others.

- *Integrity.* This refers to the leader's truthfulness and tendency to translate words into deeds. This characteristic is sometimes called *authentic leadership* because the individual acts consistently with his or her beliefs and values. He or she has a higher moral capacity to judge dilemmas based on sound values and to act accordingly. Several large-scale studies have reported that integrity or honesty is the most important leadership characteristic. Employees want honest leaders whom they can trust.[11] Unfortunately, surveys report that most employees don't trust their leaders and don't think they have integrity.

- *Drive.* Leaders have a high need for achievement. This drive represents the inner motivation that leaders possess to pursue their goals and encourage others to move forward with theirs. Drive inspires an inquisitiveness and need to learn.

- *Leadership motivation.* Leaders have a strong need for power because they want to influence others. However, they tend to have a need for *socialized power* because their motivation is directed by a strong sense of altruism and social responsibility.[13] In other words, effective leaders try to gain power

Greg Trantor (right in this photo) stood before 500 information technology professionals under his leadership as chief information officer at Allmerica Financial Corp. and gave them the bad news: Even though the group had intensively cut costs and 42 colleagues had been laid off the year before, 65 more people would be laid off immediately. At the end of Trantor's presentation, the group applauded. Why would employees applaud such devastating news? They were showing support to Trantor for his integrity in doing all he could to minimize the pain. Unfortunately, few employees in other organizations are applauding the integrity of their leaders. Although improving, still only about half of employees in one survey said they have trust and confidence in senior management. In another poll, 73 percent said chief executives of large corporations could not be trusted.[12]

so that they can influence others to accomplish goals that benefit the team or organization.

- *Self-confidence.* Procter & Gamble CEO A. G. Lafley and other leaders believe in their leadership skills and ability to achieve objectives. Effective leaders are typically extroverted—outgoing, sociable, talkative, and assertive—although not necessarily so (P&G's Lafley is apparently a counterexample).

- *Intelligence.* Leaders have above-average cognitive ability to process enormous amounts of information. Leaders aren't necessarily geniuses; rather, they have superior ability to analyze alternate scenarios and identify potential opportunities.

- *Knowledge of the business.* Effective leaders know the business environment in which they operate. For instance, Lafley has thorough knowledge of Procter & Gamble products and its markets. This assists the leader's intuition to recognize opportunities and understand the organization's capacity to capture those opportunities.

Although the competency perspective is gaining popularity (again), it assumes that all leaders have the same personal characteristics and that all of these qualities are equally important in all situations. This is probably a false assumption; leadership is far too complex to have a universal list of traits that apply to every condition. Some competencies might not be important all the time. Another limitation is that alternative combinations of competencies may be equally successful. In other words, people with two different sets of competencies might be equally good leaders.[14]

The competency perspective of leadership does not necessarily imply that people are born as great leaders. On the contrary, competencies only indicate leadership potential, not leadership performance. People with these characteristics become effective leaders only after they have developed and mastered the necessary leadership behaviors. People with somewhat lower leadership competencies may become very effective leaders because they have leveraged their potential more fully. This means that companies must do more than hire people with certain competencies; they must also develop their potential through leadership development programs and practical experience in the field.

>Behavioral Perspective of Leadership

In the 1940s and 1950s, leadership experts at several universities launched an intensive research investigation to answer the question: What behaviors make leaders effective? Questionnaires were administered to subordinates, asking them to rate their supervisors on a large number of behaviors. These studies distilled two clusters of leadership behaviors from literally thousands of leadership behavior items.[15]

One cluster represented people-oriented behaviors. This included showing mutual trust and respect for subordinates, demonstrating a genuine concern for their needs, and having a desire to look out for their welfare. Leaders with a strong people-oriented style listen to employee suggestions, do personal favors for employees, support their interests when required, and treat employees as equals.

The other cluster represented a task-oriented leadership style and included behaviors that define and structure work roles. Task-oriented leaders assign employees to specific tasks, clarify their work duties and procedures, ensure that they follow company rules, and push them to reach their performance capacity. They establish stretch goals and challenge employees to push beyond those high standards.

Choosing Task- versus People-Oriented Leadership

Should leaders be task-oriented or people-oriented? This is a difficult question to answer because each style has its advantages and disadvantages. Recent evidence suggests that both styles are positively associated with leader effectiveness, but differences are often apparent only in very high or very low levels of each style. Generally, absenteeism, grievances, turnover, and job dissatisfaction are higher among employees who work with supervisors with very low levels of people-oriented leadership. Job performance is lower among employees who work for supervisors with low levels of task-oriented leadership.[16] College students seem to value task-oriented instructors because they want clear objectives and well-prepared lectures that abide by the unit's objectives.[17]

One problem with the behavioral leadership perspective is that the two categories are broad generalizations that mask specific behaviors within each category. For instance, task-oriented leadership includes planning work activities, clarifying roles, and monitoring operations and performance. Each of these clusters of activities is fairly distinct and likely has different effects on employee well-being and performance. A second concern is that the behavioral approach assumes that high levels of both styles are best in all situations. In reality, the best leadership style depends on the situation.[18] This contingency perspective of leadership is discussed next.

>Contingency Perspective of Leadership

The contingency perspective of leadership is based on the idea that the most appropriate leadership style depends on the situation. Most, although not all, contingency leadership theories assume that effective leaders must be both insightful and flexible.[19] They must be able to adapt their behaviors and styles to the immediate situation. This isn't easy to do, however. Leaders typically have a preferred style. It takes considerable effort for leaders to learn when and how to alter their styles to match the situation. As we noted earlier, leaders must have a high emotional intelligence, so they can diagnose the circumstances and match their behaviors accordingly.

Path-Goal Theory of Leadership

Several contingency theories have been proposed over the years, but **path-goal leadership theory** has withstood scientific critique better than the others. The theory has its roots in the expectancy theory of motivation (see Chapter 5).[20] Early research incorporated expectancy theory into the study of how leader behaviors influence employee perceptions of expectancies (paths) between employee effort and performance (goals). Out of this early work was born path-goal theory as a contingency leadership model.

Path-goal theory states that effective leaders strengthen the performance-to-outcome expectancy and valences of those outcomes by ensuring that employees who perform their jobs well have a higher degree of need fulfillment than employees who perform poorly. Effective leaders strengthen the effort-to-performance expectancy by providing the information, support, and other resources necessary to help employees complete their tasks.[21] In other words, path-goal theory advocates **servant leadership.**[22] Servant leaders do not view leadership as a position of power; rather, they are coaches, stewards, and facilitators. Leadership is an obligation to understand employee needs and to facilitate their work performance and personal wellbeing. Servant leaders ask, "How can I help you?" rather than expect employees to serve them.

path-goal leadership theory
A contingency theory of leadership, based on expectancy theory of motivation, that relates several leadership styles to specific employee and situational contingencies.

servent leadership
The belief that leaders serve followers by understanding their needs and facilitating their work performance.

[Exhibit 11.2]   Path-Goal Leadership Theory

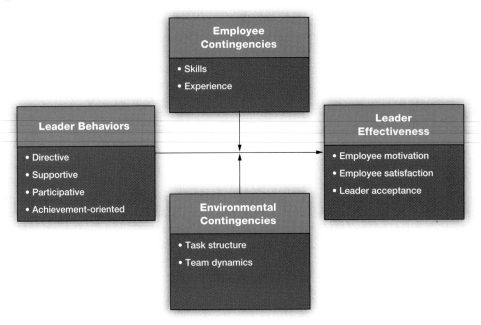

Leadership Styles

Exhibit 11.2 presents the path-goal theory of leadership. This model specifically highlights four leadership styles and several contingency factors leading to three indicators of leader effectiveness. The four leadership styles are[23]

- *Directive.* These are clarifying behaviors that provide a psychological structure for subordinates. The leader clarifies performance goals, the means to reach those goals, and the standards against which performance will be judged. It also includes judicious use of rewards and disciplinary actions. Directive leadership is the same as task-oriented leadership described earlier and echoes our discussion in Chapter 2 on the importance of clear role perceptions in employee performance.

- *Supportive.* These behaviors provide psychological support for subordinates. The leader is friendly and approachable; makes the work more pleasant; treats employees with equal respect; and shows concern for the status, needs, and well-being of employees. Supportive leadership is the same as people-oriented leadership described earlier and reflects the benefits of social support to help employees cope with stressful situations.

- *Participative.* These behaviors encourage and facilitate subordinate involvement in decisions beyond their normal work activities. The leader consults with employees, asks for their suggestions, and takes these ideas into serious consideration before making a decision. Participative leadership relates to involving employees in decisions.

- *Achievement-oriented.* These behaviors encourage employees to reach their peak performance. The leader sets challenging goals, expects employees to perform at their highest level, continuously seeks improvement in employee performance, and shows a high degree of confidence that employees will assume responsibility and accomplish challenging goals. Achievement-oriented leadership applies goal-setting theory as well as positive expectations in self-fulfilling prophecy.

Tom LaSorda (shown here with Chrysler employees in Mexico) sets tough goals and looks for ways to improve efficiency by clocking how much time employees lose moving from one station to the next. "With every second, you've lost productivity," explains LaSorda, who recently became CEO of Chrysler Group. "That's kind of how my mind works." A few years before joining Chrysler, LaSorda was a General Motors executive responsible for a troubled plant in Eisenbach, Germany. His combination of directive and achievement-oriented leadership, as well as self-taught knowledge of lean manufacturing practices, helped the Eisenbach plant become one of GM's most efficient operations. Still, some observers believe that as Chrysler CEO, LaSorda needs to shift from these transactional leadership styles to something more transformational. "Tom LaSorda, who's more of a nuts-and-bolts type of guy, needs to take it to the next level and set Chrysler up for the next decade," suggests an auto consultant.[24]

The path-goal model contends that effective leaders are capable of selecting the most appropriate behavioral style (or styles) for that situation. Leaders might simultaneously use more than one style at a time. For example, they might be both supportive and participative in a specific situation.

Contingencies of Path-Goal Theory

As a contingency theory, path-goal theory states that each of these four leadership styles will be effective in some situations but not in others. The path-goal leadership model specifies two sets of situational variables that moderate the relationship between a leader's style and effectiveness: (1) employee characteristics and (2) characteristics of the employee's work environment. Several contingencies have already been studied within the path-goal framework, and the model is open for more variables in the future.[25] However, we will examine only three contingencies here.

- *Skill and experience.* A combination of directive and supportive leadership is best for employees who are, or perceive themselves to be, inexperienced and unskilled. Directive leadership gives subordinates information about how to accomplish the task, whereas supportive leadership helps them cope with the uncertainties of unfamiliar work situations. Directive leadership is detrimental when employees are skilled and experienced because it introduces too much supervisory control.

- *Task structure.* Leaders should adopt the directive style when the task is not routine, because this style minimizes role ambiguity that tends to occur in these complex work situations, particularly for inexperienced employees.[26] The directive style is ineffective when employees have routine and simple tasks because the manager's guidance serves no purpose and may be viewed as unnecessarily close control. Employees in highly routine and simple jobs may require supportive leadership to help them cope with the tedious nature of the work and lack of control over the pace of work. Participative leadership is preferred for employees performing nonroutine tasks because the lack of rules and procedures gives them more discretion to achieve challenging goals. The participative style is ineffective for employees in routine tasks because they lack discretion over their work.

- *Team dynamics.* Cohesive teams with performance-oriented norms act as a substitute for most leader interventions. High team cohesiveness substitutes for supportive leadership, whereas performance-oriented team norms substitute for directive and possibly achievement-oriented leadership. Thus, when team cohesiveness is low, leaders should use the supportive style. Leaders should apply the directive style to counteract team norms that oppose the team's formal objectives. For example, the team leader may need to use legitimate power if team members have developed a norm to "take it easy" rather than get a project completed on time.

Path-goal theory has received considerably research support, certainly more than other contingency leadership models. However, one or two contingencies (i.e., task structure) have found limited research support. Other contingencies and leadership styles in the path-goal leadership model haven't received research investigation at all.[27] Another concern is that as path-goal theory expands, the model may become too complex for practical use. Few people would be able to remember all the contingencies and appropriate leadership styles for those contingencies. In spite of these limitations, path-goal theory remains a relatively robust contingency leadership theory.

Leadership Substitutes

leadership substitutes
A theory that identifies contingencies that either limit the leader's ability to influence subordinates or make that particular leadership style unnecessary.

Unlike path-goal leadership, which recommends different leadership styles in various situations, the **leadership substitutes** approach identifies conditions that either limit the leader's ability to influence subordinates or make that particular leadership style unnecessary. The literature identifies several conditions that possibly substitute for task-oriented or people-oriented leadership. For example, performance-based reward systems keep employees directed toward organizational goals, so they might replace or reduce the need for task-oriented leadership. Task-oriented leadership is also less important when employees are skilled and experienced. Notice how these propositions are similar to path-goal leadership theory, namely that directive leadership is unnecessary, and may be detrimental, when employees are skilled or experienced.[28]

Some research suggests that effective leaders help team members learn to lead themselves through leadership substitutes, which makes co-workers substitutes for leadership in high involvement team structures.[29] Co-workers instruct new employees, thereby providing directive leadership. They also provide social support, which reduces stress among fellow employees. Teams with norms that support organizational goals may substitute for achievement-oriented leadership, because employees encourage, or pressure, co-workers to stretch their performance levels.[30]

Self-leadership—the process of influencing oneself to establish the self-direction and self-motivation needed to perform a task—is another possible leadership substitute in self-directed work teams.[31] Employees with high self-leadership set their own goals, reinforce their own behavior, maintain positive thought processes, and monitor their own performance, thereby managing both personal motivation and abilities. As employees become more proficient in self-leadership, they presumably require less supervision to keep them focused and energized toward organizational objectives.

The leadership substitutes model has intuitive appeal, but the evidence so far is mixed. Some studies show that a few substitutes do replace the need for task- or people-oriented leadership, but others do not. The messiness of statistically testing for leadership substitutes may account for some problems, but a few writers contend that the limited support is evidence that leadership plays a critical role regardless of the situation.[32] At this point, we can conclude that a few conditions such as self-directed work teams, self-leadership, and reward systems might reduce the importance of task- or people-oriented leadership but probably won't completely replace leaders in these situations.

>Transformational Perspective of Leadership

The opening story to this chapter described how A. G. Lafley has reversed Procter & Gamble's precipitous decline and put the household goods company on a better footing for the future. By any measure, Lafley is a transformational leader. Through his vision, communication, and actions, he has transformed P&G into a more effective organization. Transformational leaders are agents of change. They develop a vision for the organization or work unit, inspire and collectively bond employees to that vision, and give them a can-do attitude that makes the vision achievable.[33]

Transformational versus Transactional Leadership

Transformational leadership differs from **transactional leadership.**[34] Transactional leadership is *managing*—helping organizations achieve their current objectives more efficiently, such as by linking job performance to valued rewards and ensuring that employees have the resources needed to get the job done. The contingency and behavioral theories described earlier adopt the transactional perspective because they focus on leader behaviors that improve employee performance and satisfaction. In contrast, **transformational leadership** is about *leading*—changing the organization's strategies and culture so that they have a better fit with the surrounding environment.[35] Transformational leaders are change agents who energize and direct employees to a new set of corporate values and behaviors.

Organizations require both transactional and transformational leadership.[36] Transactional leadership improves organizational efficiency, whereas transformational leadership steers companies onto a better course of action. Transformational leadership is particularly important in organizations that require significant alignment with the external environment. Unfortunately, too many leaders get trapped in the daily managerial activities that represent transactional leadership.[37] They lose touch with the transformational aspect of effective leadership. Without transformational leaders, organizations stagnate and eventually become seriously misaligned with their environments.

Transformational versus Charismatic Leadership

One topic that has generated some confusion and controversy is the distinction between transformational and charismatic leadership.[38] Many researchers either use the words interchangeably, as if they have the same meaning, or view charismatic leadership as an essential ingredient of transformational leadership. Others take this view further by suggesting that charismatic leadership is the highest degree of transformational leadership.

However, the emerging view, which we adopt in this book, comes from a third group of experts who contend that charisma is distinct from transformational leadership. These academics point out that charisma is a personal trait that provides referent power over followers, whereas transformational leadership is a set of behaviors that people use to lead the change process.[39] Charismatic leaders might be transformational leaders; indeed, their personal power through charisma is a tool to change the behavior of followers. However, some research points out that charismatic or "heroic" leaders easily build allegiance in followers, but they do not necessarily change the organization. Other research suggests that charismatic leaders produce dependent followers, whereas transformational leaders have the opposite effect—they support follower empowerment, which tends to reduce dependence on the leader.[40]

It is also possible to be a transformational leader without being charismatic. Consider Alan G. Lafley, the CEO of Proctor & Gamble described at the beginning of this chapter. The word *charismatic* does not come to mind when you see Lafley in a meeting. Yet the

transactional leadership
Leadership that helps organizations achieve their current objectives more efficiently, such as linking job performance to valued rewards and ensuring that employees have the resources needed to get the job done.

transformational leadership
A leadership perspective that explains how leaders change teams or organizations by creating, communicating, and modeling a vision for the organization or work unit and by inspiring employees to strive for that vision.

quiet-spoken leader has transformed the household products company and energized employees more than anyone can remember.[41] In contrast, there are many recent stories of executives who have mesmerized boards of directors into hiring them with generous salaries, yet did nothing to steer the corporate ship in new directions. Thus, we will focus on transformational leadership as a set of behaviors that change organizations, leaving charismatic leadership as a distinct source of personal power, whether used for personal gain or to benefit the organization.

Elements of Transformational Leadership

There are several descriptions of transformational leadership, but most include the four elements illustrated in Exhibit 11.3. These elements include creating a strategic vision, communicating the vision, modeling the vision, and building commitment toward the vision.

Creating a Strategic Vision

Transformational leaders shape a strategic vision of a realistic and attractive future that bonds employees together and focuses their energy toward a superordinate organizational goal. Strategic vision represents the substance of transformational leadership. It reflects a future for the company or work unit that is ultimately accepted and valued by organizational members. Strategic vision creates a "higher purpose" or superordinate goal that energizes and unifies employees.[42] A strategic vision might originate with the leader, but it is just as likely to emerge from employees, clients, suppliers, or other constituents. A shared strategic vision plays an important role in organizational effectiveness.[43] Visions offer the motivational benefits of goal setting, but they are compelling future states that bond employees and motivate them to strive for those objectives. Visions are typically described in a way that distinguishes them from the current situation yet makes the goal both appealing and achievable.

Communicating the Vision

If vision is the substance of transformational leadership, then communicating that vision is the process. Transformational leaders communicate meaning and elevate the importance

[Exhibit 11.3]   Elements of Transformational Leadership

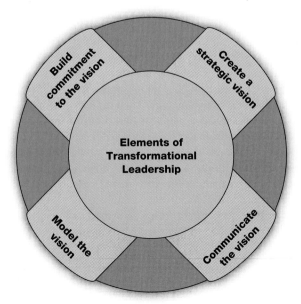

of the visionary goal to employees. They frame messages around a grand purpose with emotional appeal that captivates employees and other corporate stakeholders. Framing helps transformational leaders establish a common mental model so that the group or organization will act collectively toward the desirable goal.[44]

Transformational leaders bring their visions to life through symbols, metaphors, stories, and other vehicles that transcend plain language. Metaphors borrow images of other experiences, thereby creating richer meaning of the vision that has not yet been experienced. When George Cohen faced the difficult challenge of opening McDonald's restaurants in Moscow, he frequently reminded his team members that they were establishing "hamburger diplomacy."[45]

Modeling the Vision

Transformational leaders not only talk about a vision; they enact it. Just as P&G CEO Lafley visits customers around the world, transformational leaders "walk the talk" by stepping outside the executive suite and doing things that symbolize the vision.[46] Moreover, they are reliable and persistent in their actions, thereby legitimizing the vision and providing further evidence that they can be trusted. Leaders walk the talk through significant events, but they also alter mundane activities—meeting agendas, office locations, executive schedules—so they are consistent with the vision and its underlying values.

Modeling the vision is important because employees and other stakeholders are executive watchers who look for behaviors to symbolize values and expectations. The greater the consistency between the leader's words and actions, the more employees will believe and follow the leader. Walking the talk also builds employee trust because trust is partly determined by the consistency of the person's actions.

Building Commitment toward the Vision

Transforming a vision into reality requires employee commitment. Transformational leaders build this commitment in several ways. Their words, symbols, and stories build a contagious enthusiasm that energizes people to adopt the vision as their own. Leaders demonstrate a can-do attitude by enacting their vision and staying on course. Their persistence and consistency reflect an image of honesty, trust, and integrity. Finally, leaders build commitment by involving employees in the process of shaping the organization's vision.

When Karen Gilles Larson became CEO of Synovis Life Technologies (called Bio-Vascular at the time), she discovered a demoralized workforce that was embroiled in conflict rather than working toward a better company. So Larson met all 100 employees in the cafeteria and emphasized the need for mutual respect to turn around the beleaguered St. Paul, Minnesota, medical products manufacturer. "We're all in a boat, and we're going to row together," she said. Over the next few years, Larson transformed Synovis by investing in research and development and diversifying the company's product range, all the while keeping employees involved and informed. Today, Synovis is one of Minnesota's top business success stories. "Now we've got cash in the bank, we're growing the revenue and profits, and it's been under her leadership," says a longtime Synovis director.[47]

Evaluating the Transformational Leadership Perspective

Transformational leaders do make a difference. Subordinates are more satisfied and have higher affective organizational commitment under transformational leaders. They also perform their jobs better, engage in more organizational citizenship behaviors, and make better or more creative decisions. One study also reported that organizational commitment and financial performance seem to increase in branches of a bank where the branch manager completed a transformational leadership training program.[48]

Transformational leadership is currently the most popular leadership perspective, but it faces a number of challenges. One problem is that some writers engage in circular logic by defining transformational leadership in terms of the leader's success.[49] They suggest that leaders are transformational when they successfully bring about change, rather than whether they engage in certain behaviors we call transformational. Another concern is that the transformational leadership model seems to be universal rather than contingency-oriented. Only very recently have writers begun to explore the idea that transformational leadership is more appropriate in some situations than others.[50] For instance, transformational leadership is probably more appropriate when organizations need to adapt than when environmental conditions are stable. Preliminary evidence suggests that the transformational leadership perspective is relevant across cultures. However, there may be specific elements of transformational leadership, such as the way visions are formed and communicated, that are more appropriate in North America than other cultures.

>Implicit Leadership Perspective

The competency, behavior, contingency, and transformational leadership perspectives make the basic assumption that leaders make a difference. Certainly, there is evidence that senior executives do influence organizational performance. However, leaders might have less influence than most of us would like to believe. Some leadership experts suggest that people inflate the importance of leadership in explaining organizational events. These processes are collectively called **implicit leadership theory.**[51]

Implicit leadership theory states that everyone has preconceived notions about the features and behaviors of an effective leader. These perceptions are stereotypes or prototypes of idealized leadership that develop through socialization within the family and society.[52] Mental images of an ideal leader shape our expectations and acceptance of people as leaders, which in turn affect their ability to influence us as followers. We rely on leadership stereotypes partly because a leader's success might not be known for months or possibly years. Consequently, employees depend on immediate information to decide whether the leader is performing well. If the leader fits the mold, then employees are more confident that the leader is effective.[53]

Implicit leadership is also influenced by attribution errors. Research has found that, at least in Western cultures, people tend to attribute organizational events to the leader, even when those events are largely caused by factors beyond the leader's control. This attribution is partly caused by fundamental attribution error (see Chapter 3) in which leaders are given credit or blame for the company's success or failure because employees do not readily see the external forces that also influence these events. Leaders reinforce this belief by taking credit for organizational successes.[54] This attribution process is further reinforced by followers' needs to simplify life events and believe that life events are generated more from people than from uncontrollable natural forces.

The implicit leadership perspective questions the importance of leadership, but it also provides valuable advice to improve leadership acceptance. This approach highlights the

implicit leadership theory
The theory that people rely on preconceived traits to evaluate others as leaders, and that they tend to inflate the influence of leadership on organizational events.

fact that leadership is a perception of followers as much as the actual behaviors and characteristics of people calling themselves leaders. Potential leaders must be sensitive to this fact, understand what followers expect, and act accordingly. Individuals who do not make an effort to fit leadership prototypes will have more difficulty bringing about necessary organizational change.

>Cross-Cultural and Gender Issues in Leadership

Along with the five perspectives of leadership presented throughout this chapter, we need to be aware that leadership is affected by cultural values and gender dynamics. Culture shapes the leader's values and norms, which influence his or her decisions and actions. These cultural values also shape the expectations that followers have of their leaders. An executive who acts inconsistently with cultural expectations is more likely to be perceived as an ineffective leader. Furthermore, leaders who deviate from those values may experience various forms of influence to get them to conform to the leadership norms and expectations of that society. In other words, implicit leadership theory described in the previous section of this chapter explains differences in leadership practices across cultures.

With respect to gender, studies in field settings have generally found that male and female leaders do not differ in their levels of task-oriented or people-oriented leadership. The main explanation is that real-world jobs require similar behavior from male and female job incumbents.[55] However, women do adopt a participative leadership style more readily than their male counterparts. One possible reason why women are more participative is that, compared with boys, girls are often raised to be more egalitarian and less status oriented. There is also some evidence that women have somewhat better interpersonal skills than men, and this translates into their relatively greater use of the participative leadership style. A third explanation is that subordinates expect female leaders to be more participative, based on their own sex stereotypes, so female leaders comply with follower expectations to some extent.

Several recent surveys report that women are rated higher than men on the emerging leadership qualities of coaching, teamwork, and empowering employees.[56] Yet research also suggests that women are evaluated negatively when they try to apply the full range of leadership styles, particularly more directive and autocratic approaches. Ironically, women may be well suited to contemporary leadership roles, yet they often continue to face limitations of leadership through the gender stereotypes and prototypes of followers.[57] Overall, both male and female leaders must be sensitive to the fact that followers have expectations about how leaders should act, and negative evaluations may go to leaders who deviate from those expectations.

>chapter summary

Leadership is a complex concept that is defined as the ability to influence, motivate, and enable others to contribute toward the effectiveness and success of the organizations of which they are members. Leaders use influence to motivate followers, and arrange the work environment so that they do the job more effectively. Leaders exist throughout the organization, not just in the executive suite.

The competency perspective tries to identify the characteristics of effective leaders. Recent writing suggests that leaders have emotional intelligence, integrity, drive, leadership motivation, self-confidence, above-average intelligence, and knowledge of the business.

The behavioral perspective of leadership identified two clusters of leader behavior: people-oriented and task-oriented. People-oriented behaviors include showing mutual trust and respect for subordinates, demonstrating a genuine concern for their needs, and having a desire to look out for their welfare. Task-oriented behaviors include assigning employees to specific tasks, clarifying their work duties and procedures, ensuring that they follow company rules, and pushing them to reach their performance capacity.

The contingency perspective of leadership takes the view that effective leaders diagnose the situation and adapt their style to fit that situation. The path-goal model is the prominent contingency theory that identifies four leadership styles—directive, supportive, participative, and achievement-oriented—and several contingencies relating to the characteristics of the employee and of the situation. Leadership substitutes theory identifies contingencies that either limit the leader's ability to influence subordinates or make that particular leadership style unnecessary.

Transformational leaders create a strategic vision, communicate that vision through framing and use of metaphors, model the vision by "walking the talk" and acting consistently, and build commitment toward the vision. This contrasts with transactional leadership, which involves linking job performance to valued rewards and ensuring that employees have the resources needed to get the job done. The contingency and behavioral perspectives adopt the transactional view of leadership.

According to the implicit leadership perspective, people identify and evaluate leaders based on how well they fit into their preconceived mental model of a leader. This perspective also recognizes that people attribute organizational events to leaders more than actually occurs.

Women generally do not differ from men in the degree of people-oriented or task-oriented leadership. However, female leaders more often adopt a participative style. Research also suggests that people evaluate female leaders based on gender stereotypes, which may result in higher or lower ratings.

>key.terms

>critical.thinking.questions

1. Why is it important for top executives to value and support leadership demonstrated at all levels of the organization?

2. Find two newspaper ads for management or executive positions. What leadership competencies are mentioned in these ads? If you were on the selection panel, what methods would you use to identify these competencies in job applicants?

3. Consider your favorite teacher. What people-oriented and task-oriented leadership behaviors did he or she use effectively? In general, do you think students prefer an instructor who is more people-oriented or task-oriented? Explain your preference.

4. Your employees are skilled and experienced customer service representatives who perform nonroutine tasks, such as solving unique customer problems or special

needs with the company's equipment. Use path-goal theory to identify the most appropriate leadership style(s) you should use in this situation. Be sure to fully explain your answer and discuss why other styles are inappropriate.

5. Transformational leadership is currently the most popular perspective of leadership. However, it is far from perfect. Discuss the limitations of transformational leadership.

6. This chapter emphasized that charismatic leadership is not the same as transformational leadership. Still, charisma is often mentioned in the discussions about leadership. In your opinion, how does charisma relate to leadership?

7. Identify a current political leader (e.g., president, governor, mayor) and his or her recent accomplishments.

Now, using the implicit leadership perspective, think of ways that these accomplishments of the leader may be overstated. In other words, explain why they may be due to factors other than the leader.

8. You hear two people debating the merits of women as leaders. One person claims that women make better leaders than do men because women are more sensitive to their employees' needs and involve them in organizational decisions. The other person counters that although these leadership styles may be increasingly important, most women have trouble gaining acceptance as leaders when they face tough situations in which a more autocratic style is required. Discuss the accuracy of the comments made in this discussion.

>case study:skillbuilder11.1

Josh Martin

By Joseph C. Santora and James C. Sarros

Josh Martin, a 41-year-old administrator at the Center Street Settlement House, a nonprofit social service agency with 70 employees and more than $6 million in assets, sat pensively at his desk located outside the executive suite. He thought to himself, No, it can't be. I can't have been working here for 20 years. Where did the time go?

Martin has spent his entire adult life working at the Center Settlement House. He began his career there immediately after graduating from college with a degree in economics and very slowly climbed the narrow administrative ladder from his initial position as the director of a government-funded project to his current position as the deputy agency administrator. In addition, for the past five years, he has been serving as the president of the agency's for-profit construction company. He reports directly to Tom Saunders, the autocratic executive director of the agency.

Martin, a competent administrator, often gets things done through his participative leadership style. In the last few years, Martin's job responsibilities have increased exponentially. He fills many informational, decisional, and interpersonal managerial roles for the agency. Six months ago, he was given the added responsibility of processing invoices for agency vendors and consultants, authority he shares in common with Saunders and the agency's accountant.

Martin is rewarded handsomely for his role in the nonprofit agency. Last year, he earned $90,000, plus a liberal fringe benefits package that included an agency car, a pension plan, a medical health plan (including dental), a month's vacation, 15 paid holidays, and unlimited sick

time. Although he has received an annual cost-of-living allowance (COLA), Martin has no written contractual agreement and essentially serves at the pleasure of Saunders.

Martin pays a high personal price for his attractive compensation package. He is on call 24 hours a day, complete with a beeper. Each Sunday morning, Martin attends a mandatory agency strategy meeting required of all agency managers.

Over the years, Martin has tolerated Saunders's erratic mood swings and his inattentiveness to agency details. Tension between the two men reached a high point in recent months. For example, two months ago, Martin called in sick because he was suffering from a severe bout of the flu. Martin's absence forced Saunders to cancel an important meeting to supervise an agency fiscal audit. Saunders responded to Martin's absence in an irrational fashion by focusing on a small piece of tile missing from the cafeteria floor. He screamed at two employees who were eating lunch in the cafeteria.

"You see," he said, "Martin doesn't give a damn about anything in this agency. I always have to make sure things get done around here. Just look at the floor! There's a piece of tile missing!" Mary Thompson and Elizabeth Duncan, two veteran employees, seemed shocked by Saunders's reaction to the missing piece of title. As Saunders stormed out of the cafeteria throwing his hands in the air, Mary turned to Elizabeth and whispered, "Saunders is really going off the deep end. Without Josh nothing would get done around here. I don't see how Saunders can blame Josh for every little problem. I wonder how long Josh can take this unfair treatment." Elizabeth nodded her head in agreement.

A month after this incident, Martin recommended pay increases for two employees who had received excellent performance appraisals by their supervisors. Martin believed that a 2 percent raise, admittedly only a symbolic raise, would provide motivation, would increase morale, and would not seriously jeopardize the agency's budget. When Martin proposed his recommendations for employee raises to Saunders at the Thursday weekly fiscal meeting, Saunders vehemently rejected Martin's proposal and countered it by ranting, "Everybody wants a raise around here. It's about time people started doing more work and stopped whining about money. Let's move on to the next agenda item."

Saunders closed the weekly staff meeting by saying, "I'm the leader of this agency. I have to manage everything for this agency to run effectively." Phil Jones, the director of field operations, turned to Paul Lindstrom, the fiscal officer, and whispered, "Sure, Saunders is the director of this agency alright, but he couldn't manage his way out of a paper bag. Without Josh, this place would be in total chaos. Besides, at least Josh listens to us and tries to implement some of our ideas to make life simpler around here."

Martin has often contemplated resigning from the agency to seek other public sector employment. However, he believes such opportunities are rare since he is a middle-aged, white male. Besides, Saunders knows just about every agency CEO in the public sector. Martin believes that Saunders would find out that he applied for a job as soon as his résumé reached an agency personnel department. Moreover, Martin feels that his long tenure with the agency may be detrimental; most prospective employers would be suspicious of his motives for leaving the settlement house after some two decades of service. Martin mused, "Perhaps,

I stayed too long at the dance." Finally, given the present economic conditions in the state, many public sector agencies would be reluctant to match his salary and benefits package—at least not in his first few years of service.

Martin is uncertain of his options at this point. On a personal note, although his wife is gainfully employed and possesses good technical skills and experience in the printing industry, Martin still needs to maintain his present standard of living to support his family, including his two college-age daughters, a $100,000 mortgage on his home, and other financial obligations. He has significant nonprofit and for-profit experience and excellent managerial and leadership skills. Yet he wonders if there is any way out of his current situation.

Discussion Questions

1. Describe the two different leadership styles used by Josh Martin and Tom Saunders. Do these two different styles tell you anything about leadership traits? Do you think there is any resolution to the organizational problems resulting from the conflicting leadership styles?

2. What are the characteristics/elements of an effective leader? Do you think Saunders is an effective leader? Why or why not? Is Martin an effective leader? Why or why not?

3. Does Josh Martin have any way out of his current situation? What would you do if you were Josh Martin?

Written by Joseph C. Santora, Essex County College and TSTDCG, Inc., and James C. Sarros, Monash University.

>team.exercise:skillbuilder11.2

Leadership Diagnostic Analysis

Purpose   To help students learn about the different path-goal leadership styles and when to apply each style.

Instructions

- *Step 1:* Students individually write down two incidents in which someone had been an effective manager or leader over them. The leader and situation might be from work, a sports team, a student work group, or any other setting where leadership might emerge. For example, students might describe how their supervisor in a summer job pushed them to reach higher performance goals than they would have done otherwise. Each incident should state the actual behaviors that the leader used, not just general statements (e.g., "My boss sat down with me and we agreed on specific targets and deadlines, then he said several times over the next few weeks that I was capable of reaching those goals.") Each incident only requires two or three sentences.

- *Step 2:* After everyone has written their two incidents, the instructor will form small groups (typically between four or five students). Each team will answer the following questions for each incident presented in that team:

  1. Which path-goal theory leadership style(s)—directive, supportive, participative, or achievement-oriented—did the leader apply in this incident?

  2. Ask the person who wrote the incident about the conditions that made this leadership style (or these styles, if more than one was used) appropriate in this situation? The team should list these contingency factors clearly and, where possible, connect them to the contingencies described in path-goal theory. (*Note*: the team might identify path-goal leadership contingencies that are not described in the book. These, too, should be noted and discussed.)

- *Step 3:* After the teams have diagnosed the incidents, each team will describe to the entire class the most interesting incidents as well as its diagnosis of that incident. Other teams will critique the diagnosis. Any leadership contingencies not mentioned in the textbook should also be presented and discussed.

>self-assessment.skillbuilder11.3

Leadership Dimensions Instrument

This assessment is designed to help you to understand two important dimensions of leadership and to identify which of these dimensions is more prominent in your supervisor, team leader, coach, or other person to whom you are accountable. Read each of the statements in this instrument and select the response that you believe best describes your supervisor. You may substitute "supervisor" with anyone else to whom you are accountable, such as a team leader, CEO, course instructor, or sports coach. After completing this assessment, be prepared to discuss in class the distinctions between these leadership dimensions.

Find the full self-assessments on the OLC at
www.mhhe.com/mcshaneess

>**part 4**:

Organizational Processes

chapter 12

Organizational Structure

W. L. Gore & Associates Inc. has a team-based organizational structure that eliminates the traditional hierarchy. "There's no fear of any person going over another's head," says Gore sales veteran Tom Erickson, shown here (left) with co-worker John Cusick in Gore's testing room.

>**learning**objectives

After reading this chapter, you should be able to

- Describe three types of coordination in organizational structures.

- Explain why firms can have flatter structures than previously believed.

- Discuss the dynamics of centralization and formalization as organizations get larger and older.

- Contrast functional structures with divisional structures.

- Explain why geographic divisional structures are becoming less common than other divisional structures.

- Outline the features and advantages of the matrix structure.

- Describe four features of team-based organizational structures.

- Summarize three contingencies of organizational design.

Diane Davidson admits that her first few months at W. L. Gore & Associates Inc. were a bit frustrating. "When I arrived at Gore, I didn't know who did what," recalls the apparel industry sales executive hired to market Gore-Tex fabrics to brand name designers. "I wondered how anything got done here. It was driving me crazy." Davidson kept asking her "starting sponsor" who her boss was, but the sponsor firmly replied, "Stop using the B-word." Gore must have managers, she thought, but they probably downplay their status. But there really aren't any bosses, not in the traditional sense. "Your team is your boss, because you don't want to let them down," Davidson eventually learned. "Everyone's your boss, and no one's your boss."

From its beginnings in 1958, the Newark, Delaware–based manufacturer of fabrics (Gore-Tex), electronics, industrial, and medical products has adopted an organizational structure where most employees (or "associates" as they are known) are organized around self-directed teams. The company has an incredibly flat hierarchy with a high degree of decentralized authority. Associates make day-to-day decisions within their expertise without approval from anyone higher up. Bigger issues, such as hiring and compensating staff, are decided by teams. "We make our own decisions and everything is discussed as well," explains Phyllis Tait, a medical business support leader at Gore's U.K. business unit.

The company has a divisional structure, organized around products and clients, such as Fabrics, Medical, Electronics, and Industrial. But most of Gore's 7,000 associates work at 45 self-sufficient manufacturing and sales offices around the world. Each facility is deliberately limited to about 200 people so they can coordinate more effectively through informal communication. Within those units, new projects are started through individual initiative and support from others. "There is no positional power," explains a Gore team leader. "You are only a leader if teams decide to respect and follow you."

As Diane Davidson discovered, Gore operates without job titles, job descriptions, or a formal chain of command. This ambiguous structure was established so associates can be creative and responsive by coordinating directly with people in other areas of the organization. "You go to whomever you need to get things done," says Gore sales veteran Tom Erickson (left in photo with colleague John Cusick). "If I want to talk to a person on the manufacturing line about a particular job, I just go out and talk to him. That's one thing that sets us apart. There's no fear of any person going over another's head."[1]

W. L. Gore & Associates Inc. and many other companies are throwing out the old organizational structures and trying out new designs that will hopefully achieve corporate objectives more effectively. **Organizational structure** refers to the division of labor as well as the patterns of coordination, communication, workflow, and formal power that direct organizational activities. An organizational structure reflects its culture and power relationships.

We begin this chapter by considering the two fundamental processes in organizational structure: division of labor and coordination. This is followed by a detailed investigation of the four main elements of organizational structure: span of control, centralization, formalization, and departmentalization. The latter part of this chapter examines the contingencies of organizational design, including external environment organizational size, technology, and strategy.

organizational structure
The division of labor and the patterns of coordination, communication, work flow, and formal power that direct organizational activities.

>Division of Labor and Coordination

All organizational structures include two fundamental requirements: the division of labor into distinct tasks and the coordination of that labor so that employees are able to accomplish common goals.[2] Organizations are groups of people who work interdependently toward some purpose. To efficiently accomplish their goals, these groups typically divide the work into manageable chunks, particularly when there are many different tasks to perform. They also introduce various coordinating mechanisms to ensure that everyone is working effectively toward the same objectives.

Division of Labor

Division of labor refers to the subdivision of work into separate jobs assigned to different people. Subdivided work leads to job specialization, because each job now includes a narrow subset of the tasks necessary to complete the product or service. For example, designing and manufacturing an aircraft at Boeing Corp. requires thousands of specific tasks that are divided among thousands of people. Tasks are also divided vertically, such as having supervisors coordinate work while employees perform the work.

Work is divided into specialized jobs because it potentially increases work efficiency.[3] Job incumbents can master their tasks quickly because work cycles are very short. Less time is wasted changing from one task to another. Training costs are reduced because employees require fewer physical and mental skills to accomplish the assigned work. Finally, job specialization makes it easier to match people with specific aptitudes or skills to the jobs for which they are best suited.

Coordinating Work Activities

As soon as people divide work among themselves, coordinating mechanisms are needed to ensure that everyone works in concert. Every organization—from the two-person corner convenience store to the largest corporate entity—uses one or more of the following coordinating mechanisms:[4] informal communication, formal hierarchy, and standardization.

Coordination through Informal Communication

Informal communication is a coordinating mechanism in all organizations. This includes sharing information on mutual tasks as well as forming common mental models so that employees synchronize work activities using the same mental road map.[5] Informal communication is vital in nonroutine and ambiguous situations because employees can exchange a large volume of information through face-to-face communication and other media-rich channels.

Coordination through informal communication is easiest in small firms, although information technologies have further leveraged this coordinating mechanism in large organizations. Larger organizations such as W. L. Gore & Associates (described in the opening story) and automobile parts maker Magna International also support informal communication by keeping each workplace small (around 200 employees). Toyota and other automakers further support this coordinating mechanism by moving dozens of employees responsible for developing a new product into one large room.[6]

Coordination through Formal Hierarchy

Informal communication is the most flexible form of coordination, but it can be time-consuming. Consequently, as organizations grow, they develop a second coordinating mechanism: formal hierarchy. Hierarchy assigns legitimate power to individuals, who then use this power to direct work processes and allocate resources. In other words, work is coordinated through direct supervision. Any organization with a formal structure coordinates work to some extent through the formal hierarchy. For instance, team leaders at W. L. Gore & Associates coordinate work by ensuring that associates in their group remain on schedule and that their respective tasks are compatible with tasks completed by others in the group. At Gore, the team grants the leader authority to schedule work activities and resolve conflicts.

The formal hierarchy also coordinates work among executives through the division of organizational activities. If the organization is divided into geographic areas, the structure gives those regional group leaders legitimate power over executives responsible for production, customer service, and other activities in those areas. If the organization is divided into product groups, then the heads of those groups have the right to coordinate work across regions. The formal hierarchy has traditionally been applauded as the optimal coordinating mechanism for large organizations. However, as we'll see later in this chapter, formal hierarchy is not as agile as other forms of coordination.

Coordination through Standardization

Standardization, the third means of coordination, involves creating routine patterns of behavior or output. This coordinating mechanism takes three distinct forms:

- *Standardized processes.* Quality and consistency of a product or service can often be improved by standardizing work activities through job descriptions and procedures.[7] This coordinating mechanism is feasible when the work is routine (such as mass production) or simple (such as making pizzas), but it is less effective in nonroutine and complex work such as product design.

- *Standardized outputs.* This form of standardization involves ensuring that individuals and work units have clearly defined goals and output measures (e.g., customer satisfaction, production efficiency). For instance, to coordinate the work of salespeople, companies assign sales targets rather than specific behaviors.

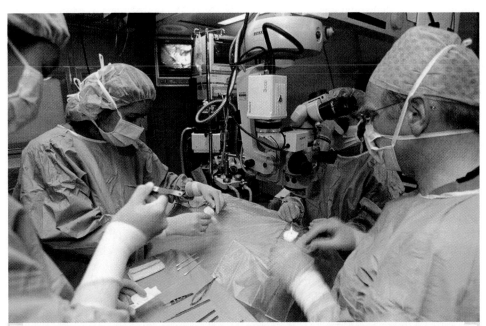

Flying to developing nations around the world, the ORBIS Flying Eye Hospital is a nonprofit service that trains local professionals and provides eye care education. Medical professionals on board the converted DC-10 also conduct an average of four eye operations each day, including the surgery shown in this photo on a young girl in Costa Rica. To some extent, these professionals coordinate their surgical work activities through informal communication. However, much of the operation occurs without discussion because team members also coordinate through standardization of skills. Through extensive training, each person has learned precise role behaviors so that his or her task activities are coordinated with others on the surgical team.[8]

• *Standardized skills.* When work activities are too complex to standardize through processes or goals, companies often coordinate work effort by extensively training employees or hiring people who have learned precise role behaviors from educational programs. This form of coordination is used in hospital operating rooms. Surgeons, nurses, and other operating room professionals coordinate their work more through training than goals or company rules.

Division of labor and coordination of work represent two fundamental ingredients of all organizations. How work is divided, who makes decisions, which coordinating mechanisms are emphasized, and other issues are related to the four elements of organizational structure.

>Elements of Organizational Structure

Every company is configured in terms of four basic elements of organizational structure. This section introduces three of them: span of control, centralization, and formalization. The fourth element—departmentalization—is presented in the next section.

Span of Control

span of control
The number of people directly reporting to the next level in the organizational hierarchy.

Span of control refers to the number of people directly reporting to the next level in the hierarchy. Almost 100 years ago, French engineer and administrative theorist Henri Fayol strongly recommended the formal hierarchy as the primary coordinating mechanism. Consequently, he prescribed a relatively narrow span of control, typically no more than 20 employees per supervisor and six supervisors per manager. These prescriptions were based on the assumption that managers simply cannot monitor and control any more subordinates closely enough. Today, we know better. The best performing manufacturing facilities currently have an average of 31 employees per supervisor.[9]

What's the secret here? Did Fayol and others miscalculate the optimal span of control? The answer is that Fayol and many other scholars sympathetic to hierarchical control believed that employees should "do" the work, whereas supervisors and other management personnel should monitor employee behavior and make most of the decisions. In contrast, the best-performing manufacturing operations today rely on self-directed work teams, so direct supervision (formal hierarchy) is just a backup coordinating mechanism. In extreme cases, such as W. L. Gore & Associates, there is almost no supervision at all. Associates manage themselves, thereby releasing leaders from the time-consuming tasks of monitoring behavior and making everyone else's decisions.

The underlying principle here is that the optimal span of control depends on the presence of other coordinating mechanisms. Self-directed work teams supplement direct supervision with informal communication and specialized knowledge. This also explains why dozens of surgeons and other medical professionals may report to just one head surgeon in a major hospital. The head surgeon doesn't engage in much direct supervision because the standardized skills of medical staff coordinate the unit's work.[10]

Tall and Flat Structures
BASF's European Seal Sands plant recently organized employees into self-directed work teams and dramatically restructured the work process. These actions did much more than increase efficiency and lower costs at the bulk chemical plant. They also chopped out several layers of hierarchy. "Seven levels of management have been cut basically to two," says a BASF executive.[11]

The main reasons BASF and other companies are moving toward flatter organizational structures are that this "delayering" potentially cuts overhead costs and puts decision makers closer to frontline staff and information about customer needs. However, some organizational experts warn that corporate leaders may be cutting out too much hierarchy. They argue that the much-maligned "middle managers" serve a valuable function by controlling work activities and managing corporate growth. Moreover, companies will always need hierarchy because someone has to make quick decisions and represent a source of appeal over conflicts.[12] The conclusion here is that there is an optimal level of delayering in most organizations. Flatter structures offer several benefits, but cutting out too much management can offset these benefits.

One last point before leaving this topic: The size of an organization's hierarchy depends on both the average span of control and the number of people employed by the organization. A tall structure has many hierarchical levels, each with a relatively narrow span of control, whereas a flat structure has few levels, each with a wide span of control. Larger organizations that depend on hierarchy for coordination necessarily develop taller structures.

Centralization and Decentralization

Centralization and decentralization represents a second element of organizational design. **Centralization** means that formal decision-making authority is held by a small group of people, typically those at the top of the organizational hierarchy. Most organizations begin with centralized structures, as the founder makes most of the decisions and tries to direct the business toward his or her vision. But as organizations grow, they diversify and their environments become more complex. Senior executives aren't able to process all the decisions that significantly influence the business. Consequently, larger organizations tend to *decentralize,* that is, they disperse decision authority and power throughout the organization.

centralization
The degree to which formal decision authority is held by a small group of people, typically those at the top of the organizational hierarchy.

The optimal level of centralization or decentralization depends on several contingencies that we will examine later in this chapter. However, we also need to keep in mind that different degrees of decentralization can occur simultaneously in different parts of the organization. Nestlé has decentralized marketing decisions to remain responsive to local markets. At the same time, the Swiss-based food company has centralized production, logistics, and supply chain management activities to improve cost efficiencies and avoid having too much complexity across the organization.[13]

Formalization

Formalization is the degree to which organizations standardize behavior through rules, procedures, formal training, and related mechanisms.[14] In other words, formalization represents the establishment of standardization as a coordinating mechanism. McDonald's Restaurants has a formalized structure because it relies heavily on standardization of work processes as a coordinating mechanism. Employees have precisely defined roles, right down to how much mustard should be dispensed, how many pickles should be applied, and how long each hamburger should be cooked. In contrast, W. L. Gore & Associates has relatively little formalization because associates have no defined job descriptions or standardized output.

formalization
The degree to which organizations standardize behavior through rules, procedures, formal training, and related mechanisms.

Companies tend to become formalized as they get older and larger. External influences, such as government safety legislation and strict accounting rules, also encourage formalization. Formalization may increase efficiency and compliance, but it can also create problems. Rules and procedures reduce organizational flexibility, so employees follow prescribed behaviors even when the situation clearly calls for a customized response. Some work rules become so convoluted that organizational efficiency would decline if they were actually followed as prescribed. Formalized structures are also a source of job dissatisfaction, particularly among younger employees, and these rules tend to undermine performance of self-directed work teams as well as creativity among employees.

Mechanistic versus Organic Structures

mechanistic structure
An organizational structure with a narrow span of control and high degrees of formalization and centralization.

organic structure
An organizational structure with a wide span of control, little formalization, and decentralized decision making.

We have discussed span of control, centralization, and formalization together because they usually cluster into two forms: mechanistic and organic structures.[15] A **mechanistic structure** is characterized by a narrow span of control and high degree of formalization and centralization. Mechanistic structures have many rules and procedures, limited decision making at lower levels, tall hierarchies of people in specialized roles, and vertical rather than horizontal communication flows. Tasks are rigidly defined and are altered only when sanctioned by higher authorities.

Companies with an **organic structure** have the opposite characteristics. W. L. Gore & Associates, described at the beginning of this chapter, is a clear example of an organic structure because it has a wide span of control, decentralized decision making, and little formalization. Tasks are fluid, adjusting to new situations and organizational needs. The organic structure values knowledge and takes the view that information may be located anywhere in the organization rather than among senior executives. Thus, communication flows in all directions with little concern for the formal hierarchy.

Mechanistic structures operate best in stable environments because they rely on efficiency and routine behaviors. However, as we have emphasized throughout this book, most organizations operate in a world of dramatic change. Information technology, globalization, a changing workforce, and other factors have strengthened the need for more organic structures that are flexible and responsive to these changes. Organic structures are also more compatible with knowledge management because they emphasize information sharing rather than hierarchy and status.[17]

>Forms of Departmentalization

Span of control, centralization, and formalization are important elements of organizational structure, but most people think about organizational charts when the discussion of organizational structure arises. The organizational chart represents the fourth element in the

Harbinger Partners is a "manager-free zone." That's because the business intelligence and creative services company has no bosses. All 20 employees (actually, they're partners) own a piece of the company and are involved in making company decisions. Harbinger doesn't even have a formal headquarters, just a post office box number in St. Paul, Minnesota. The company's partners work either from their homes or in clients' offices. This arrangement might give some executives sleepless nights, but not Scott Grausnick (center), who founded Harbinger in 1999. Instead, he deliberately created this highly organic structure so staff could cater more effectively to customer needs while satisfying their entrepreneurial spirit. The structure seems to work; Harbinger Partners weathered the downturn that affected other firms, and it receives very high satisfaction ratings from customers and staff alike.[16]

structuring of organizations, called *departmentalization.* Departmentalization specifies how employees and their activities are grouped together. It is a fundamental strategy for coordinating organizational activities because it influences organizational behavior in the following ways.[18]

- Departmentalization establishes the chain of command, that is, the system of common supervision among positions and units within the organization. It frames the membership of formal work teams and typically determines which positions and units must share resources. Thus, departmentalization establishes interdependencies among employees and subunits.

- Departmentalization focuses people around common mental models or ways of thinking, such as serving clients, developing products, or supporting a particular skill set. This focus is typically anchored around the common budgets and measures of performance assigned to employees within each departmental unit.

- Departmentalization encourages coordination through informal communication among people and subunits. With common supervision and resources, members within each configuration typically work near each other, so they can use frequent and informal interaction to get the work done.

There are almost as many organizational charts as there are businesses, but we can identify five pure types of departmentalization: simple, functional, divisional, matrix, and team-based.

Simple Structure

Most companies begin with a *simple structure.*[19] They employ only a few people and typically offer only one distinct product or service. There is minimal hierarchy—usually just employees reporting to the owner(s). Employees are grouped into broadly defined roles because there are insufficient economies of scale to assign them to specialized roles. Simple structures are flexible, yet they usually depend on the owner's direct supervision to coordinate work activities. Consequently, this structure is very difficult to operate as the company grows and becomes more complex.

Functional Structure

Organizations that grow large enough use functional structures at some level of the hierarchy or at some time in their history. A **functional structure** organizes employees around specific knowledge or other resources. Employees with marketing expertise are grouped into a marketing unit, those with production skills are located in manufacturing, engineers are found in product development, and so on. The functional structure encourages specialization and increases employees' identity with their profession. Direct supervision is easier, because managers have backgrounds in that functional area and employees approach them with common problems and issues. Finally, the functional structure creates common pools of talent that typically serve everyone in the organization. This provides more economies of scale than if functional specialists are spread over different parts of the organization.[20]

functional structure
An organizational structure that organizes employees around specific knowledge or other resources.

The functional structure also has limitations.[21] Grouping employees around their skills tends to focus attention on those skills and related professional needs rather than on the company's product/service or client needs. Unless people are transferred from one function to the next, they might not develop a broader understanding of the business. Compared with other structures, the functional structure usually produces higher dysfunctional conflict and poorer coordination in serving clients or developing products. These problems occur because employees need to work with co-workers in other departments to complete organizational tasks, yet they have different subgoals and mental models of ideal work. To-gether, these problems require substantial formal controls and coordination when people are organized around functions.

Divisional Structure

divisional structure
An organizational structure that groups employees around geographic areas, clients, or outputs.

The **divisional structure** groups employees around geographic areas, clients, or outputs (products/services). This type of structure creates mini-businesses that may operate as sub-sidiaries rather than departments (sometimes called *strategic business units*); they are far more autonomous than functional departments. Exhibit 12.1 illustrates the three pure forms of divisional structure. The *geographic structure* organizes employees around dis-tinct regions of the country or globe. Exhibit 12.1*a* illustrates a geographic divisionalized structure similar to McDonald's Restaurants global structure. The *product/service struc-ture* organizes work around distinct outputs. Exhibit 12.1*b* illustrates this type of structure at Philips. The Dutch electronics company divides its workforce mainly into five product divisions, ranging from consumer electronics to semiconductors. The *client structure* rep-resents the third form of divisional structure, in which employees are organized around specific customer groups. Exhibit 12.1*c* illustrates the customer-focused structure similar to one adopted by the U.S. Internal Revenue Service.[22]

[**Exhibit 12.1**]   Three Types of Divisional Structure

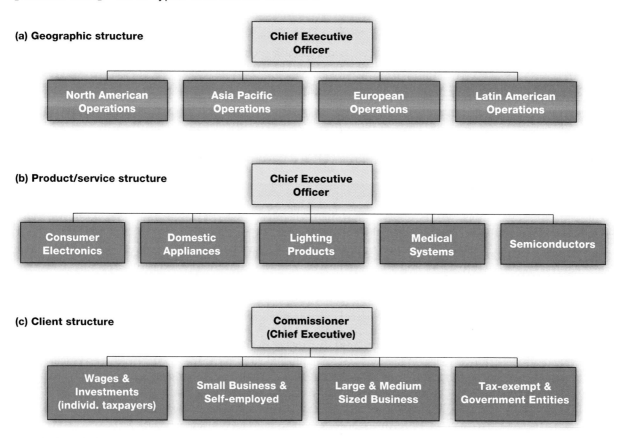

Note: Diagram (a) is similar to the global geographic divisional structure of McDonald's Restaurants; diagram (b) is similar to the product divisions at Philips; diagram (c) is similar to the customer-focused structure at the U.S. Internal Revenue Service.

Which form of divisionalization should large organizations adopt? The answer depends mainly on the primary source of environmental diversity or uncertainty.[23] Suppose an organization has one type of product sold to people across the country. If customer needs vary across regions, or if state governments impose different regulations on the product, then a geographic structure would be best to be more vigilant of this diversity. On the other hand, if the company sells several types of products across the country and customer preferences and government regulations are similar everywhere, then a product structure would likely work best.

Coca-Cola, Nestlé, and many other food and beverage companies are organized mainly around geographic regions because consumer tastes and preferred marketing strategies vary considerably around the world. Even though McDonald's makes the same Big Mac around the planet, it has more fish products in Hong Kong and more vegetarian products in India in line with traditional diets in those countries. Philips, on the other hand, is organized around products because consumer preferences are similar within each group. Hospitals from Geneva, Switzerland, to Santiago, Chile, purchase similar medical equipment from Philips, whereas manufacturing and sales of these products are quite different from Philips' semiconductor business.

Many divisionalized companies are moving away from geographical structures.[24] One reason is that information technology reduces the need for local representation. Clients can purchase online and communicate with businesses from almost anywhere in the world, so local representation is less critical. Reduced geographic variation is another reason for the shift away from geographical structures; freer trade has reduced government intervention for many products, and consumer preferences for many products and services are becoming more similar (converging) around the world. The third reason is that large companies increasingly have global business customers who demand one global point of purchase, not one in every country or region.

Evaluating the Divisionalized Structure

The divisional form is a building block structure, because it accommodates growth relatively easily. Related products or clients can be added to existing divisions with little need for additional learning. Completely different products, services, or clients can be accommodated by sprouting a new division. These advantages are offset by a number of limitations. First, the divisionalized structure tends to duplicate resources, such as production equipment and engineering or information technology expertise. Also, unless the division is quite large, resources are not used as efficiently as in functional structures where resources are pooled across the entire organization. The divisionalized structure also creates silos of knowledge. Expertise is spread throughout the various business units, which reduces the ability and perhaps motivation of these people to share their knowledge with counterparts in other divisions. In contrast, a functional structure groups experts together, which supports knowledge sharing.

Matrix Structure

Ralph Szygenda faced a dilemma when he became General Motors' first corporate chief information officer.[25] His group had to serve the company's regional divisions, and each region's information technology needs differed to some extent. At the same time, GM has five diverse IT services, such as product development and supply chain management. Each of these services requires deep expertise, so staff providing one service would have quite different knowledge than staff providing one of the other IT services. The dilemma was whether to organize GM's hundreds of IT employees around a geographic or process structure.

matrix structure
A type of departmentalization that overlays two organizational forms in order to leverage the benefits of both.

Szygenda's solution was to do both by adopting a **matrix structure.** A matrix structure overlays two organizational forms in order to leverage the benefits that each has to offer. GM's IT group is organized around both geography and processes, as illustrated in Exhibit 12.2. The processes dimension is led by five process information officers (PIOs), each of whom is responsible for specific IT processes around the world. These PIOs report only to Szygenda. The geographic dimension is led by five regional chief information officers (CIOs) who are responsible for IT functions in each of General Motors' five regions around the world. These CIOs report to Szygenda as well as to the heads of their respective geographic business division. For example, the North American CIO reports to Szygenda and to the president of GM North America. Because they work closely with GM's regional executives and understand their priorities, the regional CIOs control the region's IT budget. This means that GM's PIOs compete with each other for financial resources toward IT projects in their specialization.

The matrix structure that organizes hundreds of IT professionals at General Motors is just one of many possible matrix structure combinations. Most global firms with a matrix structure have geography on one dimension, but the other dimension might be products/services (such as GM's IT processes) or client groups. Instead of combining two divisional forms, some matrix structures overlap a functional structure with project teams.[26] Employees are assigned to a cross-functional project team, yet they also belong to a permanent functional unit (e.g., engineering, marketing, etc.) to which they return when a project is completed.

[Exhibit 12.2]   Simplified General Motors' IT Division Matrix Structure

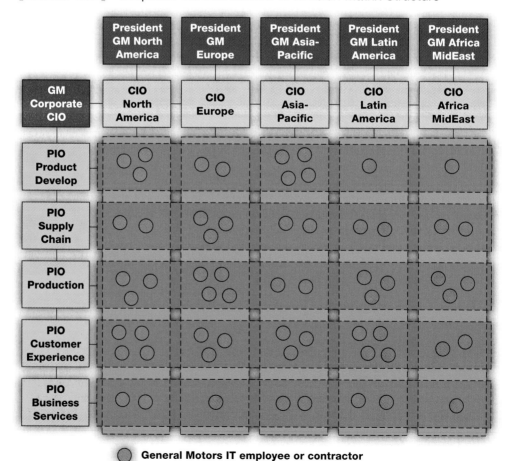

○ **General Motors IT employee or contractor**

Evaluating the Matrix Structure

The matrix structure usually optimizes the use of resources and expertise, making it ideal for project-based organizations with fluctuating workloads. When properly managed, it improves communication efficiency, project flexibility, and innovation compared to purely functional or divisional designs. It focuses employees on serving clients or creating products, yet keeps expertise organized around their specialization so knowledge sharing improves and resources are used more efficiently. The matrix structure is also a logical choice when, as in the case of GM's IT group, two different dimensions are equally important. Structures determine executive power and what is important; the matrix structure works when two different dimensions deserve equal attention.

In spite of these advantages, the matrix structure has several well-known problems.[27] One concern is that it increases goal conflict and ambiguity. Employees working at the matrix level have two bosses and, consequently, two sets of priorities that aren't always aligned with each other. At GM, the IT process people want to spend more money on their projects, whereas the regional IT people have different goals based on the needs of regional line management. A second problem is that it isn't always clear who should give approval for various decisions. A related challenge is that the existence of two bosses can dilute accountability. In a functional or divisionalized structure, one manager is responsible for everything, even the most unexpected issues. But in a matrix structure, the unusual problems don't get resolved because neither manager takes ownership for them.[28] The result of conflict and ambiguity in matrix structures is that some employees experience more stress, and some managers are less satisfied with their work arrangements.

Team-Based Structure

W. L. Gore & Associates, described in the opening story to this chapter, is an example of a **team-based structure.** Gore relies on teams throughout the organization, whereas most team-based structures are found within divisionalized structures. For example, aircraft components maker Pratt & Whitney has a divisionalized structure, but some of the manufacturing plants within those divisions are organized as team-based structures.

The team-based structure has a few distinguishing features from other organizational forms. First, it is built around self-directed work teams (SDWTs) rather than traditional teams or departments. SDWTs complete an entire piece of work requiring several interdependent tasks, and they have substantial autonomy over the execution of their tasks. The teams operating throughout Gore plan, organize, and control their own work activities without traditional supervision. These teams are typically organized around work processes, such as making a specific product or serving a specific client group.

The team-based structure flattens the organization's overall hierarchy. This flatter structure is possible because self-directed teams do not rely on direct supervision to coordinate their work. Finally, the team-based structure has very little formalization. The executive team typically assigns output goals, but teams are typically given relatively few rules about how to organize their work to achieve those goals.

> **team-based structure**
> A type of departmentalization with a flat hierarchy and relatively little formalization, consisting of self-directed work teams responsible for various work processes.

Evaluating the Team-Based Structure

The team-based organization represents an increasingly popular structure because it is usually more responsive and flexible.[29] It tends to reduce costs because teams have less reliance on formal hierarchy (direct supervision). A cross-functional team structure improves communication and cooperation across traditional boundaries. With greater autonomy, this structure also allows quicker and more informed decision making.[30]

Against these benefits, the team-based structure can be difficult to maintain due to the need for ongoing interpersonal skills training. Teamwork potentially takes more time to coordinate than formal hierarchy during the early stages of team development. Employees may experience more stress due to increased ambiguity in their roles. Team leaders also experience more stress due to increased conflict, loss of functional power, and unclear career progression ladders.[31]

>Contingencies of Organizational Design

Most organizational behavior theories and concepts have contingencies—ideas that work well in one situation might not work as well in another situation. This contingency approach is certainly relevant when choosing the most appropriate organizational structure.[32] In this section, we introduce four contingencies of organizational design: external environment, size, technology, and strategy.

External Environment

The best structure for an organization depends on its external environment. The external environment includes anything outside the organization, including most stakeholders (e.g., clients, suppliers, government), resources (e.g., raw materials, human resources, information, finances), and competitors. Four characteristics of external environments influence the type of organizational structure best suited to a particular situation: dynamism, complexity, diversity, and hostility.[33]

- *Dynamic versus stable environments.* Dynamic environments have a high rate of change, leading to novel situations and a lack of identifiable patterns. Organic structures, including the team-based structure at Gore, are better suited to this type of environment so that the organization can adapt more quickly to changes.[34] In contrast, stable environments are characterized by regular cycles of activity and steady changes in supply and demand for inputs and outputs. Events are more predictable, enabling the firm to apply rules and procedures. Mechanistic structures tend to work best under these conditions because they are more efficient when the environment is predictable.

- *Complex versus simple environments.* Complex environments have many elements, whereas simple environments have few things to monitor. As an example, a major university library operates in a more complex environment than a small town public library. The university library's clients require several types of services—book borrowing, online full-text databases, research centers, course reserve collections, and so on. A small town public library has fewer of these demands placed on it. The more complex the environment, the more decentralized the organization should become. Decentralization is a logical response to complexity because decisions are pushed down to people and subunits with the necessary information to make informed choices.

- *Diverse versus integrated environments.* Organizations located in diverse environments have a greater variety of products or services, clients, and regions. In contrast, an integrated environment has only one client, product, and geographic area. The more diversified the environment, the more the firm needs to use a divisionalized form aligned with that diversity. If it sells a single product around the world, a geographic divisionalized structure would align best with the firm's geographic diversity, for example.

7-Eleven tries to leverage the buying power and efficiencies of its 25,000 stores in 19 countries by centralizing decisions about information technology and supplier purchasing. At the same time, the convenience store chain's customers have diverse preferences around the United States and internationally, and product demand at each store can change rapidly due to weather or special events. To thrive in this diverse and complex environment, 7-Eleven's has what it calls a "centrally decentralized" structure in which store managers make local inventory decisions. Along with ongoing product training and guidance from regional consultants, store managers have the best information about their customers and can respond quickly to local market needs. For instance, when a hurricane recently hit Annapolis, Maryland, residents could count on the local 7-Eleven store for supplies. That's because Pinto Soin, who operates four stores in the area, monitored the storm's track and adjusted his supplies to take the inclement weather into account. "We could never predict a busload of football players on a Friday night, but the store manager can," explains 7-Eleven president and CEO Jim Keyes, shown in this photo.[35]

- *Hostile versus munificent environments.* Firms located in a hostile environment face resource scarcity and more competition in the marketplace. Hostile environments are typically dynamic ones because they reduce the predictability of access to resources and demand for outputs. Organic structures tend to be best in hostile environments. However, when the environment is extremely hostile—such as a severe shortage of supplies or lower market share—organizations tend to temporarily centralize so that decisions can be made more quickly and executives feel more comfortable being in control.[36] Ironically, centralization may result in lower-quality decisions during organizational crises, because top management has less information, particularly when the environment is complex.

Organizational Size

Larger organizations should have different structures from smaller organizations.[37] As the number of employees increases, job specialization increases due to a greater division of labor. This greater division of labor requires more elaborate coordinating mechanisms. Thus, larger firms make greater use of standardization (particularly, work processes and outcomes) to coordinate work activities. These coordinating mechanisms create an administrative hierarchy and greater formalization. Historically, larger organizations make less use of informal communication as a coordinating mechanism. However, emerging information technologies and increased emphasis on empowerment have caused informal communication to regain its importance in large firms.[38]

Larger organizations also tend to be more decentralized. Executives have neither sufficient time nor expertise to process all the decisions that significantly influence the business as it grows. Therefore, decision-making authority is pushed down to lower levels, where incumbents are able to cope with the narrower range of issues under their control.

Technology

Technology is another factor to consider when designing the best organizational structure for the situation.[39] Technology refers to the mechanisms or processes by which an organization turns out its products or services. One technological contingency is its *variability*—the number of exceptions to standard procedure that tend to occur. In work processes with low variability (such as assembly lines), jobs are routine and follow standard operating procedures. Generally, high variability calls for an organic structure, whereas low variability calls for a mechanistic structure.

Another contingency is *analyzability*—the predictability or difficulty of the required work. The less analyzable the work, the more it requires experts with sufficient discretion to address the work challenges. Research teams operate under conditions of low analyzability because they are discovering knowledge from unknown conditions. This low analyzability situation requires less formalization and more use of informal communication as a coordinating mechanism. In contrast, technological activities with high analyzability should have a more formalized structure with standardized work processes as a coordinating mechanism.

Organizational Strategy

organizational strategy
The way an organization positions itself in its setting in relation to its stakeholders, given the organization's resources, capabilities, and mission.

Organizational strategy refers to the way the organization positions itself in its setting in relation to its stakeholders, given the organization's resources, capabilities, and mission.[40] In other words, strategy represents the decisions and actions applied to achieve the organization's goals. Although size, technology, and environment influence the optimal organizational structure, these contingencies do not necessarily determine structure. Instead, corporate leaders formulate and implement strategies that shape both the characteristics of these contingencies as well as the organization's resulting structure.

This concept is summed up with the simple phrase: structure follows strategy.[41] Organizational leaders decide how large to grow and which technologies to use. They take steps to define and manipulate their environments, rather than let the organization's fate be entirely determined by external influences. Furthermore, organizational structures don't evolve as a natural response to these contingencies. Instead, they result from organizational decisions. Thus, organizational strategy influences both the contingencies of structure and the structure itself.

The structure follows strategy thesis has become the dominant perspective of business policy and strategic management. An important aspect of this view is that organizations can choose the environments in which they want to operate. Some businesses adopt a *differentiation strategy* by bringing unique products to the market or attracting clients who want customized goods and services. They try to distinguish their outputs from those provided by other firms through marketing, providing special services, and innovation. Others adopt a *cost leadership strategy,* in which they maximize productivity and, consequently, are able to offer popular products or services at a competitive price.[42]

The type of organizational strategy selected leads to the best organizational structure to adopt.[43] Organizations with a cost leadership strategy should adopt a mechanistic, functional structure with high levels of job specialization and standardized work processes. A differentiation strategy, on the other hand, requires more customized relations with clients. A matrix or team-based structure with decentralization and less formalization is most appropriate here so that technical specialists are able to coordinate their work activities more closely with the client's needs. Overall, it is now apparent that organizational structure is influenced by size, technology, and environment, but the organization's strategy may reshape these elements and loosen their connection to organizational structure.

>chapter summary

Organizational structure refers to the division of labor as well as the patterns of coordination, communication, work flow, and formal power that direct organizational activities. All organizational structures divide labor into distinct tasks and coordinate that labor to accomplish common goals. The primary means of coordination are informal communication, formal hierarchy, and standardization.

The four basic elements of organizational structure include span of control, centralization, formalization, and departmentalization. At one time, experts suggested that firms should have a tall hierarchy with a narrow span of control. Today, most organizations have a flatter hierarchy because they rely on informal communication and standardization, rather than mainly direct supervision, to coordinate work processes.

Centralization occurs when formal decision authority is held by a small group of people, typically senior executives. Many companies decentralize as they become larger and more complex because senior executives lack the necessary time and expertise to process all the decisions that significantly influence the business. Formalization is the degree to which organizations standardize behavior through rules, procedures, formal training, and related mechanisms. Companies become more formalized as they get older and larger.

Span of control, centralization, and formalization cluster into mechanistic and organic structures. Mechanistic structures are characterized by a narrow span of control and high degree of formalization and centralization. Companies with an organic structure have the opposite characteristics.

Departmentalization specifies how employees and their activities are grouped together. It establishes the chain of command, focuses people around common mental models, and encourages coordination through informal communication among people and subunits. A functional structure organizes employees around specific knowledge or other resources. This fosters greater specialization and improves direct supervision, but it increases conflict in serving clients or developing products. It also focuses employee attention on functional skills rather than on the company's product/service or client needs.

A divisional structure groups employees around geographic areas, clients, or outputs. This structure accommodates growth and focuses employee attention on products or customers rather than tasks. However, this structure creates silos of knowledge and duplication of resources. The matrix structure combines two structures to leverage the benefits of both structures. However, this approach requires more coordination than functional or pure divisional structures, may dilute accountability, and increases conflict. Team-based structures are very flat with low formalization; they organize self-directed teams around work processes rather than functional specialties.

The best organizational structure depends on the firm's external environment, size, technology, and strategy. The optimal structure depends on whether the environment is dynamic or stable, complex or simple, diverse or integrated, and hostile or munificent. As organizations increase in size, they become more decentralized and more formalized, with greater job specialization and elaborate coordinating mechanisms. The work unit's technology—including variety of work and analyzability of problems—influences whether to adopt an organic or mechanistic structure. These contingencies influence but do not necessarily determine structure. Instead, corporate leaders formulate and implement strategies that shape both the characteristics of these contingencies as well as the organization's resulting structure.

>key.terms

centralization 237	organic structure 238
divisional structure 240	organizational strategy 246
formalization 237	organizational structure 233
functional structure 239	span of control 236
matrix structure 242	team-based structure 243
mechanistic structure 238	

>critical.thinking.questions

1. W. L. Gore & Associates has a team-based structure throughout the organization. What coordinating mechanism dominates in this type of organizational structure? To what extent, and in what ways, would the other two types of coordination exist at Gore?

2. Think about the business school or other organizational unit whose classes you are currently attending. What is the dominant coordinating mechanism used to guide or control the instructor? Why is this coordinating mechanism used the most here?

3. Administrative theorists concluded many decades ago that the most effective organizations have a narrow span of control. Yet today's top-performing manufacturing firms have a wide span of control. Why is this possible? Under what circumstances, if any, should manufacturing firms have a narrow span of control?

4. One trend in organizational structure seems to be decentralization. Why is decentralization becoming more common in contemporary organizations? What should companies consider when determining the degree of decentralization?

5. Diversified Technologies, Inc. (DTI) makes four types of products, each type to be sold to different types of clients. For example, one product is sold exclusively to automobile repair shops, whereas another is used mainly in hospitals. Customer expectations and needs are surprisingly similar throughout the world. However, the company has separate marketing, product design, and manufacturing facilities in North America, Europe, Asia, and South America because, until recently, each jurisdiction had unique regulations governing the production and sales of these products. However, several governments have begun the process of deregulating the products that DTI designs and manufactures, and trade agreements have opened several markets to foreign-made products. Which form of departmentalization might be best for DTI if deregulation and trade agreements occur?

6. Why are many organizations moving away from the geographic divisional structures?

7. From an employee perspective, what are the advantages and disadvantages of working in a matrix structure?

8. Suppose that you have been hired as a consultant to diagnose the environmental characteristics of your college or university. How would you describe the school's external environment? Is the school's existing structure appropriate for this environment?

>case.study:skillbuilder12.1

The Rise and Fall of PMC AG

Founded in 1930, PMC AG is a German manufacturer of high-priced sports cars. During the early years, PMC was a small consulting engineering firm that specialized in solving difficult automotive design problems for clients. At the end of World War II, however, the son of PMC's founder decided to expand the business beyond consulting engineering. He was determined that PMC would build its own precision automobiles.

In 1948, the first PMC prototypes rolled out of the small manufacturing facility. Each copy was hand made by highly-skilled craftspeople. For several years, parts and engine were designed and built by other companies and assembled at the PMC plant. By the 1960s, however, PMC had begun to design and build its own parts.

PMC grew rapidly during the 1960s to mid-1980s. The company designed a completely new car in the early 1960s, launched a lower-priced model in 1970, and added a mid-priced model in 1977. By the mid-1980s, PMC had become very profitable as its name became an icon for wealthy entrepreneurs and jetsetters. In 1986, the year of highest production, PMC sold 54,000 cars. Nearly two-thirds of these were sold in North America.

PMC's Structure

PMC's organizational structure expanded with its success. During the early years, the company consisted only of an engineering department and a production department. By the 1980s, employees were divided into more than 10 functional departments representing different stages of the production process as well as upstream (e.g., design, purchasing) and downstream (e.g., quality control, marketing) activities. Employees worked exclusively in one department. It was almost considered mutiny for an employee to voluntarily move into another department.

PMC's production staff were organized into a traditional hierarchy. Front line employees reported to work group leaders, who reported to supervisors, who reported to group supervisors in each area. Group supervisors reported to production managers, who reported to production directors, who reported to PMC's executive vice-president of manufacturing. At one point in time, nearly 20 percent of production staff members was involved in supervisory tasks. In the early 1990s, for example, there were 48 group supervisors, 96 supervisors, 162 work group leaders supervising about 2,500 front-line production employees.

PMC's Craft Tradition

PMC had a long tradition and culture that supported craft expertise. This appealed to Germany's skilled workforce because it gave employees an opportunity to test and further develop their skills. PMC workers were encouraged to master long work cycles, often as much as 15 minutes per unit. Their ideal was to build as much of the automobile as possible alone. For example, a few masters were able to assemble an entire engine. Their reward was to personally sign their name on the completed component.

The design engineers worked independently of the production department, with the result that production employees had to adjust designs to fit the available parts. Rather than being a nuisance, the production employees viewed this as a challenge that would further test their well-developed craft skills. Similarly, manufacturing engineers occasionally redesigned the product to fit manufacturing capabilities.

To improve efficiency, a moving track assembly system was introduced until 1977. Even then, the emphasis on craft skills was apparent. Employees were encouraged to quickly put all the parts on the car, knowing that highly skilled troubleshooting craftspeople would discover and repair defects after the car came off the line. This was much more costly and time consuming than assembling the vehicle correctly the first time, but it provided yet another challenging set of tasks for skilled craftspeople. And to support their position, PMC vehicles were known for their few defects by the time they were sold to customers.

The End of Success?

PMC sports cars filled a small niche in the automobile market for those who wanted a true sports car just tame enough for everyday use. PMCs were known for their superlative performance based on excellent engineering technology, but they were also becoming very expensive. Japanese sports cars were not quite in the same league as a PMC, the cost of manufacturing the Japanese vehicles was a small fraction of the cost of manufacturing a vehicle at PMC.

This cost inefficiency hit PMC's sales during the late 1980s and early 1990s. First, the German currency appreciated against the U.S. dollar, which made PMC sports cars even more expensive in the North American market. By 1990, PMC was selling half of the number of cars it sold just four years earlier. Then, the North American recession hit, driving PMC sales down further. In 1993, PMC sold just 14,000 vehicles, compared to 54,000 in 1987. And although sales rebounded to 20,000 by 1995, the high price tag put PMCs out of reach of many potential customers. It was clear to PMC's founding family that changes were needed, but they weren't sure where to begin.

Discussion Questions

1. Describe PMC's organizational structure in terms of the four organizational design features (i.e., span of control, centralization, formalization, and departmentalization.

2. Discuss the problems with PMC's current structure.

3. Identify and justify an organizational structure that, in your opinion, would be more appropriate for PMC.

Source: Written by Steven L. McShane based on information from several sources about "PMC." The company name and some details of actual events have been altered to provide a fuller case discussion.

>team.exercise:skillbuilder12.2

Organizational Structure and Design: The Club Ed Exercise

By Cheryl Harvey and Kim Morouney, Wilfred Laurier University

Purpose   This exercise is designed to help you understand the issues to consider when designing organizations at various stages of growth.

Materials   Each student team should have enough overhead transparencies or flip chart sheets to display several organizational charts.

Instructions

Each team discusses the scenario presented. The first scenario is presented below. The instructor will facilitate discussion and notify teams when to begin the next step. The exercise and debriefing require approximately 90 minutes, although fewer scenarios can reduce the time somewhat.

- *Step 1:* Students are placed in teams (typically four or five people).

- *Step 2:* After reading scenario 1 presented below, each team will design an organizational chart (departmentalization) that is most appropriate for this situation. Students should be able to describe the type of

structure drawn and explain why it is appropriate. The structure should be drawn on an overhead transparency or flip chart for others to see during later class discussion. The instructor will set a fixed time (e.g., 15 minutes) to complete this task.

> *Scenario 1.* Determined never to shovel snow again, you are establishing a new resort business on a small Caribbean island. The resort is under construction and is scheduled to open one year from now. You decide it is time to draw up an organizational chart for this new venture, called Club Ed.

- *Step 3:* At the end of the time allowed, the instructor will present scenario 2 and each team will be asked to draw another organizational chart to suit that situation. Again, students should be able to describe the type of structure drawn and explain why it is appropriate.

- *Step 4:* At the end of the time allowed, the instructor will present scenario 3 and each team will be asked to draw another organizational chart to suit that situation.

- *Step 5:* Depending on the time available, the instructor might present a fourth scenario. The class will gather to present their designs for each scenario. During each presentation, teams should describe the type of structure drawn and explain why it is appropriate.

Source: Adapted from C. Harvey and K. Morouney, *Journal of Management Education* 22 (June 1998), pp. 425–29. Used with permission of the authors.

>self-assessment.skillbuilder12.3

Identifying Your Preferred Organizational Structure

Personal values influence how comfortable you are working in different organizational structures. You might prefer an organization with clearly defined rules or no rules at all. You might prefer a firm where almost any employee can make important decisions, or where important decisions are screened by senior executives. This self-assessment is designed to help you understand how an organization's

structure influences the personal needs and values of people working in that structure. Read each statement and indicate the extent to which you would like to work in an organization with that characteristic. This self-assessment is completed alone so students will complete this self-assessment honestly without concerns of social comparison. However, class discussion will focus on the elements of organizational structure and their relationship to personal needs and values.

**Find the full self-assessments on the OLC at
www.mhhe.com/mcshaneess**

[chapter 13]

Organizational Culture

Charles Schwab (left) and other executives at discount brokerage firm Charles Schwab & Co. didn't anticipate the clash of organizational cultures when they acquired U.S. Trust, led by CEO H. Marshall Schwarz (right).

>learningobjectives

After reading this chapter, you should be able to

- Describe the elements of organizational culture.
- Discuss the importance of organizational subcultures.
- List four categories of artifacts through which corporate culture is deciphered.
- Identify three functions of organizational culture.
- Discuss the conditions under which cultural strength improve corporate performance.
- Compare and contrast four strategies for merging organizational cultures.
- Identify five strategies to strengthen an organization's culture.
- Describe the stages of organizational socialization.
- Explain how realistic job previews assist the socialization process.

During the peak of the dot-com boom, Charles Schwab & Co. executives were convinced that as investors got wealthier they would migrate from the San Francisco–based discount broker to full-service firms that offered more personalized service. So Schwab paid top dollar to acquire U.S. Trust, a highbrow New York–based private bank that only served clients with at least $10 million to invest. Schwab customers who got wealthy would be shunted over to U.S. Trust for more personalized service.

The strategy backfired, partly because Schwab's customers still wanted cheap trades as they got wealthier, and partly because Schwab ignored the acquisition's cultural dynamics. Schwab's culture values rapid change, cost-cutting frugality, process efficiency, and egalitarianism. Schwab employees see themselves as nimble nonconformists who empower millions of people through low-cost Internet-based stock trading. In contrast, U.S. Trust was an exclusive club that was slow to adopt technology and preferred to admit new clients through referrals from existing clients. Clients were pampered by "wealth advisers" who earned huge bonuses and worked in an environment that reeked of luxury.

While negotiating the takeover, U.S. Trust executives expressed concern about these cultural differences, so Schwab agreed to leave the firm as a separate entity. This separation strategy didn't last very long. Schwab cut U.S. Trust's lucrative bonuses and tied annual rewards to Schwab's financial performance. U.S. Trust executives were pushed to cut costs and set more aggressive goals. Schwab even tried to acculturate several hundred U.S. Trust employees with a board game that used a giant mat showing hills, streams, and a mountain with founder Charles Schwab's face carved into the side. U.S. Trust staff complained that the game was demeaning, particularly wearing smocks as they played the role of investors.

In meetings immediately following the acquisition, U.S. Trust executives winced when Schwab frequently used the term *customers.* They reminded Schwab's staff that U.S. Trust has *clients,* which implies much more of a long-term relationship. U.S. Trust advisors also resisted Schwab's referrals of newly minted millionaires in blue jeans. "We were flabbergasted," said one Schwab board member of the cultural clash. "Some of the U.S. Trust officers simply refused to accept our referrals."

When the depth of cultural intransigence became apparent, U.S. Trust's CEO was replaced with Schwab executive Alan Weber. Weber later insisted that "there is no culture clash," because Schwab "never tried to change the nature of the organization." Meanwhile, sources say that more than 300 U.S. Trust wealth advisers have defected to competitors since the acquisition, taking many valued clients with them. Schwab's CEO was fired, in part because the U.S. Trust acquisition stumbled. The acquisition is now worth less than half of its original purchase price.

"Here are two first-class companies, but structural and cultural problems keep the combination from the kind of success they expected," explains a financial adviser in Florida.[1]

Schwab's acquisition of U.S. Trust is a classic tale of the perils of ignoring organizational culture. **Organizational culture** is the basic pattern of shared assumptions, values, and beliefs considered to be the correct way of thinking about and acting on problems and opportunities facing the organization. It defines what is important and unimportant in the company. You might think of it as the organization's DNA—invisible to the naked eye, yet a powerful template that shapes what happens in the workplace.[2]

This chapter begins by examining the elements of organizational culture and how culture is deciphered through artifacts. This is followed by a discussion of the relationship between organizational culture and corporate performance, including the effects of cultural strength, fit, and adaptability. Then we turn to the issue of mergers and corporate culture, followed by specific strategies for maintaining a strong organizational culture. The last section of this chapter zooms in on employee socialization, which is one of the more important ways to strengthen organizational culture.

organizational culture
The basic pattern of shared assumptions, values, and beliefs considered to be the correct way of thinking about and acting on problems and opportunities facing the organization.

>Elements of Organizational Culture

As Exhibit 13.1 illustrates, the assumptions, values, and beliefs that represent organizational culture operate beneath the surface of behavior. *Assumptions* are the shared mental models that people rely on to guide their perceptions and behaviors. They represent the deepest part of organizational culture because they are unconscious and taken for granted. At Schwab, for example, efficiency and low cost aren't just valued; they are assumed to be the best way to serve most customers and ensure the company's success. *Beliefs* represent the individual's perceptions of reality. *Values* are more stable, evaluative beliefs that guide our preferences for outcomes or courses of action in a variety of situations.[3] They help us define what is right or wrong, or good or bad, in the world.

Content of Organizational Culture

Organizations differ in their cultural content, that is, the relative ordering of beliefs, values, and assumptions. The culture of Charles Schwab & Co. values rapid change, cost-cutting frugality, process efficiency, and egalitarianism. At U.S. Trust, employees embrace stability, dedicated service, status, and reputation. Some writers like to classify corporate culture into four or five easy-to-remember groups. However, this is an unfortunate oversimplification because there are dozens of individual and cross-cultural values, so there are likely as many organizational values.

[**Exhibit 13.1**]   Elements of Organizational Culture

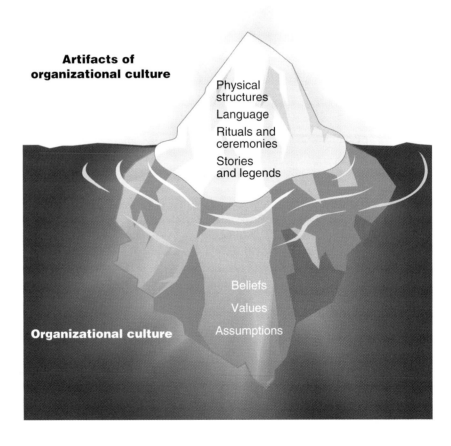

Organizational Subcultures

When discussing organizational culture, we are actually referring to the *dominant culture,* that is, the themes shared most widely by the organization's members. However, organizations are also comprised of *subcultures* located throughout their various divisions, geographic regions, and occupational groups.[4] Some subcultures enhance the dominant culture by espousing parallel assumptions, values, and beliefs; others are called *countercultures* because they directly oppose the organization's core values.

Subcultures, particularly countercultures, potentially create conflict and dissension among employees, but they also serve two important functions.[5] First, they maintain the organization's standards of performance and ethical behavior. Employees who hold countercultural values are an important source of surveillance and critique over the dominant order. They encourage constructive conflict and more creative thinking about how the organization should interact with its environment. By preventing employees from blindly following one set of values, subcultures help the organization to abide by society's ethical values.

The second function of subcultures is that they are the spawning grounds for emerging values that keep the firm aligned with the needs of customers, suppliers, society, and other stakeholders. Companies eventually need to replace their dominant values with ones that are more appropriate for the changing environment. If subcultures are suppressed, the organization may take longer to discover and adopt values aligned with the emerging environment.

>Deciphering Organizational Culture through Artifacts

We can't directly see an organization's cultural assumptions, values, and beliefs. Instead, as Exhibit 13.1 illustrated earlier, organizational culture is deciphered indirectly through **artifacts.** Artifacts are the observable symbols and signs of an organization's culture, such as the way visitors are greeted, the physical layout, and how employees are rewarded.[6] Understanding an organization's culture requires painstaking assessment of many artifacts because they are subtle and often ambiguous.[7] The process is very much like an anthropological investigation of a new society. Thus, discovering a company's culture requires more than surveying employees. It involves observing workplace behavior, listening for unique language in everyday conversations, studying written documents, and interviewing staff about corporate stories. Four broad categories of artifacts are organizational stories and legends, rituals and ceremonies, language, and physical structures and symbols.

artifacts
The observable symbols and signs of an organization's culture.

Organizational Stories and Legends

Stories permeate strong organizational cultures. Some tales recount heroic deeds by employees; others ridicule past events that deviated from the firm's core values. These stories and legends serve as powerful social prescriptions of the way things should, or should not, be done. They provide human realism to corporate expectations, individual performance standards, and the criteria for getting fired. These stories also create emotions in listeners, which tends to improve their memory of the lesson within the story. Stories have the greatest effect at communicating corporate culture when they describe real people, are assumed to be true, and are remembered by employees throughout the organization. Stories are also prescriptive—they advise people what to do or not to do.[8]

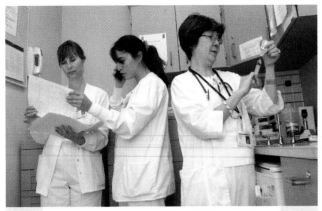

The Mayo Clinic has a well-established culture at its original clinic in Rochester, Minnesota, but maintaining that culture in its expanding operations in Jacksonville, Florida, and Scottsdale, Arizona, has been challenging. "We were struggling with growing pains [and] we didn't want to lose the culture, [so] we were looking at how to keep the heritage alive," explains Matt McElrath, Mayo Clinic human resources director in Scottsdale. The Mayo Clinic retained anthropologist Linda Catlin to decipher Mayo's culture and identify ways to reinforce it at the two newer sites. Catlin shadowed employees and posed as a patient to observe what happens in waiting rooms. "She did countless interviews, joined physicians on patient visits, and even spent time in the operating room," says McElrath. At the end of her six-week cultural expedition, Catlin submitted a report outlining Mayo's culture and how its satellite operations varied from that culture. The Mayo Clinic adopted all of Catlin's 11 recommendations, such as requiring all new physicians at the three sites to attend an orientation in Rochester where they learn about Mayo's history and values.[9]

Rituals and Ceremonies

Rituals are the programmed routines of daily organizational life that dramatize the organization's culture. They include how visitors are greeted, how often senior executives visit subordinates, how people communicate with each other, how much time employees take for lunch, and so on. **Ceremonies** are more formal artifacts than rituals. Ceremonies are planned activities conducted specifically for the benefit of an audience, such as publicly rewarding, or punishing, employees or celebrating the launch of a new product or newly won contract.

Organizational Language

The language of the workplace speaks volumes about the company's culture. How employees address co-workers, describe customers, express anger, and greet stakeholders are all verbal symbols of cultural values. This was apparent in the opening story to this chapter, where U.S. Trust executives insisted on using the term *clients* rather than *customers*, the term that Schwab executives used freely. This language reflects the long-term and deep relationship that U.S. Trust staff have with their clients, compared with the more impersonal connection between Schwab's staff and their customers.

Language also highlights values held by organizational subcultures. For instance, consultants working at Whirlpool kept hearing employees talk about the appliance company's "PowerPoint culture." This phrase, which names Microsoft's presentation software, is a critique of Whirlpool's hierarchical culture in which communication is one-way (from executives to employees).[10]

rituals
The programmed routines of daily organizational life that dramatize the organization's culture.

ceremonies
Planned and usually dramatic displays of organizational culture, conducted specifically for the benefit of an audience.

Physical Structures and Symbols

Winston Churchill once said, "We shape our buildings; thereafter, they shape us."[11] The former British prime minister was reminding us that buildings both reflect and influence an organization's culture. The size, shape, location, and age of buildings might suggest the company's emphasis on teamwork, environmental friendliness, flexibility, or any other set of values. An extreme example is the "interplanetary headquarters" of Oakley, Inc. The ultrahip eyewear and clothing company built a vaultlike structure in Foothills Ranch, California, complete with towering metallic walls studded with oversize bolts, to represent its secretive and protective culture. "We've always had a fortress mentality," says an Oakley executive. "What we make is gold, and people will do anything to get it, so we protect it."[12]

Even if the building doesn't make much of a statement, there is a treasure trove of physical artifacts inside. Desks, chairs, office space, and wall hangings, or lack of them, are just a few of the items that might convey cultural meaning. Stroll through IDEO's offices in Palo Alto, California, and you soon realize that the industrial design firm has an innovative, team-oriented, egalitarian culture. Employees have similarly sized cubicles grouped into neighborhoods facing an asymmetrical table that serves as a central "park" for the team.[13]

>Organizational Culture and Performance

Does organizational culture affect corporate performance? Herb Kelleher, the founder and chairman of Southwest Airlines, thinks so. "Culture is one of the most precious things a company has, so you must work harder on it than anything else."[14] Several writers concur with Kelleher's statement, claiming that companies with strong cultures are more likely to be successful.[15] A *strong* organizational culture exists when most employees across all subunits hold the dominant values. The company's values are also institutionalized through well-established artifacts, thereby making it difficult for those values to change. Furthermore, strong cultures tend to be long lasting, sometimes traced back to the beliefs and values established by the company's founder. In contrast, companies have weak cultures when the dominant values are short lived and held mainly by a few people at the top of the organization.

A strong corporate culture is potentially good for business because it serves three important functions:

1. Organizational culture is a deeply embedded form of social control that influences employee decisions and behavior.[16] Culture is pervasive and operates unconsciously. You might think of it as an automatic pilot, directing employees in ways that are consistent with organizational expectations.

2. Organizational culture is the "social glue" that bonds people together and makes them feel part of the organizational experience.[17] Employees are motivated to internalize the organization's dominant culture because it fulfills their need for social identity. This social glue is increasingly important as a way to attract new staff and retain top performers.

3. Organizational culture assists the sense-making process.[18] It helps employees understand what goes on and why things happen in the company. Corporate culture also makes it easier to understand what is expected of them and to interact with other employees who know the culture and believe in it.

Organizational Culture: Strength and Fit

Strong cultures are *potentially* good for business, as we explained above, but this isn't always true. On the contrary, studies have found only a modestly positive relationship between culture strength and success.[19]

One reason for the weak relationship is that a strong culture increases organizational performance only when the cultural content is appropriate for the organization's environment. When a firm's strong culture is misaligned with its environment, it is unable to effectively serve customers and other dominant stakeholders. For instance, a frugal and egalitarian culture helped Charles Schwab & Co. succeed as a discount broker. But when this culture was imposed on U.S. Trust, top-performing brokers defected with their clients. U.S. Trust's existing culture was not perfectly adapted to the times (it lagged competitors with new financial products and was fined for poor recordkeeping), but Schwab's culture would have been an even worse fit for U.S. Trust's competitive space.

A second concern why companies with strong cultures aren't necessarily more effective is that strong cultures lock decision makers into mental models that blind them to new opportunities and unique problems. Thus, strong cultures might cause decision makers to

Citibank Japan director Koichiro Kitade thrived in Citigroup's bottom-line culture. Each year, his group handily exceeded the ever-increasing targets set by Citigroup's top executives in New York. Over six years, Citibank Japan outscored all other private banks in the company's huge network by increasing its clientele tenfold and delivering record profits. Unfortunately, the Japanese government's financial watchdog recently concluded that Citibank's culture also encouraged Kitade to push aside ethical and financial compliance rules. Japan's regulator accused Citibank of constructing "a law-evading sales system," citing infractions ranging from grossly overcharging clients to helping them to falsify profit and manipulate stock. With 83 infractions, Citigroup was told to close some of its Japanese operations. "It's our fault, because all we talk about is delivering the numbers. We've done this forever," admits Citigroup chief executive Charles Prince. This photo shows Prince (right) with a colleague at a Tokyo news conference bowing in apology for the violations. Prince fired several top executives in Tokyo and New York and is now on a mission to change Citibank's culture. He has a major challenge ahead of him. The Japan affair occurred after Citigroup paid dearly for its involvement in the Enron accounting disaster. Dow Jones news service reports that Citigroup has an "established reputation for pushing the limits of acceptable banking behavior."[20]

overlook or incorrectly define subtle misalignments between the organization's activities and the changing environment. A third issue is that very strong cultures tend to suppress dissenting subcultural values. As we noted earlier, subcultures encourage constructive conflict, which improves creative thinking and offers some level of ethical vigilance over the dominant culture. In the long run, the subculture's nascent values could become important dominant values as the environment changes. Strong cultures suppress subcultures, thereby undermining these benefits.

Adaptive Cultures

adaptive culture
An organizational culture in which employees focus on the changing needs of customers and other stakeholders, and support initiatives to keep pace with those changes.

So far, we have learned that strong cultures are more effective when the cultural values are aligned with the organization's environment. Also, no corporate culture should be so strong that it blinds employees to alternative viewpoints or completely suppresses dissenting subcultures. One last point to add to this discussion is that organizations are more likely to succeed when they have an adaptive culture.[21] An **adaptive culture** exists when employees focus on the changing needs of customers and other stakeholders and support initiatives to keep pace with these changes. Adaptive cultures have an external focus, and employees assume responsibility for the organization's performance. As a result, they are proactive and quick. Employees seek out opportunities rather than wait for them to arrive.

>Merging Organizational Cultures

4C, Corporate Culture Clash & Chemistry, is a company with an unusual name and mandate. The Dutch consulting firm helps clients to determine whether their culture is aligned (chemistry) or incompatible with (clash) a potential acquisition or merger partner. The firm also compares the company's culture with its strategy. There should be plenty of demand for 4C's expertise. According to various studies, the majority of corporate mergers and acquisitions fail, mostly because corporate leaders are so focused on the financial or marketing logistics of a merger that they fail to conduct due-diligence audits on their respective corporate cultures.[22]

The corporate world is littered with mergers that failed or had a difficult gestation because of clashing organizational cultures. Schwab's acquisition of U.S. Trust, described at the beginning of this chapter, is one example. The marriage of Internet firm AOL with media giant Time Warner is another. AOL's culture valued youthful, high-flying, quick deal-making, whereas Time Warner had a button-down, hierarchical, and systematic culture.[23] These differences between AOL and Time Warner produced a colossal culture clash that undermined job performance, increased dysfunctional conflict, and resulted in lost talent.

Bicultural Audit

Organizational leaders can minimize these cultural collisions and fulfill their duty of due diligence by conducting a bicultural audit. A **bicultural audit** diagnoses cultural relations between the companies and determines the extent to which cultural clashes will likely occur.[24] The bicultural audit process begins by identifying cultural differences between the merging companies. Next, the bicultural audit data are analyzed to determine which differences between the two firms will result in conflict and which cultural values provide common ground on which to build a cultural foundation in the merged organization. The final stage involves identifying strategies and preparing action plans to bridge the two organizations' cultures.

bicultural audit
Diagnoses cultural relations between companies prior to a merger and determines the extent to which cultural clashes are likely to occur.

Strategies to Merge Different Organizational Cultures

In some cases, the bicultural audit results in a decision to end merger talks because the two cultures are too different to merge effectively. However, even with substantially different cultures, two companies may form a workable union if they apply the appropriate merger strategy. The four main strategies for merging different corporate cultures are assimilation, deculturation, integration, and separation (see Exhibit 13.2).[25]

Assimilation

Assimilation occurs when employees at the acquired company willingly embrace the cultural values of the acquiring organization. Typically, this strategy works best when the acquired company has a weak dysfunctional culture, whereas the acquiring company's culture is strong and aligned with the external environment. Culture clash is rare with

[Exhibit 13.2] Strategies for Merging Different Organizational Culture

Merger Strategy	Description	Works Best When
Assimilation	Acquired company embraces acquiring firm's culture.	Acquired firm has a weak culture.
Deculturation	Acquiring firm imposes its culture on unwilling acquired firm.	Rarely works—may be necessary only when acquired firm's culture doesn't work but employees don't realize it.
Integration	Combining the two or more cultures into a new composite culture.	Existing cultures can be improved.
Separation	Merging companies remain distinct entities with minimal exchange of culture or organizational practices.	Firms operate successfully in different businesses requiring different cultures.

Source: Based on ideas in K. W. Smith, "A Brand-New Culture for the Merged Firm," *Mergers and Acquisitions,* 35 (June 2000), pp. 45–50; and A. R. Malekazedeh and A. Nahavandi, "Making Mergers Work by Managing Cultures," *Journal of Business Strategy,* May–June 1990, pp. 55–57.

assimilation because the acquired firm's culture is weak and employees are looking for better cultural alternatives.

Deculturation

Assimilation is rare. Employees usually resist organizational change, particularly when they are asked to throw away personal and organizational values. Under these conditions, some acquiring companies apply a *deculturation* strategy by imposing their culture and business practices on the acquired organization. The acquiring firm strips away artifacts and reward systems that support the old culture. People who cannot adopt the acquiring company's culture are often terminated.

Deculturation may be necessary when the acquired firm has a dysfunctional culture, yet its employees continue to embrace that culture. However, this strategy is difficult to apply effectively because the acquired firm's employees resist the cultural intrusions from the buying firm, thereby delaying or undermining the merger process. These problems were apparent at U.S. Trust after it was acquired by Charles Schwab & Co.

Integration

A third strategy is to combine the two or more cultures into a new composite culture that preserves the best features of the previous cultures. Integration is slow and potentially risky, because there are many forces preserving the existing cultures. Still, this strategy should be considered when the companies have relatively weak cultures, or when their cultures include several overlapping values. Integration also works best when people realize that their existing cultures are ineffective and are, therefore, motivated to adopt a new set of dominant values.

Separation

A separation strategy occurs where the merging companies agree to remain distinct entities with minimal exchange of culture or organizational practices. This strategy is most appropriate when the two merging companies are in unrelated industries or operate in different countries, because the most appropriate cultural values tend to differ by industry and national culture. Schwab tried to apply a separation strategy with U.S. Trust. However, as with many companies that attempt this approach, executives in the acquiring firm have difficulty keeping their hands off the acquired firm. It's not surprising, therefore, that only 15 percent of acquisitions leave the purchased organization as a stand-alone unit.[26]

>Changing and Strengthening Organizational Culture

Whether merging two cultures or reshaping the firm's existing values, corporate leaders need to understand how to change and strengthen the organization's dominant culture. Indeed, some organizational scholars conclude that the only way to ensure any lasting change is to realign cultural values with those changes. In words of one eminent scholar, changes "stick" when they become "the way we do things around here."[27]

Changing organizational culture requires the change management toolkit that we will learn about in the next chapter. Corporate leaders need to make employees aware of the urgency for change. Then they need to "unfreeze" the existing culture by removing artifacts that represent that culture and "refreeze" the new culture by introducing artifacts that communicate and reinforce the new values.

Strengthening Organizational Culture

Artifacts communicate and reinforce the new corporate culture, but we also need to consider ways to further strengthen that culture. Five approaches that are commonly cited in the literature are the actions of founders and leaders, introducing culturally consistent rewards, maintaining a stable workforce, managing the cultural network, and selecting and socializing new employees.

Actions of Founders and Leaders

Founders establish an organization's culture.[28] You can see this at Charles Schwab & Co., where founder Charles Schwab has established a culture that is frugal, egalitarian, and fast-paced. Founders develop the systems and structures that support their personal values. They are also typically the visionaries whose energetic style provides a powerful role model for others to follow. In spite of the founder's effect, subsequent leaders can break the organization away from the founder's values if they apply the transformational leadership concepts that were described in Chapter 11. Transformational leaders alter and strengthen organizational culture by communicating and enacting their vision of the future.[29]

Introducing Culturally Consistent Rewards

Reward systems strengthen corporate culture when they are consistent with cultural values. For example, when John Deere was reorganized around a team-based organization a few years ago, it replaced its individual-oriented incentive plan with a team-based continuous improvement plan. The team bonus helped to shift the equipment manufacturer's cultural values such that employees now think in terms of team dynamics and work flow efficiencies.[30]

Maintaining a Stable Workforce

An organization's culture is embedded in the minds of its employees. Organizational stories are rarely written down; rituals and ceremonies do not usually exist in procedure

Ray Anderson (shown in photo) admits that he didn't pay much attention to environmentalism when he launched Atlanta-based Interface Inc. in 1973. But after reading *The Ecology of Commerce* in 1994, Anderson's newfound belief in sustainability has reshaped the corporate culture of the world's largest floor covering company. "Every part of the business, from the factory floor to upper management, is busy turning Interface into a forerunner of a new industrial revolution," says Anderson. Although critics note that Interface didn't achieve complete sustainability by 2000 (the target is now 2020), the company has clearly shifted to a "green" culture, thanks to Anderson's persistence. He formed a "Dream Team" task force and introduced an employee involvement program to identify ways to cut emissions and waste. Over the first decade, the company cut waste by half, smokestack emissions by 39 percent, and energy consumption by 31 percent. The company uses natural (such as corn oil) rather than petroleum-based raw materials where possible and is an early adopter of solar and biomass power systems.[31]

manuals; organizational metaphors are not found in corporate directories. Thus, organizations depend on a stable workforce to communicate and reinforce the dominant beliefs and values. The organization's culture can literally disintegrate during periods of high turnover and precipitous downsizing because the corporate memory leaves with these employees.[32] Conversely, corporate leaders who want to change the corporate culture have accelerated the turnover of senior executives and older employees who held the cultural values in place.

Managing the Cultural Network

Organizational culture is learned through informal communication, so an effective network of cultural transmission is necessary to strengthen the company's underlying assumptions, values, and beliefs. According to Max De Pree, former CEO of furniture manufacturer Herman Miller Inc., every organization needs "tribal storytellers" to keep the organization's history and culture alive.[33] The cultural network exists through the organizational grapevine. It is also supported through frequent opportunities for interaction so employees can share stories and reenact rituals. Senior executives must tap into the cultural network, sharing their own stories and creating new ceremonies and other opportunities to demonstrate shared meaning. Company magazines and other media can also strengthen organizational culture by communicating cultural values and beliefs more efficiently.

Selecting and Socializing Employees

Organizational culture is strengthened by hiring people who already embrace the cultural values. A good person-organization fit reinforces the culture; it also improves job satisfaction and organizational loyalty because new hires with values compatible to the corporate culture adjust more quickly to the organization.[34] Job applicants also pay attention to corporate culture during the hiring process. They look at corporate culture artifacts to determine whether the company's values are compatible to their own.

Along with selecting people with compatible values, companies maintain strong cultures through the process of organizational socialization. **Organizational socialization** refers to the process by which individuals learn the values, expected behaviors, and social knowledge necessary to assume their roles in the organization.[35] By communicating the company's dominant values, job candidates and new hires tend to more quickly and deeply internalize these values. Socialization is an important process for absorbing corporate culture as well as helping newcomers to adjust to co-workers, work procedures, and other corporate realities. Thus, the final section of this chapter looks more closely at the organizational socialization process.

organizational socialization
The process by which individuals learn the values, expected behaviors, and social knowledge necessary to assume their roles in the organization.

>Organizational Socialization

Bill Rainford was all set for summer employment at a financial services firm in New York City. Then Microsoft called the Boston University student with the offer of a possible internship. In January, after a successful interview in Boston, Rainford flew at Microsoft's expense to Redmond, Washington, for several more interviews and a tour of the company's lush campuslike headquarters. Microsoft even gave him a car rental so he could explore Seattle. But Rainford's real learning process occurred several months later as one of 800 interns, discovering firsthand what it's like to work at Microsoft.[36]

Microsoft successfully brings people into the organization by going beyond selecting applicants with the right competencies. It relies on internships and other organizational socialization practices to help newcomers learn about and adjust to the company's culture, physical layout, procedures, and so on. Research indicates that when employees are effectively socialized into the organization, they tend to perform better and have higher job satisfaction.[37]

Organizational socialization is a process of both learning and adjustment. It is a learning process because newcomers try to make sense of the company's physical workplace, social dynamics, and strategic/cultural environment. They learn about the organization's performance expectations, power dynamics, corporate culture, company history, and jargon. Organizational socialization is also a process of adjustment, because individuals need to adapt to their new work environment. They develop new work roles that reconfigure their social identity, adopt new team norms, and practice new behaviors.[38]

Newcomers absorb the organization's dominant culture to varying degrees. Some people deeply internalize the company's culture; a few others rebel against these attempts to change their mental models and values. Ideally, newcomers adopt a level of "creative individualism" in which they accept the essential elements of the organization's culture and team norms yet also had other values that add to the company's diversity.

Stages of Socialization

Socialization is a continuous process, beginning long before the first day of employment and continuing throughout one's career within the company. However, it is most intense when people move across organizational boundaries, such as when they first join a company or get transferred to an international assignment. Each of these transitions is a process that can be divided into three stages. Our focus here is on the socialization of new employees, so the three stages are called preemployment socialization, encounter, and role management (see Exhibit 13.3). These stages parallel the individual's transition from outsider, to newcomer, and then to insider.[39]

Stage 1: Preemployment Socialization

Think back to the months and weeks before you began working in a new job (or attending a new school). You actively searched for information about the company, formed expectations about working there, and felt some anticipation about fitting into that environment. The preemployment socialization stage encompasses all of the learning and adjustment that occurs prior to the first day of work in a new position. In fact, a large part of the socialization adjustment process occurs prior to the first day of work.[40] This is not an easy process, however. Individuals are outsiders, so they must rely on indirect information to form expectations about what it is like to work in the organization.

Stage 2: Encounter

The first day on the job typically marks the beginning of the encounter stage of organizational socialization. This is the stage in which newcomers test their prior expectations with the perceived realities. Many jobs fail the test, resulting in varying degrees of

[**Exhibit 13.3**]   Stages of Organizational Socialization

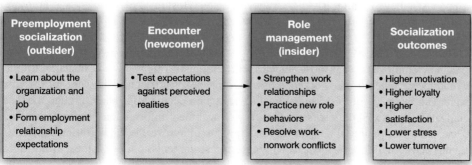

Preemployment socialization (outsider)	Encounter (newcomer)	Role management (insider)	Socialization outcomes
• Learn about the organization and job • Form employment relationship expectations	• Test expectations against perceived realities	• Strengthen work relationships • Practice new role behaviors • Resolve work-nonwork conflicts	• Higher motivation • Higher loyalty • Higher satisfaction • Lower stress • Lower turnover

reality shock
Occurs when
newcomers perceive
discrepancies between
pre-employment
expectations and on-
the-job reality.

reality shock. Reality shock occurs when newcomers perceive discrepancies between their preemployment expectations and on-the-job reality.[41] The larger the gap, the stronger the reality shock. Reality shock doesn't necessarily occur on the first day; it might develop over several weeks or even months as newcomers form a better understanding of their new work environment. Along with experiencing unmet expectations, reality shock occurs when newcomers are overwhelmed by the experience of sudden entry into a new work environment. They experience the stress of information overload and have difficulty adjusting quickly to their new role.

Stage 3: Role Management

During the role management stage in the socialization process, employees settle in as they make the transition from newcomers to insiders. They strengthen relationships with co-workers and supervisors, practice new role behaviors, and adopt attitudes and values consistent with their new position and organization. Role management also involves resolving the conflicts between work and nonwork activities. In particular, employees must redistribute their time and energy between work and family, reschedule recreational activities, and deal with changing perceptions and values in the context of other life roles. They must address any discrepancies between their existing values and those emphasized by the organizational culture. New social identities are formed that are more compatible with the work environment.

Improving the Socialization Process

Before hiring people for its new computer assembly plant in Winston-Salem, North Carolina, Dell, Inc., invited applicants to understand the company and the jobs better. "We will discuss the soul of Dell, give them a realistic job preview, and give them the opportunity to complete a job application," explains Ann Artzer, Dell's human resource manager for the plant. "It will be a chance to determine the mutual interest between the candidates and Dell."[42]

realistic job preview
Giving job applicants a
balance of positive and
negative information
about the job and work
context.

Dell has tried to improve the socialization process by providing a **realistic job preview (RJP)**, a balance of positive and negative information about the job and work context.[43] Companies often exaggerate positive features of the job and neglect to mention the undesirable elements in the hope that the best applicants will get "stuck" on the organization. In contrast, an RJP helps job applicants to decide for themselves whether their skills, needs, and values are compatible with the job and organization.

Although RJPs scare away some applicants, they tend to reduce turnover and increase job performance.[44] This occurs because RJPs help applicants develop more accurate preemployment expectations that, in turn, minimize reality shock. RJPs represent a type of vaccination by preparing employees for the more challenging and troublesome aspects of work life. There is also some evidence that RJPs increase organizational loyalty. A possible explanation for this is that companies providing candid information are easier to trust. They also show respect for the employment relationship and concern for employee welfare.[45]

Socialization Agents

Ask new employees what most helped them to adjust to their job and chances are they would mention helpful co-workers, bosses, or maybe even friends who work for the company. The fact is, a lot of organizational socialization occurs informally through these socialization agents. Supervisors tend to provide technical information, performance feedback, and information about job duties. They also improve the socialization process by giving newcomers reasonably challenging first assignments, buffering them from excessive demands, and helping them form social ties with co-workers.[46]

Co-workers are important socialization agents because they are easily accessible, can answer questions when problems arise, and serve as role models for appropriate behavior. New employees tend to receive this information and support when co-workers integrate them into the work team. Co-workers also aid the socialization process by being flexible and tolerant in their interactions with these new hires.

Several organizations rely on a "buddy system" whereby newcomers are assigned to co-workers for sources of information and social support. Progressive Inc., the Mayfield, Ohio–based insurance firm, relies on current employees to recruit and socialize job applicants. "I think candidates can trust and respect people who already work here," says Jennifer Cohen, Progressive's national employment director. "They get a lot of honest information about the company." ExtendMedia also has a formal buddy system, but equally valuable is the box of doughnuts put on every newcomer's desk on the first day of work. "The [doughnuts] are there to break the ice so that other people come and talk to them. We are introducing people through their stomachs," explains an executive at the interactive media company.[47]

Newcomers who quickly form social relations with co-workers tend to have a less traumatic socialization experience and are less likely to quit their jobs within the first year of employment.[48] However, companies need to help all employees through resocialization as they experience change in the workplace. The next chapter investigates the dynamics of organizational change.

>chapter summary

Organizational culture is the basic pattern of shared assumptions, values, and beliefs that govern behavior within a particular organization. Assumptions are the shared mental models or theories-in-use that people rely on to guide their perceptions and behaviors. Beliefs represent the individual's perceptions of reality. Values are more stable, long-lasting beliefs about what is important. They help us define what is right or wrong, or good or bad, in the world. Culture content refers to the relative ordering of beliefs, values, and assumptions.

Organizations have subcultures as well as the dominant culture. Subcultures maintain the organization's standards of performance and ethical behavior. They are also the source of emerging values that replace aging core values.

Artifacts are the observable symbols and signs of an organization's culture. Four broad categories of artifacts include organizational stories and legends, rituals and ceremonies, language, physical structures and symbols. Understanding an organization's culture requires assessment of many artifacts because they are subtle and often ambiguous.

Organizational culture has three main functions. It is a deeply embedded form of social control. It is also the social glue that bonds people together and makes them feel part of the organizational experience. Third, corporate culture helps employees make sense of the workplace.

Companies with strong cultures generally perform better than those with weak cultures, but only when the cultural content is appropriate for the organization's environment. Also, the culture should not be so strong that it drives out dissenting values, which may form emerging values for the future. Organizations should have adaptive cultures so that employees focus on the need for change and support initiatives and leadership that keeps pace with these changes.

Mergers should include a bicultural audit to diagnose the compatibility of the organizational cultures. The four main strategies for merging different corporate cultures are integration, deculturation, assimilation, and separation.

Organizational culture may be strengthened through the actions of founders and leaders, introducing culturally consistent rewards, maintaining a stable workforce, managing the cultural network, and selecting and socializing employees.

Organizational socialization is the process by which individuals learn the values, expected behaviors, and social knowledge necessary to assume their roles in the organization. It is a process of both learning about the work context and adjusting to new work roles, team norms, and behaviors. Employees typically pass through three socialization stages: preemployment, encounter, and role management. To improve the socialization process, organizations should introduce realistic job previews (RJPs) and recognize the value of socialization agents in the process.

>key.terms

adaptive culture 258

artifacts 255

bicultural audit 259

ceremonies 256

organizational culture 253

organizational socialization 262

realistic job preview (RJP) 264

reality shock 264

rituals 256

>critical.thinking.questions

1. Superb Consultants have submitted a proposal to analyze the cultural values of your organization. The proposal states that Superb has developed a revolutionary new survey to tap the company's true culture. The survey takes just 10 minutes to complete, and the consultants say results can be based on a small sample of employees. Discuss the merits and limitations of this proposal.

2. Some people suggest that the most effective organizations have the strongest cultures. What do we mean by the "strength" of organizational culture, and what possible problems are there with a strong organizational culture?

3. The CEO of a manufacturing firm wants everyone to support the organization's dominant culture of lean efficiency and hard work. The CEO has introduced a new reward system to reinforce this culture and personally interviews all professional and managerial applicants to ensure that they bring similar values to the organization. Some employees who criticized these values had their careers sidelined until they left. Two mid-level managers were fired for supporting contrary values, such as work/life balance. Based on your knowledge of organizational subcultures, what potential problems is the CEO creating?

4. Identify at least two artifacts you have observed in your department where you work or are a student from each

of the four broad categories: (*a*) organizational stories and legends, (*b*) rituals and ceremonies, (*c*) language, and (*d*) physical structures and symbols.

5. "Organizations are more likely to succeed when they have an adaptive culture." What can an organization do to foster an adaptive culture?

6. Acme Corp. is planning to acquire Beta Corp., which operates in a different industry. Acme's culture is entrepreneurial and fast-paced, whereas Beta employees value slow, deliberate decision making by consensus. Which merger strategy would you recommend to minimize culture shock when Acme acquires Beta? Explain your answer.

7. Suppose you are asked by senior officers of a city government to identify ways to reinforce a new culture of teamwork and collaboration. The senior executive group clearly supports these values, but it wants everyone in the organization to embrace them. Identify four types of activities that would strengthen these cultural values.

8. Progressive, Inc., ExtendMedia, and other organizations rely on current employees to socialize new recruits. What are the advantages of relying on this type of socialization agent? What problems can you foresee (or you have personally experienced) with co-worker socialization practices?

>case.study:skillbuilder13.1

AssetOne Bank

AssetOne Bank is one of Asia's largest financial institutions, but it had difficulty entering the personal investment business where several other companies dominate the market. To gain entry to this market, AssetOne decided to acquire TaurusBank, a much smaller financial institution that had aggressively developed investment funds (unit trusts) and online banking in the region. Taurus was owned by a European conglomerate that wanted to exit the financial sector, so the company was quietly put up for sale. The opportunity to acquire Taurus seemed like a perfect fit to AssetOne's executives, who saw the purchase as an opportunity to finally gain a competitive position in the personal investment market. In particular, the acquisition would give AssetOne valuable talent in online banking and investment fund businesses.

Negotiations between AssetOne and TaurusBank occurred secretly, except for communication with government regulatory agencies, and took several months as AssetOne's executive team deliberated over the purchase. When AssetOne finally decided in favor of the acquisition, employees of both companies were notified only a few minutes before the merger was announced publicly. During the public statement, AssetOne's CEO boldly announced that TaurusBank would become a "seamless extension of AssetOne." He explained that, like AssetOne, Taurus employees would learn the value of detailed analysis and cautious decision making.

The comments by AssetOne's CEO shocked many employees at Taurus, which was an aggressive and entrepreneurial competitor in online banking and personal investments. Taurus was well known for its edgy marketing, innovative products, and tendency to involve employees to generate creative ideas. The company didn't hesitate to hire people from other industries who would bring different ideas to the investment and online banking business. AssetOne, on the other hand, almost completely promoted its executives from within the ranks. Every one of the senior executive team had started at AssetOne. The company also emphasized decision making at the top to maintain better control and consistency.

Frustration was apparent within a few months after the merger. Several Taurus executives quit after repeated failure of AssetOne's executive team to decide quickly on critical online banking initiatives. For example, at the time of the acquisition, Taurus was in the process of forming affinity alliances with several companies. Yet, six months later, AssetOne's executive team still had not decided whether to proceed with these partnerships.

The biggest concerns occurred in the investment fund business where 20 of TaurusBank's 60 fund managers were lured away by competitors within the first year. Some left for better opportunities. Six fund managers left with the Taurus executive in charge of the investment fund business, who joined an investment firm that specializes in investment funds. Several employees left Taurus after AssetOne executives insisted that all new investment funds must be approved by AssetOne's executive group. Previous, Taurus had given the investment fund division enough freedom to launch new products without approval of the entire executive team.

Two years later, AssetOne's CEO admitted that the acquisition of TaurusBank did not gain the opportunities that they had originally hoped. AssetOne had more business in this area, but many of the more talented people in investment funds and online banking had left the firm. Overall, the merged company had not kept pace with other innovative financial institutions in the market.

Discussion Questions

1. Based on your understanding of mergers and organizational culture, discuss the problems that occurred in this case.

2. What strategies would you recommend to AssetOne's executives to avoid these corporate culture clashes in future mergers and acquisitions?

>web.exercise:skillbuilder13.2

Diagnosing Corporate Culture Proclamations

Purpose   To understand the importance and contents in which corporate culture is identified and discussed in organizations.

Instructions

This exercise is a take-home activity, although it can be completed in classes with computers and Internet connections. The instructor will divide the class into small teams (typically four or five people per team). Each team is assigned a specific industry—such as energy, biotechnology, or computer hardware.

The team's task is to search Web sites of several companies in the selected industry for company statements about their corporate culture. Use the company Web site search engine (if one exists) to find documents with key phrases such as "corporate culture" or "company values."

In the next class, or at the end of the time allotted in the current class, students will report on their observations by answering the following three discussion questions:

Discussion Questions
1. What values seem to dominate the corporate culture of the companies you searched? Are these values similar or diverse across companies in the industry?
2. What was the broader content of the Web pages where these companies described or mentioned its corporate culture?
3. Do companies in this industry refer to their corporate culture on the Web sites more or less than companies in other industries searched by team in this class?

>team.exercise:skillbuilder13.3

Truth in Advertising

Purpose   This team activity is designed to help you to diagnose the degree to which recruitment advertisements and brochures provide realistic previews of the job or organization, or both.

Materials   The instructor will bring to class either recruiting brochures or newspaper advertisements.

Instructions
The instructor will place students into teams and give them copies of recruiting brochures or advertisements. The instructor might assign one lengthy brochure; alternatively, several newspaper advertisements may be assigned. All teams should receive the same materials so that everyone is familiar with the items and results can be compared. Teams will evaluate the recruiting material(s) and answer the following questions for each item:

Discussion Questions
1. What information in the text of this brochure or advertisement identifies conditions or activities in this organization or job that some applicants may not like?
2. If there are photographs or images of people at work, do they show only positive conditions, or do any show conditions or events that some applicants may not like?
3. After reading this item, would you say that it provides a realistic preview of the job or organization?

>self-assessment.skillbuilder13.4

Corporate Culture Preference Scale

This self-assessment is designed to help you to identify a corporate culture that fits most closely with your personal values and assumptions. The scale does not attempt to measure your preference for every corporate culture, just a few of the more common varieties. Read each pair of the statements, and select the statement that describes the organization in which you would prefer to work. Keep in mind none of these corporate cultures is inherently good or bad. The focus here is on how well you fit within each of them.

Students should complete this self-assessment alone in order to assess themselves honestly without concerns of social comparison. However, class discussion will focus on the importance of matching job applicants to the organization's dominant values.

Find the full self-assessments on the OLC at
www.mhhe.com/mcshaneess

[chapter 14]

Organizational Change

>**learning**objectives

After reading this chapter, you should be able to

- Describe the elements of Lewin's force field analysis model.
- Outline six reasons why people resist organizational change.
- Discuss six strategies to minimize resistance to change.
- Outline the conditions for effectively diffusing change from a pilot project.
- Describe the action research approach to organizational change.
- Outline the Four-D model of appreciative inquiry and explain how this approach differs from action research.

Carlos Ghosn launched a turnaround at Nissan Motor Company that saved the Japanese automaker and relied on change management practices rarely seen in Japan.

Nissan Motor Company was on the brink of bankruptcy when French automaker Renault purchased a controlling interest and installed Carlos Ghosn as the effective head of the Japanese automaker. Along with Nissan's known problems of high debt and plummeting market share, Ghosn (pronounced "gone") saw that Nissan managers had no apparent sense of urgency to change. "Even though the evidence is against them, they sit down and they watch the problem a little bit longer," says Ghosn.

Ghosn's challenge was to act quickly, yet minimize the inevitable resistance that arises when an outsider tries to change traditional Japanese business practices. "I was non-Nissan, non-Japanese," he says. "I knew that if I tried to dictate changes from above, the effort would backfire, undermining morale and productivity. But if I was too passive, the company would simply continue its downward spiral."

To resolve this dilemma, Ghosn formed nine cross-functional teams of 10 middle managers each and gave them the mandate to identify innovative proposals for a specific area (marketing, manufacturing, etc.) within three months. Each team could form subteams with additional people to analyze issues in more detail. In all, more than 500 middle managers and other employees were involved in the so-called "Nissan Revival Plan."

After a slow start—Nissan managers weren't accustomed to such authority or working with colleagues across functions or cultures—ideas began to flow as Ghosn stuck to his deadline, reminded team members of the automaker's desperate situation, and encouraged teams to break traditions. Three months later, the nine teams submitted a bold plan to close three assembly plants, eliminate thousands of jobs, cut the number of suppliers by half, reduce purchasing costs by 20 percent, return to profitability, cut the company's debt by half, and introduce 22 new models within the next two years.

Although risky, Ghosn accepted all of the proposals. Moreover, when revealing the plan publicly on the eve of the annual Tokyo Motor Show, Ghosn added his own commitment to the plan: "If you ask people to go through a difficult period of time, they have to trust that you're sharing it with them," Ghosn explains. "So I said that if we did not fulfill our commitments, I would resign."

Ghosn's strategy for organizational change and the Nissan Revival Plan worked. Within 12 months, the automaker had increased sales and market share and posted its first profit in seven years. The company has introduced innovative models and expanded operations. Ghosn has received high praise throughout Japan and abroad and has since become head of Renault.[1]

Change is difficult enough in small firms. At Nissan Motor Co. and other large organizations, it requires monumental effort and persistence. Organizational change is also very messy. The change that Carlos Ghosn launched at Nissan sounds like a smooth process, but it was buffeted by uncertain consequences, organizational politics, and various forms of resistance from employees and suppliers. This chapter examines ways to bring about meaningful change in organizations. We begin by introducing Lewin's model of change and its component parts. This includes sources of resistance to change, ways to minimize this resistance, and stabilizing desired behaviors. Next, this chapter examines three approaches to organizational change: action research, appreciative inquiry, and parallel learning structures. The last section of this chapter considers both cross-cultural and ethical issues in organizational change.

>Lewin's Force Field Analysis Model

force field analysis
Kurt Lewin's model of systemwide change that helps change agents diagnose the forces that drive and restrain proposed organizational change.

Social psychologist Kurt Lewin developed the force field analysis model to help us understand how the change process works (see Exhibit 14.1).[2] Although developed more than 50 years ago, Lewin's **force field analysis** model remains the prominent way of viewing this process.

[Exhibit 14.1]   Lewin's Force Field Analysis Model

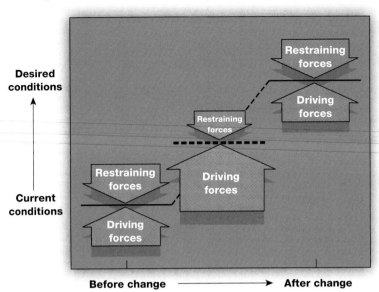

One side of the force field model represents the *driving forces* that push organizations toward a new state of affairs. Chapter 1 described some of the driving forces in the external environment, including globalization, virtual work, and a changing workforce. Along with these external forces, corporate leaders create driving forces within the organization so the organization anticipates the external forces. These internally originating forces are difficult to apply because they lack external justifications, so effective transformational leadership as well as structural change mechanisms are necessary to legitimate and support internal driving forces.

The other side of Lewin's model represents the *restraining forces* that maintain the status quo. These restraining forces are commonly called *resistance to change* because they appear as employee behaviors that block the change process. Stability occurs when the driving and restraining forces are roughly in equilibrium, that is, they are of approximately equal strength in opposite directions.

Lewin's force field model emphasizes that effective change occurs by **unfreezing** the current situation, moving to a desired condition, and then **refreezing** the system so that it remains in this desired state. Unfreezing involves producing disequilibrium between the driving and restraining forces. As we will describe later, this may occur by increasing the driving forces, reducing the restraining forces, or having a combination of both. Refreezing occurs when the organization's systems and structures are aligned with the desired behaviors. They must support and reinforce the new role patterns and prevent the organization from slipping back into the old way of doing things. Over the next few pages, we use Lewin's model to understand why change is blocked and how the process can evolve more smoothly.

unfreezing
The first part of the change process, whereby the change agent produces disequilibrium between the driving and restraining forces.

refreezing
The latter part of the change process, in which systems and conditions are introduced that reinforce and maintain the desired behaviors.

Restraining Forces

According to various surveys, more than 40 percent of executives identify employee resistance as the most important barrier to corporate restructuring or improved performance.[3] This resistance takes many forms, including passive noncompliance, complaints, absenteeism, turnover, and collective action (e.g., strikes, walkouts). In extreme cases of resistance, such as at Ford, Xerox, and EDS, the chief change agent eventually leaves or is pushed out.

In 1993, following the first terrorist attacks on the World Trade Center, the Federal Bureau of Investigation (FBI) promised to refocus from a reactive law-enforcement agency (solving crimes) to a proactive domestic intelligence agency (preventing terrorism). Yet two government reports recently concluded that resistance from FBI staff has hampered this change process for more than a decade. One report even stated that both the CIA and FBI "seem to be working harder and harder just to maintain a status quo that is increasingly irrelevant to the new challenges." The reports claim that FBI employees and managers are unable or unwilling to change because solving crimes (rather than intelligence gathering) is burned into their mindset, routines, career paths, and decentralized structure. Most FBI field managers were trained in law enforcement, so they continue to give preferential treatment and resources to enforcement than terrorist prevention initiatives. An information access barrier—called "the wall"—further isolates FBI intelligence officers from the mainstream criminal investigation staff. Turf wars with the CIA have also undermined FBI respect for the bureau's intelligence gathering initiative. "One of the most difficult things one has to do is to bring an entity through the development of a change of business practices," FBI director Robert Mueller recently admitted.[4]

Employee resistance is a symptom of deeper problems in the change process, so change agents need to investigate and remove the causes of resistance.[5] Rather than directly correcting incidences of passive noncompliance, leaders need to understand why employees are not changing their behavior in the desired ways. In some situations, employees may be worried about the *consequences* of change, such as how the new conditions will take away their power and status. In other situations, employees show resistance because of concerns about the *process* of change itself, such as the effort required to break old habits and learn new skills. The main reasons why people resist change are described below:[6]

- *Direct costs.* People tend to block actions that result in higher direct costs or lower benefits than the existing situation. For instance, Nissan suppliers actively lobbied the public and government to prevent Ghosn from implementing the Nissan Revival Plan because it threatened their highly profitable contracts with the automaker and, in some cases, put their own companies in jeopardy.

- *Saving face.* Some people resist change as a political strategy to "prove" that the decision is wrong or that the person encouraging change is incompetent. For example, senior executives in a manufacturing firm bought a computer other than the system recommended by the information systems department. Soon after the system was in place, several information systems employees let minor implementation problems escalate to demonstrate that senior management had made a poor decision.

- *Fear of the unknown.* People resist change because they are worried that they cannot adopt the new behaviors. This fear of the unknown increases the *risk* of personal loss. For example, one company owner wanted sales staff to telephone rather than personally visit prospective customers. With no experience in telephone sales, they complained about the changes. Some even avoided the training program that taught them how to make telephone sales.[7]

- *Breaking routines.* Chapter 1 described how organizations need to unlearn, not just learn. This means that employees need to abandon the behavioral routines that are no longer appropriate. Unfortunately, people are creatures of habit. They like to stay within the comfort zones by continuing routine role patterns that make life predictable. Consequently, many people resist organizational changes that force them out of their comfort zones and require investing time and energy learning new role patterns.

- *Incongruent organizational systems.* Rewards, selection, training, and other control systems ensure that employees maintain desired role patterns. Yet the organizational systems that maintain stability also discourage employees from adopting new ways. The implication, of course, is that organizational systems must be altered to fit the desired change. Unfortunately, control systems can be difficult to change, particularly when they have supported role patterns that worked well in the past.[8]

- *Incongruent team dynamics.* Teams develop and enforce conformity to a set of norms that guide behavior. However, conformity to existing team norms may discourage employees from accepting organizational change. Team norms that conflict with the desired changes need to be altered.

<Unfreezing, Changing, and Refreezing

According to Lewin's force field analysis model, effective change occurs by unfreezing the current situation, moving to a desired condition, and then refreezing the system so that it remains in this desired state. Unfreezing occurs when the driving forces are stronger than the restraining forces. Thus, unfreezing takes place when we strengthen the driving forces, weaken or remove the restraining forces, or a combination of both.

With respect to the first option, driving forces must certainly increase enough to motivate change. Change rarely occurs by increasing driving forces alone, however, because the restraining forces often adjust to counterbalance the driving forces. It is rather like the coils of a mattress. The harder corporate leaders push for change, the stronger the restraining forces push back. This antagonism threatens the change effort by producing tension and conflict within the organization. The preferred option is to both increase the driving forces and reduce or remove the restraining forces. Increasing the driving forces creates an urgency for change, whereas reducing the restraining forces minimizes resistance to change.

Creating an Urgency for Change

It is almost cliché to say that organizations today operate in more dynamic fast-paced environments than they did a few decades ago. These environmental pressures represent the driving forces that push employees out of their comfort zones. They energize people to face the risks that change creates. In many organizations, however, external driving forces are hardly felt by anyone below the top-executive level. As we read in the opening story to this chapter, Nissan employees had no sense of urgency, no sense that the Japanese automaker would actually go bankrupt in a very short time. The problem is that corporate leaders tend to buffer employees from the external environment, yet are surprised when change does not occur. Thus, the change process must begin by informing employees about competitors, changing consumer trends, impending government regulations, and other driving forces.[9]

Some companies fuel the urgency to change by putting employees in direct contact with customers. Dissatisfied customers represent a compelling driving force for change because of the adverse consequences for the organization's survival and success. Customers also provide a human element that further energizes employees to change current behavior patterns.[10]

Urging Change without External Forces

Exposing employees to external forces can strengthen the urgency for change, but leaders often need to begin the change process before problems come knocking at the company's door. "You want to create a burning platform for change even when there isn't a need for one," says Intuit CEO Steve Bennett.[11] Creating an urgency for change when the organization is riding high requires a lot of persuasive influence that helps employees visualize future competitive threats and makes environmental shifts ever present.

For instance, Apple Computer's iPod dominates the digital music market, but Steve Jobs wants the company to be its own toughest competitor. Just when sales of the iPod Mini were soaring, Jobs advised a gathering of 100 top executives and engineers that the company must develop a better product to replace it. "Playing it safe is the most dangerous thing we can do," Jobs warned. Nine months later, the company launched the iPod Nano, which replaced the still-popular iPod Mini before competitors could offer a better alternative.[12]

Reducing the Restraining Forces

Effective change requires more than making employees aware of the driving forces. It also involves reducing or removing the restraining forces. Exhibit 14.2 summarizes six ways to overcome employee resistance. Communication, learning, employee involvement, and stress management try to reduce the restraining forces and, if feasible, should be attempted

[Exhibit 14.2] Methods for Dealing with Resistance to Change

Strategy	Example	When Used	Problems
Communication	Customer complaint letters shown to employees.	When employees don't feel an urgency for change or don't know how the change will affect them.	Time-consuming and potentially costly.
Learning	Employees learn how to work in teams as company adopts a team-based structure.	When employees need to break old routines and adopt new role patterns.	Time-consuming and potentially costly.
Employee involvement	Company forms task force to recommend new customer service practices.	When the change effort needs more employee commitment, some employees need to save face, or employee ideas would improve decisions about the change strategy.	Very time-consuming; might also lead to conflict and poor decisions if employees' interests are incompatible with organizational needs.
Stress management	Employees attend sessions to discuss their worries about the change.	When communication, training, and involvement do not sufficiently ease employee worries.	Time-consuming and potentially expensive; some methods may not reduce stress for all employees.
Negotiation	Employees agree to replace strict job categories with multiskilling in return for increased job security.	When employees will clearly lose something of value from the change and would not otherwise support the new conditions; also necessary when the company must change quickly.	May be expensive, particularly if other employees want to negotiate their support; also tends to produce compliance but not commitment to the change.
Coercion	Company president tells managers to "get on board" the change or leave.	When other strategies are ineffective and the company needs to change quickly.	Can lead to more subtle forms of resistance, as well as long-term antagonism with the change agent.

Sources: Adapted from J. P. Kotter and L. A. Schlesinger, "Choosing Strategies for Change," Harvard Business Review 57 (1979), pp. 106–14; and P. R. Lawrence, "How to Deal with Resistance to Change," Harvard Business Review, May–June 1954, pp. 49–57.

first.[13] However, negotiation and coercion are necessary for people who will clearly lose something from the change and when the speed of change is critical.

Communication

Honest and frequent communication is the highest priority and first strategy required for any organizational change.[14] Communication improves the change process in at least two ways. First, it is the conduit through which employees typically learn about the driving forces for change. Whether through town hall meetings with senior management or by directly meeting with disgruntled customers, employees become energized to change. Second, communication can potentially reduce fear of the unknown. The more corporate leaders communicate their images of the future, the more easily employees can visualize their own role in that future. This effort may also begin the process of adjusting team norms to be more consistent with the new reality.

Learning

Learning is an important process in most change initiatives because employees require new knowledge and skills. When a company introduces a new sales database, for instance, representatives need to learn how to adapt their previous behavior patterns to benefit from the new system. Action learning, which was described in Chapter 3, is a potentially powerful learning process for organizational change because it develops management skills while discovering ways to improve the organization.[15] Coaching is another form of learning that provides more personalized feedback and direction during the learning process. Coaching and other forms of learning are time-consuming, but they help employees break routines by learning new role patterns.

Employee Involvement

The open vignette to this chapter described how Carlos Ghosn minimized resistance to change by forming cross-functional teams to identify and recommend changes at Nissan Motor Co. Ghosn had previously implemented similar task forces to turnaround failing businesses at Michelin and Renault. As a form of employee involvement, these cross-functional teams offer better solutions to problems, but they also minimize resistance to change by creating a psychological ownership of the decision. Rather than viewing themselves as agents of someone else's decision, participants feel personally responsible for the success of the change effort. Cross-functional task forces and other forms of employee involvement also minimize resistance to change by reducing problems of saving face and fear of the unknown.[16]

Minimizing resistance to change through employee involvement is also possible in large organizations through **future search** conferences. Future search events "put the entire system in the room," meaning that they try to involve as many employees and other stakeholders as possible associated with the organizational system. These multiday gatherings ask participants to identify trends or issues and establish strategic solutions for those conditions. Every five years, Whole Foods Market gathers together several hundred employees, shoppers, and shareholders for a future search conference to help identify new directions for the Austin, Texas–based food retailer.[17]

future search
Systemwide group sessions, usually lasting a few days, in which participants identify trends and the ways to adapt to those changes.

Stress Management

Organizational change is a stressful experience for many people because it threatens self-esteem and creates uncertainty about the future. Communication, learning, and employee involvement can reduce some of these stressors. However, research indicates that companies also need to introduce stress management practices to help employees cope with the changes.[18] For instance, stress management can minimize resistance by removing some of the direct costs and fear of the unknown of the change process. Stress also saps energy, so minimizing stress potentially increases employee motivation to support the change process.

Negotiation

As long as people resist change, organizational change strategies will require some influence tactics. Negotiation is a form of influence that involves the promise of benefits or resources in exchange for the target person's compliance with influencer's request. This strategy potentially activates those who would otherwise lose out from the change. However, it merely gains compliance rather than commitment to the change effort, so it might not be effective in the long term.

Coercion

If all else fails, leaders rely on coercion to change organizations. Coercion can include persistently reminding people of their obligations, frequently monitoring behavior to ensure compliance, confronting people who do not change, and using threats of sanctions to force compliance. Firing people who will not support the change is an extreme step, but it is not uncommon. Replacing staff is a radical form of organizational "unlearning" (see Chapter 1) because replacing executives removes knowledge of the organization's past routines. This potentially opens up opportunities for new practices to take hold.[19] At the same time, coercion is a risky strategy because survivors (employees who are not fired) may have less trust in corporate leaders and engage in more political tactics to protect their own job security.

Refreezing the Desired Conditions

Unfreezing and changing behavior patterns won't result in lasting change. People are creatures of habit, so they easily slip back into past patterns. Therefore, leaders need to refreeze the new behaviors by realigning organizational systems and team dynamics with the desired changes.[20] One of the most popular refreezing strategies is to realign the reward system around desired behavior and outcomes.[21] At Nissan Motor Company, described at the

A few years ago, test results at Sun Valley Middle School were so low that the San Fernando Valley campus was put on a federal government watch list for closer scrutiny. The Los Angeles Unified School District tried to help the principal and staff to improve, but to no avail. When a state audit reported that the school suffered from poor management, unsanitary conditions, and uneven classroom instruction, the school district applied a more radical change strategy: It replaced Sun Valley's principal and four assistant principals with new leaders. Sun Valley's new principal, Jeff Davis (shown here with Sun Valley students), introduced extra English language instruction, reorganized class locations, and launched team teaching to foster a more collegial atmosphere among staff. Sun Valley still has a long way to go, but student test scores in math and English have tripled over the past three years. "That school is absolutely headed in the right direction," says Sue Shannon, superintendent of schools in the eastern San Fernando Valley.[22]

beginning of this chapter, Carlos Ghosn replaced seniority-based pay with performance-based reward systems to refreeze employee behaviors consistent with this performance orientation. Feedback, information systems, organizational structures, and physical layout of buildings are among the other tools used to refreeze desired behaviors.

<Strategic Visions and Change Agents

Lewin's force field analysis model provides a rich understanding of the dynamics of organizational change, but it overlooks three other ingredients in effective change processes: strategic visions, change agents, and diffusing change. Every successful change requires a clear, well-articulated vision of the desired future state.[23] This vision provides a sense of direction and establishes the critical success factors against which the real changes are evaluated. It also minimizes employee fear of the unknown and provides a better understanding about what behaviors employees must learn for the future state.

Change Agents

change agent
Anyone who possesses enough knowledge and power to guide and facilitate the organizational change effort.

Every organizational change, whether large or small, requires one or more change agents. A **change agent** is anyone who possesses enough knowledge and power to guide and facilitate the change effort. Change agents come in different forms, and more than one person is often required to serve these different roles. Transformational leaders are the primary agents of change because they form a vision of the desired future state, communicate that vision in ways that are meaningful to others, behave in ways that are consistent with the vision, and build commitment to the vision.[24] Transformational leaders are the architects who shape the overall direction for the change effort and motivate employees to achieve that objective.

Organizational change also requires transactional leaders who implement the change by aligning the behavior of individual employees on a day-to-day basis with the organization's new goals.[25] If a company wants to provide better customer service, then supervisors and other transactional leaders need to arrange rewards, resources, feedback, and other conditions that support better customer service behaviors in employees. Consultants from either inside or outside the organization represent a third change agent role. Consultants typically bring unique expertise to the change process through a toolkit of change processes, some of which we introduce later in this chapter. Finally, just as employees are encouraged to become leaders anytime and anywhere, they also assist the change process as role models for others to follow in the change process.

<Three Approaches to Organizational Change

So far, we have looked at the dynamics of change that occur every day in organizations. However, organizational change agents and consultants also apply various approaches to organizational change. This section introduces three of the leading approaches to organizational change: action research, appreciative inquiry, and parallel learning structures.

action research
A data-based, problem-oriented process that diagnoses the need for change, introduces the intervention, and then evaluates and stabilizes the desired changes.

Action Research Approach

Along with introducing the force field model, Lewin recommended an **action research** approach to the change process. Action research takes the view that meaningful change is a combination of action orientation (changing attitudes and behavior) and research orientation (testing theory).[26] On the one hand, the change process needs to be action-oriented because the ultimate goal is to bring about change. An action orientation involves diagnosing current problems and applying interventions that resolve those problems. On the other hand, the change process is a research study because change agents apply a conceptual framework (such as team dynamics or organizational culture) to a real situation. As with any good research, the change process involves collecting data to diagnose problems more effectively and to systematically evaluate how well the theory works in practice. In other words, action research embraces the notion of organizational learning and knowledge management (see Chapter 1).[27]

Within this dual framework of action and research, the action research approach adopts an open systems view. It recognizes that organizations have many interdependent parts, so change agents need to anticipate both the intended and unintended consequences of their interventions. Action research is also a highly participative process because changing an open system requires both the knowledge and commitment of members within that system. Indeed, employees are essentially co-researchers as well as participants in the intervention. Overall, action research is a data-based, problem-oriented process that diagnoses the need for change, introduces the intervention, and then evaluates and stabilizes the desired changes.[28]

1. *Form client–consultant relationship.* Action research usually assumes that the change agent originates outside the system (such as a consultant), so the process begins by forming the client–consultant relationship. Consultants need to determine the client's readiness for change, including whether people are motivated to participate in the process, are open to meaningful change, and possess the abilities to complete the process.

2. *Diagnose the need for change.* Action research is a problem-oriented activity that carefully diagnoses the problem through systematic analysis of the situation. Organizational diagnosis identifies the appropriate direction for the change effort by gathering and analyzing data about an ongoing system, such as through interviews and surveys of employees and other stakeholders. Organizational diagnosis also includes employee involvement in agreeing on the appropriate change method, the schedule for these actions, and the expected standards of successful change.

3. *Introduce intervention.* This stage in the action research model applies one or more actions to correct the problem. It may include any of the prescriptions mentioned in this textbook, such as building more effective teams, managing conflict, building a better organizational structure, or changing the corporate culture. An important issue is how quickly the changes should occur.[29] Some experts recommend *incremental change* in which the organization fine-tunes the system and takes small steps toward a desired state. Others claim that *quantum change* is often required, in which the system is overhauled decisively and quickly. Quantum change, such as at Nissan Motor Company (see opening vignette to this chapter), is usually traumatic to employees and offers little opportunity for correction. But incremental change is also risky when the organization is seriously misaligned with its environment, thereby threatening its survival.

4. *Evaluate and stabilize change.* Action research recommends evaluating the effectiveness of the intervention against the standards established in the diagnostic stage. Unfortunately, even when these standards are clearly stated, the effectiveness of an intervention might not be apparent for several years, or might be difficult to separate from other factors. If the activity has the desired effect, then the change agent and participants need to stabilize the new conditions. This refers to the refreezing process that we described earlier. Rewards, information systems, team

norms, and other conditions are redesigned so that they support the new values and behaviors.

The action research approach has dominated organizational change thinking ever since it was introduced in the 1940s. However, some experts complain that the problem-oriented nature of action research—in which something is wrong that must be fixed—focuses on the negative dynamics of the group or system rather than its positive opportunities and potential. This concern with action research has led to the development of a more positive approach to organizational change, called appreciative inquiry.[30]

Appreciative Inquiry Approach

appreciative inquiry
An organizational change process that directs attention away from the group's own problems and focuses participants on the group's potential and positive elements.

Appreciative inquiry tries to break out of the problem-solving mentality of traditional change management practices by reframing relationships around the positive and the possible. It searches for organizational (or team) strengths and capabilities, then adapts or applies that knowledge for further success and well-being. Appreciative inquiry is therefore deeply grounded in the emerging philosophy of *positive organizational behavior*, which suggests that focusing on the positive rather than negative aspects of life will improve organizational success and individual well-being.[31]

Appreciative inquiry typically directs its inquiry toward successful events and successful organizations or work units. This external focus becomes a form of behavioral modeling, but it also increases open dialogue by redirecting the group's attention away from its own problems. Appreciative inquiry is especially useful when participants are aware of their "problems" or already suffer from enough negativity in their relationships. The positive orientation of appreciative inquiry enables groups to overcome these negative tensions and build a more hopeful perspective of their future by focusing on what is possible. [32]

The Four-D model of appreciative inquiry shown in Exhibit 14.3 begins with *discovery*—identifying the positive elements of the observed events or organization.[33] This might involve documenting positive experiences elsewhere in the organization. Or it might include interviewing members of another organization to discover its fundamental strengths. As participants discuss their findings, they shift into the *dreaming* stage by envisioning what might be possible in an ideal organization. By directing their attention to a theoretically ideal organization or situation, participants feel safer revealing their hopes and aspirations than if they were discussing their own organization or predicament.

As participants make their private thoughts public to the group, the process shifts into the third stage, called *designing*. Designing involves the process of dialogue, in which participants listen with selfless receptivity to each other's models and assumptions and eventually form a collective model for thinking within the team. In effect, they create a com-

[Exhibit 14.3]   The Appreciative Inquiry Process

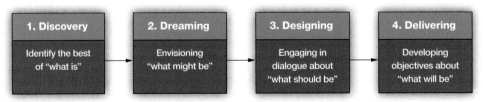

Sources: Based on J. M. Watkins and B. J. Mohr, *Appreciative Inquiry: Change at the Speed of Imagination* (San Francisco: Jossey-Bass, 2001), pp. 25, 42–45; D. Whitney and C. Schau, "Appreciative Inquiry: An Innovative Process for Organization Change," *Employment Relations Today* 25 (Spring 1998), pp. 11–21; F. J. Barrett and D. L. Cooperrider, "Generative Metaphor Intervention: A New Approach for Working with Systems Divided by Conflict and Caught in Defensive Perception," *Journal of Applied Behavioral Science* 26 (1990), p. 229.

Hunter Douglas Windows Fashion Division (WFD) in Broomfield, Colorado, applied the appreciative inquiry process a few years ago to help the organization establish a more positive mind-set following a rapid expansion of production and change in leadership. An advisory team spent a week learning about the Four-D process, then communicated this appreciative inquiry process to employees through a series of town hall meetings. The discovery phase consisted of more than 500 interviews with employees, customers, suppliers, and community members. These results were reviewed at an Appreciative Summit, where WFD employees worked through the dream, design, and deliver stages. A second wave of interviews became background data for a subsequent search conference–type of strategic planning summit. WFD executives say that appreciative inquiry improved productivity and cross-departmental collaboration and created a can-do attitude toward the company's quality management initiative. "Historically, American businesses look at problem solving with a mind-set of 'what's wrong,'" says a Hunter Douglas executive. "If you look at everything else that's right, 17 production lines are working well."[34]

mon image of what should be. As this model takes shape, group members shift the focus back to their own situation. In the final stage of appreciative inquiry, called *delivering*, participants establish specific objectives and direction for their own organization based on their model of what will be.

Appreciative inquiry is a relatively new approach to organization change, but it has already generated success stories at Avon Mexico, American Express, Green Mountain Coffee Roasters, and Hunter Douglas, among others. At the same time, this approach has not always been successful, and experts warn that it is not always the best approach to changing teams or organizations.[35] It requires a particular mind-set in which participants are willing to let go of the problem-oriented approach and leaders are willing to accept appreciative inquiry's less-structured process. Another concern is that research has not yet examined the contingencies of this approach.[36] Specifically, we don't yet know the conditions under which appreciative inquiry is the best approach to organizational change, and under what conditions it is less effective. Overall, appreciative inquiry has much to offer the organizational change process, but we are just beginning to understand it potential and limitations.

Parallel Learning Structure Approach

parallel learning structures

Highly participative groups constructed alongside (i.e. parallel to) the formal organization with the purposes of increasing the organization's learning and producing meaningful organizational change.

Parallel learning structures are highly participative arrangements, composed of people from most levels of the organization who follow the action research model to produce meaningful organizational change. They are social structures developed alongside the formal hierarchy with the purpose of increasing the organization's learning.[37] Ideally, parallel learning structure participants are sufficiently free from the constraints of the larger organization so they can more effectively solve organizational issues.

Royal Dutch/Shell relied on a parallel learning structure to introduce a more customer-focused organization.[38] Rather than try to change the entire organization at once, executives held weeklong "retail boot camps" with six country teams of frontline people (e.g., gas station managers, truck drivers, marketing professionals). Participants learned about competitive trends in their regions and were taught powerful marketing tools to identify new opportunities. The teams then returned home to study their market and develop proposals for improvement.

Four months later, boot camp teams returned for a second workshop during which each proposal was critiqued by Royal/Dutch Shell executives. Each team had 60 days to put its ideas into action, then return for a third workshop to analyze what worked and what didn't. This parallel learning process did much more than introduce new marketing ideas. It created enthusiasm in participants that spread contagiously to their co-workers, including managers above them, when they returned to their home countries.

<Cross-Cultural and Ethical Issues in Organizational Change

One significant concern with organizational change interventions or philosophies originating from North America is that they potentially conflict with cultural values in some other countries.[39] A few experts point out that change practices in the United States assume a linear model of change, as shown earlier in the force field analysis, that is punctuated by tension and overt conflict. Indeed, some organizational change practices encourage the open display of conflict. But these assumptions are incompatible with cultures that view change as a natural cyclical process with harmony and equilibrium as the objectives.[40]

For instance, people in many Asian countries try to minimize conflict in order to respect others and save face.[41] These concerns do not mean that Western-style change interventions are necessarily ineffective elsewhere. Rather, it suggests that we need to develop a more contingency-oriented perspective with respect to the cultural values of its participants.

Some organizational change practices also face ethical concerns.[42] One ethical concern is the threat to the privacy rights of individuals. The action research model is built on the idea of collecting information from organizational members, yet this requires employees to provide personal information that they may not want to divulge. Another ethical concern is that some change activities potentially increase management's power by inducing compliance and conformity in organizational members. For instance, although action research purports to embrace employee involvement, it also emphasizes the need to "bring onside" those who are reluctant to engage in the process. A third concern is that some organizational change interventions undermine the individual's self-esteem. The unfreezing process requires participants to disconfirm their existing beliefs, sometimes including their own competence at certain tasks or interpersonal relations.

Organizational change is a complex process with a variety of approaches and issues. Many corporate leaders have promised more change than they were able to deliver because they underestimated the time and challenges involved with this process. Yet the dilemma is that most organizations operate in hyperfast environments that demand continuous and rapid adaptation. Successful organizations have mastered the complex dynamics of moving people through the continuous process of change.

<Organizational Behavior: The Journey Continues

Nearly 100 years ago, industrialist Andrew Carnegie said, "Take away my people, but leave my factories, and soon grass will grow on the factory floors. Take away my factories, but leave my people, and soon we will have a new and better factory." Carnegie's statement reflects the message woven throughout this textbook that organizations are not buildings, machinery, or financial assets. Rather, they are the people in them. Organizations are human entities, full of life, sometimes fragile, always exciting.

<chapter summary

Lewin's force field analysis model states that all systems have driving and restraining forces. Change occurs through the process of unfreezing, changing, and refreezing. Unfreezing produces disequilibrium between the driving and restraining forces. Refreezing realigns the organization's systems and structures with the desired behaviors.

Restraining forces are manifested as employee resistance to change. The main reasons people resist change are direct costs, saving face, fear of the unknown, breaking routines, incongruent organizational systems, and incongruent team dynamics. Resistance to change may be minimized by keeping employees informed about what to expect from the change effort (communicating); teaching employees valuable skills for the desired future (learning); involving them in the change process; helping employees cope with the stress of change; negotiating trade-offs with those who will clearly lose from the change effort; and using coercion (sparingly and as a last resort).

Organizational change also requires driving forces. This means that employees need to have an urgency to change by becoming aware of the environmental conditions that demand change in the organization. The change process also requires refreezing the new behaviors by realigning organizational systems and team dynamics with the desired changes.

Every successful change requires a clear, well-articulated vision of the desired future state. Change agents rely on transformational leadership to develop a vision, communicate that vision, and build commitment to the vision of a desirable future state.

Action research is a highly participative, open systems approach to change management that combines an action orientation (changing attitudes and behavior) with a research orientation (testing theory). It is a data-based, problem-oriented process that diagnoses the need for change, introduces the intervention, and then evaluates and stabilizes the desired changes.

Appreciative inquiry embraces the positive organizational behavior philosophy by focusing participants on the positive and possible. It tries to break out of the problem-solving mentality that dominates organizational change through the action research model. The four stages of appreciative inquiry include discovery, dreaming, designing, and delivering. A third approach, called parallel learning structures, relies on social structures developed alongside the formal hierarchy with the purpose of increasing the organization's learning. They are highly participative arrangements, composed of people from most levels of the organization who follow the action research model to produce meaningful organizational change.

One significant concern with organizational change methods originating from North America is that they potentially conflict with cultural values in some other countries. Also, organizational change practices can raise one or more ethical concerns, including increasing management's power over employees, threatening individual privacy rights, and undermining individual self-esteem.

>key.terms

action research 278

appreciative inquiry 280

change agent 278

force field analysis 271

future search, 276

parallel learning structure 282

refreezing 272

unfreezing 272

>critical.thinking.questions

1. Chances are that the school you are attending is currently undergoing some sort of change to adapt more closely with its environment. Discuss the external forces that are driving these changes. What internal drivers for change also exist?

2. Use Lewin's force field analysis to describe the dynamics of organizational change at Nissan Motor Company (opening vignette to this chapter).

3. Employee resistance is a *symptom,* not a *problem,* in the change process. What are some of the real problems that may underlie employee resistance?

4. Senior management of a large multinational corporation is planning to restructure the organization. Currently, the organization is decentralized around geographical areas so that the executive responsible for each area has considerable autonomy over manufacturing and sales. The new structure will transfer power to the executives responsible for different product groups; the executives responsible for each geographic area will no longer be responsible for manufacturing in their area but will retain control over sales activities. Describe two types of resistance senior management might encounter from this organizational change.

5. Discuss the role of reward systems in organizational change. Specifically, identify where reward systems relate to Lewin's force field model and where they serve as a toll in the organizational change process.

6. Web Circuits, Inc. is a Singapore-based manufacturer of computer circuit boards for high-technology companies. Senior management wants to introduce value-added management practices to reduce production costs and remain competitive. A consultant has recommended that the company start with a pilot project in one department and, when successful, diffuse these practices to other areas of the organization. Discuss the advantages of this recommendation, and identify three ways (other than the pilot project's success) to make diffusion of the change effort more successful.

7. Suppose that you are vice president of branch services at the Bank of East Lansing. You notice that several branches have consistently low customer service ratings even though there are no apparent differences in resources or staff characteristics. Describe an appreciative inquiry process in one of these branches that might help to overcome these problems.

8. This chapter suggests that some organizational change activities face ethical concerns. Yet several consultants actively use these processes because they believe they benefit the organization and do less damage to employees than it seems on the surface. For example, some activities try to open up the employee's hidden area (see Johari Window in Chapter 3) to improve mutual understanding with co-workers. Discuss this argument and identify where you think organizational change interventions should limit this process.

>case.study:skillbuilder14.1

The Excellent Employee

By Mary J. Gander, Winona State University

Emily, who has the reputation of being an excellent worker, is a machine operator in a furniture manufacturing plant that has been growing at a rate of between 15 and 20 percent each year for the past decade. New additions have been built onto the plant, new plants opened in the region, workers hired, new product lines developed, lots of expansion, but with no significant change in overall approach to operations, plant layout, ways of managing workers, or in the design processes. Plant operations as well as organizational culture are rooted in traditional Western management practices and logic, based largely on the notion of mass production and economies of scale. Over the past four years, the company has been growing in number and variety of products produced and in market penetration, however, profitability has been flattening and showing signs of decline. As a result, management is beginning to focus on production operations (internal focus) rather than mainly focusing on new market strategies, new products, and new market segments (external focus), in developing their strategic plans. They hope to get manufacturing costs down, improve consistency of quality and ability to meet delivery times better, while decreasing inventory and increasing flexibility.

One of several new programs initiated by management in this effort to improve flexibility and lower costs was to get workers cross-trained. However, when a representative from Human Resources explained this program to Emily's supervisor, Jim, he reluctantly agreed to cross-train most of his workers but not Emily.

Jim explained to the HR person that Emily works on a machine that is very complex and not easy to effectively operate. She has to "babysit" it much of the time. He has tried many workers on it, and tried to train them, but Emily is the only one who can consistently get product through the machine that is within specification and still meet production schedules. When anyone else tries to operate the machine, which performs a key function in the manufacturing process, it either ends up being a big bottleneck or producing excessive waste, which creates a lot of trouble for Jim.

Jim goes on to explain that Emily knows this sophisticated and complicated machine inside and out, she has been running it for five years. She likes the challenge and says it makes the day go by faster, too. She is a meticulous, very skilled employee who really cares about the quality of her work. Jim told the HR person that he wished all of his workers were like Emily. In spite of the difficulty of running this machine, Emily can run it so well that product piles up at the next work station downstream in the production process—they can't keep up with her!

Jim was adamant about keeping Emily on this machine and not cross-training her. The HR person was frustrated. He could see Jim's point, but he had to follow executive orders: "Get these people cross-trained."

Around the same period of time, a university student was doing a field study in the section of the plant where Emily worked and Emily was one of the workers he interviewed. Emily told the student that, in spite of the fact that the plant had some problems with employee morale and excessive employee turnover, she really liked working there. She liked the piece-rate pay system very much and hoped that she did not have to participate in the recent "Program of the Month" that was having operators learn each other's jobs. She told the student that it would just create more waste if they tried to have other employees run her machine. She told him that other employees had tried to learn how to operate her machine but couldn't do it as well as she could.

Emily seemed to take a special liking for the student and began to open up to him. She told him that her machine really didn't need to be so difficult and touchy to operate; with a couple of rather minor design changes in the machine and better maintenance, virtually anyone could run it. She had tried to explain this to her supervisor a couple of years ago, but he just told her to "do her work and leave operations to the manufacturing engineers." She also said that if workers upstream in the process would spend a little more time and care to keep the raw material in slightly tighter specifications, it would go through her machine much more easily and trouble free, but that they were too focused on going fast and making more piece-rate pay. She expressed a lack of respect for the managers who couldn't see this and even joked about how "managers didn't know anything."

Discussion Questions

1. Identify the sources of resistance to change in this case study.

2. Discuss whether this resistance is justified or could be overcome.

3. Recommend ways to minimize resistance to change in this incident or in future incidents.

>team.exercise:skillbuilder14.2

Strategic Change Incidents

Purpose   This exercise is designed to help you to identify strategies to facilitate organizational change in various situations.

Instructions

- *Step 1:* The instructor will place students into teams, and each team will be assigned one of the scenarios presented below.

- *Step 2:* Each team will diagnose its assigned scenario to determine the most appropriate set of change management practices. Where appropriate, these practices should (*a*) create an urgency to change, (*b*) minimize resistance to change, and (*c*) refreeze the situation to support the change initiative. Each of these scenarios is based on real events.

- *Step 3:* Each team will present and defend its change management strategy. Class discussion regarding the appropriateness and feasibility of each strategy will occur after all teams assigned the same scenario have presented. The instructor will then describe what the organizations actually did in these situations.

Scenario 1: Greener Telco
The board of directors at a large telephone company wants its executives to make the organization more environmentally friendly by encouraging employees to reduce waste in the workplace. Government and other stakeholders have high expectations for the company to take this action and be publicly successful. Consequently, the board and senior executive group wants to significantly reduce the use of paper, refuse, and other waste throughout the company's many widespread offices. Unfortunately, a survey indicates that employees do not value environmental objectives and do not know how to "reduce, reuse, recycle." As the executive responsible for this change, you have been asked to develop a strategy that might bring about meaningful behavioral change toward these environmental goals. What would you do?

Scenario 2: Go Forward Airline
A major airline had experienced a decade of rough turbulence, including two bouts of bankruptcy protection, 6 chief executives, and morale so low that employees had ripped off company logos from their uniforms out of embarrassment. Service was terrible, and the airplanes rarely arrived or left the terminal on time. This was costing the airline significant amounts of money in passenger layovers. Managers were paralyzed by anxiety, and many had been with the firm so long that they didn't know how to set strategic goals that worked. One-fifth of all flights were losing money, and the company overall was near financial collapse (just three months to defaulting on payroll obligations). The newly hired CEO and you (the chief operating officer) must get employees to quickly improve operational efficiency and customer service. What actions would you take to bring about these changes in time?

>self-assessment.skillbuilder14.3

Tolerance of Change Scale

Some people are naturally less comfortable than other people with the complexity and uncertainty of change. This self-assessment provides an estimate of how tolerant you are of change. Read each of the statements and select the response that best fits your personal belief. This self-assessment is completed alone so students rate themselves honestly without concerns of social comparison. However, class discussion will focus on the meaning of the concept measured by this scale and its implications for managing change in organizational settings.

Find the full self-assessments on the OLC at
www.mhhe.com/mcshaneess

>additionalcases

[case.1] Arctic Mining Consultants

By Steven L. McShane and Tim Neale

Tom Parker enjoyed working outdoors. At various times in the past, he worked as a ranch hand, high steel rigger, headstone installer, prospector, and geological field technician. Now 43, Parker is a geological field technician and field coordinator with Arctic Mining Consultants. He has specialized knowledge and experience in all nontechnical aspects of mineral exploration, including claim staking, line cutting and grid installation, soil sampling, prospecting, and trenching. He is responsible for hiring, training, and supervising field assistants for all of Arctic Mining Consultants' programs. Field assistants are paid a fairly low daily wage (no matter how long they work, which may be up to 12 hours or more) and are provided meals and accommodation. Many of the programs are operated by a project manager who reports to Parker.

Parker sometimes acts as a project manager, as he did on a job that involved staking 15 claims near Eagle Lake, Alaska. He selected John Talbot, Greg Boyce, and Brian Millar, all of whom had previously worked with Parker, as the field assistants. To stake a claim, the project team marks a line with flagging tape and blazes along the perimeter of the claim, cutting a claim post every 500 yards (called a *length*). The 15 claims would require almost 60 miles of line in total. Parker had budgeted seven days (plus mobilization and demobilization) to complete the job. This meant that each of the four stakers (Parker, Talbot, Boyce, and Millar) would have to complete a little more than seven lengths each day. The following is a chronology of the project.

Day 1

The Arctic Mining Consultants crew assembled in the morning and drove to Eagle Lake, from where they were flown by helicopter to the claim site. On arrival, they set up tents at the edge of the area to be staked and agreed on a schedule for cooking duties. After supper, they pulled out the maps and discussed the job—how long it would take, the order in which the areas were to be staked, possible helicopter landing spots, and areas that might be more difficult to stake.

Parker pointed out that with only a week to complete the job, everyone would have to average seven and a half lengths per day. "I know that is a lot," he said, "but you've all staked claims before and I'm con-

fident that each of you is capable of it. And it's only for a week. If we get the job done in time, there's a $300 bonus for each man." Two hours later, Parker and his crew members had developed what seemed to be a workable plan.

Day 2

Millar completed six lengths, Boyce six lengths, Talbot eight, and Parker eight. Parker was not pleased with Millar's or Boyce's production. However, he didn't make an issue of it, thinking that they would develop their rhythm quickly.

Day 3

Millar completed five and a half lengths, Boyce four, and Talbot seven. Parker, who was nearly twice as old as the other three, completed eight lengths. He also had enough time remaining to walk over and check the quality of stakes that Millar and Boyce had completed, then walk back to his own area for helicopter pickup back to the tent site.

That night Parker exploded with anger. "I thought I told you that I wanted seven and a half lengths a day!" he shouted at Boyce and Millar. Boyce said that he was slowed down by unusually thick underbrush in his assigned area. Millar said that he had done his best and would try to pick up the pace. Parker did not mention that he had inspected their work. He explained that as far as he was concerned, the field assistants were supposed to finish their assigned area for the day, no matter what.

Talbot, who was sharing a tent with Parker, talked to him later. "I think that you're being a bit hard on them, you know. I know that it has been more by luck than anything else that I've been able to do my quota. Yesterday I only had five lengths done after the first seven hours and there was only an hour before I was supposed to be picked up. Then I hit a patch of really open bush, and was able to do three lengths in 70 minutes. Why don't I take Millar's area tomorrow and he can have mine? Maybe that will help."

"Conditions are the same in all of the areas," replied Parker, rejecting Talbot's suggestion. "Millar just has to try harder."

Day 4

Millar did seven lengths and Boyce completed six and a half. When they reported their production that evening, Parker grunted uncommunicatively. Parker and Talbot did eight lengths each.

Day 5

Millar completed six lengths, Boyce six, Talbot seven and a half, and Parker eight. Once again Parker blew up, but he concentrated his diatribe on Millar. "Why don't you do what you say you are going to do? You know that you have to do seven and a half lengths a day. We went over that when we first got here, so why don't you do it? If you aren't willing to do the job then you never should have taken it in the first place!"

Millar replied by saying that he was doing his best, that he hadn't even stopped for lunch, and that he didn't know how he could possibly do any better. Parker launched into him again: "You have got to work harder! If you put enough effort into it, you will get the area done!"

Later Millar commented to Boyce, "I hate getting dumped on all the time! I'd quit if it didn't mean that I'd have to walk 50 miles to the highway. And besides, I need the bonus money. Why doesn't he pick on you? You don't get any more done than me; in fact, you usually get less. Maybe if you did a bit more he wouldn't be so bothered about me."

"I only work as hard as I have to," Boyce replied.

Day 6

Millar raced through breakfast, was the first one to be dropped off by the helicopter, and arranged to be the last one picked up. That evening the production figures were Millar eight and a quarter lengths, Boyce seven, and Talbot and Parker eight each. Parker remained silent when the field assistants reported their performance for the day.

Day 7

Millar was again the first out and last in. That night, he collapsed in an exhausted heap at the table, too tired to eat. After a few moments, he announced in an abject tone, "Six lengths. I worked like a dog all day and I only got a lousy six lengths!" Boyce completed five lengths, Talbot seven, and Parker seven and a quarter.

Parker was furious. "That means we have to do a total of 34 lengths tomorrow if we are to finish this job on time!" With his eyes directed at Millar, he added, "Why is it that you never finish the job? Don't you realize that you are part of a team, and that you are letting the rest of the team down? I've been checking your lines and you're doing too much blazing and wasting too much time making picture-perfect claim posts! If you worked smarter, you'd get a lot more done!"

Day 8

Parker cooked breakfast in the dark. The helicopter drop-offs began as soon as morning light appeared on the horizon. Parker instructed each assistant to complete eight lengths and, if they finished early, to help the others. Parker said that he would finish the other 10 lengths. Helicopter pickups were arranged for one hour before dark.

By noon, after working as hard as he could, Millar had only completed three lengths. "Why bother," he thought to himself, "I'll never be able to do another five lengths before the helicopter comes, and I'll catch the same amount of abuse from Parker for doing six lengths as for seven and a half." So he sat down and had lunch and a rest. "Boyce won't finish his eight lengths either, so even if I did finish mine, I still wouldn't get the bonus. At least I'll get one more day's pay this way."

That night, Parker was livid when Millar reported that he had completed five and a half lengths. Parker had done ten and a quarter lengths, and Talbot had completed eight. Boyce proudly announced that he finished seven and a half lengths, but sheepishly added that Talbot had helped him with some of it. All that remained were the two and a half lengths that Millar had not completed.

The job was finished the next morning and the crew demobilized. Millar has never worked for Arctic Mining Consultants again, despite being offered work several times by Parker. Boyce sometimes does staking for Arctic, and Talbot works full-time with the company.

Steven L. McShane and Tim Neale. © Copyright. This case is based on actual events, but names and some characteristics have been changed to maintain anonymity.

[case.2] A Week to Remember

By Trudy Somers, Pfeiffer University

Lee entered the corporate training center, meeting Paul as he waited for the elevator. They rode in silence to the top floor. Lee eyed Paul circumspectly. New shoes. New suit. Good briefcase. New haircut. Nice tie. Paul breathed, "Good luck." Lee responded, "You, too." The door opened onto a flurry of activity. Secretaries in designer suits handed out leather-bound schedules and program guides, found printed brass name badges, and welcomed the management trainee applicants to Corporate University for a weeklong assessment center.

Lee put the name tag firmly on her right lapel and noticed the I/O psychologist standing discreetly against the wall, watching the trainees select coffee, juice, fruit, bagels, muffins, or pastry from an attractive buffet laid out in the hallway to the plenary session. She cheerfully nodded and spoke, casually putting something on her plate as she remembered the whispered rumor last year that David had been dismissed from the program because he complained about the buffet selection that first morning. Or was it that he had not complained? She found a seat and took a deep breath as she looked around.

Lee had worked six years for Pharmazing, a pharmaceutical manufacturing firm. She joined just out of undergraduate school, completing graduate school on evenings and weekends. She had been rotated through assignments in customer support, technical support, product development, distribution systems, accounts payable/receivable, production scheduling, and quality control. She recognized many of the faces around her. Paul, for instance, had been her transition link in the production scheduling job. David had trained her in accounts payable/receivables languages. There was some chatter, but Lee, like most of her peers, knew that at the end of the week 20 to 40 of these bright young faces would be removed from the "promotable to executive rank," another 10 percent would be directly promoted to an executive track, and half of the remainder would lose their executive promotion potential within a year. The others would be groomed and promoted as replacement chart fillers.

The lights dimmed and the CEO himself narrated the multimedia show about the vision for the firm over the next five years and the strategic place of this annual class in that plan. The screen was filled with charts of market shares, global expansion, human capital, dis-ease projections, revenue streams, patent goals, and other trappings of corporate growth. Lee remembered when Ron, her second supervisor, had suggested her nomination for the management training program. She was an enthusiastic employee, capable and committed to making a difference in lives. She had been initially drawn to Pharmazing because of its reputation as an industry leader, a caring employer, and a solid community citizen. Ron told her that her values matched the corporate values, and if she successfully completed the management training program, she could be in a position to influence decisions and policies for the entire organization. The notion of making a difference for more lives was a compelling one for Lee. This opportunity would be more than her onetime thought of working for a city shelter and soup kitchen. Ron had started the process, and here she sat, part of the 25th management training class.

After the multimedia show, the CEO answered some canned questions and gave his personal statement. He had been part of the first management training class. Lee looked carefully around the room. Two guys were asleep. Kurt was fiddling absently with his coffee cup and spoon. They would be the first three out of the program. The CEO smiled and told the group that the week would provide lots of good opportunity to get to know each other, to find out what values lay beneath the mottoes and the vision statements. He promised that the class would find out what was most important, what was really in the hearts and minds of Pharmazing executives. He urged them to listen, to meet people during the session breaks, and to find the one person they could identify with most closely. Lee had especially looked forward to this part of the program. Work was all about money on most days—schedules, budgets, profits, or risk management. But the business was about life-saving, life-changing medicines and procedures to move people to health and wellness. Lee thought about the "professional front" she projected—detailed, calm, friendly, rational, competent, enthusiastic—to meet expectations of clients and co-workers alike. It was not a lie, but it was just a part of her. Executives were the same, she assumed, only more so.

The CEO attributed his own success to a long-standing relationship with Phil, the recently retired chairman of the board of directors. She listened as the

CEO finished with comments that the firm had been good to him. He made lots of money, belonged to lots of important clubs and groups. He was very satisfied with life. Lee noted that the head of the organization had just described his heart and mind in financial terms.

The group was quickly divided into a number of teams. Lee headed for the group that had ribbons that matched hers and dismissed a doubt about how much the CEO had really shared about his personal values. Lee and 10 of her classmates were Team Red River. They headed to a big room divided into cubicles. She was led to a desk with an in-basket full of papers, an empty out-basket, a computer, a notepad, and pens and pencils. The top in-basket memo was addressed to her. It said,

> You have a staff meeting in one hour. Before that meeting begins, you need to go through your in-basket. Make a record on this attachment of the disposition of each item.

She looked at her watch, jotted down the time, and picked up a memo that announced a parking lot resurfacing sometime next month that would affect her assigned parking spot.

After the break Lee took a series of psychological tests in another room at another cubicle. Lunch tasted like cardboard. It looked like it was a lovely seafood buffet. She went back to the psychological tests after lunch.

The next morning, the plenary session speaker was the vice president of research and development. A serious looking man with advanced degrees in biochemistry and biotechnology, he talked about the patents and breakthroughs that had come out of his shop in recent years. He confided that he enjoyed a balanced life with many benefits, a health club membership, lucrative retirement and bonus packages, and flexible work and vacation schedules. Lee wondered about the heart and mind of the man.

Team Red River went outside to the "woods." They were told they had the morning to get from "Here" to "There" on a torn map. They were to transport what looked like a phone pole, some trash bags with ropes in them, some bottled water, and a box with assorted items (protein bars, insect repellant, a knife) with them. Lee was handed the hiking clothes she had sent in a month earlier, as requested. "Good thing I layered," she muttered as she put on the T-shirt. It was a lot hotter now than it was when she packed. Rodney, an ex-military man, said they'd have time for a nap before lunch as he started trotting down the road, dragging the pole behind him. Don stuffed his trash bag into a tree

and sauntered along, talking to Lee about a project they had completed last year in the customer support area. They laughed until they came to a gorge with a broken rope bridge. Rodney shouted, "Who has the ropes?" They all sat down as Don headed back to the start. They arrived late for lunch, mad at Don, glad Rodney was with them.

The afternoon located them in a large wood-paneled room with a large oval table in the center. There was a folder, each with the name on it. They were instructed that this was the final preparation meeting for a major competitive presentation. Each of them had specific information. They were to develop a video presentation for the vice president of marketing at 7 P.M. that evening. All of them groaned when they were told that Don was in charge.

The next morning Lee and Paul again rode the elevator to the large meeting room on the top floor. They grinned faintly at each other and sat as the vice president of marketing told them of his 30-year career with the organization. He had started with a competitor but quickly learned that he could make more money here. Lee thought, Money? Is that all this is about? Lee followed the vice president to the refreshment area after his talk and asked him to identify the five most important events, the real milestones, in his career with Pharmazing. He smiled for a moment, and then told her about introducing a life-saving drug in a third world country, launching an antidepressant in the United States, and initiating limited offerings of three life-enhancing drugs in Western Europe. The contribution to society was measured, each time, in benefits for humanity. It was validated, he explained, with financial gain for the organization.

His response preoccupied Lee all day as she went through more individual and group assessments with Red River. They spent the afternoon making paper houses in competition with Team Green Tree and Team Blue Cloud. Blue Cloud won, but Red River came in second.

Lee was happy with this career, with this company, because she was aware of their many humanitarian outreach efforts. She had rebuilt porches on Saturdays one year with a group from work. She had "walked for a cure" for several diseases and to end community blights of violence and neglect. However, it was not evident to her that societal benefit could be translated to corporate profit.

She looked forward to the last session on the last day. Phil, the retired chairman of the board who had mentored the current CEO, was the keynote speaker at the celebration dinner. Lee's father had served with

Phil on a board for a woman's shelter. Lee knew his reputation for philanthropy and caring. His speech recounted 50 years of financial success. Lee made a mental note: So all good deeds are rewarded—with money.

She went home that Friday night and asked her husband, "What is wrong with me? Does everyone just want money? Why did all these people talk about their lives in terms of dollars and not people? Why is that not OK with me? What is wrong with me? What should I do?"

Her husband said, "Don't worry about it. The phone call tomorrow may put you out of your misery."

Lee asked, "Why would they do all those outreach programs? Remember when we met?"

Her husband nodded, "Pharmazing teamed up with First Bank. We built wheelchair ramps together for those old duplexes on the west side. You looked great with that hammer!"

She smiled at him, "You are still the best plywood handler in the city. So why do all these companies do community service?"

Her husband asked, "Do you think it helps them make money?"

The phone rang at 8 A.M. the next morning. Lee made her husband answer. He handed it to her with a face that said, "Big news." Lee heard the vice president of marketing congratulate her on successful completion of the management assessment week. He told her to report to his office Monday morning, as his new assistant-to.

She hung up and said, "Now what?"

[case.3] Diana's Disappointment: The Promotion Stumbling Block

By Rosemary Maellaro, University of Dallas

Diana Gillen had an uneasy feeling of apprehension as she arrived at the Cobb Street Grille corporate offices. Today she was meeting with her supervisor, Julie Spencer, and regional director, Tom Miner, to learn the outcome of her promotion interview for the district manager position. Diana had been employed by this casual dining restaurant chain for 12 years and had worked her way up from waitress to general manager. Based on her track record, she was the obvious choice for the promotion; and her friends assured her that the interview process was merely a formality. Diana was still anxious, though, and feared that the news might not be positive. She knew she was more than qualified for the job, but that didn't guarantee anything these days.

Nine months ago, when Diana interviewed for the last district manager opening, she thought her selection for the job was inevitable. She was shocked when that didn't happen. Diana was so upset about not getting promoted then that she initially decided not to apply for the current opening. She eventually changed her mind—after all, the company had just named her Restaurant Manager of the Year and entrusted her with managing their flagship location. Diana thought her chances had to be really good this time.

A multi-unit management position was a desirable move up for any general manager and was a goal to which Diana had aspired since she began working in the industry. When she had not been promoted the last time, Julie, her supervisor, explained that her people skills needed to improve. But Diana knew that explanation had little to do with why she hadn't gotten the job—the real reason was corporate politics. She heard that the person they hired was some superstar from the outside, a district manager from another restaurant company who supposedly had strong multi-unit management experience and a proven track record of developing restaurant managers. Despite what she was told, she was convinced that Tom, her regional manager, had been unduly pressured to hire this person, who had been referred by the CEO.

The decision to hire the outsider may have impressed the CEO, but it enraged Diana. With her successful track record as a store manager for the Cobb Street Grille, she was much more capable, in her opinion, of overseeing multiple units than someone who was new to the operation. Besides, district managers had always been promoted internally among the store managers and she was unofficially designated as the next one to move up to a district position. Tom had hired the outside candidate as a political maneuver to put himself in a good light with management, even though it meant overlooking a loyal employee like her in the process. Diana had no patience with people who made business decisions for the wrong reasons. She worked very hard to avoid politics, and it especially irritated her when the political actions of others negatively affected her.

Diana was ready to be a district manager nine months ago and thought she was even more qualified today, provided the decision was based on performance. She ran a tight ship, managing her restaurant completely by the book. She meticulously adhered to policies and procedures and rigorously controlled expenses. Her sales were growing, in spite of new competition in the market, and she received relatively few customer complaints. The only number that was a little out of line was the higher turnover among her staff.

Diana was not too concerned about the increasing number of terminations, however; there was a perfectly logical explanation for this. It was because she had high standards—for herself and her employees. Any employee who delivered less than 110 percent at all times would be better off finding a job somewhere else. Diana didn't think she should bend the rules for anyone, for whatever reason. A few months ago, for example, she had to fire three otherwise good employees who decided to try a new customer service tactic—a so-called innovation they dreamed up—rather than complying with the established process. As the general manager, it was her responsibility to make sure that the restaurant was managed strictly in accordance with the operations manual, and she could not allow deviations. This by-the-book approach to managing had served her well for many years. It got her promoted in the past, and she was not about to jinx that now. Losing a few employees now and then—particularly those who had difficulty following the rules—was simply the cost of doing business.

During a recent store visit, Julie suggested that Diana might try creating a friendlier work environment because she seemed aloof and interacted with employees somewhat mechanically. Julie even told her that she overheard employees refer to Diana as the "Ice Maiden" behind her back. Diana was surprised that

Julie brought this up because her boss rarely criticized her. They had an unspoken agreement: Since Diana was so technically competent and always met her financial targets, Julie didn't need to give her much input. Diana was happy to be left alone to run her restaurant without needless advice.

At any rate, Diana rarely paid attention to what employees said about her. She wasn't about to let something as childish as a silly name cause her to modify a successful management strategy. What's more, even though she had recently lost more than the average number of employees due to "personality differences" or "miscommunications" over her directives, her superiors did not seem to mind when she consistently delivered strong bottom-line results every month.

As she waited in the conference room for the others, Diana worried that she was not going to get this promotion. Julie had sounded different in the voice-mail message she left to inform her about this meeting, but Diana couldn't put her finger on exactly what it was. She would be very angry if she was passed over again and wondered what excuse they would have this time. Then her mind wandered to how her employees would respond to her if she did not get the promotion. They all knew how much she wanted the job, and she cringed at how embarrassed she would be if she didn't get it. Her eyes began to mist over at the sheer thought of having to face them if she was not promoted today.

Julie and Tom entered the room then and the meeting was under way. They told Diana, as kindly as they could, that she would not be promoted at this time; one of her colleagues would become the new district manager. She was incredulous. The individual who got promoted had only been with the company three years—and Diana had trained her! She tried to comprehend how this happened, but it did not make sense. Before any further explanation could be offered, she burst into tears and left the room. As she tried in vain to regain her composure, Diana was overcome with crushing disappointment.

[case.4] MexFabrics

Martha Burkle, Monterrey Institute of Technology*

Juan Diego Martinez watched the sunset over the city of Guadalajara. It was not only the heat that made the human resources manager at MexFabrics sweat during that day. Production orders from headquarters in Mexico City were far more a problem for him. After the Easter holiday, another seven workers quit work without a particular reason. High turnover of MexFabrics' production employees, most of whom are women, has been a constant problem ever since Martinez started his job two years ago. Now the problem has turned into a serious matter that threatens the company's reputation. How could he finish orders on time and also maintain high standards of quality without the experienced people he needed? The work was highly dependent on handwork, since automation was almost nonexistent in most of the small manufacturing plants in Mexico, and MexFabrics' most important competitive advantage was the high quality of their products.

People at the head office in Mexico City expected excellent results this year, and Juan Diego Martinez was now very aware that this could not be achieved until he had solved the problem of the high turnover of staff. He thought that this was especially difficult, considering the personal situations of many of his female workers and the specific context in Mexico. A strategy had to be developed whereby the situation was radically improved and a stable, well-trained and experienced workforce established.

MexFabrics: The Company

The company started its operation in 1938 with the imports of fine Italian, French, and Spanish ties under the name of several recognized brands. Years after that, the group MexFabrics decided to manufacture high-quality ties in Mexico. By the 1970s, the company's production became an addition to the already large clothes manufacturing industry in Mexico, which had begun in 1966 with the purpose of promoting foreign investment and technology transfer in the country. Manufacturing industries in Mexico have had a large growth during the 1990s, supported by the implementation of NAFTA, foreign investment from other countries (particularly the United States, Canada, and Japan), and cheap hand labor. Currently, there are more than 4,500 garment manufacturing plants employing more than 2 million people in Mexico. So MexFabrics entered an already large industry sector. Over the years, compatible products were added to the line of ties, fine shirts, trousers, cuff links, belts, and scarves.

Today, MexFabrics is one of the largest and best-known manufacturers of fine clothes in Mexico. The company manufactures and markets 30 different high-quality products for men. In total, the company employs 1,000 people in Mexico, of which almost 400 manufacture 80 percent of the products in Guadalajara. The operations are divided into two divisions, formal and casual wear, which are then further divided into several subgroups. In both fields, shirts and ties were among the most important products. Last year, Mex-

Fabrics sold around one million articles with a sales volume of more than 300 million Mexican pesos (30 million U.S. dollars). Shirts represent 35 percent of sales, followed by ties with 30 percent and trousers with 15 percent. MexFabrics is number one in the two largest mall chains in Mexico in terms of sales and prestige.

The work performed at MexFabrics could appear to be easy and repetitive; employees simply receive raw materials, and after sewing and cutting, a final piece of work is produced. But nothing is further from the truth. In fact, being an employee at MexFabrics is a challenging task. The manufacture of quality clothing demands employees with high levels of skills and special abilities supported by regular training to be able to produce a high-quality piece in a short period of time.

Operations and Human Resources Challenges for Group MexFabrics

In 1991, the first shirt factory of the group was built in Guadalajara in response to the company's need to offer a better service to the group and to have the capacity to improve quality control standards. In 1994, the leather and ties factory was transferred from Mexico City to Guadalajara, and, in 1997, the plant for casual shirts and trousers began operations. Daily production in these plants consists of approximately 1,300 shirts, 1,200 ties, 300 trousers, and 950 leather products such as belts and wallets.

The production process starts with the production order, which documents the specifications and quantities, and the reception of the raw materials, which are imported from Italy, France, or Spain and received at the general warehouse in Mexico City. After the first quality inspection, the raw materials are sent to production where the forms are designed and the product fabricated. Product quality is maintained by frequently inspecting random samples throughout the production process.

After packing, products are sent to the distribution center in Guadalajara and then shipped to the different outlets around Mexico.

MexFabrics has recently experienced a number of challenges and opportunities regarding employees. The high turnover among personnel (up to 20 percent per month by the end of 2004) has threatened product quality as inexperienced employees fill jobs vacated by qualified staff. The problem of fulfilling the planned production output, together with the time required for the recruitment of new personnel, is also putting a great deal of pressure on plant managers and on the human resources manager.

MexFabrics receives a large number of job applicants, but selecting the appropriate personnel for the demanding production process is a difficult task. Out of every 100 applications, the human resources department in Guadalajara selects about 50 for individual interviews and about 10 people for employment in the plants. There, they receive specific training on manufacturing the different products MexFabrics produces, from shirts to trousers. After about two weeks of this training, the new recruits begin working in assigned production jobs but receive ongoing advice and instruction for several more weeks. It takes about six months for a typical worker to be fully trained.

All workers receive salary increases based on the number of weeks they have worked for the company. These increases are proportionate to the country general inflation. To give an example, during the first semester last year, inflation was 0.8 percent. So after 8 weeks, the salary increases 0.5 percent, and this increase reaches 1 percent after 48 weeks. After that, the salary increase policy is substituted by a policy of bonus that encourages employee's loyalty to the company over a period of 18 months. Employees also receive bonuses for punctuality and attendance. Moreover, there is an incentive for the different operation units, trousers or belts for example, in which workers earn more money by improving productivity (total pieces produced per person hour). However, employees seldom receive these productivity bonuses because high turnover keeps productivity too low.

MexFabrics Organizational Culture

Buses operate on specific routes every morning to facilitate workers' transportation to the plant. For those who live far away from the bus route, a certain amount of money is designated to pay for public transportation. Since the workforce consists of a high percentage of women, MexFabrics has a child care center, a service offered to workers who have been employed for at least five years in the company and have a good work record.

This strategy has resulted in satisfaction among those women who could enjoy the benefit, but not those who are still new to the company. Moreover, to reduce the turnover of workers during the first weeks, while still in training, MexFabrics pays a special bonus for those who learn their jobs quickly.

An internal magazine promotes MexFabrics organizational culture. Boards across the plant also state the company's values and mission—to be a flexible, dynamic, and efficient company that responds to market needs. Distributed information also promotes employees' loyalty to the company. However, promoting loyalty is a difficult task for the HR department. Low literacy skills and lack of responsibility seems to be a constant characteristic among many manufacturing employees in developing countries. Coming from poor families, employees just want to survive from day to day; they have no vision of the possibilities that working in the sector could give them, such as skills development and economic stability.

Personal problems among the workers or social problems within their households are seen as the main reasons for the high turnover, resulting in a shortage of experienced personnel. Many employees lack the necessary education to perform the work; others lack commitment to the company. Often without any reason, people would fail to show up for work or would quit from one day to another. There was an urgent need to analyze and overcome these problems. Juan Diego Martinez, MexFabric's HR manager, was not too keen to go to bed that night, since he knew the problem of chronic employee turnover would not let him sleep well. A meeting is scheduled on Monday morning, when MexFabric's directors expect Martinez to outline a decisive strategy to significantly reduce turnover. He would certainly present them some things that he thought were crucial. But within the context of the firm, the economic and social climate of Mexican industry, and the day-to-day personal and social challenges experienced by the mainly female workers, things were not always so easy to realize.

*Jaschar Saedi, of the Otto Beisheim Graduate School of Management, Germany, assisted in developing this case study.

>videosummaries

>**video**summary/**for:**part one

Video Cases For Part One

Global Giant

Wal-Mart has grown from one Arkansas store in the 1960s into the largest company in the world. But with such a ruthless focus on prices and productivity, Wal-Mart is now experiencing numerous ethical problems, including a massive class action suit alleging that the retailer favors men over women in promotion to store management. Critics also charge that Wal-Mart's low-wage policy forces employees to rely on public services. Wal-Mart argues that most of its employees are college students or senior citizens employed to supplement their incomes. A third complaint is that Wal-Mart's manufacturing operations are rolling back wages and benefits, whereas Wal-Mart claims that it is monitoring its suppliers and raising working standards.

Discussion Questions
1. Identify the ethical and corporate social responsibility concerns that various groups are raising against Wal-Mart in this video program.

2. If you were the CEO of Wal-Mart, how would you address each of these concerns? What effect, if any, would your actions have on the company's competitiveness in the marketplace?

New Belgium Brewery

This video program outlines the various ways in which New Belgium Brewery in Fort Collins, Colorado, tries to operate an environmentally sustainable business. The company accomplishes impressive environmental standards through new technology, alternative forms of energy, and waste minimization. The program reveals these environmentally sustainable strategies and describes how employees buy into this model of doing business.

Discussion Questions
1. Describe the various ways that New Belgium Brewery supports environmental sustainability.

2. How did New Belgium Brewery's founders gain employee support for environmental sustainability?

>**video**summary/**for:**part two

Video Cases For Part Two

Child Care Help

This video program highlights work/life initiatives at both IBM and Abbott Laboratories. In spite of job cuts, IBM offers its employees a variety of work/life balance options, including unpaid leave, maternity leave, telecommuting, and on-site child care facilities. Abbott Laboratories also invests heavily in child care and other employee work/life benefits because management knows these benefits have a meaningful payback in terms of employee morale and productivity.

Discussion Questions
1. Executives at both IBM and Abbott Laboratories refer to the payback of these work/life benefits. Explain how this payback tends to occur.

2. This program specifically shows on-site child care as a work/life initiative. Use concepts on stress and employee emotions to explain how on-site child care might improve morale and productivity.

Money and Ethics

Is *business ethics* an oxymoron? Although stock manipulation and other forms of business fraud have occurred for hundreds of years, Barbara Toffler, an ethics professor and former

ethics consultant at Arthur Andersen, believes that business can be more ethical. Still, she acknowledges that being ethical isn't easy. Most executives know right from wrong, yet they make unethical decisions when the financial rewards and pressure to perform are high enough. This video case study documents Toffler's experience at Arthur Andersen, where greed overwhelmed ethical values. It also tells the story of grocer Stew Leonard, Sr., who was jailed for tax fraud just two years after being featured in an ethics video.

Discussion Questions
1. Identify the various strategies described in this video program to encourage ethical conduct and discourage or punish wrongdoing. Explain why each of these practices is, or is not, effective.

2. Use the expectancy theory of motivation model, discussed in Chapter 5, to explain why people engage in unethical behavior even though they know it is wrong.

Now Who's Boss?

Jonathan Tisch, CEO of Loews Hotels, had plenty of opportunity to empathize with staff when he spent five days performing a variety of frontline jobs. Although Tisch began his career working on the front desk, times have changed. Tisch discovered the complexities of computer technology as well as the challenges of greeting irritable guests, making beds, and working in sweaty polyester outfits. In this video program Tisch recalls his five-day experience.

Discussion Questions
1. Relate the frontline experience that Tisch went through to the Johari Window model.

2. Is working on the front lines an effective way for executives to understand the business? Why or why not?

Pike Place Fish Market

Fifteen years ago, Pike Place Fish Market in Seattle had unhappy employees and was in financial trouble. Rather than close shop, owner John Yokoyama sought help from consultant Jim Bergquist to improve his leadership and energize the workforce. Rather than rule as a tyrant, Yokoyama learned how to actively involve employees in the business. Soon, staff felt more empowered and gained more enjoyment from their work. They also began to actively have fun at work, including setting goals as a game, throwing fish to each other as sport, and pretending they are "world famous." Today, thanks to these and other strategies described in this video case, Pike Place *is* world famous. The little shop has become a tourist attraction and customers from California to New York call in orders.

Discussion Questions
1. Based on the model of emotions and attitudes in Chapter 4, explain how the changes at Pike Place Fish Market improved job satisfaction and reduced turnover. How did these attitude changes affect customer satisfaction?

2. Goal setting is discussed as an important activity at Pike Place. Evaluate the effectiveness of this goal-setting process in the context of the characteristics of effective goals described in Chapter 5 of this textbook.

3. How is coaching applied at Pike Place, and how does this coaching influence employee performance?

Stress in Japan

Stress from overwork has become an epidemic in Japan. This video program consists of two segments that illustrate the degree to which some Japanese employees are overworked, as well as the consequences of their overwork. The first segment follows a typical day of a Japanese manager, from his two-hour morning commute to his late-night working hours. The program also shows how he is under constant pressure to improve efficiency and experiences a heavy burden and responsibility to do better. The second segment describes how *karoshi*—death from overwork—took the life of 23-year-old Yoshika. It reconstructs Yoshika's work life as a graphic artist up to the time when she died suddenly on the job due to a brain hemorrhage.

Discussion Questions
1. Identify the various sources of stress (i.e., stressors) that the Japanese manager in the first segment likely experiences each day. Does he do anything to try to manage his stress?

2. What conditions led up to the *karoshi* of Yoshika? Are these conditions commonly found in the country where you live?

>videosummary/for:part three

Video Cases For Part Three

Bully Broads

Women executives in Silicon Valley who seem to be overaggressive are sent to, or voluntarily join, a reform program called the Bully Broads Program. The program provides executive coaching as well as group activities to curb the impulse to influence others through too much assertiveness. But while the program tries to change women, its founder and participants also believe there is a double standard; aggressive male executives aren't sent to similar programs, whereas women are expected to act more gentile.

Discussion Questions
1. Use your knowledge of leadership theories to explain why aggressive women are told to be less aggressive whereas this behavior is acceptable in men.

2. Are there situations where employees are more likely to accept aggressive female leaders?

Celebrity CEO Charisma

Does the cult of CEO charisma really make a difference to company profits? This NBC program takes a brief look at chief executives who acted like superheroes but failed to deliver, as well as a few low-key executives who really made a difference. The program features Harvard business school professor Rakesh Khurana, author of *Searching for a Corporate Savior,* a book warning that charismatic leaders are not necessarily effective leaders.

Discussion Questions
1. Why do company boards tend to hire charismatic CEOs?

2. What can corporate boards do to minimize the charisma effect when filling chief executive officer and other senior executive positions?

>**video**summary/**for:**part four

Video Cases For Part Four

JetBlue Airways

JetBlue Airways is one of America's great aviation success stories. In just a few short years after its start-up, the New York–based discount airline has become both profitable and highly popular among customers. Founder David Neeleman claims that the notion of a "JetBlue experience" emerged from customer feedback about their travels on JetBlue. This unique experience is based on the company's customer-focused culture and the many decisions focused on giving customers the best possible encounters.

Discussion Questions

1. Identify the activities or conditions that have developed and maintained JetBlue's customer-focused culture.

2. How has JetBlue's culture and explicit values influenced its decision making?

A

ability Both the natural aptitudes and learned capabilities required to successfully complete a task.

achievement-nurturing orientation A competitive versus cooperative view of relations with other people.

action learning Occurs when employees, usually in teams, investigate and apply solutions to a situation that is both real and complex, with immediate relevance to the company.

action research A data-based, problem-oriented process that diagnoses the need for change, introduces the intervention, and then evaluates and stabilizes the desired changes.

adaptive culture An organizational culture in which employees focus on the changing needs of customers and other stakeholders and support initiatives to keep pace with those changes.

appreciative inquiry An organizational change process that directs attention away from the group's own problems and focuses participants on the group's potential and positive elements.

artifacts The observable symbols and signs of an organization's culture.

attitudes The cluster of beliefs, assessed feelings, and behavioral intentions toward an object.

attribution process The perceptual process of deciding whether an observed behavior or event is caused largely by internal or by external factors.

autonomy The degree to which a job gives employees the freedom, independence, and discretion to schedule their work and determine the procedures used in completing it.

B

behavior modification A theory that explains learning in terms of the antecedents and consequences of behavior.

bicultural audit Diagnoses cultural relations between companies prior to a merger and determines the extent to which cultural clashes are likely to occur.

Big Five personality dimensions The five abstract dimensions representing most personality traits: conscientiousness, agreeableness, neuroticism, openness to experience, and extroversion (CANOE).

bounded rationality Processing limited and imperfect information and satisficing rather than maximizing when choosing among alternatives.

brainstorming A freewheeling, face-to-face meeting where team members aren't allowed to criticize, but are encouraged to speak freely, generate as many ideas as possible, and build on the ideas of others.

C

categorical thinking The mostly unconscious process of organizing people and objects into preconceived categories that are stored in our long-term memory.

centrality The degree and nature of interdependence between the powerholder and others.

centralization The degree to which formal decision authority is held by a small group of people, typically those at the top of the organizational hierarchy.

ceremonies Planned and usually dramatic displays of organizational culture, conducted specifically for the benefit of an audience.

change agent Anyone who possesses enough knowledge and power to guide and facilitate the organizational change effort.

coalition A group that attempts to influence people outside the group by pooling the resources and power of its members.

cognitive dissonance Occurs when people perceive an inconsistency between their beliefs, feelings, and behavior.

collectivism The extent to which people value duty to groups to which they belong as well as group harmony.

communication The process by which information is transmitted and understood between two or more people.

competencies The abilities, values, personality traits, and other characteristics of people that lead to superior performance.

conflict The process in which one party perceives that its interests are being opposed or negatively affected by another party.

conflict management Interventions that alter the level and form of conflict in ways that maximize its benefits and minimize its dysfunctional consequences.

constructive conflict Occurs when team members debate their different perceptions about an issue in a way that keeps the conflict focused on the task rather than people.

contingency approach The idea that a particular action may have different consequences in different situations.

contingent work Any job in which the individual does not have an explicit or implicit contract for long-term employment, or one in which the minimum hours of work can vary in a nonsystematic way.

continuance commitment A bond felt by an employee that motivates him or her to stay only because leaving would be costly.

corporate social responsibility (CSR) An organization's moral obligation toward its stakeholders.

counterpower The capacity of a person, team, or organization to keep a more powerful person or group in the exchange relationship.

counterproductive work behaviors (CWBs) Voluntary behaviors that have the potential to directly or indirectly harm the organization.

creativity The development of original ideas that make a socially recognized contribution.

D

decision making A conscious process of making choices among one or more alternatives with the intention of moving toward some desired state of affairs.

distributive justice principle The moral principle stating that people who are similar should be rewarded similarly, and those dissimilar should be rewarded differently.

divergent thinking Reframing a problem in a unique way and generating different approaches to the issue.

divisional structure An organizational structure that groups employees around geographic areas, clients, or outputs.

drives Instinctive or innate tendencies to seek certain goals or maintain internal stability.

E

electronic brainstorming Using special computer software, participants share ideas while minimizing the team dynamics problems inherent in traditional brainstorming sessions.

emotional dissonance The conflict between required and true emotions.

emotional intelligence (EI) The ability to perceive and express emotion, assimilate emotion and thought, understand and reason with emotion, and regulate emotion in oneself and others.

emotional labor The effort, planning, and control needed to express organizationally desired emotions during interpersonal transactions.

emotions Physiological, behavioral, and psychological episodes experienced toward an object, person, or event that create a state of readiness.

empathy A person's ability to understand and be sensitive to the feelings, thoughts, and situations of others.

employability An employment relationship in which people are expected to continuously develop their skills to remain employed.

employee engagement How much employees identify with and are emotionally committed to their work, are cognitively focused on that work, and possess the ability and resources to do so.

employee involvement The degree to which employees influence how their work is organized and carried out.

empowerment A psychological concept in which people experience more self-determination, meaning, competence, and impact regarding their role in the organization.

enacted values Values we rely on to guide our decisions and actions.

equity theory A theory that explains how people develop perceptions of fairness in the distribution and exchange of resources.

escalation of commitment The tendency to repeat an apparently bad decision or allocate more resources to a failing course of action.

espoused values Values that we say we use and think we use.

ethical sensitivity A personal characteristic that enables people to recognize the presence and determine the relative importance of an ethical issue.

ethics The study of moral principles or values that determine whether actions are right or wrong and outcomes are good or bad.

evaluation apprehension When individuals are reluctant to mention ideas that seem silly because they believe (often correctly) that other team members are silently evaluating them.

exit-voice-loyalty-neglect (EVLN) model The four ways, as indicated in the name, employees respond to job dissatisfaction.

expectancy theory The motivation theory based on the idea that work effort is directed toward behaviors that people believe will lead to desired outcomes.

extinction Occurs when the target behavior decreases because no consequence follows it.

extroversion A "Big Five" personality dimension that characterizes people who are outgoing, talkative, sociable, and assertive.

F

feedback Any information that people receive about the consequences of their behavior.

flaming The act of sending an emotionally charged electronic mail message to others.

force field analysis Kurt Lewin's model of systemwide change that helps change agents diagnose the forces that drive and restrain proposed organizational change.

formalization The degree to which organizations standardize behavior through rules, procedures, formal training, and related mechanisms.

four-drive theory A motivation theory based on the innate drives to acquire, bond, learn, and defend that incorporates both emotions and rationality.

functional structure An organizational structure that organizes employees around specific knowledge or other resources.

fundamental attribution error The tendency to attribute the behavior of other people more to internal than to external factors.

future search Systemwide group sessions, usually lasting a few days, in which participants identify trends and ways to adapt to those changes.

G

general adaptation syndrome A model of the stress experience, consisting of three stages: alarm reaction, resistance, and exhaustion.

globalization Economic, social, and cultural connectivity (and interdependence) with people in other parts of the world.

goal setting The process of motivating employees and clarifying their role perceptions by establishing performance objectives.

grapevine An unstructured and informal communication network founded on social relationships rather than organizational charts or job descriptions.

groups Two or more people with a unifying relationship.

groupthink The tendency of highly cohesive groups to value consensus at the price of decision quality.

H

heterogeneous teams Teams that include members with diverse personal characteristics and backgrounds.

homogeneous teams Teams that include members with common technical expertise, demographics (age, gender), ethnicity, experiences, or values.

I

implicit favorite The decision maker's preferred alternative against which all other choices are judged.

implicit leadership theory A theory stating that people rely on preconceived traits to evaluate others as leaders and that they tend to inflate the influence of leadership on organizational events.

impression management The practice of actively shaping our public image.

individual rights principle The moral principle stating that every person is entitled to legal and human rights.

individualism The extent to which people value independence and personal uniqueness.

influence Any behavior that attempts to alter another person's attitudes or behavior.

information overload A condition in which the volume of information received exceeds the person's capacity to process it.

ingratiation Any attempt to increase the extent to which a target person likes us or perceives that he or she is similar to us.

inoculation effect A persuasive communication strategy of warning listeners that others will try to influence them in the future and that they should be wary about the opponent's arguments.

intellectual capital The sum of an organization's human capital, structural capital, and relationship capital.

introversion A "Big Five" personality dimension that characterizes people who are territorial and solitary.

intuition The ability to know when a problem or opportunity exists and select the best course of action without conscious reasoning.

J

jargon Technical language and acronyms as well as recognized words with specialized meanings in specific organizations or groups.

job characteristics model A job design model that relates the motivational properties of jobs to specific personal and organizational consequences of those properties.

job design The process of assigning tasks to a job, including the interdependency of those tasks with other jobs.

job enrichment Occurs when employees are given more responsibility for scheduling, coordinating, and planning their own work.

job satisfaction A person's attitude regarding his or her job and work content.

job specialization The result of division of labor in which each job includes a subset of the tasks required to complete the product or service.

Johari Window The model of personal and interpersonal understanding that encourages disclosure and feedback to increase the open area and reduce the blind, hidden, and unknown areas of oneself.

K

knowledge management Any structured activity that improves an organization's capacity to acquire, share, and use knowledge in ways that improve its survival and success.

L

leadership Influencing, motivating, and enabling others to contribute toward the effectiveness and success of the organizations of which they are members.

leadership substitutes A theory that identifies contingencies that either limit the leader's ability to influence subordinates or make that particular leadership style unnecessary.

learning A relatively permanent change in behavior that occurs as a result of a person's interaction with the environment.

learning orientation The extent that an organization or individual supports knowledge management, particularly opportunities to acquire knowledge through experience and experimentation.

legitimate power The capacity to influence others through formal authority.

M

Machiavellian values The belief that deceit is a natural and acceptable way to influence others.

management by walking around (MBWA) A communication practice in which executives get out of their offices and learn from others in the organization through face-to-face dialogue.

Maslow's needs hierarchy A motivation theory of needs arranged in a hierarchy, whereby people are motivated to fulfill a higher need as a lower one becomes gratified.

matrix structure A type of departmentalization that overlays two organizational forms in order to leverage the benefits of both.

mechanistic structure An organizational structure with a narrow span of control and high degrees of formalization and centralization.

media richness The data-carrying capacity of a communication medium, including the volume and variety of information it can transmit.

mental models The broad worldviews or "theories in use" that people rely on to guide their perceptions and behaviors.

moral intensity The degree to which an issue demands the application of ethical principles.

motivation The forces within a person that affect his or her direction, intensity, and persistence of voluntary behavior.

Myers-Briggs Type Indicator (MBTI) A personality test that measures each of the traits in Jung's model.

N

needs Deficiencies that energize or trigger behaviors to satisfy those needs.

negative reinforcement Occurs when the removal or avoidance of a consequence increases or maintains the frequency or future probability of a behavior.

networking Cultivating social relationships with others to accomplish one's goals.

nominal group technique A structured team decision-making process whereby team members independently write down ideas, describe and clarify them to the group, and then independently rank or vote on them.

norms The informal rules and expectations that groups establish to regulate the behavior of their members.

O

open systems Organizations that take their sustenance from the environment and, in turn, affect that environment through their output.

organic structure An organizational structure with a wide span of control, little formalization, and decentralized decision making.

organizational (affective) commitment The employee's emotional attachment to, identification with, and involvement in a particular organization.

organizational behavior (OB) The study of what people think, feel, and do in and around organizations.

organizational citizenship Behaviors that extend beyond the employee's normal job duties.

organizational culture The basic pattern of shared assumptions, values, and beliefs considered to be the correct way of thinking about and acting on problems and opportunities facing the organization.

organizational learning The knowledge management process in which organizations acquire, share, and use knowledge to succeed.

organizational memory The storage and preservation of intellectual capital.

organizational politics Behaviors that others perceive as self-serving tactics for personal gain at the expense of other people and possibly the organization.

organizational socialization The process by which individuals learn the values, expected behaviors, and social knowledge necessary to assume their roles in the organization.

organizational strategy The way an organization positions itself in its setting in relation to its stakeholders, given the organization's resources, capabilities, and mission.

organizational structure The division of labor and the patterns of coordination, communication, work flow, and formal power that direct organizational activities.

organizations Groups of people who work interdependently toward some purpose.

P

parallel learning structures Highly participative groups constructed alongside (i.e., parallel to) the formal organization with the purpose of increasing the organization's learning and producing meaningful organizational change.

path-goal leadership theory A contingency theory of leadership based on expectancy theory of motivation that relates several leadership styles to specific employee and environmental contingencies.

perception The process of selecting, organizing, and interpreting information in order to make sense of the world around us.

personality The relatively stable pattern of behaviors and consistent internal states that explain a person's behavioral tendencies.

persuasion Using logical arguments, facts, and emotional appeals to encourage people to accept a request or message.

positive reinforcement Occurs when the introduction of a consequence increases or maintains the frequency or future probability of a behavior.

power The capacity of a person, team, or organization to influence others.

power distance The extent to which people accept unequal distribution of power in a society.

process losses Resources (including time and energy) expended toward team development and maintenance rather than the task.

production blocking A time constraint in team decision making due to the procedural requirement that only one person may speak at a time.

prospect theory An effect in which losing a particular amount is more disliked than gaining the same amount.

psychological harassment Repeated and hostile or unwanted conduct, verbal comments, actions or gestures that affect an employee's dignity or psychological or physical integrity and that result in a harmful work environment for the employee.

punishment Occurs when a consequence decreases the frequency or future probability of a behavior.

R

realistic job preview (RJP) Giving job applicants a balance of positive and negative information about the job and work context.

reality shock Occurs when newcomers perceive discrepancies between pre-employment expectations and on-the-job reality.

referent power The capacity to influence others based on the identification and respect they have for the powerholder.

refreezing The latter part of the change process in which systems and conditions are introduced that reinforce and maintain the desired behaviors.

resilience The capability of individuals to cope successfully in the face of significant change, adversity, or risk.

rituals The programmed routines of daily organizational life that dramatize the organization's culture.

S

satisficing Selecting a solution that is satisfactory or "good enough" rather than optimal or "the best."

scenario planning A systematic process of thinking about alternative futures, and what the organization should do to anticipate and react to those environments.

scientific method A set of principles and procedures that help researchers to systematically understand previously unexplained events and conditions.

selective attention The process of filtering information received by our senses.

self-actualization The need for self-fulfillment in reaching one's potential.

self-directed work teams (SDWTs) Cross-functional work groups organized around work processes, that complete an entire piece of work requiring several interdependent tasks, and that have substantial autonomy over the execution of those tasks.

self-fulfilling prophecy Occurs when our expectations about another person cause that person to act in a way that is consistent with those expectations.

self-reinforcement Occurs whenever someone has control over a reinforcer but delays it until a self-set goal has been completed.

self-serving bias A perceptual error whereby people tend to attribute their favorable outcomes to internal factors and their failures to external factors.

servant leadership The belief that leaders serve followers by understanding their needs and facilitating their work performance.

sexual harassment Unwelcome conduct of a sexual nature that detrimentally affects the work environment or leads to adverse job-related consequences for its victims.

skill variety The extent to which employees must use different skills and talents to perform tasks within their job.

social identity theory States that self-perception and social perception are shaped by a person's unique characteristics (personal identity) and membership in various social groups (social identity).

social learning theory A theory stating that much learning occurs by observing others and then modeling the behaviors that lead to favorable outcomes and avoiding the behaviors that lead to punishing consequences.

social loafing A situation in which people exert less effort (and usually perform at a lower level) when working in groups than when working alone.

socioemotional conflict Any situation where people view their differences as personal attacks rather than attempts to resolve an issue.

span of control The number of people directly reporting to the next level in the organizational hierarchy.

stakeholders Shareholders, customers, suppliers, governments, and any other groups with a vested interest in the organization.

stereotyping The process of assigning traits to people based on their membership in a social category.

stress An individual's adaptive response to a situation that is perceived as challenging or threatening to the person's well-being.

stressors The causes of stress, including any environmental conditions that place a physical or emotional demand on the person.

substitutability The extent to which people dependent on a resource have alternatives.

superordinate goal A common objective held by conflicting parties that is more important than their conflicting departmental or individual goals.

T

tacit knowledge Knowledge embedded in our actions and ways of thinking, and transmitted only through observation and experience.

task identity The degree to which a job requires completion of a whole or an identifiable piece of work.

task interdependence The degree to which a task requires employees to share common inputs or outcomes, or to interact in the process of executing their work.

task performance Goal-directed activities that are under the individual's control.

task significance The degree to which the job has a substantial impact on the organization and/or larger society.

team cohesiveness The degree of attraction people feel toward the team and their motivation to remain members.

team effectiveness The extent to which a team achieves its objectives, achieves the needs and objectives of its members, and sustains itself over time.

team-based structure A type of departmentalization with a flat hierarchy and relatively little formalization, consisting of self-directed work teams responsible for various work processes.

teams Groups of two or more people who interact and influence each other, are mutually accountable for achieving common objectives, and perceive themselves as a social entity within an organization.

third-party conflict resolution Any attempt by a relatively neutral person to help the parties resolve their differences.

transactional leadership Leadership that helps organizations achieve their current objectives more efficiently, such as linking job performance to valued rewards and ensuring that employees have the resources needed to get the job done.

transformational leadership A leadership perspective that explains how leaders change teams or organizations by creating, communicating, and modeling a vision for the organization or work unit, and inspiring employees to strive for that vision.

trust A psychological state comprising the intention to accept vulnerability based upon positive expectations of the intent or behavior of another person.

U

uncertainty avoidance The degree to which people tolerate ambiguity or feel threatened by ambiguity and uncertainty.

unfreezing The first part of the change process whereby the change agent produces disequilibrium between the driving and restraining forces.

upward appeal A type of coalition in which one or more members is someone with higher authority or expertise.

utilitarianism The moral principle stating that decision makers should seek the greatest good for the greatest number of people when choosing among alternatives.

V

values Stable, long-lasting beliefs about what is important in a variety of situations.

values congruence A situation wherein two or more entities have similar value systems.

virtual teams Cross-functional teams that operate across space, time, and organizational boundaries with members who communicate mainly through information technologies.

virtual teams Teams whose members operate across space, time, and organizational boundaries and are linked through information technologies to achieve organizational tasks.

virtual work Employees perform work away from the traditional physical workplace using information technology.

W

win–lose orientation The belief that conflicting parties are drawing from a fixed pie, so the more one party receives, the less the other party will receive.

win–win orientation The belief that the parties will find a mutually beneficial solution to their disagreement.

work/life balance The minimization of conflict between work and nonwork demands.

>endnotes

chapter 1

1. J. McHugh, "Google vs. Evil," *Wired,* January 2003; A. Hermida, "Google Looks to See Off Rivals," *BBC News Online,* March 30, 2004; M. Liedtke, "Google vs. Yahoo: Heavyweights Attack from Different Angles," *Associated Press Newswires,* December 18, 2004; F. Vogelstein, "Google @ $165," *Fortune,* December 13, 2004, pp. 98–104; R. Basch, "Doing Well by Doing Good," *Searcher Magazine,* January 2005, pp. 18–28; and K. Coughlin, "Goooood Move," *Star-Ledger* (Newark, NJ), June 5, 2005, p. 1.

2. M. Warner, "Organizational Behavior Revisited," *Human Relations* 47 (October 1994), pp. 1151–66; and R. Westwood and S. Clegg, "The Discourse of Organization Studies: Dissensus, Politics, and Paradigms," in *Debating Organization: Point-Counterpoint in Organization Studies,* ed. R. Westwood and S. Clegg (Malden, MA: Blackwood, 2003), pp. 1–42.

3. D. K. Katz and R. L. Kahn, *The Social Psychology of Organizations* (New York: Wiley, 1966), Chap. 2; and R. N. Stern and S. R. Barley, "Organizations as Social Systems: Organization Theory's Neglected Mandate," *Administrative Science Quarterly* 41 (1996), pp. 146–62.

4. B. Schlender, "The Three Faces of Steve," *Fortune,* November 9, 1998, pp. 96–101.

5. S. A. Mohrman, C. B. Gibson, and A. M. Mohrman Jr., "Doing Research That Is Useful to Practice: A Model and Empirical Exploration," *Academy of Management Journal* 44 (April 2001), pp. 357–75.

6. B. N. Pfau and I. T. Kay, *The Human Capital Edge* (New York: McGraw-Hill, 2002); I. S. Fulmer, B. Gerhart, and K. S. Scott, "Are the 100 Best Better? An Empirical Investigation of the Relationship between Being a 'Great Place to Work' and Firm Performance," *Personnel Psychology* 56, no. 4 (Winter 2003), pp. 965–93. However, one study warns that organizational success might cause better OB practices, not the other way around. See P. M. Wright et al., "The Relationship between HR Practices and Firm Performance: Examining Causal Order," *Personnel Psychology* 58, no. 2 (Summer 2005), pp. 409–46.

7. J. Guyon, "David Whitwam (CEOs on Managing Globally)," *Fortune,* July 26, 2004, p. 174; P. Loewe and J. Rufat-Latre, "The Changing Face of Global Business," *Optimize,* June 2004, pp. 32–37; L. Uchitelle, "Globalization: It's Not Just Wages," *The New York Times,* June 17, 2005, pp. C1, C4.

8. V. Kopytoff, "Google Making Its Mark Worldwide," *San Francisco Chronicle,* September 20, 2004, p. H1.

9. S. Fischer, "Globalization and Its Challenges," *American Economic Review,* May 2003, pp. 1–29. For discussion of the diverse meanings of *globalization,* see M. F. Guillén, "Is Globalization Civilizing, Destructive or Feeble? A Critique of Five Key Debates in the Social Science Literature," *Annual Review of Sociology* 27 (2001), pp. 235–60.

10. The ongoing debate regarding the advantages and disadvantages of globalization are discussed in Guillén, "Is Globalization Civilizing, Destructive or Feeble?"; D. Doane, "Can Globalization Be Fixed?" *Business Strategy Review* 13, no. 2 (2002), pp. 51–58; J. Bhagwati, *In Defense of Globalization* (New York: Oxford University Press, 2004); and M. Wolf, *Why Globalization Works* (New Haven, CT: Yale University Press, 2004).

11. Verizon, *Making Connections: Verizon Corporate Responsibility Report 2004* (New York: Verizon, December 2004); and P. Goffney, "Champions of Diversity: The Path to Corporate Enlightenment," *Essence,* May 2005, pp. 149–57.

12. M. F. Riche, "America's Diversity and Growth: Signposts for the 21st Century," *Population Bulletin,* June 2000, pp. 3–43; and U.S. Census Bureau, *Statistical Abstract of the United States: 2004–2005* (Washington: U.S. Census Bureau, May 2005).

13. Association of American Medical Colleges, "Table 1: Women Applicants, Enrollees—Selected Years 1949–50 through 2002–2003," July 14, 2003, www.aamc.org/members/wim/statistics/stats03/start.htm, accessed June 20, 2005; and U.S. Census Bureau, *Statistical Abstract of the United States: 2004–2005,* Table no. 570, p. 371.

14. R. Zemke, C. Raines, and B. Filipczak, *Generations at Work: Managing the Clash of Veterans, Boomers, Xers, and Nexters in Your Workplace* (New York: Amacom,

2000); M. R. Muetzel, *They're Not Aloof, Just Generation X* (Shreveport, LA: Steel Bay, 2003); and S. H. Applebaum, M. Serena, and B. T. Shapiro, "Generation X and the Boomers: Organizational Myths and Literary Realities," *Management Research News* 27, no. 11/12 (2004), pp. 1–28.

15. O. C. Richard, "Racial Diversity, Business Strategy, and Firm Performance: A Resource-Based View," *Academy of Management Journal* 43 (2000), pp. 164–77; D. D. Frink et al., "Gender Demography and Organization Performance: A Two-Study Investigation with Convergence," *Group & Organization Management* 28 (March 2003), pp. 127–47; T. Kochan et al., "The Effects of Diversity on Business Performance: Report of the Diversity Research Network," *Human Resource Management* 42 (2003), pp. 3–21; and N. R. Lockwood, "Workplace Diversity: Leveraging the Power of Difference for Competitive Advantage," *HR Magazine,* June 2005, pp. A1–A10.

16. Sempra Energy, "Case History: Putting Diversity to Work," (San Diego: Sempra Energy, 2005), www.sempra.com/diversity.htm, accessed June 21, 2005.

17. R. J. Ely and D. A. Thomas, "Cultural Diversity at Work: The Effects of Diversity Perspectives on Work Group Processes and Outcomes," *Administrative Science Quarterly* 46 (June 2001), pp. 229–73; and D. van Knippenberg and S. A. Haslam, "Realizing the Diversity Dividend: Exploring the Subtle Interplay between Identity, Ideology and Reality," in *Social Identity at Work: Developing Theory for Organizational Practice,* ed. S. A. Haslam et al. (New York: Taylor and Francis, 2003), pp. 61–80.

18. M. Fugate, A. J. Kinicki, and B. E. Ashforth, "Employability: A Psycho-Social Construct, Its Dimensions, and Applications," *Journal of Vocational Behavior* 65, no. 1 (2004), pp. 14–38; and R. W. McQuaid and C. Lindsay, "The Concept of Employability," *Urban Studies* 42, no. 2 (February 2005), pp. 197–219. The quotation is from M. Jenkins, "Yours for the Taking," *Boeing Frontiers,* June 2004, www.boeing.com/news/frontiers/index.html.

19. A. E. Polivka, "Contingent and Alternative Work Arrangements, Defined," *Monthly Labor Review* 119 (October 1996),

pp. 3–10; D. H. Pink, *Free Agent Nation* (New York: Time Warner, 2002); and D. G. Gallagher and M. Sverke, "Contingent Employment Contracts: Are Existing Employment Theories Still Relevant?" *Economic and Industrial Democracy* 26, no. 2 (May 2005), pp. 181–203.

20. B. A. Lautsch, "Uncovering and Explaining Variance in the Features and Outcomes of Contingent Work," *Industrial & Labor Relations Review* 56 (October 2002), pp. 23–43; S. Ang, L. Van Dyne, and T. M. Begley, "The Employment Relationships of Foreign Workers versus Local Employees: A Field Study of Organizational Justice, Job Satisfaction, Performance, and OCB," *Journal of Organizational Behavior* 24 (2003), pp. 561–83; and C. E. Connelly and D. G. Gallagher, "Emerging Trends in Contingent Work Research," *Journal of Management* 30, no. 6 (2004), pp. 959–83.

21. W. G. Bennis and R. J. Thomas, *Geeks and Geezers* (Boston: Harvard Business School Press, 2002), pp. 74–79; and E. D. Y. Greenblatt, "Work/Life Balance: Wisdom or Whining," *Organizational Dynamics* 31, no. 2 (2002), pp. 177–93. Surveys on the importance of work/life balance are reported in PricewaterhouseCoopers, *International Student Survey: Summary Findings Report* (New York: PricewaterhouseCoopers, May 1999); and Ipsos-Reid, *Canadian Families and the Internet,* Report to the Royal Bank of Canada, January 2002.

22. J. Gannon, "The Perfect Commute," *Post-Gazette* (Pittsburgh, PA), April 24, 2003, p. E1.

23. J. Cummings, "Masters of a Virtual World," *Network World,* April 25, 2005, pp. 76–77. Another survey puts the figure at 27 percent; see "Broadband-Enhanced Teleworking Options Fuel Work-Life Balance Growth for Americans," *Business Wire,* June 30, 2003.

24. D. E. Bailey and N. B. Kurland, "A Review of Telework Research: Findings, New Directions, and Lessons for the Study of Modern Work," *Journal of Organizational Behavior* 23 (2002), pp. 383–400; L. Duxbury and C. Higgins, "Telecommute: A Primer for the Millennium Introduction," in *The New World of Work: Challenges and Opportunities,* ed. C. L. Cooper and R. J. Burke (Oxford: Blackwell, 2002), pp. 157–99; D. W. McCloskey and M. Igbaria, "Does 'Out of Sight' Mean 'Out of Mind'? An Empirical Investigation of the Career Advancement Prospects of Telecommuters," *Information Resources Management Journal* 16 (April–June 2003),

pp. 19–34; V. Illegems and A. Verbeke, "Telework: What Does It Mean for Management?" *Long Range Planning* 37 (2004), pp. 319–34; and S. Raghuram and B. Wiesenfeld, "Work-Nonwork Conflict and Job Stress among Virtual Workers," *Human Resource Management* 43, no. 2/3 (Summer/Fall 2004), pp. 259–77.

25. J. Lipnack and J. Stamps, *Virtual Teams: People Working across Boundaries with Technology* (New York: John Wiley & Sons, 2001); L. L. Martins, L. L. Gilson, and M. T. Maynard, "Virtual Teams: What Do We Know and Where Do We Go from Here?" *Journal of Management* 30, no. 6 (2004), pp. 805–35; and G. Hertel, S. Geister, and U. Konradt, "Managing Virtual Teams: A Review of Current Empirical Research," *Human Resource Management Review* 15, no. 1 (2005), pp. 69–95.

26. B. M. Meglino and E. C. Ravlin, "Individual Values in Organizations: Concepts, Controversies, and Research," *Journal of Management* 24, no. 3 (1998), pp. 351–89; B. R. Agle and C. B. Caldwell, "Understanding Research on Values in Business," *Business and Society* 38, no. 3 (September 1999), pp. 326–87; and S. Hitlin and J. A. Pilavin, "Values: Reviving a Dormant Concept," *Annual Review of Sociology* 30 (2004), pp. 359–93.

27. Middle East Company News, "Accountability, Teamwork, and Continuous Improvement Define Core Operating Values at DED," news release, Dubai, January 4, 2005.

28. The role of values as a control system is discussed in T. M. Begley and D. P. Boyd, "Articulating Corporate Values through Human Resource Policies," *Business Horizons* 43, no. 4 (July 2000), pp. 8–12; and M. G. Murphy and K. M. Davey, "Ambiguity, Ambivalence and Indifference in Organisational Values," *Human Resource Management Journal* 12 (2002), pp. 17–32.

29. This cynicism of executive ethics is beautifully captured in D. Olive, "How Celebrity CEOs Failed to Deliver," *Toronto Star,* August 24, 2002, p. A1.

30. Vector Research, "Analysis of the Public Opinion Poll Conducted for the Canadian Democracy and Corporate Accountability Commission," Toronto, 2001; and V. Matthews, "Corps Values," *Director* 58, no. 10 (May 2005), pp. 50–54. The quotation by Friedman is cited in S. Zadek, *The Civil Corporation: The New Economy of Corporate Citizenship* (London: Earthscan, 2001), pp. 50–51.

31. M. van Marrewijk, "Concepts and Definitions of CSR and Corporate Sustainability: Between Agency and

Communion," *Journal of Business Ethics* 44 (May 2003), pp. 95–105; and E. Garriga and D. Melé, "Corporate Social Responsibility Theories: Mapping the Territory," *Journal of Business Ethics* 53 (2004), pp. 51–71.

32. Zadek, *The Civil Corporation,* Chap. 9; and S. Zambon and A. Del Bello, "Towards a Stakeholder Responsible Approach: The Constructive Role of Reporting," *Corporate Governance* 5, no. 2 (2005), pp. 130–42.

33. M. N. Zald, "More Fragmentation? Unfinished Business in Linking the Social Sciences and the Humanities," *Administrative Science Quarterly* 41 (1996), pp. 251–61. Concerns about the "trade deficit" in OB are raised in C. Heath and S. B. Sitkin, "Big-B versus Big-O: What Is Organizational about Organizational Behavior?" *Journal of Organizational Behavior* 22 (2001), pp. 43–58.

34. C. M. Christensen and M. E. Raynor, "Why Hard-Nosed Executives Should Care about Management Theory," *Harvard Business Review,* September 2003, pp. 66–74. For excellent critique of the "one best way" approach in early management scholarship, see P. F. Drucker, "Management's New Paradigms," *Forbes,* October 5, 1998, pp. 152–77.

35. H. L. Tosi and J. W. Slocum Jr., "Contingency Theory: Some Suggested Directions," *Journal of Management* 10 (1984), pp. 9–26.

36. D. M. H. Rousseau, R. J., "Meso Organizational Behavior: Avoiding Three Fundamental Biases," in *Trends in Organizational Behavior,* ed. C. L. Cooper and D. M. Rousseau (Chichester, UK: John Wiley & Sons, 1994), pp. 13–30.

37. F. E. Kast and J. E. Rosenzweig, "General Systems Theory: Applications for Organization and Management," *Academy of Management Journal* 4 (1972), pp. 47–65; A. De Geus, *The Living Company* (Boston: Harvard Business School Press, 1997); and R. T. Pascale, M. Millemann, and L. Gioja, *Surfing on the Edge of Chaos* (London: Texere, 2000).

38. V. P. Rindova and S. Kotha, "Continuous 'Morphing': Competing through Dynamic Capabilities, Form, and Function," *Academy of Management Journal* 44 (2001), pp. 1263–80; and J. McCann, "Organizational Effectiveness: Changing Concepts for Changing Environments," *Human Resource Planning* 27, no. 1 (2004), pp. 42–50.

39. G. Huber, "Organizational Learning: The Contributing Processes and Literature," *Organizational Science* 2 (1991), pp. 88–115; E. C. Nevis, A. J. DiBella, and J. M. Gould, "Understanding Organizations

as Learning Systems," *Sloan Management Review* 36 (1995), pp. 73–85; G. Miles et al., "Some Conceptual and Research Barriers to the Utilization of Knowledge," *California Management Review* 40 (Spring 1998), pp. 281–88; and D. A. Garvin, *Learning in Action: A Guide to Putting the Learning Organization to Work* (Boston: Harvard Business School Press, 2000).

40. T. A. Stewart, *Intellectual Capital: The New Wealth of Organizations* (New York: Currency/Doubleday, 1997); H. Saint-Onge and D. Wallace, *Leveraging Communities of Practice for Strategic Advantage* (Boston: Butterworth-Heinemann, 2003), pp. 9–10; and J.-A. Johannessen, B. Olsen, and J. Olaisen, "Intellectual Capital as a Holistic Management Philosophy: A Theoretical Perspective," *International Journal of Information Management* 25, no. 2 (2005), pp. 151–71.

41. There is no complete agreement on the meaning of *organizational learning* (or *learning organization*), and the relationship between organizational learning and knowledge management is still somewhat ambiguous. For example, see S. C. Goh, "The Learning Organization: An Empirical Test of a Normative Perspective," *International Journal of Organization Theory & Behavior* 4, no. 3/4 (August 2001), pp. 329–55; and B. R. McElyea, "Knowledge Management, Intellectual Capital, and Learning Organizations: A Triad of Future Management Integration," *Futurics* 26 (2002), pp. 59–65.

42. C. W. Wick and L. S. Leon, "From Ideas to Actions: Creating a Learning Organization," *Human Resource Management* 34 (Summer 1995), pp. 299–311; and L. Falkenberg et al., "Knowledge Acquisition Processes for Technology Decisions," in *Proceedings of the Academy of Management 2002 Annual Conference,* 2002, pp. J1–J6.

43. R. Garud and A. Kumaraswamy, "Vicious and Virtuous Circles in the Management of Knowledge: The Case of Infosys Technologies," *MIS Quarterly* 29, no. 1 (March 2005), pp. 9–33.

44. H. Beazley, J. Boenisch, and D. Harden, "Knowledge Continuity: The New Management Function," *Journal of Organizational Excellence* 22 (2003), pp. 65–81.

45. D. Cline, "On a Roll," *Augusta Chronicle,* February 2, 2003, p. D1.

chapter 2

1. J. Harter, F. L. Schmidt, and T. L. Hayes, "Business-Unit-Level Relationship between Employee Satisfaction, Employee Engagement, and Business Outcomes: A Meta-Analysis," *Journal of Applied Psychology* 87, no. 2 (2002), pp. 268–79; Towers Perrin, *Working Today: Understanding What Drives Employee Engagement* (Stamford, CT: 2003); "Owens Corning Makes Smart Investments in Employee Training," *The Resource* (newsletter of Jackson State's Division of Economic and Community Development), Fall 2004, p. 1; M. Millar, "Getting the Measure of Its People," *Personnel Today,* December 14, 2004, p. 6; J. Robison, "ASB Bank: Good Isn't Good Enough," *Gallup Management Journal,* August 12, 2004; D. Welch, "Mutual of Omaha's Healthy Preoccupation with Talent," *Gallup Management Journal,* May 13, 2004; and K. Ockenden, "Inside Story," *Utility Week,* January 28, 2005, p. 26.

2. Thanks to senior officers in the Singapore Armed Forces for discovering the handy MARS acronym. Thanks also to Chris Perryer at the University of Western Australia for pointing out that the full model should be called the "MARS BAR" because the outcomes are "behavior and results"! The MARS model is a variation of earlier models and writing by several sources, including E. E. Lawler III and L. W. Porter, "Antecedent Attitudes of Effective Managerial Performance," *Organizational Behavior and Human Performance* 2, no. 2 (1967), pp. 122–42; and K. F. Kane, "Special Issue: Situational Constraints and Work Performance," *Human Resource Management Review* 3 (Summer 1993), pp. 83–175.

3. C. C. Pinder, *Work Motivation in Organizational Behavior* (Upper Saddle River, NJ: Prentice Hall, 1998); and G. P. Latham and C. C. Pinder, "Work Motivation Theory and Research at the Dawn of the Twenty-First Century," *Annual Review of Psychology* 56 (2005), pp. 485–516.

4. L. M. Spencer and S. M. Spencer, *Competence at Work: Models for Superior Performance* (New York: Wiley, 1993); and J. A. Conger and D. A. Ready, "Rethinking Leadership Competencies," *Leader to Leader,* Spring 2004, pp. 41–47.

5. Kane, "Special Issue"; S. B. Bacharach and P. Bamberger, "Beyond Situational Constraints: Job Resources Inadequacy and Individual Performance at Work," *Human Resource Management Review* 5, no. 2 (1995), pp. 79–102; and G. Johns, "Commentary: In Praise of Context," *Journal of Organizational Behavior* 22 (2001), pp. 31–42.

6. J. P. Campbell, "The Definition and Measurement of Performance in the New Age," in *The Changing Nature of Performance: Implications for Staffing, Motivation, and Development,* ed. D. R. Ilgen and E. D. Pulakos (San Francisco: Jossey-Bass, 1999), pp. 399–429.

7. J. A. LePine, A. Erez, and D. E. Johnson, "The Nature and Dimensionality of Organizational Citizenship Behavior: A Critical Review and Meta-Analysis," *Journal of Applied Psychology* 87 (February 2002), pp. 52–65; B. Erickson, "Nature Times Nurture: How Organizations Can Optimize Their People's Contributions," *Journal of Organizational Excellence* 24, no. 1 (Winter 2004), pp. 21–30; and M. A. Vey and J. P. Campbell, "In-Role or Extra-Role Organizational Citizenship Behavior: Which Are We Measuring?" *Human Performance* 17, no. 1 (2004), pp. 119–35.

8. W. Ferchland, "Going the Extra Mile," *Tahoe Daily Tribune,* May 31, 2005.

9. P. D. Dunlop and K. Lee, "Workplace Deviance, Organizational Citizenship Behavior, and Business Unit Performance: The Bad Apples Do Spoil the Whole Barrel," *Journal of Organizational Behavior* 25 (2004), pp. 67–80; and R. W. Griffin and A. O'Leary-Kelly, eds., *The Dark Side of Organizational Behavior* (San Francisco: Jossey-Bass, 2004).

10. R. Athey, *It's 2008: Do You Know Where Your Talent Is?* (Deloitte & Touche USA, November 2004).

11. Employment Policy Foundation, "Employee Turnover Rises, Increasing Costs," *EPF Fact Sheet,* March 22, 2005, 1; and F. Hansen, "The Turnover Myth," *Workforce,* June 2005, pp. 34–39.

12. T. R. Mitchell, B. C. Holtom, and T. W. Lee, "How to Keep Your Best Employees: Developing an Effective Retention Policy," *Academy of Management Executive* 15 (November 2001), pp. 96–108.

13. D. A. Harrison and J. J. Martocchio, "Time for Absenteeism: A 20-Year Review of Origins, Offshoots, and Outcomes," *Journal of Management* 24 (Spring 1998), pp. 305–50; and A. Vaananen et al., "Job Characteristics, Physical and Psychological Symptoms, and Social Support as Antecedents of Sickness Absence among Men and Women in the Private Industrial Sector," *Social Science & Medicine* 57, no. 5 (2003), pp. 807–24.

14. R. Woolnough, "The 'My Way' Code," *Financial Management,* July 2003, p. 20; and K. Walters, "Define Your Values," *Business Review Weekly,* April 21, 2005, p. 95.

15. Some of the more popular books that encourage executives to develop values statements include J. C. Collins and J. I. Porras, *Built to Last: Successful Habits of Visionary Companies* (London: Century, 1995); C. A. O'Reilly III and J. Pfeffer, *Hidden Value* (Cambridge, MA: Harvard Business School Press, 2000); and J. M. Kouzes and B. Z. Posner, *The Leadership Challenge,* 3rd ed. (San Francisco: Jossey-Bass, 2002).

16. B. M. Meglino and E. C. Ravlin, "Individual Values in Organizations: Concepts, Controversies, and Research," *Journal of Management* 24, no. 3 (1998), pp. 351–89; B. R. Agle and C. B. Caldwell, "Understanding Research on Values in Business," *Business and Society* 38, no. 3 (September 1999), pp. 326–87; and S. Hitlin and J. A. Pilavin, "Values: Reviving a Dormant Concept," *Annual Review of Sociology* 30 (2004), pp. 359–93.

17. D. Lubinski, D. B. Schmidt, and C. P. Benbow, "A 20-Year Stability Analysis of the Study of Values for Intellectually Gifted Individuals from Adolescence to Adulthood," *Journal of Applied Psychology* 81 (1996), pp. 443–51.

18. B. Kabanoff and J. Daly, "Espoused Values in Organisations," *Australian Journal of Management* 27, special issue (2002), pp. 89–104.

19. S. H. Schwartz, "Universals in the Content and Structure of Values: Theoretical Advances and Empirical Tests in 20 Countries," *Advances in Experimental Social Psychology* 25 (1992), pp. 1–65; D. Spini, "Measurement Equivalence of 10 Value Types from the Schwartz Value Survey across 21 Countries," *Journal of Cross-Cultural Psychology* 34, no. 1 (January 2003), pp. 3–23; and S. H. Schwartz and K. Boehnke, "Evaluating the Structure of Human Values with Confirmatory Factor Analysis," *Journal of Research in Personality* 38, no. 3 (2004), pp. 230–55.

20. G. R. Maio and J. M. Olson, "Values as Truisms: Evidence and Implications," *Journal of Personality and Social Psychology* 74, no. 2 (1998), pp. 294–311; G. R. Maio et al., "Addressing Discrepancies between Values and Behavior: The Motivating Effect of Reasons," *Journal of Experimental Social Psychology* 37, no. 2 (2001), pp. 104–17; B. Verplanken and R. W. Holland, "Motivated Decision Making: Effects of Activation and Self-Centrality of Values on Choices and Behavior," *Journal of Personality and Social Psychology* 82, no. 3 (2002), pp. 434–47; A.

Bardi and S. H. Schwartz, "Values and Behavior: Strength and Structure of Relations," *Personality and Social Psychology Bulletin* 29, no. 10 (October 2003), pp. 1207–20; and M. M. Bernard and G. R. Maio, "Effects of Introspection about Reasons for Values: Extending Research on Values-as-Truisms," *Social Cognition* 21, no. 1 (2003), pp. 1–25.

21. "Keeping Values Top-of-Mind," *Chemical Engineering Progress* 100, no. 9 (September 2004), p. 64.

22. A. L. Kristof, "Person-Organization Fit: An Integrative Review of Its Conceptualizations, Measurement, and Implications," *Personnel Psychology* 49, no. 1 (Spring 1996), pp. 1–49; M. L. Verquer, T. A. Beehr, and S. H. Wagner, "A Meta-Analysis of Relations between Person-Organization Fit and Work Attitudes," *Journal of Vocational Behavior* 63 (2003), pp. 473–89; and J. W. Westerman and L. A. Cyr, "An Integrative Analysis of Person-Organization Fit Theories," *International Journal of Selection and Assessment* 12, no. 3 (September 2004), pp. 252–61.

23. K. F. Alam, "Business Ethics in New Zealand Organizations: Views from the Middle and Lower Level Managers," *Journal of Business Ethics* 22 (November 1999), pp. 145–53; and Aspen Institute, "Scandals, Economy Alter Attitudes of Next Generation Business Leaders, MBA Student Survey Shows," news release, May 20, 2003.

24. T. Simons, "Behavioral Integrity: The Perceived Alignment between Managers' Words and Deeds as a Research Focus," *Organization Science* 13, no. 1 (January–February 2002), pp. 18–35.

25. T. A. Joiner, "The Influence of National Culture and Organizational Culture Alignment on Job Stress and Performance: Evidence from Greece," *Journal of Managerial Psychology* 16 (2001), pp. 229–42; and Z. Aycan, R. N. Kanungo, and J. B. P. Sinha, "Organizational Culture and Human Resource Management Practices: The Model of Culture Fit," *Journal Of Cross-Cultural Psychology* 30 (July 1999), pp. 501–26.

26. D. Oyserman, H. M. Coon, and M. Kemmelmeier, "Rethinking Individualism and Collectivism: Evaluation of Theoretical Assumptions and Meta-Analyses," *Psychological Bulletin 128* (2002), pp. 3–72; C. P. Earley and C. B. Gibson, "Taking Stock in Our Progress on Individualism-Collectivism: 100 Years of Solidarity and Community," *Journal of Management* 24 (May 1998), pp. 265–304;

and F. S. Niles, "Individualism-Collectivism Revisited," *Cross-Cultural Research* 32 (November 1998), pp. 315–41.

27. Oyserman, Coon, and Kemmelmeier, "Rethinking Individualism and Collectivism." The relationship between individualism and collectivism is still being debated. Some researchers suggest that there are different types of individualism and collectivism, and some of these types may be opposites. Others say the lack of association is due to the way we measure these concepts. See E. G. T. Green, J.-C. Deschamps, and D. Paez, "Variation of Individualism and Collectivism within and between 20 Countries," *Journal of Cross-Cultural Psychology* 36, no. 3 (May 2005), pp. 321–39; and S. Oishi et al., "The Measurement of Values across Cultures: A Pairwise Comparison Approach," *Journal of Research in Personality* 39, no. 2 (2005), pp. 299–305.

28. G. Hofstede, *Culture's Consequences: Comparing Values, Behaviors, Institutions, and Organizations across Nations,* 2nd ed. (Thousand Oaks, CA: Sage, 2001).

29. J. Chao, "Culture Clash Looms as Lenovo Gobbles IBM Unit," *Palm Beach Post,* December 19, 2004, p. 3F; and D. Roberts and L. Lee, "East Meets West, Big Time," *Business Week,* May 9, 2005, p. 74.

30. G. Hofstede, *Cultures and Organizations: Software of the Mind* (New York: McGraw-Hill, 1991). Hofstede used the terms *masculinity* and *femininity* for achievement and nurturing orientation, respectively. We have adopted the latter to minimize the sexist perspective of these concepts.

31. J. S. Osland et al., "Beyond Sophisticated Stereotyping: Cultural Sensemaking in Context," *Academy of Management Executive* 14 (February 2000), pp. 65–79; and M. Voronov and J. A. Singer, "The Myth of Individualism-Collectivism: A Critical Review," *Journal of Social Psychology* 142 (August 2002), pp. 461–80.

32. R. B. Wickman, "Interest in Ethics Courses Increases after Corporate Scandals," *Kansas City Star,* July 20, 2003.

33. P. L. Schumann, "A Moral Principles Framework for Human Resource Management Ethics," *Human Resource Management Review* 11 (Spring–Summer 2001), pp. 93–111; J. Boss, *Analyzing Moral Issues,* 3rd ed. (New York: McGraw-Hill, 2005), Chap. 1; and M. G. Velasquez, *Business Ethics: Concepts and Cases,* 6th ed. (Upper Saddle River, NJ: Prentice Hall, 2006), Chap. 2.

34. J. R. Sparks and S. D. Hunt, "Marketing Researcher Ethical Sensitivity: Conceptualization, Measurement, and Exploratory Investigation," *Journal of Marketing* 62 (April 1998), pp. 92–109.

35. Alam, "Business Ethics in New Zealand Organizations"; K. Blotnicky, "Is Business in Moral Decay?" *Chronicle-Herald* (Halifax), June 11, 2000; and B. Stoneman and K. K. Holliday, "Pressure Cooker," *Banking Strategies,* January–February 2001, p. 13.

36. M. S. Schwartz, "A Code of Ethics for Corporate Code of Ethics," *Journal of Business Ethics* 41 (2002), pp. 27–43; and M. S. Schwartz, "Effective Corporate Codes of Ethics: Perceptions of Code Users," *Journal of Business Ethics* 55 (2004), pp. 323–43.

37. P. J. Gnazzo and G. R. Wratney, "Are You Serious About Ethics?" *Across the Board* 40 (July–August 2003), pp. 46ff; B. Schultz, "Ethics under Investigation," *Network World,* April 26, 2004 ; and K. Tyler, "Do the Right Thing," *HR Magazine* 50, no. 2 (February 2005), pp. 99–103.

38. S. Greengard, "Golden Values," *Workforce Management,* March 2005, pp. 52–53.

39. E. Aronson, "Integrating Leadership Styles and Ethical Perspectives," *Canadian Journal of Administrative Sciences* 18 (December 2001), pp. 266–76; and D. R. May et al., "Developing the Moral Component of Authentic Leadership," *Organizational Dynamics* 32 (2003), pp. 247–60. The Vodafone director quotation is from R. Van Lee, L. Fabish, and N. McGaw, "The Value of Corporate Values," *Strategy+Business,* Summer 2005, pp. 1–13.

40. S. Roccas et al., "The Big Five Personality Factors and Personal Values," *Personality and Social Psychology* 28 (June 2002), pp. 789–801.

41. B. Reynolds and K. Karraker, "A Big Five Model of Disposition and Situation Interaction: Why a 'Helpful' Person May Not Always Behave Helpfully," *New Ideas in Psychology* 21 (April 2003), pp. 1–13; and W. Mischel, "Toward an Integrative Science of the Person," *Annual Review of Psychology* 55 (2004), pp. 1–22.

42. K. M. DeNeve and H. Cooper, "The Happy Personality: A Meta-Analysis of 137 Personality Traits and Subjective Well-Being," *Psychological Bulletin* 124 (September 1998), pp. 197–229; T. A. Judge et al., "Personality and Leadership: A Qualitative and Quantitative Review," *Journal of Applied Psychology* 87, no. 4

(2002), pp. 765–80; and T. A. Judge and R. Illies, "Relationship of Personality to Performance Motivation: A Meta-Analytic Review," *Journal of Applied Psychology* 87, no. 4 (2002), pp. 797–807.

43. This historical review and the trait descriptions in this section are discussed in J. M. Digman, "Personality Structure: Emergence of the Five-Factor Model," *Annual Review of Psychology* 41 (1990), pp. 417–40; M. K. Mount and M. R. Barrick, "The Big Five Personality Dimensions: Implications for Research and Practice in Human Resources Management," *Research in Personnel and Human Resources Management* 13 (1995), pp. 153–200; and R. J. Schneider and L. M. Hough, "Personality and Industrial/Organizational Psychology," *International Review of Industrial and Organizational Psychology* 10 (1995), pp. 75–129.

44. Judge and Illies, "Relationship of Personality to Performance Motivation"; and A. Witt, L. A. Burke, and M. R. Barrick, "The Interactive Effects of Conscientiousness and Agreeableness on Job Performance," *Journal of Applied Psychology* 87 (February 2002), pp. 164–69.

45. C. G. Jung, *Psychological Types,* trans. H. G. Baynes (Princeton, NJ: Princeton University Press, 1971); and I. B. Myers, *The Myers-Briggs Type Indicator* (Palo Alto, CA: Consulting Psychologists Press, 1987).

46. M. Gladwell, "Personality Plus," *New Yorker,* September 20, 2004, pp. 42–48; and R. B. Kennedy and D. A. Kennedy, "Using the Myers-Briggs Type Indicator in Career Counseling," *Journal of Employment Counseling* 41, no. 1 (March 2004), pp. 38–44.

47. R. M. Capraro and M. M. Capraro, "Myers-Briggs Type Indicator Score Reliability across Studies: A Meta-Analytic Reliability Generalization Study," *Educational and Psychological Measurement* 62 (August 2002), pp. 590–602; and J. Michael, "Using the Myers-Briggs Type Indicator as a Tool for Leadership Development? Apply with Caution," *Journal of Leadership & Organizational Studies* 10 (Summer 2003), pp. 68–81.

chapter 3

1. J. Lynch and M. Dagostino, "Man in Motion," *People,* August 26, 2002, p. 89; E. Pope, "Domino's Puts Execs on the Line," *Detroit News,* August 1, 2003; D. Knight, "Hands-on CEO Gets IPL Back on Track," *Indianapolis Star,* November 21, 2004; and W. Frey, "Rubbish Boy Doing Well as Junk

Man," *Metro-Vancouver,* April 25, 2005, p. 11.

2. The effect of the target in selective attention is known as *bottom-up selection;* the effect of the perceiver's psychodynamics on this process is known as *top-down selection.* C. E. Connor, H. E. Egeth, and S. Yantis, "Visual Attention: Bottom-up versus Top-Down," *Current Biology* 14, no. 19 (2004), pp. R850-52.

3. A. Mack et al., "Perceptual Organization and Attention," *Cognitive Psychology* 24, no. 4 (1992), pp. 475–501; A. R. Damasio, *Descartes' Error: Emotion, Reason, and the Human Brain* (New York: Putnam Sons, 1994); C. Frith, "A Framework for Studying the Neural Basis of Attention," *Neuropsychologia* 39, no. 12 (2001), pp. 1367–71; and N. Lavie, "Distracted and Confused? Selective Attention under Load," *Trends in Cognitive Sciences* 9, no. 2 (2005), pp. 75–82.

4. C. N. Macrae and G. V. Bodenhausen, "Social Cognition: Thinking Categorically about Others," *Annual Review of Psychology* 51 (2000), pp. 93–120. For literature on the automaticity of the perceptual organization and interpretation process, see J. A. Bargh and M. J. Ferguson, "Beyond Behaviorism: On the Automaticity of Higher Mental Processes," *Psychological Bulletin* 126, no. 6 (2000), pp. 925–45; and M. Gladwell, *Blink: The Power of Thinking without Thinking* (New York: Little, Brown, 2005).

5. E. M. Altmann and B. D. Burns, "Streak Biases in Decision Making: Data and a Memory Model," *Cognitive Systems Research* 6, no. 1 (2005), pp. 5–16. For discussion of cognitive closure and perception, see A. W. Kruglanski and D. M. Webster, "Motivated Closing of the Mind: 'Seizing' and 'Freezing,'" *Psychological Review* 103, no. 2 (1996), pp. 263–83.

6. N. Ambady and R. Rosenthal, "Half a Minute: Predicting Teacher Evaluations from Thin Slices of Nonverbal Behavior and Physical Attractiveness," *Journal of Personality and Social Psychology* 64, no. 3 (March 1993), pp. 431–41. For other research on thin slices, see N. Ambady and R. Rosenthal, "Thin Slices of Expressive Behavior as Predictors of Interpersonal Consequences: A Meta-Analysis," *Psychological Bulletin* 111, no. 2 (1992), pp. 256–74; and N. Ambady et al., "Surgeons' Tone of Voice: A Clue to Malpractice History," *Surgery* 132, no. 1 (July 2002), pp. 5–9.

7. P. M. Senge, *The Fifth Discipline: The Art and Practice of the Learning Organization* (New York: Doubleday

Currency, 1990), Chap. 10; P. N. Johnson-Laird, "Mental Models and Deduction," *Trends in Cognitive Sciences* 5, no. 10 (2001), pp. 434–42; A. B. Markman and D. Gentner, "Thinking," *Annual Review of Psychology* 52 (2001), pp. 223–47; and T. J. Chermack, "Mental Models in Decision Making and Implications for Human Resource Development," *Advances in Developing Human Resources* 5, no. 4 (2003), pp. 408–22.

8. B. E. Ashforth and F. Mael, "Social Identity Theory and the Organization," *Academy of Management Review* 14 (1989), pp. 20–39; M. A. Hogg and D. J. Terry, "Social Identity and Self-Categorization Processes in Organizational Contexts," *Academy of Management Review* 25 (January 2000), pp. 121–40; and S. A. Haslam, R. A. Eggins, and K. J. Reynolds, "The Aspire Model: Actualizing Social and Personal Identity Resources to Enhance Organizational Outcomes," *Journal of Occupational and Organizational Psychology* 76 (2003), pp. 83–113. Although this topic is labeled "social identity theory," it also incorporates an extension of social identity theory, called *self-categorization theory.*

9. J. E. Dutton, J. M. Dukerich, and C. V. Harquail, "Organizational Images and Member Identification," *Administrative Science Quarterly* 39 (June 1994), pp. 239–63; and B. Simon and C. Hastedt, "Self-Aspects as Social Categories: The Role of Personal Importance and Valence," *European Journal of Social Psychology* 29 (1999), pp. 479–87.

10. M. A. Hogg et al., "The Social Identity Perspective: Intergroup Relations, Self-Conception, and Small Groups," *Small Group Research* 35, no. 3 (June 2004), pp. 246–76.

11. S. T. Fiske, "Stereotyping, Prejudice, and Discrimination," in *Handbook of Social Psychology,* ed. D. T. Gilbert, S. T. Fiske, and G. Lindzey, 4th ed. (New York: McGraw-Hill, 1998), 357–411; and Macrae and Bodenhausen, "Social Cognition."

12. C. N. Macrae, A. B. Milne, and G. V. Bodenhausen, "Stereotypes as Energy-Saving Devices: A Peek inside the Cognitive Toolbox," *Journal of Personality and Social Psychology* 66 (1994), pp. 37–47; J. A. Bargh and T. L. Chartrand, "The Unbearable Automaticity of Being," *American Psychologist* 54, no. 7 (July 1999), pp. 462–79; and L. Sinclair and Z. Kunda, "Motivated Stereotyping of Women: She's Fine if She Praised Me but Incompetent if She Criticized Me," *Personality and Social*

Psychology Bulletin 26 (November 2000), pp. 1329–42.

13. A. L. Friedman and S. R. Lyne, "The Beancounter Stereotype: Towards a General Model of Stereotype Generation," *Critical Perspectives on Accounting* 12, no. 4 (2001), pp. 423–51. For discussion of stereotype accuracy, see Y. Lee, L. J. Jussim, and C. R. McCauley, *Stereotype Accuracy: Toward Appreciating Group Differences* (Washington, DC: American Psychological Association, 1996).

14. S. O. Gaines and E. S. Reed, "Prejudice: From Allport to Dubois," *American Psychologist* 50 (February 1995), pp. 96–103; and M. Billig, "Henri Tajfel's 'Cognitive Aspects of Prejudice' and the Psychology of Bigotry," *British Journal of Social Psychology* 41 (2002), pp. 171–88.

15. Bargh and Chartrand, "The Unbearable Automaticity of Being"; and S. T. Fiske, "What We Know Now about Bias and Intergroup Conflict, the Problem of the Century," *Current Directions in Psychological Science* 11, no. 4 (August 2002), pp. 123–28. For recent evidence that shows that intensive training can minimize stereotype activation, see K. Kawakami et al., "Just Say No (to Stereotyping): Effects of Training in the Negation of Stereotypic Associations on Stereotype Activation," *Journal of Personality and Social Psychology* 78, no. 5 (2000), pp. 871–88; and E. A. Plant, B. M. Peruche, and D. A. Butz, "Eliminating Automatic Racial Bias: Making Race Non-Diagnostic for Responses to Criminal Suspects," *Journal of Experimental Social Psychology* 41, no. 2 (2005), pp. 141–56.

16. J. Sinclair, "Breaking Down the Barriers," *The Age* (Melbourne, Australia), January 30, 2002, p. 14; L. Giovanelli, "Gender Divide," *Winston-Salem Journal,* July 3, 2005, p. 1; and V. Reitman, "Caltech to Harvard: Redo the Math," *Los Angeles Times,* June 20, 2005.

17. H. H. Kelley, *Attribution in Social Interaction* (Morristown, NJ: General Learning Press, 1971).

18. R. E. Ployhart and K. H. Ehrhart, "Using Attributions to Understand the Effects of Explanations on Applicant Reactions: Are Reactions Consistent with the Covariation Principle?" *Journal of Applied Social Psychology* 35, no. 2 (February 2005), pp. 259–96.

19. Fundamental attribution error is part of a larger phenomenon known as correspondence bias. See D. T. Gilbert and P. S. Malone, "The Correspondence Bias,"

Psychological Bulletin 117, no. 1 (1995), pp. 21–38.

20. D. S. Krull et al., "The Fundamental Fundamental Attribution Error: Correspondence Bias in Individualist and Collectivist Cultures," *Personality and Social Psychology Bulletin* 25, no. 10 (October 1999), pp. 1208–19; and R. E. Nisbett, *The Geography of Thought: How Asians and Westerners Think Differently—and Why* (New York: Free Press, 2003), Chap. 5.

21. E. W. K. Tsang, "Self-Serving Attributions in Corporate Annual Reports: A Replicated Study," *Journal of Management Studies* 39, no. 1 (January 2002), pp. 51–65.

22. A. R. Remo, "Nurture the Good to Create an Asset," *Philippine Daily Inquirer,* December 6, 2004.

23. Similar models are presented in D. Eden, "Self-Fulfilling Prophecy as a Management Tool: Harnessing Pygmalion," *Academy of Management Review* 9 (1984), pp. 64–73; R. H. G. Field and D. A. Van Seters, "Management by Expectations (MBE): The Power of Positive Prophecy," *Journal of General Management* 14 (Winter 1988), pp. 19–33; and D. O. Trouilloud et al., "The Influence of Teacher Expectations on Student Achievement in Physical Education Classes: Pygmalion Revisited," *European Journal of Social Psychology* 32 (2002), pp. 591–607.

24. D. Eden, "Interpersonal Expectations in Organizations," in *Interpersonal Expectations: Theory, Research, and Applications* (Cambridge, UK: Cambridge University Press, 1993), 154–78.

25. D. Eden, "Pygmalion Goes to Boot Camp: Expectancy, Leadership, and Trainee Performance," *Journal of Applied Psychology* 67 (1982), pp. 194–99; and R. P. Brown and E. C. Pinel, "Stigma on My Mind: Individual Differences in the Experience of Stereotype Threat," *Journal of Experimental Social Psychology* 39, no. 6 (2003), pp. 626–33.

26. S. Madon, L. Jussim, and J. Eccles, "In Search of the Powerful Self-Fulfilling Prophecy," *Journal of Personality and Social Psychology* 72, no. 4 (April 1997), pp. 791–809; A. E. Smith, L. Jussim, and J. Eccles, "Do Self-Fulfilling Prophecies Accumulate, Dissipate, or Remain Stable over Time?" *Journal of Personality and Social Psychology* 77, no. 3 (1999), pp. 548–65; and S. Madon et al., "Self-Fulfilling Prophecies: The Synergistic Accumulative Effect of Parents' Beliefs on Children's Drinking Behavior,"

Psychological Science 15, no. 12 (2005), pp. 837–45.

27. S. S. White and E. A. Locke, "Problems with the Pygmalion Effect and Some Proposed Solutions," *Leadership Quarterly* 11 (Autumn 2000), pp. 389–415. For literature on positive organizational behavior, see K. Cameron, J. E. Dutton, and R. E. Quinn, *Positive Organizational Scholarship: Foundations of a New Discipline* (San Francisco: Berrett Koehler, 2003).

28. T. F. Pettigrew, "Intergroup Contact Theory," *Annual Review of Psychology* 49 (1998), pp. 65–85; S. Brickson, "The Impact of Identity Orientation on Individual and Organizational Outcomes in Demographically Diverse Settings," *Academy of Management Review* 25 (January 2000), pp. 82–101; and J. Dixon and K. Durrheim, "Contact and the Ecology of Racial Division: Some Varieties of Informal Segregation," *British Journal of Social Psychology* 42 (March 2003), pp. 1–23.

29. T. Phillips, "UPS Sends Executives on Diversity Sabbaticals," *Indianapolis Business Journal,* November 2004, p. 10; S. Teicher, "Corner-Office Volunteers," *Christian Science Monitor,* July 19, 2004, pp. 14–15; "Walking in Their Shoes," *Training,* June 2005, p. 19; and C. Darden, "Pursuing Excellence-Constructive Dissatisfaction," *Executive Speeches,* February 2005, p. 1.

30. W. G. Stephen and K. A. Finlay, "The Role of Empathy in Improving Intergroup Relations," *Journal of Social Issues* 55 (Winter 1999), pp. 729–43; S. K. Parker and C. M. Axtell, "Seeing Another Viewpoint: Antecedents and Outcomes of Employee Perspective Taking," *Academy of Management Journal* 44 (December 2001), pp. 1085–100; and G. J. Vreeke and I. L. van der Mark, "Empathy, an Integrative Model," *New Ideas in Psychology* 21, no. 3 (2003), pp. 177–207.

31. T. W. Costello and S. S. Zalkind, *Psychology in Administration: A Research Orientation* (Englewood Cliffs, NJ: Prentice Hall, 1963), pp. 45–46; and J. M. Kouzes and B. Z. Posner, *The Leadership Challenge,* 3rd ed. (San Francisco: Jossey-Bass, 2002), Chap. 3.

32. J. Luft, *Group Processes* (Palo Alto: Mayfield Publishing, 1984). For a variation of this model, see J. Hall, "Communication Revisited," *California Management Review* 15 (Spring 1973), pp. 56–67.

33. L. C. Miller and D. A. Kenny, "Reciprocity of Self-Disclosure at the Individual and Dyadic Levels: A Social Relations Analysis," *Journal of Personality and Social Psychology* 50 (1986), pp. 713–19.

34. Teicher, "Corner-Office Volunteers."

35. "Wipro: Leadership in the Midst of Rapid Growth," *Knowledge@Wharton,* February 2005.

36. I. Nonaka and H. Takeuchi, *The Knowledge-Creating Company* (New York: Oxford University Press, 1995); and P. Duguid, " 'The Art of Knowing': Social and Tacit Dimensions of Knowledge and the Limits of the Community of Practice," *The Information Society* 21 (2005), pp. 109–18.

37. B. F. Skinner, *About Behaviorism* (New York: Alfred A. Knopf, 1974); J. Komaki, T. Coombs, and S. Schepman, "Motivational Implications of Reinforcement Theory," in *Motivation and Leadership at Work,* ed. R. M. Steers, L. W. Porter, and G. A. Bigley (New York: McGraw-Hill, 1996), pp. 34–52; and R. G. Miltenberger, *Behavior Modification: Principles and Procedures* (Pacific Grove, CA: Brooks/Cole, 1997).

38. T. K. Connellan, *How to Improve Human Performance* (New York: Harper & Row, 1978), pp. 48–57; and F. Luthans and R. Kreitner, *Organizational Behavior Modification and Beyond* (Glenview, IL: Scott, Foresman, 1985), pp. 85–88.

39. Miltenberger, *Behavior Modification,* Chaps. 4–6.

40. T. R. Hinkin and C. A. Schriesheim, "If You Don't Hear from Me You Know You Are Doing Fine," *Cornell Hotel & Restaurant Administration Quarterly* 45, no. 4 (November 2004), pp. 362–72.

41. L. K. Trevino, "The Social Effects of Punishment in Organizations: A Justice Perspective," *Academy of Management Review* 17 (1992), pp. 647–76; and L. E. Atwater et al., "Recipient and Observer Reactions to Discipline: Are Managers Experiencing Wishful Thinking?" *Journal of Organizational Behavior* 22, no. 3 (May 2001), pp. 249–70.

42. G. P. Latham and V. L. Huber, "Schedules of Reinforcement: Lessons from the Past and Issues for the Future," *Journal of Organizational Behavior Management* 13 (1992), pp. 125–49; and B. A. Williams, "Challenges to Timing-Based Theories of Operant Behavior," *Behavioural Processes* 62 (April 2003), pp. 115–23.

43. ExxonMobil, *UK and Ireland Corporate Citizenship,* August 2004; and "ExxonMobil Recognises Employees, Contractors for Outstanding Performances," *Bernama Daily Malaysian News,* June 27, 2005.

44. T. C. Mawhinney, "Philosophical and Ethical Aspects of Organizational Behavior Management: Some Evaluative Feedback," *Journal of Organizational Behavior Management* 6 (Spring 1984), pp. 5–13; and "New Warnings on the Fine Points of Safety Incentives," *Pay for Performance Report,* September 2002.

45. A. Bandura, *Social Foundations of Thought and Action: A Social Cognitive Theory* (Englewood Cliffs, NJ: Prentice Hall, 1986).

46. A. Pescuric and W. C. Byham, "The New Look of Behavior Modeling," *Training & Development* 50 (July 1996), pp. 24–30.

47. M. E. Schnake, "Vicarious Punishment in a Work Setting," *Journal of Applied Psychology* 71 (1986), pp. 343–45; Trevino, "The Social Effects of Punishment in Organizations"; and J. B. DeConinck, "The Effect of Punishment on Sales Managers' Outcome Expectancies and Responses to Unethical Sales Force Behavior," *American Business Review* 21, no. 2 (June 2003), pp. 135–40.

48. A. Bandura, "Self-Reinforcement: Theoretical and Methodological Considerations," *Behaviorism* 4 (1976), pp. 135–55; C. A. Frayne and J. M. Geringer, "Self-Management Training for Improving Job Performance: A Field Experiment Involving Salespeople," *Journal of Applied Psychology* 85, no. 3 (June 2000), pp. 361–72; and J. B. Vancouver and D. V. Day, "Industrial and Organisation Research on Self-Regulation: From Constructs to Applications," *Applied Psychology* 54, no. 2 (April 2005), pp. 155–85.

49. D. A. Kolb, *Experiential Learning* (Englewood Cliffs, NJ: Prentice Hall, 1984); S. Gherardi, D. Nicolini, and F. Odella, "Toward a Social Understanding of How People Learn in Organizations," *Management Learning* 29 (September 1998), pp. 273–97; and D. A. Kolb, R. E. Boyatzis, and C. Mainemelis, "Experiential Learning Theory: Previous Research and New Directions," in *Perspectives on Thinking, Learning, and Cognitive Styles,* ed. R. J. Sternberg and L. F. Zhang (Mahwah, NJ: Lawrence Erlbaum, 2001), 227–48.

50. W. E. Baker and J. M. Sinkula, "The Synergistic Effect of Market Orientation and Learning Orientation," *Journal of the Academy of Marketing Science* 27, no. 4 (Fall 1999), pp. 411–27; and R. J. Calantone, S. T. Cavusgil, and Y. Zhao, "Learning Orientation, Firm Innovation Capability, and Firm Performance,"

Industrial Marketing Management 31, no. 6 (September 2002), pp. 515–24.

51. R. W. Revans, *The Origin and Growth of Action Learning* (London: Chartwell Bratt, 1982), pp. 626–27; and M. J. Marquardt, *Optimizing the Power of Action Learning: Solving Problems and Building Leaders in Real Time* (Palo Alto, CA: Davies-Black, 2004).

chapter 4

1. S. C. Lundin, H. Paul, and J. Christensen, *Fish! A Remarkable Way to Boost Morale and Improve Results* (New York: Hyperion Press, 2000); S. C. Lundin, H. Paul, and J. Christensen, *Fish! Tales: Bite-Sized Stories, Unlimited Possibilities* (New York: Hyperion Press, 2002); V. Watson, "Having Fun while Improving Customer Service," Sprint news release, June 13, 2002; K. Mellen, "Fish! Tackles Workplace Morale," *Daily Hampshire Gazette.* February 24 2003; and E. D. Thompson, "Motivating Employees," *Credit Union Magazine* 69 (April 2003), p. 56.

2. A. R. Damasio, *Descartes' Error: Emotion, Reason, and the Human Brain* (New York: Putnam Sons, 1994); P. Ekman, "Basic Emotions," in *Handbook of Cognition and Emotion,* ed. T. Dalgleish and M. Power (San Francisco: Jossey-Bass, 1999), pp. 45–60; and D. S. Massey, "A Brief History of Human Society: The Origin and Role of Emotion in Social Life," *American Sociological Review* 67 (February 2002), pp. 1–29.

3. The definition presented here is constructed from information in the following sources: N. M. Ashkanasy, W. J. Zerbe, and C. E. J. Hartel, "Introduction: Managing Emotions in a Changing Workplace," in *Managing Emotions in the Workplace,* ed. N. M. Ashkanasy, W. J. Zerbe, and C. E. J. Hartel (Armonk, NY: M. E. Sharpe, 2002), pp. 3–18; and H. M. Weiss, "Conceptual and Empirical Foundations for the Study of Affect at Work," in *Emotions in the Workplace,* ed. R. G. Lord, R. J. Klimoski, and R. Kanfer (San Francisco: Jossey-Bass, 2002), pp. 20–63.

4. R. B. Zajonc, "Emotions," in *Handbook of Social Psychology,* ed. D. T. Gilbert, S. T. Fiske, and L. Gardner (New York: Oxford University Press, 1998), pp. 591–634.

5. A. H. Eagly and S. Chaiken, *The Psychology of Attitudes* (Orlando, FL: Harcourt Brace Jovanovich, 1993); and A. P. Brief, *Attitudes in and around Organizations* (Thousand Oaks, CA: Sage, 1998).

6. H. M. Weiss and R. Cropanzano, "Affective Events Theory: A Theoretical

Discussion of the Structure, Causes, and Consequences of Affective Experiences at Work," *Research in Organizational Behavior* 18 (1996), pp. 1–74; C. D. Fisher, "Mood and Emotions While Working: Missing Pieces of Job Satisfaction?" *Journal of Organizational Behavior* 21 (2000), pp. 185–202; M. Perugini and R. P. Bagozzi, "The Role of Desires and Anticipated Emotions in Goal-Directed Behaviors: Broadening and Deepening the Theory of Planned Behavior," *British Journal of Social Psychology* 40 (March 2001), pp. 79–98; and J. D. Morris et al., "The Power of Affect: Predicting Intention," *Journal of Advertising Research* 42 (May–June 2002), pp. 7–17.

7. We refer to a singular "cognitive (logical reasoning) center" and "emotional center" to simplify the discussion, whereas an emerging view is that both the emotional and rational "centers" are distributed throughout the brain.

8. J. A. Bargh and M. J. Ferguson, "Beyond Behaviorism: On the Automaticity of Higher Mental Processes," *Psychological Bulletin* 126, no. 6 (2000), pp. 925–45; R. H. Fazio, "On the Automatic Activation of Associated Evaluations: An Overview," *Cognition and Emotion* 15, no. 2 (2001), pp. 115–41; and M. Gladwell, *Blink: The Power of Thinking without Thinking* (New York: Little, Brown, 2005).

9. Damasio, *Descartes' Error;* J. E. LeDoux, "Emotion Circuits in the Brain," *Annual Review of Neuroscience* 23 (2000), pp. 155–84; and R. J. Dolan, "Emotion, Cognition, and Behavior," *Science* 298, no. 5596 (November 8, 2002), pp. 1191–94.

10. B. Niedt, "Wegmans Reaches No. 1 on List of Workplaces," *Post Standard* (Syracuse), January 11, 2005, p. A1; and M. Sommer and J. F. Bonfatti, "Wegmans Employees Feel Challenged, Valued," *Buffalo News,* January 16, 2005, p. B7.

11. G. R. Maio, V. M. Esses, and D. W. Bell, "Examining Conflict between Components of Attitudes: Ambivalence and Inconsistency Are Distinct Constructs," *Canadian Journal of Behavioural Science* 32, no. 2 (2000), pp. 71–83.

12. P. C. Nutt, *Why Decisions Fail* (San Francisco: Berrett-Koehler, 2002); S. Finkelstein, *Why Smart Executives Fail* (New York: Viking, 2003); and P. C. Nutt, "Search during Decision Making," *European Journal of Operational Research* 160 (2005), pp. 851–76.

13. L. Festinger, *A Theory of Cognitive Dissonance* (Evanston, IL: Row, Peterson, 1957); and A. D. Galinsky, J. Stone, and

J. Cooper, "The Reinstatement of Dissonance and Psychological Discomfort Following Failed Affirmation," *European Journal of Social Psychology* 30, no. 1 (2000), pp. 123–47.

14. B. E. Ashforth and R. H. Humphrey, "Emotional Labor in Service Roles: The Influence of Identity," *Academy of Management Review* 18 (1993), pp. 88–115. For a recent review of the emotional labor concept, see T. M. Glomb and M. J. Tews, "Emotional Labor: A Conceptualization and Scale Development," *Journal of Vocational Behavior* 64, no. 1 (2004), pp. 1–23.

15. J. Strasburg, "The Making of a Grand Hotel," *San Francisco Chronicle,* March 25 2001, p. B1. The antecedents of emotional labor are discussed in J. A. Morris and D. C. Feldman, "The Dimensions, Antecedents, and Consequences of Emotional Labor," *Academy of Management Review* 21 (1996), pp. 986–1010; and D. Zapf, "Emotion Work and Psychological Well-Being: A Review of the Literature and Some Conceptual Considerations," *Human Resource Management Review* 12 (2002), pp 237–68.

16. E. Forman, "'Diversity Concerns Grow as Companies Head Overseas,' Consultant Says," *Sun-Sentinel* (Fort Lauderdale, FL), June 26, 1995. Cultural differences in emotional expression are discussed in F. Trompenaars, "Resolving International Conflict: Culture and Business Strategy," *Business Strategy Review* 7, no. 3 (Autumn 1996), pp. 51–68; and F. Trompenaars and C. Hampden-Turner, *Riding the Waves of Culture,* 2nd ed. (New York: McGraw-Hill, 1998), Chap. 6.

17. R. Hallowell, D. Bowen, and C.-I. Knoop, "Four Seasons Goes to Paris," *Academy of Management Executive* 16, no. 4 (November 2002), pp. 7–24.

18. This relates to the automaticity of emotion, which is summarized in P. Winkielman and K. C. Berridge, "Unconscious Emotion," *Current Directions in Psychological Science* 13, no. 3 (2004), pp. 120–23; and K. N. Ochsner and J. J. Gross, "The Cognitive Control of Emotions," *Trends in Cognitive Sciences* 9, no. 5 (May 2005), pp. 242–49.

19. W. J. Zerbe, "Emotional Dissonance and Employee Well-Being," in *Managing Emotions in the Workplace,* ed. N. M. Ashkanasy, W. J. Zerbe, and C. E. J. Hartel (Armonk, NY: M. E. Sharpe, 2002), pp. 189–214; and R. Cropanzano, H. M. Weiss, and S. M. Elias, "The Impact of Display Rules and Emotional Labor on Psychological Well-Being at Work,"

Research in Occupational Stress and Well Being 3 (2003), pp. 45–89.

20. C. M. Brotheridge and A. A. Grandey, "Emotional Labor and Burnout: Comparing Two Perspectives of 'People Work," *Journal of Vocational Behavior* 60 (2002), pp. 17–39; Zapf, "Emotion Work and Psychological Well-Being"; and J. M. Diefendorff, M. H. Croyle, and R. H. Gosserand, "The Dimensionality and Antecedents of Emotional Labor Strategies," *Journal of Vocational Behavior* 66, no. 2 (2005), pp. 339–57.

21. A. Schwitzerlette, "Cici's Pizza Coming to Beckley," *Register-Herald* (Beckley, WV), August 24, 2003.

22. J. Stuller, "Unconventional Smarts," *Across the Board* 35 (January 1998), pp. 22–23; and T. Schwartz, "How Do You Feel?" *Fast Company,* June 2000, p. 296.

23. J. D. Mayer, P. Salovey, and D. R. Caruso, "Models of Emotional Intelligence," in *Handbook of Human Intelligence,* ed. R. J. Sternberg, 2nd ed. (New York: Cambridge University Press, 2000), pp. 396–420. This definition is also recognized in C. Cherniss, "Emotional Intelligence and Organizational Effectiveness," in *The Emotionally Intelligent Workplace,* ed. C. Cherniss and D. Goleman (San Francisco: Jossey-Bass, 2001), pp. 3–12.

24. These four dimensions of emotional intelligence are discussed in detail in D. Goleman, R. Boyatzis, and A. McKee, *Primal Leadership* (Boston: Harvard Business School Press, 2002), Chap. 3. Slight variations of this model are presented in R. Boyatzis, D. Goleman, and K. S. Rhee, "Clustering Competence in Emotional Intelligence," in *The Handbook of Emotional Intelligence,* ed. R. Bar-On and J. D. A. Parker (San Francisco: Jossey-Bass, 2000), pp. 343–62; and D. Goleman, "An EI-Based Theory of Performance," in *The Emotionally Intelligent Workplace,* ed. C. Cherniss and D. Goleman (San Francisco: Jossey-Bass, 2001), pp. 27–44.

25. H. A. Elfenbein and N. Ambady, "Predicting Workplace Outcomes from the Ability to Eavesdrop on Feelings," *Journal of Applied Psychology* 87, no. 5 (2002), pp. 963–71.

26. The hierarchical nature of the four EI dimensions is discussed by Goleman but is more explicit in the Salovey and Mayer model. See D. R. Caruso and P. Salovey, *The Emotionally Intelligent Manager* (San Francisco: Jossey-Bass, 2004).

27. P. N. Lopes et al., "Emotional Intelligence and Social Interaction," *Personality and Social Psychology Bulletin*

30, no. 8 (August 2004), pp. 1018–34; and C. S. Daus and N. M. Ashkanasy, "The Case for the Ability-Based Model of Emotional Intelligence in Organizational Behavior," *Journal of Organizational Behavior* 26 (2005), pp. 453–66. Not all studies have found that EI predicts job performance. See S. Newsome, A. L. Day, and V. M. Catano, "Assessing the Predictive Validity of Emotional Intelligence," *Personality and Individual Differences,* no. 29 (December 2000), pp. 1005–16.

28. S. C. Clark, R. Callister, and R. Wallace, "Undergraduate Management Skills Courses and Students' Emotional Intelligence," *Journal of Management Education* 27, no. 1 (February 2003), pp. 3–23; and B. Carey, "Measuring Emotions," *Journal Gazette* (Fort Wayne, IN), April 20, 2004, p. 8B.

29. E. A. Locke, "The Nature and Causes of Job Satisfaction," in *Handbook of Industrial and Organizational Psychology,* ed. M. Dunnette (Chicago: Rand McNally, 1976), pp. 1297–350; and H. M. Weiss, "Deconstructing Job Satisfaction: Separating Evaluations, Beliefs and Affective Experiences," *Human Resource Management Review,* no. 12 (2002), pp. 173–94.

30. T. Lemke, "Poll Data Show Americans' Long-Term Positive Attitude toward Jobs," *Washington Times,* August 28, 2001, p. B8; and F. Newport, "Most American Workers Satisfied with Their Jobs," *Gallup News Service,* August 29, 2002.

31. M. J. Withey and W. H. Cooper, "Predicting Exit, Voice, Loyalty, and Neglect," *Administrative Science Quarterly,* no. 34 (1989), pp. 521–39; W. H. Turnley and D. C. Feldman, "The Impact of Psychological Contract Violations on Exit, Voice, Loyalty, and Neglect," *Human Relations,* no. 52 (July 1999), pp. 895–922; and L. Van Dyne, S. Ang, and I. C. Botero, "Conceptualizing Employee Silence and Employee Voice as Multidimensional Constructs," *Journal of Management Studies* 40, no. 6 (2003), pp. 1359–92.

32. T. R. Mitchell, B. C. Holtom, and T. W. Lee, "How to Keep Your Best Employees: Developing an Effective Retention Policy," *Academy of Management Executive* 15 (November 2001), pp. 96–108; and C. P. Maertz and M. A. Campion, "Profiles of Quitting: Integrating Process and Content Turnover Theory," *Academy of Management Journal* 47, no. 4 (2004), pp. 566–82.

33. M. J. Withey and I. R. Gellatly, "Situational and Dispositional Determinants of Exit, Voice, Loyalty and Neglect," *Proceedings of the Administrative Sciences*

Association of Canada, Organizational Behaviour Division, June 1998; and M. J. Withey and I. R. Gellatly, "Exit, Voice, Loyalty and Neglect: Assessing the Influence of Prior Effectiveness and Personality," *Proceedings of the Administrative Sciences Association of Canada, Organizational Behaviour Division* 20 (1999), pp. 110–19.

34. T. A. Judge et al., "The Job Satisfaction-Job Performance Relationship: A Qualitative and Quantitative Review," *Psychological Bulletin* 127 (2001), pp. 376–407; and L. Saari and T. A. Judge, "Employee Attitudes and Job Satisfaction," *Human Resource Management* 43, no. 4 (Winter 2004), pp. 395–407.

35. "The Greatest Briton in Management and Leadership," *Personnel Today,* February 18, 2003, p. 20. The Wegmans motto is mentioned in R. Levering and M. Moskowitz, "The Best 100 Companies to Work For," *Fortune,* January 24, 2005, pp. 90–96.

36. J. I. Heskett, W. E. Sasser, and L. A. Schlesinger, *The Service Profit Chain* (New York: Free Press, 1997); W.-C. Tsai and Y.-M. Huang, "Mechanisms Linking Employee Affective Delivery and Customer Behavioral Intentions," *Journal of Applied Psychology* 87, no. 5 (2002), pp. 1001–8; and G. A. Gelade and S. Young, "Test of a Service Profit Chain Model in the Retail Banking Sector," *Journal of Occupational & Organizational Psychology* 78 (2005), pp. 1–22.

37. P. Guenzi and O. Pelloni, "The Impact of Interpersonal Relationships on Customer Satisfaction and Loyalty to the Service Provider," *International Journal of Service Industry Management* 15, no. 3–4 (2004). pp. 365–84; and S. J. Bell, S. Auh, and K. Smalley, "Customer Relationship Dynamics: Service Quality and Customer Loyalty in the Context of Varying Levels of Customer Expertise and Switching Costs," *Journal of the Academy of Marketing Science* 33, no. 2 (Spring 2005), pp. 169–83.

38. T. DeCotiis et al., "How Outback Steakhouse Created a Great Place to Work, Have Fun, and Make Money," *Journal of Organizational Excellence* 23, no. 4 (Autumn 2004), pp. 23–33.

39. R. T. Mowday, L. W. Porter, and R. M. Steers, *Employee Organization Linkages: The Psychology of Commitment, Absenteeism, and Turnover* (New York: Academic Press, 1982); and J. P. Meyer and N. J. Allen, *Commitment in the Workplace: Theory, Research, and Application* (Thousand Oaks, CA: Sage, 1997).

40. A. A. Luchak and I. R. Gellatly, "What Kind of Commitment Does a Final-Earnings Pension Plan Elicit?" *Relations Industrielles* 56 (Spring 2001), pp. 394–417.

41. J. P. Meyer et al., "Affective, Continuance, and Normative Commitment to the Organization: A Meta-Analysis of Antecedents, Correlates, and Consequences," *Journal of Vocational Behavior* 61 (2002), pp. 20–52; and M. Riketta, "Attitudinal Organizational Commitment and Job Performance: A Meta-Analysis," *Journal of Organizational Behavior* 23 (2002), pp. 257–66.

42. J. P. Meyer et al., "Organizational Commitment and Job Performance: It's the Nature of the Commitment That Counts," *Journal of Applied Psychology* 74 (1989), pp. 152–56; Z. X. Chen and A. M. Francesco, "The Relationship between the Three Components of Commitment and Employee Performance in China," *Journal of Vocational Behavior* 62, no. 3 (2003), pp. 490–510; and D. M. Powell and J. P. Meyer, "Side-Bet Theory and the Three-Component Model of Organizational Commitment," *Journal of Vocational Behavior* 65, no. 1 (2004), pp. 157–77.

43. J. E. Finegan, "The Impact of Person and Organizational Values on Organizational Commitment," *Journal of Occupational and Organizational Psychology* 73 (June 2000), pp. 149–69; and B. Kuvaas, "Employee Ownership and Affective Organizational Commitment: Employees' Perceptions of Fairness and Their Preference for Company Shares over Cash," *Scandinavian Journal of Management* 19 (2003), pp. 193–212.

44. T. J. Kalliath, A. C. Bluedorn, and M. J. Strube, "A Test of Value Congruence Effects," *Journal of Organizational Behavior* 20, no. 7 (1999), pp. 1175–98; and J. W. Westerman and L. A. Cyr, "An Integrative Analysis of Person-Organization Fit Theories," *International Journal of Selection and Assessment* 12, no. 3 (September 2004), pp. 252–61.

45. S. Ashford, C. Lee, and P. Bobko, "Content, Causes, and Consequences of Job Insecurity: A Theory-Based Measure and Substantive Test," *Academy of Management Journal* 32 (1989), pp. 803–29; and D. M. Rousseau et al., "Not So Different after All: A Cross-Discipline View of Trust," *Academy of Management Review* 23 (1998), pp. 393–404.

46. T. S. Heffner and J. R. Rentsch, "Organizational Commitment and Social Interaction: A Multiple Constituencies Approach," *Journal of Vocational Behavior* 59 (2001), pp. 471–90.

47. E. Frauenheim, "For Developers, It's Not All Fun and Games," *CNET News.com,* November 18, 2004; and A. Pham, "Video Game Programmers Get Little Time to Play," *Houston Chronicle,* November 21, 2004, p. 6.

48. J. C. Quick et al., *Preventive Stress Management in Organizations* (Washington, DC: American Psychological Association, 1997), pp. 3–4; and R. S. DeFrank and J. M. Ivancevich, "Stress on the Job: An Executive Update," *Academy of Management Executive* 12 (August 1998), pp. 55–66.

49. Quick et al., *Preventive Stress Management in Organizations,* pp. 5–6; and B. L. Simmons and D. L. Nelson, "Eustress at Work: The Relationship between Hope and Health in Hospital Nurses," *Health Care Management Review* 26, no. 4 (October 2001), pp. 7ff.

50. H. Selye, *Stress without Distress* (Philadelphia: J. B. Lippincott, 1974).

51. S. E. Taylor, R. L. Repetti, and T. Seeman, "Health Psychology: What Is an Unhealthy Environment and How Does It Get under the Skin?" *Annual Review of Psychology* 48 (1997), pp. 411–47.

52. D. Ganster, M. Fox, and D. Dwyer, "Explaining Employees' Health Care Costs: A Prospective Examination of Stressful Job Demands, Personal Control, and Physiological Reactivity," *Journal of Applied Psychology* 86 (May 2001), pp. 954–64; M. Kivimaki et al., "Work Stress and Risk of Cardiovascular Mortality: Prospective Cohort Study of Industrial Employees," *British Medical Journal* 325 (October 19, 2002), pp. 857–60; and A. Rosengren et al., "Association of Psychosocial Risk Factors with Risk of Acute Myocardial Infarction in 11,119 Cases and 13,648 Controls from 52 Countries (the Interheart Study): Case-Control Study," *The Lancet* 364, no. 9438 (September 11, 2004), pp. 953–62.

53. R. C. Kessler, "The Effects of Stressful Life Events on Depression," *Annual Review of Psychology* 48 (1997), pp. 191–214; L. Greenburg and J. Barling, "Predicting Employee Aggression against Coworkers, Subordinates and Supervisors: The Roles of Person Behaviors and Perceived Workplace Factors," *Journal of Organizational Behavior* 20 (1999), pp. 897–913; M. Jamal and V. V. Baba, "Job Stress and Burnout among Canadian Managers and Nurses: An Empirical Examination," *Canadian Journal of Public Health* 91, no. 6 (November–December 2000), pp. 454–58; and L. Tourigny, V. V. Baba, and T. R.

Lituchy, "Job Burnout among Airline Employees in Japan: A Study of the Buffering Effects of Absence and Supervisory Support," *International Journal of Cross Cultural Management* 5, no. 1 (April 2005), pp. 67–85.

54. K. Danna and R. W. Griffin, "Health and Well-Being in the Workplace: A Review and Synthesis of the Literature," *Journal of Management,* Spring 1999, pp. 357–84.

55. T. Goldenberg, "Thousands of Workers Intimidated on Job: Study," *Montreal Gazette,* June 11, 2005, p. A9. The definition presented here is a slight variation of the Quebec anti-harassment legislation. See www.cnt.gouv.qc.ca. For related definitions and discussion of workplace incivility, see H. Cowie et al., "Measuring Workplace Bullying," *Aggression and Violent Behavior* 7 (2002), pp. 33–51; C. M. Pearson and C. L. Porath, "On the Nature, Consequences and Remedies of Workplace Incivility: No Time for 'Nice'? Think Again," *Academy of Management Executive* 19, no. 1 (February 2005), pp. 7–18.

56. V. Schultz, "Reconceptualizing Sexual Harassment," *Yale Law Journal* 107 (April 1998), pp. 1683–805; and M. Rotundo, D.-H. Nguyen, and P. R. Sackett, "A Meta-Analytic Review of Gender Differences in Perceptions of Sexual Harassment," *Journal of Applied Psychology* 86 (October 2001), pp. 914–22.

57. B. K. Hunnicutt, *Kellogg's Six-Hour Day* (Philadelphia: Temple University Press, 1996); E. Galinsky et al., *Overwork in America: When the Way We Work Becomes Too Much* (New York: Families and Work Institute, March 2005); and R. G. Netemeyer, J. G. Maxham III, and C. Pullig, "Conflicts in the Work-Family Interface: Links to Job Stress, Customer Service Employee Performance, and Customer Purchase Intent," *Journal of Marketing* 69 (April 2005), pp. 130–45.

58. J. Ryall, "Japan Wakes up to Fatal Work Ethic," *Scotland on Sunday,* June 15, 2003, p. 22; and C. B. Meek, "The Dark Side of Japanese Management in the 1990s: Karoshi and Ijime in the Japanese Workplace," *Journal of Managerial Psychology* 19, no. 3 (2004), pp. 312–31.

59. L. Wahyudi S., "'Traffic Congestion Makes Me Crazy," *Jakarta Post,* March 18, 2003. The effect of traffic congestion on stress is reported in G. W. Evans, R. E. Wener, and D. Phillips, "The Morning Rush Hour: Predictability and Commuter Stress," *Environment and Behavior* 34 (July 2002), pp. 521–30.

60. F. Kittel et al., "Job Conditions and Fibrinogen in 14,226 Belgian Workers: The Belstress Study," *European Heart Journal* 23 (2002), pp. 1841–48; and S. K. Parker, "Longitudinal Effects of Lean Production on Employee Outcomes and the Mediating Role of Work Characteristics," *Journal of Applied Psychology* 88, no. 4 (2003), pp. 620–34.

61. S. J. Havlovic and J. P. Keenen, "Coping with Work Stress: The Influence of Individual Differences; Handbook on Job Stress [Special Issue]," *Journal of Social Behavior and Personality* 6 (1991), pp. 199–212.

62. S. S. Luthar, D. Cicchetti, and B. Becker, "The Construct of Resilience: A Critical Evaluation and Guidelines for Future Work," *Child Development* 71, no. 3 (May–June 2000), pp. 543–62; F. Luthans, "The Need for and Meaning of Positive Organizational Behavior," *Journal of Organizational Behavior* 23 (2002), pp. 695–706; and G. A. Bonanno, "Loss, Trauma, and Human Resilience: Have We Underestimated the Human Capacity to Thrive after Extremely Aversive Events?" *American Psychologist* 59, no. 1 (2004), pp. 20–28.

63. M. Beasley, T. Thompson, and J. Davidson, "Resilience in Response to Life Stress: The Effects of Coping Style and Cognitive Hardiness," *Personality and Individual Differences* 34, no. 1 (2003), pp. 77–95; M. M. Tugade, B. L. Fredrickson, and L. Feldman Barrett, "Psychological Resilience and Positive Emotional Granularity: Examining the Benefits of Positive Emotions on Coping and Health," *Journal of Personality* 72, no. 6 (2004), pp. 1161–90; I. Tsaousis and I. Nikolaou, "Exploring the Relationship of Emotional Intelligence with Physical and Psychological Health Functioning," *Stress and Health* 21, no. 2 (2005), pp. 77–86; and L. Campbell-Sills, S. L. Cohan, and M. B. Stein, "Relationship of Resilience to Personality, Coping, and Psychiatric Symptoms in Young Adults," *Behaviour Research and Therapy,* in press (2006).

64. Y. Kim and L. Seidlitz, "Spirituality Moderates the Effect of Stress on Emotional and Physical Adjustment," *Personality and Individual Differences* 32, no. 8 (June 2002), pp. 1377–90; and G. E. Richardson, "The Metatheory of Resilience and Resiliency," *Journal of Clinical Psychology* 58, no. 3 (2002), pp. 307–21.

65. L. T. Eby et al., "Work and Family Research in IO/OB: Content Analysis and Review of the Literature (1980–2002)," *Journal of Vocational Behavior* 66, no. 1 (2005), pp. 124–97.

66. Y. Iwasaki et al., "A Short-Term Longitudinal Analysis of Leisure Coping Used by Police and Emergency Response Service Workers," *Journal of Leisure Research* 34 (July 2002), pp. 311–39.

67. M. Waung, "The Effects of Self-Regulatory Coping Orientation on Newcomer Adjustment and Job Survival," *Personnel Psychology* 48 (1995), pp. 633–50; and A. M. Saks and B. E. Ashforth, "Proactive Socialization and Behavioral Self-Management," *Journal of Vocational Behavior* 48 (1996), pp. 301–23.

68. The effectiveness of these program are reported in numerous studies, including V. A. Barnes, F. A. Treiber, and M. H. Johnson, "Impact of Transcendental Meditation on Ambulatory Blood Pressure in African-American Adolescents," *American Journal of Hypertension* 17, no. 4 (2004), pp. 366–69; and W. M. Ensel and N. Lin, "Physical Fitness and the Stress Process," *Journal of Community Psychology* 32, no. 1 (January 2004), pp. 81–101.

69. S. Moreland, "Strike up Creativity," *Crain's Cleveland Business,* April 14, 2003, p. 3.

70. S. E. Taylor et al., "Biobehavioral Responses to Stress in Females: Tend-and-Befriend, Not Fight-or-Flight," *Psychological Review* 107, no. 3 (July 2000), pp. 411–29; and R. Eisler and D. S. Levine, "Nurture, Nature, and Caring: We Are Not Prisoners of Our Genes," *Brain and Mind* 3 (2002), pp. 9–52.

chapter 5

1. British Columbia Government, "Recognition Best Practices," www.bcpublicservice.ca/awards/best_practices/best_practices_index.htm, accessed April 10 2005; K. Rives, "Ways to Thank Your Colleagues," *News & Observer* (Raleigh), March 30, 2003, p. E1; J. Weiss, "Romney Offers Surprise Calls Governor Enjoys Getting Personal to Salute Workers," *Boston Globe,* March 14, 2003, p. B1; D. Creelman, "Interview: Bob Catell & Kenny Moore," *HR.com,* February 2005; and T. J. Ryan, "Just Rewards," *Sporting Goods Business,* June 2005.

2. C. C. Pinder, *Work Motivation in Organizational Behavior* (Upper Saddle River, NJ: Prentice Hall, 1998); and R. M. Steers, R. T. Mowday, and D. L. Shapiro, "The Future of Work Motivation Theory," *Academy of Management Review* 29 (2004), pp. 379–87.

3. T. V. Sewards and M. A. Sewards, "Fear and Power-Dominance Drive Motivation: Neural Representations and Pathways Mediating Sensory and Mnemonic Inputs, and Outputs to Premotor Structures," *Neuroscience and Biobehavioral Reviews* 26 (2002), pp. 553–79; and K. C. Berridge, "Motivation Concepts in Behavioral Neuroscience," *Physiology & Behavior* 81, no. 2 (2004), pp. 179–209.

4. R. J. Lowry, *The Journals of A. H. Maslow* (Monterey, CA: Brooks-Cole, 1979).

5. A. H. Maslow, "A Preface to Motivation Theory," *Psychosomatic Medicine* 5 (1943), pp. 85–92.

6. A. H. Maslow, "A Theory of Human Motivation," *Psychological Review* 50 (1943), pp. 370–96; and A. H. Maslow, *Motivation and Personality* (New York: Harper & Row, 1954).

7. D. T. Hall and K. E. Nougaim, "An Examination of Maslow's Need Hierarchy in an Organizational Setting," *Organizational Behavior and Human Performance* 3, no. 1 (1968), p. 12; M. A. Wahba and L. G. Bridwell, "Maslow Reconsidered: A Review of Research on the Need Hierarchy Theory," *Organizational Behavior and Human Performance* 15 (1976), pp. 212–40; E. L. Betz, "Two Tests of Maslow's Theory of Need Fulfillment," *Journal of Vocational Behavior* 24, no. 2 (1984), pp. 204–20; and P. A. Corning, "Biological Adaptation in Human Societies: A 'Basic Needs' Approach," *Journal of Bioeconomics* 2, no. 1 (2000), pp. 41–86.

8. B. A. Agle and C. B. Caldwell, "Understanding Research on Values in Business," *Business and Society* 38 (September 1999), pp. 326–87; B. Verplanken and R. W. Holland, "Motivated Decision Making: Effects of Activation and Self-Centrality of Values on Choices and Behavior," *Journal of Personality and Social Psychology* 82, no. 3 (2002), pp. 434–47; and S. Hitlin and J. A. Pilavin, "Values: Reviving a Dormant Concept," *Annual Review of Sociology* 30 (2004), pp. 359–93.

9. P. R. Lawrence and N. Nohria, *Driven: How Human Nature Shapes Our Choices* (San Francisco: Jossey-Bass, 2002).

10. R. E. Baumeister and M. R. Leary, "The Need to Belong: Desire for Interpersonal Attachments as a Fundamental Human Motivation," *Psychological Bulletin* 117 (1995), pp. 497–529.

11. This explanation refers to a singular "rational center" and "emotional center." While many scholars do refer to a single

location for most emotional transactions, an emerging view is that both the emotional and rational centers are distributed throughout the brain. See J. Schulkin, B. L. Thompson, and J. B. Rosen, "Demythologizing the Emotions: Adaptation, Cognition, and Visceral Representations of Emotion in the Nervous System," *Brain and Cognition* 52, no. 1 (2003), pp. 15–23.

12. A. R. Damasio, *Descartes' Error: Emotion, Reason, and the Human Brain* (New York: Putnam Sons, 1994); J. E. LeDoux, "Emotion Circuits in the Brain," *Annual Review of Neuroscience* 23 (2000), pp. 155–84; and P. Winkielman and K. C. Berridge, "Unconscious Emotion," *Current Directions in Psychological Science* 13, no. 3 (2004), pp. 120–23.

13. Lawrence and Nohria, *Driven,* pp. 145–47.

14. Lawrence and Nohria, *Driven,* Chap. 11.

15. Human Resources and Skill Development Canada, "Organizational Profiles: Pancanadian Petroleum," Ottawa, July 2005, www.hrsdc.gc.ca/en/lp/spila/wlb/ell/12pancanadian_petroleum.shtml, accessed July 2005.

16. Expectancy theory of motivation in work settings originated in V. H. Vroom, *Work and Motivation* (New York: Wiley, 1964). The version of expectancy theory presented here was developed by Edward Lawler. Lawler's model provides a clearer presentation of the model's three components. P-to-O expectancy is similar to "instrumentality" in Vroom's original expectancy theory model. The difference is that instrumentality is a correlation whereas P-to-O expectancy is a probability. See J. P. Campbell et al., *Managerial Behavior, Performance, and Effectiveness* (New York: McGraw-Hill, 1970); E. E. Lawler III, *Motivation in Work Organizations* (Monterey, CA: Brooks-Cole, 1973); and D. A. Nadler and E. E. Lawler, "Motivation: A Diagnostic Approach," in *Perspectives on Behavior in Organizations,* ed. J. R. Hackman, E. E. Lawler III, and L. W. Porter, 2nd ed. (New York: McGraw-Hill, 1983), pp. 67–78.

17. M. Zeelenberg et al., "Emotional Reactions to the Outcomes of Decisions: The Role of Counterfactual Thought in the Experience of Regret and Disappointment," *Organizational Behavior and Human Decision Processes* 75, no. 2 (1998), pp. 117–41; B. A. Mellers, "Choice and the Relative Pleasure of Consequences," *Psychological Bulletin* 126, no. 6 (November 2000), pp. 910–24; and R. P.

Bagozzi, U. M. Dholakia, and S. Basuroy, "How Effortful Decisions Get Enacted: The Motivating Role of Decision Processes, Desires, and Anticipated Emotions," *Journal of Behavioral Decision Making* 16, no. 4 (October 2003), pp. 273–95.

18. Nadler and Lawler, "Motivation: A Diagnostic Approach."

19. T. Janz, "Manipulating Subjective Expectancy through Feedback: A Laboratory Study of the Expectancy-Performance Relationship," *Journal of Applied Psychology* 67 (1982), pp. 480–85; K. A. Karl, A. M. O' Leary-Kelly, and J. J. Martoccio, "The Impact of Feedback and Self-Efficacy on Performance in Training," *Journal of Organizational Behavior* 14 (1993), pp. 379–94; and R. G. Lord, P. J. Hanges, and E. G. Godfrey, "Integrating Neural Networks into Decision-Making and Motivational Theory: Rethinking Vie Theory," *Canadian Psychology* 44, no. 1 (2003), pp. 21–38.

20. A. G. Marshall et al., "Cross-Cultural Comparisons: Using Expectancy Theory to Assess Student Motivation: An International Replication," *Issues in Accounting Education* 13, no. 1 (1998), pp. 139–56; M. L. Ambrose and C. T. Kulik, "Old Friends, New Faces: Motivation Research in the 1990s," *Journal of Management* 25 (May 1999), pp. 231–92; C. L. Haworth and P. E. Levy, "The Importance of Instrumentality Beliefs in the Prediction of Organizational Citizenship Behaviors," *Journal of Vocational Behavior* 59 (August 2001), pp. 64–75; and Y. Chen, A. Gupta, and L. Hoshower, "Marketing Students' Perceptions of Teaching Evaluations: An Application of Expectancy Theory," *Marketing Education Review* 14, no. 2 (Summer 2004), pp. 23–36.

21. L. Hollman, "Seeing the Writing on the Wall," *Call Center,* August 2002, p. 37.

22. G. P. Latham, "Goal Setting: A Five-Step Approach to Behavior Change," *Organizational Dynamics* 32, no. 3 (2003), pp. 309–18; and E. A. Locke and G. P. Latham, *A Theory of Goal Setting and Task Performance* (Englewood Cliffs, NJ: Prentice Hall, 1990). Some practitioners rely on the acronym "SMART" goals, referring to goals that are specific, measurable, acceptable, relevant, and timely. However, this list overlaps key elements (e.g., specific goals *are* measurable), overlooks the key elements of challenging and feedback-related, and includes "timely," which usually applies to feedback, not the goals themselves.

23. A. Prayag, "All Work And More Play," *Business Line (The Hindu),* June 13, 2005, p. 4; S. Rajagopalan, "Bangalore to Hawaii, an All-Paid Holiday," *Hindustan Times,* May 7, 2005; and J. A. Singh, "Hola for Success!" *Business Standard* (India), June 4, 2005.

24. K. R. Thompson, W. A. Hochwarter, and N. J. Mathys, "Stretch Targets: What Makes Them Effective?" *Academy of Management Executive* 11 (August 1997), pp. 48–60; and S. Kerr and S. Landauer, "Using Stretch Goals to Promote Organizational Effectiveness and Personal Growth: General Electric and Goldman Sachs," *Academy of Management Executive* 18, no. 4 (2004), pp. 134–38.

25. A. Li and A. B. Butler, "The Effects of Participation in Goal Setting and Goal Rationales on Goal Commitment: An Exploration of Justice Mediators," *Journal of Business and Psychology* 19, no. 1 (Fall 2004): 37–51

26. Locke and Latham, *A Theory of Goal Setting and Task Performance,* Chaps. 6 and 7; and J. Wegge, "Participation in Group Goal Setting: Some Novel Findings and a Comprehensive Model as a New Ending to an Old Story," *Applied Psychology: An International Review* 49 (2000), pp. 498–516.

27. M. London, E. M. Mone, and J. C. Scott, "Performance Management and Assessment: Methods for Improved Rater Accuracy and Employee Goal Setting," *Human Resource Management* 43, no. 4 (Winter 2004), pp. 319–36; and G. P. Latham and C. C. Pinder, "Work Motivation Theory and Research at the Dawn of the Twenty-First Century," *Annual Review of Psychology* 56 (2005), pp. 485–516.

28. S. P. Brown, S. Ganesan, and G. Challagalla, "Self-Efficacy as a Moderator of Information-Seeking Effectiveness," *Journal of Applied Psychology* 86, no. 5 (2001), pp. 1043–51; P. A. Heslin and G. P. Latham, "The Effect of Upward Feedback on Managerial Behaviour," *Applied Psychology: An International Review* 53, no. 1 (2004), pp. 23–37; D. Van-Dijk and A. N. Kluger, "Feedback Sign Effect on Motivation: Is It Moderated by Regulatory Focus?" *Applied Psychology: An International Review* 53, no. 1 (2004), pp. 113–35; and J. E. Bono and A. E. Colbert, "Understanding Responses to Multi-Source Feedback: The Role of Core Self-Evaluations," *Personnel Psychology* 58, no. 1 (Spring 2005), pp. 171–203.

29. J. B. Miner, "The Rated Importance, Scientific Validity, and Practical Usefulness

of Organizational Behavior Theories: A Quantitative Review," *Academy of Management Learning and Education* 2, no. 3 (2003), pp. 250–68. Also see C. C. Pinder, *Work Motivation in Organizational Behavior* (Upper Saddle River, NJ: Prentice Hall, 1997), p. 384.

30. P. M. Wright, "Goal Setting and Monetary Incentives: Motivational Tools That Can Work Too Well," *Compensation and Benefits Review* 26 (May–June 1994), pp. 41–49; and E. A. Locke and G. P. Latham, "Building a Practically Useful Theory of Goal Setting and Task Motivation: A 35-Year Odyssey," *American Psychologist* 57, no. 9 (2002), pp. 705–17.

31. A. Lue, "Women Seethe over Gender Gap in Salaries," *Taipei Times,* March 6, 2003.

32. J. S. Adams, "Toward an Understanding of Inequity," *Journal of Abnormal and Social Psychology* 67 (1963), pp. 422–36; R. T. Mowday, "Equity Theory Predictions of Behavior in Organizations," in *Motivation and Work Behavior,* ed. L. W. Porter and R. M. Steers, 5th ed. (New York: McGraw-Hill, 1991), pp.111–31; R. G. Cropanzano and J. Greenberg, "Progress in Organizational Justice: Tunneling through the Maze," in *International Review of Industrial and Organizational Psychology,* ed. C. L. Cooper and I. T. Robertson (New York: Wiley, 1997), pp. 317–72; and L. A. Powell, "Justice Judgments as Complex Psychocultural Constructions: An Equity-Based Heuristic for Mapping Two- and Three-Dimensional Fairness Representations in Perceptual Space," *Journal of Cross-Cultural Psychology* 36, no. 1 (January 2005), pp. 48–73.

33. C. T. Kulik and M. L. Ambrose, "Personal and Situational Determinants of Referent Choice," *Academy of Management Review* 17 (1992), pp. 212–37; and G. Blau, "Testing the Effect of Level and Importance of Pay Referents on Pay Level Satisfaction," *Human Relations* 47 (1994), pp. 1251–68.

34. T. P. Summers and A. S. DeNisi, "In Search of Adams' Other: Reexamination of Referents Used in the Evaluation of Pay," *Human Relations* 43 (1990), pp. 497–511.

35. Y. Cohen-Charash and P. E. Spector, "The Role of Justice in Organizations: A Meta-Analysis," *Organizational Behavior and Human Decision Processes* 86 (November 2001), pp. 278–321.

36. M. Ezzamel and R. Watson, "Pay Comparability across and within UK Boards: An Empirical Analysis of the Cash Pay Awards to CEOs and Other Board Members," *Journal of Management Studies* 39, no. 2 (March 2002), pp. 207–32; and J. Fizel, A. C. Krautman, and L. Hadley, "Equity and Arbitration in Major League Baseball," *Managerial and Decision Economics* 23, no. 7 (October–November 2002), pp. 427–35.

37. Cohen-Charash and Spector, "The Role of Justice in Organizations: A Meta-Analysis"; J. A. Colquitt et al., "Justice at the Millennium: A Meta-Analytic Review of 25 Years of Organizational Justice Research," *Journal of Applied Psychology* 86 (2001), pp. 425–45.

38. J. Greenberg and E. A. Lind, "The Pursuit of Organizational Justice: From Conceptualization to Implication to Application," in *Industrial and Organizational Psychology: Linking Theory with Practice,* ed. C. L. Cooper and E. A. Locke (London: Blackwell, 2000), pp. 72–108. For recent studies of voice and injustice, see K. Roberts and K. S. Markel, "Claiming in the Name of Fairness: Organizational Justice and the Decision to File for Workplace Injury Compensation," *Journal of Occupational Health Psychology* 6 (October 2001), pp. 332–47; and J. B. Olson-Buchanan and W. R. Boswell, "The Role of Employee Loyalty and Formality in Voicing Discontent," *Journal of Applied Psychology* 87, no. 6 (2002), pp. 1167–74.

39. J. R. Edwards, J. A. Scully, and M. D. Brtek, "The Nature and Outcomes of Work: A Replication and Extension of Interdisciplinary Work-Design Research," *Journal of Applied Psychology* 85, no. 6 (2000), pp. 860–68; F. P. Morgeson and M. A. Campion, "Minimizing Tradeoffs When Redesigning Work: Evidence from a Longitudinal Quasi-Experiment," *Personnel Psychology* 55, no. 3 (Autumn 2002), pp. 589–612.

40. D. Whitford, "A Human Place to Work," *Fortune,* January 8, 2001, pp. 108–19.

41. H. Fayol, *General and Industrial Management,* trans. C. Storrs (London: Pitman, 1949); E. E. Lawler III, *Motivation in Work Organizations* (Monterey, CA: Brooks-Cole, 1973), Chap. 7; and M. A. Campion, "Ability Requirement Implications of Job Design: An Interdisciplinary Perspective," *Personnel Psychology* 42 (1989),pp. 1–24.

42. C. R. Walker and R. H. Guest, *The Man on the Assembly Line* (Cambridge, MA: Harvard University Press, 1952); W. F. Dowling, "Job Redesign on the Assembly Line: Farewell to Blue-Collar Blues?" *Organizational Dynamics* (Autumn 1973), pp. 51–67; and E. E. Lawler III, *High-Involvement Management* (San Francisco: Jossey-Bass, 1986).

43. J. R. Hackman and G. Oldham, *Work Redesign* (Reading, MA: Addison-Wesley, 1980).

44. J. E. Champoux, "A Multivariate Test of the Job Characteristics Theory of Work Motivation," *Journal of Organizational Behavior* 12, no. 5 (September 1991), pp. 431–46; and R. B. Tiegs, L. E. Tetrick, and Y. Fried, "Growth Need Strength and Context Satisfactions as Moderators of the Relations of the Job Characteristics Model," *Journal of Management* 18, no. 3 (September 1992), pp. 575–93.

45. M. A. Campion and C. L. McClelland, "Follow-up and Extension of the Interdisciplinary Costs and Benefits of Enlarged Jobs," *Journal of Applied Psychology* 78 (1993), pp. 339–51; and N. G. Dodd and D. C. Ganster, "The Interactive Effects of Variety, Autonomy, and Feedback on Attitudes and Performance," *Journal of Organizational Behavior* 17 (1996), pp. 329–47.

46. J. R. Hackman et al., "A New Strategy for Job Enrichment," *California Management Review* 17, no. 4 (1975), pp. 57–71; and R. W. Griffin, *Task Design: An Integrative Approach* (Glenview, IL: Scott Foresman, 1982).

47. P. E. Spector and S. M. Jex, "Relations of Job Characteristics from Multiple Data Sources with Employee Affect, Absence, Turnover Intentions, and Health," *Journal of Applied Psychology* 76 (1991), pp. 46–53; P. Osterman, "How Common Is Workplace Transformation and Who Adopts It?" *Industrial and Labor Relations Review* 47 (1994), pp. 173–88; and R. Saavedra and S. K. Kwun, "Affective States in Job Characteristics Theory," *Journal of Organizational Behavior* 21 (2000), pp. 131–46.

48. Hackman and Oldham, *Work Redesign,* pp. 137–38.

49. A. Hertting et al., "Personnel Reductions and Structural Changes in Health Care: Work-Life Experiences of Medical Secretaries," *Journal of Psychosomatic Research* 54 (February 2003), pp. 161–70.

50. Business Wire, "WKRN-TV and KRON-TV to Become First U.S. Broadcast Stations to Utilize Video Journalism Model to Maximize News Gathering Capabilities and Branding," news release, San Francisco, June 29, 2005; and DV Dojo, "Michael Rosenblum," www.dvdojo.com/who.php, accessed 27 July 2005.

51. B. Lewis, "Westjet—a Crazy Idea That Took Off," *Vancouver Province,* October 21,

2001; and P. Grescoe, *Flight Path* (Toronto: John Wiley & Sons Canada, 2004).

52. This definition is based on G. M. Spreitzer and R. E. Quinn, *A Company of Leaders: Five Disciplines for Unleashing the Power in Your Workforce* (San Francisco: Jossey-Bass, 2001). However, most elements of this definition appear in other discussions of empowerment. See, for example, R. Forrester, "Empowerment: Rejuvenating a Potent Idea," *Academy of Management Executive* 14 (August 2000), pp. 67–80; W. A. Randolph, "Re-Thinking Empowerment: Why Is It So Hard to Achieve?" *Organizational Dynamics* 29 (November 2000), pp. 94–107; and S. T. Menon, "Employee Empowerment: An Integrative Psychological Approach," *Applied Psychology: An International Review* 50 (2001), pp. 153–80.

53. C. S. Koberg et al., "Antecedents and Outcomes of Empowerment," *Group and Organization Management* 24 (1999), pp. 71–91; and Y. Melhem, "The Antecedents of Customer-Contact Employees' Empowerment," *Employee Relations* 26, no. 1/2 (2004), pp. 72–93.

54. B. J. Niehoff et al., "The Influence of Empowerment and Job Enrichment on Employee Loyalty in a Downsizing Environment," *Group and Organization Management* 26 (March 2001), pp. 93–113; J. Yoon, "The Role of Structure and Motivation for Workplace Empowerment: The Case of Korean Employees," *Social Psychology Quarterly* 64 (June 2001), pp. 195–206; and T. D. Wall, J. L. Cordery, and C. W. Clegg, "Empowerment, Performance, and Operational Uncertainty: A Theoretical Integration," *Applied Psychology: An International Review* 51 (2002), pp. 146–69.

55. G. M. Spreitzer, "Social Structural Characteristics of Psychological Empowerment," *Academy of Management Journal* 39 (April 1996), pp. 483–504; J. Godard, "High Performance and the Transformation of Work? The Implications of Alternative Work Practices for the Experience and Outcomes of Work," *Industrial & Labor Relations Review* 54 (July 2001), pp. 776–805; and P. A. Miller, P. Goddard, and H. K. Spence Laschinger, "Evaluating Physical Therapists' Perception of Empowerment Using Kanter's Theory of Structural Power in Organizations," *Physical Therapy* 81 (December 2001). pp. 1880–88.

56. J.-C. Chebat and P. Kollias, "The Impact of Empowerment on Customer Contact Employees' Role in Service Organizations," *Journal of Service Research* 3 (August 2000), pp. 66–81; and H. K. S. Laschinger,

J. Finegan, and J. Shamian, "The Impact of Workplace Empowerment, Organizational Trust on Staff Nurses' Work Satisfaction and Organizational Commitment," *Health Care Management Review* 26 (Summer 2001), pp. 7–23.

chapter 6

1.   "NASA Managers Differed over Shuttle Strike," *Reuters,* July 22, 2003; Columbia Accident Investigation Board, *Report, Volume 1* (Washington, DC: Government Printing Office, August 2003); C. Gibson, "Columbia: The Final Mission," *NineMSN,* July 13, 2003; S. Jefferson, "NASA Let Arrogance on Board," *Palm Beach Post,* August 30, 2003; and R. J. Smith, "NASA Culture, Columbia Probers Still Miles Apart," *Washington Post,* August 22, 2003, p. A3.

2.   F. A. Shull Jr., A. L. Delbecq, and L. L. Cummings, *Organizational Decision Making* (New York: McGraw-Hill, 1970), p. 31.

3.   This model is adapted from several sources, including P. F. Drucker, *The Practice of Management* (New York: Harper & Brothers, 1954); H. A. Simon, *The New Science of Management Decision* (New York: Harper & Row, 1960); H. Mintzberg, D. Raisinghani, and A. Théorét, "The Structure of 'Unstructured' Decision Processes," *Administrative Science Quarterly* 21 (1976), pp. 246–75. Greek, Roman, and Chinese history on rational choice is described in R. E. Nisbett, *The Geography of Thought: How Asians and Westerners Think Differently—and Why* (New York: Free Press, 2003).

4.   Drucker, *The Practice of Management,* pp. 353–57; and B. M. Bass, *Organizational Decision Making* (Homewood, IL: Irwin, 1983), Chap. 3.

5.   I. L. Janis, *Crucial Decisions* (New York: Free Press, 1989), pp. 35–37; and W. Zhongtuo, "Meta-Decision Making: Concepts and Paradigm," *Systematic Practice and Action Research* 13, no. 1 (February 2000), pp. 111–15.

6.   J. G. March and H. A. Simon, *Organizations* (New York: John Wiley & Sons, 1958).

7.   N. Schwarz, "Social Judgment and Attitudes: Warmer, More Social, and Less Conscious," *European Journal of Social Psychology* 30 (2000), pp. 149–76; and N. M. Ashkanasy and C. E. J. Hartel, "Managing Emotions in Decision-Making," in *Managing Emotions in the Workplace,* ed. N. M. Ashkanasy, W. J. Zerbe, and C. E. J. Hartel (Armonk, NY: M. E. Sharpe, 2002).

8.   A. Howard, "Opinion," *Computing,* July 8, 1999, p. 18.

9.   P. Winkielman and K. C. Berridge, "Unconscious Emotion," *Current Directions in Psychological Science* 13, no. 3 (2004), pp. 120–23; and A. Bechara and A. R. Damasio, "The Somatic Marker Hypothesis: A Neural Theory of Economic Decision," *Games and Economic Behavior* 52, no. 2 (2005), pp. 336–72.

10. T. K. Das and B. S. Teng, "Cognitive Biases and Strategic Decision Processes: An Integrative Perspective," *Journal Of Management Studies* 36, no. 6 (November 1999), pp. 757–78; P. Bijttebier, H. Vertommen, and G. V. Steene, "Assessment of Cognitive Coping Styles: A Closer Look at Situation-Response Inventories," *Clinical Psychology Review* 21, no. 1 (2001), pp. 85–104; and P. C. Nutt, "Expanding the Search for Alternatives during Strategic Decision-Making," *Academy of Management Executive* 18, no. 4 (November 2004), pp. 13–28.

11. A. Hertzfeld, "1984," www.folklore.org, accessed July 31, 2005; and M. McCarthy, "Top 20 in 20 Years: Apple Computer— 1984," www.adweek.com/adweek/creative/top20_20years/index.jsp, accessed January 16, 2003.

12. P. C. Nutt, *Why Decisions Fail* (San Francisco: Berrett-Koehler, 2002); and S. Finkelstein, *Why Smart Executives Fail* (New York: Viking, 2003).

13. E. Witte, "Field Research on Complex Decision-Making Processes—the Phase Theorum," *International Studies of Management and Organization,* 1972, pp. 156–82; and J. A. Bargh and T. L. Chartrand, "The Unbearable Automaticity of Being," *American Psychologist* 54, no. 7 (July 1999), pp. 462–79.

14. H. A. Simon, *Administrative Behavior,* 2nd ed. (New York: Free Press, 1957); and H. A. Simon, "Rational Decision Making in Business Organizations," *American Economic Review* 69, no. 4 (September 1979), pp. 493–513.

15. D. Sandahl and C. Hewes, "Decision Making at Digital Speed," *Pharmaceutical Executive* 21 (August 2001), p. 62.

16. Simon, *Administrative Behavior,* pp. xxv, 80–84.

17. A. L. Brownstein, "Biased Predecision Processing," *Psychological Bulletin* 129, no. 4 (2003), pp. 545–68.

18. H. A. Simon, "Rational Choice and the Structure of Environments," *Psychological Review* 63 (1956), pp. 129–38; and H. Schwartz, "Herbert Simon and Behavioral

Economics," *Journal of Socio-Economics* 31 (2002), pp. 181–89.

19. J. P. Forgas and J. M. George, "Affective Influences on Judgments and Behavior in Organizations: An Information Processing Perspective," *Organizational Behavior and Human Decision Processes* 86 (September 2001), pp. 3–34; and G. Loewenstein and J. S. Lerner, "The Role of Affect in Decision Making," in *Handbook of Affective Sciences,* ed. R. J. Davidson, K. R. Scherer, and H. H. Goldsmith (New York: Oxford University Press, 2003), pp. 619–42.

20. M. T. Pham, "The Logic of Feeling," *Journal of Consumer Psychology* 14 (September 2004), pp. 360–69; and N. Schwarz, "Metacognitive Experiences in Consumer Judgment and Decision Making," *Journal of Consumer Psychology* 14 (September 2004), pp. 332–49.

21. L. Sjöberg, "Intuitive vs. Analytical Decision Making: Which Is Preferred?" *Scandinavian Journal of Management* 19 (2003), pp. 17–29.

22. G. Klein, *Intuition at Work* (New York: Currency/Doubleday, 2003), pp. 3–7.

23. W. H. Agor, "The Logic of Intuition," *Organizational Dynamics,* Winter 1986, pp. 5–18; H. A. Simon, "Making Management Decisions: The Role of Intuition and Emotion," *Academy of Management Executive,* February 1987, pp. 57–64; and O. Behling and N. L. Eckel, "Making Sense out of Intuition," *Academy of Management Executive* 5 (February 1991), pp. 46–54.

24. M. D. Lieberman, "Intuition: A Social Cognitive Neuroscience Approach," *Psychological Bulletin* 126 (2000), pp. 109–37; Klein, *Intuition at Work;* and E. Dane and M. G. Pratt, "Intuition: Its Boundaries and Role in Organizational Decision Making" in *Academy of Management Best Papers Proceedings,* New Orleans, 2004, pp. A1–A6.

25. Y. Ganzach, A. H. Kluger, and N. Klayman, "Making Decisions from an Interview: Expert Measurement and Mechanical Combination," *Personnel Psychology* 53 (Spring 2000), pp. 1–20; and A. M. Hayashi, "When to Trust Your Gut," *Harvard Business Review* 79 (February 2001), pp. 59–65. Evidence of high failure rates from quick decisions is reported in P. C. Nutt, "Search during Decision Making," *European Journal of Operational Research* 160 (2005), pp. 851–76.

26. P. Goodwin and G. Wright, "Enhancing Strategy Evaluation in Scenario Planning: A Role for Decision Analysis," *Journal of Management Studies* 38 (January 2001), pp.

1–16; and R. Bradfield et al., "The Origins and Evolution of Scenario Techniques in Long Range Business Planning," *Futures* 37, no. 8 (2005), pp. 795–812.

27. G. Whyte, "Escalating Commitment to a Course of Action: A Reinterpretation," *Academy of Management Review* 11 (1986), pp. 311–21; and J. Brockner, "The Escalation of Commitment to a Failing Course of Action: Toward Theoretical Progress," *Academy of Management Review* 17, no. 1 (January 1992), pp. 39–61.

28. P. Ayton and H. Arkes, "Call It Quits," *New Scientist,* June 20, 1998; M. Fackler, "Tokyo's Newest Subway Line a Saga of Hubris, Humiliation," *Associated Press Newswires,* July 20, 1999; and M. Keil and R. Montealegre, "Cutting Your Losses: Extricating Your Organization When a Big Project Goes Awry," *Sloan Management Review,* no. 41 (Spring 2000), pp. 55–68. An excellent overview of the Scottish parliament affair is available at "Holyrood Inquiry," BBC News, news.bbc.co.uk/1/hi/scotland/3619533.stm, accessed May 4, 2004.

29. F. D. Schoorman and P. J. Holahan, "Psychological Antecedents of Escalation Behavior: Effects of Choice, Responsibility, and Decision Consequences," *Journal of Applied Psychology* 81 (1996), pp. 786–93.

30. G. Whyte, "Escalating Commitment in Individual and Group Decision Making: A Prospect Theory Approach," *Organizational Behavior and Human Decision Processes* 54 (1993), pp. 430–55; and D. J. Sharp and S. B. Salter, "Project Escalation and Sunk Costs: A Test of the International Generalizability of Agency and Prospect Theories," *Journal of International Business Studies* 28, no. 1 (1997), pp. 101–21.

31. J. D. Bragger et al., "When Success Breeds Failure: History, Hysteresis, and Delayed Exit Decisions," *Journal of Applied Psychology* 88, no. 1 (2003), pp. 6–14. A second logical reason for escalation, called the martingale strategy, is described in J. A. Aloysius, "Rational Escalation of Costs by Playing a Sequence of Unfavorable Gambles: The Martingale," *Journal of Economic Behavior & Organization* 51 (2003), pp. 111–29.

32. I. Simonson and B. M. Staw, "De-Escalation Strategies: A Comparison of Techniques for Reducing Commitment to Losing Courses of Action," *Journal of Applied Psychology* 77 (1992), pp. 419–26; and M. Keil and D. Robey, "Turning around Troubled Software Projects: An Exploratory Study of the Deescalation of Commitment to Failing Courses of Action," *Journal of*

Management Information Systems (Spring 1999), pp. 63–87.

33. M. Fenton-O'Creevy, "Employee Involvement and the Middle Manager: Saboteur or Scapegoat?" *Human Resource Management Journal* 11 (2001), pp. 24–40. Also see V. H. Vroom and A. G. Jago, *The New Leadership: Managing Participation in Organizations* (Englewood Cliffs, NJ: Prentice Hall, 1988).

34. K. T. Dirks, L. L. Cummings, and J. L. Pierce, "Psychological Ownership in Organizations: Conditions under Which Individuals Promote and Resist Change," *Research in Organizational Change and Development* 9 (1996), pp. 1–23; A. Kleingeld, H. Van Tuijl, and J. A. Algera, "Participation in the Design of Performance Management Systems: A Quasi-Experimental Field Study," *Journal of Organizational Behavior* 25, no. 7 (2004), pp. 831–51; and A. G. Robinson and D. M. Schroeder, *Ideas Are Free* (San Francisco: Berrett-Koehler, 2004).

35. M. Bruno, "Macon: Big Acclaim for a Small Facility," *Boeing Frontiers Online,* June 2005.

36. G. P. Latham, D. C. Winters, and E. A. Locke, "Cognitive and Motivational Effects of Participation: A Mediator Study," *Journal of Organizational Behavior* 15 (1994), pp. 49–63; and J. A. Wagner III et al., "Cognitive and Motivational Frameworks in U.S. Research on Participation: A Meta-Analysis of Primary Effects," *Journal of Organizational Behavior,* no. 18 (1997), pp. 49–65.

37. B. Nussbaum, "Get Creative! How to Build Innovative Companies," *Business Week,* August 1, 2005, p. 60; and J. Tylee, "Procter's Creative Gamble," *Campaign,* March 18, 2005, pp. 24–26.

38. J. Zhou and C. E. Shalley, "Research on Employee Creativity: A Critical Review and Directions for Future Research," *Research in Personnel and Human Resources Management* 22 (2003), pp. 165–217; and M. A. Runco, "Creativity," *Annual Review of Psychology* 55 (2004), pp. 657–87.

39. B. Kabanoff and J. R. Rossiter, "Recent Developments in Applied Creativity," *International Review of Industrial and Organizational Psychology* 9 (1994), pp. 283–324.

40. R. S. Nickerson, "Enhancing Creativity," in *Handbook of Creativity,* ed. R. J. Sternberg (New York: Cambridge University Press, 1999), pp. 392–430.

41. For a thorough discussion of insight, see R. J. Sternberg and J. E. Davidson, *The*

Nature of Insight (Cambridge, MA: MIT Press, 1995).

42. R. J. Sternberg and L. A. O' Hara, "Creativity and Intelligence," in *Handbook of Creativity,* ed. R. J. Sternberg (New York: Cambridge University Press, 1999), pp. 251–72; and S. Taggar, "Individual Creativity and Group Ability to Utilize Individual Creative Resources: A Multilevel Model," *Academy of Management Journal* 45 (April 2002), pp. 315–30.

43. G. J. Feist, "The Influence of Personality on Artistic and Scientific Creativity," in *Handbook of Creativity,* ed. R. J. Sternberg (New York: Cambridge University Press, 1999), pp. 273–96; and R. I. Sutton, *Weird Ideas That Work* (New York: Free Press, 2002), pp. 8–9, Chap. 10.

44. R. W. Weisberg, "Creativity and Knowledge: A Challenge to Theories," in *Handbook of Creativity,* ed. R. J. Sternberg (New York: Cambridge University Press, 1999), pp. 226–50.

45. Sutton, *Weird Ideas That Work,* pp. 121, 153–54; and C. Andriopoulos, "Six Paradoxes in Managing Creativity: An Embracing Act," *Long Range Planning* 36 (2003), pp. 375–88.

46. D. K. Simonton, "Creativity: Cognitive, Personal, Developmental, and Social Aspects," *American Psychologist* 55 (January 2000), pp. 151–58.

47. M. D. Mumford, "Managing Creative People: Strategies and Tactics for Innovation," *Human Resource Management Review* 10 (Autumn 2000), pp. 313–51; T. M. Amabile et al., "Leader Behaviors and the Work Environment for Creativity: Perceived Leader Support," *Leadership Quarterly* 15, no. 1 (2004), pp. 5–32; and C. E. Shalley, J. Zhou, and G. R. Oldham, "The Effects of Personal and Contextual Characteristics on Creativity: Where Should We Go from Here?" *Journal of Management* 30, no. 6 (2004), pp. 933–58.

48. T. M. Amabile, "Motivating Creativity in Organizations: On Doing What You Love and Loving What You Do," *California Management Review* 40 (Fall 1997), pp. 39–58; and A. Cummings and G. R. Oldham, "Enhancing Creativity: Managing Work Contexts for the High Potential Employee," *California Management Review,* no. 40 (Fall 1997), pp. 22–38.

49. P. Withers, "Few Rules Rule," *B.C. Business,* January 2002, p. 24; G. Huston, I. Wilkinson, and D. Kellogg, "Dare to Be Great," *B.C. Business,* May 2004, pp. 28–29; and P. Withers and L. Kloet, "The Best Companies to Work for in B.C.," *B.C. Business,* December 2004, pp. 37–53.

50. T. M. Amabile, "Changes in the Work Environment for Creativity During Downsizing," *Academy of Management Journal* 42 (December 1999), pp. 630–40.

51. J. M. Howell and K. Boies, "Champions of Technological Innovation: The Influence of Contextual Knowledge, Role Orientation, Idea Generation, and Idea Promotion on Champion Emergence," *Leadership Quarterly* 15, no. 1 (2004), pp. 123–43; and Shalley, Zhou, and Oldham, "The Effects of Personal and Contextual Characteristics on Creativity."

52. A. Hiam, "Obstacles to Creativity—and How You Can Remove Them," *Futurist* 32 (October 1998), pp. 30–34.

53. M. A. West, *Developing Creativity in Organizations* (Leicester, UK: BPS Books, 1997), pp. 33–35.

54. L. Chappell, "Honda Spurs Suppliers to Compete," *Automotive News,* November 22, 2004, p. 24; and T. Nudd, "All Work and Some Play," *Adweek,* March 8, 2004, p. 37.

55. J. Neff, "At Eureka Ranch, Execs Doff Wing Tips, Fire up Ideas," *Advertising Age,* March 9, 1998, pp. 28–29.

56. A. Hargadon and R. I. Sutton, "Building an Innovation Factory," *Harvard Business Review* 78 (May–June 2000), pp. 157–66; and T. Kelley, *The Art of Innovation* (New York: Currency Doubleday, 2001), pp. 158–62.

57. K. S. Brown, "The Apple of Jonathan Ive's Eye," *Investor's Business Daily,* September 19, 2003.

chapter 7

1. S. Konig, "The Challenge of Teams," *On Wall Street,* August 2003; D. Jamieson, "8 Most Common Myths about Teams," *On Wall Street,* May 2005; H. J. Stock, "A 'Cheat Sheet' to Cross Sell," *Bank Investment Consultant,* April 2005, p. 28; and L. Wei, "Brokers Increasingly Use Teamwork," *The Wall Street Journal,* February 23, 2005, p. 1.

2. This definition and very similar variations are found in M. E. Shaw, *Group Dynamics,* 3rd ed. (New York: McGraw-Hill, 1981), p. 8; S. A. Mohrman, S. G. Cohen, and A. M. Mohrman Jr., *Designing Team-Based Organizations: New Forms for Knowledge Work* (San Francisco: Jossey-Bass, 1995), pp. 39–40; and E. Sundstrom, "The Challenges of Supporting Work Team Effectiveness," in *Supporting Work Team Effectiveness,* ed. E. Sundstrom and Associates (San Francisco: Jossey-Bass, 1999), pp. 6–9.

3. C. R. Emery and L. D. Fredenhall, "The Effect of Teams on Firm Profitability and Customer Satisfaction," *Journal of Service Research* 4 (February 2002), pp. 217–29; and G. S. Van der Vegt and O. Janssen, "Joint Impact of Interdependence and Group Diversity on Innovation," *Journal of Management* 29 (2003), pp. 729–51. Early research on teams is discussed in M. Moldaschl and W. Weber, "The 'Three Waves' of Industrial Group Work: Historical Reflections on Current Research on Group Work," *Human Relations* 51 (March 1998), pp. 347–88.

4. B. D. Pierce and R. White, "The Evolution of Social Structure: Why Biology Matters," *Academy of Management Review* 24 (October 1999), pp. 843–53; P. R. Lawrence and N. Nohria, *Driven: How Human Nature Shapes Our Choices* (San Francisco: Jossey-Bass, 2002); and J. R. Spoor and J. R. Kelly, "The Evolutionary Significance of Affect in Groups: Communication and Group Bonding," *Group Processes & Intergroup Relations* 7, no. 4 (2004), pp. 398–412.

5. M. A. Hogg et al., "The Social Identity Perspective: Intergroup Relations, Self-Conception, and Small Groups," *Small Group Research* 35, no. 3 (June 2004), pp. 246–76; N. Michinov, E. Michinov, and M.-C. Toczek-Capelle, "Social Identity, Group Processes, and Performance in Synchronous Computer-Mediated Communication," *Group Dynamics: Theory, Research, and Practice* 8, no. 1 (2004), pp. 27–39; and M. Van Vugt and C. M. Hart, "Social Identity as Social Glue: The Origins of Group Loyalty," *Journal of Personality and Social Psychology* 86, no. 4 (2004), pp. 585–98.

6. S. Schacter, *The Psychology of Affiliation* (Stanford, CA: Stanford University Press, 1959), pp. 12–19; R. Eisler and D. S. Levine, "Nurture, Nature, and Caring: We Are Not Prisoners of Our Genes," *Brain and Mind* 3 (2002), pp. 9–52; and A. C. DeVries, E. R. Glasper, and C. E. Detillon, "Social Modulation of Stress Responses," *Physiology & Behavior* 79, no. 3 (August 2003), pp. 399–407.

7. M. A. West, C. S. Borrill, and K. L. Unsworth, "Team Effectiveness in Organizations," *International Review of Industrial and Organizational Psychology* 13 (1998), pp. 1–48; R. Forrester and A. B. Drexler, "A Model for Team-Based Organization Performance," *Academy of Management Executive* 13 (August 1999), pp. 36–49; J. E. McGrath, H. Arrow, and J. L. Berdahl, *"The Study of Groups: Past, Present, and Future,"* Personality & Social Psychology Review 4, no. 1 (2000), pp.

95–105; and M. A. Marks, J. E. Mathieu, and S. J. Zaccaro, "A Temporally Based Framework and Taxonomy of Team Processes," *Academy of Management Review* 26, no. 3 (July 2001), pp. 356–76.

8. G. P. Shea and R. A. Guzzo, "Group Effectiveness: What Really Matters?" *Sloan Management Review* 27 (1987), pp. 33–46; and J. R. Hackman et al., "Team Effectiveness in Theory and in Practice," in *Industrial and Organizational Psychology: Linking Theory with Practice,* ed. C. L. Cooper and E. A. Locke (Oxford, UK: Blackwell, 2000), pp. 109–29.

9. J. N. Choi, "External Activities and Team Effectiveness: Review and Theoretical Development," *Small Group Research* 33 (April 2002), pp. 181–208; and T. L. Doolen, M. E. Hacker, and E. M. Van Aken, "The Impact of Organizational Context on Work Team Effectiveness: A Study of Production Team," *IEEE Transactions on Engineering Management* 50, no. 3 (August 2003), pp. 285–96.

10. J. S. DeMatteo, L. T. Eby, and E. Sundstrom, "Team-Based Rewards: Current Empirical Evidence and Directions for Future Research," *Research in Organizational Behavior* 20 (1998), pp. 141–83; and E. E. Lawler III, *Rewarding Excellence: Pay Strategies for the New Economy* (San Francisco: Jossey-Bass, 2000), pp. 207–14.

11. R. Wageman, "Case Study: Critical Success Factors for Creating Superb Self-Managing Teams at Xerox," *Compensation and Benefits Review* 29 (September–October 1997), pp. 31–41; and G. Gard, K. Lindström, and M. Dallner, "Towards a Learning Organization: The Introduction of a Client-Centered Team-Based Organization in Administrative Surveying Work," *Applied Ergonomics* 34 (2003), pp. 97–105.

12. A. Niimi, "The Slow and Steady Climb toward True North," Toyota Motor Manufacturing North America news release, August 7, 2003; and B. Andrews, "Room with Many Views," *Business Review Weekly,* January 15, 2004, p. 68.

13. M. A. Campion, E. M. Papper, and G. J. Medsker, "Relations between Work Team Characteristics and Effectiveness: A Replication and Extension," *Personnel Psychology* 49 (1996), pp. 429–52; and D. C. Man and S. S. K. Lam, "The Effects of Job Complexity and Autonomy on Cohesiveness in Collectivistic and Individualistic Work Groups: A Cross-Cultural Analysis," *Journal of Organizational Behavior* 24 (2003), pp. 979–1001.

14. R. Wageman, "Interdependence and Group Effectiveness," *Administrative Science Quarterly* 40 (1995), pp. 145–80; G. S. Van der Vegt, J. M. Emans, and E. Van de Vliert, "Patterns of Interdependence in Work Teams: A Two-Level Investigation of the Relations with Job and Team Satisfaction," *Personnel Psychology* 54 (Spring 2001), pp. 51–69; and R. Wageman, "The Meaning of Interdependence," in *Groups at Work: Theory and Research,* ed. M. E. Turner (Mahwah, NJ: Lawrence Erlbaum Associates, 2001), pp. 197–217.

15. S. E. Nedleman, "Recruiters Reveal Their Top Interview Questions," *Financial News Online,* February 16, 2005.

16. M. R. Barrick et al., "Relating Member Ability and Personality to Work-Team Processes and Team Effectiveness," *Journal of Applied Psychology* 83 (1998), pp. 377–91; and S. Sonnentag, "Excellent Performance: The Role of Communication and Cooperation Processes," *Applied Psychology: An International Review* 49 (2000), pp. 483–97.

17. C. M. Riodan, "Relational Demography within Groups: Past Developments, Contradictions, and New Directions," in *Research in Personnel and Human Resources Management,* ed. G. R. Ferris (Greenwich, CT: JAI, 2000), pp. 131–73; S. E. Jackson and A. Joshi, "Diversity in Social Context: A Multi-Attribute, Multilevel Analysis of Team Diversity and Sales Performance," *Journal of Organizational Behavior* 25 (2004), pp. 675–702; D. van Knippenberg, C. K. W. De Dreu, and A. C. Homan, "Work Group Diversity and Group Performance: An Integrative Model and Research Agenda," *Journal of Applied Psychology* 89, no. 6 (2004), pp. 1008–22; and D. C. Lau and J. K. Murnighan, "Interactions within Groups and Subgroups: The Effects of Demographic Faultlines," *Academy of Management Journal* 48, no. 4 (August 2005), pp. 645–59.

18. B. W. Tuckman and M. A. C. Jensen, "Stages of Small-Group Development Revisited," *Group and Organization Studies* 2 (1977), pp. 419–42.

19. D. L. Miller, "The Stages of Group Development: A Retrospective Study of Dynamic Team Processes," *Canadian Journal of Administrative Sciences* 20, no. 2 (2003), pp. 121–34.

20. D. C. Feldman, "The Development and Enforcement of Group Norms," *Academy of Management Review* 9 (1984), pp. 47–53; and E. Fehr and U. Fischbacher, "Social Norms and Human Cooperation," *Trends in Cognitive Sciences* 8, no. 4 (2004), pp. 185–90.

21. N. Ellemers and F. Rink, "Identity in Work Groups: The Beneficial and Detrimental Consequences of Multiple Identities and Group Norms for Collaboration and Group Performance," *Advances in Group Processes* 22 (2005), pp. 1–41.

22. J. J. Dose and R. J. Klimoski, "The Diversity of Diversity: Work Values Effects on Formative Team Processes," *Human Resource Management Review* 9, no. 1 (Spring 1999), pp. 83–108.

23. R. Hallowell, D. Bowen, and C.-I. Knoop, "Four Seasons Goes to Paris," *Academy of Management Executive* 16, no. 4 (November 2002), pp. 7–24.

24. L. Grant, "Container Store's Workers Huddle up to Help you Out," *USA Today,* 30 April 2002, p. B1; S. F. Gale, "Swanky Dinners, Trips and EveryDay Praise are Part of The Container Store's Culture," *Workforce Management,* August 2003, pp. 80–82.

25. A. P. Hare, "Types of Roles in Small Groups: A Bit of History and a Current Perspective," *Small Group Research* 25 (1994), pp. 443–48.

26. S. H. N. Leung, J. W. K. Chan, and W. B. Lee, "The Dynamic Team Role Behavior: The Approaches of Investigation," *Team Performance Management* 9 (2003), pp. 84–90.

27. B. Mullen and C. Copper, "The Relation between Group Cohesiveness and Performance: An Integration," *Psychological Bulletin* 115 (1994), pp. 210–27; A. V. Carron et al., "Cohesion and Performance in Sport: A Meta-Analysis," *Journal of Sport and Exercise Psychology* 24 (2002), pp. 168–88; and D. J. Beal et al., "Cohesion and Performance in Groups: A Meta-Analytic Clarification of Construct Relations," *Journal of Applied Psychology* 88, no. 6 (2003), pp. 989–1004.

28. K. A. Jehn, G. B. Northcraft, and M. A. Neale, "Why Differences Make a Difference: A Field Study of Diversity, Conflict, and Performance in Workgroups," *Administrative Science Quarterly* 44, no. 4 (1999), pp. 741–63. For evidence that diversity/similarity does not always influence cohesion, see S. S. Webber and L. M. Donahue, "Impact of Highly and Less Job-Related Diversity on Work Group Cohesion and Performance: A Meta-Analysis," *Journal of Management* 27, no. 2 (2001), pp. 141–62.

29. E. Aronson and J. Mills, "The Effects of Severity of Initiation on Liking for a

Group," *Journal of Abnormal and Social Psychology* 59 (1959), pp. 177–81; and J. E. Hautaluoma and R. S. Enge, "Early Socialization into a Work Group: Severity of Initiations Revisited," *Journal of Social Behavior & Personality* 6 (1991), pp. 725–48.

30. M. Rempel and R. J. Fisher, "Perceived Threat, Cohesion, and Group Problem Solving in Intergroup Conflict," *International Journal of Conflict Management* 8 (1997), pp. 216–34; and M. E. Turner and T. Horvitz, "The Dilemma of Threat: Group Effectiveness and Ineffectiveness under Adversity," in *Groups at Work: Theory and Research,* ed. M. E. Turner (Mahwah, NJ: Lawrence Erlbaum Associates, 2001), pp. 445–70.

31. W. Piper et al., "Cohesion as a Basic Bond in Groups," *Human Relations* 36 (1983), pp. 93–108; C. A. O'Reilly, D. E. Caldwell, and W. P. Barnett, "Work Group Demography, Social Integration, and Turnover," *Administrative Science Quarterly* 34 (1989), pp. 21–37; and P. Sullivan, J. and D. L. Feltz, "The Relationship between Intrateam Conflict and Cohesion within Hockey Teams," *Small Group Research* 32 (June 2001), pp. 34–55.

32. C. Langfred, "Is Group Cohesiveness a Double-Edged Sword? An Investigation of the Effects of Cohesiveness on Performance," *Small Group Research* 29 (1998), pp. 124–143; and K. L. Gammage, A. V. Carron, and P. A. Estabrooks, "Team Cohesion and Individual Productivity: The Influence of the Norm for Productivity and the Identifiability of Individual Effort," *Small Group Research* 32 (February 2001), pp. 3–18.

33. E. A. Locke et al, "The Importance of the Individual in an Age of Groupism," in *Groups at Work: Theory and Research,* ed. M. E. Turner (Mahwah, NJ: Lawrence Erbaum Associates, 2001), pp. 501–28; and N. J. Allen and T. D. Hecht, "The 'Romance of Teams': Toward an Understanding of Its Psychological Underpinnings and Implications," *Journal of Occupational and Organizational Psychology* 77 (2004), pp. 439–61.

34. I. D. Steiner, *Group Process and Productivity* (New York: Academic Press, 1972); and N. L. Kerr and S. R. Tindale, "Group Performance and Decision Making," *Annual Review of Psychology* 55 (2004), pp. 623–55.

35. F. P. Brooks, ed., *The Mythical Man-Month: Essays on Software Engineering,* 2nd ed. (Reading, MA: Addison-Wesley, 1995).

36. R. Cross, "Looking before You Leap: Assessing the Jump to Teams in Knowledge-Based Work," *Business Horizons,* September 2000, pp. 29–36; and Q. R. Skrabec Jr., "The Myth of Teams," *Industrial Management* (September–October 2002), pp. 25–27.

37. S. J. Karau and K. D. Williams, "Social Loafing: A Meta-Analytic Review and Theoretical Integration," *Journal of Personality and Social Psychology* 65 (1993), pp. 681–706; and R. C. Liden et al., "Social Loafing: A Field Investigation," *Journal of Management* 30 (2004), pp. 285–304.

38. E. Kidwell and N. Bennett, "Employee Propensity to Withhold Effort: A Conceptual Model to Intersect Three Avenues of Research," *Academy of Management Review* 19 (1993), pp. 429–56; J. M. George, "Asymmetrical Effects of Rewards and Punishments: The Case of Social Loafing," *Journal of Occupational and Organizational Psychology* 68 (1995), pp. 327–38; and T. A. Judge and T. D. Chandler, "Individual-Level Determinants of Employee Shirking," *Relations Industrielles* 51 (1996), pp. 468–86.

39. C. Eberting, "The Harley Mystique Comes to Kansas City," *Kansas City Star,* January 6, 1998, p. A1; D. Fields, "Harley Teams Shoot for Better Bike," *Akron Beacon Journal,* June 15, 1998; J. Singer and S. Duvall, "High-Performance Partnering by Self-Managed Teams in Manufacturing," *Engineering Management Journal* 12 (December 2000), pp. 9–15; and P. A. Chansler, P. M. Swamidass, and C. Cammann, "Self-Managing Work Teams: An Empirical Study of Group Cohesiveness in 'Natural Work Groups' at a Harley-Davidson Motor Company Plant," *Small Group Research* 34 (February 2003), pp. 101–20.

40. S. A. Mohrman, S. G. Cohen, and J. Mohrman, A. M., *Designing Team-Based Organizations: New Forms for Knowledge Work* (San Francisco: Jossey-Bass, 1995); B. L. Kirkman and D. L. Shapiro, "The Impact of Cultural Values on Employee Resistance to Teams: Toward a Model of Globalized Self-Managing Work Team Effectiveness," *Academy of Management Review* 22 (July 1997), pp. 730–57; and D. E. Yeatts and C. Hyten, *High-Performing Self-Managed Work Teams: A Comparison of Theory and Practice* (Thousand Oaks, CA: Sage, 1998).

41. C. R. Emery and L. D. Fredendall, "The Effect of Teams on Firm Profitability and Customer Satisfaction," *Journal of Service Research* 4 (February 2002), pp. 217–29;

I. M. Kunii, "He Put the Flash Back in Canon," *Business Week,* September 16, 2002, p. 40; and A. Krause and H. Dunckel, "Work Design and Customer Satisfaction: Effects of the Implementation of Semi-Autonomous Group Work on Customer Satisfaction, Considering Employee Satisfaction and Group Performance" (translated abstract), *Zeitschrift fur Arbeits-und Organisationspsychologie* 47, no. 4 (2003), pp. 182–93.

42. C. C. Manz, D. E. Keating, and A. Donnellon, "Preparing for an Organizational Change to Employee Self-Management: The Managerial Transition," *Organizational Dynamics* 19 (Autumn 1990), pp. 15–26; and J. D. Orsburn and L. Moran, *The New Self-Directed Work Teams: Mastering the Challenge* (New York: McGraw-Hill, 2000), Chap. 11.

43. D. Stafford, "Sharing the Driver's Seat," *Kansas City Star,* June 11, 2002, p. D1.

44. M. Fenton-O'Creevy, "Employee Involvement and the Middle Manager: Saboteur or Scapegoat?" *Human Resource Management Journal* 11 (2001), pp. 24–40; R. Wageman, "How Leaders Foster Self-Managing Team Effectiveness," *Organization Science* 12, no. 5 (September–October 2001), pp. 559–77; and C. Douglas and W. L. Gardner, "Transition to Self-Directed Work Teams: Implications of Transition Time and Self-Monitoring for Managers' Use of Influence Tactics," *Journal of Organizational Behavior* 25 (2004), pp. 47–65.

45. C. E. Nicholls, H. W. Lane, and M. B. Brechu, "Taking Self-Managed Teams to Mexico," *Academy of Management Executive* 13 (August 1999), pp. 15–25; and B. L. Kirkman and D. L. Shapiro, "The Impact of Cultural Values on Job Satisfaction and Organizational Commitment in Self-Managing Work Teams: The Mediating Role of Employee Resistance," *Academy of Management Journal* 44 (June 2001), pp. 557–69.

46. C. Pavett and T. Morris, "Management Styles within a Multinational Corporation: A Five Country Comparative Study," *Human Relations* 48 (1995), pp. 1171–91; Kirkman and Shapiro, "The Impact of Cultural Values on Employee Resistance to Teams"; and C. Robert and T. M. Probst, "Empowerment and Continuous Improvement in the United States, Mexico, Poland, and India," *Journal of Applied Psychology* 85 (October 2000), pp. 643–58.

47. J. Gordon, "Do Your Virtual Teams Deliver Only Virtual Performance?" *Training,* June 2005, pp. 20–24.

48. J. Lipnack and J. Stamps, *Virtual Teams: People Working across Boundaries with Technology* (New York: John Wiley and Sons, 2001); B. S. Bell and W. J. Kozlowski, "A Typology of Virtual Teams: Implications for Effective Leadership," *Group & Organization Management* 27 (March 2002), pp. 14–49; and G. Hertel, S. Geister, and U. Konradt, "Managing Virtual Teams: A Review of Current Empirical Research," *Human Resource Management Review* 15 (2005), pp. 69–95.

49. D. Robey, H. M. Khoo, and C. Powers, "Situated Learning in Cross-Functional Virtual Teams," *Technical Communication* (February 2000), pp. 51–66; L. L. Martins, L. L. Gilson, and M. T. Maynard, "Virtual Teams: What Do We Know and Where Do We Go From Here?" *Journal of Management* 30, no. 6 (2004), pp. 805–35; and Hertel, Geister, and Konradt, "Managing Virtual Teams."

50. Gordon, "Do Your Virtual Teams Deliver Only Virtual Performance?"

51. V. H. Vroom and A. G. Jago, *The New Leadership* (Englewood Cliffs, NJ: Prentice Hall, 1988), pp. 28–29.

52. M. Diehl and W. Stroebe, "Productivity Loss in Idea-Generating Groups: Tracking Down the Blocking Effects," *Journal of Personality and Social Psychology* 61 (1991), pp. 392–403; R. B. Gallupe et al., "Blocking Electronic Brainstorms," *Journal of Applied Psychology* 79 (1994), pp. 77–86; and B. A. Nijstad, W. Stroebe, and H. F. M. Lodewijkx, "Production Blocking and Idea Generation: Does Blocking Interfere with Cognitive Processes?" *Journal of Experimental Social Psychology* 39, no. 6 (November 2003), pp. 531–48.

53. B. E. Irmer, P. Bordia, and D. Abusah, "Evaluation Apprehension and Perceived Benefits in Interpersonal and Database Knowledge Sharing," *Academy of Management Proceedings* (2002), pp. B1–B6.

54. I. L. Janis, *Groupthink: Psychological Studies of Policy Decisions and Fiascoes,* Second ed. (Boston: Houghton Mifflin, 1982); and J. K. Esser, "Alive and Well after 25 Years: A Review of Groupthink Research," *Organizational Behavior and Human Decision Processes* 73, no. 2–3 (1998), pp. 116–41.

55. J. N. Choi and M. U. Kim, "The Organizational Application of Groupthink and Its Limitations in Organizations," *Journal of Applied Psychology* 84, no. 2 (April 1999), pp. 297–306; and Kerr and Tindale, "Group Performance and Decision Making."

56. D. Miller, *The Icarus Paradox: How Exceptional Companies Bring About Their Own Downfall* (New York: HarperBusiness, 1990); S. Finkelstein, *Why Smart Executives Fail* (New York: Viking, 2003); and K. Tasa and G. Whyte, "Collective Efficacy and Vigilant Problem Solving in Group Decision Making: A Non-Linear Model," *Organizational Behavior and Human Decision Processes* 96, no. 2 (March 2005), pp. 119–29.

57. For three of the many contrasting studies on the effects of constructive conflict, see C. K. W. De Dreu and L. R. Weingart, "Task versus Relationship Conflict, Team Performance, and Team Member Satisfaction: A Meta-Analysis," *Journal of Applied Psychology* 88 (August 2003), pp. 587–604; P. Hinds and D. E. Bailey, "Out of Sight, Out of Sync: Understanding Conflict in Distributed Teams," *Organization Science* 14, no. 6 (2003), pp. 615–32; and C. J. Nemeth et al., "The Liberating Role of Conflict in Group Creativity: A Study in Two Countries," *European Journal of Social Psychology* 34, no. 4 (2004), pp. 365–74.

58. K. Darce, "Ground Control: NASA Attempts a Cultural Shift," *Seattle Times,* April 24, 2005, p. A3; and R. Shelton, "NASA Attempts to Change Mindset in Wake of Columbia Tragedy," *Macon Telegraph* (Macon, GA), July 7, 2005.

59. B. Mullen, C. Johnson, and E. Salas, "Productivity Loss in Brainstorming Groups: A Meta-Analytic Integration," *Basic and Applied Psychology* 12 (1991), pp. 2–23. The original description of brainstorming appeared in A. F. Osborn, *Applied Imagination* (New York: Scribner, 1957).

60. R. I. Sutton and A. Hargadon, "Brainstorming Groups in Context: Effectiveness in a Product Design Firm," *Administrative Science Quarterly* 41 (1996), pp. 685–718; T. Kelley, *The Art of Innovation* (New York: Currency Doubleday, 2001); V. R. Brown and P. B. Paulus, "Making Group Brainstorming More Effective: Recommendations from an Associative Memory Perspective," *Current Directions in Psychological Science* 11, no. 6 (2002), pp. 208–12; and K. Leggett Dugosh and P. B. Paulus, "Cognitive and Social Comparison Processes in Brainstorming," *Journal of Experimental Social Psychology* 41, no. 3 (2005), pp. 313–20.

61. R. B. Gallupe, L. M. Bastianutti, and W. H. Cooper, "Unblocking Brainstorms," *Journal of Applied Psychology* 76 (1991), pp. 137–42; P. Bordia, "Face-to-Face Versus Computer-Mediated Communication: A Synthesis of the Experimental Literature," *Journal of Business Communication* 34 (1997), pp. 99–120; A. R. Dennis, B. H. Wixom, and R. J. Vandenberg, "Understanding Fit and Appropriation Effects in Group Support Systems Via Meta-Analysis," *MIS Quarterly* 25, no. 2 (June 2001), pp. 167–93; and D. S. Kerr and U. S. Murthy, "Divergent and Convergent Idea Generation in Teams: A Comparison of Computer-Mediated and Face-to-Face Communication," *Group Decision and Negotiation* 13, no. 4 (July 2004), pp. 381–99.

62. A. L. Delbecq, A. H. Van de Ven, and D. H. Gustafson, *Group Techniques for Program Planning: A Guide to Nominal Group and Delphi Processes* (Middleton, WI: Green Briar Press, 1986).

63. S. Frankel, "NGT + MDS: An Adaptation of the Nominal Group Technique for Ill-Structured Problems," *Journal of Applied Behavioral Science* 23 (1987), pp. 543–51; and H. Barki and A. Pinsonneault, "Small Group Brainstorming and Idea Quality: Is Electronic Brainstorming the Most Effective Approach?" *Small Group Research* 32, no. 2 (April 2001), pp. 158–205.

chapter 8

1. E. Cone, "Rise of the Blog," *CIO Insight,* April 2005, p. 54; M. Delio, "The Enterprise Blogosphere," *InfoWorld,* March 28, 2005, pp. 42–47; N. Z. Dizon, "Corporations Entering New World of Blogs," *Associated Press Newswires,* June 6, 2005; and V. Galt, "Top-Down Communication with an Interactive Twist," *Globe & Mail,* August 20, 2005, p. B10.

2. I. Nonaka and H. Takeuchi, *The Knowledge-Creating Company* (New York: Oxford University Press, 1995); R. T. Barker and M. R. Camarata, "The Role of Communication in Creating and Maintaining a Learning Organization: Preconditions, Indicators, and Disciplines," *Journal of Business Communication* 35 (October 1998), pp. 443–67; and D. Te'eni, "A Cognitive-Affective Model of Organizational Communication for Designing It," *MIS Quarterly* 25 (June 2001), pp. 251–312.

3. "What Are the Bottom Line Results of Communicating?" *Pay for Performance Report,* June 2003, p. 1; and R. Maitland, "Bad Drivers," *People Management,* May 29 2003, p. 49.

4. C. E. Shannon and W. Weaver, *The Mathematical Theory of Communication*

(Urbana, IL: University of Illinois Press, 1949); and K. J. Krone, F. M. Jablin, and L. L. Putnam, "Communication Theory and Organizational Communication: Multiple Perspectives," in *Handbook of Organizational Communication: An Interdisciplinary Perspective,* ed. F. M. Jablin et al. (Newbury Park, CA: Sage, 1987), pp. 18–40.

5. W. Lucas, "Effects of E-Mail on the Organization," *European Management Journal* 16, no. 1 (February 1998), pp. 18–30; D. A. Owens, M. A. Neale, and R. I. Sutton, "Technologies of Status Management Status Dynamics in E-Mail Communications," *Research on Managing Groups and Teams* 3 (2000), pp. 205–30; and N. Ducheneaut and L. A. Watts, "In Search of Coherence: A Review of E-Mail Research," *Human-Computer Interaction* 20, no. 1–2 (2005), pp. 11–48.

6. G. Hertel, S. Geister, and U. Konradt, "Managing Virtual Teams: A Review of Current Empirical Research," *Human Resource Management Review* 15 (2005), pp. 69–95; and H. Lee, "Behavioral Strategies for Dealing with Flaming in an Online Forum," *Sociological Quarterly* 46, no. 2 (2005), pp. 385–403.

7. "Does E-Mail Really Help Us Get the Message?" *Leicester Mercury* (UK), August 31, 2002, p. 15; and M. Greenwood, "I Have Banned Emails: They Are a Cancer of Modern Business," *The Mirror* (London, UK), September 19, 2003, p. 11.

8. C. Meyer and S. Davis, *Blur: The Speed of Change in the Connected Economy* (Reading, MA: Addison-Wesley, 1998); and S. Stellin, "Intranets Nurture Companies from the Inside," *The New York Times,* January 29, 2001, p. C4.

9. D. Robb, "Ready or Not . . . Instant Messaging Has Arrived as a Financial Planning Tool," *Journal of Financial Planning,* July 2001, pp. 12–14; J. Black, "Why Offices Are Now Open Secrets," *Business Week Online,* September 17, 2003; and A. F. Cameron and J. Webster, "Unintended Consequences of Emerging Communication Technologies: Instant Messaging in the Workplace," *Computers in Human Behavior* 21, no. 1 (2005), pp. 85–103.

10. L. Z. Tiedens and A. R. Fragale, "Power Moves: Complementarity in Dominant and Submissive Nonverbal Behavior," *Journal of Personality and Social Psychology* 84, no. 3 (2003), pp. 558–68.

11. P. Ekman and E. Rosenberg, *What the Face Reveals: Basic and Applied Studies of Spontaneous Expression Using the Facial Action Coding System* (Oxford, England: Oxford University Press, 1997); and P. Winkielman and K. C. Berridge, "Unconscious Emotion," *Current Directions in Psychological Science* 13, no. 3 (2004), pp. 120–23.

12. R. L. Daft and R. H. Lengel, "Information Richness: A New Approach to Managerial Behavior and Organization Design," *Research in Organizational Behavior* 6 (1984), pp. 191–233; and R. H. Lengel and R. L. Daft, "The Selection of Communication Media as an Executive Skill," *Academy of Management Executive* 2 (1988), pp. 225–32.

13. R. E. Rice, "Task Analyzability, Use of New Media, and Effectiveness: A Multi-Site Exploration of Media Richness," *Organization Science* 3 (1992), pp. 475–500.

14. D. Goleman, R. Boyatzis, and A. McKee, *Primal Leaders* (Boston: Harvard Business School Press, 2002), pp. 92–95.

15. T. Koski, "Reflections on Information Glut and Other Issues in Knowledge Productivity," *Futures* 33 (August 2001), pp. 483–95; D. D. Dawley and W. P. Anthony, "User Perceptions of E-Mail at Work," *Journal of Business and Technical Communication* 17, no. 2 (April 2003), pp. 170–200; and "Email Brings Costs and Fatigue," *Western News* (University of Western Ontario, London, Ontario), July 9, 2004.

16. A. G. Schick, L. A. Gordon, and S. Haka, "Information Overload: A Temporal Approach," *Accounting, Organizations & Society* 15 (1990), pp. 199–220; and A. Edmunds and A. Morris, "The Problem of Information Overload in Business Organisations: A Review of the Literature," *International Journal of Information Management* 20 (2000), pp. 17–28.

17. D. Kirkpatrick, "Gates and Ozzie: How to Escape E-Mail Hell," *Fortune,* June 27, 2005, pp. 169–71.

18. D. C. Thomas and K. Inkson, *Cultural Intelligence: People Skills for Global Business* (San Francisco: Berrett-Koehler, 2004), Chap. 6. The "catastrophe" example is mentioned in D. Woodruff, "Crossing Culture Divide Early Clears Merger Paths," *Asian Wall Street Journal,* May 28, 2001, p. 9.

19. S. Ohtaki, T. Ohtaki, and M. D. Fetters, "Doctor-Patient Communication: A Comparison of the USA and Japan," *Family Practice* 20 (June 2003), pp. 276–82; and M. Fujio, "Silence during Intercultural Communication: A Case Study," *Corporate Communications* 9, no. 4 (2004), pp. 331–39.

20. H. Yamada, *American and Japanese Business Discourse: A Comparison of Interaction Styles* (Norwood, NJ: Ablex, 1992), Chap. 2; and H. Yamada, *Different Games, Different Rules* (New York: Oxford University Press, 1997), pp. 76–79.

21. P. Harris and R. Moran, *Managing Cultural Differences* (Houston: Gulf, 1987); H. Blagg, "A Just Measure of Shame?" *British Journal of Criminology* 37 (Autumn 1997), pp. 481–501; and R. E. Axtell, *Gestures: The Do's and Taboos of Body Language around the World,* revised ed. (New York: Wiley, 1998).

22. M. Griffin, "The Office, Australian Style," *Sunday Age.* June 22, 2003, p. 6.

23. This stereotypic notion is prevalent throughout J. Gray, *Men Are from Mars, Women Are from Venus* (New York: Harper Collins, 1992). For a critique of this view, see J. T. Wood, "A Critical Response to John Gray's Mars and Venus Portrayals of Men and Women," *Southern Communication Journal* 67 (Winter 2002), pp. 201–10.

24. D. Tannen, *You Just Don't Understand: Men and Women in Conversation* (New York: Ballentine Books, 1990); D. Tannen, *Talking from 9 to 5* (New York: Avon, 1994); and L. L. Namy, L. C. Nygaard, and D. Sauerteig, "Gender Differences in Vocal Accommodation: The Role of Perception," *Journal of Language and Social Psychology* 21, no. 4 (December 2002), pp. 422–32.

25. A. Mulac et al., "Uh-Huh. What's That All About?' Differing Interpretations of Conversational Backchannels and Questions as Sources of Miscommunication across Gender Boundaries," *Communication Research* 25 (December 1998), pp. 641–68; N. M. Sussman and D. H. Tyson, "Sex and Power: Gender Differences in Computer-Mediated Interactions," *Computers in Human Behavior* 16 (2000), pp. 381–94; and D. R. Caruso and P. Salovey, *The Emotionally Intelligent Manager* (San Francisco: Jossey-Bass, 2004), p. 23.

26. P. Tripp-Knowles, "A Review of the Literature on Barriers Encountered by Women in Science Academia," *Resources for Feminist Research* 24 (Spring–Summer 1995), pp. 28–34.

27. Cited in K. Davis and J. W. Newstrom, *Human Behavior at Work: Organizational Behavior,* 7th ed. (New York: McGraw-Hill, 1985), p. 438.

28. The three components of listening discussed here are based on several recent studies in the field of marketing, including

S. B. Castleberry, C. D. Shepherd, and R. Ridnour, "Effective Interpersonal Listening in the Personal Selling Environment: Conceptualization, Measurement, and Nomological Validity," *Journal of Marketing Theory and Practice* 7 (Winter 1999), pp. 30–38; L. B. Comer and T. Drollinger, "Active Empathetic Listening and Selling Success: A Conceptual Framework," *Journal of Personal Selling & Sales Management* 19 (Winter 1999), pp. 15–29; and K. de Ruyter and M. G. M. Wetzels, "The Impact of Perceived Listening Behavior in Voice-to-Voice Service Encounters," *Journal of Service Research* 2 (February 2000), pp. 276–84.

29. G. Evans and D. Johnson, "Stress and Open-Office Noise," *Journal of Applied Psychology* 85 (2000), pp. 779–83; and F. Russo, "My Kingdom for a Door," *Time,* October 23, 2000, p. B1.

30. S. P. Means, "Playing at Pixar," *Salt Lake Tribune* (Utah), May 30, 2003, p. D1; and G. Whipp, "Swimming against the Tide," *Daily News of Los Angeles,* May 30, 2003, p. U6.

31. B. Sosnin, "Digital Newsletters 'E-Volutionize' Employee Communications," *HRMagazine,* May 2001, pp. 99–107.

32. K. Swisher, "Boomtown: 'Wiki' May Alter How Employees Work Together," *The Wall Street Journal,* July 29, 2004, p. B1; and Delio, "The Enterprise Blogosphere."

33. S. Greengard, "Employee Surveys: Ask the Right Questions, Probe the Answers for Insight," *Workforce Management,* December 2004, p. 76.

34. The original term is "management by *wandering* around," but this has been replaced with "walking" over the years. See W. Ouchi, *Theory Z* (New York: Avon Books, 1981), pp. 176–77; and T. Peters and R. Waterman, *In Search of Excellence* (New York: Harper and Row, 1982), p. 122.

35. R. Rousos, "Trust in Leaders Lacking at Utility," *The Ledger* (Lakeland, FL), July 29, 2003, p. B1; and B. Whitworth and B. Riccomini, "Management Communication: Unlocking Higher Employee Performance," *Communication World,* March–April 2005, pp. 18–21.

36. K. Davis, "Management Communication and the Grapevine," *Harvard Business Review* 31 (September–October 1953), pp. 43–49; and W. L. Davis and J. R. O'Connor, "Serial Transmission of Information: A Study of the Grapevine," *Journal of Applied Communication Research* 5 (1977), pp. 61–72.

37. H. Mintzberg, *The Structuring of Organizations* (Englewood Cliffs, NJ:

Prentice Hall, 1979), pp. 46–53; and D. Krackhardt and J. R. Hanson, "Informal Networks: The Company Behind the Chart," *Harvard Business Review* 71 (July–August 1993), pp. 104–11.

38. C. J. Walker and C. A. Beckerle, "The Effect of State Anxiety on Rumor Transmission," *Journal of Social Behaviour & Personality* 2 (August 1987), pp. 353–60; R. L. Rosnow, "Inside Rumor: A Personal Journey," *American Psychologist* 46 (May 1991), pp. 484–96; and M. Noon and R. Delbridge, "News from behind My Hand: Gossip in Organizations," *Organization Studies* 14 (1993), pp. 23–36.

39. N. Nicholson, "Evolutionary Psychology: Toward a New View of Human Nature and Organizational Society," *Human Relations* 50 (September 1997), pp. 1053–78.

chapter 9

1. United States Bankruptcy Court, Southern District of New York, In Re: WorldCom, Inc., et al., Debtors, Chapter 11, Case No. 02-15533 (Ajg) Jointly Administered Second Interim Report of Dick Thornburgh, Bankruptcy Court Examiner, June 9, 2003; Report of Investigation by the Special Investigative Committee of the Board of Directors of Worldcom, Inc. Dennis R. Beresford, Nicholas Deb. Katzenbach, C. B. Rogers, Jr., Counsel, Wilmer, Cutler & Pickering, Accounting Advisors, Pricewaterhousecoopers LLP, March 31, 2003. Also see T. Catan et al., "Before the Fall," *Financial Times* (London), December 19, 2002, p. 17; J. O'Donnell and A. Backover, "Ebbers' High-Risk Act Came Crashing Down on Him," *USA Today,* December 12, 2002, p. B1; C. Stern, "Ebbers Dominated Board, Report Says," *Washington Post,* November 5, 2002, p. E1; D. S. Hilzenrath, "How a Distinguished Roster of Board Members Failed to Detect Company's Problems," *Washington Post,* June 16, 2003, p. E1; S. Pulliam and A. Latour, "Lost Connection," *The Wall Street Journal,* January 12, 2005, p. A1; and S. Rosenbush, "Five Lessons of the Worldcom Debacle," *Business Week Online,* March 16, 2005.

2. For a discussion of the definition of power, see H. Mintzberg, *Power in and around Organizations* (Englewood Cliffs, NJ: Prentice Hall, 1983), Chap. 1; J. Pfeffer, *Managing with Power* (Boston: Harvard Business University Press, 1992), pp. 17, 30; J. Pfeffer, *New Directions in Organizational Theory* (New York: Oxford

University Press, 1997), Chap. 6; and J. M. Whitmeyer, "Power through Appointment," *Social Science Research* 29 (2000), pp. 535–55.

3. R. A. Dahl, "The Concept of Power," *Behavioral Science* 2 (1957), pp. 201–18; R. M. Emerson, "Power-Dependence Relations," *American Sociological Review* 27 (1962), pp. 31–41; and A. M. Pettigrew, *The Politics of Organizational Decision-Making* (London: Tavistock, 1973).

4. K. M. Bartol and D. C. Martin, "When Politics Pays: Factors Influencing Managerial Compensation Decisions," *Personnel Psychology* 43 (1990), pp. 599–614; and D. J. Brass and M. E. Burkhardt, "Potential Power and Power Use: An Investigation of Structure and Behavior," *Academy of Management Journal* 36 (1993), pp. 441–70.

5. J. R. P. French and B. Raven, "The Bases of Social Power," in *Studies in Social Power,* ed. D. Cartwright (Ann Arbor, MI: University of Michigan Press, 1959), pp. 150–67; P. Podsakoff and C. Schreisheim, "Field Studies of French and Raven's Bases of Power: Critique, Analysis, and Suggestions for Future Research," *Psychological Bulletin* 97 (1985), pp. 387–411; and P. P. Carson and K. D. Carson, "Social Power Bases: A Meta-Analytic Examination of Interrelationships and Outcomes," *Journal of Applied Social Psychology* 23 (1993), pp. 1150–69.

6. C. Barnard, *The Function of the Executive* (Cambridge, MA: Harvard University Press, 1938); and C. Hardy and S. R. Clegg, "Some Dare Call It Power," in *Handbook of Organization Studies,* ed. S. R. Clegg, C. Hardy, and W. R. Nord (London: Sage, 1996), pp. 622–41.

7. A. I. Shahin and P. L. Wright, "Leadership in the Context of Culture: An Egyptian Perspective," *Leadership & Organization Development Journal* 25, no. 5/6 (2004), pp. 499–511; and Y. J. Huo et al., "Leadership and the Management of Conflicts in Diverse Groups: Why Acknowledging versus Neglecting Subgroup Identity Matters," *European Journal of Social Psychology* 35, no. 2 (2005), pp. 237–54.

8. C. Mabin, "Steeling Themselves: Workers Burned by a Dwindling Industry," *Journal Gazette* (Fort Wayne, IN), July 3, 2005, p. 1H.

9. P. F. Drucker, "The New Workforce," *The Economist,* November 3, 2001, pp. 8–12.

10. J. D. Kudisch and M. L. Poteet, "Expert Power, Referent Power, and Charisma:

Toward the Resolution of a Theoretical Debate," *Journal of Business & Psychology* 10 (Winter 1995), pp. 177–95; and H. L. Tosi et al., "CEO Charisma, Compensation, and Firm Performance," *Leadership Quarterly* 15, no. 3 (2004), pp. 405–20.

11. G. Yukl and C. M. Falbe, "Importance of Different Power Sources in Downward and Lateral Relations," *Journal of Applied Psychology* 76 (1991), pp. 416–23; and B. H. Raven, "Kurt Lewin Address: Influence, Power, Religion, and the Mechanisms of Social Control," *Journal of Social Issues* 55 (Spring 1999), pp. 161–86.

12. C. R. Hinings et al., "Structural Conditions of Intraorganizational Power," *Administrative Science Quarterly* 19 (1974), pp. 22–44. Also see C. S. Saunders, "The Strategic Contingency Theory of Power: Multiple Perspectives," *Journal of Management Studies* 27 (1990), pp. 1–21.

13. S. Elliott, "Hunting for the Next Cool in Advertising," *The New York Times,* December 1, 2003, p. C19; S. Delaney, "Predicting the Birth of the Cool," *The Independent* (London), September 5, 2005, p. 15; and A. McMains, "Trend-Spotting Division Adds to Lowe's Evolution," *Adweek,* April 11, 2005, p. 11.

14. D. J. Hickson et al., "A Strategic Contingencies' Theory of Intraorganizational Power," *Administrative Science Quarterly* 16 (1971), pp. 216–27; Hinings et al., "Structural Conditions of Intraorganizational Power"; and R. M. Kanter, "Power Failure in Management Circuits," *Harvard Business Review,* July–August 1979, pp. 65–75.

15. Hickson et al., "A Strategic Contingencies' Theory of Intraorganizational Power"; J. D. Hackman, "Power and Centrality in the Allocation of Resources in Colleges and Universities," *Administrative Science Quarterly* 30 (1985), pp. 61–77; and Brass and Burkhardt, "Potential Power and Power Use."

16. Kanter, "Power Failure in Management Circuits"; B. E. Ashforth, "The Experience of Powerlessness in Organizations," *Organizational Behavior and Human Decision Processes* 43 (1989), pp. 207–42; and L. Holden, "European Managers: HRM and an Evolving Role," *European Business Review* 12 (2000), pp. 251–260.

17. J. Voight, "When Credit Is Not Due," *Adweek,* March 1, 2004, p. 24.

18. D. Krackhardt and J. R. Hanson, "Informal Networks: The Company behind the Chart," *Harvard Business Review* 71 (July–August 1993), pp. 104–11; and P. S.

Adler and S.-W. Kwon, "Social Capital: Prospects for a New Concept," *Academy of Management Review* 27, no. 1 (2002), pp. 17–40.

19. A. Mehra, M. Kilduff, and D. J. Brass, "The Social Networks of High and Low Self-Monitors: Implications for Workplace Performance," *Administrative Science Quarterly* 46 (March 2001), pp. 121–46.

20. K. Atuahene-Gima and H. Li, "Marketing's Influence Tactics in New Product Development: A Study of High Technology Firms in China," *Journal of Product Innovation Management* 17 (2000), pp. 451–70; and A. Somech and A. Drach-Zahavy, "Relative Power and Influence Strategy: The Effects of Agent/Target Organizational Power on Superiors' Choices of Influence Strategies," *Journal of Organizational Behavior* 23 (2002), pp. 167–79.

21. D. Kipnis, S. M. Schmidt, and I. Wilkinson, "Intraorganizational Influence Tactics: Explorations in Getting One's Way," *Journal of Applied Psychology* 65 (1980), pp. 440–52; A. Rao and K. Hashimoto, "Universal and Culturally Specific Aspects of Managerial Influence: A Study of Japanese Managers," *Leadership Quarterly* 8 (1997), pp. 295–312; W. A. Hochwarter et al., "A Reexamination of Schriesheim and Hinkin's (1990) Measure of Upward Influence," *Educational and Psychological Measurement* 60 (October 2000), pp. 755–71; and L. A. McFarland, A. M. Ryan, and S. D. Kriska, "Field Study Investigation of Applicant Use of Influence Tactics in a Selection Interview," *Journal of Psychology* 136 (July 2002), pp. 383–98.

22. R. B. Cialdini and N. J. Goldstein, "Social Influence: Compliance and Conformity," *Annual Review of Psychology* 55 (2004), pp. 591–621.

23. S. F. Pasa, "Leadership Influence in a High Power Distance and Collectivist Culture," *Leadership & Organization Development Journal* 21 (2000), pp. 414–26.

24. "Be Part of the Team If You Want to Catch the Eye," *Birmingham Post* (UK), August 31, 2000, p. 14; and S. Maitlis, "Taking It from the Top: How CEOs Influence (and Fail to Influence) Their Boards," *Organization Studies* 25, no. 8 (2004), pp. 1275–311.

25. A. T. Cobb, "Toward the Study of Organizational Coalitions: Participant Concerns and Activities in a Simulated Organizational Setting," *Human Relations* 44 (1991), pp. 1057–79; E. A. Mannix,

"Organizations as Resource Dilemmas: The Effects of Power Balance on Coalition Formation in Small Groups," *Organizational Behavior and Human Decision Processes* 55 (1993), pp. 1–22; and D. J. Terry, M. A. Hogg, and K. M. White, "The Theory of Planned Behavior: Self-Identity, Social Identity and Group Norms," *British Journal of Social Psychology* 38 (September 1999), pp. 225–44.

26. Rao and Hashimoto, "Universal and Culturally Specific Aspects of Managerial Influence."

27. D. Strutton and L. E. Pelton, "Effects of Ingratiation on Lateral Relationship Quality within Sales Team Settings," *Journal of Business Research* 43 (1998), pp. 1–12; and R. Vonk, "Self-Serving Interpretations of Flattery: Why Ingratiation Works," *Journal of Personality and Social Psychology* 82 (2002), pp. 515–26.

28. C. A. Higgins, T. A. Judge, and G. R. Ferris, "Influence Tactics and Work Outcomes: A Meta-Analysis," *Journal of Organizational Behavior* 24 (2003), pp. 90–106.

29. D. Strutton, L. E. Pelton, and J. Tanner, J. F., "Shall We Gather in the Garden: The Effect of Ingratiatory Behaviors on Buyer Trust in Salespeople," *Industrial Marketing Management* 25 (1996), pp. 151–62; and J. O' Neil, "An Investigation of the Sources of Influence of Corporate Public Relations Practitioners," *Public Relations Review* 29 (June 2003), pp. 159–69.

30. A. Rao and S. M. Schmidt, "Upward Impression Management: Goals, Influence Strategies, and Consequences," *Human Relations* 48 (1995), pp. 147–67.

31. A. P. J. Ellis et al., "The Use of Impression Management Tactics in Structured Interviews: A Function of Question Type?" *Journal of Applied Psychology* 87 (December 2002), pp. 1200–8; and M. C. Bolino and W. H. Tunley, "More than One Way to Make an Impression: Exploring Profiles of Impression Management," *Journal of Management* 29 (2003), pp. 141–60.

32. A. P. Brief, *Attitudes in and around Organizations* (Thousand Oaks, CA: Sage, 1998), pp. 69–84; and D. J. O'Keefe, *Persuasion: Theory and Research* (Thousand Oaks, CA: Sage, 2002).

33. L. A. Conger, *Winning 'Em Over: A New Model for Managing in the Age of Persuasion* (New York: Simon & Schuster, 1998); and J. J. Jiang, G. Klein, and R. G. Vedder, "Persuasive Expert Systems: The Influence of Confidence and Discrepancy,"

Computers in Human Behavior 16 (March 2000), pp. 99–109.

34. S. Gilmor, "Ahead of the Curve," *Infoworld,* January 13, 2003, p. 58; and M. Hiltzik, "Apple CEO's Visions Don't Guarantee Sustained Gains," *Los Angeles Times,* April 14, 2003, p. C1. The origin of "reality distortion field" is described at www.folklore.org.

35. These and other features of message content in persuasion are detailed in R. Petty and J. Cacioppo, *Attitudes and Persuasion: Classic and Contemporary Approaches* (Dubuque, Iowa: W. C. Brown, 1981); D. G. Linz and S. Penrod, "Increasing Attorney Persuasiveness in the Courtroom," *Law and Psychology Review* 8 (1984), pp. 1–47; M. Pfau, E. A. Szabo, and J. Anderson, "The Role and Impact of Affect in the Process of Resistance to Persuasion," *Human Communication Research* 27 (April 2001), pp. 216–52; and O'Keefe, *Persuasion: Theory and Research,* Chap. 9.

36. N. Rhodes and W. Wood, "Self-Esteem and Intelligence Affect Influenceability: The Mediating Role of Message Reception," *Psychological Bulletin* 111, no. 1 (1992), pp. 156–71.

37. A. W. Gouldner, "The Norm of Reciprocity: A Preliminary Statement," *American Sociological Review* 25 (1960), pp. 161–78.

38. Y. Fan, "Questioning Guanxi: Definition, Classification, and Implications," *International Business Review* 11 (2002), pp. 543–61; D. Tan and R. S. Snell, "The Third Eye: Exploring Guanxi and Relational Morality in the Workplace," *Journal of Business Ethics* 41 (December 2002), pp. 361–84; and W. R. Vanhonacker, "When Good Guanxi Turns Bad," *Harvard Business Review* 82, no. 4 (April 2004), pp. 18–19.

39. C. M. Falbe and G. Yukl, "Consequences for Managers of Using Single Influence Tactics and Combinations of Tactics," *Academy of Management Journal* 35 (1992), pp. 638–52.

40. Falbe and Yukl, "Consequences for Managers of Using Single Influence Tactics and Combinations of Tactics"; and Atuahene-Gima and Li, "Marketing's Influence Tactics in New Product Development."

41. R. C. Ringer and R. W. Boss, "Hospital Professionals' Use of Upward Influence Tactics," *Journal of Managerial Issues* 12 (2000), pp. 92–108.

42. G. Blickle, "Do Work Values Predict the Use of Intraorganizational Influence Strategies?" *Journal of Applied Social*

Psychology 30, no. 1 (January 2000), pp. 196–205; and P. P. Fu et al., "The Impact of Societal Cultural Values and Individual Social Beliefs on the Perceived Effectiveness of Managerial Influence Strategies: A Meso Approach," *Journal of International Business Studies* 35, no. 4 (July 2004), pp. 284–305.

43. G. R. Ferris and K. M. Kacmar, "Perceptions of Organizational Politics," *Journal of Management* 18 (1992), pp. 93–116; R. Cropanzano et al., "The Relationship of Organizational Politics and Support to Work Behaviors, Attitudes, and Stress," *Journal of Organizational Behavior* 18 (1997), pp. 159–80; and E. Vigoda and A. Cohen, "Influence Tactics and Perceptions of Organizational Politics: A Longitudinal Study," *Journal of Business Research* 55 (2002), pp. 311–24. For the older perspective of organizational politics as any discretionary behavior, see J. Pfeffer, *Power in Organizations* (Boston: Pitman, 1981); and Mintzberg, *Power in and around Organizations.*

44. K. M. Kacmar and R. A. Baron, "Organizational Politics: The State of the Field, Links to Related Processes, and an Agenda for Future Research," in *Research in Personnel and Human Resources Management,* ed. G. R. Ferris (Greenwich, CT: JAI Press, 1999), pp. 1–39; and E. Vigoda, "Stress-Related Aftermaths to Workplace Politics: The Relationships among Politics, Job Distress, and Aggressive Behavior in Organizations," *Journal of Organizational Behavior* 23 (2002), pp. 571–91.

45. C. Hardy, *Strategies for Retrenchment and Turnaround: The Politics of Survival* (Berlin: Walter de Gruyter, 1990), Chap. 14; and M. C. Andrews and K. M. Kacmar, "Discriminating among Organizational Politics, Justice, and Support," *Journal of Organizational Behavior* 22 (2001), pp. 347–66.

46. S. Blazejewski and W. Dorow, "Managing Organizational Politics for Radical Change: The Case of Beiersdorf-Lechia S.A., Poznan," *Journal of World Business* 38 (August 2003), pp. 204–23.

47. L. W. Porter, R. W. Allen, and H. L. Angle, "The Politics of Upward Influence in Organizations," *Research in Organizational Behavior* 3 (1981), pp. 120–22; and R. J. House, "Power and Personality in Complex Organizations," *Research in Organizational Behavior* 10 (1988), pp. 305–57.

48. R. Christie and F. Geis, *Studies in Machiavellianism* (New York: Academic Press, 1970); S. M. Farmer et al., "Putting

Upward Influence Strategies in Context," *Journal of Organizational Behavior* 18 (1997), pp. 17–42; and K. S. Sauleya and A. G. Bedeian, "Equity Sensitivity: Construction of a Measure and Examination of Its Psychometric Properties," *Journal of Management* 26 (September 2000), pp. 885–910.

49. R. Gluyas, "Fear and Loathing in NAB's Forex Fiasco," *The Australian,* August 6, 2005, p. 35; E. Johnston, "Expletives and Stench in Hothouse of NAB Dealers," *Australian Financial Review,* August 6, 2005, p. 3; and E. Johnston, "'Anything Goes,' Ex-Trader Says," *Australian Financial Review,* August 2, 2005, p. 3.

50. G. R. Ferris et al., "Perceptions of Organizational Politics: Prediction, Stress-Related Implications, and Outcomes," *Human Relations* 49 (1996), pp. 233–63.

chapter 10

1. Based on information in B. L. Toffler, *Final Accounting: Ambition, Greed, and the Fall of Arthur Andersen* (New York: Broadway Books, 2003).

2. J. A. Wall and R. R. Callister, "Conflict and Its Management," *Journal of Management,* 21 (1995), pp. 515–58; and M. A. Rahim, "Toward a Theory of Managing Organizational Conflict," *International Journal of Conflict Management* 13, no. 3 (2002), pp. 206–35.

3. L. Pondy, "Organizational Conflict: Concepts and Models," *Administrative Science Quarterly* 2 (1967), pp. 296–320; and K. W. Thomas, "Conflict and Negotiation Processes in Organizations," in *Handbook of Industrial and Organizational Psychology,* ed. M. D. Dunnette and L. M. Hough, 2nd ed. (Palo Alto, CA: Consulting Psychologists Press, 1992), pp. 651–718.

4. M. A. Von Glinow, D. L. Shapiro, and J. M. Brett, "Can We Talk, and Should We? Managing Emotional Conflict in Multicultural Teams," *Academy of Management Review* 29, no. 4 (2004), pp. 578–92.

5. G. E. Martin and T. J. Bergman, "The Dynamics of Behavioral Response to Conflict in the Workplace," *Journal of Occupational & Organizational Psychology* 69 (December 1996), pp. 377–87; and J. M. Brett, D. L. Shapiro, and A. L. Lytle, "Breaking the Bonds of Reciprocity in Negotiations," *Academy of Management Journal* 41 (August 1998), pp. 410–24.

6. H. Witteman, "Analyzing Interpersonal Conflict: Nature of Awareness, Type of Initiating Event, Situational Perceptions, and

Management Styles," *Western Journal of Communications* 56 (1992), pp. 248–80; and Wall and Callister, "Conflict and Its Management."

7. M. Rempel and R. J. Fisher, "Perceived Threat, Cohesion, and Group Problem Solving in Intergroup Conflict," *International Journal of Conflict Management* 8 (1997), pp. 216–34.

8. D. Tjosvold, *The Conflict-Positive Organization* (Reading, MA: Addison-Wesley, 1991); K. M. Eisenhardt, J. L. Kahwajy, and L. J. Bourgeois III, "Conflict and Strategic Choice: How Top Management Teams Disagree," *California Management Review* 39 (Winter 1997), pp. 42–62; L. H. Pelled, K. M. Eisenhardt, and K. R. Xin, "Exploring the Black Box: An Analysis of Work Group Diversity, Conflict, and Performance," *Administrative Science Quarterly* 44 (March 1999), pp. 1–28; and S. Schulz-Hardt, M. Jochims, and D. Frey, "Productive Conflict in Group Decision Making: Genuine and Contrived Dissent as Strategies to Counteract Biased Information Seeking," *Organizational Behavior and Human Decision Processes* 88 (2002), pp. 563–86.

9. R. Birchfield, "The Management Interview: Jim Syme," *New Zealand Management,* May 1, 2004, p. 32; Trans-Tasman Business Circle, "Waste Management New Zealand—A Formula for Success," from www.transtasmanbusiness.com.au/syme_akl.html, accessed October 5, 2005.

10. C. K. W. De Dreu and L. R. Weingart, "Task versus Relationship Conflict, Team Performance, and Team Member Satisfaction: A Meta-Analysis," *Journal of Applied Psychology* 88 (August 2003), pp. 587–604.

11. J. Yang and K. W. Mossholder, "Decoupling Task and Relationship Conflict: The Role of Intergroup Emotional Processing," *Journal of Organizational Behavior* 25 (2004), pp. 589–605.

12. R. E. Walton and J. M. Dutton, "The Management of Conflict: A Model and Review," *Administrative Science Quarterly* 14 (1969), pp. 73–84.

13. R. Zemke and B. Filipczak, *Generations at Work: Managing the Clash of Veterans, Boomers, Xers, and Nexters in Your Workplace* (New York: Amacom, 1999); and P. Harris, "Boomers vs. Echo Boomer: The Work War," *T+D* (May 2005), pp. 44–49.

14. P. C. Earley and G. B. Northcraft, "Goal Setting, Resource Interdependence, and Conflict Management," in *Managing Conflict: An Interdisciplinary Approach,* ed.

M. A. Rahim (New York: Praeger, 1989), pp. 161–70; and K. Jelin, "A Multimethod Examination of the Benefits and Detriments of Intragroup Conflict," *Administrative Science Quarterly* 40 (1995), pp. 245–82.

15. A. Risberg, "Employee Experiences of Acquisition Processes," *Journal of World Business* 36 (March 2001), pp. 58–84.

16. K. A. Jehn and C. Bendersky, "Intragroup Conflict in Organizations: A Contingency Perspective on the Conflict-Outcome Relationship," *Research in Organizational Behavior* 25 (2003), pp. 187–242.

17. J. Jetten, R. Spears, and T. Postmes, "Intergroup Distinctiveness and Differentiation: A Meta-Analytic Integration," *Journal of Personality and Social Psychology* 86, no. 6 (2004), pp. 862–79.

18. J. M. Brett, *Negotiating Globally: How to Negotiate Deals, Resolve Disputes, and Make Decisions across Cultural Boundaries* (San Francisco: Jossey-Bass, 2001); and R. J. Lewicki et al., *Negotiation,* 4th ed. (Burr Ridge, IL: McGraw-Hill/Irwin, 2003), Chap. 4.

19. Jelin, "A Multimethod Examination of the Benefits and Detriments of Intragroup Conflict."

20. C. K. W. De Dreu et al., "A Theory-Based Measure of Conflict Management Strategies in the Workplace," *Journal of Organizational Behavior* 22 (2001), pp. 645–68.

21. D. Cox, "Goodenow's Downfall," *Toronto Star,* July 29, 2005, p. A1; A. Maki, "NHLPA's New Leader Is a Peacemaker, Not Warrior," *Globe & Mail,* July 29, 2005, p. S1; and M. Spector, "Players: He Is Your Father," *National Post,* July 29, 2005, p. B8.

22. D. W. Johnson et al., "Effects of Cooperative, Competitive, and Individualistic Goal Structures on Achievement: A Meta-Analysis," *Psychological Bulletin* 89 (1981), pp. 47–62; D. Tjosvold, *Working Together to Get Things Done* (Lexington, MA: Lexington, 1986); and C. K. W. De Dreu, E. Giebels, and E. Van de Vliert, "Social Motives and Trust in Integrative Negotiation: The Disruptive Effects of Punitive Capability," *Journal of Applied Psychology* 83, no. 3 (June 1998), pp. 408–22.

23. C. K. W. De Dreu and A. E. M. Van Vianen, "Managing Relationship Conflict and the Effectiveness of Organizational Teams," *Journal of Organizational Behavior* 22 (2001), pp. 309–28; and Lewicki et al., *Negotiation,* pp. 35–36.

24. M. W. Morris and H.-Y. Fu, "How Does Culture Influence Conflict Resolution? Dynamic Constructivist Analysis," *Social Cognition* 19 (June 2001), pp. 324–49; S. Ting-Toomey, J. G. Oetzel, and K. Yee-Jung, "Self-Construal Types and Conflict Management Styles," *Communication Reports* 14 (Summer 2001), pp. 87–104; and C. H. Tinsley, "How Negotiators Get to Yes: Predicting the Constellation of Strategies Used across Cultures to Negotiate Conflict," *Journal of Applied Psychology* 86, no. 4 (2001), pp. 583–93.

25. C. H. Tinsley and E. Weldon, "Responses to a Normative Conflict among American and Chinese Managers," *International Journal of Conflict Management* 3, no. 2 (2003), pp. 183–94. Also see D. A. Cai and E. L. Fink, "Conflict Style Differences between Individualists and Collectivists," *Communication Monographs* 69 (March 2002), pp. 67–87.

26. N. Brewer, P. Mitchell, and N. Weber, "Gender Role, Organizational Status, and Conflict Management Styles," *International Journal of Conflict Management* 13 (2002), pp. 78–95; and N. B. Florea et al., "Negotiating from Mars to Venus: Gender in Simulated International Negotiations," *Simulation & Gaming* 34 (June 2003), pp. 226–48.

27. M. Sherif, "Superordinate Goals in the Reduction of Intergroup Conflict," *American Journal of Sociology* 68 (1958), pp. 349–58; K. M. Eisenhardt, J. L. Kahwajy, and L. J. Bourgeois III, "How Management Teams Can Have a Good Fight," *Harvard Business Review,* July–August 1997, pp. 77–85; and X. M. Song, J. Xile, and B. Dyer, "Antecedents and Consequences of Marketing Managers' Conflict-Handling Behaviors," *Journal of Marketing* 64 (January 2000), pp. 50–66.

28. H. C. Triandis, "The Future of Workforce Diversity in International Organisations: A Commentary," *Applied Psychology: An International Journal* 52, no. 3 (2003), pp. 486–95.

29. E. Elron, B. Shamir, and E. Bem-Ari, "Why Don't They Fight Each Other? Cultural Diversity and Operational Unity in Multinational Forces," *Armed Forces & Society* 26 (October 1999), pp. 73–97; and "Teamwork Polishes This Diamond," *Philippine Daily Inquirer,* October 4, 2000, p. 10.

30. K. R. Lewis, "(Drum) Beatings Build Corporate Spirit," *Star Tribune* (Minneapolis), June 3, 2003, p. 3E; "Oh What a Feeling!" *Music Trades,* May 2004, pp. 94–95; and D. Cole, "Joining the Tom-

Tom Club," *U.S. News & World Report,* March 22, 2004, p. D12.

31. T. F. Pettigrew, "Intergroup Contact Theory," *Annual Review of Psychology* 49 (1998), pp. 65–85; S. Brickson, "The Impact of Identity Orientation on Individual and Organizational Outcomes in Demographically Diverse Settings," *Academy of Management Review* 25 (January 2000), pp. 82–101; and J. Dixon and K. Durrheim, "Contact and the Ecology of Racial Division: Some Varieties of Informal Segregation," *British Journal of Social Psychology* 42 (March 2003), pp. 1–23.

32. Triandis, "The Future of Workforce Diversity in International Organisations."

33. Von Glinow, Shapiro, and Brett, "Can We Talk, and Should We?"

34. P. O. Walker, "Decolonizing Conflict Resolution: Addressing the Ontological Violence of Westernization," *American Indian Quarterly* 28, no. 3/4 (July 2004), pp. 527–49; and Native Dispute Resolution Network, "Glossary of Terms," http://nativenetwork.ecr.gov, accessed September 15, 2005.

35. E. Horwitt, "Knowledge, Knowledge, Who's Got the Knowledge," *Computerworld,* April 8, 1996, pp. 80, 81, 84.

36. L. L. Putnam, "Beyond Third-Party Role: Disputes and Managerial Intervention," *Employee Responsibilities and Rights Journal* 7 (1994), pp. 23–36; and A. R. Elangovan, "The Manager as the Third Party: Deciding How to Intervene in Employee Disputes," in *Negotiation: Readings, Exercises, and Cases,* ed. R. J. Lewicki, J. A. Litterer, and D. Saunders, 3rd ed. (New York: McGraw-Hill, 1999), pp. 458–69. For a somewhat different taxonomy of managerial conflict intervention, see P. G. Irving and J. P. Meyer, "A Multidimensional Scaling Analysis of Managerial Third-Party Conflict Intervention Strategies," *Canadian Journal of Behavioural Science* 29, no. 1 (January 1997), pp. 7–18.

37. B. H. Sheppard, "Managers as Inquisitors: Lessons from the Law," in *Bargaining inside Organizations,* ed. M. H. Bazerman and R. J. Lewicki (Beverly Hills, CA: Sage, 1983); and N. H. Kim, D. W. Sohn, and J. A. Wall, "Korean Leaders' (and Subordinates') Conflict Management," *International Journal of Conflict Management* 10, no. 2 (April 1999), pp. 130–53.

38. R. Karambayya and J. M. Brett, "Managers Handling Disputes: Third-Party Roles and Perceptions of Fairness," *Academy of Management Journal* 32 (1989), pp. 687–704; and R. Cropanzano et al., "Disputant Reactions to Managerial Conflict Resolution Tactics," *Group & Organization Management* 24 (June 1999), pp. 124–53.

39. A. R. Elangovan, "Managerial Intervention in Organizational Disputes: Testing a Prescriptive Model of Strategy Selection," *International Journal of Conflict Management* 4 (1998), pp. 301–35; and P. S. Nugent, "Managing Conflict: Third-Party Interventions for Managers," *Academy of Management Executive* 16, no. 1 (February 2002), pp. 139–54.

40. J. P. Meyer, J. M. Gemmell, and P. G. Irving, "Evaluating the Management of Interpersonal Conflict in Organizations: A Factor-Analytic Study of Outcome Criteria," *Canadian Journal of Administrative Sciences* 14 (1997), pp. 1–13.

chapter 11

1. K. Brooker and J. Schlosser, "The Un-CEO," *Fortune,* September 16, 2002, pp. 88–93; B. Nussbaum, "The Power of Design," *Business Week,* May 17, 2004, p. 86; N. Buckley, "The Calm Reinventor," *Financial Times* (London), January 29, 2005, p. 11; S. Ellison, "Women's Touch Guides P&G Chief's Firm Hand in Company Turnaround," *The Wall Street Journal Europe,* June 1, 2005, p. A1; S. Hill Jr., "P&G's Turnaround Proves Listening to Customer Pays," *Manufacturing Business Technology,* July 2005, p. 64; and J. Tylee, "Procter's Creative Gamble," *Campaign,* March 18, 2005, pp. 24–26.

2. R. House, M. Javidan, and P. Dorfman, "Project Globe: An Introduction," *Applied Psychology: An International Review* 50 (2001), pp. 489–505; and R. House et al., "Understanding Cultures and Implicit Leadership Theories across the Globe: An Introduction to Project Globe," *Journal of World Business* 37 (2002), pp. 3–10.

3. R. G. Issac, W. J. Zerbe, and D. C. Pitt, "Leadership and Motivation: The Effective Application of Expectancy Theory," *Journal of Managerial Issues* 13 (Summer 2001), pp. 212–26; C. L. Pearce and J. A. Conger, eds., *Shared Leadership: Reframing the Hows and Whys of Leadership* (Thousand Oaks, CA: Sage, 2003); and J. S. Nielson, *The Myth of Leadership* (Palo Alto, CA: Davies-Black, 2004).

4. C. L. Cole, "Eight Values Bring Unity to a Worldwide Company," *Workforce,* March 2001, pp. 44–45.

5. J. Raelin, "Preparing for Leaderful Practice," *T+D,* March 2004, p. 64.

6. Many of these perspectives are summarized in R. N. Kanungo, "Leadership in Organizations: Looking Ahead to the 21st Century," *Canadian Psychology* 39 (Spring 1998), pp. 71–82; and G. A. Yukl, *Leadership in Organizations,* 6th ed. (Upper Saddle River, NJ: Pearson Education, 2006).

7. R. M. Stogdill, *Handbook of Leadership* (New York: Free Press, 1974), Chap. 5.

8. M. D. Mumford et al., "Leadership Skills for a Changing World: Solving Complex Social Problems," *Leadership Quarterly* 11, no. 1 (2000), pp. 11–35; J. A. Conger and D. A. Ready, "Rethinking Leadership Competencies," *Leader to Leader* (Spring 2004), pp. 41–47; and S. J. Zaccaro, C. Kemp, and P. Bader, "Leader Traits and Attributes," in *The Nature of Leadership,* ed. J. Antonakis, A. T. Cianciolo, and R. J. Sternberg (Thousand Oaks, CA: Sage, 2004), pp. 101–24.

9. This list is based on S. A. Kirkpatrick and E. A. Locke, "Leadership: Do Traits Matter?" *Academy of Management Executive* 5 (May 1991), pp. 48–60; R. M. Aditya, R. J. House, and S. Kerr, "Theory and Practice of Leadership: Into the New Millennium," in *Industrial and Organizational Psychology: Linking Theory with Practice,* ed. C. L. Cooper and E. A. Locke (Oxford, UK: Blackwell, 2000), pp. 130–65; D. Goleman, R. Boyatzis, and A. McKee, *Primal Leaders* (Boston: Harvard Business School Press, 2002); T. A. Judge et al., "Personality and Leadership: A Qualitative and Quantitative Review," *Journal of Applied Psychology* 87, no. 4 (August 2002). pp. 765–80; and T. A. Judge, A. E. Colbert, and R. Ilies, "Intelligence and Leadership: A Quantitative Review and Test of Theoretical Propositions," *Journal of Applied Psychology* 89, no. 3 (June 2004), pp. 542–52.

10. J. George, "Emotions and Leadership: The Role of Emotional Intelligence," *Human Relations* 53 (August 2000), pp. 1027–55; Goleman, Boyatzis, and McKee, *Primal Leaders;* and R. G. Lord and R. J. Hall, "Identity, Deep Structure and the Development of Leadership Skill," *Leadership Quarterly* 16, no. 4 (August 2005), pp. 591–615.

11. D. R. May et al., "The Moral Component of Authentic Leadership," *Organizational Dynamics* 32 (August 2003), pp. 247–60; W. L. Gardner et al., "'Can You See the Real Me?' A Self-based Model of Authentic Leader and Follower Development," *Leadership Quarterly* 16 (2005), pp. 343–72. The large-scale studies are reported in C. Savoye, "Workers Say

Honesty Is Best Company Policy," *Christian Science Monitor,* June 15, 2000, p. 3; J. M. Kouzes and B. Z. Posner, *The Leadership Challenge,* 3rd ed. (San Francisco: Jossey-Bass, 2002), Chap. 2; and J. Schettler, "Leadership in Corporate America," *Training & Development,* September 2002, pp. 66–73.

12. J. Norman, "Ethical Fallout," *Orange County Register* (CA), August 5, 2002, p. 1; K. Melymuka, "Layoff Survivors," *Computerworld,* June 9, 2003, p. 26; A. Sidimé, "Company Ethics on Mend," *Express-News* (San Antonio), September 1, 2003; and Watson Wyatt, "Workers' Attitudes toward Leaders Rebounded Strongly between 2002 and 2004, Watson Wyatt Survey Finds," Watson Wyatt news release, Washington, DC, December 14, 2004.

13. R. J. House and R. N. Aditya, "The Social Scientific Study of Leadership: Quo Vadis?" *Journal of Management* 23 (1997), pp. 409–73.

14. R. Jacobs, "Using Human Resource Functions to Enhance Emotional Intelligence," in *The Emotionally Intelligent Workplace,* ed. C. Cherniss and D. Goleman (San Francisco: Jossey-Bass, 2001), pp. 161–63; and Conger and Ready, "Rethinking Leadership Competencies."

15. P. G. Northouse, *Leadership: Theory and Practice,* 3rd ed. (Thousand Oaks, CA: Sage, 2004), Chap. 4; and Yukl, *Leadership in Organizations,* Chap. 3.

16. A. K. Korman, "Consideration, Initiating Structure, and Organizational Criteria—A Review," *Personnel Psychology* 19 (1966), pp. 349–62; E. A. Fleishman, "Twenty Years of Consideration and Structure," in *Current Developments in the Study of Leadership,* ed. E. A. Fleishman and J. C. Hunt (Carbondale, IL: Southern Illinois University Press, 1973), pp. 1–40; T. A. Judge, R. F. Piccolo, and R. Ilies, "The Forgotten Ones? The Validity of Consideration and Initiating Structure in Leadership Research," *Journal of Applied Psychology* 89, no. 1 (2004), pp. 36–51; and Yukl, *Leadership in Organizations,* pp. 62–75.

17. V. V. Baba, "Serendipity in Leadership: Initiating Structure and Consideration in the Classroom," *Human Relations* 42 (1989), pp. 509–25.

18. S. Kerr et al., "Towards a Contingency Theory of Leadership Based upon the Consideration and Initiating Structure Literature," *Organizational Behavior and Human Performance* 12 (1974), pp. 62–82; and L. L. Larson, J. G. Hunt, and R. N.

Osborn, "The Great Hi–Hi Leader Behavior Myth: A Lesson from Occam's Razor," *Academy of Management Journal* 19 (1976), pp. 628–41.

19. R. Tannenbaum and W. H. Schmidt, "How to Choose a Leadership Pattern," *Harvard Business Review,* May–June 1973, pp. 162–80.

20. For a thorough study of how expectancy theory of motivation relates to leadership, see R. G. Isaac, W. J. Zerbe, and D. C. Pitt, "Leadership and Motivation: The Effective Application of Expectancy Theory," *Journal of Managerial Issues* 13 (Summer 2001), pp. 212–26.

21. R. J. House, "A Path-Goal Theory of Leader Effectiveness," *Administrative Science Quarterly* 16 (1971), pp. 321–38; M. G. Evans, "Extensions of a Path-Goal Theory of Motivation," *Journal of Applied Psychology* 59 (1974), pp. 172–78; R. J. House and T. R. Mitchell, "Path-Goal Theory of Leadership," *Journal of Contemporary Business* (Autumn 1974), pp. 81–97; and M. G. Evans, "Path-Goal Theory of Leadership," in *Leadership,* ed. L. L. Neider and C. A. Schriesheim (Greenwich, CT: Information Age Publishing, 2002), pp. 115–38.

22. Various thoughts on servant leadership are presented in L. C. Spears and M. Lawrence, eds., *Focus on Leadership: Servant-Leadership* (New York: John Wiley & Sons, 2002).

23. R. J. House, "Path-Goal Theory of Leadership: Lessons, Legacy, and a Reformulated Theory," *Leadership Quarterly* 7 (1996), pp. 323–52.

24. D.-A. Durbin, "New Chrysler Boss LaSorda Gears up to Improve Efficiency," *St. Louis Post-Dispatch,* August 21, 2005, p. E1.

25. J. Indvik, "Path-Goal Theory of Leadership: A Meta-Analysis," *Academy of Management Proceedings* (1986), pp. 189–92; and J. C. Wofford and L. Z. Liska, "Path-Goal Theories of Leadership: A Meta-Analysis," *Journal of Management* 19 (1993), pp. 857–76.

26. R. T. Keller, "A Test of the Path-Goal Theory of Leadership with Need for Clarity as a Moderator in Research and Development Organizations," *Journal of Applied Psychology* 74 (1989), pp. 208–12.

27. C. A. Schriesheim and L. L. Neider, "Path-Goal Leadership Theory: The Long and Winding Road," *Leadership Quarterly* 7 (1996), pp. 317–21.

28. This observation has also been made by C. A. Schriesheim, "Substitutes-for-

Leadership Theory: Development and Basic Concepts," *Leadership Quarterly* 8 (1997), pp. 103–8.

29. D. F. Elloy and A. Randolph, "The Effect of Superleader Behavior on Autonomous Work Groups in a Government Operated Railway Service," *Public Personnel Management* 26 (Summer 1997). pp. 257–72; and C. C. Manz and H. Sims Jr., *The New SuperLeadership: Leading Others to Lead Themselves* (San Francisco: Berrett-Koehler, 2001).

30. M. L. Loughry, "Coworkers Are Watching: Performance Implications of Peer Monitoring," *Academy of Management Proceedings* (2002), pp. O1–O6.

31. C. C. Manz and C. Neck, *Mastering Self-Leadership,* 3rd ed. (Upper Saddle River, NJ: Prentice Hall, 2004).

32. P. M. Podsakoff and S. B. MacKenzie, "Kerr and Jermier's Substitutes for Leadership Model: Background, Empirical Assessment, and Suggestions for Future Research," *Leadership Quarterly* 8 (1997), pp. 117–32; S. D. Dionne et al., "Neutralizing Substitutes for Leadership Theory: Leadership Effects and Common-Source Bias," *Journal of Applied Psychology* 87, no. 3 (June 2002), pp. 454–64; J. R. Villa et al., "Problems with Detecting Moderators in Leadership Research Using Moderated Multiple Regression," *Leadership Quarterly* 14, no. 1 (February 2003), pp. 3–23; and S. D. Dionne et al., "Substitutes for Leadership, or Not," *Leadership Quarterly* 16, no. 1 (2005), pp. 169–93.

33. J. M. Burns, *Leadership* (New York: Harper & Row, 1978); B. M. Bass, *Transformational Leadership: Industrial, Military, and Educational Impact* (Hillsdale, NJ: Erlbaum, 1998); and B. J. Avolio and F. J. Yammarino, eds., *Transformational and Charismatic Leadership: The Road Ahead* (Greenwich, CT: JAI Press, 2002).

34. V. L. Goodwin, J. C. Wofford, and J. L. Whittington "A Theoretical and Empirical Extension to the Transformational Leadership Construct," *Journal of Organizational Behavior* 22 (November 2001), pp. 759–74.

35. A. Zaleznik, "Managers and Leaders: Are They Different?" *Harvard Business Review* 55, no. 5 (1977), pp. 67–78; W. Bennis and B. Nanus, *Leaders: The Strategies for Taking Charge* (New York: Harper & Row, 1985); and R. H. G. Field, "Leadership Defined: Web Images Reveal the Differences between Leadership and Management" in *Annual Conference of the*

Administrative Sciences Association of Canada, Organizational Behavior Division, ed. P. Mudrack (Winnipeg, Manitoba, May 25–28, 2002), p. 93.

36. Both transformational and transactional leadership improve work unit performance. See B. M. Bass et al., "Predicting Unit Performance by Assessing Transformational and Transactional Leadership," *Journal of Applied Psychology* 88 (April 2003), pp. 207–18.

37. For discussion on the tendency to slide from transformational to transactional leadership, see W. Bennis, *An Invented Life: Reflections on Leadership and Change* (Reading, MA: Addison-Wesley, 1993).

38. R. J. House, "A 1976 Theory of Charismatic Leadership," in *Leadership: The Cutting Edge,* ed. J. G. Hunt and L. L. Larson (Carbondale, IL.: Southern Illinois University Press, 1977), pp. 189–207; and J. A. Conger, "Charismatic and Transformational Leadership in Organizations: An Insider's Perspective on These Developing Streams of Research," *Leadership Quarterly* 10 (Summer 1999), pp. 145–79.

39. J. E. Barbuto, "Taking the Charisma out of Transformational Leadership," *Journal of Social Behavior & Personality* 12 (September 1997), pp. 689–97; Y. A. Nur, "Charisma and Managerial Leadership: The Gift That Never Was," *Business Horizons* 41 (July 1998), pp. 19–26; and M. D. Mumford and J. R. Van Doorn, "The Leadership of Pragmatism—Reconsidering Franklin in the Age of Charisma," *Leadership Quarterly* 12, no. 3 (Fall 2001), pp. 279–309.

40. R. E. De Vries, R. A. Roe, and T. C. B. Taillieu, "On Charisma and Need for Leadership," *European Journal of Work and Organizational Psychology* 8 (1999), pp. 109–33; and R. Khurana, *Searching for a Corporate Savior: The Irrational Quest for Charismatic CEOs* (Princeton, NJ: Princeton University Press, 2002).

41. K. L. Miller, "The Quiet CEOs," *Newsweek,* December 20, 2004, pp. E10– E12.

42. Bennis and Nanus, *Leaders,* pp. 27–33, 89; I. M. Levin, "Vision Revisited," *Journal of Applied Behavioral Science* 36 (March 2000), pp. 91–107; J. R. Sparks and J. A. Schenk, "Explaining the Effects of Transformational Leadership: An Investigation of the Effects of Higher-Order Motives in Multilevel Marketing Organizations," *Journal of Organizational Behavior* 22 (2001), pp. 849–69; D. Christenson and D. H. T. Walker, "Understanding the Role of 'Vision' in

Project Success," *Project Management Journal* 35, no. 3 (September 2004), pp. 39–52; and R. E. Quinn, *Building the Bridge as You Walk on It: A Guide for Leading Change* (San Francisco: Jossey-Bass, 2004), Chap. 11.

43. J. R. Baum, E. A. Locke, and S. A. Kirkpatrick, "A Longitudinal Study of the Relation of Vision and Vision Communication to Venture Growth in Entrepreneurial Firms," *Journal of Applied Psychology* 83 (1998), pp. 43–54; and S. L. Hoe and S. L. McShane, "Leadership Antecedents of Informal Knowledge Acquisition and Dissemination," *International Journal of Organisational Behaviour* 5 (2002), pp. 282–91.

44. J. A. Conger, "Inspiring Others: The Language of Leadership," *Academy of Management Executive* 5 (February 1991), pp. 31–45; G. T. Fairhurst and R. A. Sarr, *The Art of Framing: Managing the Language of Leadership* (San Francisco, CA: Jossey-Bass, 1996); and A. E. Rafferty and M. A. Griffin, "Dimensions of Transformational Leadership: Conceptual and Empirical Extensions," *Leadership Quarterly* 15, no. 3 (2004), pp. 329–54.

45. L. Black, "Hamburger Diplomacy," *Report on Business Magazine,* August 1988, pp. 30–36.

46. D. E. Berlew, "Leadership and Organizational Excitement," *California Management Review* 17, no. 2 (Winter 1974), pp. 21–30; Bennis and Nanus, *Leaders,* pp. 43–55; and T. Simons, "Behavioral Integrity: The Perceived Alignment between Managers' Words and Deeds as a Research Focus," *Organization Science* 13, no. 1 (January–February 2002), pp. 18–35.

47. "Most Influential Women and Women to Watch: Karen Gilles Larson," *Minneapolis–St. Paul Business Journal,* July 26, 2002, p. S31; "Underpaid Women CEOs Say Pay Meets Standards," *Minneapolis–St. Paul Business Journal,* July 18, 2003, p. 23; and N. St. Anthony, "CEO Led Synovis Back from Brink," *Star Tribune* (Minneapolis), February 16, 2003, p. D1.

48. J. Barling, T. Weber, and E. K. Kelloway, "Effects of Transformational Leadership Training on Attitudinal and Financial Outcomes: A Field Experiment," *Journal of Applied Psychology* 81 (1996), pp. 827–32.

49. A. Bryman, "Leadership in Organizations," in *Handbook of Organization Studies,* ed. S. R. Clegg, C. Hardy, and W. R. Nord (Thousand Oaks, CA: Sage, 1996), pp. 276–92.

50. B. S. Pawar and K. K. Eastman, "The Nature and Implications of Contextual Influences on Transformational Leadership: A Conceptual Examination," *Academy of Management Review* 22 (1997), pp. 80–109; and C. P. Egri and S. Herman, "Leadership in the North American Environmental Sector: Values, Leadership Styles, and Contexts of Environmental Leaders and Their Organizations," *Academy of Management Journal* 43, no. 4 (2000), pp. 571–604.

51. J. R. Meindl, "On Leadership: An Alternative to the Conventional Wisdom," *Research in Organizational Behavior* 12 (1990), pp. 159–203; L. R. Offermann, J. J. K. Kennedy, and P. W. Wirtz, "Implicit Leadership Theories: Content, Structure, and Generalizability," *Leadership Quarterly* 5, no. 1 (1994), pp. 43–58; R. J. Hall and R. G. Lord, "Multi-Level Information Processing Explanations of Followers' Leadership Perceptions," *Leadership Quarterly* 6 (1995), pp. 265–87; and O. Epitropaki and R. Martin, "Implicit Leadership Theories in Applied Settings: Factor Structure, Generalizability, and Stability over Time," *Journal of Applied Psychology* 89, no. 2 (2004), pp. 293–310.

52. L. M. A. Chong and D. C. Thomas, "Leadership Perceptions in Cross-Cultural Context: Pakeha and Pacific Islanders in New Zealand," *Leadership Quarterly* 8 (1997), pp. 275–93; R. G. Lord et al., "Contextual Constraints on Prototype Generation and Their Multilevel Consequences for Leadership Perceptions," *Leadership Quarterly* 12, no. 3 (2001), pp. 311–38; and T. Keller, "Parental Images as a Guide to Leadership Sensemaking: An Attachment Perspective on Implicit Leadership Theories," *Leadership Quarterly* 14 (2003), pp. 141–60.

53. S. F. Cronshaw and R. G. Lord, "Effects of Categorization, Attribution, and Encoding Processes on Leadership Perceptions," *Journal of Applied Psychology* 72 (1987), pp. 97–106; and J. L. Nye and D. R. Forsyth, "The Effects of Prototype-Based Biases on Leadership Appraisals: A Test of Leadership Categorization Theory," *Small Group Research* 22 (1991), pp. 360–79.

54. M. A. Hogg, "A Social Identity Theory of Leadership," *Personality and Social Psychology Review* 5, no. 3 (August 2001), pp. 184–200; and N. Ensari and S. E. Murphy, "Cross-Cultural Variations in Leadership Perceptions and Attribution of Charisma to the Leader," *Organizational Behavior and Human Decision Processes* 92 (2003), pp. 52–66.

55. G. N. Powell, "One More Time: Do Female and Male Managers Differ?" *Academy of Management Executive* 4 (1990), pp. 68–75; and M. L. van Engen and T. M. Willemsen, "Sex and Leadership Styles: A Meta-Analysis of Research Published in the 1990s," *Psychological Reports* 94, no. 1 (February 2004), pp. 3–18.

56. R. Sharpe, "As Leaders, Women Rule," *Business Week,* November 20, 2000, p. 74; M. Sappenfield and J. F. Day, "Women, It Seems, Are Better Bosses," *Christian Science Monitor,* January 16, 2001, p. 1; A. H. Eagly and L. L. Carli, "The Female Leadership Advantage: An Evaluation of the Evidence," *Leadership Quarterly* 14, no. 6 (December 2003), pp. 807–34; and A. H. Eagly, M. C. Johannesen-Schmidt, and M. L. van Engen, "Transformational, Transactional, and Laissez-Faire Leadership Styles: A Meta-Analysis Comparing Women and Men," *Psychological Bulletin* 129 (July 2003), pp. 569–91.

57. A. H. Eagly, S. J. Karau, and M. G. Makhijani, "Gender and the Effectiveness of Leaders: A Meta-Analysis," *Psychological Bulletin* 117 (1995), pp. 125–45; J. G. Oakley, "Gender-Based Barriers to Senior Management Positions: Understanding the Scarcity of Female CEOs," *Journal of Business Ethics* 27 (2000), pp. 321–34; and N. Z. Stelter, "Gender Differences in Leadership: Current Social Issues and Future Organizational Implications," *Journal of Leadership Studies* 8 (2002), pp. 88–99; and A. H. Eagly, "Achieving Relational Authenticity in Leadership: Does Gender Matter?" *Leadership Quarterly* 16, no. 3 (June 2005), pp. 459–74.

chapter 12

1. "The Firm That Lets Staff Breathe," *Sunday Times* (London), March 24, 2002; A. Brown, "Satisfaction All in a Day's Work for Top 3," *Evening News* (Edinburgh, Scotland), March 23, 2002, p. 13; M. Weinreb, "Power to the People," *Sales & Marketing Management,* April 2003, pp. 30–35; A. Deutschman, "The Fabric of Creativity," *Fast Company,* December 2004, pp. 54–59; and L. D. Maloney, "Smiles in the Workplace," *Test & Measurement World,* March 2004, p. 5.

2. H. Mintzberg, *The Structuring of Organizations* (Englewood Cliffs, NJ: Prentice Hall, 1979), pp. 2–3.

3. E. E. Lawler III, *Motivation in Work Organizations* (Monterey, CA: Brooks-Cole, 1973); and M. A. Campion, "Ability Requirement Implications of Job Design:

An Interdisciplinary Perspective," *Personnel Psychology* 42 (1989), pp. 1–24.

4. Mintzberg, *The Structuring of Organizations,* pp. 2–8; and D. A. Nadler and M. L. Tushman, *Competing by Design: The Power of Organizational Architecture* (New York: Oxford University Press, 1997), Chap. 6.

5. C. Downs, P. Clampitt, and A. L. Pfeiffer, "Communication and Organizational Outcomes," in *Handbook of Organizational Communication,* ed. G. Goldhaber and G. Barnett (Norwood, NJ: Ablex, 1988), pp. 171–211; and I. Nonaka and H. Takeuchi, *The Knowledge-Creating Company* (New York: Oxford University Press, 1995).

6. A. L. Patti, J. P. Gilbert, and S. Hartman, "Physical Co-Location and the Success of New Product Development Projects," *Engineering Management Journal* 9 (September 1997), pp. 31–37; and M. Hoque, M. Akter, and Y. Monden, "Concurrent Engineering: A Compromise Approach to Develop a Feasible and Customer-Pleasing Product," *International Journal of Production Research* 43, no. 8 (April 15, 2005), pp. 1607–24.

7. Y.-M. Hsieh and A. Tien-Hsieh, "Enhancement of Service Quality with Job Standardisation," *Service Industries Journal* 21 (July 2001), pp. 147–66.

8. A. Krisnakumar, "A Hospital on Wings," *Frontline,* November 23, 2002; and B. Batz, "Orbis Flying Hospital a Site for Sore Eyes," *Dayton Daily News* (Ohio), July 17, 2003.

9. J. H. Sheridan, "Lessons from the Best," *Industry Week,* February 20 1995, pp. 13–22.

10. D. D. Van Fleet and B. A. G., "A History of the Span of Management," *Academy of Management Review* 2 (1977), pp. 356–72; and Mintzberg, *The Structuring of Organizations,* Chap. 8.

11. "BASF Culling Saves (GBP) 4m," *Personnel Today,* February 19, 2002, p. 3.

12. Q. N. Huy, "In Praise of Middle Managers," *Harvard Business Review* 79 (September 2001), pp. 72–79; and H. J. Leavitt, *Top Down: Why Hierarchies Are Here to Stay and How to Manage Them More Effectively* (Cambridge, MA: Harvard Business School Press, 2005).

13. P. Brabeck, "The Business Case against Revolution: An Interview with Nestle's Peter Brabeck," *Harvard Business Review* 79 (February 2001), p. 112; H. A. Richardson et al., "Does Decentralization Make a Difference for the Organization? An

Examination of the Boundary Conditions Circumscribing Decentralized Decision-Making and Organizational Financial Performance," *Journal of Management* 28, no. 2 (2002), pp. 217–44; and G. Masado, "To Centralize or Decentralize?" *Optimize,* May 2005, p. 58.

14. Mintzberg, *The Structuring of Organizations,* Chap. 5.

15. T. Burns and G. Stalker, *The Management of Innovation* (London: Tavistock, 1961).

16. D. Youngblood, "Computer Consultants Win Business with Creative Strategies," *Star Tribune* (Minneapolis), July 15, 2001; S. Brouillard, "Right at Home," *Minneapolis–St. Paul Business Journal,* August 23, 2002; and J. Fure, "Staying Connected," *Minneapolis–St. Paul Business Journal,* August 20, 2004.

17. J. Tata, S. Prasad, and R. Thom, "The Influence of Organizational Structure on the Effectiveness of TQM Programs," *Journal of Managerial Issues* 11, no. 4 (Winter 1999), pp. 440–53; and A. Lam, "Tacit Knowledge, Organizational Learning and Societal Institutions: An Integrated Framework," *Organization Studies* 21 (May 2000), pp. 487–513.

18. Mintzberg, *The Structuring of Organizations,* p. 106.

19. Ibid., Chap. 17.

20. J. R. Galbraith, *Designing Organizations* (San Francisco: Jossey-Bass, 2002), pp. 23–25.

21. E. E. Lawler III, *Rewarding Excellence: Pay Strategies for the New Economy* (San Francisco: Jossey-Bass, 2000), pp. 31–34.

22. These structures were identified from corporate websites and annual reports. These companies include a mixture of other structures, so the charts shown are adapted for learning purposes.

23. M. Goold and A. Campbell, "Do You Have a Well-Designed Organization," *Harvard Business Review* 80 (March 2002), pp. 117–24.

24. J. R. Galbraith, "Structuring Global Organizations," in *Tomorrow's Organization,* ed. S. A. Mohrman et al. (San Francisco: Jossey-Bass, 1998), pp. 103–29; C. Homburg, J. P. Workman Jr., and O. Jensen, "Fundamental Changes in Marketing Organization: The Movement toward a Customer-focused Organizational Structure," *Academy of Marketing Science. Journal* 28 (Fall 2000), pp. 459–78; T. H. Davenport, J. G. Harris, and A. K. Kohli, "How Do They Know Their Customers So Well?" *Sloan Management Review* 42

(Winter 2001), pp. 63–73; and J. R. Galbraith, "Organizing to Deliver Solutions," *Organizational Dynamics* 31 (2002), pp. 194–207.

25. J. Teresko, "Transforming GM," *Industry Week,* December–January 2002, pp. 34–38; and E. Prewitt, "GM's Matrix Reloads," *CIO Magazine,* September 1, 2003.

26. R. C. Ford and W. A. Randolph, "Cross-Functional Structures: A Review and Integration of Matrix Organization and Project Management," *Journal of Management* 18 (1992), pp. 267–94.

27. G. Calabrese, "Communication and Co-Operation in Product Development: A Case Study of a European Car Producer," *R & D Management* 27 (July 1997), pp. 239–52; and T. Sy and L. S. D'Annunzio, "Challenges and Strategies of Matrix Organizations: Top-Level and Mid-Level Managers' Perspectives," *Human Resource Planning* 28, no. 1 (2005), pp. 39–48.

28. Nadler and Tushman, *Competing by Design,* Chap. 6; and M. Goold and A. Campbell, "Structured Networks: Towards the Well-Designed Matrix," *Long Range Planning* 36, no. 5 (October 2003), pp. 427–39.

29. J. R. Galbraith, E. E. Lawler III, and Associates, *Organizing for the Future: The New Logic for Managing Complex Organizations* (San Francisco: Jossey-Bass, 1993); and R. Bettis and M. Hitt, "The New Competitive Landscape," *Strategic Management Journal* 16 (1995), pp. 7–19.

30. P. C. Ensign, "Interdependence, Coordination, and Structure in Complex Organizations: Implications for Organization Design," *Mid-Atlantic Journal of Business* 34 (March 1998), pp. 5–22.

31. R. Cross, "Looking before You Leap: Assessing the Jump to Teams in Knowledge-Based Work," *Business Horizons,* September 2000, pp. 29–36; M. Fenton-O'Creevy, "Employee Involvement and the Middle Manager: Saboteur or Scapegoat?" *Human Resource Management Journal* 11 (2001), pp. 24–40; G. Garda, K. Lindstrom, and M. Dallnera, "Towards a Learning Organization: The Introduction of a Client-Centered Team-Based Organization in Administrative Surveying Work," *Applied Ergonomics* 34 (2003), pp. 97–105; and C. Douglas and W. L. Gardner, "Transition to Self-Directed Work Teams: Implications of Transition Time and Self-Monitoring for Managers' Use of Influence Tactics," *Journal of Organizational Behavior* 25 (2004), pp. 47–65.

32. L. Donaldson, *The Contingency Theory of Organizations* (Thousand Oaks, CA: Sage, 2001); and J. Birkenshaw, R. Nobel, and J. Ridderstrâle, "Knowledge as a Contingency Variable: Do the Characteristics of Knowledge Predict Organizational Structure?" *Organization Science* 13, no. 3 (May–June 2002), pp. 274–89.

33. P. R. Lawrence and J. W. Lorsch, *Organization and Environment* (Homewood, IL: Irwin, 1967); and Mintzberg, *The Structuring of Organizations,* Chap. 15.

34. Burns and Stalker, *The Management of Innovation;* and Lawrence and Lorsch, *Organization and Environment.*

35. J. G. Kelley, "Slurpees and Sausages: 7-Eleven Holds School," *Richmond (VA) Times-Dispatch,* March 12, 2004, p. C1; and S. Marling, "The 24-Hour Supply Chain," *InformationWeek,* January 26, 2004, p. 43.

36. Mintzberg, *The Structuring of Organizations,* p. 282.

37. D. S. Pugh and C. R. Hinings, *Organizational Structure: Extensions and Replications* (Farnborough, England: Lexington Books, 1976); and Mintzberg, *The Structuring of Organizations,* Chap. 13.

38. G. Hertel, S. Geister, and U. Konradt, "Managing Virtual Teams: A Review of Current Empirical Research," *Human Resource Management Review* 15 (2005), pp. 69–95.

39. C. Perrow, "A Framework for the Comparative Analysis of Organizations," *American Sociological Review* 32 (1967), pp. 194–208; D. Gerwin, "The Comparative Analysis of Structure and Technology: A Critical Appraisal," *Academy of Management Review* 4, no. 1 (1979), pp. 41–51; and C. C. Miller et al., "Understanding Technology-Structure Relationships: Theory Development and Meta-Analytic Theory Testing," *Academy of Management Journal* 34, no. 2 (1991), pp. 370–99.

40. R. H. Kilmann, *Beyond the Quick Fix* (San Francisco: Jossey-Bass, 1984), p. 38.

41. A. D. Chandler, *Strategy and Structure* (Cambridge, MA: MIT Press, 1962).

42. A. M. Porter, *Competitive Strategy* (New York: Free Press, 1980).

43. D. Miller, "Configurations of Strategy and Structure," *Strategic Management Journal* 7 (1986), pp. 233–49.

chapter 13

1. F. Vogelstein and E. Florian, "Can Schwab Get Its Mojo Back?" *Fortune,* September 17, 2001, p. 93; B. Morris, "When Bad Things Happen to Good Companies," *Fortune,* December 8, 2003, p. 78; S. Craig and K. Brown, "Schwab Ousts Pottruck as CEO," *The Wall Street Journal,* July 21, 2004, p. A1; R. Frank, "U.S. Trust Feels Effects of Switch," *The Wall Street Journal,* July 21, 2004, p. A8; R. Frank and S. Craig, "White-Shoe Shuffle," *The Wall Street Journal,* September 15, 2004, p. A1; C. Harrington, "Made in Heaven? Watching the Wachovia-Tanager Union," *Accounting Today,* December 20, 2004, p. 18; and J. Kador, "Cultures in Conflict," *Registered Rep,* October 2004, p. 43.

2. A. Williams, P. Dobson, and M. Walters, *Changing Culture: New Organizational Approaches* (London: Institute of Personnel Management, 1989); and E. H. Schein, "What Is Culture?" in *Reframing Organizational* Culture, ed. P. J. Frost et al. (Beverly Hills: Sage, 1991), pp. 243–53.

3. B. M. Meglino and E. C. Ravlin, "Individual Values in Organizations: Concepts, Controversies, and Research," *Journal of Management* 24, no. 3 (1998), pp. 351–89; B. R. Agle and C. B. Caldwell, "Understanding Research on Values in Business," Business and Society 38, no. 3 (September 1999), pp. 326–87; and S. Hitlin and J. A. Pilavin, "Values: Reviving a Dormant Concept," *Annual Review of Sociology* 30 (2004), pp. 359–93.

4. J. S. Ott, *The Organizational Culture Perspective* (Pacific Grove, CA: Brooks/Cole, 1989), pp. 45–47; and S. Sackmann, "Culture and Subcultures: An Analysis of Organizational Knowledge," *Administrative Science Quarterly* 37 (1992), pp. 140–61.

5. A. Sinclair, "Approaches to Organizational Culture and Ethics," *Journal of Business Ethics* 12 (1993), pp. 63–73; and A. Boisnier and J. Chatman, "The Role of Subcultures in Agile Organizations," in *Leading and Managing People in Dynamic Organizations,* ed. R. Petersen and E. Mannix (Mahwah, NJ: Lawrence Erlbaum Associates, 2003), pp. 87–112.

6. Ott, *The Organizational Culture Perspective,* Chap. 2; J. S. Pederson and J. S. Sorensen, *Organizational Cultures in Theory and Practice* (Aldershot, England: Gower, 1989), pp. 27–29; and M. O. Jones, *Studying Organizational Symbolism: What, How, Why?* (Thousand Oaks, CA: Sage, 1996).

7. E. H. Schein, "Organizational Culture," *American Psychologist,* February 1990, pp. 109–19; A. Furnham and B. Gunter, "Corporate Culture: Definition, Diagnosis, and Change," *International Review of*

Industrial and Organizational Psychology 8 (1993), pp. 233–61; and E. H. Schein, *The Corporate Culture Survival Guide* (San Francisco: Jossey-Bass, 1999), Chap. 4.

8. A. L. Wilkins, "Organizational Stories as Symbols Which Control the Organization," in *Organizational Symbolism,* ed. L. R. Pondy et al. (Greenwich, CT: JAI Press, 1984), pp. 81–92; R. Zemke, "Storytelling: Back to a Basic," *Training* 27 (March 1990), pp. 44–50; J. C. Meyer, "Tell Me a Story: Eliciting Organizational Values from Narratives," *Communication Quarterly* 43 (1995), pp. 210–24; and W. Swap et al., "Using Mentoring and Storytelling to Transfer Knowledge in the Workplace," *Journal of Management Information Systems* 18 (Summer 2001), pp. 95–114.

9. M. Doehrman, "Anthropologists—Deep in the Corporate Bush," *Daily Record* (Kansas City, MO), July 19, 2005, p. 1.

10. R. E. Quinn and N. T. Snyder, "Advance Change Theory: Culture Change at Whirlpool Corporation," in *The Leader's Change Handbook,* ed. J. A. Conger, G. M. Spreitzer, and E. E. Lawler III (San Francisco: Jossey-Bass, 1999), pp. 162–93.

11. Churchill apparently made this statement on October 28, 1943, in the British House of Commons, when London, damaged by bombings in World War II, was about to be rebuilt.

12. P. Roberts, "The Empire Strikes Back," *Fast Company,* no. 22 (February–March 1999), pp. 122–31. Some details also found at www.oakley.com and americahurrah. com/oakley/entry.htm.

13. T. Kelley, *The Art of Innovation* (New York: Currency Doubleday, 2001), Chap. 7.

14. T. E. Deal and A. A. Kennedy, *The New Corporate Cultures* (Cambridge, MA: Perseus Books, 1999).

15. T. E. Deal and A. A. Kennedy, *Corporate Cultures* (Reading, MA: Addison-Wesley, 1982); J. B. Barney, "Organizational Culture: Can It Be a Source of Sustained Competitive Advantage?" *Academy of Management Review* 11 (1986), pp. 656–65; and C. Siehl and J. Martin, "Organizational Culture: A Key to Financial Performance?" in *Organizational Climate and Culture,* ed. B. Schneider (San Francisco: Jossey-Bass, 1990), pp. 241–81.

16. C. A. O'Reilly and J. A. Chatman, "Culture as Social Control: Corporations, Cults, and Commitment," *Research in Organizational Behavior* 18 (1996), pp. 157–200; J. C. Helms Mills and A. J. Mills, "Rules, Sensemaking, Formative Contexts,

and Discourse in the Gendering of Organizational Culture," in *International Handbook of Organizational Climate and Culture,* ed. N. Ashkanasy, C. Wilderom, and M. Peterson (Thousand Oaks, CA: Sage, 2000), pp. 55–70; and J. A. Chatman and S. E. Cha, "Leading by Leveraging Culture," *California Management Review* 45 (Summer 2003), pp. 20–34.

17. B. Ashforth and F. Mael, "Social Identity Theory and the Organization," *Academy of Management Review* 14 (1989), pp. 20–39.

18. M. R. Louis, "Surprise and Sensemaking: What Newcomers Experience in Entering Unfamiliar Organizational Settings," *Administrative Science Quarterly* 25 (1980), pp. 226–51; and S. G. Harris, "Organizational Culture and Individual Sensemaking: A Schema-Based Perspective," *Organization Science* 5 (1994), pp. 309–21.

19. D. R. Denison, *Corporate Culture and Organizational Effectiveness* (New York: Wiley, 1990); G. G. Gordon and N. DiTomasco, "Predicting Corporate Performance from Organizational Culture," *Journal of Management Studies* 29 (1992), pp. 783–98; and J. P. Kotter and J. L. Heskett, *Corporate Culture and Performance* (New York: Free Press, 1992).

20. "Japanese Officials Order Citibank to Halt Some Operations," *Dow Jones Business News,* September 17, 2004; "Citigroup CEO Prince Holds Press Conference in Japan," *Business Wire* (Tokyo), October 25, 2004; A. Morse, "Citigroup Extends Apology to Japan," *The Wall Street Journal,* October 26, 2004, p. A3; and M. Pacelle, M. Fackler, and A. Morse, "Mission Control," *The Wall Street Journal,* December 22, 2004, p. A1.

21. Kotter and Heskett, *Corporate Culture and Performance;* and J. P. Kotter, "Cultures and Coalitions," *Executive Excellence* 15 (March 1998), pp. 14–15.

22. M. L. Marks, "Adding Cultural Fit to Your Diligence Checklist," *Mergers & Acquisitions.* 34 (November–December 1999), pp. 14–20; Schein, *The Corporate Culture Survival Guide,* Chap. 8; M. L. Marks, "Mixed Signals," *Across the Board,* May 2000, pp. 21–26; and J. P. Daly, R. W. Pouder, and B. Kabanoff, "The Effects of Initial Differences in Firms' Espoused Values on Their Postmerger Performance," *Journal of Applied Behavioral Science* 40, no. 3 (September 2004), pp. 323–43.

23. A. Klein, "A Merger Taken AO-Ill," *Washington Post,* October 21 2002, p. E1; and A. Klein, *Stealing Time: Steve Case,*

Jerry Levin, and the Collapse of AOL Time Warner (New York: Simon & Shuster, 2003).

24. S. Greengard, "Due Diligence: The Devil in the Details," *Workforce,* October 1999, p. 68; and Marks, "Adding Cultural Fit to Your Diligence Checklist."

25. A. R. Malekazedeh and A. Nahavandi, "Making Mergers Work by Managing Cultures," *Journal of Business Strategy,* May–June 1990, pp. 55–57; and K. W. Smith, "A Brand-New Culture for the Merged Firm," *Mergers and Acquisitions* 35 (June 2000), pp. 45–50.

26. Hewitt Associates, "Mergers and Acquisitions May Be Driven by Business Strategy—but Often Stumble over People and Culture Issues," news release Lincolnshire, IL, August 3, 1998.

27. J. P. Kotter, "Leading Change: The Eight Steps of Transformation," in *The Leader's Change Handbook,* ed. J. A. Conger, G. M. Spreitzer, and E. E. Lawler III (San Francisco: Jossey-Bass, 1999), pp. 87–99.

28. E. H. Schein, "The Role of the Founder in Creating Organizational Culture," *Organizational Dynamics* 12, no. 1 (Summer 1983), pp. 13–28; R. House, M. Javidan, and P. Dorfman, "Project Globe: An Introduction," *Applied Psychology: An International Review* 50 (2001), pp. 489–505; and R. House et al., "Understanding Cultures and Implicit Leadership Theories across the Globe: An Introduction to Project Globe," *Journal of World Business* 37 (2002), pp. 3–10.

29. T. J. Peters, "Symbols, Patterns, and Settings: An Optimistic Case for Getting Things Done," *Organizational Dynamics* 7, no. 2 (Autumn 1978), pp. 2–23; and E. H. Schein, *Organizational Culture and Leadership* (San Francisco: Jossey-Bass, 1985), Chap. 10.

30. J. Kerr and J. W. Slocum Jr., "Managing Corporate Culture through Reward Systems," *Academy of Management Executive* 1 (May 1987), pp. 99–107; and K. R. Thompson and F. Luthans, "Organizational Culture: A Behavioral Perspective," in *Organizational Climate and Culture,* ed. B. Schneider (San Francisco: Jossey-Bass, 1990), pp. 319–44. John Deere's reward system is described in G. B. Sprinkle and M. G. Williamson, "The Evolution from Taylorism to Employee Gainsharing: A Case Study Examining John Deere's Continuous Improvement Pay Plan," *Issues in Accounting Education* 19, no. 4 (November 2004), pp. 487–503.

31. R. Anderson, "Climbing Mount Sustainability," *Quality Progress* 37, no. 2

(February 2004), pp. 32–37; M. Conlin, "From Plunderer to Protector," *Business Week,* July 19, 2004, p. 60; and P. Foster, "Heaven Can Wait," *National Post,* July 2, 2005, p. FP17.

32. K. McNeil and J. D. Thompson, "The Regeneration of Social Organizations," *American Sociological Review* 36 (1971), pp. 624–37; and W. G. Ouchi and A. M. Jaeger, "Type Z Organization: Stability in the Midst of Mobility," *Academy of Management Review* 3 (1978), pp. 305–14.

33. M. De Pree, *Leadership Is an Art* (East Lansing, MI: Michigan State University Press, 1987).

34. D. M. Cable and T. A. Judge, "Person-Organization Fit, Job Choice Decisions, and Organizational Entry," *Organizational Behavior and Human Decision Processes* 67, no. 3 (1996), p. 294; A. E. M. Van Vianen, "Person-Organization Fit: The Match between Newcomers' and Recruiters' Preferences for Organizational Cultures," *Personnel Psychology* 53 (Spring 2000), pp. 113–49; K. J. Lauver and A. Kristof-Brown, "Distinguishing between Employees' Perceptions of Person-Job and Person-Organization Fit," *Journal of Vocational Behavior* 59, no. 3 (December 2001), pp. 454–70; and J. W. Westerman and L. A. Cyr, "An Integrative Analysis of Person-Organization Fit Theories," *International Journal of Selection and Assessment* 12, no. 3 (September 2004), pp. 252–61.

35. J. Van Maanen, "Breaking In: Socialization to Work," in *Handbook of Work, Organization, and Society,* ed. R. Dubin (Chicago: Rand McNally, 1976), pp. 67–130.

36. S. Hirsch, "Software King Builds Young Careers, Too," *Baltimore Sun,* March 9, 2003, p. D1; and D. E. Lewis, "Internships Are Key Resumé Booster," *Boston Globe,* April 13, 2003, p. G1.

37. C. L. Adkins, "Previous Work Experience and Organizational Socialization: A Longitudinal Examination," *Academy of Management Journal* 38 (1995), pp. 839–62; and J. D. Kammeyer-Mueller and C. R. Wanberg, "Unwrapping the Organizational Entry Process: Disentangling Multiple Antecedents and Their Pathways to Adjustment," *Journal of Applied Psychology* 88, no. 5 (2003), pp. 779–94.

38. J. M. Beyer and D. R. Hannah, "Building on the Past: Enacting Established Personal Identities in a New Work Setting," *Organization Science* 13 (November–December 2002), pp. 636–52; and H. D. C. Thomas and N. Anderson, "Newcomer Adjustment: The Relationship between Organizational Socialization Tactics, Information Acquisition and Attitudes," *Journal of Occupational and Organizational Psychology* 75 (December 2002), pp. 423–37.

39. L. W. Porter, E. E. Lawler III, and J. R. Hackman, *Behavior in Organizations* (New York: McGraw-Hill, 1975), pp. 163–67; Van Maanen, "Breaking In: Socialization to Work"; and D. C. Feldman, "The Multiple Socialization of Organization Members," *Academy of Management Review* 6 (1981), pp. 309–18.

40. B. E. Ashforth and A. M. Saks, "Socialization Tactics: Longitudinal Effects on Newcomer Adjustment," *Academy of Management Journal* 39 (1996), pp. 149–78; and Kammeyer-Mueller and Wanberg, "Unwrapping the Organizational Entry Process."

41. Louis, "Surprise and Sensemaking: What Newcomers Experience in Entering Unfamiliar Organizational Settings."

42. R. Craver, "Dell Thinning out List of Job Candidates," *Winston-Salem Journal,* April 23, 2005.

43. J. A. Breaugh, *Recruitment: Science and Practice* (Boston: PWS-Kent, 1992); and J. P. Wanous, Organizational Entry (Reading, MA: Addison-Wesley, 1992).

44. J. M. Phillips, "Effects of Realistic Job Previews on Multiple Organizational Outcomes: A Meta-Analysis," *Academy of Management Journal* 41 (December 1998), pp. 673–90.

45. Y. Ganzach et al., "Social Exchange and Organizational Commitment: Decision-Making Training for Job Choice as an Alternative to the Realistic Job Preview," *Personnel Psychology* 55 (Autumn 2002), pp. 613–37.

46. C. Ostroff and S. W. J. Koslowski, "Organizational Socialization as a Learning Process: The Role of Information Acquisition," *Personnel Psychology* 45 (1992), pp. 849–74; E. W. Morrison, "Newcomer Information Seeking: Exploring Types, Modes, Sources, and Outcomes," *Academy of Management Journal* 36 (1993), pp. 557–89; and U. Anakwe and J. H. Greenhaus, "Effective Socialization of Employees: Socialization Content Perspective," *Journal of Managerial Issues* 11, no. 3 (Fall 1999), pp. 315–29.

47. D. Francis, "Work Is a Warm Puppy," *National Post,* May 27, 2000, p. W20; and C. Goforth, "Still Recruiting Staff," *Akron (OH) Beacon Journal,* July 15, 2001.

48. S. L. McShane, *Effect of Socialization Agents on the Organizational Adjustment of New Employees* (Big Sky, MT: Annual Conference of the Western Academy of Management, March 1988).

chapter 14

1. C. Lebner, "Nissan Motor Co.," *Fast Company,* July 2002, p. 80; C. Dawson, "On Your Marks," *Business Week,* March 17, 2003, p. 52; D. Magee, *Turn Around: How Carlos Ghosn Rescued Nissan* (New York: HarperCollins, 2003); and C. Ghosn and P. Riès, *Shift: Inside Nissan's Historic Revival* (New York: Currency Doubleday, 2005).

2. K. Lewin, *Field Theory in Social Science* (New York: Harper & Row, 1951).

3. C. O. Longenecker, D. J. Dwyer, and T. C. Stansfield, "Barriers and Gateways to Workforce Productivity," *Industrial Management,* March–April 1998, pp. 21–28; and J. Seifman, "Middle Managers—the Meat in the Corporate Sandwich," *China Staff,* June 2002, p. 7.

4. "The Wrong People Doing the Right Job: Reforming the FBI," *The Economist,* April 17, 2004, p. 371; National Commission on Terrorist Attacks upon the United States, *The 9/11 Commission Report* (Washington, DC: U.S. Government Printing Office, July 2004); D. Eggen, "FBI Fails to Transform Itself, Panel Says," *Washington Post,* June 7, 2005, p. A04; C. Ragavan and C. S. Hook, "Fixing the FBI," *U.S. News & World Report,* March 28, 2005, pp. 18–24, 26, 29–30; and Commission on the Intelligence Capabilities of the United States Regarding Weapons of Mass Destruction, *Report to the President of the United States* (Washington, DC.: U.S. Government Printing Office, March 31, 2005).

5. E. B. Dent and S. G. Goldberg, "Challenging 'Resistance to Change'," *Journal of Applied Behavioral Science* 35 (March 1999), pp. 25–41.

6. D. A. Nadler, "The Effective Management of Organizational Change," in *Handbook of Organizational Behavior,* ed. J. W. Lorsch (Englewood Cliffs, NJ: Prentice Hall, 1987), pp. 358–69; R. Maurer, *Beyond the Wall of Resistance: Unconventional Strategies to Build Support for Change* (Austin, TX: Bard Books, 1996); P. Strebel, "Why Do Employees Resist Change?" *Harvard Business Review,* May–June 1996, pp. 86–92; and D. A. Nadler, *Champions of Change* (San Francisco: Jossey-Bass, 1998).

7. "Making Change Work for You—Not against You," *Agency Sales Magazine* 28 (June 1998), pp. 24–27.

8. D. Miller, "What Happens after Success: The Perils of Excellence," *Journal of Management Studies* 31 (1994), pp. 325–58.

9. T. G. Cummings, "The Role and Limits of Change Leadership," in *The Leader's Change Handbook*, ed. J. A. Conger, G. M. Spreitzer, and E. E. Lawler III (San Francisco: Jossey-Bass, 1999), pp. 301–20; and J. P. Kotter and D. S. Cohen, *The Heart of Change* (Boston: Harvard Business School Press, 2002), pp. 15–36.

10. L. D. Goodstein and H. R. Butz, "Customer Value: The Linchpin of Organizational Change," *Organizational Dynamics* 27 (June 1998), pp. 21–35.

11. D. Darlin, "Growing Tomorrow," *Business 2.0*, May 2005, p. 126.

12. L. Grossman and S. Song, "Stevie's Little Wonder," *Time*, September 19, 2005, p. 63; and S. Levy, "Honey, I Shrunk the iPod. A Lot," *Newsweek*, September 19, 2005, p. 58.

13. J. P. Kotter and L. A. Schlesinger, "Choosing Strategies for Change," *Harvard Business Review*, March–April 1979, pp. 106–14.

14. B. Nanus and S. M. Dobbs, *Leaders Who Make a Difference* (San Francisco: Jossey-Bass, 1999); and Kotter and Cohen, *The Heart of Change*, pp. 83–98.

15. M. J. Marquardt, *Optimizing the Power of Action Learning: Solving Problems and Building Leaders in Real Time* (Palo Alto, CA: Davies-Black, 2004).

16. K. T. Dirks, L. L. Cummings, and J. L. Pierce, "Psychological Ownership in Organizations: Conditions under Which Individuals Promote and Resist Change," *Research in Organizational Change and Development* 9 (1996), pp. 1–23.

17. B. B. Bunker and B. T. Alban, *Large Group Interventions: Engaging the Whole System for Rapid Change* (San Francisco: Jossey-Bass, 1996); M. Weisbord and S. Janoff, *Future Search: An Action Guide to Finding Common Ground in Organizations and Communities* (San Francisco: Berrett-Koehler, 2000); and Darlin, "Growing Tomorrow."

18. M. McHugh, "The Stress Factor: Another Item for the Change Management Agenda?" *Journal of Organizational Change Management* 10 (1997), pp. 345–62; and D. Buchanan, T. Claydon, and M. Doyle, "Organisation Development and Change: The Legacy of the Nineties," *Human Resource Management Journal* 9 (1999), pp. 20–37.

19. D. Nicolini and M. B. Meznar, "The Social Construction of Organizational Learning: Conceptual and Practical Issues in the Field," *Human Relations* 48 (1995), pp. 727–46.

20. Kotter and Cohen, *The Heart of Change*, pp. 161–77.

21. R. H. Miles, "Leading Corporate Transformation: Are You up to the Task?" in *The Leader's Change Handbook*, ed. J. A. Conger, G. M. Spreitzer, and E. E. Lawler III (San Francisco: Jossey-Bass, 1999), pp. 221–67; and E. E. Lawler III, "Pay Can Be a Change Agent," *Compensation & Benefits Management* 16 (Summer 2000), pp. 23–26.

22. D. Helfand, "School Is Down but Looking Up," *Los Angeles Times*, October 14, 2004, p. B1; and "Mrs. Bush Remarks on Helping America's Youth in Sun Valley, California," White House news release, www.whitehouse.gov/news/releases/2005/04/20050427-5.html.

23. R. E. Quinn, *Building the Bridge as You Walk on It: A Guide for Leading Change* (San Francisco: Jossey-Bass, 2004), Chap. 11.

24. J. P. Kotter, "Leading Change: Why Transformation Efforts Fail," *Harvard Business Review*, March–April 1995, pp. 59–67; and J. P. Kotter, "Leading Change: The Eight Steps to Transformation," in *The Leader's Change Handbook*, ed. J. A. Conger, G. M. Spreitzer, and E. E. Lawler III (San Francisco: Jossey-Bass, 1999), pp. 221–67.

25. R. Caldwell, "Models of Change Agency: A Fourfold Classification," *British Journal of Management* 14 (June 2003), pp. 131–42.

26. P. Reason and H. Bradbury, *Handbook of Action Research* (London: Sage, 2001); D. Coghlan and T. Brannick, "Kurt Lewin: The 'Practical Theorist' for the 21st Century," *Irish Journal of Management* 24, no. 2 (2003), pp. 31–37; and C. Huxham and S. Vangen, "Researching Organizational Practice through Action Research: Case Studies and Design Choices," *Organizational Research Methods* 6 (July 2003), pp. 383–403.

27. V. J. Marsick and M. A. Gephart, "Action Research: Building the Capacity for Learning and Change," *Human Resource Planning* 26 (2003), pp. 14–18.

28. L. Dickens and K. Watkins, "Action Research: Rethinking Lewin," *Management Learning* 30 (June 1999), pp. 127–40; and J. Heron and P. Reason, "The Practice of Co-Operative Inquiry: Research 'with' Rather than 'on' People," in *Handbook of Action Research*, ed. P. Reason and H. Bradbury (Thousand Oaks, CA: Sage, 2001), pp. 179–88.

29. D. A. Nadler, "Organizational Frame Bending: Types of Change in the Complex Organization," in *Corporate Transformation: Revitalizing Organizations for a Competitive World*, ed. R. H. Kilmann, T. J. Covin, and Associates (San Francisco: Jossey-Bass, 1988), pp. 66–83; and K. E. Weick and R. E. Quinn, "Organizational Change and Development," *Annual Review of Psychology* (1999), pp. 361–86.

30. T. M. Egan and C. M. Lancaster, "Comparing Appreciative Inquiry to Action Research: OD Practitioner Perspectives," *Organization Development Journal* 23, no. 2 (Summer 2005), pp. 29–49.

31. F. Luthans, "The Need for and Meaning of Positive Organizational Behavior," *Journal of Organizational Behavior* 23 (2002), pp. 695–706; N. Turner, J. Barling, and A. Zacharatos, "Positive Psychology at Work," in *Handbook of Positive Psychology*, ed. C. R. Snyder and S. Lopez (Oxford, UK: Oxford University Press, 2002), pp. 715–30; K. Cameron, J. E. Dutton, and R. E. Quinn, eds., *Positive Organizational Scholarship: Foundation of a New Discipline* (San Francisco: Berrett Koehler Publishers, 2003); and J. I. Krueger and D. C. Funder, "Towards a Balanced Social Psychology: Causes, Consequences, and Cures for the Problem-Seeking Approach to Social Behavior and Cognition," *Behavioral and Brain Sciences* 27, no. 3 (June 2004), pp. 313–27.

32. D. Whitney and D. L. Cooperrider, "The Appreciative Inquiry Summit: Overview and Applications," *Employment Relations Today* 25 (Summer 1998), pp. 17–28; and J. M. Watkins and B. J. Mohr, *Appreciative Inquiry: Change at the Speed of Imagination* (San Francisco: Jossey-Bass, 2001).

33. F. J. Barrett and D. L. Cooperrider, "Generative Metaphor Intervention: A New Approach for Working with Systems Divided by Conflict and Caught in Defensive Perception," *Journal of Applied Behavioral Science* 26 (1990), pp. 219–39; Whitney and Cooperrider, "The Appreciative Inquiry Summit"; and Watkins and Mohr, *Appreciative Inquiry*, pp. 15–21.

34. M. LeJeune, "Companies Turning to 'Appreciative Inquiry' to Ask Staff What's Right," *Boulder County Business Report*, February 1999, p. 7; A. Trosten-Bloom, ed., *Case Study: Hunter Douglas Window Fashions Division* (San Francisco: Jossey-Bass, 2001); and D. Whitney and A. Trosten-Bloom, *The Power of Appreciative*

Inquiry: A Practical Guide to Positive Change (San Francisco: Berrett-Koehler Publishers, 2003).

35. T. F. Yaeger, P. F. Sorensen, and U. Bengtsson, "Assessment of the State of Appreciative Inquiry: Past, Present, and Future," *Research in Organizational Change and Development* 15 (2004), pp. 297–319; and G. R. Bushe and A. F. Kassam, "When Is Appreciative Inquiry Transformational? A Meta-Case Analysis," *Journal of Applied Behavioral Science* 41, no. 2 (June 2005), pp. 161–81.

36. G. R. Bushe, "Five Theories of Change Embedded in Appreciative Inquiry" in *18th Annual World Congress of Organization Development,* Dublin, Ireland, July 14–18, 1998.

37. G. R. Bushe and A. B. Shani, *Parallel Learning Structures* (Reading, MA: Addison-Wesley, 1991); and E. M. Van Aken, D. J. Monetta, and D. S. Sink, "Affinity Groups: The Missing Link in Employee Involvement," *Organization Dynamics* 22 (Spring 1994), pp. 38–54.

38. D. J. Knight, "Strategy in Practice: Making It Happen," *Strategy & Leadership* 26 (July–August 1998), pp. 29–33; R. T. Pascale, "Grassroots Leadership—Royal Dutch/Shell," *Fast Company,* no. 14 (April–May 1998), pp. 110–20; R. T. Pascale, "Leading from a Different Place," in *The Leader's Change Handbook,* ed. J. A. Conger, G. M. Spreitzer, and E. E. Lawler III (San Francisco: Jossey-Bass, 1999), pp. 301–20; and R. Pascale, M. Millemann, and L. Gioja, *Surfing on the Edge of Chaos* (London: Texere, 2000).

39. C.-M. Lau, "A Culture-Based Perspective of Organization Development Implementation," *Research in Organizational Change and Development* 9 (1996), pp. 49–79.

40. T. C. Head and P. F. Sorenson, "Cultural Values and Organizational Development: A Seven-Country Study," *Leadership and Organization Development Journal* 14 (1993), pp. 3–7; R. J. Marshak, "Lewin Meets Confucius: A Review of the OD Model of Change," *Journal of Applied Behavioral Science* 29 (1993), pp. 395–415; and C. M. Lau and H. Y. Ngo, "Organization Development and Firm Performance: A Comparison of Multinational and Local Firms," *Journal of International Business Studies* 32, no. 1 (2001), pp. 95–114.

41. For an excellent discussion of conflict management and Asian values, see several articles in K. Leung and D. Tjosvold, eds., *Conflict Management in the Asia Pacific: Assumptions and Approaches in Diverse Cultures* (Singapore: John Wiley & Sons, 1998).

42. M. McKendall, "The Tyranny of Change: Organizational Development Revisited," *Journal of Business Ethics* 12 (February 1993), pp. 93–104; and C. M. D. Deaner, "A Model of Organization Development Ethics," *Public Administration Quarterly* 17 (1994), pp. 435–46.

>**photo**credits

chapter 1

P1.1, page 2, AP/Wide World Photos
P1.2, page 5, Hans Rudolf Oeser/The New York Times
P1.3, page 9, Department of Economic Development, Government of Dubai
P1.4, page 14, © The Augusta Chronicle

chapter 2

P2.1, page 22, Reprinted with permission of Owens Corning. All Rights Reserved.
P2.2, page 26, Chad Lunquist, Tahoe Daily Tribune
P2.3, page 32, Photo by Cancan Chu/Getty Images
P2.4, page 35, Courtesy of Molson Coors

chapter 3

P3.1, page 44, Photo provided by Indianapolis Power & Light Company
P3.2, page 49, © Mel Melcon, 2005, Los Angeles Times. Reprinted with permission.
P3.3, page 52, Melanie Stetson Freeman/The Christian Science Monitor/Getty Images
P3.4, page 57, Courtesy of Exxon Mobil

chapter 4

P4.1, page 66, AP/Wide World Photos
P4.2, page 70, Photo courtesy of Wegmans Food Markets
P4.3, page 72, Courtesy of Four Seasons Hotels and Resorts
P4.4, page 77, Photo courtesy of Outback Steakhouse
P4.5, page 83, Photo Courtesy of Liggett-Stashower

chapter 5

P5.1, page 90, © H. Lynch/Raleigh News and Observer
P5.2, page 95, Photo Courtesy of EnCana Corporation
P5.3, page 98, Photo courtesy of Akamai
P5.4, page 101, © The New Yorker Collection 2001 Barbara Smaller from cartoonbank.com. All rights reserved.
P5.5, page 105, Photo by Kevin Adler, KRON 4

chapter 6

P6.1, page 112, Photo courtesy of NASA
P6.2, page 115, © Apple Computer, Inc. Use with permission. All rights reserved. Apple ® and the Apple logo are registered trademarks of Apple Computer, Inc.
P6.3, page 121, Photo by Ken Krakow/ © Boeing. Used under license.
P6.4, page 124, Ron Sangha Photography Ltd./Used by permission of Radical Entertainment Inc.

chapter 7

P7.1, page 132, © Paul Thomas/Getty Images
P7.2, page 137, © Chamussy/Sipa Press.

P7.3, page 140, © H. Darr Beiser, USA Today. Reprinted with permission of The Journal News
P7.4, page 145, Photo Courtesy of Standard Motor Company
P7.5, page 149, Johnson Space Center/NASA

chapter 8

P8.1, page 156, Photo Courtesy of Sun Microsystems, Inc.
P8.2, page 160, © UK Out Epa-Photo/PA Files/Phil Noble
P8.3, page 164, © Mark M. Lawrence/Corbis
P8.4, page 167, Photo courtesy of www.aintitcool.com

chapter 9

P9.1, page 174, © Martin H. Simon/Corbis
P9.2, page 178, Photo courtesy of Lowe Worldwide
P9.3, page 183, AFP/Getty Images
P9.4, page 187, Craig Abraham/Fairfax Photos

chapter 10

P10.1, page 194, AP/Wide World Photos
P10.2, page 197, *Management* magazine, www.management.co.nz
P10.3, page 202, AP/Wide World Photos
P10.4, page 204, Edward Carreon/Newhouse News Service

chapter 11

P11.1, page 212, AP/Wide World Photos
P11.2, page 215, © Tracy Powell
P11.3, page 219, AP/Wide World Photos
P11.4, page 223, © BBN Publishing

chapter 12

P12.1, page 232, © Bill Cramer
P12.2, page 235, AP/Wide World Photos
P12.3, page 238, The Minnesota Business Journal/Used with permission by Harbinger Partners Inc.
P12.4, page 245, Photo courtesy of 7-Eleven, Inc.

chapter 13

P13.1, page 252, AP/Wide World Photos
P13.2, page 256, Courtesy of Mayo Clinic
P13.3, page 258, Yuriko Nakao/Reuters
P13.4, page 261, © 2000, Pierre Roussel

chapter 14

P14.1, page 270, © Eriko Sugita/Reuters/Corbis
P14.2, page 273, AP / Wide World Photos
P14.3, page 277, © Brian Vander Brug, 2004, Los Angeles Times. Reprinted with permission
P14.4, page 281, Courtesy of Amanda Troston-Bloom, Corporation for Positive Change, Golden, CO

>**company**index

>**url**index